Numerical Methods
Algorithms and Applications

Laurene Fausett
Georgia Southern University

Pearson Education, Inc.
Upper Saddle River, New Jersey 07458

Library of Congress Cataloging-in-Publication Data

Fausett, Laurene V.
    Numerical methods : algorithms and applications / Laurene Fausett.
    p. cm.
  Includes bibliographical references and index.
  ISBN 0-13-031400-5
  1. Numerical analysis   I. Title.
  QA297.F382 2003
  519.4—dc21   2002006376

Vice Presidential and Editorial Director, ECS: *Marcia J. Horton*
Acquisitions Editor: *Eric Frank*
Associate Editor: *Alice Dworkin*
Editorial Assistant: *Jessica Romeo*
Vice President and Director of Production
  and Manufacturing, ESM: *David W. Riccardi*
Executive Managing Editor: *Vince O'Brien*
Managing Editor: *David A. George*
Production Editor: *Patty Donovan*

Director of Creative Services: *Paul Belfanti*
Creative Director: *Carole Anson*
Art Director: *Jayne Conte*
Art Editor: *Greg Dulles*
Cover Designer: *Bruce Kenselaar*
Manufacturing Manager: *Trudy Pisciotti*
Manufacturing Buyer: *Lynda Castillo*
Marketing Manager: *Holly Stark*

About the Cover: Image from *Colors Dance*, a quilt by Susan Webb Lee, 1985, Weddington, NC. From the collection of the artist.

2003 by Pearson Education, Inc.
Pearson Education, Inc.
Upper Saddle River, New Jersey 07458

The author and publisher of this book have used their best efforts in preparing this book. These efforts include the development, research, and testing of the theories and programs to determine their effectiveness. The author and publisher make no warranty of any kind, expressed or implied, with regard to these programs or the documentation contained in this book. The author and publisher shall not be liable in any event for incidental or consequential damages in connection, or arising out of, the furnishing, performance, or use of these programs.

Printed in the United States of America

10 9 8 7 6 5 4 3 2

ISBN 0-13-031400-5

Pearson Education Ltd., *London*
Pearson Education Australia Pty. Ltd., *Sydney*
Pearson Education Singapore, Pte. Ltd.
Pearson Education North Asia Ltd., *Hong Kong*
Pearson Education Canada, Inc., *Toronto*
Pearson Educacíon de Mexico, S.A. de C.V.
Pearson Education—Japan, *Tokyo*
Pearson Education Malaysia, Pte. Ltd.
Pearson Education, Inc., *Upper Saddle River, New Jersey*

Books extend our world through time and space.
In that spirit, I dedicate this work to all of my teachers
and all of my students.

Contents

3   SOLVING SYSTEMS OF LINEAR EQUATIONS: DIRECT METHODS   95

4   LU AND QR FACTORIZATION   131

6 SOLVING SYSTEMS OF LINEAR EQUATIONS: ITERATIVE METHODS   207

7 NONLINEAR FUNCTIONS OF SEVERAL VARIABLES   241

10 FOURIER METHODS   369

11 NUMERICAL DIFFERENTIATION AND INTEGRATION   407

12   ORDINARY DIFFERENTIAL EQUATIONS: INITIAL-VALUE PROBLEMS   449

13   ORDINARY DIFFERENTIAL EQUATIONS: HIGHER ORDER EQUATIONS AND FIRST-ORDER SYSTEMS   491

14 ORDINARY DIFFERENTIAL EQUATIONS: BOUNDARY-VALUE PROBLEMS   529

15 PARTIAL DIFFERENTIAL EQUATIONS   559

Lists of Examples/Algorithms

Examples

Chapter 1

Chapter 2

Chapter 3

Chapter 4 LU and QR Factorization

Chapter 5

Algorithms

Preface

The purpose of this text is to present the fundamental numerical techniques used in engineering, applied mathematics, computer science, and the physical and life sciences in a manner that is both interesting and understandable to undergraduate and beginning graduate students in those fields. The organization of the chapters, and of the material within each chapter, is designed with student learning as the primary objective. A detailed algorithm is given for each method presented, so that students can write simple programs implementing the technique in the computer language of their choice. Numerous examples of the use of the methods are also included.

The first chapter sets the stage for the material in the rest of the text, giving a brief introduction to the long history of numerical techniques and a "preview of coming attractions" for some of the recurring themes in the remainder of the text. It also presents a summary of the key components of a computer program for solving problems involving numerical techniques such as those given in the text. The trapezoid rule for numerical integration is used to illustrate the relationship between a numerical algorithm and a computer program implementing the algorithm. Sample programs are given in several different languages.

Each of the subsequent chapters begins with a one page overview of the subject matter, together with an indication as to how the topics presented in the chapter are related to those in previous and subsequent chapters. Introductory examples are presented to suggest a few of the types of problems for which the topics of the chapter may be used. Following the sections in which the methods are presented, each chapter concludes with a summary of the most important formulas, of suggestions for further reading, and an extensive set of exercises. The first group of problems provides fairly routine practice of the techniques; the second group includes applications adapted from a variety of fields, and the final group of problems encourages students to extend their understanding of either the theoretical or the computational aspects of the methods.

The presentation of each numerical technique is based on the successful teaching methodology of providing examples and geometric motivation for a method, and a concise statement of the steps to carry out the computation, before giving a mathematical derivation of the process or a discussion of the more theoretical issues that are relevant to the use and understanding of the topic. Each topic is illustrated by examples that range in complexity from very simple to moderate. Geometrical or graphical illustrations are included whenever they are appropriate. The last section of each chapter gives a brief discussion of more advanced methods for solving the kinds of problems covered in the chapter, including methods used in MATLAB, Mathcad, *Mathematica*, and various software libraries.

The chapters are arranged according to the following general areas:

Chapter 2 deals with solving nonlinear equations of a single variable.

Chapters 3–6 treat topics from numerical linear algebra.

Chapter 7 considers nonlinear functions of several variables

Chapters 8–10 cover numerical methods for data interpolation and approximation.

Chapter 11 presents numerical differentiation and integration.

Chapters 12–15 introduce numerical techniques for solving differential equations.

For much of the material, a calculus sequence that includes an introduction to differential equations and linear algebra provides adequate background. For more in-depth coverage of the topics from linear algebra (especially the QR method for eigenvalues), a linear algebra course would be an appropriate prerequisite. The coverage of Fourier approximation and FFT (Chapter 10) and partial differential equations (Chapter 15) assumes that the students have somewhat more mathematical maturity since the material in intrinsically more challenging. The subject matter included is suitable for a two-semester sequence of classes, or for any of several different one-term courses, depending on the desired emphasis, student background, and selection of topics.

Many people have contributed to the development of this text. My colleagues at Florida Institute of Technology, the Naval Postgraduate School, the University of South Carolina Aiken, and Georgia Southern University have provided support, encouragement, and suggestions. I especially wish to thank Sharon Barrs, Jacalyn Huband, and Gary Huband for writing the sample programs in Chapter 1, and Pierre Larochelle for the example of robot motion in Ch 13. Thanks also to Jane Lybrand and Jack Leifer, who provided data for several examples and exercises. I also appreciate the many contributions my students have made to this text, which was after all written with them in mind. The comments made by the reviewers of the text have helped greatly in the fine-tuning of the final presentation. The editorial and production staff at Prentice Hall, as well as Patty Donovan and the rest of the staff at Pine Tree Composition have my heartfelt gratitude for their efforts in insuring that the text is as accurate and well designed as possible. And, saving the most important for last, I thank my husband and colleague, Don Fausett, for his patience and support.

LAURENE FAUSETT

Foundations

From the earliest times, the search for solutions of real-world problems has been an important aspect of mathematical study. In many interesting applications, an exact solution may be unattainable, or it may not give the answer in a convenient form. Useful answers may involve finding good approximate results with a reasonable amount of computational effort.

Many numerical methods have a very long history. There is evidence that the Babylonians (more than 3,700 years ago) knew how to find numerical solutions of quadratic equations and approximations to the square root of an integer. They also used linear interpolation to solve problems involving compound interest.

An example of the method of solving systems of linear equations that we know as Gaussian elimination appears in a Chinese manuscript (the *Nine Chapters*) from the Han Dynasty (approximately 2,000 years ago); matrix notation was used. The famous German mathematician Carl Friedrich Gauss (1777–1855) indicated that the method was well known.

Chinese mathematics during the Sung dynasty (960–1279) generalized the method of successive approximations from the *Nine Chapters* to find numerical solutions of higher degree equations. Matrix solution techniques for linear systems were also extended to equations of higher degree (an approach similar to work in the West in the 19th century).

Greek mathematics included methods of calculating areas based on approximating the desired quantity by a large number of regions of known area. (A similar process was used for volumes.) A letter from Archimedes to Eratosthenes (c. 250 B.C.) describes one of these methods; the letter was discovered in 1906.

The continuation of the Greek mathematical traditions by Middle Eastern scholars tended to stress computational and practical aspects. Omar Khayyam, who lived 900 years ago, wrote a treatise on algebra that includes a systematic investiga-tion of cubic equations. (He is perhaps better known as the author of the *Rubaiyat of Omar Khayyam*.) Jemshid Al-Kashi (who died about 1436), another Persian mathematician, solved cubic equations by iterative and trigonometric methods and also knew the method for solving general algebraic equations, which is now usually called Horner's method. W. G. Horner published the method in 1819, presumably without being aware of its previous history.

Leonardo Fibonacci (c. 1200) showed that certain cubic equations cannot be solved in terms of square roots, but that very accurate approximate solutions can be generated.

The first tables of logarithms were published by the Scotsman John Napier in 1614; they were revised by Henry Briggs (based on Napier's suggestions) in 1624 and provided a great tool for improving computation.

The connection between mathematics and astronomy has been extremely close throughout history. Leaders of the Copernican revolution ventured into a number of areas of mathematics. For example, Johannes Kepler published the *New solid geometry of wine barrels* in 1615, in which he used geometric approximations to calculate the volume of a solid of revolution.

A widely known method for approximating the roots of an equation, called Newton's method (or the Newton-Raphson method), is a generalization of an iterative approach to finding the roots of polynomials published in the early 1700s. According to recent research, Thomas Simpson (well known for Simpson's rule for the numerical approximation of definite integrals) extended Newton's method to more general functions and published the results in 1740.

Taylor's formula is the theoretical basis for many numerical techniques. Taylor polynomials were introduced in an article by Brook Taylor published in 1715; the remainder term first appeared in a book by Joseph Louis Lagrange in 1797.

One of the most popular approaches to finding numerical approximations to ordinary differential equations, the Runge-Kutta method, was developed 100 years ago by the German applied mathematicians Carl Runge (1856–1927) and M. W. Kutta (1867–1944). Runge is also known for his work on the Zeeman effect and Kutta for his contributions to the theory of airfoil lift in aerodynamics.

Our modern-day calculators follow the basic design introduced in Blaise Pascal's adding machine (1642) and Gottfried Wilhelm Leibniz's multiplication machine (1671). The origin of computers, on the other hand, is usually traced to Charles Babbage's analytical engine (developed in the 1830s). However, essentially the entire development of the personal computer (PC or Mac) dates from about 1980.

Although the classical numerical methods mentioned above continue to be important in the development of computer software, many of the preferred methods of modern computing include relatively recent innovations and refinements. Some of these, with the date of publication of the primary reference for the method, are summarized here. They are discussed in more detail in the appropriate section of the text. For finding the root of a single equation, software packages often use relatively recent methods, such as Brent's method (1973) or Ridders' method (1979). For constrained linear optimization problems, the simplex method (1948) is the standard method. For general nonlinear least-squares problems, the Levenberg-Marquardt method (1963) provides an elegant algorithm for combining two more classical approaches. Other important methods for these problems are the conjugate gradient methods, such as the Polak-Ribiere method (1971) or the closely related Fletcher-Reeves method. The routines for finding eigenvalues and eigenvectors that are widely used in software libraries and packages are generally based on routines published by Wilkinson and Reinsch (1971). For function interpolation, the work by DeBoor on cubic splines (1978) is the standard. For rational function interpolation, the Bulirsch-Stoer algorithm (1980) is important. The existence of fast methods for computing discrete Fourier transforms (DFT) became widely known in the 1960s through the work of Cooley and Tukey; however, Danielson and Lancoz had also developed such methods (early 1940s). In fact, Gauss (1805) led the list of perhaps a dozen people who discovered efficient methods for the DFT independently over the years. There have also been numerous improvements in recent years in the numerical methods for finding derivatives, integrals, and solutions to ordinary and partial differential equations.

Many of the issues that confront a scientist or engineer who uses numerical methods are the same today as throughout the history of the subject, although the relative importance of the competing considerations may change, depending on the computational resources available. Two primary considerations are the computational effort required and the accuracy of the resulting solution. Numerical methods for solving a problem may be classified as either direct or iterative. A direct method, such as Gaussian elimination, produces an answer to a problem in a fixed number of computational steps. An iterative method produces a sequence of approximate answers (designed to converge ever closer to the true solution, under the proper conditions).

For a direct method that would give an exact result if the computations were carried out in exact arithmetic, such as Gaussian elimination, the effect of numerical round-off may be significant. Also, since the linear systems that occur in modern applications may be extremely large, efficiency of computation is a critical aspect of choosing a solution technique for these types of problems. Other direct methods, such as techniques for numerical integration, are developed by replacing the given function by an approximating function (such as a Taylor polynomial) for which the integral can be found. The accuracy of the method depends in part on the number of terms that are retained before the Taylor series is truncated.

For iterative techniques, it is imperative that questions of convergence be understood. Do the successive approximate answers actually approach the true answer? If so, how quickly? How should the decision be made to terminate the process?

In the next section, we present three problems that illustrate basic types of numerical methods. We then summarize some significant issues, such as convergence and computational effort, which form the recurring themes of subsequent chapters. We conclude this chapter with an introduction to the basic components of simple computer programs for solving numerical problems.

In the remainder of the text, numerical methods are grouped according to the types of problems for which they are intended. Techniques for solving nonlinear equations of a single variable and systems of linear or nonlinear equations are presented in Chapters 2 and 3 and Chapter 6 and 7. Some basic methods from numerical linear algebra are given in Chapters 4 and 5. Functional approximation, including interpolation, least squares approximation, and Fourier methods, are discussed in Chapters 8–10. Numerical approximation of differentiation and integration, the basic operations of calculus, are the subject of Chapter 11. Numerical solutions of ordinary and partial differential equations are considered in Chapters 12–15.

To illustrate the types of problems for which a numerical solution may be desired, we consider three examples. The simple problems presented in these examples can be solved exactly by techniques that are well known in algebra or calculus. However, there are closely related problems for which no exact solution can be found. There are many numerical methods for solving problems such as these examples. We introduce one method for each problem presented, to illustrate some of the basic issues and themes that recur throughout numerical analysis.

1.1.1 Roots of Nonlinear Equations

Although the zeros of a quadratic function such as $f(x) = x^2 - 3$ can be found exactly by the quadratic formula, no such exact methods exist for most nonlinear functions. The formula for finding the zeros of a cubic function is much more complicated, and Niels Henrik Abel (1802–1829) proved that no formula exists for fifth-order polynomials. (A translation of Abel's paper appears in Smith [1959].)

There are many methods for finding approximate zeros of nonlinear functions. The simplest, the bisection method, is a systematic searching technique; the secant, false-position, and Newton's methods use a straight-line approximation to the function whose zero is sought. More powerful methods use a quadratic approximation to the function or a combination of these techniques. Each approach produces a succession of approximations. One consideration in choosing such a technique is whether, and how rapidly, these approximations approach the desired solution. The computational effort required for each iteration may also be important.

Finding the zeros of $f(x) = x^2 - 3$ is equivalent to the problem of finding the square root of 3. A simple iterative method for finding square roots is illustrated in Section 1.2. The graph of $y = x^2 - 3$ is shown in Fig. 1.1.

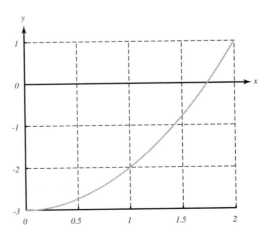

FIGURE 1.1   Graph of $y = x^2 - 3$ on the interval $[\,0, 2\,]$.

1.1.2 Fixed-Point Iteration

To find the square root of a positive number c, it is convenient to rewrite the equation $x^2 = c$ as the implicit equation

$$x = \frac{1}{2}\left(x + \frac{c}{x}\right);$$

this form provides the basis for an iterative solution technique by using the right-hand side of the equation to generate an updated estimate for the desired value of x.

A solution of an implicit equation of the form $x = g(x)$ is called a *fixed point*. In more detail, starting with an initial guess x_0, we evaluate

$$x_1 = \frac{1}{2}\left(x_0 + \frac{c}{x_0}\right); \quad x_2 = \frac{1}{2}\left(x_1 + \frac{c}{x_1}\right); \ldots \quad x_k = \frac{1}{2}\left(x_{k-1} + \frac{c}{x_{k-1}}\right).$$

Geometrically this corresponds to finding the intersection of the line $y = x$ and the curve $y = \frac{1}{2}\left(x + \frac{c}{x}\right) = g(x)$. The method is known as fixed-point iteration, since we are seeking a value of x for which $x_k = x_{k+1} = g(x_k)$.

Example 1.1 Fixed-Point Iterations to Find $\sqrt{3}$

The first two iterations in the procedure for finding a root of $x^2 = 3$ give

$$x_1 = \frac{1}{2}\left(1 + \frac{3}{1}\right) = 2; \quad x_2 = \frac{1}{2}\left(2 + \frac{3}{2}\right) = \frac{7}{4}.$$

The process of generating x_1 from $x_0 = 1$ is illustrated in Fig. 1.2.

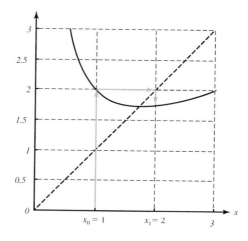

FIGURE 1.2   First step of fixed-point iteration.

1.1.3 Linear Systems

If a linear system of equations has a unique solution, then a (nonzero) linear combination of two of the equations produces another linear equation that also passes through the same solution point. The well-known Gaussian elimination method systematically transforms the original system into an equivalent system (with the same solution) for which the solution point can be more easily identified. The process is illustrated in Example 1.2 for two equations in two unknowns. The graphs of the following two linear equations are illustrated in Fig. 1.3:

L_1: $4x_1 + x_2 = 6,$

M_1: $-x_1 + 5x_2 = 9.$

Linear systems can be written more compactly in matrix-vector form. Thus, the foregoing system is written as $\mathbf{A}\,\mathbf{x} = \mathbf{b}$, where

$$\mathbf{A} = \begin{bmatrix} 4 & 1 \\ -1 & 5 \end{bmatrix}, \quad \mathbf{x} = \begin{bmatrix} x_1 \\ x_2 \end{bmatrix}, \quad \mathbf{b} = \begin{bmatrix} 6 \\ 9 \end{bmatrix}.$$

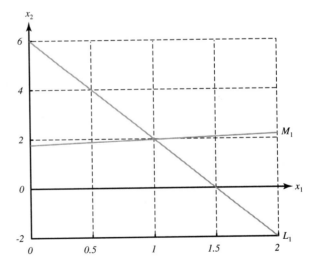

FIGURE 1.3   Graphs of $4x_1 + x_2 = 6$ and $-x_1 + 5x_2 = 9$ on $[0, 2]$.

The linear systems for which numerical methods are required are frequently very large. In many important applications, the coefficient matrix has a particular structure that allows specialized solution techniques, which reduce computation and memory requirements.

1.1.4 Gaussian Elimination

Basic Gaussian elimination systematically transforms a system of linear equations into an equivalent system for which the solution is easier to find.

Example 1.2 Solving a Linear System

To illustrate this process, consider the following simple system:

L_1: $\qquad\qquad\qquad\qquad\qquad 4x + y = 6,$

M_1: $\qquad\qquad\qquad\qquad\qquad -x + 5y = 9.$

Using basic Gaussian elimination, we multiply the first equation by 0.25 and add the result to the second equation to give the new (equivalent) system:

L_1: $\qquad\qquad\qquad\qquad\qquad 4x + \quad y = 6,$

M_2: $\qquad\qquad\qquad\qquad\qquad\quad + 5.25y = 10.5.$

Solving the second equation gives $y = 2$; substituting that value for y into the first equation yields $x = 1$.

The original two equations are shown as lines L_1 and M_1 in Fig. 1.4. The modified second equation is shown as M_2. The solution for y is found from M_2; substituting into the first equation gives $x = 1$.

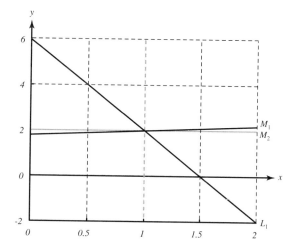

FIGURE 1.4 Geometric representation of Gaussian elimination for two equations.

If the computations in Gaussian elimination could be carried out exactly, then the main issue would be computational efficiency. However, not all numbers are represented in exact form in computer calculations; the extent of the difficulties this causes depends on certain characteristics of the coefficient matrix of the linear system.

1.1.5 Numerical Integration

The fundamental theorem of calculus states that the definite integral of a function may be found from the antiderivative of the function. However, for many functions, it is much easier to show that they have a definite integral than it is to find an expression for the antiderivative in terms of elementary functions. Several numerical techniques for finding definite integrals are based on approximating the function to be integrated by a simpler function whose antiderivative can be found exactly. The accuracy of the approximate integral depends on the form of the approximating function and the number of function evaluations. The basic numerical methods for integration may be improved by subdividing the interval of integration and using the fact that the integral over the entire interval is the sum of the integrals over the subintervals.

1.1.6 Trapezoid Rule

The basic trapezoid rule for integration is based on approximating the function to be integrated by a straight line connecting the points $(a, f(a))$ and $(b, f(b))$. We denote the length of the interval of integration as $h = b - a$. The formula for the basic trapezoid rule is

$$\int_a^b f(x)\, dx \approx \frac{h}{2}[f(a) + f(b)].$$

In order to obtain a useful formula for approximate integration based on trapezoidal regions, it is necessary to subdivide the interval of integration into relatively small subintervals and apply the basic trapezoid rule to each subinterval. We take n subintervals, each of the same length, so that each subinterval is of length $h = (b - a)/n$. For $n = 2$, the first subinterval is $[a, m]$ and the second subinterval is $[m, b]$ where $m = (a + b)/2$.

To apply the trapezoid rule to approximate a definite integral using two subintervals, write

$$\int_a^b f(x)\, dx = \int_a^m f(x)\, dx + \int_m^b f(x)\, dx$$

and apply the basic trapezoid to each of the integrals on the right-hand side.

$$\int_a^b f(x)\, dx \approx \frac{h}{2}[f(a) + f(m)] + \frac{h}{2}[f(m) + f(b)] = \frac{h}{2}[f(a) + 2\, f(m) + f(b)].$$

Note that h is the length of each subinterval, namely, $(b-a)/2$.

In general, the subintervals are $[a, x_1]$, $[x_1, x_2]$, . . . $[x_{n-1}, b]$, where $x_1 = a + h$, $x_2 = a + 2h$, etc. It is often convenient to set $x_0 = a$ and $x_n = b$. The trapezoid rule is

$$\int_a^b f(x)\, dx \approx \frac{h}{2}[f(x_0) + 2\, f(x_1) + 2\, f(x_2) + \ldots + 2\, f(x_{n-1}) + f(x_n)].$$

Example 1.3 Approximating an Integral

Using the basic trapezoid rule approximation to the definite integral

$$I = \int_1^3 \frac{1}{x^3}\, dx$$

gives

$$I \approx \frac{h}{2}[f(a) + f(b)] = 1 + 1/27 = 28/27 \approx 1.037037$$

Taking two subintervals, we have $m = x_1 = 2$, $f(2) = 1/8$, $h = 1$, and

$$I \approx \frac{h}{2}[f(a) + 2f(m) + f(b)] = \frac{1}{2}(1 + 2(1/8) + 1/27) \approx 0.6435185.$$

With four subintervals, we have $x_1 = 3/2$, $x_2 = 2$, $x_3 = 5/2$, and $h = 1/2$,

$$I \approx \frac{h}{2}[f(a) + 2f(x_1) + 2f(x_2) + 2f(x_3) + f(b)]$$

$$= \frac{1}{4}(1 + 2(8/27) + 2(1/8) + 2(8/125) + 1/27) \approx 0.5019074$$

The exact value of this integral is $4/9 \approx 0.444444$

The graph of the function $f(x) = \dfrac{1}{x^3}$, and the straight line approximations used in the trapezoid rule and the trapezoid rule with $n = 2$, are shown in Figure 1.5. As the graphs suggest, the value of the integral given by the basic trapezoid rule is much larger than the true value of the integral, since the area under the straight line is larger than the area under the curve.

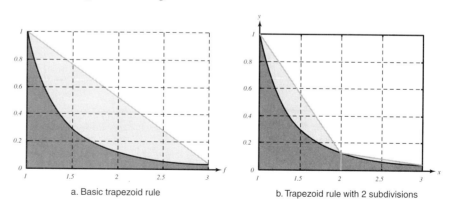

a. Basic trapezoid rule   b. Trapezoid rule with 2 subdivisions

FIGURE 1.5   The areas given by $\displaystyle\int_1^3 \frac{1}{x^3}\, dx$ and by the trapezoid rule approximations.

We now introduce some of the recurring themes in the analysis of numerical methods; these ideas are revisited in various settings in the remainder of the text. First we consider the two primary issues for iterative methods: "Does the process converge?" and "When do we stop?" We then discuss some issues related to the question of how good the result of a numerical method is, and how the result can be improved.

1.2.1   Key Issues for Iterative Methods

For iterative techniques, it is imperative to know whether the method converges, that is, whether the sequence of approximate results approaches the true solution. If the method does converge, we must decide when to terminate the process. For an important class of methods, the convergence depends on the eigenvalues of the iteration matrix; a useful theorem for bounds on the eigenvalues is given below.

Convergence of Iterative Methods

For some iterative techniques, the convergence, or divergence, of the method can be illustrated geometrically. The sequence of points generated by the fixed-point formula $x_k = g(x_{k-1})$ is shown in the next example.

Example 1.4 Fixed-Point Iteration

Figure 1.6a shows the first two steps of the convergent fixed-point iteration for $x = cos(x)$, starting with $x_0 = 0.5$. Figure 1.6b shows the first two steps of the divergent fixed-point iteration for $x = g(x) = 1 - x^3$ with $x_0 = 0.5$

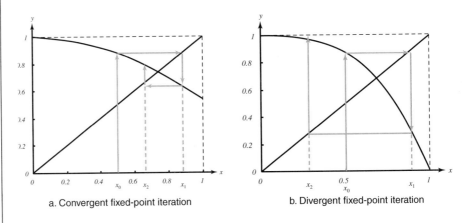

a. Convergent fixed-point iteration   b. Divergent fixed-point iteration

FIGURE 1.6   Fixed-point iterations.

It is very useful to be able to analyze algebraically whether a fixed-point formula will converge, and if so, to estimate how rapidly. The following theorem states conditions which guarantee that

(a) the equation $x = g(x)$ has a fixed point in the interval $I = [a, b]$, and

(b) the iterative procedure $x_k = g(x_{k-1})$ will converge to that fixed point.

Fixed-point Convergence Theorem

If

1. $g(x)$ maps $[a, b]$ into $[a, b]$,
2. $g'(x)$ is continuous on $[a, b]$, and
3. there is a number $N < 1$ such that $|g'(x)| \le N$ for all x in $[a, b]$;

then

1. $x = g(x)$ has exactly one solution (call it x^*) in the interval $[a, b]$, and
2. the fixed-point iteration $x_k = g(x_{k-1})$ converges to x^*, for any starting estimate in $[a, b]$.

Furthermore, the value of N gives an estimate of the error at any stage of the iteration, in that the error $e_k = x_k - x^*$ satisfies the inequalities

$$|e_{k+1}| \le N |e_k| \text{ and } |e_{k+1}| \le N^{k+1} |e_0|.$$

It is easy to construct examples of functions $g(x)$ that do not map a given interval $I = [a, b]$ into I and for which the curves $y = x$ and $y = g(x)$ do not cross (at least for x in I). If g is continuous and does map I into I, then the curves will cross (at least once) in the interval. The guarantee of convergence of the iterative process hinges on the magnitude of $g'(x)$ being less than 1, at least near the fixed point.

To illustrate what this theorem says, consider the fixed-point iteration $x = \cos(x)$ illustrated in Example 1.4. For $0 \le x \le 1$, $\cos(x)$ is also between 0 and 1, so $g(x)$ does map $[0, 1]$ into $[0, 1]$. Furthermore, $g'(x) = -\sin(x)$ ranges between 0 and $-\sin(1)$, so $|g'(x)| \le 0.85$ for all x in $[0, 1]$, and the theorem guarantees convergence of the iterations.

On the other hand, for $x = g(x) = 1 - x^3$, $g'(x) = -3x^2$, which is not bounded by a number less than 1 on $[0, 1]$. Although there is a fixed point in the interval (and $g(x)$ does map $[0, 1]$ into $[0, 1]$), the conditions of the theorem are not satisfied, and in fact, the iterations do not converge. The difficulty is that in any neighborhood of the fixed point, $|g'(x)| > 1$.

Estimating Eigenvalues

A number λ is an eigenvalue of matrix $\mathbf{M}$ (with a corresponding nonzero eigenvector $\mathbf{v}$) if and only if $\mathbf{Mv} = \lambda\mathbf{v}$. The convergence of iterative methods based on repeated multiplication by a matrix often depends on the eigenvalues of $\mathbf{M}$; methods for calculating eigenvalues are discussed in Chapter 7. However, in some situations it is sufficient to be able to estimate the eigenvalues. The following theorem gives bounds on the location of the eigenvalues of $\mathbf{M}$.

If, for $i = 1, \ldots, n$, C_i is the circle in the complex plane with center at $(m_{ii}, 0)$ and radius $r_i = \sum_{j \in I} |m_{ij}|$, where I indicates the index set $\{1, 2, \ldots, i-1, i+1, \ldots, n\}$, then all of the eigenvalues of $\mathbf{M}$ lie within the union of the disks bounded by these circles.

Furthermore, if there are k disks, the union of which is disjoint from the other disks, then exactly k eigenvalues lie within that union.

Example 1.5 Bounds on Eigenvalues

To illustrate the Gerschgorin circle theorem, consider the problem of finding bounds on the eigenvalues of the matrix

$$M = \begin{bmatrix} 2 & -1/2 & 0 \\ -1/2 & 3 & 1/2 \\ 0 & 1/2 & 6 \end{bmatrix}.$$

We find that

C_1 has center $(2, 0)$ and radius $|-1/2| + |0| = 1/2$;
C_2 has center $(3, 0)$ and radius $|-1/2| + |1/2| = 1$;
C_3 has center $(6, 0)$ and radius $|0| + |1/2| = 1/2$.

The union of the interiors of circles C_1 and C_2 is disjoint from the disk bounded by circle C_3, so we know that there are exactly two eigenvalues in the union of the regions enclosed by circles C_1 and C_2. Furthermore, there is one eigenvalue in the region bounded by circle C_3. These regions are illustrated in Fig. 1.7.

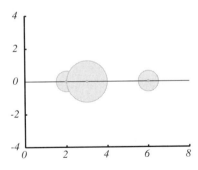

FIGURE 1.7   Gerschgorin disks.

Termination Conditions

A variety of conditions can be used for deciding when to stop an iterative procedure; however, there is no perfect test for a "stopping condition." The conditions may be characterized as being of three general types: the problem is "solved," the iteration has "converged," or the iteration process has continued "long enough." For the example of finding the zero of $f(x) = x^2 - 3$, with the true zero denoted x^*, possible convergence tests include the following:

The problem is "solved":

$$|f(x_k)| \leq f_{\text{tol}} \qquad \text{(function value reduced to specified tolerance)}.$$

The iteration has "converged":

$$|x_{k+1} - x_k| \leq \text{tol} \quad \text{(absolute change is within specified tolerance)};$$

if tol $= 10^{-n}$, then x_{k+1} should approximate x^* to n decimal places.

$$|x_{k+1} - x_k| \leq \text{tol } x_{k+1} \text{ (relative change is within specified tolerance)};$$

if tol $= 10^{-n}$, then x_{k+1} should approximate x^* to n significant digits.

The iterations have gone on "long enough":

$$k \geq \text{max\_it} \qquad \text{(iteration counter exceeds a specified limit)}.$$

It may also be desirable to check whether "the solution is looking bad":

$$|f(x_k)| \geq f_{\text{big}} \qquad \text{(function value exceeds a specified limit)};$$

$$|x_k| \geq x_{\text{big}} \qquad \text{(value of iterated variable exceeds a specified limit)}.$$

Caveats

It is important to realize that none of these tests guarantees the desired result, namely that $|x_k - x^*| < \text{tol}$.

In addition, an iterative process could pass the successive iterates test at the same time that the iterates were diverging to ∞. As an example, consider a process in which $x_k = 1 + \dfrac{1}{2} + \dfrac{1}{3} + \ldots + \dfrac{1}{k}$. The difference, $|x_{k+1} - x_k| = \dfrac{1}{k+1} \to 0$, as $k \to \infty$, but $x_{k+1} \to \infty$ as $k \to \infty$.

Choosing an Appropriate Test

The relative-change test is appropriate for problems in which the desired roots may be of greatly differing magnitudes. It is not suitable, however, if $x = 0$ is a desired root and the method is converging rapidly, since that would produce a relatively large change in the iterates.

1.2.2 How Good Is the Result?

There are several reasons that the results of a numerical solution to a problem from the "real world" may not be the exact answer. Simplifying assumptions made in modeling the original problem are one source of inaccuracies. Errors arising from data collection are another.

In this section we illustrate several basic types of errors that are more directly linked to the numerical solution of the stated problem. We first define some standard terminology for describing errors that occur in numerical methods. We then summarize the fundamentals of computer arithmetic and illustrate two types of errors that arise because computers do not represent most numbers in an exact form; that is, they do not do exact arithmetic. The third example in this section illustrates one common form of error introduced in replacing a continuous process by a discrete approximation.

Measuring Error

If x is our approximate result, and the exact (but usually unknown) result is denoted x^*, then the error in using the approximate result is

$$\text{Error}(x) = x^* - x$$

However, especially for problems in which the magnitude of the true value may be very large, or very small, the relative error may be more important than the actual error.

$$\text{Rel Error}(x) = \frac{x^* - x}{x^*}$$

In computing the relative error, the approximate value is often used in the denominator in place of the unknown true value x^*.

Significant Digits

The number x is said to approximate x^* to t significant digits if t is the largest nonnegative integer for which $\left| \dfrac{x^* - x}{x} \right| < 5 \cdot 10^{-t}$.

Big Oh Approximation

For errors that come from using a finite step size, h, in approximating a continuous process by a discrete one, it is often useful to describe how the error depends on h, as h approaches zero. We say that a function $f(h)$ is "Big Oh" of h if $|f(h)| \le c |h|$ for some constant c, when h is near 0. This is written $f(h) = O(h)$. Similarly, $f(h) = O(h^2)$ means that $|f(h)| \le c |h^2|$ for some constant c, when h is near 0. If a method has an error term that is $O(h^k)$, the method is often called a kth order method.

For example, if we use a Taylor polynomial to approximate the function f at $x = a + h$, we have

$$f(x) = f(a + h) = f(a) + h f'(a) + \frac{h^2}{2!} f''(a) + \frac{h^3}{3!} f'''(\eta); \text{ for some } \eta \in [a, a + h].$$

Assuming that f is sufficiently smooth, we can let M be the maximum of $f'''(x)$ for $a \leq x \leq a + h$. Then this approximation is $O(h^3)$, since the error, $\frac{h^3}{3!} f'''(\eta)$ satisfies

$$\left| \frac{h^3}{3!} f'''(\eta) \right| \leq c \left| h^3 \right|$$

where $c = \frac{1}{3!} M$.

Computer Representation of Real Numbers

Computers represent real numbers in a form, called floating point, that is similar to scientific notation. For example, a number N is stored as

$$N = \pm .d_1 d_2 d_3 \ldots d_p B^e,$$

where B is the base and the d_i's are the digits. For a computer, the base is usually 2, 8, or 16; in scientific notation, the base is 10. Each digit is an integer between 0 and $B - 1$. There are a fixed number of digits, p, and the integer exponent, e, is restricted to a range of values; that is, $e \in [\text{emin}, \text{emax}]$. If, as is generally the case, it is required that $d_1 \neq 0$, the system is called a *normalized floating-point system*. Note that for a binary system, this means that $d_1 = 1$, so there is in fact no need to store its value.

In a binary floating-point system, the decimals correspond to sums of negative powers of 2. To illustrate these ideas, consider the numbers that can be expressed exactly in this form, for very small values of p and e, for base 2. (The opposite of each number listed can also be represented.)

It is important to note that the numbers that can be represented exactly are not evenly distributed between the largest and smallest such numbers. The numbers that can be represented exactly, using base 2 with 3 digits and exponents of $-1, 0$, and 1 are illustrated in Figure 1.8

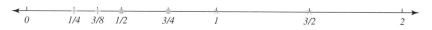

FIGURE 1.8   Exact numbers in base 2.

Base 2 numbers expressible using three digits (leading digit is 1)

Exponent	Binary decimal	Expansion	Decimal
0	0.100_2	$(1)\dfrac{1}{2} + (0)\dfrac{1}{4} + (0)\dfrac{1}{8}$	0.5
	0.101_2	$(1)\dfrac{1}{2} + (0)\dfrac{1}{4} + (1)\dfrac{1}{8}$	0.625
	0.110_2	$(1)\dfrac{1}{2} + (1)\dfrac{1}{4} + (0)\dfrac{1}{8}$	0.75
	0.111_2	$(1)\dfrac{1}{2} + (1)\dfrac{1}{4} + (1)\dfrac{1}{8}$	0.875
1	1.00_2	$(1)\,1 + (0)\dfrac{1}{2} + (0)\dfrac{1}{4}$	1.0
	1.01_2	$(1)\,1 + (0)\dfrac{1}{2} + (1)\dfrac{1}{4}$	1.25
	1.10_2	$(1)\,1 + (1)\dfrac{1}{2} + (0)\dfrac{1}{4}$	1.5
	1.11_2	$(1)\,1 + (1)\dfrac{1}{2} + (1)\dfrac{1}{4}$	1.75
−1	0.0100_2	$(1)\dfrac{1}{4} + (0)\dfrac{1}{8} + (0)\dfrac{1}{16}$	0.25
	0.0101_2	$(1)\dfrac{1}{4} + (0)\dfrac{1}{8} + (1)\dfrac{1}{16}$	0.3125
	0.0110_2	$(1)\dfrac{1}{4} + (1)\dfrac{1}{8} + (0)\dfrac{1}{16}$	0.375
	0.0111_2	$(1)\dfrac{1}{4} + (1)\dfrac{1}{8} + (1)\dfrac{1}{16}$	0.4375

Precision

The precision with which numbers can be stored, and computations carried out, depends on the number of digits and the range of exponents used to represent a real number. In *single precision*, a real variable is stored in four words, or 32 bits. A *bit* is a binary digit (0 or 1); a *byte* is 4 bits (so a byte can have $2^4 = 16$ possible values); a word is 2 bytes (8 bits). Of the 32 bits, 23 are used for the digits, 8 for the exponent, and 1 for the sign. The 8 bits for the exponent can take on 256 possible values, from $0 = 00000000_2$ to $255 = 11111111_2$. In *double precision*, each floating-point number occupies eight words (64 bits, 11 for the exponent, 52 for the digits, and 1 for the sign.)

How Many?

In general, the total number of values, V, that can be represented (assuming that $d_1 \neq 0$) is given by

$$V = 2 \, (B - 1) \, (B^{p-1}) \, (\text{total number of exponents}) + 1.$$

The factor of 2 corresponds to the sign bit; the factor of $(B - 1)$ gives the number of possible values for the first digit. Each of the digits $d_2 \ldots d_p$ can take on B different values. The bit required to store zero accounts for the one additional value not counted in the product.

For a base 10 system, with two digits and exponents of 0 or 1, we have

$$V = 2 \, (10 - 1) \, (10^{2-1}) \, (2) + 1.2 \, (9)(10)(2) + 1 = 361.$$

The maximum value is $.99 \times 10 = 9.9$ and the minimum value is -9.9. The positive numbers that can be represented with the exponent 1 are of the form 1.0, 1.1, 1.2, . . . 2.0, 2.1, 2.3, . . . 9.9; the positive numbers represented with the exponent 0 are 0.10, 0.11, 0.12, . . . , 0.20, 0.21, 0.23, . . . , 0.99. Thus, there are 91 values in the interval [0, 0.99], but only 10 values in the interval [1.0, 1.9].

In a binary floating-point system, with two digits and exponents of 0 or 1, we have

$$V = 2 \, (2 - 1) \, (2^{2-1}) \, (2) + 1 = 2 \, (2 - 1) \, (2^1) \, (2) + 1 = 9.$$

The positive numbers (with their decimal equivalents in parentheses) that can be represented with exponent 0 are 0.10_2 ($= 0.5$) and 0.11_2 ($= 0.75$); those with exponent 1 are 1.0_2 ($=1.0$) and 1.1_2 ($=1.5$). Thus, the largest value is 1.5 and the minimum value is -1.5. For binary representation, the uneven distribution of representation is more evident when there are more digits and exponents, as in Figure 1.8.

How Large and How Small?

The range of exponents that are available determines the smallest and largest numbers (in magnitude) that can be represented. For single precision, the binary numbers in the interval $[00000000_2, 11111111_2]$ are mapped to the interval $[-128, 127]$, so the smallest number is approximately 0.14693×10^{-38}; the largest number is approximately 0.9414×10^{127}. Numbers smaller than 10^{-38} cause *underflow* (which is often set to be zero). Numbers larger than 10^{127} (or 10^{1023} for double precision) cause *overflow* (which usually halts the program).

Errors from Inexact Representation

There are two approaches to shortening a number that has more digits than can be represented by the available floating-point system. The simplest is to *chop* the number, by discarding any digits beyond what the system can accommodate. The second method is to *round* the number; the result depends on the value of the first digit to be discarded. If the system allows for n digits, rounding produces the same result as chopping if the $(n + 1)^{st}$ digit is 0, 1, 2, 3, or 4. If the $(n + 1)^{st}$ digit is 6, 7, 8, or 9, the nth digit is increased by 1. If the $(n + 1)^{st}$ digit is 5, it is common to round so that the nth digit is even, rounding up about half of the time. The errors that occur from rounding are less likely to accumulate during repeated calculations, since the true value is larger than the rounded value about half of the time and smaller about half of the time. Furthermore, the largest absolute error that can occur is twice as large for chopping as for rounding. On the other hand, chopping requires no decisions as to whether to change the last retained digit. The inaccuracies that result from either rounding or chopping are known as round-off errors. We now consider some examples of the difficulties that can occur due to inexact computations.

Example 1.6 Effect of Order of Operations

As an example of the effect of round-off, consider the following addition problem:

$$0.99 + 0.0044 + 0.0042.$$

With exact arithmetic, the result is 0.9986, regardless of the order in which the additions are performed. However, if we have three-digit arithmetic, and the operations are nested from left to right, we find that

$$(0.99 + 0.0044) + 0.0042 = 0.994 + 0.0042 = 0.998.$$

On the other hand, if we change the nesting so that the small numbers are added together first, we have

$$0.99 + (0.0044 + 0.0042) = 0.99 + 0.0086 = 0.999.$$

Using the definition of x approximating x^* to t significant digits, we see that 0.998 approximates the true solution, $x^* = 0.9986$ to three significant digits, since

$$\left| \frac{0.998 - 0.9986}{0.998} \right| = 6.012 \cdot 10^{-4} < 5 \cdot 10^{-3}.$$

On the other hand, 0.999 approximates the true solution, $x^* = 0.9986$ to four significant digits, since

$$\left| \frac{0.999 - 0.09986}{0.999} \right| = 4.004 \cdot 10^{-4} < 5 \cdot 10^{-4}$$

For cases with greater difference in the sizes of the numbers, and with more terms, the loss of significance can be extreme.

Cancellation Error

A second example of the effect of inexact calculations occurs when a computation involves the subtraction of two nearly equal numbers. It is advisable to rewrite the formula to avoid the difficulty, if possible. Consider the problem of using the quadratic formula to solve the quadratic equation

$$x^2 - bx + 1 = 0$$

The effect of rounding the discriminant $r = \sqrt{b^2 - 4}$ is illustrated in this example; note that for large b ($b \gg 4$), r is quite close to b.

The quadratic formula gives $x_1 = \dfrac{b + r}{2}$ and $x_2 = \dfrac{b - r}{2}$.

If b is positive, x_2 will involve the difference of two numbers that are very close to each other, a dangerous situation. This difficulty can be avoided by rationalizing the numerator in the quadratic formula,

$$x_2 = \frac{(b - r)}{2}\frac{(b + r)}{(b + r)} = \frac{(b^2 - r^2)}{2(b + r)} = \frac{4}{2(b + r)} = \frac{2}{(b + r)}.$$

If the same process is applied to the formula for x_1 (with which the standard quadratic formula does not have a problem), the rationalized numerator formula results in division by a quantity that is close to zero, which is a much worse situation.

Example 1.7 Cancellation Errors

To illustrate the effect of rounding, consider the problem of solving the quadratic equation $x^2 - 97\, x + 1 = 0$. The exact roots (shown to nine digits) and the approximations computed with rounding to five digits are summarized in the following table.

Effect of Rounding for Roots of Quadratic Equation

	x_1	x_2
Exact	96.9896896	0.0103103743
Standard quadratic formula rounded	96.990	0.01050
Rationalized quadratic formula rounded	95.238	0.01031

For the standard quadratic formula, rounding has a much larger effect on x_2 than on x_1, as expected. Using the rationalized quadratic formula for x_2 gives the correct result to the number of digits used in the rounded computation. On the other hand, if the rationalized formula is used for x_1, for which it is not appropriate, the results for the rounded computations approximate the true solution only to two digits.

Errors from Mathematical Approximations

Many numerical methods are based on a Taylor series expansion or on a Taylor polynomial approximation with remainder:

$$f(a + h) = f(a) + h f'(a) + \frac{h^2}{2!} f''(c), \text{ for some } c \in [a, a + h] \qquad (***)$$

In analyzing the error associated with using the trapezoid rule, a Taylor polynomial approximation is used for both the function being integrated and for the function defined as the indefinite integral.

Local Truncation Error

To introduce the analysis of the error produced by approximating a function by a simpler function, consider again the basic trapezoid rule for numerical integration, which we write now as

$$\int_a^{a+h} f(x)\, dx \approx \frac{h}{2} [f(a) + f(a + h)].$$

Define the function
$$F(t) = \int_a^t f(x)\, dx.$$

We can represent F by its Taylor polynomial with remainder, as follows

$$F(a + h) = F(a) + h F'(a) + \frac{h^2}{2!} F''(a) + \frac{h^3}{3!} F'''(c_1), \text{ for some } c_1 \in [a, a + h].$$

Since $F' = f$, $F'' = f'$, $F''' = f''$, . . . , and $F(a) = 0$, we have

$$\int_a^{a+h} f(x)\, dx = F(a + h) = h f(a) + \frac{h^2}{2!} f'(a) + \frac{h^3}{3!} f''(c_1) \qquad (1.1)$$

On the other hand, the Taylor polynomial with remainder for f is given by $(***)$, which gives after a little algebra, with the remainder evaluated at c_2

$$\frac{h}{2} [f(a + h) + f(a)] = h f(a) + \frac{h^2}{2} f'(a) + \frac{h^3}{4} f''(c_2) \qquad (1.2)$$

The error in the trapezoid rule is the difference of eqs. (1.1) and (1.2), or

$$\int_a^{a+h} f(x)\, dx - \frac{h}{2} [f(a + h) + f(a)] = \frac{h^3}{6} f''(c_1) - \frac{h^3}{4} f''(c_2)$$

We now show that if f is sufficiently smooth; that is, f'' is continuous and bounded on $[a, a + h]$, we can combine these two remainder terms.

If

$$m \le f''(x) \le M, \text{ for all } x \text{ on } [a, a + h]$$

then

$$\frac{h^3}{6} m \le \frac{h^3}{6} f''(c_1) \le \frac{h^3}{6} M,$$

and

$$\frac{h^3}{4} m \le \frac{h^3}{4} f''(c_2) \le \frac{h^3}{4} M,$$

so

$$\frac{-h^3}{12} m \le \frac{h^3}{6} f''(c_1) - \frac{h^3}{4} f''(c_2) \le \frac{-h^3}{12} M.$$

By the Intermediate Value Theorem (applied to f'') there is some point η in the interval $[a, a + h]$ such that

$$f''(\eta) = \frac{-12}{h^3} \left[\frac{h^3}{6} f''(c_1) - \frac{h^3}{4} f''(c_2) \right].$$

Thus we have

$$\int_a^{a+h} f(x)\, dx - \frac{h}{2} [f(a + h) + f(a)] = \frac{-h^3}{12} f''(\eta),$$

for some $\eta \in [a, a + h]$.

This is the local truncation error, which comes from truncating the Taylor series expansions, for one step of the trapezoid rule.

Global Truncation Error

To improve the results, it is useful to subdivide the interval into n equal subintervals $[a, x_1], [x_1, x_2], \ldots [x_{n-1}, b]$ and apply the method in each region. The length of each subinterval is $h = (b - a)/n$. This gives the more general (composite) trapezoid rule:

$$\int_a^b f(x)\, dx \approx \frac{h}{2} [f(a) + 2f(x_1) + \ldots + 2f(x_{n-1}) + f(b)] = T(h)$$

The global error is the result of adding the local error in each of the regions. If f is sufficiently smooth, the global error can be represented as $\dfrac{-(b - a)h^2}{12} f''(\eta)$ for some $a \le \eta \le b$. Thus, the global error for the trapezoid rule is proportional to h^2, and the method is $O(h^2)$. This means that if the step size is cut in half, the bound on the global truncation error is reduced by a factor of one-fourth.

Using the Truncation Error

Representation of the approximation error in terms of a term that depends on a derivative of the function, evaluated at some (unknown) point in the interval, and a power of the step size, are useful in several ways. It is sometimes not too difficult to find bounds on the derivative, so that the error term gives bounds on how large or how small the error can be on the interval. Even without finding bounds on the derivative, the power of the step size that occurs in the error term (that is, the order of the method) gives some indication as to how different methods may be expected to compare. A higher order method does not always give better results than a lower order method, but in general one can at least expect to obtain more improvement in the results by reducing the step size in a higher order method.

For some analysis it is useful to represent the truncation error as a series, by retaining all of the terms in the Taylor series expansion used in deriving the method. For some methods, including the trapezoid rule, the series can be expressed as a power series in h with coefficients that do not depend on the derivatives of the function. Especially if that power series depends only on even powers of h, as is the case for the trapezoid rule, and several other important numerical methods, there is a technique, known as acceleration (or extrapolation) by which two applications of the method may be combined to obtain an even more accurate result. The series form for the error in the trapezoid rule can be written as

$$\int_a^b f(x)\,dx - T(h) = a_2\,h^2 + a_4\,h^4 + a_6\,h^6 + \dots$$

1.2.3   Getting Better Results

Two of the important issues in judging a numerical method are the accuracy of the results and the amount of computational effort required to achieve them. For many methods, the accuracy of the results can be improved by reducing the step size; for example, taking more subdivisions of the interval of integration for the trapezoid method. However, the increased computational effort may be an unacceptably high price to pay for the improvement. Carried to an extreme, this approach also leads to round-off errors. We begin this section with a method, acceleration, which can be used to improve the results of certain basic approximation formulas (one of which is the trapezoid rule); it is considered further in Chapter 11. We also illustrate the effect on the results when an algorithm (such as Gaussian elimination) is applied carefully, or in an unwise manner. Finally, we introduce some of the ideas of computational efficiency.

Acceleration

A technique known as acceleration provides a method of improving the accuracy of an approximation formula $A(h)$ whose error can be expressed as

$$A - A(h) = a_2 h^2 + a_4 h^4 + a_6 h^6 + \dots,$$

where A is the true (unknown) value of the quantity being approximated by $A(h)$ and the coefficients of the error terms do not depend on the step size h. The trapezoid rule for integration is one such formula.

To apply acceleration, we form approximations to A using steps h and $h/2$. Let A_1 be the approximation using (the larger) step $h_1 = h$, and let A_2 be the approximation using step $h_2 = h/2$. Thus, we have

$$A - A_1 = a_2 h^2 + a_4 h^4 + a_6 h^6 + \dots$$

and

$$A - A_2 = a_2 (h/2)^2 + a_4 (h/2)^4 + a_6 (h/2)^6 + \dots$$

$$= \frac{1}{4} a_2 h^2 + \frac{1}{16} a_4 h^4 + \frac{1}{64} a_6 h^6 + \dots$$

After some simple algebra, these equations can be written as

$$A = A_1 + a_2 h^2 + a_4 h^4 + a_6 h^6 + \dots$$

and

$$4A = 4A_2 + a_2 h^2 + \frac{1}{4} a_4 h^4 + \frac{1}{16} a_6 h^6 + \dots$$

Subtracting the first equation from the second gives

$$3A = 4A_2 - A_1 + \frac{-3}{4} a_4 h^4 + \text{higher order terms}$$

Solving for A yields

$$A = \frac{4A_2 - A_1}{3} - \frac{1}{4} a_4 h^4 + \text{higher order terms}$$

Thus, the linear combination

$$A \approx \frac{4A_2 - A_1}{3}$$

of two applications of the $O(h^2)$ approximation, using step sizes h and $h/2$, gives an $O(h^4)$ approximation to A.

Acceleration may give very good results with only a simple application, but in fact the process can be repeated for even more improvement. To see how the second stage works, call the approximation generated by the first stage of acceleration, with step sizes h and $h/2$, B_1. Furthermore, we apply the original formula with $h_3 = h/4$, and call the result A_3. We call the result of combining A_2 and A_3 using first stage acceleration B_2. Thus

$$B_1 = \frac{4A_2 - A_1}{3} \quad \text{and} \quad B_2 = \frac{4A_3 - A_2}{3}$$

The error in using B_1 is a power series in even powers of h, starting with the h^4 term. We do not need the explicit form of the coefficients, so we write

$$A = B_1 + b_4 h^4 + b_6 h^6 + \dots$$

and

$$A = B_2 + b_4 (h/2)^4 + b_6 (h/2)^6 + \dots$$

$$= B_2 + \frac{1}{16} b_4 h^4 + \frac{1}{64} b_6 h^6 + \dots$$

since B_2 is produced by the same formula as B_1 but with the step sizes cut in half. Some simple algebra yields

$$A = \frac{16B_2 - B_1}{15} + c_6 h^6 + \text{higher order terms}$$

Thus, three applications of the original formula, with error $O(h^2)$, together with three linear combinations of those results has produced an approximation with error $O(h^6)$.

Example 1.8 Improving an Integral by Acceleration

To illustrate the use of acceleration for the trapezoid rule (generally known as *Richardson extrapolation*), we use the results obtained in Example 1.3. It is often convenient to show the results of acceleration as additional columns in a table. The first and second stages of acceleration are shown in the following table.

Step	Approx. integral	1st stage accel.	2nd stage accel.
$h = 2$	$A_1 = 1.037037$		
		$B_1 = 0.51233$	
$h = 1$	$A_2 = 0.6435185$		$C_1 = 0.4508619$
		$B_2 = 0.457037$	
$h = 1/2$	$A_3 = 0.5019074$		

Efficient Computations

Problems of interest for numerical methods often require many applications of certain computations that individually are not too time consuming. As computing capabilities have developed, the time required for basic operations, such as addition, subtraction, multiplication, and division, has been reduced dramatically. Not too many years ago multiplication and division required significantly more computational effort than addition and subtraction; it was common then to analyze algorithms based on counting only multiplications and divisions. The differential between multiplication and addition is much less now, and effort is usually evaluated in terms of floating-point operations (flops). In this section, we consider the computational effort (flops) for polynomial evaluation.

The straightforward evaluation of each term in the polynomial

$$P(x) = a_n x^n + a_{n-1} x^{n-1} + \ldots + a_1 x + a_0$$

requires n multiplications for the highest (n^{th} degree) term and one less for each lower term. The total number of multiplications for the polynomial is

$$\sum_{k=1}^{n} k = \frac{n(n+1)}{2}$$

There are n additions, giving the final count for the individual term evaluation as

$$\text{flops} = \frac{n(n+3)}{2}.$$

Of course, no one would evaluate each term independently if he or she were doing it by hand. Each power of x would utilize the value of the previous power; that is, $x^k = x \cdot x^{k-1}$. This approach requires $n-1$ multiplications by x, n multiplications by the coefficients, and n additions. The corresponding count of operations is flops $= 3n - 1$.

A more efficient algorithm, Horner's method for evaluating polynomials, is based on expressing $P(x)$ as $(x-c)Q(x) + P(c)$, where

$$P(x) = a_n x^n + a_{n-1} x^{n-1} + \ldots + a_1 x + a_0,$$

$$Q(x) = b_n x^{n-1} + b_{n-1} x^{n-2} + \ldots + b_2 x + b_1, \text{ and } b_0 = P(c).$$

Horner's Algorithm

Define $b_n = a_n$.
For $k = n - 1, \ldots 0$, compute
$b_k = a_k + b_{k+1} c$.
End $(b_0 = P(c))$

Each of the n stages requires one multiplication and one addition, giving flops $= 2n$. In some applications, the value of the derivative of P is also required. Since $P'(x) = (x - c)Q'(x) + Q(x)$, we have $P'(c) = Q(c)$, which can be found by applying Horner's algorithm to $Q(x)$.

Apply the Algorithm Carefully

The next example illustrates the fact that the way in which an algorithm is applied may affect the quality of the result.

Example 1.9 Careful Use of Algorithm Reduces Error

Consider again the system introduced in Example 1.2, but assume now that there is some error in the values on the right-hand side of the equation:

$$L_1: \qquad\qquad 4x + y = 6 \pm 0.4 \qquad\qquad (1.3)$$
$$M_1: \qquad\qquad -x + 5y = 9 \pm 0.4 \qquad\qquad (1.4)$$

After Gaussian elimination, the system becomes

$$L_1: \qquad\qquad 4x + y = 6 \pm 0.4, \qquad\qquad (1.3)$$
$$M_2: \qquad\qquad 5.25y = 10.5 \pm 0.5. \qquad\qquad (1.5)$$

Solving eq. (1.5) for y gives $y = 2 \pm 0.0952 \ldots$; thus (to four decimal places) $y = 2.0952$ or 1.9048 and backsubstitution gives the four points that determine the parallelogram containing the solution (as shown in Figure 1.9b).

$$(1.0762, 2.0952), (0.8762, 2.0952), (1.1238, 1.9048), (0.9238, 1.9048).$$

This region is very close to the region containing the actual solution, shown in Figure 1.9a. The true solution of this system is contained within the parallelogram determined by the points

$$(1.0762, 2.0952), (0.8857, 2.057), (1.1143, 1.9420), (0.9238, 1.9048).$$

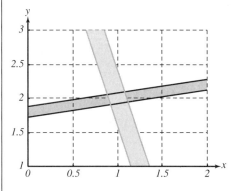

FIGURE 1.9a   Graphical representation of a linear system.

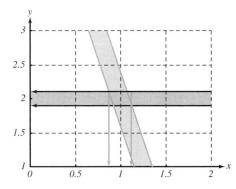

FIGURE 1.9b   Graph of eqs. (1.3) and (1.5).

On the other hand, if the equations are listed in the opposite order, and the computations of Gaussian elimination are carried out without modification, the final result is much less accurate. The system is now

M_1: $\qquad\qquad\qquad -x + 5y = 9 \pm 0.4,$ $\qquad\qquad$ (1.4)
L_1: $\qquad\qquad\qquad 4x + y = 6 \pm 0.4.$ $\qquad\qquad$ (1.3)

After Gaussian elimination, the system becomes

M_1: $\qquad\qquad\qquad -x + 5y = 9 \pm 0.4$ $\qquad\qquad$ (1.4)
L_2: $\qquad\qquad\qquad\quad 21y = 42 \pm 2$ $\qquad\qquad$ (1.6)

Solving eq. (1.6) for y gives $y = 2 \pm 0.0952$, so (to four decimal places) $y = 2.0952$ or 1.9048, as before. However, now backsubstitution results in the four points

$$(1.076, 2.0952), (0.124, 1.9048), (1.876, 2.0952), (0.9238, 1.9048).$$

As shown in Figure 1.10b, the region determined by these points is not very close to the region containing the actual solution, shown in Figure 1.10a. The true solution of this system is contained within the parallelogram determined by the points

$$(1.0762, 2.0952), (0.8857, 2.057), (1.1143, 1.9420), (0.9238, 1.9048).$$

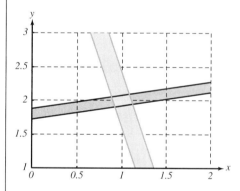

FIGURE 1.10a   Graphical representation of a linear system with uncertainties.

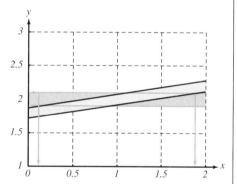

FIGURE 1.10b   Graph of eqs. (1.4) and (1.6).

Note that as in the previous solution, two of the points are the same for the true solution and the solution by Gaussian elimination. However, the other two points are much more different in this solution.

A numerical algorithm is a systematic procedure for carrying out a set of computations. The numerical methods described in the remainder of this text are presented as detailed algorithms. These algorithms may serve as the basis for solving simple problems by hand (or calculator). They also provide the framework for writing simple computer programs to implement the methods, using any of a wide variety of programming languages (e.g., Basic, C, Fortran, Java, etc.) or computing environments (e.g., MATLAB, Mathcad, *Mathematica*, etc.).

There are several fundamental structures that occur frequently in computer programs that implement numerical methods. These are summarized in section 1.3.1. The notation used in the algorithms is discussed in section 1.3.2. Finally, we conclude with some simple examples of computer programs (in a variety of languages) to implement an algorithm for the trapezoid rule for numerical integration.

1.3.1   Fundamental Elements of a Computer Program

Input/Output

A computer program to implement a numerical method must specify the input values for various parameters, the definitions of other functions used in the procedure, and the computed value(s) of the variable(s). Together these parts of the program are often called the I/O (input/output). In the algorithms given throughout this text, I/O is indicated as *Input* (followed by a list of variable and function names and descriptions) at the beginning of the algorithm and *Return* (followed by a list of variables whose values should be returned from the procedure) at the end of the algorithm. Depending on the programming language used for implementing the algorithm, and the level of generality desired for the program, input values may be defined in the program, or passed as arguments in the call to the program.

Declarations

In many programming languages, it is necessary to specify a type for each variable used in the program (integer, real, complex, etc.). In some languages there is a default type (which may depend on the name of the variable); in other languages every variable type must be declared. Also, again depending on the language, it may be necessary to specify the dimensions of any arrays (vectors or matrices) before they are used in the program.

Computation

Loops

The main body of a computer program consists of statements that perform the computations to implement the algorithm. In many cases these computations are performed repeatedly, either for a specified range of values for some variable, or until some condition is satisfied. Such repeated computation is usually controlled by a looping structure. The algorithms given in this text are presented using two types of loops: *For-loops* or *While-loops.* A For-loop is executed for a specified range of values of the looping index (unless some condition is encountered that causes the program to exit the loop.) A While-loop is executed as long as the controlling condition is true.

Conditional Execution

There are also cases in which a statement (or group of statements) are to be executed under certain conditions, and not under other conditions. The algorithms presented in this text assume the existence of several forms of conditional execution. These are the *If* statement (or the more general *If/Else* statement), the *If/Break,* and the *If/Return* (or *If/Error*) statements. The If statement executes the statements that follow if the condition is true. The Break statement causes the program to exit the loop in which the break occurs. The Return or Error statements cause the program to terminate (with an error message in the case of the Error statement). Examples of the form each of these takes in the algorithms are given in the next section.

Matrix and Vector Computation

Many mathematical procedures are described in terms of vector and matrix operations. Computer programs vary greatly in the ease with which they carry out such operations. In the following algorithms, we assume that the computer language being used either supports standard matrix-vector operations, or that subroutines are available (provided by the user, if necessary) for these operations. More details are given in the next section on the operations.

1.3.2   Algorithms

The algorithms given throughout this text are designed to facilitate implementing the numerical method in a simple computer program. Each algorithm follows the same general structure described above for programs.

Comments

Comments are shown in italics.

Input/Output

Input

Values of parameters, and the names of other functions used by the program implementing the algorithm, are listed at the beginning of each algorithm. These would usually be passed to the program as input arguments. These input values may also be given in the program if desired, but that would make the program much less general.

Return

The value (or values) to be returned by a program implementing the algorithm are listed at the end of the algorithm. In addition, intermediate output could be displayed or written to a file, as desired.

Declarations

The dimensions of any matrix (vector or two-dimensional array) input to the algorithm are given in the comment statements defining the matrix. Since the requirements for declarations of variable type and array dimensions vary greatly from one computer language to another, the algorithms do not include such declarations explicitly.

Computation

Initializations

Parameters that are derived from input values are computed at the beginning of each algorithm.

Looping Structures

Most numerical methods involve carrying out a set of computations for a range of values of some variable. We assume that two such structures are supported, which we designate as "For-loops" and "While-loops."

For-loops. In a For-loop, the computations are carried out for all values of the looping index, from the beginning value to the ending value, unless some condition occurs (conditional execution is discussed next) that causes the process to exit the loop. In general, if such an exit occurs, the value of the looping index is not preserved outside the loop. We indicate a For-loop as

```
For i = 1 to max
        Statement 1
        . . .
        Statement k
End
```

While-loops. In a While-loop, the computations are continued as long as the specified condition is true. Care should be taken that the computations will eventually terminate. We indicate a While-loop as

```
While (condition)
        Statement 1
        . . .
        Statement k
End
```

Conditional Execution

Another key feature of any computer programming environment or language that is suitable for implementing numerical methods is the ability to control execution of one or more statements, depending on certain conditions. We use three types of conditional execution statements in the algorithms. They are If (or If/Else), If/Break, and If/Return (or If/Error).

If and If/Else. The basic If/Then statement allows a statement or group of statements to be executed if a specified condition is true. The statements are skipped if the condition is false. It is indicated as

    If (condition)
       Statement 1
       . . .
       Statement k
    End

If only a single statement is to be executed if the condition is true, it is common to use a condensed (single line) form, given as

    If (condition) Statement

A slightly more detailed form may be designated as If/Then/Else. This form allows a statement or group of statements to be executed if a specified condition is true, and a second statement or group of statements to be executed if the condition is false. It is indicated as

    If (condition)
       Statement 1
       . . .
       Statement k
    Else
       Statement k+1
       . . .
       Statement m
    End

If/Break and If/Return. The If/Break and If/Return (or If/Error) structures allow the program execution to jump out of a Loop, or to Return (with an error message if appropriate). The If/Break structure exits from the loop in which it occurs. They are indicated as

    If (condition) Break

    If (condition) Return

Or

    If (condition) Error "message"

Matrix and Vector Computation

Vector and matrix operations are extremely important in many numerical methods. In the following algorithms, we assume that all basic matrix operations are defined. If they are not supported in the particular programming language one is using, then the corresponding parts of the algorithm will need to be expanded to carry out the required operations.

For simplicity, we assume that the element in the ith row, j^{th} column of matrix M may be accessed as

$$M(i, j)$$

Furthermore, we assume that the entire i^{th} row can be accessed as

$$M(i, :)$$

Similarly, the jth column is indicated as

$$M(:, j)$$

If it is important to indicate that a vector is a row vector, we may do so by designating it as a 1-by-n matrix, that is, as

$$v(1, :)$$

Similarly, a column vector would be given as

$$v(:, 1)$$

However, in other settings, we will indicate a vector with only one index, so that the ith element would be

$$v(i)$$

We assume that arrays may be indexed beginning with either 0 or 1, (or any other value) depending what is most convenient for a particular method.

Arithmetic Operations

Multiplication is shown by the symbol *
Exponentiation is shown by the symbol ^

Mathematical Functions

Absolute value is indicated as | x |
Natural exponential is indicated as exp(x)
Natural logarithm is indicated as ln(x)

Sample Algorithms for the Trapezoid Rule

Many of the elements described above are illustrated in the following algorithms, which describe the process of computing the numerical approximation to the integral of a function $f(x)$, using the trapezoid rule.

In order to incorporate a test for convergence, the first algorithm computes a sequence of values of the integral, using more and more subdivisions of the interval of integration. This could form the basis for using acceleration to obtain even better approximations.

The second algorithm describes the standard trapezoid rule, computing an approximation to the integral using a specified number of subintervals.

Trapezoid Rule (Iterative Form)

Input

f	*name of function to be integrated*	
	definition supplied in separate program/function	
a	*left-hand end of interval of integration*	
b	*right-hand end of interval of integration*	
kmax	*program will compute integral for* $n = 2, 2^2, \ldots 2^{kmax}$	
tol	*program will terminate computation if the difference*	
	between two successive approximate integrals is less than tol	

Compute
For k = 1 to kmax
    n = 2^k
    h = (b−a)/n
    S = f(a) + **f**(b)

    For *i* = 1 to n−1
        x(i) = a + h i
        S = S + 2*f(x(i))
    End

    I(k) = h*S/2

    If((k>1)&(| I(k) − I(k−1) | < tol)) Break

End

Return
    I   *vector of values of trapezoid approximation to the integral*

Input

    f   *name of function to be integrated*
                   definition supplied in separate program/function
    a   *left-hand end of interval of integration*
    b   *right-hand end of interval of integration*
    n   *number of subintervals to be used in integration*

Initialize

$$h = (b-a)/n$$
$$S = f(a) + f(b)$$

Compute

For i = 1 to n−1
        x(i) = a + h i
        S = S + 2*f(x(i))
End

    I = h*S/2

Return

    I   *trapezoid approximation to the integral*

1.3.3   Sample Programs

To illustrate the variety of ways in which the algorithms in this text may be implemented, we give simple programs for the trapezoid rule (either standard or iterative) in several different computer languages. Fortran and C continue to be the most common languages for large-scale numerical computing. Java and Basic are widely used in introductory programming classes. Software packages such as MATLAB, Mathcad, and *Mathematica* include built-in programs for many numerical methods, as well as the capability for the user to write simple programs. MATLAB is especially well suited for a wide range of numerical applications. Finally, programmable calculators and spreadsheets are suitable for many small numerical problems.

Visual Basic Program for the Trapezoid Rule (Iterative Form)

```
'Demonstrate trapezoidal integration of the function x^-3

Option Explicit

Private Sub cmdIntegrate_Click()
    Dim a As Double, b As Double, tol As Double
    Dim kmax As Integer

    'get the values from the text boxes
    a = txtStart
    b = txtEnd
    kmax = txtIterations
    tol = txtTolerance

    'calculate and print the results
    picResult.Print IntegrateTrapz(a, b, kmax, tol)
End Sub

'trapezoidal integration
Private Function IntegrateTrapz(a As Double, b As Double, kmax As
                               Integer, _tol As Double) As Double
    Dim n As Integer, k As Integer, i As Integer
    Dim h As Double, S As Double, last As Double
    Dim x As Double, diff As Double

    'start iterations
    Do
        n = 2 ^ k
        h = (b - 1) / n
        S = f(a) - f(b)

        For i = 1 To n - 1
            x = a + h * i
            S = S + 2 * f(x)
        Next i

        IntegrateTrapz = h * S / 2
        diff = Abs(i - last)
        last = IntegrateTrapz

        k = k + 1
    Loop While k <= kmax And diff > tol

End Function

'function definition
Private Function f(x As Double) As Double
    f - x ^ ( 3)
End Function
```

Java Program for Trapezoid Rule (Iterative Form)

```
/*
   Trapezoid.java

   main for demo of Trapezoid Rule Algorithm in Java

      f - function to integrate,
      a - left hand end of the interval of integration
      b - right hand end of the interval of integration
      kmax - maximum iterations
      tol - tolerance to stop iterations

      My_Function - class defining function to integrate
      IntegrateTrapz - class to perform trapezoidal rule integration
*/

public class Trapezoid {

   public static void main(String[] args) {

      double a = 1.0;
      double b = 3.0;
      int kmax = 20;
      double tol = 0.00001;
      My_Function f = new My_Function();
      IntegrateTrapz t = new IntegrateTrapz();
      double result = t.integrate(f, a, b, kmax, tol);
      System.out.println("Trapezoidal integration of "
         + f.toString() + " from a = " + a + " to b = " + b + " is
         " + result);
   }
}

/*
   IntegrateTrapz.java

   Uses the trapezoidal rule to integrate a function.

   f - function to integrate,
   a - left hand end of the interval of integration
   b - right hand end of the interval of integration
   kmax - maximum iterations
   tol - tolerance to stop iterations
*/

public class IntegrateTrapz {
```

```java
public double integrate(My_Function f, double a, double b, int
    kmax, double tol) {

    double x, diff, I, lastI=0.0;
    int n;
    int k = 1;

    do {
        n = (int)Math.pow(2,k);
        double h = (b-a)/n;
        double S = f.valueAt(a) + f.valueAt(b);

        for(int i=1; i <= n-1; i++) {
            x = a + h*i;
            S += 2*f.valueAt(x);
        }

        I = h*S/2;
        diff = Math.abs(I-lastI);
        System.out.println("I, diff = " + I + " " + diff);
        lastI = I;

        k++;

    } while(k<= kmax && diff > tol);

    return I;

  }

}

/*
   MyFunction.java

   Returns the double value of the function evaluated at x.
*/

public class My_Function {

public double valueAt(double x) {
return Math.pow(x, -3);
}

public String toString() {
return "x^-3";
}
}
```

C++ Program for Trapezoid Rule (Iterative Form)

```cpp
/*
    Trapezoid.cpp
    Defines the entry point for the console application.
*/

#include "IntegrateTrapz.h"
#include "My_Function.h"
#include <iostream>
using namespace std;

int main()
{
    double a = 1.0;
    double b = 3.0;
    int kmax = 20;
    double tol = 0.00001;

    My_Function f;
    IntegrateTrapz t;

    double result = t.integrate(f, a, b, kmax, tol);
    cout << "Trapezoidal integration of " << f.toString() << "
        from a = "
        << a << " to b = " << b << " is " << result << endl;
    return (0);
}

/*
My_Function.h
Returns the double value of the function evaluated at x.
*/
#include <string>
#include <cmath>
using namespace std;

#ifndef MYFUNCTION_H
#define MYFUNCTION_H

//class declaration
class My_Function {

public:
    My_Function() {};
    double valueAt(double x);
    string toString(void);
};

//class methods
double My_Function::valueAt(double x) {
    return (pow(x,-3.0));
```

```
    }
    string My_Function::toString() {
        return ("x^-3");
    }
    #endif

    // IntegrateTrapz.h
    #include "My_Function.h"
    #include <iostream>
    #include <cmath>
    using namespace std;

    #ifndef INTEGRATETRAPZ_H
    #define INTEGRATETRAPZ_H

    //class definition
    class IntegrateTrapz
    {
    public:
        IntegrateTrapz() {};
        double integrate(My_Function f, double a, double b, int kmax,
            double tol);
    };

    //class methods
    double IntegrateTrapz::integrate(My_Function f, double a, double
    b, int kmax, double tol)
    {
        double x, diff, I, lastI=0.0;
        int n;
        int k = 1;

        do {
            n = pow(2,k);
            double h = (b-a)/n;
            double S = f.valueAt(a) + f.valueAt(b);

            for(int i=1; i <= n-1; i++) {
                x = a + h*i;
                S += 2*f.valueAt(x);
            }

            I = h*S/2;
            diff = fabs(I-lastI);
            cout << "I, diff = " << I << " " << diff << endl;
            lastI = I;

            k++;
        } while(k<= kmax && diff > tol);
        return (I);
    }
    #endif
```

C Program for Trapezoid Rule (Iterative Form)

```c
#include <stdio.h
#include <math.h
double valueAt(double x);
double integrate(double a, double b, int kmax, double tol);
int main()
{
    double a = 1.0;
    double b = 3.0;
    int kmax = 20;
    double tol = 0.00001;
    double result = integrate(a, b, kmax, tol);
    printf("Trapezoidal integration of x^-3 from a = %3.2f to
        b = %3.2f is %8.8f\n" , a, b, result);
    return (0);
}
double valueAt(double x)
{
    return (pow(x,-3.0));
}
double integrate(double a, double b, int kmax, double tol)
{
    double x, diff, I, lastI=0.0;
    int n;
    int k = 1;
    do {
        n = pow(2,k);
        double h = (b-a)/n;
        double S = valueAt(a) + valueAt(b);
        for(int i=1; i <= n-1; i++) {
            x = a + h*i;
            S += 2*valueAt(x); }
            I = h*S/2;
            diff = fabs(I-lastI);
            printf("I, diff = %8.8f %8.8f\n", I, diff);
            lastI = I; k++; }
    while(k<= kmax && diff tol);
    return (I);
}
```

Fortran Program for Trapezoid Rule (iterative form)

```fortran
C*****************************************************************
C       Sample program that calls trap_rule
C*****************************************************************
      external f
      real g(100)
      n=15
      call trap_rule(f,1.0,3.0,n,0.0001,g)
      do i=1,n
        write(*,*)g(i)
      enddo
      stop
      end
C*****************************************************************
      subroutine trap_rule(f,a,b,kmax,tol,g)
C*****************************************************************
C  Input:  f:      a function, defined externally, to be integrated
C          a:      a real value for the lower limit of integration
C          b:      a real value for the upper limit of integration
C          kmax:   an integer value for the maximum number of iterations
C          tol:    a real value for the closeness of approximation
C  Output: g:      array of real values for the intermediate integral values.
C*********************************************************************
      real g(kmax)
      external f
C  Initialize local variables
      k=1
      delf=10.0*tol
C  Begin iterative loop
      do while ((k.le.kmax).and.(delf.ge.tol))
        n=2**k
        h=(b-a)/n
        S=f(a)+f(b)
        do i=1,n-1
           x=a+h*i
           S=S+2.0*f(x)
        enddo
        g(k)=h*S/2.0
        if (k.gt.1) delf=abs(g(k)-g(k-1))
      k=k+1
      enddo
      return
      end
C
      real function f(x)
C*********************************************************************
C   Input:    x:      the value at which f is evaluated
C   Output:   f:      the value of the function at x
C*********************************************************************
      f=x**(-3.0)
      return
      end
```

Chapter 1 Foundations

MATLAB Program for Trapezoid Rule (Iterative Form)

The following function returns the vector I. In calling the function, the name of the function to be integrated is enclosed in single quotes. Values for the parameters a, b, and *kmax* may be specified before the function is called, or the values may be given in the function call.

```
function I = Trap( f, a, b, kmax, tol)
%     f        function to be integrated
%              definition given in separate function
%     a        left hand end of interval of integration
%     b        right hand end of interval of integration
%     kmax     compute for n = 2,... 2^kmax, unless change is less
%              than tol
%     tol      terminate computation if abs(I(k) - I(k-1)) < tol

for k = 1:kmax
      n = 2^k
      h = (b-a)/n
      S = feval(f, a) + feval(f,b)
      for i = 1 : n-1
          x(i) = a + h*i
          S = S + 2*feval(f, x(i))
      end
      I(k) = h*S/2
      if ((k>1)&(abs(I(k)-I(k-1))<tol)
            disp('trapezoid method has converged')
            break
      end
end
```

The following function evaluates the function $y = 1/x^3$.

```
function y = my_func( x)
%    example function for trapezoid rule
y = x.^(-3)
```

Mathcad Function for Trapezoid Rule (Standard Form)

$$\text{Trap}(f,a,b,n) := \begin{vmatrix} h \leftarrow \dfrac{(b-a)}{n} \\[2mm] S \leftarrow f(a) \\[2mm] \text{for } i \in 1..n-1 \qquad \text{if } n > 1 \\[2mm] \qquad \begin{vmatrix} x_i \leftarrow a + h \cdot i \\[2mm] S \leftarrow S + 2 \cdot f\left(x_i\right) \end{vmatrix} \\[2mm] S \leftarrow S + f(b) \\[2mm] I \leftarrow \dfrac{h \cdot S}{2} \\[2mm] I \end{vmatrix}$$

Mathematica Module for the Trapezoid Rule (Standard Form)

The following functions implement the more basic form of the trapezoid rule, in which the number of subintervals n is given. The use of a Module allows one or more variables to be local to the function TrapezoidSum. The local variables are listed enclosed in brackets in the first line of the Module. In this case the variables *h*, *S*1, and *S*2 are declared to be local.

```
TrapezoidSum[f_, a_, b_, n_] :=
    Module[ { h, S1, S2},
            h = (b-a)/n;
            S1 = f[a] + f[b]  ;
            S2 = 2*Sum[(f[a+i*h] ), {i, 1, n-1}];
            N[ (S1 + S2)*h/2]     ]
```

The following function plots the function *f*, and the straight-line approximations to *f* used in forming the trapezoid rule approximation to the integral. In this case, *h* is declared to be local, and given the value $(b - a)/n$ simultaneously.

```
TrapezoidDisplay[f_,a_,b_,n_ ]:=
    Module[   {h = (b-a)/n},
            Show[Plot[f[x], {x,a,b}, DisplayFunction->Identity],
                Graphics[Table[Line[{{a+h*i,0},
                                        {a+delx*i,f[a+h*i]},
                                        {a+h*(i+1),f[a+h*(i+1)]},
                                        {a+h*(i+1),0},
                                        {a+h*i,0}}],
                            {i,0,n-1}]],
                    DisplayFunction->$DisplayFunction]   ]
```

TI-83 Program for the Trapezoid Rule (Standard Form)

The following program implements the trapezoid rule on a TI-83 calculator.

```
ClrHome
Disp "TRAPEZOIDAL RULE"
Input "A=",A
Input "B=",B
Input "N=",N
(B-A)/N→H
Y/(A)+Y/(B)→S
For(I,1,N-1)
A+H*I→T
S+2*Y/(T)→S
End
H*S/2→I
ClrHome
Disp "TRAP AREA",I
Disp "APPROX AREA",fnIntY/,X,A,B)
Stop
```

The following calculator screens show the definition of the function to be integrated, the required input to the function, and the results from the program.

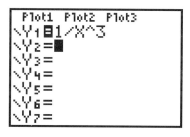

TI-92 Program for the Trapezoid Rule (Standard Form)

The following program implements the trapezoid rule on a TI-92 calculator.

```
( )
Prgm
©Program written by Sharon Barrs
ClrDraw
ClrGraph
ClrIO
FnOff
Disp "This program approximates the"
Disp "net signed area between a function"
Disp "and the x-axis on an interval [a,b]"
Disp "using the trapezoidal rule with"
Disp "n subintervals."
Disp ""
Disp "Press <ENTER> to continue."
Pause
ClrIO
InputStr "Enter the function of x.",w
expr(w)y1(x)
Input "Enter the value of a.",a
Input "Enter the value of b.",b
Input "Enter the value of n.",n
ClrIO
(b-a)/n→h
y1(a)+y1(b) → s
For i,1,n-1
a+h*iØxi
s+2*y1(xi) → s
EndFor
h*s/2→i
Disp "The approximate net signed area is"
Disp string(i)&" or"
Disp string(approx(i))&"."
∫(y1(x),x,a,b) →i
Disp "The actual net signed area is"
Disp string(i)&" or"
Disp string(approx(i))&"."
Disp "Press <ENTER> to continue."
Pause
ClrIO
Disp "Press <2nd> <ESC> to QUIT and return to"
Disp "the home screen."
EndPrgm
```

The screens below show the calculator display as the program is called, and executed.

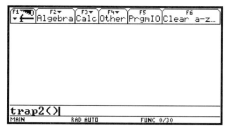

call the program

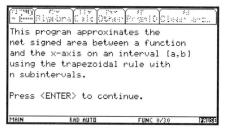

brief description of the program

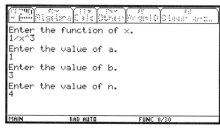

interactive instructions

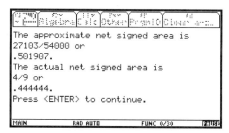

results from trapezoid rule,
and from antidifferentiation if possible

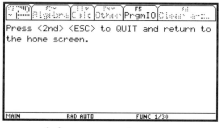

end of program execution

Fixed-Point Iteration

To find a numerical approximation to $\sqrt{c}$ by fixed-point iteration, use

$$x = g(x) = \frac{1}{2}\left(x + \frac{c}{x}\right),$$

so that the iteration formula is

$$x_k = \frac{1}{2}\left(x_{k-1} + \frac{c}{x_{k-1}}\right).$$

Trapezoid Rule

$$\int_a^b f(x)\,dx \approx \frac{b-a}{2}[f(a) + f(b)].$$

Horner's Algorithm

A computationally efficient method of evaluating the polynomial

$$P(x) = a_n x^n + a_{n-1} x^{n-1} + \ldots + a_1 x + a_0,$$

at $x = c$ is given by Horner's algorithm:

> Begin by setting $b_n = a_n$.
> For $k = n-1, \ldots, 0$,
> $$b_k = a_k + b_{k+1} c.$$
> The result is $b_0 = P(c)$.

$P(x) = (x-c)\,Q(x) + P(c)$; the coefficients of $Q(x)$, are $b_n, \ldots b_1$. $P'(c)$ can be found by evaluating $Q(c)$ using Horner's method.

Gerschgorin Circle Theorem

All eigenvalues of the matrix A lie within the union of the disks bounded by the n circles, $C_1, \ldots C_n$, where circle C_i has center at a_{ii} and radius $r_i = -|a_{ii}| + \sum_{j=1}^{n}|a_{ij}|$.

Acceleration

The order of convergence for some approximation formulas, including the trapezoid rule for numerical integration, can be improved by combining the approximate values obtained with step size h and step size $h/2$. If we denote these approximations as $T(h)$ and $T(h/2)$, respectively, a better estimate of the desired result is given by

$$T \approx \frac{1}{3}[4\,T(h/2) - T(h)].$$

The trapezoid rule is a formula of order $O(h^2)$, but the extrapolated value is an approximation of order $O(h^4)$.

Much of the historical discussion in the introduction to this chapter is based on material in the following excellent books:

Eves, H., *Great Moments in Mathematics* (v. 1, before 1650; v. 2, after 1650). Mathematical Association of America, Washington, DC, 1983.

Smith, D. E., *A Source Book in Mathematics.* Dover, New York, 1959.

Struik, D. J., *A Concise History of Mathematics*, 4th ed., Dover, New York, 1987.

For historical notes related to calculus or differential equations, the following books are especially recommended:

Boyer, C. B., *The History of the Calculus and Its Conceptual Development,* Dover, New York, 1949.

Simmons, G. F., *Calculus with Analytic Geometry.* McGraw-Hill, New York, 1985.

Simmons, G. F., *Differential Equations with Applications and Historical Notes,* McGraw-Hill, New York, 1972.

Among the references for more theoretical and advanced treatments of numerical methods are:

Atkinson, K. E., *An Introduction to Numerical Analysis*, 2d ed., John Wiley, New York, 1989.

Dahlquist. G., and A. Bjorck, *Numerical Methods* (Trans. by Ned Anderson), Prentice-Hall, Englewood Cliffs, NJ, 1974.

Isaacson, E., and H. B. Keller, *Analysis of Numerical Methods.* Dover, New York, 1994 (Originally published by Wiley, 1966).

Ralston, A., and P. Rabinowitz, *A First Course in Numerical Analysis*, 2d ed., McGraw-Hill, New York, 1978.

Press, W. H., S. A. Teukolsky, W. T. Vetterling, and B. P. Flannery, *Numerical Recipes in C: The Art of Scientific Computing*, 2d ed. Cambridge University Press, Cambridge, 1992.

For further discussion on programming languages, see

Chapman, S. J., *Fortran 90/95 for Scientists and Engineers,* McGraw-Hill, New York, 1997.

Deitel, H. M., and P. J. Deitel, *C++ How to Program*, 3rd ed., Prentice-Hall, Upper Saddle River, NJ, 2001.

Deitel, H. M., and P. J. Deitel, *Java How to Program*, 4th ed., Prentice-Hall, Upper Saddle River, NJ, 2001.

Deitel, H. M., P. J., Deitel, and T. R. Nieto, *Visual Basic 6 How to Program,* Prentice-Hall, Upper Saddle River, NJ, 1998.

Ellis, T. M. R., I. R. Phillips, and T. M. Lahey, *Fortran 90 Programming,* Addison-Wesley, Reading, MA, 1994.

Ettcr, D. M., *Engineering Problem Solving with Ansi C,* Prentice-Hall, Englewood Cliffs, NJ, 1999.

Etter, D. M. and D. C. Kuncicky, *Introduction to Matlab,* Prentice-Hall, Englewood Cliffs, NJ, 1999.

Larsen, R. W., *Introduction to Mathcad 2000,* Prentice-Hall, Upper Saddle River, NJ, 2001.

Nyhoff, L. R., *Fortran 90 for Engineers and Scientists,* Prentice-Hall, Upper Saddle River, NJ, 1996.

For problems P1.1 to P1.5, investigate the use of Gaussian elimination to solve systems of two equations in two unknowns.

   a.   Solve the system as given.
   b.   Graph the given equations, and graph the transformed second equation after the elimination step.
   c.   Repeat Parts a and b for the system consisting of the same two equations, but given in reverse order.

P1.1 $4x + y = 6$,
       $-x + 2y = 3$.

P1.2 $4x + y = 9$,
       $x + 2y = 4$.

P1.3 $3x + y = 4$,
       $6x + 7y = 13$

P1.4 $5x + y = 17$,
       $-10x + 17y = 4$.

P1.5 $3x + y = 6$,
       $x + 5y = 16$.

For problems P1.6 to 1.10, investigate the convergence of the given fixed-point iteration formula.

   a.   Show the first three iterations graphically.
   b.   Compute the first three iterates algebraically
   c.   Determine whether the conditions of the fixed-point convergence theorem are satisfied.

P1.6 $x = g(x) = 0.5\, x^3 + 0.3$.

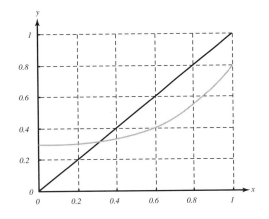

P1.7 $x = g(x) = \sin(2x)$.

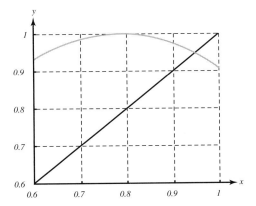

P1.8 $x = g(x) = -0.5x^3 + 0.8$.

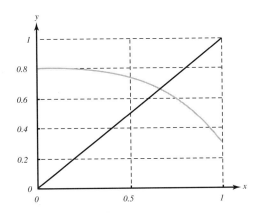

P1.9 $x = g(x) = 1 - x^2$.

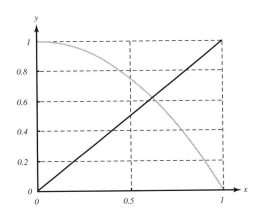

P1.10 $x = g(x) = \dfrac{1}{2} + \dfrac{1}{2} + \sin(3x)$

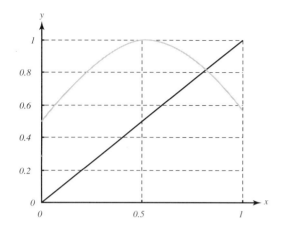

Problems P1.11 to P1.15 illustrate the use of the Gerschgorin theorem to find bounds on the eigenvalues of a matrix. Find the Gerschgorin circles for each row of the given matrix. Graph the regions, and give bounds on the eigenvalues.

P1.11 $\mathbf{A} = \begin{bmatrix} 1 & 1/8 & 1/4 \\ 1/2 & 2 & 0 \\ 0 & 0 & 3 \end{bmatrix}$.

P1.12 $\mathbf{A} = \begin{bmatrix} 1 & 3/4 & 0 \\ 1/2 & 2 & -1/8 \\ 0 & 1/8 & 3 \end{bmatrix}$.

P1.13 $\mathbf{A} = \begin{bmatrix} 1 & 1/4 & 0 \\ 1/4 & 2 & 1/4 \\ 0 & 1/4 & 3 \end{bmatrix}$.

P1.14 $\mathbf{A} = \begin{bmatrix} 1 & 1/3 & 1/3 \\ 1/4 & 2 & 1/4 \\ 1/2 & 1/4 & 3 \end{bmatrix}$.

P1.15 $\mathbf{A} = \begin{bmatrix} 1 & -1/2 & 0 \\ 1/2 & 2 & 1/8 \\ 0 & 1/8 & 3 \end{bmatrix}$.

P1.16 to P1.17 illustrate the effect of round-off error in adding numbers of differing magnitudes.
  a. Add from left to right, rounding to three digits at each step.
  b. Add from right to left, rounding to three digits at each step.
  c. Compare the relative error for the results from parts a and b.

P1.16 $100 + 0.49 + 0.49$

P1.17 $10.0 + 0.333 + 0.333 + 0.333$

Problems P1.18 to P1.20 illustrate the effect of round-off in the quadratic formula.
  a. Use the standard quadratic formula with rounding.
  b. Use the rationalized-numerator quadratic formula with rounding.
  c. Compare the results from parts a and b with the results found without rounding.

P1.18 $x^2 - 973\,x + 1 = 0$. (Round to three digits.)
P1.19 $x^2 - 57\,x + 1 = 0$. (Round to four digits.)
P1.20 $x^2 - 23\,x + 1 = 0$. (Round to four digits.)

Problems P1.21 to P1.25 illustrate the use of the trapezoid rule for numerical integration.
  a. Approximate the given integral, using the basic trapezoid rule with $h = b - a$.
  b. Approximate the integral, using the composite trapezoid rule with $h = \dfrac{b - a}{2}$.
  c. Improve the approximation by acceleration, using results from parts a and b.

P1.21 Find $\displaystyle\int_0^2 \frac{1}{1 + x^2}\,dx$.

P1.22 Find $\displaystyle\int_0^{\pi/2} \sin(x)\,dx$.

P1.23 Find $\displaystyle\int_0^2 2^x\,dx$.

P1.24 Find $\displaystyle\int_0^2 e^{-x^2}\,dx$.

P1.25 Find $\displaystyle\int_0^{\pi/2} \frac{3}{1 + \sin(x)}\,dx$.

Problems P1.26 to P1.30 illustrate the effect of the order of the equations in Gaussian elimination (with error).

   a. Solve the equations in the order given; determine bounds on x and y.
Graph the given equations, and the transformed second equation

   b. Solve the equations in reverse order; determine bounds on x and y.
Graph the given equations, and the transformed second equation

   c. Compare the relative error in the values of x and y found in parts a and b.

P1.26 $4x + y = 6 \pm 0.1$,
$-x + 2y = 3 \pm 0.1$.

P1.27 $4x + y = 9 \pm 0.1$,
$x + 2y = 4 \pm 0.1$.

P1.28 $3x + y = 4 \pm 0.1$,
$6x + 7y = 13 \pm 0.1$.

P1.29 $5x + y = 17 \pm 0.2$,
$-10x + 17y = 4 \pm 0.2$.

P1.30 $3x + y = 6 \pm 0.2$,
$x + 5y = 16 \pm 0.2$.

EXTEND YOUR UNDERSTANDING

U1.1 For each of the Problems P1.6 to P1.10 for which the conditions of the theorem are not satisfied on [0, 1], investigate the following questions.

   a. Is there a starting value of x for which the iterations do not converge? (Show this on the graph.)

   b. Is there a subinterval on which the conditions are satisfied?

U1.2 Use the Gerschgorin circle theorem to show that, for any matrix

$$\mathbf{A} = \begin{bmatrix} 1+2r & -r & 0 \\ -r & 1+2r & -r \\ 0 & -r & 1+2r \end{bmatrix},$$

any eigenvalue m satisfies $|m| \ge 1$, regardless of the value of r. This result is used in Chapter 15. Extend the pattern to larger dimension matrices (e.g.,tridiagonal, with $1 + 2r$ on the diagonal, and $-r$ on the subdiagonal and superdiagonal).

U1.3 Show that Horner's method is equivalent to synthetic division.

U1.4 Show that Horner's method for evaluating polynomials can be viewed as rearranging the polynomial such that

$$P(x) = a_n x^n + a_{n-1} x^{n-1} + \ldots + a_1 x + a_0$$
$$= (\ldots((a_n x + a_{n-1})x + a_{n-1})x$$
$$+ \ldots + a_1)x + a_0$$

If only the value of P(c) is required, it is not necessary to save the intermediate quantities (the b_i in the statement of the algorithm in the text). Write an algorithm for Horner's method using a single temporary variable.

U1.5 Consider a very limited binary normalized floating point system in which there are four bits to store the positive numbers. What exponents can be represented if 2 bits are used? What numbers can be represented if 2 bits are used for digits, and 2 for exponents? What numbers can be represented if 3 bits are used for digits and 1 for the exponents?

U1.6 Find the positive numbers that can be represented with only 1 digit and exponents of 0 or 1 in a base-10 normalized floating-point system.

2

··

Solving Equations
of One Variable

As discussed in Chapter 1, the problem of finding the zeros of a nonlinear function (or roots of a nonlinear equation) has a long history. Although quadratic equations of one variable can be solved analytically, numerical estimation of the zeros may be desired. For many other types of equations, it is either difficult or impossible to find an exact solution. In this chapter, we investigate several techniques for finding roots or zeros of nonlinear equations of a single variable.

The first technique presented, bisection, is a systematic approach to subdividing an interval on which we know the function has a zero. In addition to being simple and intuitive, this method can be used to obtain an adequate initial estimate of the zero that will be refined by more powerful methods. The second group of solution techniques—the *regula falsi,* secant, and Newton methods—are based on approximating the function whose zero is desired by a straight-line approximation, either a secant line through two points on the function or a tangent line to the function. We then investigate a technique, known as Muller's method, that is based on a quadratic approximation to the function.

The presentation of each technique includes several simple examples and a detailed algorithm for implementing the method.

Applications of zero-finding techniques occur throughout science and engineering. We begin with two examples, which we also use to illustrate the techniques throughout the chapter. Further examples from fields such as statics occur in the exercises.

In Chapters 3, 4, and 6 we consider some methods for solving systems of linear equations; Chapter 7 presents techniques for dealing with systems of nonlinear equations.

Example 2-A Floating Sphere

According to Archimedes, if a solid that is lighter than a fluid is placed in the fluid, the solid will be immersed to such a depth that the weight of the solid is equal to the weight of the displaced fluid. For example, a spherical ball of unit radius will float in water at a depth x (the distance from the bottom of the ball to the water line) determined by ρ, the specific gravity of the ball ($\rho < 1$).

The volume of the submerged segment of the sphere is

$$V = \pi x (3r^2 + x^2) / 6,$$

where r and x are related by the Pythagorean theorem, $r^2 + (1 - x)^2 = 1$. (See Fig. 2.1.)

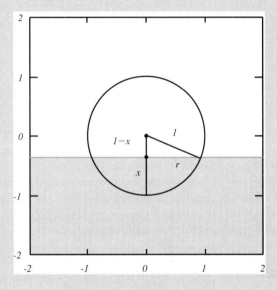

FIGURE 2.1   Floating sphere.

To find the depth at which the ball floats, we must solve the equation stating that the volume of the submerged segment is ρ times the volume of the entire sphere; i.e.,

$$\pi x (3r^2 + x^2) / 6 = \rho (4\pi / 3),$$

which simplifies to

$$x^3 - 3x^2 + 4\rho = 0.$$

In general, the zero that is of physical interest is between 0 and 2 (since the ball is of unit radius and x is measured up from the bottom of the ball).

Representative values of specific gravity include $\rho \approx 0.25$ for cork and $0.33 < \rho < 0.99$ for air-dried timber, depending on the type of wood. We investigate several methods of solving the preceding equation in this chapter.

Example 2-B Planetary Orbits

The position of a moon that revolves around a planet in an elliptical orbit can be described by Kepler's equation, which gives the central angle θ as a function of time. The relationship between time t and the central angle is given by

$$2\pi t = P(\theta - e \sin \theta),$$

where P is the period of revolution of the moon about the planet, e is the eccentricity of the moon's orbit, and the moon is at $(a, 0)$ at $t = 0$. The planet is located at a focus of the ellipse, $(a\,e, 0)$. To find the central angle for any given time t, we must find the root of the equation

$$2\pi t - P\theta + Pe \sin \theta = 0.$$

If the period of revolution is 100 days, and the eccentricity is 0.5, then, for any specified time, t, the central angle can be found from the relation

$$2\pi t - 100\theta + 50 \sin \theta = 0.$$

Kepler's law says that the orbit sweeps out equal areas in equal times. The position of the planet at 10-day intervals and the areas swept out between $t = 0$ and $t = 10$, and between $t = 60$ and $t = 70$ are illustrated in Fig. 2.2.

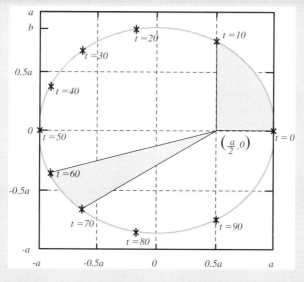

FIGURE 2.2   Position of the moon at 10-day intervals and areas swept out from day 0 to 10 and day 60 to 70.

The equation of the ellipse is $x(\theta) = a \cos(\theta)$, $y(\theta) = b \sin(\theta)$, where the coefficients a and b and the eccentricity e are related by the equation

$$b^2 = a^2 (1 - e^2).$$

Bisection is a systematic search technique for finding a zero of a continuous function. The method is based on first finding an interval in which a zero is known to occur because the function has opposite signs at the ends of the interval, then dividing the interval into two equal subintervals, and determining which subinterval contains a zero, and continuing the computations on the subinterval that contains the zero.

Suppose that an interval $[a, b]$ has been located which is known to contain a zero, since the function changes signs between a and b. The midpoint of the interval is

$$m = \frac{a + b}{2},$$

and a zero must lie in either $[a, m]$ or $[m, b]$. The appropriate subinterval is determined by testing the function to see whether it changes sign on $[a, m]$. If so, the search continues on that interval; otherwise, it continues on the interval $[m, b]$. Figure 2.3 illustrates the first approximation to the zero of the function $y = f(x) = x^2 - 3$, starting with the interval $[1, 2]$.

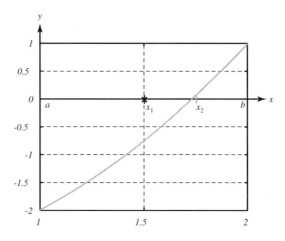

FIGURE 2.3   Graph of $y = x^2 - 3$ and first approximation to the zero on $[1, 2]$.

2.1.1 Algorithm for Bisection Method

The algorithmic statement of the bisection method given here consists of input variables, an initialization step, and a block of steps which may be repeated several times depending on the accuracy desired for the result. These steps can be carried out conveniently by hand, as illustrated in Example 2.1. The algorithm can also be used as the foundation for writing a simple computer program to implement the method.

Bisection Method

Input
- f   *function whose zero is desired (define here or in separate program)*
- a   *left-hand end of interval containing the zero*
- b   *right-hand end of interval containing the zero*
- max   *maximum number of iterations*
- tol   *stop if absolute value of function is less than tol*

Initialize
    ya = f(a)
    yb = f(b)
    If (ya*yb) $\geq$ 0) Error   *test to be sure there is a zero in [a,b]*
Begin Iterations
    For i = 1 to max
         xm = (a + b)/2   *compute midpoint of interval*
         ym = f(xm)
         If (|ym| < tol) Break   *solution is good enough*
         If ya*ym < 0)   *solution is in left half interval*
            b = xm
            yb = ym
         Else
            a = xm
            ya = ym
         End
    End
Return
    xm   *approximation to zero of f(x)*

2.1.2 Applications of Bisection Method

Example 2.1 Square Root of 3, Using Bisection

It is often helpful to graph the function whose zero is desired before proceeding with the computations. The graph of $y = f(x) = x^2 - 3$ is shown in Figure 2.3. We illustrate in detail the computation for the first iteration of the algorithm, taking the initial interval to be $[1, 2]$, so that $a = 1$ and $b = 2$.

Initialize
  ya $= f(1) = 1^2 - 3 = -2$
  yb $= f(2) = 2^2 - 3 = 1$
  ya*yb $= (-2)(1) < 0$, so there is a zero in the interval $[1, 2]$
First iteration
  xm $= (1 + 2)/2 = 3/2$
  ym $= f(3/2) = (3/2)^2 - 3 = -3/4$
  ya*ym $= (-2)(-3/4) > 0$, so the zero is not in the interval $[1, 3/2]$
  Since the zero must be in the interval $[3/2, 2]$, we set
    a $= 3/2$
    ya $=$ 3/4
  (and leave the current values of b and yb unchanged).

It is convenient to keep track of the calculations in tabular form. The following table shows the results of five iterations through this process.

Calculation of $\sqrt{3}$ using bisection.

step	a	b	x_m	y(a)	y(b)	y_m
1	1.0000	2.0000	1.5000	−2.0000	1.0000	−0.7500
2	1.5000	2.0000	1.7500	−0.7500	1.0000	0.0625
3	1.5000	1.7500	1.6250	−0.7500	0.0625	−0.3594
4	1.6250	1.7500	1.6875	−0.3594	0.0625	−0.1523
5	1.6875	1.7500	1.7188	−0.1523	0.0625	−0.0459

As indicated by the values of the function at the approximate zeros, it is possible to be quite close to the true zero at some stage of the iteration and then move away from the zero before returning to a good approximation later (with a smaller error bracket for the zero). In the foregoing calculations, we had a better approximation at step 2 than we had at step 3 or step 4.

Example 2.2 Floating Depth for a Cork Ball

To find the floating depth for a cork ball of radius 1 whose density is one-fourth that of water, we must find the zero (between 0 and 1) of

$$y = x^3 - 3x^2 + 1.$$

The function is shown in Fig. 2.4 for the region of interest. The computations using a simple function implementing the bisection algorithm are shown below.

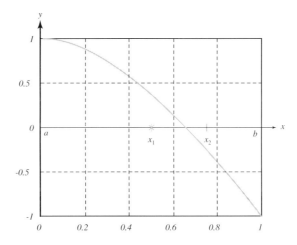

FIGURE 2.4   Graph of $y = x^3 - 3x^2 + 1$ and the first two approximations to its zero in [0, 1].

A summary of the calculations for the first 10 iterations is given in the following table (without the values for the endpoints of the interval at each stage). Note that the approximation was actually better at step 5 than at step 6, as indicated by the magnitude of y_i.

Calculation of floating depth using bisection method.

i	x_i	y_i
1	0.5	0.375
2	0.75	−0.26562
3	0.625	0.072266
4	0.6875	−0.093018
5	0.65625	−0.0093689
6	0.64062	0.031712
7	0.64844	0.011236
8	0.65234	0.00094932
9	0.6543	−0.0042058
10	0.65332	−0.0016273

2.1.3 Discussion

The bisection method is based on a well-known property of continuous functions, the intermediate value theorem. Applied specifically to the cases we are interested in, the theorem states that if $f(a) > 0$ and $f(b) < 0$, or if $f(a) < 0$ and $f(b) > 0$, then there is a number c between a and b such that $f(c) = 0$.

It is helpful to know how good our answers are for any numerical technique. In general, bisection is slow, but sure. At the first stage, the length of the interval is $b - a$. The furthest that our estimated zero (the midpoint of the interval) can be from the true solution is $(b - a)/2$. At each stage the length of the interval is halved, so the maximum possible error is reduced by a factor of one-half. The error at stage k is at most $(b - a)/2^k$.

In many cases, we would not choose to retain the entire sequence of values of the endpoints of the interval bracketing the zero, but the values could be stored in vectors **a** and **b** if desired.

One definition of linear convergence is that the inequality

$$|x^* - x_k| \le r^k \, |x^* - x_1|$$

holds for some constant $r < 1$, where x^* is the true zero, r is the convergence rate, x_k is the approximate zero at the kth stage, and $x_1 = (a + b)/2$ is the first approximate zero. Thus, bisection is linearly convergent with rate $1/2$.

As indicated by the values of the function at the approximate zeros in Example 2.1, it is possible to be quite close to the true zero at some stage of the iteration and then move away from the zero before returning to a good approximation later (with a smaller error bracket for the zero). In computing the square root of 3, we had a better approximation at the second bisection step than we had at step 3 or step 4.

Bisection works well with problems that cause difficulties for other methods. It is also useful as a preprocessing algorithm for the methods we discuss in the remainder of the chapter.

Bisection makes no use of information about the shape of the function $y = f(x)$ whose zero is desired. The first way to incorporate such information is to consider a straight-line approximation to the function. Since we know how to find the zero of a linear function, it is not much more work to find our approximation to the zero of $f(x)$ not as the midpoint of the interval, but as the point where the straight-line approximation to f crosses the x-axis. In this section, we consider two closely related methods based on straight-line approximations using two initial values of the independent variable that bracket the desired zero (as with the bisection method).

The *regula falsi* and secant methods start with two points, $(a, f(a))$ and $(b, f(b))$, satisfying the condition that $f(a) \cdot f(b) < 0$. The next approximation to the zero is the value of x where the straight line through the initial points crosses the x-axis; this approximate solution is

$$s = b - \frac{b - a}{f(b) - f(a)} f(b).$$

The *regula falsi* and secant methods may differ in the choice of the points to be used to define the next iteration.

The geometric basis for this new approximate zero is illustrated in Fig. 2.5.

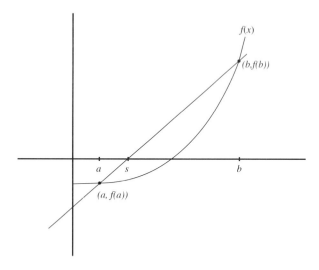

FIGURE 2.5   New approximate zero.

2.2.1 Algorithm for *Regula Falsi*

The *regula falsi* method, or the rule of false position, proceeds as in bisection to find the subinterval $[a, s]$ or $[s, b]$ that contains the zero by testing for a change of sign of the function, i.e., testing whether $f(a) \cdot f(s) < 0$ or $f(s) \cdot f(b) < 0$. If there is a zero in the interval $[a, s]$, we leave the value of a unchanged and set $b = s$. On the other hand, if there is no zero in $[a, s]$, the zero must be in the interval $[s, b]$; so we set $a = s$ and leave b unchanged.

The stopping condition may test the size of y, the amount by which the approximate solution s has changed on the last iteration, or whether the process has continued too long. Typically, a combination of these conditions is used. The following algorithm allows for a maximum number of iterations, but stops if the magnitude of the function at the approximate solution becomes sufficiently small. The algorithm as stated only returns the final approximate solution. With minor modifications, all intermediate values could be retained in a vector and returned, or intermediate results could be printed or displayed as they are calculated.

Regula Falsi Method ──────────────────────────────────────

Input
    f   *function whose zero is desired*
                (define here or in separate program)
    a   *left-hand end of interval containing the zero*
    b   *right-hand end of interval containing the zero*
    max   *maximum number of iterations*
    tol   *stop if absolute value of function is less than tol*

Initialize
    ya = f(a)
    yb = f(b)
    If (ya*yb) $\geq$ 0) Error   *test to be sure there is a zero in [a,b]*

Begin Iterations
    For i = 1 to max
            s = b − yb*(b−a)/(yb−ya) *compute approximate solution*
            ys = f(s)
            If (|ys| < tol) Break   *solution is good enough*
            If (ya*ys < 0)   *solution is in left half interval*
                 b = s
                 yb = ys
            Else   *solution is in the right half interval*
                 a = s
                 ya = ys
            End
    End

Return
    s   *approximation to zero of f(x)*

2.2.2 Applications of *Regula Falsi*

Example 2.3 Cube Root of 2, Using *Regula Falsi*

To find a numerical approximation to $\sqrt[3]{2}$, we seek the zero of $y = f(x) = x^3 - 2$, illustrated, with the first approximation, in Fig. 2.6.

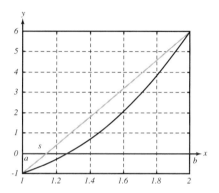

FIGURE 2.6   Graph of $y = x^3 - 2$ and approximation line on the interval $[1, 2]$.

Since $f(1) = -1$ and $f(2) = 6$, we take $a = 1$ and $b = 2$; the corresponding function values are $y(a) = -1$ and $y(b) = 6$. The first approximation to the zero is

$$s = b - \frac{b - a}{y(b) - y(a)}(y(b)) = 2 - \frac{2 - 1}{6 + 1}(6) = 2 - 6/7 = 8/7 \approx 1.1429.$$

We then find the value of the function, $ys = f(s) = (8/7)^3 - 2 \approx -0.5073$. Since $y(a)$ and ys are both negative, but ys and $y(b)$ have opposite signs, we know that there is a zero in the interval $[8/7, 2]$. We repeat the process, setting $a = 8/7$. Now $y(a) \approx -0.5073$; the right-hand end of the interval remains unchanged, so $b = 2$ and $y(b) = 6$. The computations are summarized in the following table.

	Calculation of $\sqrt[3]{2}$ using regula falsi.			
step	a	b	x	y
1	1	2	1.1429	−0.50729
2	1.1429	2	1.2097	−0.22986
3	1.2097	2	1.2388	−0.098736
4	1.2388	2	1.2512	−0.041433
5	1.2512	2	1.2563	−0.017216
6	1.2563	2	1.2584	−0.0071216
7	1.2584	2	1.2593	−0.0029429
8	1.2593	2	1.2597	−0.0012148

The next example demonstrates the use of a simple computer program implementing the *regula falsi* method by investigating the solution to the problem introduced in Example 2-B.

Example 2.4 Central Angle of an Elliptical Orbit, Day 10

To find the central angle θ at $t = 10$ days (see Example 2-B), we must find the zero of the equation $y = 10\pi - 50\theta + 25 \sin \theta$, which is illustrated in Fig. 2.7. The approximate value of the desired zero for steps 1, . . . 6 of the *regula falsi* method are summarized in the following table. The *regula falsi* method has converged, with tol = 0.0001.

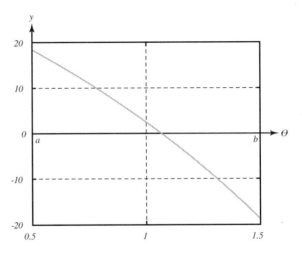

FIGURE 2.7 Graph of $y = 10\pi - 50\theta + 25 \sin \theta$.

	Calculation of central angle at day 10, using *regula falsi*.			
step	**a**	**b**	**θ**	**y(θ)**
1	0.5	1.5	0.99669	2.5733
2	0.99669	1.5	1.0577	0.31063
3	1.0577	1.5	1.065	0.036638
4	1.065	1.5	1.0658	0.0043094
5	1.0658	1.5	1.0659	0.0005067
6	1.0659	1.5	1.0659	5.9575e-05

2.2.3 Algorithm for Secant Method

The secant method, closely related to the *regula falsi* method, results from a slight modification of the latter. Instead of choosing the subinterval that must contain the zero, we form the next approximation from the two most recently generated points:

$$x_2 = x_1 - \frac{x_1 - x_0}{y_1 - y_0} \, y_1$$

At the kth stage, the new approximation to the zero is

$$x_{k+1} = x_k - \frac{x_k - x_{k-1}}{y_k - y_{k-1}} \, y_k.$$

This process does not require any testing to determine the action to take at the next step. It also converges more rapidly than the *regula falsi* method, in general, even though the zero is not required to lie within the interval at each stage.

Secant Method

Input
- f   *function whose zero is desired*
- a   *left-hand end of interval (not required to contain a zero)*
- b   *right-hand end of interval*
- max   *maximum number of iterations*
- tol   *stop if absolute value of function is less than* tol

Initialize
- x(0) = a
- x(1) = b
- y(0) = f(a)
- y(1) = f(b)

Begin Iterations
    For i = 1 to max
        x(i+1) = x(i) − y(i)*(x(i) − x(i−1))/(y(i) − y(i−1))   *approximate solution*
        y(i+1) = f(x(i+1))
        If (|y(i+1)| < tol) Break   *solution is good enough*
    End

Return
- x   *vector of approximations to zero of f(x)*

2.2.4 Applications of Secant Method

> ## Example 2.5 Square Root of 3, Using Secant Method
>
> To find a numerical approximation to $\sqrt{3}$ we seek the zero of $y = f(x) = x^2 - 3$. Since $f(1) = -2$ and $f(2) = 1$, we take as our starting estimates of the zero $x_0 = 1$ and $x_1 = 2$; the corresponding function values are $y_0 = -2$ and $y_1 = 1$. The first approximation to the zero is
>
> $$x_2 = x_1 - \frac{x_1 - x_0}{y_1 - y_0}\, y_1$$
>
> $$= 2 - \frac{2 - 1}{1 - (-2)}\,(1) = 5/3 \approx 1.667$$
>
> The secant method does not require that the points used to compute the next approximation bracket the zero (or even that $x_0 < x_1$). It is convenient to keep track of the calculations in tabular form; the results of four iterations through the process are shown in the following table. The secant method has converged with a tolerance of 10^{-4}. Note that the first two steps in the table list the initial values for x and y and therefore do not actually represent iterations.
>
> Calculation of $\sqrt{3}$ using secant method.
>
> | step | x | y |
> |------|--------|-------------|
> | 0 | 1 | -2 |
> | 1 | 2 | 1 |
> | 2 | 1.6667 | -0.22222 |
> | 3 | 1.7273 | -0.016529 |
> | 4 | 1.7321 | 0.00031888 |
> | 5 | 1.7321 | $-4.4042\text{e-}07$ |
>
> The graph of the function is shown in Figure 2.1. Comparing the results found here with the secant method to those found in Example 2.1 using the bisection method clearly illustrates the superior results that are typical for the secant method.

Example 2.6 Central Angle of an Elliptical Orbit, Day 20

As introduced in Example 2-B, the central angle (at any specified time, t) of an elliptical orbit, with period of revolution = 100 days and eccentricity = 0.5, can be found by solving

$$f(\theta, t) = 2\pi t - 100\theta + 50 \sin \theta = 0.$$

The graphs of $f(\theta, t)$ for several values of t are shown in Figure 2.8.

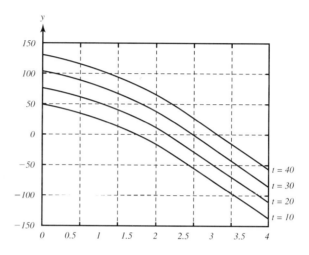

FIGURE 2.8   Graph of $f(\theta, t) = 2\pi t - 100\theta + 50 \sin\theta$, for $t = 10, 20, 30, 40$.

The calculations to find the central angle θ at $t = 20$ days (see Example 2-B) using the secant method are summarized in the following table.

Finding a zero of $y = 20\pi - 50\theta + 25\sin\theta$ using the secant method.

k	θ_k	y_k
1	1	33.869
2	2	−14.436
3	1.7012	2.5622
4	1.7462	0.13835
5	1.7488	−0.0015105
6	1.7487	8.6907e-07

2.2.5   Discussion

The standard method of comparing how fast various iterative zero finding methods converge is to investigate the behavior of $\dfrac{|x_k - x^*|}{|x_{k-1} - x^*|^p}$ for large values of k; as in the discussion of the bisection method, we denote the true zero x^*.

Rate of Convergence

If

$$\lim_{k \to \infty} \frac{|x_k - x^*|}{|x_{k-1} - x^*|^p} = \lambda \text{ for some } \lambda > 0,$$

we say that the sequence x_k converges to x^* with order $p > 0$; the number λ is called the *asymptotic error constant*. In general, higher values of p give faster convergence.

> If a sequence converges with $p = 1$, we say it is linearly convergent;
> If a sequence converges with $p = 2$, we say it converges quadratically.

It is not too hard to see that if a function is concave up on the interval $[a_k, b_k]$, the point $(b_k, y(b_k))$ will not change during the *regula falsi* iterations $(k + 1, \ldots)$ (as illustrated in Fig. 2.9); similarly, if the function is concave down, the point $(a_k, y(a_k))$ does not change. At some stage, one or the other of these conditions will be met, and from that stage onward, the convergence is linear. The *regula falsi* method can be modified to improve the convergence order to 1.4 or 1.6. (See Ralston and Rabinowitz, 1978, for further discussion.)

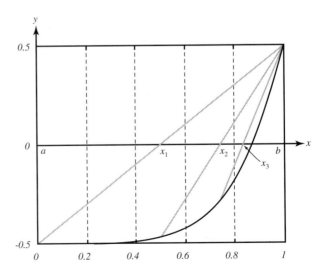

FIGURE 2.9   A function that is concave near the zero.

Although it is appealing to know that the zero is bracketed at each step of the process, some effort is required to find the appropriate subinterval at each stage. Also, an iterative process in which the form of the function being iterated can change at each stage (as is the case for a process where a choice must be made as to which subinterval to pursue) is more difficult to analyze.

The calculation of the update formula for the secant method is the same as that for the *regula falsi* method; only the choice of which two of the x values are used for the next iteration differs. Because the secant method does not bracket the zero at each iteration (as do the bisection and *regula falsi* methods), the secant method is not guaranteed to converge. However, when it does, the convergence is usually more rapid than for either bisection or *regula falsi*. Typically, as the iterations progress, the secants become increasingly more accurate approximations to $f(x)$.

The rate of convergence is $p = \dfrac{1 + \sqrt{5}}{2} \approx 1.62$, so convergence is faster than linear, but less than quadratic. The asymptotic error constant is

$$\lambda = \left| \frac{f''(x^*)}{2f'(x^*)} \right|^{\beta}, \text{ with } \beta \frac{\sqrt{5} - 1}{2}.$$

Convergence Theorem for the Secant Method

If

1. $f(x)$, $f'(x)$ and $f''(x)$ are continuous on $I = [x^* - e, x^* + e]$
2. $f'(x^*) \neq 0$, and
3. the initial estimates x_0 and x_1 (in I) are sufficiently close to x^*, then the secant method will converge.

The requirements for "sufficiently close" can be made more precise by defining $M = \dfrac{\max |f''|}{2 \min |f'|}$, where max and min are for all x in the interval $I = [x^* - e, x^* + e]$. Then if $\max \{M | x^* - x_0 |, M | x^* - x_1 |\} < 1$, the secant method will converge. It may converge for starting values that do not satisfy this inequality, but in general, the larger the value of M (if it can be computed), the closer the starting values should be to the zero. (See Atkinson, 1989, pp. 65–73, for a development of these results.)

We conclude our discussion of the *regula falsi* and secant methods by considering the challenging problem of finding the zero of a function that is quite flat near the desired zero.

Example 2.7 A Challenging Problem

To illustrate the difficulties that may occur when a function is relatively flat near a zero, consider the simple example of finding the positive real zero of $y = x^5 - 0.5$. The function and the first three straight-line approximations are illustrated in Fig. 2.10.

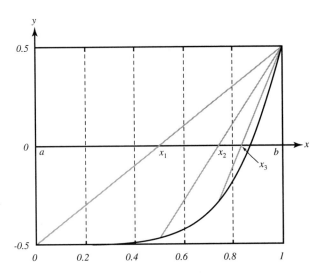

FIGURE 2.10   Graph of $y = x^5 - 0.5$ and first three approximations using *regula falsi*.

The results of the calculations using *regula falsi* are summarized in the following table. The *regula falsi* method converges in nine iterations with tol = 0.0001.

Calculation of $\sqrt[5]{0.5}$ using *regula falsi*.				
step	a	b	x	y
1	0	1	0.5	−0.46875
2	0.5	1	0.74194	−0.27518
3	0.74194	1	0.83355	−0.09761
4	0.83355	1	0.86801	−0.0072543
6	0.86801	1	0.8699	−0.0018732
7	0.8699	1	0.87038	−0.00048132
8	0.87038	1	0.87051	−0.00012352
9	0.87051	1	0.87054	− 3.1687e-05

Now consider the problem of finding the positive real zero of $y = x^5 - 0.5$ using the secant method (see Fig. 2.11.)

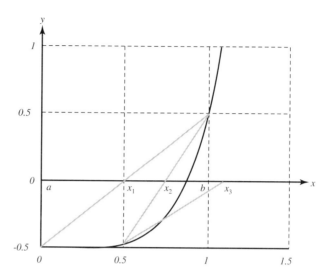

FIGURE 2.11 Graph of $y = x^5 - 0.5$ and first three approximations using secant method.

As shown in the following table, the third approximation is outside the original interval that contains the root. Nevertheless, after seven iterations, the method has achieved essentially the same result as *regula falsi*.

Calculation of $\sqrt[5]{0.5}$ using the secant method.		
step	x	y
1	0.5	-0.46875
2	0.74194	-0.27518
3	1.0859	1.0098
4	0.81559	-0.13911
5	0.84832	-0.060656
6	0.87362	0.008891
7	0.87039	-0.00046064

On the other hand, if we give the starting values as $x_0 = 1$ and $x_1 = 0$, we again find $x_2 = 0.5$, but the calculation of x_3 is based on a straight line with almost zero slope (the line determined by the points $(0, -0.5)$ and $(0.5, -0.46875)$). There are extreme oscillations before the method converges to the correct value. Although it may seem contrived to give the starting estimates in this "nonnatural" order, completely analogous behavior occurs for $y = x^5 + 0.5$ when the starting estimates are $x_0 = -1$ and $x_1 = 0$.

Like the *regula falsi* and secant methods, Newton's method uses a straight-line approximation to the function whose zero we wish to find, but in this case the line is the tangent to the curve. The next approximation to the zero is the value of x where the tangent crosses the x-axis. This requires additional information about the function (i.e., its derivative). The secant method discussed in the previous section can be viewed as Newton's method with the derivative approximated by a difference quotient.

Given an initial estimate of the zero, x_0; the value of the function at x_0, $y_0 = f(x_0)$; and the value of the derivative at x_0, $y'_0 = f'(x_0)$; the x intercept of the tangent line, which is the new approximation to the zero, is

$$x_1 = x_0 - \frac{y_0}{y'_0}.$$

The tangent line at (x_0, y_0) has slope $m = f'(x_0)$, so the equation of the tangent line can be written as

$$y - y_0 = m(x - x_0).$$

To find the value of x where this line crosses the x-axis, set $y = 0$ and solve for x:

$$0 - y_0 = m\,x - m\,x_0$$

$$m\,x_0 - y_0 = m\,x$$

$$x = x_0 - \frac{y_0}{m}$$

This value of x is the new approximate zero, since $m = f'(x_0) = y'_0$.

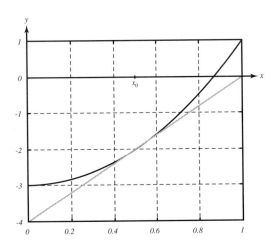

FIGURE 2.12 Graph of f(x) and tangent line at $x = 0.5$.

2.3.1 Algorithm for Newton's Method

In general, at the kth stage, we have

$$x_{k+1} = x_k - \frac{y_k}{y'_k}$$

The process continues until the change in the approximations is sufficiently small, the magnitude of the function at the approximate solution is sufficiently small, or some other stopping condition is satisfied.

Newton's Method

Input
- f   *function whose zero is desired*
- df   *derivative of function whose zero is desired*
- x0   *initial estimate of solution*
- max   *maximum number of iterations*
- tol   *stop if absolute value of function is less than tol*

Initialize
- x(0) = x0
- y(0) = f(x0)
- dy(0) = df(x0)

Begin Iterations
- For i = 0 to max
  - x(i+1) = x(i) − y(i)/dy(i)   *next approximate solution*
  - y(i+1) = f(x(i+1))
  - If (|y(i+1)| < tol) Break   *solution is good enough*
  - dy(i+1) = df(x(i+1))
- End

Return
- x   *vector of approximations to zero of f(x)*

2.3.2   Applications of Newton's Method

<hr>

Example 2.8 Square Root of 3/4, Using Newton's Method

To find a numerical approximation to $\sqrt{3/4}$, we approximate the zero of

$$y = f(x) = 4x^2 - 3 \text{ (see Fig. 2.13)}$$

using the fact that

$$y' = f'(x) = 8x.$$

Since $f(0) = -3$ and $f(1) = 1$, we take as our starting estimate of the zero $x_0 = 0.5$; the corresponding function value is $y_0 = -2$, and the derivative value is $y'_0 = 4$. Our first approximation to the zero is

$$x_1 = x_0 - \frac{y_0}{y'_0} = 0.5 - \frac{-2}{4} = 1.$$

Continuing for one more step yields

$$x_2 = x_1 - \frac{y_1}{y'_1} = 1.0 - \frac{1}{8} = 7/8 = 0.875.$$

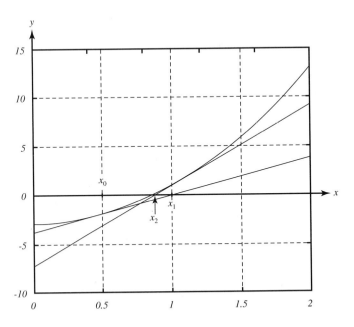

FIGURE 2.13   The graph of $y = 4x^2 - 3$ and the tangent line approximation at $x = 0.5$.

Example 2.9 Floating Depth for a Wooden Ball

To find the floating depth of a ball of unit radius, whose density is one-third that of water, we must find the zero (between 0 and 1) of $y = x^3 - 3x^2 + 4/3$. (See Fig. 2.14.) The calculations are summarized in the following table.

Floating depth of a wooden ball, using Newton's method.

step	x	y
1	0.5	0.70833
2	0.81481	−0.11746
3	0.77427	−0.00097989
4	0.77393	−8.0255e-08
5	0.77393	−4.4409e-16

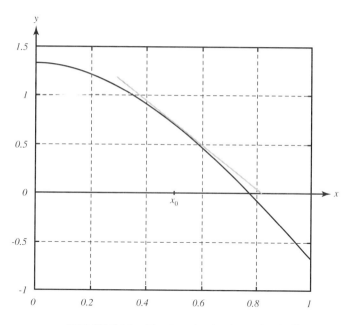

FIGURE 2.14   Floating depth of wooden ball.

2.3.3 Discussion

Newton's method is based on using the tangent line to the function $y = f(x)$ at the current approximate zero to find the new approximation to the zero.

The tangent line at (x_0, y_0) has slope $m = f'(x_0)$, so the equation of the tangent line can be written as

$$y - y_0 = m(x - x_0).$$

To find the value of x where this line crosses the x-axis, set $y = 0$ and solve for x:

$$0 - y_0 = m\,x - m\,x_0$$

$$m\,x_0 - y_0 = m\,x$$

$$x = x_0 - \frac{y_0}{m}$$

This value of x is the new approximate zero, since $m = f'(x_0) = y'_0$.

We can obtain more information about the approximation to the zero x^* if we consider the Taylor series expansion for $f(x)$ near x_k, i.e.,

$$f(x) = f(x_k) + (x - x_k)f'(x_k) + 0.5(x - x_k)^2 f''(\eta)$$

where η is some unknown point between x and x_k.

If $x = x^*$ and $f(x^*) = 0$,

then

$$0 = f(x_k) + (x^* - x_k)f'(x_k) + 0.5(x^* - x_k)^2 f''(\eta),$$

and

$$x^* = x_k - \frac{f(x_k)}{f'(x_k)} - 0.5(x^* - x_k)^2 \frac{f''(\eta)}{f'(x_k)}.$$

If we now set

$$x_{k+1} = x_k - \frac{f(x_k)}{f'(x_k)}$$

and substitute this into the previous equation, we can solve for the error at the $(k + 1)^{\text{st}}$ approximation:

$$x^* - x_{k+1} = -0.5(x^* - x_k)^2 \frac{f''(\eta)}{f'(x_k)}.$$

Convergence Theorem for Newton's Method

If

1. $f(x)$, $f'(x)$, and $f''(x)$ are continuous for all x in a neighborhood of x^*,
2. $f'(x^*) \neq 0$, and x_0 is chosen sufficiently close to x^*, then the iterates

$$x_{k+1} = x_k - \frac{f(x_k)}{f'x_k}$$

will converge to x^*.

Furthermore,

$$\lim_{k \to \infty} \frac{x_k - x^*}{(x_{k-1} - x^*)^2} = \frac{f''(x^*)}{2f'(x^*)}.$$

Some Considerations When Using Newton's Method

The convergence theorem can be used to obtain some information about how close the initial estimate x_0 must be to the actual zero. Let I be an interval around x^* such that $f'(x) \neq 0$ on I, and let

$$M = \frac{\max |f''(x)|}{2 \min |f'(x)|},$$

where the max and min are taken over all x in I; then convergence is guaranteed if the initial estimate is chosen close enough to the true zero so that $|x^* - x_0| < 1/M$. (See Atkinson, 1989, p. 60, for further discussion.)

Newton's method is quadratically convergent (the order of convergence is $p = 2$), with asymptotic error constant $\left| \frac{f''(x^*)}{2f'(x^*)} \right|$.

Newton's method has a high order of convergence and a fairly simple statement; hence, it is often the first method people use. However, the method can encounter difficulties, as illustrated in the next example.

Furthermore, the derivative must not be zero at any approximation to the zero, or Newton's method will fail. The stopping condition should be a combination of a specified maximum number of iterations and minimum tolerance on the change in the computed zero. Because of the potential for divergence, it is also wise to test for large changes in the value of the computed zero, which might signal difficulties.

Example 2.10 Oscillations in Newton's Method

Newton's method can give oscillatory results for some functions and some initial estimates. For example, consider the cubic equation

$$y = x^3 - 3x^2 + x + 3.$$

The derivative is $y' = 3x^2 - 6x + 1$. If we don't consider the graph, we might guess $x_0 = 1$ as the initial point. The calculations for the first three iterations are summarized in the following table. The tangent approximations for the first two iterations are illustrated in Fig. 2.15. It is easy to see that the process will oscillate between these two values.

Oscillations resulting from the use of Newton's method.

step	x_{i-1}	x_i	y_{i-1}	y_i
1	1	2	2	1
2	2	1	1	2
3	1	2	2	1

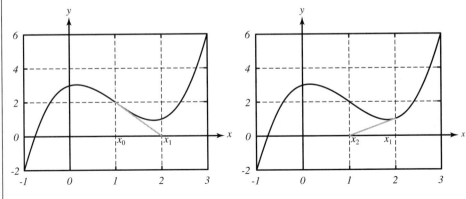

FIGURE 2.15   Oscillatory behavior of Newton's method.

A logical extension of the methods based on linear approximations to the function whose zero we are seeking is to approximate the function by a quadratic function. This method is known as Muller's method. It has the advantage of being able to generate approximations to complex zeros even if the initial estimates are real. The idea is quite simple, although the formulas are more complicated than in the previous methods. Using three points on the function, we can find the equation of the quadratic that passes through those points and then find the zeros of that quadratic. It is also possible to start with two points that bracket the zero and use the midpoint of the interval between the points as the third point. In general, Muller's method is less sensitive to starting values than Newton's method is.

The parabola passing through the points (x_a, y_a), (x_b, y_b), and (x_c, y_c) can be written as $y = y_c + q(x - x_c) + r(x - x_c)(x - x_b)$, where $p = (y_b - y_a)/(x_b - x_a)$ and the coefficients are $q = (y_c - y_b)/(x_c - x_b)$ and $r = (q - p)/(x_c - x_a)$. This somewhat strange form is closely related to Newton's form of an interpolating polynomial, which is discussed in Chapter 8. Letting $s = c_2 + r(x_3 - x_2)$ and solving for the zero that is closest to x_c gives the next approximation to the desired zero:

$$x_n = x_c - \frac{2\,y_c}{s + \text{sign}(s)\sqrt{s^2 - 4\,y_c\,r}}.$$

Of course, once the formulas for the new approximation are derived, it is not necessary to actually find the equation of the quadratic at each step.

The first step is illustrated in Fig. 2.16.

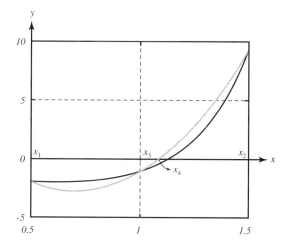

FIGURE 2.16 $y = x^6 - 2$ (black line) and parabola (grey line) for Muller's method.

2.4.1 Algorithm for Muller's Method

A step-by-step procedure for carrying out the computations for Muller's Method is given in the following algorithm. The three (distinct) initial estimates of the zero are not required to satisfy any particular relationships; however, it is good practice to take the interval $[a, c]$ so that $f(a)$ and $f(c)$ have opposite signs. It is also common to take b to be the midpoint of the interval.

Muller's Method

Input

f	*function whose zero is desired*
a, b, c	*initial three estimates of solution*
max	*maximum number of iterations*
tol	*stop if absolute value of function is less than tol*

Initialize

$x(1) = a$
$x(2) = c$
$x(3) = b$
$y(1) = f(a)$
$y(2) = f(c)$
$y(3) = f(b)$
$c(1) = (y(2) - y(1))/(x(2) - x(1))$

Begin Iterations
For i = 3 to max

$c(i-1) = (y(i) - y(i-1))/x(i) - x(i-1))$
$d(i-2) = (c(i-1) - c(i-2))/x(i) - x(i-2))$
$s = c(i-1) + (x(i) - x(i-1))*d(i-2))$
$x(i+1) = x(i) - 2*y(i)/(s + \text{sign}(s)*\text{sqrt}(s^2 - 4*y(i)*d(i-2)))$
$y(i+1) = f(x(i+1))$
If $(f(x(i+1)) < \text{tol})$ Break

End

Return

x	*vector of approximations to zero of f(x)*
	computed approximations begin with x(4)

2.4.2 Applications of Muller's Method

The use of Muller's method is illustrated in the next two examples.

Example 2.11 Sixth Root of 2, Using Muller's Method

To approximate the real zero of $y = f(x) = x^6 - 2$ (see Fig. 2.12), take as starting estimates

$$x_1 = 0.5, \; x_2 = 1.5 \text{ and } x_3 = 1.0;$$

the corresponding function values are

$$y_1 = -1.9844, \; y_2 = 9.3906, \text{ and } y_3 = -1.$$

Then, to find the next approximation to the zero, compute

$$c_1 = \frac{y_2 - y_1}{x_2 - x_1} = 11.375, \qquad c_2 = \frac{y_3 - y_2}{x_3 - x_2} = 20.781,$$

$$d_1 = \frac{c_2 - c_1}{x_3 - x_1} = 18.812,$$

$$s = c_2 + d_1(x_3 - x_2) = 20.781 + 18.812\,(-0.5) = 11.375,$$

$$x_4 = x_3 - \frac{2\,y_3}{s + \operatorname{sign}(s)\sqrt{s^2 - 4\,y_3\,d_1}}$$

$$= 1 - \frac{2(-1)}{11.375 + \sqrt{11.375^2 - 4(-1)\,18.812}} = 1.0779.$$

The results are summarized in the following table. The first two values of x are user-supplied starting estimates, and the third value of x is the midpoint of the interval defined by x_1 and x_2; values calculated by Muller's method start with x_4.

Calculation of $\sqrt[6]{2}$ using Muller's method.

i	x	y
1	0.5	−1.9844
2	1.5	9.3906
3	1	−1
4	1.0779	−0.43172
5	1.117	−0.057635
6	1.1225	0.00076162
7	1.1225	−4.7432e-07
8	1.1225	−4.8628e-13

Example 2.12 Another Challenging Problem

Consider the problem of finding a zero of $y = x^{10} - 0.5$. The function and the first parabolic approximation are shown in Fig. 2.17.

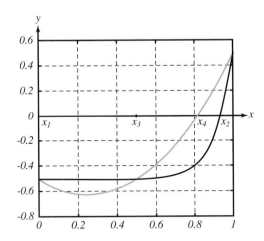

FIGURE 2.17 $y = x^{10} - 0.5$ (black line) and parabola (grey line) for Muller's method.

Calculation of $\sqrt[10]{0.5}$ using Muller's method.		
step	x	y
1	0	−0.5
2	1	0.5
3	0.5	−0.49902
4	0.80875	−0.38029
5	0.9081	−0.11862
6	0.94325	0.057542
7	0.93269	−0.0018478
8	0.93303	−6.3021e-06
9	0.93303	−3.1235e-10

2.4.3   Discussion

The parabola passing through the points (x_1, y_1), (x_2, y_2), and $(x_3 \; y_3)$ can be written as

$$y = y_3 + c_2(x - x_3) + d_1(x - x_3)(x - x_2), \tag{2.1}$$

where the coefficients are found by calculating

$$c_1 = \frac{y_2 - y_1}{x_2 - x_1}, \qquad c_2 = \frac{y_3 - y_2}{x_3 - x_2}, \qquad \text{and } d_1 = \frac{c_2 - c_1}{x_3 - x_1}.$$

We write the equation for the zeros of eq. 2.1 in terms of powers of $(x - x_3)$:

$$0 = y_3 + c_2(x - x_3) + d_1(x - x_3)(x - x_2)$$
$$0 = y_3 + c_2(x - x_3) + d_1(x - x_3)(x - x_3 + x_3 - x_2)$$
$$0 = y_3 + c_2(x - x_3) + d_1(x - x_3)(x - x_3) + d_1(x - x_3)(x_3 - x_2)$$

Letting $s = c_2 + d_1(x_3 - x_2)$, the equation becomes

$$0 = y_3 + s(x - x_3) + d_1(x - x_3)^2$$

Since we wish to find the zero of that is closest to x_3, we divide by $(x - x_3)^2$, set $z = (x - x_3)^{-1}$, and apply the quadratic formula to

$$0 = y_3 z^2 + s z + d_1.$$

We choose the zero with the largest magnitude, so that $z^{-1} = x - x_3$ will be as small as possible; this gives

$$z = \frac{-s - \text{sign}(s)\sqrt{s^2 - 4 y_3 d_1}}{2 y_3},$$

or

$$x = x_3 - \frac{2 y_3}{s + \text{sign}(s)\sqrt{s^2 - 4 y_3 d_1}}$$

In contrast to Newton's method, Muller's method requires only function values; the derivative need not be calculated. Another advantage of Muller's method is that it may be used to find complex as well as real zeros. The method fails if $f(x_1) = f(x_2) = f(x_3)$, which can occur if x is a zero of multiplicity greater than 2.

The rate of convergence of Muller's method is slightly less than quadratic, since $p \approx 1.84$; the asymptotic error constant is $\left| \dfrac{f''(x^*)}{2f'(x^*)} \right|^{\beta}$, where p is the positive root of $f(x) = x^3 - x^2 - x - 1$, and $\beta = \dfrac{p - 1}{2}$. (See Atkinson, 1989, p. 67, for a development of these results.)

In this section we consider briefly some of the methods implemented in the built-in functions for root- or zero-finding in popular software packages, such as MATLAB, Mathcad, and *Mathematica*, or included in professionally developed software libraries, such as NAG. The methods are separated into two groups, those for polynomials and those for general nonlinear functions. As mentioned earlier, mathematical terminology distinguishes between the zero of a function and the root of an equation. Software packages often do not make this distinction in naming their routines or built-in functions. Polynomials are usually input as a vector of the coefficients of $p(x)$, and the method typically returns a vector containing all of the roots of $p(x) = 0$.

2.5.1 Roots of a Polynomial Equation, $p(x) = 0$

The methods of choice for finding the roots of $p(x) = 0$ are able to find all roots, either real or complex. Some methods begin by finding a root r of $p(x)$, then find $q(x)$ such that $p(x) = (x - r) q(x)$, and then proceed to find a root of $q(x)$, continuing until all roots are found. This process of dividing $p(x)$ by $x - r$ to find $q(x)$ is called deflation. The other primary approach is to construct the companion matrix $\mathbf{M}$ for $p(x)$ and then use methods from matrix linear algebra (some of which are discussed in Chapter 7) to find the eigenvalues of $\mathbf{M}$. The eigenvalues are the roots of the polynomial.

Other important approaches to polynomial root finding include the Jenkins-Traub method (see Ralston and Rabinowitz, 1978, sect 8.9–8.13, or the IMSL Math/Library Users Manual) and the Lehmer-Schur algorithm (see Acton, 1990, Ch. 7).

Laguerre's Method

The Laguerre method with deflation and polishing is the default method in Mathcad. It is also included in the NAG software library. Laguerre's method is the most straightforward of a group of methods that are guaranteed to converge to all types of roots of a polynomial, whether real or complex, single or repeated. It requires that the computations be carried out in complex arithmetic. The motivation for the method is based on the following relationships.

If we write the polynomial as $P_n(x) = (x - x_1)(x - x_2)\ldots(x - x_n)$ and take logarithms of both sides of the equation, we obtain

$$\ln |P_n(x)| = \ln |x - x_1| + \ln |x - x_2| + \ldots + \ln |x - x_n|$$

The first derivative is

$$\frac{d}{dx}\left(\ln |P_n(x)|\right) = \frac{1}{x - x_1} + \frac{1}{x - x_2} + \ldots + \frac{1}{x - x_n}$$

and the negative of the second derivative is

$$-\frac{d^2}{dx^2}\left(\ln |P_n(x)|\right) = \frac{1}{(x - x_1)^2} + \frac{1}{(x - x_2)^2} + \ldots + \frac{1}{(x - x_n)^2}$$

We define

$$G = \frac{1}{x - x_1} + \frac{1}{x - x_2} + \ldots + \frac{1}{x - x_n}$$

and

$$H = \frac{1}{(x - x_1)^2} + \frac{1}{(x - x_2)^2} + \ldots + \frac{1}{(x - x_n)^2}$$

Let a be the approximate distance of the desired root, x_1 from the current guess x, and let the distance of each of the other roots, $x_2, \ldots x_n$ from the current guess x be b. Expressing G and H in terms of these two variables, we get

$$G = \frac{1}{a} + \frac{n - 1}{b} \quad \text{and} \quad H = \frac{1}{a^2} + \frac{n - 1}{b^2}$$

Solving for a gives

$$a = \frac{n}{G + -\sqrt{(n - 1)(nH - G^2)}}$$

where the sign in the denominator is chosen to give the largest possible magnitude for the denominator. Starting with an initial value for x, the next approximation to the root is $x + a$.

This motivation is based on a discussion in Press et al., 1992; for a more rigorous derivation, see Ralston and Rabinowitz, 1978.

Polynomial Roots via a Companion Matrix

Since the software package MATLAB is based on matrix operations (the name is a condensation of Matrix Laboratory), it is not surprising that its approach to finding the roots of a polynomial is to construct the companion matrix and then find its eigenvalues. The polynomial $c_1 x^n + \ldots + c_{n-1} x^2 + c_n x + c_{n+1}$ with $c_1 \neq 0$, is given as the vector of coefficients $\mathbf{c} = [c_1 \ldots c_{n-1} \quad c_n \quad c_{n+1}]$. If $c_{n+1} = 0$, the vector is reduced in length by one component, but the root $x = 0$ is retained. Similarly, if both $c_{n+1} = 0$ and $c_n = 0$, the vector is reduced to $[c_1 \ldots c_{n-1}]$ and $x = 0$ is identified as a double root. All trailing zeros are stripped in a similar manner, so that in forming the companion matrix, we have both the first and last components of the vector c non-zero. The companion matrix is the $(n - 1)$-by-$(n - 1)$ matrix (with sub-diagonal of 1's)

$$\mathbf{A} = \begin{bmatrix} -c_2/c_1 & & & -c_n/c_1 \\ 1 & & & \\ & 1 & & \\ & & \ldots & \\ & & 1 & 0 \end{bmatrix}$$

The roots of $p(x) = 0$ are the eigenvalues of $\mathbf{A}$, together with any roots of $x = 0$ identified before $\mathbf{A}$ was formed.

2.5.3 Zeros of a Nonlinear Function, $f(x)$

Although Newton's method is popular in many settings for finding a zero of a nonlinear function, professional software packages usually implement methods that do not require an explicit formula for the derivative of the function whose zero is sought. The methods of choice vary in terms of the initial estimate of the root which is used; some need an interval bracketing the root, others a single starting estimate, still others allow for either an interval or a single point for starting.

Mathcad allows for either an interval that brackets the root or a single starting point. The unbracketed form implements the secant and Muller methods, which have been discussed in sections 2.2.2 and 2.4. The bracketed form uses the Ridders' method, or if that fails to find a root, the Brent method. Brent's method is also the method used in MATLAB. *Mathematica* uses Newton's method and the secant method for its numerical root-finding routines. Since *Mathematica* has extensive capabilities for symbolic computation (it is one of the premier computer algebra systems), the software can find the formula for the derivative function needed for Newton's method, rather than requiring it as input from the user.

Ridders' Method

Ridders' method, a variation of the regula falsi method, uses three starting estimates of the desired root. The first two estimates must bracket the root; the third estimate is the midpoint between the first two. The derivation of Ridders' method utilizes (as an intermediate step) a quadratic equation involving an unknown exponential function. The new approximation to the root comes from applying the *regula falsi* method to a function which is a combination of the original function and this exponential function. The formula for the new approximation is independent of this unknown exponential function. For initial estimates $x_1 < x_2$ (and $x_3 = (x_1 + x_2)/2$), and the corresponding function values $y_1 = f(x_1)$, $y_2 = f(x_2)$ and $x_3 = f(x_3)$, the next estimate is

$$x_4 = x_3 + (x_3 - x_1) \frac{\text{sign}[y_1 - y_2] \, y_3}{\sqrt{y_3^2 - y_1 y_2}}$$

For the next step, one determines which of the previous estimates, x_1, x_2, or x_3, to retain, along with x_4, so that the root is still bracketed. The new midpoint, and the two new function values (for x_4 and the new midpoint) are computed, and the next approximate root is found from the formula above.

One of the nice properties of Ridders' method is that at each stage the new estimate is always within the bracketing interval (x_1, x_2) for that step. Another is that the convergence is quadratic; the number of significant digits in the solution approximately doubles with each step of the method.

For further details on this method, see Ridders, 1979, or Press et al., 1992, p. 358.

Brent's Method

Brent's method, published in 1973, is an improved version of a general root-finding method developed at the Mathematical Center in Amsterdam in the 1960s. The basic idea is to combine the guaranteed (but often slow) convergence of the bisection method with a more rapid (but not always convergent) method. In Brent's method the more rapidly convergent method is inverse quadratic interpolation. That is, the method is based on using three points on the function whose root is desired to express x as a quadratic function of y (that is the inverse quadratic interpolation). Then by setting $y = 0$, a new approximate root is obtained. Interpolation is discussed in Chapter 8. If the points to be interpolated are denoted

$$(x_a, y_a), (x_b, y_b) \text{ and } (x_c, y_c)$$

then it is straightforward to verify that they each satisfy the following quadratic function $(x = f(y))$

$$x = \frac{(y - y_b)(y - y_c)}{(y_a - y_b)(y_a - y_c)} x_a + \frac{(y - y_a)(y - y_c)}{(y_b - y_a)(y_b - y_c)} x_b + \frac{(y - y_a)(y - y_b)}{(y_c - y_a)(y_c - y_b)} x_c$$

Setting $y = 0$ gives the new approximate root x_n as

$$x_n = \frac{y_b \, y_c}{(y_a - y_b)(y_a - y_c)} x_a + \frac{y_a \, y_c}{(y_b - y_a)(y_b - y_c)} x_b + \frac{y_a \, y_b}{(y_c - y_a)(y_c - y_b)} x_c$$

The method must also perform various bookkeeping tasks in order to decide when bisection steps should be performed, and to make sure that the root remains bracketed by the appropriate approximations. For further details, see Brent, 1973, or Press et al., 1992, p. 362.

This algorithm was originated by T. Dekker. See Richard Brent in "Algorithms for Minimization Without Derivatives," Prentice-Hall, 1973 (which contains an Algol 60 version of the method). A Fortran version is in Forsythe, Malcolm, and Moler, "Computer Methods for Mathematical Computations," Prentice-Hall, 1976. This method is also implemented in the NAG software library.

2.5.3 Using Professionally Developed Software

MATLAB's Functions

MATLAB has two built-in functions for solving problems of the type discussed in this chapter. For finding the zeros of a polynomial, the function roots(p) is appropriate. The polynomial is given as the (row) vector **p** of the coefficients, in descending order of the power of the variable. The roots are returned as a column vector. The function poly(r) constructs the polynomial with the roots given in column vector **r.**

To find a zero of a function of one variable, the appropriate MATLAB function is fzero('function name', x0), where x0 is the initial estimate of the root. As is generally the case for built-in MATLAB functions, there are several options for calling fzero(f, x0) to find a zero of f, which is a string containing the name of a real-valued function of a single real variable. If the starting estimate x0 is a scalar (as in this case), fzero searches out from x0 to find (if possible) an interval where f changes sign. If x0 is a vector of length 2, fzero assumes that the sign of f(x0(1)) differs from the sign of f(x0(2)); an error occurs if this is not true.

Mathcad's Functions

Mathcad has two built-in functions for finding roots of equations of the form $f(x) = 0$. One function, polyroots, finds all roots (real or complex) of a polynomial with real or complex coefficients. The second function, root, finds one root of the specified function, *f(x)*.

To use the function polyroots to find the roots of a polynomial equation $p(x) = 0$, define the polynomial by defining the vector **v** of the coefficients of the polynomial $p(x)$, starting with the constant term and including 0's for any terms that do not explicitly appear. The function returns a vector of the n roots of the polynomial equation $p(x) = 0$.

There are two ways of using the function root to find the roots of a general equation of the form $f(x) = 0$. The *unbracketed form* requires an initial guess of the solution to begin its search for a zero of the function $f(x)$. The *bracketed form* does not require an initial guess for the solution, but as its name suggests, it does require two values of the independent variable that bracket the desired root. The bracketed form is limited to real valued functions of a real variable, and only real roots are produced.

Mathematica's Functions

Mathematica also has two functions for finding numerical solutions to equations. Nroots[lhs == rhs, x] approximates the roots of the polynomial equation, lhs==rhs. The function FindRoot[lhs==rhs, {x, x0}] searches for a numerical solution of the general equation lhs==rhs using Newton's method; it requires that symbolic derivatives of lhs and rhs can be found. Alternatively, the function can be called with two starting estimates, in which case a variant of the secant method is used.

SUMMARY

Bisection

To find a root in $[a, b]$, where $f(a) f(b) < 0$:

Find $m = (a + b)/2$;

determine whether the root is in $[a, m]$ or in $[m, b]$ by testing whether $f(a) f(m) < 0$; continue the process on an appropriate subinterval.

Regula Falsi and Secant Methods

Given two points (x_{k-1}, y_{k-1}) and (x_k, y_k), the next approximation to the root is

$$x_{k+1} = x_k - \frac{x_k - x_{k-1}}{y_k - y_{k-1}} y_k.$$

Regula falsi (false position) requires that the root is bracketed by the approximate roots at each stage, so the calculation of x_{k+1} uses x_k together with either x_{k-1} or x_{k-2}, and the corresponding y values.

The *secant method* uses x_k and x_{k-1}, and the corresponding y values to find x_{k+1}.

Newton's Method

Given the current estimate of the root, x_k, the value of the function at x_k, i.e., $y_k = f(x_k)$, and the value of the derivative at x_k, i.e., $y'_k = f'(x_k)$, it follows that

$$x_{k+1} = x_k - \frac{y_k}{y'_k}$$

Muller's Method

Given three points (x_1, y_1), (x_2, y_2) and (x_3, y_3), compute

$$c_1 = \frac{y_2 - y_1}{x_2 - x_1} \qquad c_2 = \frac{y_3 - y_2}{x_3 - x_2}, \qquad d_1 = \frac{c_2 - c_1}{x_3 - x_1}, \qquad \text{and}$$

$$s = c_2 + d_1(x_3 - x_2).$$

The next approximate root is then

$$x = x_3 - \frac{2 y_3}{s + \text{sign}(s)\sqrt{s^2 - 4 y_3 d_1}}.$$

For additional information on root-finding techniques, the following references are recommended:

Acton, F. S. *Numerical Methods That Work* (corrected edition). Mathematical Association of America, Washington, DC, 1990.

Atkinson, K. E. *An Introduction to Numerical Analysis*, 2ᵈ ed. John Wiley & Sons, New York, 1989.

Press, W. H., S. A. Teukolsky, W. T. Vetterling, and B. P. Flannery, *Numerical Recipes in C; The Art of Scientific Computing*, 2ᵈ ed. Cambridge Unversity Press, Cambridge, 1992.

Ralston, A., and P. Rabinowitz. *A First Course in Numerical Analysis.* McGraw-Hill, New York, 1978.

Rice, J. R. *Numerical Methods, Software, and Analysis.* McGraw-Hill, New York, 1983.

For a particularly nice discussion on special methods for polynomials and why they are worthwhile, see:

Hamming, R. W. *Numerical Methods for Scientists and Engineers*, 2ᵈ ed. McGraw-Hill, New York, 1973.

Examples of applications of root-finding techniques occur throughout science and engineering. A few sources are suggested here.

Edwards, C. H. Jr. and D. E. Penney. *Calculus and Analytic Geometry,* 5ᵗʰ ed. Prentice Hall, Englewood Cliffs, NJ, 1998.

Greenberg, M. D. *Foundations of Applied Mathematics*, 2ᵈ ed. Prentice Hall, Englewood Cliffs, NJ, 1998.

Hibbeler, R. C. *Engineering Mechanics: Statics and Dynamics*, 7ᵗʰ ed. Prentice Hall, Englewood Cliffs, NJ, 1995.

Details of Brent's method and Ridders' method are given in:

Brent, R. *Algorithms for Minimization Without Derivatives* Prentice-Hall, Englewood Cliffs, NJ, 1973.

Forsythe, G. E., M. A. Malcolm, and C. B. Moler. *Computer Methods for Mathematical Computations.* Prentice-Hall, Englewood Cliffs, NJ, 1976.

Ridders, C. J. F. *IEEE Transaction on Circuits and Systems,* 1979, vol. CAS-26, pp. 979–980.

For a comprehensive survey of methods, see

Householder, A. S. *The Numerical Treatment of a Single Nonlinear Equation.* McGraw-Hill, New York, 1970.

For Problems P2.1 to P2.10, find the positive real zero of the functions that follow; find consecutive integers a and b that bracket the root to use as starting values for the bisection, regula falsi, or secant method. Use $\dfrac{a + b}{2}$ as the starting value for Newton's method and as the third starting value for Muller's method.

a. Find the zero using bisection.
b. Find the zero using regula falsi.
c. Find the zero using the secant method.
d. Find the zero using Newton's method.
e. Find the zero using Muller's method.

P2.1 $f(x) = x^2 - 2$.
P2.2 $f(x) = x^2 - 5$.
P2.3 $f(x) = x^2 - 7$.
P2.4 $f(x) = x^3 - 3$.
P2.5 $f(x) = x^3 - 4$.
P2.6 $f(x) = x^3 - 6$.
P2.7 $f(x) = x^4 - 0.06$.
P2.8 $f(x) = x^4 - 0.25$.
P2.9 $f(x) = x^4 - 0.45$.
P2.10 $f(x) = x^4 - 0.65$.

For Problems P2.11 to P2.20, find all real zeros of the functions that follow; choose starting values as described for Problems P2.1 to P2.10.

a. Find the zeros using bisection.
b. Find the zeros using regula falsi.
c. Find the zeros using the secant method.
d. Find the zeros using Newton's method.
e. Find the zeros using Muller's method.

P2.11 $f(x) = x^3 + 3x^2 - 1$.
P2.12 $f(x) = x^3 - 4x + 1$.
P2.13 $f(x) = x^3 - 9x + 2$.
P2.14 $f(x) = x^3 - 2x^2 - 5$.
P2.15 $f(x) = x^3 - x^2 - 4x - 3$.
P2.16 $f(x) = x^3 - 6x^2 + 11x - 5$.
P2.17 $f(x) = x^3 - x^2 - 24x - 32$.
P2.18 $f(x)) = x^3 - 7x^2 + 14x - 7$.
P2.19 $f(x) = 6x^3 - 23x^2 + 20x$.
P2.20 $f(x) = 3x^3 - x^2 - 18x + 6$.

P2.21 For each of the following equations, use Newton's method with the specified starting value to find a root; discuss the source of the difficulty if Newton's method fails.

a. $f(x) = -5x^4 + 11x^2 - 2$ $x_0 = 1$
b. $f(x) = x^3 - 4x + 1$ $x_0 = 0$
c. $f(x) = 5x^4 - 11x^2 + 2$
    $x_0 = 1; x_0 = 1/2;$ $x_0 = 0$
d. $f(x) = x^5 - 0.5$ $x_0 = 1$

For Problems P2.22 to P2.29, use the method of your choice.

P2.22 Find the zeros of the following Legendre polynomials:

a. $P_2(x) = (3x^2 - 1)/2$.
b. $P_3(x) = (5x^3 - 3x)/2$.
c. $P_4(x) = (35x^4 - 30x^2 + 3)/8$.
d. $P_5(x) = (63x^5 - 70x^3 + 15x)/8$.

P2.23 Find the first three positive zeros of $y = x \cos x + \sin x$.

P2.24 Find the intersection(s) of $y = e^x$ and $y = x^3$; i.e., find the zeros of $f(x) = e^x - x^3$.

P2.25 Find the intersection(s) of $y = e^x$ and $y = x^2$.

P2.26 Find all intersections of $y = 2^x$ and $y = x^2$.

P2.27 Find the point(s) of intersection of x^c and c^x for different values of c.

a. $c = 3$ b. $c = 2.7$
(Note that for $c = e$, $x^c \le c^x$ for all x.)

P2.28 Find the intersection(s) of $y = -a + e^x$ and $y = b + \ln(x)$.

a. $a = 5, b = 1$.
b. $a = 3, b = 2$.
c. $a = 1, b = 5$.

P2.29 Find the zeros of $y = f(x) = \ln(x + 0.1) + 1.5$.

A2.1 To determine the displacement d of a spring of stiffness 400 *N/m* and unstretched length 6 *m* when a force of 200 N is applied, as illustrated in the following figure, two expressions are found for the tension T in each half of the spring.

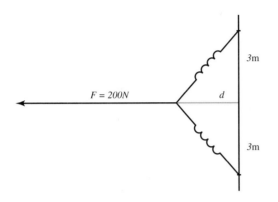

First, T is half the horizontal component of the applied force; i.e.,

$$T = 100 \sqrt{9 + d^2}/d.$$

Second, T is the product of the spring constant and the amount by which the spring is stretched; i.e.,

$$T = 400 \left(\sqrt{9 + d^2} - 3 \right).$$

Find d by finding a root of the equation

$$4 \left(\sqrt{9 + d^2} - 3 \right) - \sqrt{9 + d^2}/d = 0.$$

(See Hibbeler, *Statics,* 1995 for a discussion of similar problems.)

A2.2 A boat can travel with a speed of $v_b = 20$ in still water. (See accompanying figure.) Determine the bearing angle θ of the boat in a river flowing at $v_w = -5$. The bearing angle is measured from the longitudinal axis along which the river flows. Let v be the velocity of the boat along the desired path, which is at 60° from the transverse axis (across the river).

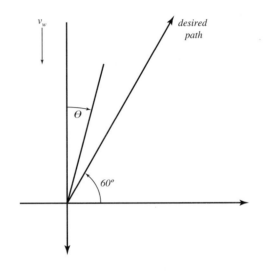

Equating the longitudinal and transverse components of the velocities, gives

$$v \cos(60°) = 20 \sin \theta$$

$$v \sin(60°) = -5 + 20 \cos \theta$$

Eliminating v, gives the equation for θ :

$$1.732 \sin \theta - \cos \theta + 0.25 = 0.$$

(See Hibbler, *Dynamics,* 1995, p. 88 for a discussion of a similar problem.)

A2.3 The van der Waals equation of state, a simple extension of the ideal gas law discovered in 1873 by the Dutch physicist Johanes Diderik van der Waals, is

$$\left(P + \frac{n^2 a}{V^2}\right)(V - nb) = nRT,$$

where the constants a and b, characteristic of the gas, are determined experimentally. For P in atmospheres, V in liters, n in moles, and T in kelvins, R is approximately 0.0820 liter atm deg^{-1} mole^{-1}. The volume of 1 mole of a perfect gas at standard conditions (1 atm, 273 K) is 22.415 liters. Find the volume occupied by 1 mole of the following gases, with given values of a and b:

Gas	a	b
O_2	1.36	0.0318
N_2O	3.78	0.0441
SO_2	6.71	0.0564

These parameter values come from Pauling, *General Chemistry,* 1989, p. 337. For further discussion of related problems, see also Himmelblau, *Basic Principles and Calculations in Chemical Engineering,* 1974, Sec 3.2.

A2.4 A simple model of oxygen diffusion around a capillary leads to an equation of the form

$$C(r) = \frac{R r^2}{4 K} + B_1 \ln(r) + B_2,$$

where R, K, B_1, and B_2 depend on the geometry, reaction rates, and other specifics of the problem. As an example, without considering realistic values of these constants, find the value of r such that

$$C(r) = 2r^2 + 3\ln(r) + 1 = 2;$$

this corresponds to finding a zero of $y(r) = 2r^2 + 3\ln(r) - 1$.

(See Simon, 1986, pp. 185–189 for a discussion of the derivation of this equation.)

A2.5 The flow rate in a pipe system connecting two reservoirs (at different surface elevations) depends on the characteristics of the pump, the roughness of the pipe, the length and diameter of the pipe, and the specific gravity of the fluid. For an

800-ft section of 6-in. pipe connecting two reservoirs (with a 5-ft differential in elevation) containing oil of specific gravity 0.8, with a 6-hp pump, the equation for the flow rate Q is

$$12 Q^3 + 5 Q - 40 = 0.$$

Approximate the real root of the equation in the interval $0 \le Q \le 2$.

(For derivation of this equation, see Ayyub and McCuen, 1996, pp. 53–59.)

A2.6 The Peng-Robinson equation of state

$$P = \frac{RT}{V - b} - \frac{a}{V(V + b) + b(V - b)}$$

is a two-parameter extension of the ideal gas law. Find the volume of 1 mole of a gas at $P = 10^4$ kPa and $T = 340$ K; take as the parameter values $a = 364$ m^{6}kPa/(kg mole)^2, $b = 0.03$ m^3/kg mole and $R = 1.618$. Use $V = 0.055$ m^3/kg mole as an initial estimate (from the ideal gas law). (See Hanna and Sandall, 1995, pp. 161ff. for discussion)

A2.7 The Beattie-Bridgeman equation of state

$$P = \frac{RT}{V} + \frac{a}{V^2} + \frac{b}{V^3} + \frac{c}{V^4}$$

is a three-parameter extension of the ideal gas law. Using $a = -1.06$, $b = 0.057$, and $c = -0.0001$, find the volume of 1 mole of a gas at $P = 25$ atm, and $T = 293$ K. The constant $R = 0.082$ liter-atm/K-g mole. (See Ayyub and McCuen, 1996, p. 91).

A2.8 For given values of s (the length of the cable) and x (the distance between the support positions of the ends, the problem of finding the deflection of the hanging cable shown in the following diagram requires (as an intermediate step) the solution (for F) of the equation

$$s = F \sinh (x/F).$$

Find F for $s = 100$, and $x = 97$. (Adapted from Hibbeler, *Statics:,* 1996.)

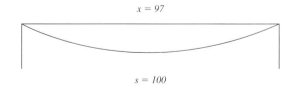

$x = 97$

$s = 100$

A2.9 The position of a ball, thrown up with a given initial velocity v_0, and initial position x_0, subject to air resistance proportional to its velocity is given by

$$x(t) = \rho^{-1}(v_0 + v_r)(1 - e^{-\rho t}) - v_r t + x_0$$

where ρ is the drag coefficient, g is the gravitational constant, and $v_r = g/\rho = mg/k$ is the terminal velocity. Find when the ball hits the ground, if $x_0 = 0$, $v_0 = 20$ m/s, $\rho = 0.35$, $g = 9.8$ m/s^2. See a differential equations text (e.g., Edwards and Penney, Boyce and DiPrima, etc.) for further discussion.

A2.10 Some techniques for solving the differential equation describing the deflection of a uniform beam with both ends fixed, subject to a load that is proportional to the distance from one end of the beam, require the positive roots of the function $f(x)$ = cosh x cos x − 1. In order to keep the function values within a reasonable range, it is better to consider the equivalent problem, of finding the zeros of $g(x)$ = cos x − 1/ cosh x. Find the first 5 roots. (For more discussion of the deflection of a beam problem, see Edwards and Penney, *Differential Equations with Boundary Value Problems,* 1996, p. 624.)

A2.11 For a cantilever beam (one end fixed, the other free) the required parameters are the positive roots of $f(x)$ = cosh x cos x + 1; in order to keep function values within a reasonable range, consider zeros of $g(x)$ = cos x + 1/ cosh x. Find the first 5 roots.

EXTEND YOUR UNDERSTANDING

U2.1 Muller's method can also be given in the following form given three initial approximations to the root:

$$(x_0, y_0), (x_1, y_1) \text{ and } (x_2, y_2)$$

find a and b:

$$b = \frac{(x_0 - x_2)^2(y_1 - y_2) - (x_1 - x_2)^2(y_0 - y_2)}{(x_0 - x_2)(x_1 - x_2)(x_0 - x_1)}$$

$$a = \frac{(x_1 - x_2)(y_0 - y_2) - (x_0 - x_2)(y_1 - y_2)}{(x_0 - x_2)(x_1 - x_2)(x_0 - x_1)}$$

the next approximation is

$$x = x_2 + \frac{-2c}{b + \text{sign}(b)\sqrt{b^2 - 4ac}}$$

compare the computational effort for performing one step of this algorithm to the effort required for the algorithm given in the text.

U2.2 Use Newton's method, or the secant method, to find a root of

$$f(x) = -0.01 + \frac{1}{1 + x^2}$$

Compare the use of a convergence test of the form $|f(x_k)| < f$tol with a test of the form

$$|x_{k+1} - x_k| < \text{tol.}$$

U2.3 Show that for the bisection method

$$\frac{|x_k - x^*|}{|x_{k-1} - x^*|} \le \frac{1}{2}$$

is equivalent to $|x^* - x_k| \le \dfrac{1}{2^k} |x^* - x_1|$, so that bisection is linearly convergent according to the general definition.

U2.4 Show that even without the initial estimates bracketing the zero, the secant method converges for Example 2.7; take $a = 2$, $b = 3$.

3

Solving Systems of Linear Equations: Direct Methods

We now extend our investigation of numerical methods for solving equations to the consideration of linear systems. In this chapter, we present the method known as Gaussian elimination.

We begin with two examples that are used to illustrate basic Gaussian elimination and two important variations. Gaussian elimination is based on the fact that if two equations have a point in common, then that point also satisfies any linear combination of the two equations. If we can find linear combinations of suitably simple form, we will be able to find the solution of the original system more easily. The form that we desire is one in which certain of the variables have been eliminated from some of the equations.

Variations of Gaussian elimination are also presented for row pivoting and tridiagonal systems. These methods are direct techniques that require a single pass through the appropriate algorithm. The specific form of the resulting (equivalent) system of equations is illustrated in the algorithms and examples that follow. We restrict our inquiry to systems in which we have the same number of equations as unknowns.

Systems of linear equations occur in a wide variety of settings, including the analysis of electrical circuits, the determination of forces on a truss, balancing the reactants in a chemical reaction, economics, traffic flow, queuing theory, and calculating the equilibrium heat distribution in a plate.

In Chapter 4 we investigate two important types of matrix factorization that can be useful in solving linear systems as well as in other applications. The first of these factorizations (LU) is closely related to the Gaussian elimination techniques presented here. The second type of factorization (QR) is important for finding the eigenvalues of a matrix; eigenvalues and eigenvectors are discussed in Chapter 5.

Example 3-A Current in an Electrical Circuit

Consider the problem of finding the currents in different parts of an electrical circuit, with resistors as shown in Fig. 3.1.

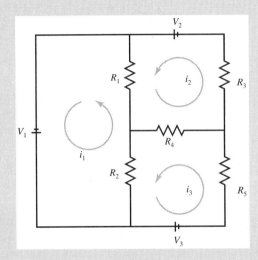

FIGURE 3.1   Simple electrical circuit.

The analysis tools come from elementary physics:

1. The sum of the voltage drops around a closed loop is zero;
2. The voltage drop across a resistor is the product of the current and the resistance.

We define each unknown current to be positive if it flows in the counterclockwise direction; if a computed current is negative, the flow is clockwise.

The analysis of the voltages around the three loops gives three equations, which we solve later in the chapter.

If $R_1 = 20$, $R_2 = 0$, $R_3 = 25$, $R_4 = 10$, $R_5 = 30$, $V_1 = 0$, $V_2 = 0$, and $V_3 = 200$, we have

Flow around left loop
$$20\,(i_1 - i_2) + 10\,(i_1 - i_3) = 0.$$

Flow around upper right loop
$$25\,i_2 + 10\,(i_2 - i_3) + 20\,(i_2 - i_1) = 0.$$

Flow around lower right loop
$$30\,i_3 + 10\,(i_3 - i_2) + 10\,(i_3 - i_1) = 200.$$

Example 3-B Forces on a Truss

A lightweight structure constructed of triangular elements may be capable of supporting large weights. To analyze the forces on such a structure, known as a *truss*, a system of linear equations describing the equilibrium of the horizontal and vertical forces on each node (or joint) of the truss must be solved. A single triangular element is shown in Fig. 3.2.

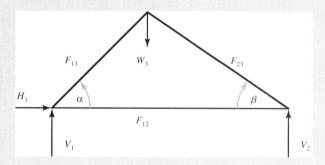

FIGURE 3.2   Element of a simple truss.

We assume that the forces in each of the members of the truss (F_{12}, F_{13}, and F_{23}) are acting to pull the structure together. V_1 and V_2 are unknown vertical forces supporting the structure (at nodes 1 and 2, respectively), H_1 is an unknown horizontal bracing force at node 1. At node 3, W_3 is a known vertical force representing the weight of the structure, and H_3 is a known horizontal force. We define the forces (that appear on the left-hand side of the linear equations below) to be positive if they act to the right, or in an upward direction. If a computed quantity is negative, it indicates that the force acts in the opposite direction. The system of equations represents the conditions for vertical and horizontal equilibrium at the three nodes.

Node 1

$$V_1 \qquad\qquad + F_{13} \sin \alpha \qquad\qquad = 0,$$

$$H_1 \quad + F_{12} + F_{13} \cos \alpha \qquad\qquad = 0.$$

Node 2

$$V_2 \qquad\qquad\qquad + F_{23} \sin \beta = 0,$$

$$- F_{12} \qquad\qquad - F_{23} \cos \beta = 0.$$

Node 3

$$- F_{13} \sin \alpha - F_{23} \sin \beta = W_3,$$

$$- F_{13} \cos \alpha + F_{23} \cos \beta = 0.$$

The process of Gaussian elimination was introduced in Chapter 1 for a system of two equations. Example 3.1 illustrates the steps for a system of three equations in three unknowns.

Example 3.1 Solving a Small Linear System

The three-by-three system

$$
\begin{array}{rcrcrcr}
x & + & 2y & + & 3z & = & 1 \\
2x & + & 6y & + & 10z & = & 0 \\
3x & + & 14y & + & 28z & = & -8
\end{array}
$$

can be solved by Gaussian elimination as described in the following steps:

Step 1
Use the first equation to eliminate x in the second and third equations.

Multiply the first equation by -2 and add it to the second equation to get a new second equation with the x variable eliminated.

Also, multiply the first equation by -3 and add it to the third equation to get a new third equation with the x variable eliminated. The resulting system is

$$
\begin{array}{rcr}
x + 2y + 3z & = & 1 \\
2y + 4z & = & -2 \\
8y + 19z & = & -11
\end{array}
$$

Step 2
Use the second equation to eliminate the y term in the third equation.

Multiply the second equation by -4 and add it to the third equation to get a new third equation with the y variable eliminated. The system now looks like this:

$$
\begin{array}{rcr}
x + 2y + 3z & = & 1 \\
2y + 4z & = & -2 \\
3z & = & -3
\end{array}
$$

This completes the "forward elimination" phase; we have an upper triangular system.

We now use "back substitution" to find the values of the unknowns:

$$
\begin{array}{lcl}
3z = -3 & & \Rightarrow z = -1 \\
2y + 4(-1) = -2 & & \Rightarrow y = 1 \\
x + 2(1) + 3(-1) = 1 & \Rightarrow & x = 2
\end{array}
$$

3.1.1 Using Matrix Notation

We see in the preceding example that all of the computations are based on the coefficients and elements of the right-hand side of the system of equations. This system is written in matrix-vector form as $\mathbf{A}\mathbf{x} = \mathbf{b}$ (see Chapter 1) with

$$\mathbf{A} = \begin{bmatrix} 1 & 2 & 3 \\ 2 & 6 & 10 \\ 3 & 14 & 28 \end{bmatrix}, \qquad \mathbf{b} = \begin{bmatrix} 1 \\ 0 \\ -8 \end{bmatrix}.$$

Since the same operations are performed on the matrix $\mathbf{A}$ and the vector $\mathbf{b}$, they are often combined in the augmented matrix:

$$\begin{bmatrix} 1 & 2 & 3 & | & 1 \\ 2 & 6 & 10 & | & 0 \\ 3 & 14 & 28 & | & -8 \end{bmatrix}.$$

A general four-by-four system of equations can be represented in matrix form as $\mathbf{A}\mathbf{x} = \mathbf{b}$, where

$$\mathbf{A} = \begin{bmatrix} a_{11} & a_{12} & a_{13} & a_{14} \\ a_{21} & a_{22} & a_{23} & a_{24} \\ a_{31} & a_{32} & a_{33} & a_{34} \\ a_{41} & a_{42} & a_{43} & a_{44} \end{bmatrix} \quad \text{and} \quad \mathbf{b} = \begin{bmatrix} b_1 \\ b_2 \\ b_3 \\ b_4 \end{bmatrix}.$$

There are a variety of ways to transform a linear system of equations into an equivalent system having the same solution. However, the basic Gaussian elimination procedure follows a specific sequence of steps and only uses operations of the following form:

Add a multiple m of row R_i onto row R_j to form a new row R_j, or

$$R_j \leftarrow mR_i + R_j$$

At the kth stage of the basic Gaussian elimination procedure, the appropriate multiples of the kth equation are used to eliminate the kth variable from equations $k + 1, \ldots n$; in terms of the coefficient matrix $\mathbf{A}$, the appropriate multiple of the kth row is used to reduce each of the entries in the kth column below the kth row to zero. The kth row is called the *pivot row*, the kth column is the *pivot column*, and the element a_{kk} is the *pivot element*. Since finding the appropriate multiplier for each row requires dividing by the pivot element for that stage, the process fails if the pivot element is zero. Possible remedies for this situation are discussed later in the chapter; they allow interchanging the order of the rows of the augmented matrix. An algorithm for basic Gaussian elimination is given in the next section.

3.1.2 Algorithm for Basic Gaussian Elimination

The steps to solve the linear system $\mathbf{M}\,\mathbf{x} = \mathbf{B}$ using Gaussian elimination are given in the following algorithm. Each column of the right-hand side matrix $\mathbf{B}$ generates a corresponding column in the solution matrix $\mathbf{X}$. When the colon symbol appears as the second index in a matrix, it indicates that computations are to be carried out for all elements in the column. (Using the colon as the first index indicates that computations apply to all elements in the row). Similarly, a range of indices is given as $k + 1{:}n$, so that the dot product $\mathbf{A}(k, k + 1{:}n)*\mathbf{X}(k + 1{:}n,j)$ is vector shorthand for

$$\mathbf{A}(k, k + 1)*\mathbf{X}(k + 1,j) + \mathbf{A}(k, k + 2)*\mathbf{X}(k + 2,j) + \ldots + \mathbf{A}(k, n)*\mathbf{X}(n,j)$$

Basic Gaussian Elimination

Input

A	*matrix of coefficients (n-by-n)*
B	*right-hand side(s) of equation, A x = B (n-by-m)*
n	*number of rows and columns in A, number of rows in B*
m	*number of columns in B*

Forward Elimination

For k = 1 to n − 1   *the pivot element is A(k,k)*
    For i = k + 1 to n
        s = −A(i, k)/A(k,k)
        A(i, :) = A(i, :) + s*A(k, :)   *update row i in A*
        B(i, :) = B(i, :) + s*B(k, :)   *update row i in B*
    End
End

Back Substitution

For j = 1 to m   *for each column in the right hand side matrix*
    X(n, j) = B(n, j)/A(n,n)   *generate solution matrix*
    For k = n − 1 to 1
        K(k, j) = (B(k, j) − A(k, k + 1{:}n)*X(k + 1{:}nj))/A(k,k)
                     dot product of part of row k of matrix A with
                     part of column j of matrix X
    End
End

Return
    X   *solution matrix*

3.1.3 Applications of Basic Gaussian Elimination

The algorithm for Gaussian elimination is illustrated in the next example using the equations for the electrical circuit in Example 3-A, and a single right-hand side.

Example 3.2 Electrical Circuit Analysis

The equations describing the electrical circuit in Example 3-A simplify to

$$+30i_1 - 20i_2 - 10i_3 = 0$$
$$-20i_1 + 55i_2 - 10i_3 = 0$$
$$-10i_1 - 10i_2 + 50i_3 = 200$$

In matrix form the system is $\mathbf{A}\,\mathbf{x} = \mathbf{b}$, with

$$\mathbf{A} = \begin{bmatrix} 30 & -20 & -10 \\ -20 & 55 & -10 \\ -10 & -10 & 50 \end{bmatrix}, \qquad \mathbf{b} = \begin{bmatrix} 0 \\ 0 \\ 200 \end{bmatrix}.$$

Step 1 The pivot is $a_{11} = 30$.
Multiply first row by $m_{21} = 20/30 = 2/3$; add result to second row to get

$$a_{21} = 0, \; a_{22} = 55 + (2/3)(-20) = 125/3, \; a_{23} = -10 + (2/3)(-10) = -50/3.$$

Transform right-hand side in the same way: $b_2 = 0 + (2/3)(0) = 0$.
Multiply first row by $m_{31} = 10/30 = 1/3$; add result to third row to get

$$a_{31} = 0, \; a_{32} = -10 + (1/3)(-20) = -50/3, \; a_{33} = 50 + (1/3)(-10) = 140/3.$$

Transform right-hand side in the same way: $b_3 = 200 + (1/3)(0) = 200$
After the first stage of Gaussian elimination,

$$\mathbf{A} = \begin{bmatrix} 30 & -20 & -10 \\ 0 & 125/3 & -50/3 \\ 0 & -50/3 & 140/3 \end{bmatrix} \qquad \mathbf{b} = \begin{bmatrix} 0 \\ 0 \\ 200 \end{bmatrix}$$

Step 2 The pivot is $a_{22} = 125/3$.
Multiply second row by $m_{32} = 2/5$; add result to third row to get

$$a_{31} = 0, \; a_{32} = 0, \; a_{33} = 140/3 + (2/5)(-50/3) = 40.$$

Transform right-hand side in the same way: $b_3 = 200 + (2/5)(0) = 200$.
After the second stage of Gaussian elimination,

$$\mathbf{A} = \begin{bmatrix} 30 & -20 & -10 \\ 0 & 125/3 & -50/3 \\ 0 & 0 & 40 \end{bmatrix} \qquad \mathbf{b} = \begin{bmatrix} 0 \\ 0 \\ 200 \end{bmatrix}$$

Back substitution

$$x_3 = b_3/a_{33} = 200/40 = 5$$

$$x_2 = \frac{b_2 - a_{23}x_3}{a_{22}} = [0 + (-50/3)\,(5)]/[125/3] = 2$$

$$x_1 = \frac{b_1 - a_{12}x_2 - a_{13}x_3}{a_{11}} = [0 - (-20)(2) - (-10)(5)]/30 = 3$$

Example 3.3 Gaussian Elimination for a Four-by-Four System

Solve $\mathbf{A}\,\mathbf{x} = \mathbf{b}$, for a general 4-by-4 matrix $\mathbf{A}$ and column vector $\mathbf{b}$.

Step 1
The pivot is a_{11}.
  Multiply the first row by $m_{21} = -a_{21}/a_{11}$ and add the result to the second row

$$a_{21} \Leftarrow 0; \qquad\qquad a_{22} \Leftarrow a_{22} + m_{21}a_{12};$$
$$a_{23} \Leftarrow a_{23} + m_{21}a_{13}; \qquad\qquad a_{24} \Leftarrow a_{24} + m_{21}a_{14}.$$

Transform the right-hand side: $b_2 \Leftarrow b_2 + m_{21}b_1$.
  Multiply the first row by $m_{31} = -a_{31}/a_{11}$ and add the result to the third row

$$a_{31} \Leftarrow 0; \qquad\qquad a_{32} \Leftarrow a_{32} + m_{31}a_{12};$$
$$a_{33} \Leftarrow a_{33} + m_{31}a_{13}; \qquad\qquad a_{34} \Leftarrow a_{34} + m_{31}a_{14}.$$

Transform the right-hand side: $b_3 \Leftarrow b_3 + m_{31}b_1$.
  Multiply the first row by $m_{41} = -a_{41}/a_{11}$ and add the result to the fourth row

$$a_{41} \Leftarrow 0; \qquad\qquad a_{42} \Leftarrow a_{42} + m_{41}a_{12};$$
$$a_{43} \Leftarrow a_{43} + m_{41}a_{13}; \qquad\qquad a_{44} \Leftarrow a_{44} + m_{41}a_{14}.$$

Transform the right-hand side: $b_4 \Leftarrow b_4 + m_{41}b_1$.

Step 2
The pivot is a_{22}.
  Multiply the second row by $m_{32} = -a_{32}/a_{22}$; add the result to the third row

$$a_{31} = 0; \quad a_{32} \Leftarrow 0; \quad a_{33} \Leftarrow a_{33} + m_{32}a_{23}; \quad a_{34} \Leftarrow a_{34} + m_{32}a_{24}.$$

Transform the right-hand side: $b_3 \Leftarrow b_3 + m_{32}b_2$.
  Multiply the second row by $m_{42} = -a_{42}/a_{22}$; add the result to the fourth row

$$a_{41} = 0; \quad a_{42} \Leftarrow 0; \quad a_{43} \Leftarrow a_{43} + m_{42}a_{23}; \quad a_{44} \Leftarrow a_{44} + m_{42}a_{24}.$$

Transform the right-hand side: $b_4 \Leftarrow b_4 + m_{42}b_2$.

Step 3
The pivot is a_{33}.
  Multiply the third row by $m_{43} = a_{43}/a_{33}$ and add the result to the fourth row

$$a_{41} = 0; \quad a_{42} = 0; \quad a_{43} \Leftarrow 0; \quad a_{44} \Leftarrow a_{44} + m_{43}a_{34}.$$

Transform the right-hand side: $b_4 \Leftarrow b_4 + m_{43}b_3$.

Back Substitution

$$x_4 = b_4/a_{44}$$
$$x_3 = (b_3 - a_{34}x_4)/a_{33}$$
$$x_2 = (b_2 - a_{23}x_3 - a_{24}x_4)/a_{22}$$
$$x_1 = (b_1 - a_{12}x_2 - a_{13}x_3 - a_{14}x_4)/a_{11}$$

Example 3.4 Forces on a Simple Truss

To illustrate the use of a simple computer program implementing Gaussian elimination, we investigate the effect of different applied forces in the single-triangle truss shown in Fig. 3.2. The first case corresponds to the case in which the only force at node 3 is the weight of the structure, W_3. The second case extends the situation to include a horizontal force applied at node 3, in addition to the weight of the structure. The matrix $\mathbf{A}$ is unchanged as long as the geometry of the structure is not modified. We take $\alpha = \pi/6$ and $\beta = \pi/3$, so that the coefficient matrix is

$$\mathbf{A} = \begin{bmatrix} 1.00 & 0 & 0 & 0 & 0.50 & 0 \\ 0 & 1.00 & 0 & 1.00 & 0.8660 & 0 \\ 0 & 0 & 1.00 & 0 & 0 & 0.8660 \\ 0 & 0 & 0 & -1.00 & 0 & -0.50 \\ 0 & 0 & 0 & 0 & -0.50 & -0.8660 \\ 0 & 0 & 0 & 0 & -0.8660 & 0.50 \end{bmatrix}$$

To find the forces for the two cases described above, we solve the linear system $\mathbf{A}\,\mathbf{x} = \mathbf{B}$ for

$$\mathbf{B} = \begin{bmatrix} 0 & 0 \\ 0 & 0 \\ 0 & 0 \\ 0 & 0 \\ 100 & 100 \\ 0 & 20 \end{bmatrix}$$

The function returns the matrix $\mathbf{X}$; the first column of $\mathbf{X}$ gives the forces for a vertical force of 100 units at node 3; note that 1/4 of the structure's weight is supported at node 1 and 3/4 of the weight is supported at node 2.

The second column gives the results for the scenario in which there is a horizontal force at node 3 in addition to the weight of the structure. The vertical support of the structure is shifted toward node 1 and a horizontal force must be applied at node 1 to balance the horizontal force at node 3.

$$\mathbf{X} = \begin{bmatrix} 25.0000 & 33.6603 \\ -0.0000 & 20.0000 \\ 75.0000 & 66.3397 \\ 43.3013 & 38.3013 \\ -50.0000 & -67.3205 \\ -86.6025 & -76.6025 \end{bmatrix}$$

3.1.4 Discussion

There are two key aspects to understanding why Gaussian elimination works. The first is to see why a linear combination of two equations passes through the point of intersection of the two equations. The second is to consider why (or when) the sequence of steps for Gaussian elimination produces a system that can be solved by back substitution. Analyzing these two questions suggests when Gaussian elimination works well, when it works poorly or fails, and when it can be improved.

If two equations have a point in common, then that point is also a solution of any equation formed as a linear combination of the equations. This result can be shown by simple algebra. Consider two linear equations,

$$S_1: a_0 + a_1 x_1 + a_2 x_2 + \ldots + a_n x_n = 0$$

and

$$T_1: b_0 + b_1 x_1 + b_2 x_2 + \ldots + b_n x_n = 0$$

and assume that the point $\mathbf{r} = (r_1, r_2, \ldots r_n)$ satisfies both equations. Then $\mathbf{r}$ also satisfies the linear combination $C = m_1 S_1 + m_2 T_1$, or

$$C: m_1 a_0 + m_1 a_1 x_1 + m_1 a_2 x_2 + \ldots + m_1 a_n x_n$$
$$+ m_2 b_0 + m_2 b_1 x_1 + m_2 b_2 x_2 + \ldots + m_2 b_n x_n = 0.$$

Substituting $(r_1, r_2, \ldots r_n)$ in the equation C and using the fact that $\mathbf{r}$ satisfies S_1 and T_1 gives the desired result.

Now consider the specific sequence of transformations on the linear system given in the basic Gaussian elimination algorithm presented earlier. The description assumes that it is possible to find the necessary multiplier to reduce each column to zero as indicated. Two situations can arise if a zero pivot element is encountered, depending on whether or not there are any nonzero elements in the pivot column below the pivot row.

If a zero pivot occurs (in an n-by-n linear system), and the entire pivot column below the pivot row is also zero, then the system of equations does not have a unique solution. The equations are either inconsistent or redundant.

On the other hand, if a zero element is encountered in a pivot position, but there is a nonzero element in the pivot column below the pivot element, the Gaussian elimination process can be modified to allow for interchanging the row whose pivot element is zero with a row below it. This process is called (partial) pivoting and is the subject of the next section.

Several considerations are operative in determining how well a particular numerical method works. Among the most important are questions dealing with the quality of the solution, the sensitivity of the method to errors (including inexact arithmetic), and the computational effort required.

Computational effort is usually measured in terms of the number of multiplications and divisions ($m + d$) or in terms of the number of floating-point operations (flops). On early computers, multiplication and division were much more time intensive than addition and subtraction, which led researchers to analyze algorithms in terms of multiplication and division. It is also typical for the number of additions and subtractions to be directly related to the number of multiplications and divisions. Today, because the difference in effort for different operations has been reduced, analysis in terms of flops has become more common. Since the linear systems that arise in practice are often very large, it is important to see how the computational effort required for Gaussian elimination is related to the size of the coefficient matrix A (assumed to be n-by-n).

At the first stage of Gaussian elimination, one division is required to find the multiplier for the second row ($m_{12} = -a_{12}/a_{11}$). Then n multiplications and n additions are required to form the new second row. Note that we must also multiply the right-hand side, but we do not have to multiply the first element in the row, since we know that the new first element in the second row will be zero. This process must be performed for each of the rows below the first row. Thus, the first stage requires $(n + 1)$ $(n - 1)$ multiplications and divisions, as well as $n(n - 1)$ additions.

At the kth stage of elimination, there is one division to form the multiplier m_{ki} and $(n - k)$ multiplications to generate the new i^{th} row (for $i = k + 1, \ldots, n$). There are also $n - k$ additions required for each new row.

The total number of multiplications and divisions is

$$\sum_{k=1}^{n-1}(n - k + 1)(n - k) = \sum_{k=1}^{n-1}(n^2 - 2nk + k^2 + n - k)$$

$$= \sum_{k=1}^{n-1}(n^2 + n) - \sum_{k=1}^{n-1}(2n + 1)k + \sum_{k=1}^{n-1}k^2$$

which simplifies to

$$= \frac{n^3}{3} - \frac{n}{3} \qquad .$$

If there is a unique solution, if computations are exact, and if the pivot element is not zero at any stage, Gaussian elimination gives the solution. However, since computer computations are not exact, we may be faced with errors in the calculations that result from round-off. We illustrate here two types of difficulties that can occur. The first can be avoided by a suitable reordering of the rows of the augmented matrix, which is the subject of the next section. The second example is indicative of a more serious problem.

Gaussian elimination works well for systems with coefficient matrices with special properties. For example, if **A** is strictly diagonally dominant, i.e., for each i,

$|a_{ii}| > \sum_{j \neq i}|a_{ij}|$, Gaussian elimination will work well (Golub and Van Loan, 1996, p. 120).

Some Difficulties Are Solvable with Pivoting

Consider the following system of two equations in two unknowns, and suppose that we have arithmetic with rounding to two digits at each stage of the Gaussian elimination process:

$$0.001x_1 + x_2 = 3,$$
$$x_1 + 2x_2 = 5.$$

Proceeding according to the basic Gaussian elimination procedure, we multiply the first equation by -1000 and add it to the second equation to give (if arithmetic were exact)

$$-998x_2 = -2995.$$

After rounding, this equation becomes $-1000\, x_2 = -3000$, which gives $x_3 = 3$. Substitution of this value in the first equation then yields $x_1 = 0$. Clearly, this is not a good approximation to a solution of the second equation. In the next section, we discuss an enhancement to Gaussian elimination to avoid such a dilemma.

An Ill-Conditioned Matrix Causes More Serious Difficulties

Consider the linear system

$$x_1 + \frac{1}{2}x_2 = \frac{3}{2},$$
$$\frac{1}{2}x_1 + \frac{1}{3}x_2 = \frac{5}{6}.$$

Using exact arithmetic gives the exact solution $x_1 = x_2 = 1$. However, if the right-hand side is modified slightly, to

$$x_1 + \frac{1}{2}x_2 = \frac{3}{2}$$
$$\frac{1}{2}x_1 + \frac{1}{3}x_2 = 1$$

the exact solution becomes $x_1 = 0$ and $x_2 = 3$.

This extreme sensitivity to small changes in the right-hand side is evidence of the fact that the coefficient matrix is "ill-conditioned." The difficulties arising from ill-conditioning cannot be solved by simple refinements in the Gaussian elimination procedure. There are several ways of defining the *condition number* of a matrix; one is to define the condition number as the ratio of the largest eigenvalue to the smallest eigenvalue. Eigenvalues are discussed in Chapter 5. Conditioning is discussed further in section 3.4.2. Regardless of the definition used for the condition number, a matrix with a large condition number is ill-conditioned.

The Hilbert matrix is a well-known example of a matrix that is very ill-conditioned. For the 2-by-2 Hilbert matrix

$$H = \begin{bmatrix} 1 & 1/2 \\ 1/2 & 1/3 \end{bmatrix}$$

the condition number has a value between 19 and 27 (depending on the specific definition used).

Basic Gaussian elimination, as presented in the previous section, fails if the pivot element at any stage of the elimination process is zero, because division by zero is not possible. In addition, difficulties that are not as easy to detect arise if the pivot element is significantly smaller than the coefficients it is being used to eliminate. In this section, we investigate an enhancement to Gaussian elimination that prevents or alleviates some of these shortcomings of the basic procedure.

In order to reduce the inaccuracies that occur in solutions computed with Gaussian elimination and avoid (if possible) the failure of the method resulting from a zero coefficient in the pivot position at some stage of the process, we may need to interchange selected rows of the augmented matrix. We illustrate this process, known as *row pivoting,* in Example 3.5.

Example 3.5   A Difficult System

Consider again the following simple system of two equations in two unknowns, to be solved by Gaussian elimination with rounding to two significant digits at each stage of the process:

$$0.001x_1 + x_2 = 3$$
$$x_1 + 2x_2 = 5$$

With basic Gaussian elimination (with rounding) we found that $x_2 = 3$ and $x_1 = 0$. This is not a good approximation to a solution of the second equation.

If, instead of solving the system with the equations in the order given, we recognize that the very small coefficient of x_1 in the first equation is dangerous (because we would be dividing by something that is close to zero), we can interchange the order of the equations as follows.

$$x_1 + 2x_2 = 5$$
$$0.001x_1 + x_2 = 3$$

Now we multiply the first equation by -0.001 and add it to the second equation to give (if arithmetic were exact)

$$0.998x_2 = 2.995$$

After rounding, this equation becomes $x_2 = 3$. Substitution of this value into the first equation yields $x_1 = -1$, a much better approximation to a solution of the system.

The small pivot element shown in the previous example could occur at any stage of elimination. Gaussian elimination with row pivoting checks all entries in the pivot column (from the current diagonal element to the bottom of the column) and chooses the largest element as the pivot. The current row and the selected pivot row are interchanged. The process is summarized in the following algorithm, and illustrated in Example 3.6.

3.2.1 Algorithm for Gaussian Elimination with Pivoting

The following algorithm to solve **M X** = **B** combines the coefficient matrix **M** and the matrix of right-hand sides, **B,** into the augmented matrix **A.** Row pivoting is performed on **A.** More sophisticated algorithms would keep a vector of indices of the pivot rows without actually performing the row interchanges.

Gaussian Elimination with Row Pivoting ═══════════════════════════════════════

Input
  M   *matrix of coefficients (n-by-n)*
  B   *right-hand side(s) of equation, M x = B (n-by-m)*
  n   *number of rows and columns in M, number of rows in B*
  m   *number of columns in B*
Initialize
  A = [M B]   *form augmented matrix*
Forward elimination
For k = 1 to n − 1
    pivot = | A(k, k) | *pivot element*
    p = k   *pivot row*
    For i = k + 1 to n
        If (|A(i,k)| > pivot)
                pivot = | A(i,k) | *update pivot element*
                p = i   *update pivot row*
        End
    End
    If (p > k)   *interchange rows k and p*
        temp = A(k, :)
        A(k, :) = A(p, :)
        A(p, :) = temp
    End
    For i = k + 1 to n
        s = −A(i, k)/A(k,k)
        A(i, :) = A(i, :) + s*A(k, :)   *update row i in A*
    End
End
Back Substitution
For j = 1 to m   *generate column j of solution matrix*
    X(n, j) = A(n, n + j)/A(n,n)
    For k = n − 1 to 1
        X(k, j) = (A(k, n + j) − A(k, k + 1:n)*X(k + 1:n, j))/A(k,k)
    End
End
Return
  X   *matrix of solution*

3.2.2 Applications of Gaussian Elimination with Row Pivoting

Example 3.6 Solving a Small System

Solve $\mathbf{M}\mathbf{x} = \mathbf{b}$, for

$$\mathbf{M} = \begin{bmatrix} 2 & 6 & 10 \\ 1 & 3 & 3 \\ 3 & 14 & 28 \end{bmatrix} \qquad \mathbf{b} = \begin{bmatrix} 0 \\ 2 \\ -8 \end{bmatrix}$$

Initialize

Create the augmented matrix $\mathbf{A} = [\mathbf{M}\,\mathbf{b}]$.

$$\mathbf{A} = \begin{bmatrix} 2 & 6 & 10 & 0 \\ 1 & 3 & 3 & 2 \\ 3 & 14 & 28 & -8 \end{bmatrix}$$

Forward Elimination

Since $A(3,1) > A(1,1)$, interchange rows 1 and 3.

$$\mathbf{A} = \begin{bmatrix} 3 & 14 & 28 & -8 \\ 1 & 3 & 3 & 2 \\ 2 & 6 & 10 & 0 \end{bmatrix}$$

Transform row 2

$$s = -A(2,1)/A(1,1) = -1/3$$
$$A(2,:) = A(2,:) + s*A(1,:) = [0 \quad -5/3 \quad -19/3 \quad 14/3]$$

Transform row 3

$$s = -A(3,1)/A(1,1) = -2/3$$
$$A(3,:) = A(3,:) + s*A(1,:) = [0 \quad -10/3 \quad -26/3 \quad 16/3]$$

$$\mathbf{A} = \begin{bmatrix} 3 & 14 & 28 & -8 \\ 0 & -5/3 & -19/3 & 14/3 \\ 0 & -10/3 & -26/3 & 16/3 \end{bmatrix}$$

Since $A(3,1) > A(1,1)$, interchange rows 2 and 3.

$$\mathbf{A} = \begin{bmatrix} 3 & 14 & 28 & -8 \\ 0 & -10/3 & -26/3 & 16/3 \\ 0 & -5/3 & -19/3 & 14/3 \end{bmatrix}$$

Transform row 3

$$s = -A(3,2)/A(2,2) = -1/2$$
$$A(3,:) = A(3,:) + s*A(2,:) = [0 \quad 0 \quad -2 \quad 2]$$

Display the current system, if desired.

$$\mathbf{A} = \begin{bmatrix} 3 & 14 & 28 & -8 \\ 0 & -10/3 & -26/3 & 16/3 \\ 0 & 0 & -2 & 2 \end{bmatrix}$$

Back Substitution

$$x(3) = A(3,4)/A(3,3) \qquad\qquad\qquad\qquad \Rightarrow x_3 = -1$$
$$x(2) = (A(2,4) - A(2,3)*X(3))/A(2,2) \qquad\qquad \Rightarrow x_2 = 1$$
$$x(1) = (A(1,4) - A(1,2)*X(2) - A(1,3)*X(3))/A(1,1) \Rightarrow x_1 = 2$$

Example 3.7 Forces in a Simple Truss

Assuming that the weight of the structure (100 kg) is localized at node 2 (bottom center of the figure), the following linear system describes the truss:

$$
\begin{array}{llllll}
V_1 & +F_{14}\sin\alpha & & & & = & 0 \\
& H_1 & +F_{12}+F_{14}\cos\alpha & & & = & 0 \\
& & & +F_{24}\sin\beta+F_{25}\sin\gamma & & = & 100 \\
& -F_{12} & +F_{23}-F_{24}\cos\beta+F_{25}\cos\gamma & & = & 0 \\
& V_3 & & +F_{35}\sin\delta & = & 0 \\
& & -F_{23} & -F_{35}\cos\delta & = & 0 \\
& -F_{14}\sin\alpha & -F_{24}\sin\beta & & = & 0 \\
& -F_{14}\cos\alpha & +F_{24}\cos\beta & +F_{45} & = & 0 \\
& & -F_{25}\sin\gamma-F_{35}\sin\delta & & = & 0 \\
& & -F_{25}\cos\gamma+F_{35}\cos\delta-F_{45} & & = & 0
\end{array}
$$

The equations, in the order written, cannot be solved without pivoting.

The results of using a simple computer program for Gaussian elimination with row pivoting show that for $\alpha = \beta = \gamma = \delta = \pi/4$, we have

$$V_1 = 50, \qquad H_1 = 0, \qquad V_3 = 50,$$

$$F_{12} = 50, \qquad F_{14} = -70.7, \qquad F_{23} = 50, \qquad F_{24} = 70.7,$$

$$F_{25} = 70.7, \qquad F_{35} = -70.7, \qquad F_{45} = -100.$$

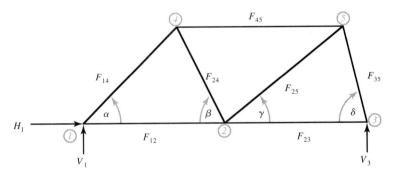

FIGURE 3.3   Triangular truss.

3.2.3 Discussion

For situations in which row pivoting is desirable because some pivot elements are significantly smaller than others, some form of row scaling should also be used, since, of course, the difficulties illustrated in Example 3.4 could be masked by multiplying the first equation by 1,000 to give

$$x_1 + 1000x_2 = 3000$$
$$x_1 + 2x_2 = 5$$

Now no row interchange occurs, because the elements in the first column are equal. However, the computational difficulties described in Example 3.5 are still present. Those difficulties were more apparent with the first equation in its original form.

Scaling strategies vary and are difficult to include in general-purpose computer codes. One possible approach is to scale each row by the appropriate power of 10 (including, of course, the corresponding right-hand side if it has been retained in a separate vector) so that the magnitude of the largest element in each row of the coefficient matrix is between 0.1 and 1. Dividing by a power of 2 is actually better, since it avoids any round-off error. An even easier method to incorporate into the foregoing functions for Gaussian elimination is to divide each row of A by the largest element in the row, making the corresponding scaling on b also. However, this may introduce additional round-off error. Scaling is sometimes suggested on the columns of the coefficient matrix also; this corresponds to changing the units in which the corresponding unknown is measured. Scaling does not generally mitigate problems caused by ill-conditioning.

The computational effort for Gaussian elimination is proportional to n^3, so, for large systems of equations more efficient methods may be desirable. Improved methods have been developed in recent years that reduce the exponent to values less than 2.5. (See Hager, 1988, or Strang, 1988.) When the system has the appropriate structure, iterative techniques, which we examine in Chapter 6, may be appropriate. In the next section, we consider Gaussian elimination for the special case of a tridiagonal matrix.

In many applications, the linear system to be solved has a banded structure. For a tridiagonal system, the only nonzero entries in the coefficient matrix are the diagonal, the subdiagonal (below the main diagonal), and the superdiagonal band above the main diagonal).

In this notation, the general tridiagonal system of equations

$$
\begin{aligned}
d_1 x_1 + a_1 x_2 && = r_1 \\
b_2 x_1 + d_2 x_2 + a_2 x_3 && = r_2 \\
& \cdots \cdots & \\
+ b_{n-1} x_{n-2} + d_{n-1} x_{n-1} + a_{n-1} x_n && = r_{n-1} \\
+ b_n x_{n-1} + d_n x_n && = r_n
\end{aligned}
$$

requires only $3n$ locations to store the vector $\mathbf{d}$ containing the **d**iagonal elements, the vector $\mathbf{a}$ containing the elements **a**bove the diagonal, and the vector $\mathbf{b}$ containing the elements **b**elow the diagonal. The right-hand side is stored as the vector $\mathbf{r}$.

3.3.1 Algorithm for the Gauss-Thomas Method

An efficient algorithm for the solution of a tridiagonal system is based on Gaussian elimination with the coefficients of the diagonal elements scaled to 1 at each stage. This algorithm takes advantage of the zero elements that are already present in the coefficient matrix and avoids unnecessary arithmetic operations. Thus, we need to store only the new vectors $\mathbf{a}$ and $\mathbf{r}$. This procedure is known in the engineering literature as the *Thomas method*. To see how this works, consider the following general 3-by-3 tridiagonal system.

$$
\begin{aligned}
d_1 x_1 + a_1 x_2 && = r_1 \\
b_2 x_1 + d_2 x_2 + a_2 x_3 && = r_2 \\
+ b_3 x_2 + d_3 x_3 && = r_3
\end{aligned}
$$

Scale the first row

$$
\begin{aligned}
x_1 + (a_1/d_1) x_2 && = r_1/d_1 \\
b_2 x_1 + d_2 x_2 + a_2 x_3 && = r_2 \\
+ b_3 x_2 + d_3 x_3 && = r_3
\end{aligned}
$$

We only need to retain the new coefficients, $\mathbf{a_1} = a_1/d_1$ and $\mathbf{r_1} = r_1/d_1$
Eliminate x_1 in second equation

$$
\begin{aligned}
x_1 + \mathbf{a_1} x_2 && = \mathbf{r_1} \\
(d_2 - b_2 \mathbf{a_1}) x_2 + a_2 x_3 && = r_2 - b_2 \mathbf{r_1} \\
+ b_3 x_2 + d_3 x_3 && = r_3
\end{aligned}
$$

Scale the second equation

$$
\begin{aligned}
x_1 + \mathbf{a_1} x_2 && = \mathbf{r_1} \\
+ x_2 + \mathbf{a_2} x_3 && = \mathbf{r_2} \\
+ b_3 x_2 + d_3 x_3 && = r_3
\end{aligned}
$$

where the new coefficients, $\mathbf{a_2}$ and $\mathbf{r_2}$ are

$$\mathbf{a_2} = a_2/(d_2 - b_2\mathbf{a_1}) \text{ and } \mathbf{r_2} = (r_2 - b_2\mathbf{r_1})/(d_2 - b_2\mathbf{a_1})$$

Eliminate x_2 in the third equation

$$x_1 + \mathbf{a_1}x_2 \qquad\qquad\qquad = \mathbf{r_1}$$
$$+ x_2 \quad + \mathbf{a_2}x_3 \qquad\quad = \mathbf{r_2}$$
$$+ (d_3 - b_3\mathbf{a_2})x_3 = r_3 - b_3\mathbf{r_2}$$

And, finally, scale the third equation

$$x_1 + \mathbf{a_1}x_2 \qquad\qquad = \mathbf{r_1}$$
$$+ x_2 \quad + \mathbf{a_2}x_3 = \mathbf{r_2}$$
$$x_3 = \mathbf{r_3}$$

where the new coefficient $\mathbf{r_3}$ is

$$\mathbf{r_3} = (r_3 - b_3\mathbf{r_2})/(d_3 - b_3\mathbf{a_2})$$

For an n-by-n system, the computations for equations 2 through n-1 follow the pattern for equation 2, as shown in the following algorithm.

Gauss-Thomas Method

```
Input
    a           vector of above diagonal elements, a(n) = 0
    d           vector of main diagonal elements
    b           vector of below diagonal elements, b(1) = 0
    r           right-hand side vector
    n           number of components in each vector
Forward Elimination
a(1) = a(1)/d(1)                                    first equation
r(1) = r(1)/d(1)
For i = 2 to n − 1                                  equations i = 2, . . ., n−1
    denom = d(i) − b(i)*a(i−1)
    If (denom = 0) Error
    a(i) = a(i)/denom
    r(i) = (r(i) − b(i)*r(i−1))/denom
End
r(n) = (r(n) − b(n)*r(n−1))/(d(n) − b(n)*a(n−1))    last equation
Back Substitution
x(n) = r(n)
For i = n − 1 to 1
    x(i) = r(i) − a(i)*x(i+1)
End
```

3.3.2 Applications of the Gauss-Thomas Method

Example 3.8 Scaled Gaussian Elimination for a Tridiagonal System

Consider the following system of equations:

$$
\begin{aligned}
2x_1 + 2x_2 &= 4 \\
2x_1 + 4x_2 + 4x_3 &= 6 \\
x_2 + 3x_3 + 3x_4 &= 7 \\
2x_3 + 5x_4 &= 10
\end{aligned}
$$

First, scale the first equation by dividing through by a_{11}:

$$
\begin{aligned}
x_1 + x_2 &= 2 \\
2x_1 + 4x_2 + 4x_3 &= 6 \\
x_2 + 3x_3 + 3x_4 &= 7 \\
2x_3 + 5x_4 &= 10
\end{aligned}
$$

Second, use the first equation to eliminate the x_1 term in the second equation:

$$
\begin{aligned}
x_1 + x_2 &= 2 \\
2x_2 + 4x_3 &= 2 \\
x_2 + 3x_3 + 3x_4 &= 7 \\
2x_3 + 5x_4 &= 10
\end{aligned}
$$

Complete this step by scaling the second equation:

$$
\begin{aligned}
x_1 + x_2 &= 2 \\
x_2 + 2x_3 &= 1 \\
x_2 + 3x_3 + 3x_4 &= 7 \\
2x_3 + 5x_4 &= 10
\end{aligned}
$$

Next, use the second equation to eliminate the x_2 term in the third equation:

$$
\begin{aligned}
x_1 + x_2 &= 2 \\
x_2 + 2x_3 &= 1 \\
x_3 + 3x_4 &= 6 \\
2x_3 + 5x_4 &= 10
\end{aligned}
$$

(The third equation does not require scaling.)
Finally, use the third equation to eliminate x_3 in the last equation:

$$
\begin{aligned}
x_1 + x_2 &= 2 \\
x_2 + 2x_3 &= 1 \\
x_3 + 3x_4 &= 6 \\
- x_4 &= -2
\end{aligned}
$$

And scale the last equation:

$$
\begin{aligned}
x_1 + x_2 &= 2 \\
x_2 + 2x_3 &= 1 \\
x_3 + 3x_4 &= 6 \\
x_4 &= 2
\end{aligned}
$$

Now solve by back substitution to obtain

$$
\begin{aligned}
x_4 &= 2 & x_3 &= 6 - (3)(2) = 0 \\
x_2 &= 1 - (2)(0) = 1 & x_1 &= 2 - (1)(1) = 1
\end{aligned}
$$

Example 3.9 Gauss-Thomas Method for a Tridiagonal System

We now illustrate the steps of the Gauss-Thomas algorithm, using the tridiagonal system from Example 3.8. The system

$$2x_1 + 2x_2 \qquad\qquad\qquad = 4$$
$$2x_1 + 4x_2 + 4x_3 \qquad\qquad = 6$$
$$x_2 + 3x_3 + 3x_4 = 7$$
$$2x_3 + 5x_4 = 10$$

is stored as the vectors

$$\mathbf{d} = (2, 4, 3, 5); \ \mathbf{a} = (2, 4, 3, 0); \ \mathbf{b} = (0, 2, 1, 2); \mathbf{r} = (4, 6, 7, 10).$$

First, form the new elements a_1 and r_1:

$$a_1 = \frac{a_1}{d_1} = \frac{2}{2} = 1 \qquad r_1 = \frac{r_1}{d_1} = \frac{4}{2} = 2$$

For the second equation,

$$a_2 = \frac{a_1}{d_2 - b_2 a_1} = \frac{4}{4 - (2)(1)} = 2$$

$$r_2 = \frac{r_2}{d_2} - \frac{b_2 r_1}{d_2 - b_2 a_1} = \frac{6}{4} - \frac{(2)(2)}{(2)(1)} = 1$$

For the third equation,

$$a_3 = \frac{a_3}{d_3 - b_3 a_2} = \frac{3}{3 - (1)(2)} = 3$$

$$r_3 = \frac{r_3 - b_3 r_2}{d_3 - b_3 a_2} = \frac{7 - (1)(1)}{3 - (1)(2)} = 6$$

For the last equation,

$$r_4 = \frac{r_4 - b_4 r_3}{d_4 - b_4 a_3} = \frac{10 - (2)(6)}{5 - (2)(3)} = 2$$

Finally, solve by back substitution to obtain

$$x_4 = r_4 = 2$$
$$x_3 = r_3 - a_3 x_4 = 6 - (3)(2) = 0$$
$$x_2 = r_2 - a_2 x_3 = 1 - (2)(0) = 1$$
$$x_1 = r_1 - a_1 x_2 = 2 - (1)(1) = 1$$

3.3.3 Discussion

The storage requirements are greatly reduced by taking advantage of the special structure of a tridiagonal matrix. The computational effort is also much less for the Thomas method than for the general form of Gaussian elimination. The required multiplications and divisions for the Thomas method are as follows:

For the first equation: 2 divisions.

For each of the next $n - 2$ equations: 2 multiplications and 2 divisions.

For the last equation: 2 multiplications and 1 division.

The total for elimination is $5 + 4(n - 2)$.

For the back substitution; $n - 1$ multiplications are needed.

The Thomas algorithm requires that $d_1 \neq 0$ and that $d_1 - b_1 a_{i-1} \neq 0$ for each i. For many applications, the structure of the tridiagonal matrix guarantees that these quantities will not be zero. In other cases, if we do encounter a zero value (but the system is, in fact, nonsingular) we can solve for the appropriate variable directly, reduce the size of the system, and solve the new reduced system, as illustrated in the next example.

In general, the Thomas method works well when the system is diagonally dominant.

Example 3.10 Recovery from a Zero-Pivot Using Gauss-Thomas

To illustrate the possibility of continuing the solution process with the Thomas method when a division by zero is encountered, consider the following system:

$$
\begin{array}{rrrrrrcr}
2x_1 & -x_2 & & & & & = & 1 \\
-x_1 & +2x_2 & -x_3 & & & & = & 0 \\
& -x_2 & +\dfrac{2}{3}x_3 & -x_4 & & & = & -\dfrac{4}{3} \\
& & -x_3 & +2x_4 & -x_5 & & = & 0 \\
& & & -x_4 & +2x_5 & -x_6 & = & 0 \\
& & & & -x_5 & +2x_6 & = & 1
\end{array}
$$

The solution begins by scaling the first equation and using the result to eliminate the x_1 term in the second equation. Scaling the second equation and using it to eliminate the x_2 term in the third equation, we obtain

$$
\begin{array}{rrrrrcr}
x_1 & -\dfrac{1}{2}x_2 & & & & = & \dfrac{1}{2} \\
& x_2 & -\dfrac{2}{3}x_3 & & & = & \dfrac{1}{3} \\
& & -x_4 & & & = & -1 \\
& & -x_3 & +2x_4 & -x_5 & = & 0 \\
& & & -x_4 & +2x_5 & -x_6 = & 0 \\
& & & & -x_5 & +2x_6 = & 1
\end{array}
$$

However, we are unable to scale the third equation so as to have 1 on the diagonal, since the coefficient of x_3 is now 0. But because the third row does have a nonzero coefficient (for variable x_4), we can solve for that variable and proceed. Thus, the third equation is solved for x_4, giving $x_4 = 1$. The fourth equation is skipped for now, and the computed value of x_4 is substituted into the fifth equation. The elimination proceeds, using the fifth equation to eliminate x_5 from the final equation:

$$
\begin{array}{rcll}
x_1 \;-\; \dfrac{1}{2}x_2 & = & \dfrac{1}{2} & \\[4pt]
x_2 \;-\; \dfrac{2}{3}x_3 & = & \dfrac{1}{3} & \\[4pt]
-x_4 & = & -1 & (\text{solve}) \\[4pt]
-x_3 \;+\; 2x_4 \;-\; x_5 & = & 0 & (\text{skip for now}) \\[4pt]
2x_5 \;-\; x_6 & = & 1 & (\text{using } x_4 = 1) \\[4pt]
-x_5 \;+\; 2x_6 & & &
\end{array}
$$

Finally, we scale the fifth equation, use it to eliminate x_5 in the last equation, and scale the last equation:

$$
\begin{array}{rcl}
x_1 \;-\; \dfrac{1}{2}x_2 & = & \dfrac{1}{2} \\[4pt]
x_2 \;-\; \dfrac{2}{3}x_3 & = & \dfrac{1}{3} \\[4pt]
-x_4 & = & -1 \\[4pt]
-x_3 \;+\; 2x_4 \;-\; x_5 & = & 0 \\[4pt]
x_5 \;-\; \dfrac{1}{2}x_6 & = & \dfrac{1}{2} \\[4pt]
x_6 & = & 1
\end{array}
$$

Solving by back substitution yields

$$x_6 = 1$$

$$x_5 = \frac{1}{2} + \frac{1}{2}x_6 = 1$$

$$x_4 = 1 \quad (\text{computed previously})$$

$$x_3 = 2x_4 - x_5 = 1 \quad (\text{skipped previously})$$

$$x_2 = \frac{1}{3} + \frac{2}{3}x_3 = 1$$

$$x_1 = \frac{1}{2} + \frac{1}{2}x_2 = 1$$

The basic routines for solving linear systems that are included in software packages and libraries are usually based on some form of Gaussian elimination with pivoting.

Factorization of a matrix into the product of a Lower triangular matrix **L** and an Upper triangular matrix **U** (discussed in Chapter 4) is closely related to Gaussian elimination, and is used in many routines for solving linear systems. It may also be convenient (but not particularly efficient) to find the inverse of a matrix, and use that to solve the linear system. Specialized routines for solving linear systems in which the coefficient matrix has a particular form (such as tridiagonal, banded, or real, symmetric, positive definite) may also be included. Some solution routines use Gauss-Jordan elimination, which is described in the next section.

3.4.1 Gauss-Jordan Elimination

Naive Gauss-Jordan elimination uses standard row reduction (as discussed in Section 3.1), along with scaling of the diagonal elements to 1, and row reduction applied to rows above the pivot row as well as below the pivot row to also reduce the above diagonal elements to 0. In this method the elimination process is carried out on all of the rows above and below the pivot row at each step. This transforms the matrix into what is generally known as *reduced row echelon form* (RREF). It is interesting to note that the operation count for naive Gauss-Jordan elimination is somewhat higher than for Gaussian elimination with back substitution $O\left(\frac{1}{2}n^3\right)$ as compared to $O\left(\frac{1}{3}n^3\right)$. The reason for the higher computational load is that elimination is more expensive than back substitution, and at each stage the elimination must be applied to all of the rows other than the pivot row.

A small modification to the naive Gauss-Jordan scheme provides a computationally more efficient process; this is the standard RREF algorithm. By performing row reduction to transform the below-diagonal elements first (forward elimination, as in standard Gauss elimination) together with scaling of the diagonal elements, followed by the reduction of the above diagonal elements (backward elimination), the operation count for RREF is of the same order as for Gaussian elimination. The reason that this small change in the algorithm (applying all of the backward elimination after the forward elimination stages are completed) makes a significant improvement on the operation count is that now each forward elimination step only involves elimination of the elements in one column. The resulting computation for backward elimination is of the same order as that for back substitution.

Pivoting (at least row pivoting, as described for Gaussian elimination) should be included for numerical stability in Gauss-Jordan elimination. Full pivoting allows for column interchange as well as row interchange, but increases the bookkeeping complexity of the method, with only slightly better stability characteristics.

The following algorithm presents the computationally preferable form of Gauss-Jordan elimination. The row updates could be made more efficient by only updating the columns in which nonzero elements could appear.

If the matrix of right-hand sides is the identity matrix, the solution matrix will be the inverse of the original coefficient matrix **M.** For a computer program for Gauss-Jordan elimination with full pivoting, in which the inverse of matrix **M** is generated along with solutions to a linear system **M X** = **B,** see Press et al., 1992, pp. 39–40.

Gauss-Jordan Elimination with Row Pivoting

Input
> M $\qquad$ *matrix of coefficients (n-by-n)*
> B $\qquad$ *right-hand side(s) of equation,* A x = B *(n-by-m)*
> n, m $\qquad$ *dimensions of input matrices*

Initialize
> A = [M B] $\qquad$ *form augmented matrix*

Forward Elimination
For k = 1 to n − 1
> pivot = | A(k,k) | $\qquad$ *pivot element*
> p = k $\qquad$ *pivot row*
> For i = k + 1 to n
> > If (|A(i,k)| > pivot)
> > > pivot = | A(i,k) | $\qquad$ *update pivot element*
> > > p = i $\qquad$ *update pivot row*
> > Endif
> End
> If (p > k) $\qquad$ *interchange rows k and p*
> > temp = A(k, :)
> > A(k, :) = A(p, :)
> > A(p, :) = temp
> Endif
> A(k, :) = A(k, :)/A(k,k) $\qquad$ *scale row k*
> For i = k + 1 to n
> > A(i, :) = A(i, :) − A(i, k)*A(k, :) $\qquad$ *update row i in A*
> End
End

Backward Elimination
For i = k − 1 to 1
> A(i, :) = A(i, :) − A(i, k)*A(k, :) $\qquad$ *update row i in A*
End
For j = 1 to m $\qquad$ *generate column j of solution matrix*
> X(:, j) − A(:, n + j)
End

3.4.2 Estimating the Condition of a Matrix

The condition number of a nonsingular matrix $\mathbf{A}$ is defined in terms of the norm of the matrix $\|\mathbf{A}\|$ and the norm of the inverse matrix, $\mathbf{A}^{-1}$. Since there are several different matrix norms, there are several different condition numbers for a matrix. Some matrix norms are derived from (or are subordinate to) a vector norm.

The three most common vector norms are

$$\|\mathbf{x}\|_1 = |x_1| + |x_2| + \ldots + |x_n|$$

$$\|\mathbf{x}\|_2 = (|x_1|^2 + |x_2|^2 + \ldots + |x_n|^2)^{1/2}$$

$$\|\mathbf{x}\|_{\text{inf}} = \text{Max} |x_i|$$

In general, if p is a real number ≥ 1, the p-norm is

$$\|\mathbf{x}\|_p = (|x_1|^p + |x_2|^p + \ldots + |x_n|^p)^{1/p}$$

The vector 2-norm is also known as the Euclidean norm.

A matrix norm that is subordinate to a vector norm is defined as

$$\|\mathbf{A}\| = \sup \|\mathbf{A}\,\mathbf{x}\| / \|\mathbf{x}\|$$

where the sup is taken over all nonzero vectors.

The matrix norm that is subordinate to the vector p-norm is denoted $\|\mathbf{A}\|_p$. The matrix norms $\|\mathbf{A}\|_1$, $\|\mathbf{A}\|_2$, and $\|\mathbf{A}\|_{\text{inf}}$ have several useful properties, which can be established directly from the definitions.

$$\|\mathbf{A}\|_1 = \text{maximum column sum}$$
$$= \text{max (over } j) \,[\text{sum of column } j]$$
$$= \text{max (over } j) \,(|a_{1j}| + |a_{2j}| + \ldots + |a_{nj}|)$$

$$\|\mathbf{A}\|_{\text{inf}} = \text{maximum row sum}$$
$$= \text{max (over } i) \,[\text{sum of row } i]$$
$$= \text{max (over } i) \,(|a_{i1}| + |a_{i2}| + \ldots + |a_{in}|)$$

$$\|\mathbf{A}\|_2 = (\text{maximum eigenvalue of } \mathbf{A}^H\mathbf{A})^{1/2}$$

The $\|\mathbf{A}\|_2$ norm is also known as the spectral norm. $\mathbf{A}^H$ is the complex conjugate of the transpose of $\mathbf{A}$. The eigenvalues of $\mathbf{A}^H\mathbf{A}$ are non-negative; the square roots of these eigenvalues are called the singular values of $\mathbf{A}$.

There are also important matrix norms that are not subordinate to any vector norm. The most important of these is the Euclidean (or Shur, or Frobenius) norm

$$\|\mathbf{A}\|_E = (\text{sum of the squares of all elements of } \mathbf{A})^{1/2}$$

See Wilkinson, 1965, for further discussion. Note that the Euclidean matrix norm is not subordinate to the Euclidean vector-norm (or to any other vector norm).

In a fairly broad sense, a computational problem is "ill-conditioned" if the solution of the problem is very sensitive to small changes in the parameters that define the problem. For problems involving a matrix (solving a linear system, finding the eigenvalues of the matrix, etc.), it may be useful to describe this sensitivity in terms of a number, called the condition number of the matrix. There are several ways of defining the condition number of a matrix, depending on the underlying matrix norm that is used. For any matrix norm, we define the condition number $\kappa(\mathbf{A}) = \|\mathbf{A}\|\|\mathbf{A}^{-1}\|$. Although the actual value found for the condition number will in general be different for different norms, a matrix that is ill-conditioned in one norm will also be ill-conditioned in all other matrix norms.

The *spectral condition number* of a matrix $\mathbf{A}$ is defined as $\kappa(\mathbf{A}) = \|\mathbf{A}\|_2 \|\mathbf{A}^{-1}\|_2$. If $\mathbf{A}$ is symmetric, it can be shown that $\kappa(\mathbf{A}) = |\lambda_1|/|\lambda_n|$ where λ_1 is the eigenvalue of largest magnitude and λ_n is the eigenvalue of smallest magnitude (Wilkinson, 1965, p. 191). If $\mathbf{A}$ is not symmetric, then instead of the eigenvalues, one would have the corresponding singular values.

The relative change in the solution to a linear system is bounded by the product of the condition number of the matrix and the relative change in the right-hand side of the system. See, e.g., Hager, 1984, p. 137. However, exact computation of the condition number of a matrix (using any of the matrix norms) is computationally quite expensive. The following algorithm (Hager, 1984, p. 139) gives an estimate of the condition number $\kappa(\mathbf{A})$ using the 1-norm. It is based on an estimate of the 1-norm of the inverse of $\mathbf{A}$, namely, $\|\mathbf{A}^{-1}\|_1$. The algorithm assumes that the test condition for the while-loop is checked at the end of the loop.

Estimate of Condition Number of A

```
A                         input the n-by-n matrix
b( : ) = 1/n              initialize each component of column vector b
p = 0
Solve A x = b
If (‖x‖ − p > 0) test = true         iterate if ‖x‖ > p
While (test = true)
      p = ‖x‖₁
      For k = 1 to n
              If (x(k) ≥ 0)
                      y(k) = 1
              Else
                      y(k) = −1
              End
End
Solve Aᵀz = y
j = index such that |z(j)| is maximal
test = false          escape iterations unless if-statement condition is true
If (|z(j)| > zᵀb)
                      b( : ) = 0
                      b(j) = 1
                      test = true        continue iterations
      End
End
c = p‖A‖₁                              ‖A‖₁ is max absolute column sum
Return
      c                               estimate of condition number of A
```

3.4.3 Using Professionally Developed Software

Many software packages have built-in functions for solving linear systems. We illustrate the features that are typical by describing briefly the functions in MATLAB, Mathcad, and *Mathematica,* as well as the routines included in the NIST index of available software. MATLAB and Mathcad also have operators that provide very convenient ways of solving linear systems.

MATLAB's Methods

There are two division symbols in MATLAB, the forwardslash (/) and the backslash (\ ). It is useful to think of each as indicating multiplication by the inverse of the quantity under the slash. In this way of interpreting the symbols, $a/b = a(b^{-1})$ and $c\backslash d = c^{-1}(d)$. Since scalar multiplication is commutative, we can write a fraction using either of these symbols. However, matrix multiplication is not commutative, and backslash division gives us a convenient way of solving the linear system $\mathbf{A}\mathbf{x} = \mathbf{b}$. The solution of $\mathbf{A}\mathbf{x} = \mathbf{b}$ is $\mathbf{x} = \mathbf{A}\backslash\mathbf{b}$, which is suggestive of $\mathbf{x} = \mathbf{A}^{-1}\mathbf{b}$, where it is important that the implied multiplication by the inverse of $\mathbf{A}$ is from the left. The backslash division operator is also called the `matrix left-division` operator.

If $\mathbf{A}$ is an n-by-n matrix and $\mathbf{b}$ is a column vector with n components (or a matrix with several such columns), then $\mathbf{x} = \mathbf{A}\backslash\mathbf{b}$ is the solution of the equation $\mathbf{A}\mathbf{x} = \mathbf{b}$, computed by Gaussian elimination (not computed by multiplying by the inverse of $\mathbf{A}$).

It is also possible to solve the linear system $\mathbf{A}\mathbf{x} = \mathbf{b}$ by using MATLAB's function for finding a matrix inverse; however, multiplication by a matrix inverse is usually not the best way to solve a linear system.

Mathcad's Methods

The Mathcad function `rref` transforms a matrix to its reduced row echelon form, which is a form in which elements above or below the diagonal are (as much as possible) reduced to 0 and the elements on the diagonal are equal to 1. To use this function to solve a linear system, $\mathbf{M}\mathbf{x} = \mathbf{b}$, form the augmented matrix of the system, $\mathbf{A} = [\mathbf{M}\,\mathbf{b}]$ and transform $\mathbf{A}$ to reduced row echelon form. The last column of the reduced matrix is the solution vector $\mathbf{x}$.

It is also very straightforward to use matrix inversion to solve a small linear system written in matrix-vector form. To solve $\mathbf{M}\mathbf{x} = \mathbf{b}$, define $\mathbf{N}:=\mathbf{M}^{-1}$ (find $\mathbf{M}^{-1}$ using the Matrix Toolbar), and compute

$$\mathbf{x} = \mathbf{N}\,\mathbf{b}$$

This is not computationally as efficient as reduction to reduced row echelon form.

Mathematica's Methods

The *Mathematica* function `LinearSolve[M, b]` gives the vector **x** that solves the linear equations $\mathbf{M\,x} = \mathbf{b}$. The matrix **M** may be square or rectangular.

The condition number of a matrix may be found by using the function `SingularValues` and taking the ratio of the largest singular value to the smallest singular value.

Using the NIST Index

The NIST (National Institute of Standards and Technology) has an extensive *Guide to Available Mathematical Software;* it can be accessed at http://gams. nist.gov. The software is cross-indexed according to four criteria: 1) the problem to be solved; 2) the package name; 3) the module name; and 4) text in the module abstract. Many of the software modules can be downloaded. The following outline of the categories for software for the solution of systems of linear equations shows the variety of special structures for which software is available.

> Solution of systems of linear equations
>> Real nonsymmetric matrices
>>> General
>>> Banded
>>>> Tridiagonal
>>> Triangular
>> Sparce
>> Real symmetric matrices
>>> General
>>>> Indefinite
>>>> Positive definite
>>> Positive definite banded
>>> Tridiagonal
>>> Sparce
>> Complex non-Hermitian matrices
>>> General
>>> Banded
>>>> Tridiagonal
>>> Triangular
>>> Sparce
>> Complex Hermitian matrices
>>> General
>>>> Indefinite
>>>> Positive definite
>>> Positive definite banded
>>> Tridiagonal
>>> Sparce

Basic Gaussian Elimination

To solve $\mathbf{A}\mathbf{x} = \mathbf{b}$, transform matrix $\mathbf{A}$ into an upper triangular matrix by systematically applying the following row transformations to the augmented matrix consisting of $\mathbf{A}$ together with $\mathbf{b}$, i.e., $[\mathbf{A} : \mathbf{b}]$.

Add a multiple m of row R_i onto row R_j to form a new row R_j:

$$R_j \leftarrow m\, R_i + R_j.$$

Solve the resulting linear system by back substitution:

$$
\begin{aligned}
x_n &= b_n/a_{nn}, \\
x_{n-1} &= (b_{n-1} - a_{n-1,n}\, x_n)/a_{n-1,n-1}, \\
&\;\;\ldots \\
x_2 &= (b_2 - a_{23}x_3 - \ldots - a_{2n}\, x_n)/a_{22}, \\
x_1 &= (b_1 - a_{12}\, x_2 - \ldots - a_{1,n-1}\, x_{n-1} - a_{1,n}\, x_n)/a_{11}.
\end{aligned}
$$

Gaussian Elimination with Row Pivoting

To solve $\mathbf{A}\mathbf{x} = \mathbf{b}$, transform matrix $\mathbf{A}$ into an upper triangular matrix by systematically performing row interchanges on the augmented matrix so that at each stage the pivot element is as large as possible, then performing the same row transformations as for basic Gaussian elimination.

Thomas Method

The tridiagonal linear system is given by the following four vectors

above diagonal: $\quad \mathbf{a} = [a_1 \quad a_2 \quad \ldots \quad a_{n-1} \quad 0]$
diagonal: $\qquad\;\; \mathbf{d} = [d_1 \quad d_2 \quad \ldots \quad d_{n-1} \quad d_n]$
below diagonal: $\quad \mathbf{b} = [0 \quad b_2 \quad \ldots \quad b_{n-1} \quad b_n]$
right-hand side: $\;\; \mathbf{r} = [r_1 \quad r_2 \quad \ldots \quad r_{n-1} \quad r_n]$

Step 1   For the first equation, form the new elements a_1 and r_1,

$$a_1 = \frac{a_1}{d_1}, \qquad\qquad r_1 = \frac{r_1}{d_1}.$$

Step 2   For each of the equations from $i = 2, \ldots, n - 1$,

$$a_i = \frac{a_i}{d_i - b_i\, a_{i-1}}, \qquad\qquad r_i = \frac{r_i - b_i\, r_{i-1}}{d_i - b_i\, a_{i-1}}.$$

Step 3   For the last equation,

$$r_n = \frac{r_n - b_n\, r_{n-1}}{d_n - b_n\, a_{n-1}}.$$

Step 4   Solve by back substitution, yielding

$$
\begin{aligned}
x_n &= r_n, \\
x_i &= r_i - a_i\, x_{i+1}, \qquad i = n - 1, n - 2, n - 3, \ldots, 2, 1.
\end{aligned}
$$

The topics introduced in this chapter are part of the field of numerical linear algebra. We consider other topics from this area in Chapters 4 and 5. For more in depth treatments of these techniques, the following are a few suggested sources:

Atkinson, K. E., *An Introduction to Numerical Analysis*, 2nd ed., John Wiley, New York, 1989.

Coleman, T. F. and C. Van Loan, *Handbook for Matrix Computations*, SIAM, Philadelphia, 1988.

Dongarra, J. J., et al., *LINPACK User's Guide*, SIAM, Philadelphia, 1979.

Forsythe, G. E. and C. B. Moler, *Computer Solution of Linear Algebraic Systems*, Prentice-Hall, Englewood Cliffs, NJ, 1967.

Gill, P. E., W. Murray, and M. H. Wright, *Numerical Linear Algebra and Optimization*, Addison-Wesley, Redwood City, CA, 1991.

Golub, G. H. and C. F. Van Loan, *Matrix Computations* , 3rd ed., Johns Hopkins University Press, Baltimore, 1996.

Hager, W. W., *Applied Numerical Linear Algebra*, Prentice Hall, Englewood Cliffs, NJ, 1988. This book includes a discussion of the relative merits of row and column pivoting.

Hager, W. W., Condition Estimates, *SIAM J. Sci. Stat. Comut.* 5 (1984), pp. 311 316.

Isaacson, E. and H. B. Keller, *Analysis of Numerical Methods*, Wiley, New York, 1966.

Jensen, J. A., and J. H. Rowland, *Methods of Computation*, Scott, Foresman and Company, Glenview, IL, 1975.

Press, W. H., S. A. Teukolsky, W. T. Vetterling, and B. P. Flannery, *Numerical Recipes in C, The Art of Scientific Computing*, 2nd ed., Cambridge Unversity Press, 1992. (Discussion of Gauss-Jordan elimination, pp. 36–41).

Ralston, A. and P. Rabinowitz, *A First Course in Numerical Analysis*, 2nd ed. McGraw Hill, New York, 1978.

Stoer, J. and R. Bulirsch, *Introduction to Numerical Analysis*, Springer-Verlag, New York, 1980.

Strang, G., *Linear Algebra and Its Applications*, 3rd ed., Harcourt Brace Jovanovich, San Diego, 1988.

Wilkinson, J. H., *The Algebraic Eigenvalue Problem*, Oxford University Press, New York, 1965.

Wilkinson, J. H. and C. Reinsch, *Linear Algebra*, vol II *of Handbook for Automatic Computation*, Springer-Verlag, New York, 1971.

For problems P3.1 to P3. 10, solve the linear system **A x = b** *using basic Gaussian elimination.*

P3.1 $A = \begin{bmatrix} 3 & -1 & 2 \\ 1 & 2 & 3 \\ 2 & -2 & -1 \end{bmatrix}$, $b = \begin{bmatrix} 1 \\ 1 \\ 1 \end{bmatrix}$

P3.2 $A = \begin{bmatrix} 2 & 5 & 3 \\ 8 & 9 & 7 \\ 4 & 6 & 1 \end{bmatrix}$ $b = \begin{bmatrix} 2 \\ 14 \\ 3 \end{bmatrix}$

P3.3 $A = \begin{bmatrix} 10 & -2 & 1 \\ -2 & 10 & -2 \\ -2 & -5 & 10 \end{bmatrix}$, $b = \begin{bmatrix} 9 \\ 12 \\ 18 \end{bmatrix}$

P3.4 $A = \begin{bmatrix} -1 & 5 & 2 \\ 2 & 3 & 1 \\ 3 & 2 & 1 \end{bmatrix}$, $b = \begin{bmatrix} -2 \\ 7 \\ 3 \end{bmatrix}$

P3.5 $A = \begin{bmatrix} 8 & 1 & -1 \\ -1 & 7 & -2 \\ 2 & 1 & 9 \end{bmatrix}$, $b = \begin{bmatrix} 8 \\ 4 \\ 12 \end{bmatrix}$

P3.6 $A = \begin{bmatrix} 2 & 0 & -2 \\ 3 & -4 & -4 \\ -2 & 2 & -1 \end{bmatrix}$ $b = \begin{bmatrix} -10 \\ -8 \\ 3 \end{bmatrix}$

P3.7 $A = \begin{bmatrix} 3 & -5 & -5 \\ 5 & -5 & -2 \\ 2 & 3 & 4 \end{bmatrix}$ $b = \begin{bmatrix} -36 \\ -15 \\ 33 \end{bmatrix}$

P3.8 $A = \begin{bmatrix} 4 & 12 & 8 & 4 \\ 1 & 7 & 18 & 9 \\ 2 & 9 & 20 & 20 \\ 3 & 11 & 15 & 14 \end{bmatrix}$ $b = \begin{bmatrix} -4 \\ -5 \\ -25 \\ -18 \end{bmatrix}$

P3.9 $A = \begin{bmatrix} 1 & 1 & 0 & 3 \\ 2 & 1 & -1 & 1 \\ 3 & -1 & -1 & 2 \\ -1 & 2 & 3 & -1 \end{bmatrix}$ $b = \begin{bmatrix} 4 \\ 1 \\ -3 \\ 4 \end{bmatrix}$

P3.10 $A = \begin{bmatrix} 1 & 1 & 1 & 1 \\ 2 & 4 & 4 & 4 \\ 3 & 11 & 14 & 14 \\ 5 & 17 & 38 & 42 \end{bmatrix}$ $b = \begin{bmatrix} 0 \\ -2 \\ -8 \\ -20 \end{bmatrix}$

For problems P3.11 to P3.15, solve the linear system, **Ax = b**, *using Gaussian elimination with row pivoting*

P3.11 $A = \begin{bmatrix} 6 & 2 & 2 \\ 6 & 2 & 1 \\ 1 & 2 & -1 \end{bmatrix}$, $b = \begin{bmatrix} 0 \\ 5 \\ 0 \end{bmatrix}$

P3.12 $A = \begin{bmatrix} 1 & 2 & 3 \\ 2 & 4 & 10 \\ 3 & 14 & 28 \end{bmatrix}$ $b = \begin{bmatrix} 0 \\ -2 \\ -8 \end{bmatrix}$

P3.13 $A = \begin{bmatrix} 2 & 6 & 10 \\ 1 & 3 & 3 \\ 3 & 14 & 28 \end{bmatrix}$ $b = \begin{bmatrix} 0 \\ 2 \\ -8 \end{bmatrix}$

P3.14 $A = \begin{bmatrix} -1 & 1 & 0 & 0 \\ 1 & -1 & 1 & 0 \\ 0 & 1 & -1 & 1 \\ 0 & 0 & 1 & -1 \end{bmatrix}$ $b = \begin{bmatrix} 1 \\ 1 \\ -1 \\ -1 \end{bmatrix}$

P3.15 $A = \begin{bmatrix} 2 & -1 & 0 & 0 & 0 & 0 \\ -1 & 2 & -1 & 0 & 0 & 0 \\ 0 & -1 & 2/3 & -1 & 0 & 0 \\ 0 & 0 & -1 & 2 & -1 & 0 \\ 0 & 0 & 0 & -1 & 2 & -1 \\ 0 & 0 & 0 & 0 & -1 & 2 \end{bmatrix}$

$b = \begin{bmatrix} 1 & 0 & -4/3 & 0 & 0 & -1 \end{bmatrix}^T$

For problems P3.16 to P3.20, solve the linear system **Ax = b** *with rounding to two digits.*

    a. using Gaussian elimination.
    b. using Gaussian elimination with row pivoting.
    c. Compare the results from Parts a and b.

P3.16 $0.001\, x_1 + 2x_2 = 4$
        $x_1 + 2x_2 = 5$

P3.17 $0.001\, x_1 + 10x_2 = 30$
        $x_1 + x_2 = 2$

P3.18 $0.001 x_1 + 2x_2 = 6$
$x_1 + 3x_2 - 8$

P3.19 $0.001 x_1 + x_2 + x_3 = 5$
$x_1 + x_2 \quad = 3$
$x_1 \quad + x_3 = 4$

P3.20 $6x_1 - 2.2x_2 + 3x_3 = 20$
$-3x_1 + x_2 - 1.1x_3 = -8.1$
$-1x_1 - 3 x_2 + 0.9x_3 = 6$

For problems P3.21 to 3.25, solve the linear system
$Ax = b$; *round to 2 digits, using*

    a. *basic Gaussian elimination.*
    b. *Gaussian elimination with row pivoting.*
    c. *Gaussian elimination with scaling and pivoting; scale each row so that the largest element is 1 before choosing the pivot element.*

P3.21 $x_1 + 2000x_2 = 4000$
$x_1 + 2x_2 = 5$

P3.22 $x_1 + 1000x_2 = 3000$
$x_1 + x_2 = 2$

P3.23 $x_1 + 2000x_2 = 6000$
$x_1 + 3x_2 = 8$

P3.24 $x_1 + 1000x_2 + 1000x_3 = 5000$
$x_1 + x_2 + \quad = 3$
$x_1 + \quad + x_3 = 4$

P3.25 $600x_1 - 220x_2 + 300x_3 = 2000$
$-300x_1 + 100x_2 - 110x_3 = -810$
$-1x_1 - 3x_2 + 0.9x_3 = 6$

For problems P3.26 to 3.35, solve the linear system
$Ax = r$

    a. *using Gaussian elimination.*
    b. *using the Thomas method for tridiagonal systems.*

P3.26 $A = \begin{bmatrix} 1 & 2 & 0 \\ 1 & 3 & 3 \\ 0 & 3 & 10 \end{bmatrix}$ $r = \begin{bmatrix} 10 & 17 & 22 \end{bmatrix}^T$

P3.27 $A = \begin{bmatrix} 1 & 2 & 0 \\ 1 & 3 & 4 \\ 0 & 3 & 13 \end{bmatrix}$ $r = \begin{bmatrix} 3 & 8 & 16 \end{bmatrix}^T$

P3.28 $A = \begin{bmatrix} -2 & 1 & 0 & 0 \\ 1 & -2 & 1 & 0 \\ 0 & 1 & -2 & 1 \\ 0 & 0 & 1 & -2 \end{bmatrix}$, $r = \begin{bmatrix} -1 \\ 0 \\ 0 \\ 0 \end{bmatrix}$.

P3.29 $A = \begin{bmatrix} 2 & 1 & 0 & 0 \\ -1 & 2 & 1 & 0 \\ 0 & 1 & 2 & -1 \\ 0 & 0 & -1 & 2 \end{bmatrix}$, $r = \begin{bmatrix} 0 \\ 0 \\ 0 \\ 11 \end{bmatrix}$

P3.30 $A = \begin{bmatrix} 5 & 1 & 0 & 0 \\ 1 & 5 & 1 & 0 \\ 0 & 1 & 5 & 1 \\ 0 & 0 & 1 & 5 \end{bmatrix}$, $r = \begin{bmatrix} 33 \\ 26 \\ 30 \\ 15 \end{bmatrix}$

P3.31 $A = \begin{bmatrix} -3 & -4 & 0 & 0 & 0 & 0 \\ -3 & 4 & 5 & 0 & 0 & 0 \\ 0 & 1 & -1 & -3 & 0 & 0 \\ 0 & 0 & 0 & 4 & -5 & 0 \\ 0 & 0 & 0 & 3 & 1 & -5 \\ 0 & 0 & 0 & 0 & -1 & 2 \end{bmatrix}$
$r = \begin{bmatrix} 14 & -36 & -6 & 14 & -9 & 6 \end{bmatrix}^T$

P3.32 $A = \begin{bmatrix} 1 & 3 & 0 & 0 & 0 & 0 & 0 \\ 5 & -4 & -1 & 0 & 0 & 0 & 0 \\ 0 & 5 & -2 & -1 & 0 & 0 & 0 \\ 0 & 0 & 2 & 3 & 1 & 0 & 0 \\ 0 & 0 & 0 & 5 & -3 & -1 & 0 \\ 0 & 0 & 0 & 0 & 1 & -1 & 0 \\ 0 & 0 & 0 & 0 & 0 & -2 & 4 \end{bmatrix}$
$r = \begin{bmatrix} 19 & 1 & 28 & 0 & -25 & 0 & 2 \end{bmatrix}^T$

P3.33 $A = \begin{bmatrix} -1 & 1 & 0 & 0 & 0 & 0 & 0 & 0 \\ -1 & 4 & 1 & 0 & 0 & 0 & 0 & 0 \\ 0 & 4 & 1 & 3 & 0 & 0 & 0 & 0 \\ 0 & 0 & 0 & -1 & -2 & 0 & 0 & 0 \\ 0 & 0 & 0 & -2 & -2 & -2 & 0 & 0 \\ 0 & 0 & 0 & 0 & -4 & -2 & -2 & 0 \\ 0 & 0 & 0 & 0 & 0 & 2 & 4 & 0 \\ 0 & 0 & 0 & 0 & 0 & 0 & 2 & 0 \end{bmatrix}$
$r = \begin{bmatrix} 7 & 13 & -3 & -2 & -4 & -28 & 26 & 10 \end{bmatrix}^T$

P3.34

$$\mathbf{A} = \begin{bmatrix} -1 & 1 & 0 & 0 & 0 & 0 & 0 & 0 & 0 \\ 2 & 3 & 1 & 0 & 0 & 0 & 0 & 0 & 0 \\ 0 & 3 & -3 & -1 & 0 & 0 & 0 & 0 & 0 \\ 0 & 0 & -4 & 3 & 4 & 0 & 0 & 0 & 0 \\ 0 & 0 & 0 & 3 & 3 & 5 & 0 & 0 & 0 \\ 0 & 0 & 0 & 0 & -1 & -5 & 0 & 0 & 0 \\ 0 & 0 & 0 & 0 & 0 & -5 & 1 & -4 & 0 \\ 0 & 0 & 0 & 0 & 0 & 0 & -2 & 2 & -4 \\ 0 & 0 & 0 & 0 & 0 & 0 & 0 & -4 & 2 \end{bmatrix}$$

$\mathbf{r} = \begin{bmatrix} -1 & 19 & 20 & -1 & -19 & 14 & 0 & -4 & -2 \end{bmatrix}^T$

P3.35

$$\mathbf{A} = \begin{bmatrix} 3 & -4 & 0 & 0 & 0 & 0 & 0 & 0 & 0 & 0 \\ 3 & 3 & 5 & 0 & 0 & 0 & 0 & 0 & 0 & 0 \\ 0 & -1 & 1 & 2 & 0 & 0 & 0 & 0 & 0 & 0 \\ 0 & 0 & -2 & -4 & 5 & 0 & 0 & 0 & 0 & 0 \\ 0 & 0 & 0 & 1 & 0 & -2 & 0 & 0 & 0 & 0 \\ 0 & 0 & 0 & 0 & 5 & -3 & -2 & 0 & 0 & 0 \\ 0 & 0 & 0 & 0 & 0 & 1 & 0 & -5 & 0 & 0 \\ 0 & 0 & 0 & 0 & 0 & 0 & -3 & 0 & -1 & 0 \\ 0 & 0 & 0 & 0 & 0 & 0 & -3 & 0 & 1 \\ 0 & 0 & 0 & 0 & 0 & 0 & 0 & -4 & 1 \end{bmatrix}$$

$\mathbf{r} = \begin{bmatrix} -13 & -11 & -6 & 25 & 6 & 29 & 1 & 0 & 3 & -12 \end{bmatrix}^T$

For Problems P3.36 to P3.39, solve the linear system $\mathbf{A}x = \mathbf{b}$.

P3.36

$$\mathbf{A} = \begin{bmatrix} -5 & 0 & -4 & 1 & 4 & 5 \\ 3 & 5 & -2 & -4 & 3 & -2 \\ -1 & -3 & 3 & 4 & 3 & 1 \\ 0 & 1 & 1 & 1 & -1 & -4 \\ -4 & -1 & -4 & -3 & 2 & 0 \\ -3 & -3 & -4 & 5 & 3 & 1 \end{bmatrix}$$

a. $\mathbf{b} = \begin{bmatrix} 14 & -26 & 0 & -16 & 0 & -17 \end{bmatrix}^T$
b. $\mathbf{b} = \begin{bmatrix} 19 & -3 & -15 & -4 & 15 & 10 \end{bmatrix}^T$
c. $\mathbf{b} = \begin{bmatrix} -16 & 29 & -4 & 2 & -13 & -31 \end{bmatrix}^T$
d. $\mathbf{b} = \begin{bmatrix} -44 & 3 & -23 & 3 & -10 & -40 \end{bmatrix}^T$

P3.37

$$\mathbf{A} = \begin{bmatrix} -4 & -2 & -1 & 4 & 5 & -2 & -1 & 5 \\ -4 & 1 & 3 & -4 & -4 & -4 & -2 & -3 \\ 2 & 1 & -2 & 3 & -4 & -1 & -3 & 0 \\ 1 & 2 & -2 & 5 & 2 & -5 & 1 & 3 \\ 0 & -4 & 4 & -2 & -1 & -3 & 1 & 4 \\ 4 & -1 & 5 & 0 & 3 & 3 & 0 & 3 \\ 4 & 3 & 2 & 2 & -1 & -3 & -1 & 1 \\ 0 & -5 & 4 & 1 & 2 & 3 & 3 & 1 \end{bmatrix}$$

a. $\mathbf{b} = \begin{bmatrix} 10 & -30 & 0 & -16 & 23 & 61 & 9 & 40 \end{bmatrix}^T$
b. $\mathbf{b} = \begin{bmatrix} 46 & -13 & -14 & 18 & 16 & 20 & 0 & 7 \end{bmatrix}^T$
c. $\mathbf{b} = \begin{bmatrix} 48 & -10 & -27 & 24 & 16 & -13 & -22 & 16 \end{bmatrix}^T$
d. $\mathbf{b} = \begin{bmatrix} -19 & -7 & 7 & 23 & -12 & -11 & 21 & -38 \end{bmatrix}^T$

P3.38

$$\mathbf{A} = \begin{bmatrix} 0 & -3 & -3 & -2 & 3 & 3 & 1 & 2 \\ 3 & 1 & 0 & -4 & 4 & -4 & 2 & -1 \\ -3 & 2 & 3 & -5 & 3 & 5 & -2 & 0 \\ -1 & 0 & -1 & 0 & 4 & -1 & -4 & -5 \\ 5 & -1 & -2 & -1 & 4 & 0 & 2 & 3 \\ -4 & -3 & -2 & -3 & 0 & -2 & -1 & 0 \\ -3 & -3 & -4 & 1 & -3 & 2 & 4 & 0 \\ -4 & 0 & -3 & 0 & 2 & 3 & 3 & -3 \end{bmatrix}$$

a. $\mathbf{b} = \begin{bmatrix} -18 & -13 & -77 & 25 & -8 & 4 & 13 & -15 \end{bmatrix}^T$
b. $\mathbf{b} = \begin{bmatrix} 3 & 14 & -53 & 3 & 14 & -7 & 36 & 25 \end{bmatrix}^T$
c. $\mathbf{b} = \begin{bmatrix} 14 & -30 & 36 & -7 & -18 & 26 & 3 & -7 \end{bmatrix}^T$
d. $\mathbf{b} = \begin{bmatrix} -28 & -3 & -36 & -49 & 5 & -24 & -6 & -37 \end{bmatrix}^T$

P3.39

$\mathbf{A} =$

$$\begin{bmatrix} 1 & -4 & 4 & 1 & 2 & 1 & 3 & -1 & -2 & 4 \\ 2 & 2 & -3 & -4 & 5 & 5 & -4 & -2 & 0 & -2 \\ 2 & 3 & 1 & 0 & -2 & 1 & -1 & 1 & -3 & 1 \\ 1 & -4 & -4 & -3 & -2 & -3 & -1 & 1 & 0 & 4 \\ 1 & 3 & -2 & 0 & -5 & -3 & 3 & -2 & 3 & -1 \\ -1 & -1 & -2 & 0 & -1 & -4 & 0 & -3 & -2 & -3 \\ 4 & -5 & 2 & 0 & 1 & -3 & -4 & 1 & -5 & -2 \\ 5 & -2 & 3 & 1 & 3 & 1 & 2 & 1 & -3 & -5 \\ 0 & -4 & 3 & -4 & -1 & -1 & -2 & -1 & -2 & -5 \\ -4 & 5 & 3 & 5 & -2 & -2 & 1 & -1 & 0 & 4 \end{bmatrix}$$

a. $\mathbf{b} = \begin{bmatrix} 14 & 42 & -3 & -22 & -28 & 21 & 38 & 34 & 31 & -16 \end{bmatrix}^T$
b. $\mathbf{b} = \begin{bmatrix} -12 & -47 & 15 & 28 & 17 & 28 & 37 & -2 & -5 & 15 \end{bmatrix}^T$
c. $\mathbf{b} = \begin{bmatrix} -16 & 6 & 14 & 20 & -16 & -10 & -10 & -44 & -46 & 26 \end{bmatrix}^T$
d. $\mathbf{b} = \begin{bmatrix} -9 & 46 & 16 & -21 & -20 & 6 & 27 & 21 & 36 & -25 \end{bmatrix}^T$

EXPLORE SOME APPLICATIONS

A3.1 Linear systems occur in many other problems involving numerical methods. The following system is a small example of the type of system encountered as part of quadratic spline interpolation problem (see Chapter 8):

$$
\begin{aligned}
a_1 - a_2 &\quad + b_1 &&= 4 \\
+ a_2 - a_3 &\quad + b_1 + b_2 &&= 12 \\
+ a_3 - a_4 &\quad + b_2 &&= -4 \\
a_1 + a_2 &\quad - b_1 &&= 0 \\
+ a_2 + a_3 &\quad + b_1 - b_2 &&= 0 \\
a_3 + a_4 &\quad + b_2 &&= 0
\end{aligned}
$$

Solve for the unknowns, a_1, a_2, a_3, b_1, b_2, and b_3.

A3.2 This is a small example of the type of system encountered as part of the cubic spline interpolation technique (discussed later in section 8.4.3). Solve for the unknowns, $a_1, a_2, ..., a_7$.

$$\frac{2}{3}a_1 + \frac{1}{6}a_2 = 1.2$$

$$\frac{1}{6}a_1 + \frac{2}{3}a_2 + \frac{1}{6}a_3 = 1.97$$

$$+ \frac{1}{6}a_2 + \frac{2}{3}a_3 + \frac{1}{6}a_4 = 2$$

$$+ \frac{1}{6}a_3 + \frac{2}{3}a_4 + \frac{1}{6}a_5 = 0$$

$$+ \frac{1}{6}a_4 + \frac{2}{3}a_5 + \frac{1}{6}a_6 = -2$$

$$+ \frac{1}{6}a_5 + \frac{2}{3}a_6 + \frac{1}{6}a_7 = -1.97$$

$$+ \frac{1}{6}a_6 + \frac{2}{3}a_7 = -1.2$$

A3.3 An 10-stage equilibrium process such as liquid extraction or gas absorption can be modeled by a tridiagonal system of linear equations; solve using $rr = 0.9$ (this depends on the ratio of flow rates (left to right and right to left) and the ratio of weight fractions of the two components that are flowing). Assume that the flow in is 0.05, and that the flow out is 0.5.

$$
\begin{aligned}
-(1 + rr)x_1 + rr\, x_2 &= -(\text{flow into compartment 1}) \\
x_{i-1} - (1 + rr)x_i + rr\, x_{i+1} &= 0 \quad i = 2, ... n - 1 \\
x_{n-1} - (1 + rr)x_n &= -(\text{flow out of compartment } n)
\end{aligned}
$$

(See Hanna and Sandall, p. 58 for a discussion of similar problems.)

A3.4 Consider the single triangle truss shown in Figure 3.2, but take $\alpha = \beta = \pi/4$, so that $\cos \alpha = \sin \alpha = \cos \beta = \sin \beta = \sqrt{2}/2$. Take $W_3 = 100$.

$$
\begin{aligned}
V_1 &\quad + \sqrt{2}/2\, F_{13} &&= 0 \\
H_1 &\quad + F_{12} + \sqrt{2}/2\, F_{13} &&= 0 \\
V_2 &\quad + \sqrt{2}/2\, F_{23} &&= 0 \\
&\quad + F_{12} - \sqrt{2}/2\, F_{23} &&= 0 \\
&\quad - \sqrt{2}/2\, F_{13} - \sqrt{2}/2\, F_{23} &&= 100 \\
&\quad - \sqrt{2}/2\, F_{13} + \sqrt{2}/2\, F_{23} &&= 0
\end{aligned}
$$

A3.5 Tridiagonal systems also occur in solutions of ordinary differential equations with boundary conditions when the equations are solved by means of finite differences. For this example, solve the system $\mathbf{Ax} = \mathbf{b}$

$\mathbf{A} =$

$$
\begin{bmatrix}
-1.99 & 1.00 & 0 & 0 & 0 & 0 & 0 & 0 & 0 \\
1.00 & -1.99 & 1.00 & 0 & 0 & 0 & 0 & 0 & 0 \\
0 & 1.00 & -1.99 & 1.00 & 0 & 0 & 0 & 0 & 0 \\
0 & 0 & 1.00 & -1.99 & 1.00 & 0 & 0 & 0 & 0 \\
0 & 0 & 0 & 1.00 & -1.99 & 1.00 & 0 & 0 & 0 \\
0 & 0 & 0 & 0 & 1.00 & -1.99 & 1.00 & 0 & 0 \\
0 & 0 & 0 & 0 & 0 & 1.00 & -1.99 & 1.00 & 0 \\
0 & 0 & 0 & 0 & 0 & 0 & 1.00 & -1.99 & 1.00 \\
0 & 0 & 0 & 0 & 0 & 0 & 0 & 1.00 & -1.99
\end{bmatrix}
$$

$\mathbf{b} = [-0.99 \quad 0.002 \quad 0.0031 \quad 0.0042 \quad 0.0055 \quad 0.0068 \quad 0.0084 \quad 0.0103 \quad -0.6874]^T$

A3.6 Consider the simple truss shown in Figure 3.3, but take the angles to be $\alpha = \pi/6$, $\beta = \pi/3$, $\gamma = \pi/6$, $\delta = \pi/3$. Solve the linear system, and compare the forces to those found in Example 3.6.

A3.7 Consider the same truss as in A 3.6, but assume that half of the load is applied at node 4, and half at node 5, instead of the entire load being localized at node 2.

A3.8 The equilibrium positions of a system of blocks coupled by springs is described by a linear system of equations. Suppose that there are 4 blocks arranged as shown below. The unstretched length of the ith spring is L_i, and its spring constant is k_i. The distance between the two walls is L. The equation stating that the ith block is in equilibrium states that the forces on the block (from the springs on either side of it) are equal. For example, for B_2, this gives

$$k_2(x_1 + L_2 - x_2) = k_3(x_2 + L_3 - x_3)$$

$$\begin{bmatrix} -k_1 - k_2 & k_2 & 0 & 0 \\ k_2 & -k_2 - k_3 & k_3 & 0 \\ 0 & k_3 & -k_3 - k_4 & k_4 \\ 0 & 0 & k_4 & -k_4 - k_5 \end{bmatrix} \begin{bmatrix} x_1 \\ x_2 \\ x_3 \\ x_4 \end{bmatrix} = \begin{bmatrix} -k_1 L_1 + k_2 L_2 \\ -k_2 L_2 + k_3 L_3 \\ -k_3 L_3 + k_4 L_4 \\ -k_4 L_4 + k_5(L_5 - L) \end{bmatrix}$$

Solve the system for $L_1 = 2$; $L_2 = 2$; $L_3 = 2$; $L_4 = 2$; $L_5 = 2$; $L_w = 8$. $k_1 = 1$; $k_2 = 1$; $k_3 = 1$; $k_4 = 1$; $k_5 = 5$. See (Garcia, p. 103) for discussion of a similar problem.

A3.9 Find the currents in the electrical circuit shown in Fig. 3.1 if the resistances are $R_1 = 12$, $R_2 = 4$, $R_3 = 5$, $R_4 = 2$, $R_5 = 10$, and the voltages are $V_1 = 100$, $V_2 = 0$, $V_3 = 0$.

A3.10 Find the currents in the electrical circuit shown in Fig. 3.1 if the resistances are $R_1 = 15$, $R_2 = 5$, $R_3 = 20$, $R_4 = 0$, $R_5 = 10$, and the voltages are $V_1 = 0$, $V_2 = 200$, $V_3 = 100$.

A3.11 Find the currents in the electrical circuit shown in Fig. 3.1 if the resistances are $R_1 = 10$, $R_2 = 5$, $R_3 = 0$, $R_4 = 10$, $R_5 = 5$, and the voltages are $V_1 = -200$, $V_2 = 0$, $V_3 = 35$.

EXTEND YOUR UNDERSTANDING

U3.1 In Gauss-Jordan elimination, elements above the diagonal are eliminated in the same manner as are elements below the diagonal, thus avoiding the back-substitution phase of the solution process. In a modified Gauss-Jordan technique, the elimination of elements below the diagonal is done in a first phase (as with basic Gaussian elimination), but the second phase eliminates elements above the diagonal (rather than using backsubstitution). Compare the number of operations (flops) required for the ordinary Gauss-Jordan and the modified Gauss-Jordan techniques to the number of flops required for basic Gaussian elimination.

U3.2 Consider the problem of solving the system $\mathbf{Ax} = \mathbf{b}$, where

$$\mathbf{A} = \begin{bmatrix} 1 & 1/2 & 1/3 \\ 1/2 & 1/3 & 1/4 \\ 1/3 & 1/4 & 1/5 \end{bmatrix}$$

and $\mathbf{b}$ is four different, but similar, right-hand sides:

$$\mathbf{b} = \begin{bmatrix} 3.0000 & 2.9000 & 3.1000 & 3.0000 \\ 1.9000 & 2.0000 & 1.8000 & 2.0000 \\ 1.4330 & 1.5000 & 1.4000 & 1.4000 \end{bmatrix}$$

Compare the solutions to $\mathbf{x} = [\, 1 \ \ 2 \ \ 3 \,]^T$, the solution to

$$\mathbf{Ax} = [3.0000 \quad 1.9167 \quad 1.4333].$$

U3.3 Solve the following tridiagonal system, performing steps of the Thomas algorithm by hand (note that the process can be separated into two parts when division by zero would occur in the basic process):

$$
\begin{aligned}
1x_1 + 1x_2 && = 2 \\
2x_1 + 3x_2 + 1x_3 && = 5 \\
+ 2x_2 + 3x_3 + 2x_4 && = 3 \\
+ 1x_3 + 2x_4 + 1x_5 && = 2 \\
+ 1x_4 + 1x_5 + 1x_6 && = 3 \\
+ 2x_5 + 1x_6 + 2x_7 && = 4 \\
+ 2x_6 + 5x_7 + 2x_8 && = 6 \\
+ 1x_7 + 1x_8 && = 3
\end{aligned}
$$

4

LU and QR Factorization

In Chapter 3 we used vector-matrix notation and operations to solve systems of linear equations. In this chapter and the next, we investigate numerical methods for carrying out several important tasks from linear algebra. In this chapter, we consider two important ways of factoring a matrix. The first is the factorization of a matrix into the product of a lower triangular matrix **L** and an upper triangular matrix **U**; this is known as LU factorization. The second, QR factorization, finds an orthogonal matrix **Q** and a right (upper) triangular matrix **R** such that **A** = **QR**. A matrix is orthogonal if the transpose of the matrix is also the inverse of the matrix.

There are two common methods of finding an LU factorization: Gaussian elimination and direct computation. The first creates an upper triangular matrix during the elimination process; the corresponding lower triangular matrix, with 1's on the diagonal, can be constructed from the multipliers used during the elimination.

The second method, direct decomposition, is somewhat more general, in that it allows for the fact that the LU factorization of a given matrix is not unique. The three most common forms correspond to three different assumptions about the diagonal elements of **L** and **U**.

An LU factorization of **A** can be used to solve linear systems of equations efficiently, especially when the system **A x** = **b** must be solved repeatedly using a given matrix **A** with different values of **b** that are not known in advance.

There are also two common methods of finding a QR factorization. One method utilizes Householder transformations; the other method is based on Givens rotations. In each case, a sequence of transformations converts the original matrix into a product of matrices with the desired characteristics. Householder transformations are also used in some settings to perform a similarity transformation of a matrix into an (upper) Hessenberg matrix. A similarity transformation preserves eigenvalues. All elements below the first subdiagonal of a Hessenberg matrix are zero.

QR factorization can be used for a number of types of problems, including solving a linear system and finding an orthonormal basis for the space spanned by a collection of vectors. We restrict our application of QR factorization to its use in finding the eigenvalues of a matrix. Methods for finding eigenvalues are presented in the next chapter.

Example 4-A Currents in an Electrical Circuit

Consider the problem of finding the currents in different parts of an electrical circuit, as shown originally in Figure 3.1. Suppose now that we want to investigate the effect of changing the size of the voltage drop and even its position, placing it perhaps in one of the other two subloops of the circuit (see Fig. 4.1). This corresponds to changing the right-hand side of the system of equations developed in Chapter 3.

The equations for the three loops can be written in a more general form as follows:

Flow around left loop

$$20(i_1 - i_2) + 10(i_1 - i_3) = V_1$$

Flow around upper right loop

$$25i_2 + 10(i_2 - i_3) + 20(i_2 - i_1) = V_2$$

Flow around lower right loop

$$30i_3 + 10(i_3 - i_2) + 10(i_3 - i_1) = V_3$$

In Figure 3.1 we had $V_1 = 0$, $V_2 = 0$, and $V_3 = 200$.

The equations simplify to

$$30i_1 - 20i_2 - 10i_3 = V_1$$
$$-20i_1 + 55i_2 - 10i_3 = V_2$$
$$-10i_1 - 10i_2 + 50i_3 = V_3$$

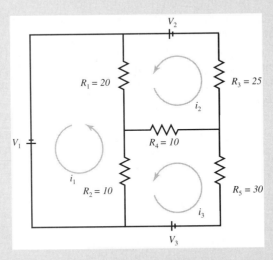

FIGURE 4.1 Simple electrical circuit.

We can solve the new circuit equations efficiently by finding the LU factorization of the coefficient matrix (which does not change as long as we do not modify the sizes or positions of the resistors). This is especially useful if we do not know in advance what the changes will be to the right-hand side of the equation.

Example 4-B LU Factorization for Tridiagonal Systems

There are a number of numerical methods that require the solution of a tridiagonal system as part of the overall process. In this example, we introduce two settings where such systems occur; these types of problems are discussed in more detail in later chapters.

Cubic Spline Interpolation

One of the most popular methods of finding a function representation for data, cubic spline interpolation, requires the solution of a tridiagonal system of equations. If the data to be interpolated are given as the points $(x_1, y_1) \ldots (x_n, y_n)$, the coefficient matrix depends only on the abcissas of the data (the x-values). The right-hand side of the system of equations is determined by the ordinates (the y-values) of the data. If the independent variable represents the times or places where measurements are taken, then it is quite possible that several sets of data, with the same abcissas, may need to be interpolated. This suggests that it may be more efficient to find the LU factorization of the coefficient matrix, and use the factors to solve the linear system, rather than using the Gauss-Thomas algorithm to solve each system separately. For n data points it is necessary to find the values of $n-2$ parameters, $a(1) \ldots a(n-1)$. If the data are given at equally spaced intervals, so that $x(j + 1) - x(j) = h$ for $j = 1 \ldots n - 1$, then the tridiagonal system (with $n = 8$) looks like

$$
\begin{bmatrix}
4 & 1 & 0 & 0 & 0 & 0 \\
1 & 4 & 1 & 0 & 0 & 0 \\
0 & 1 & 4 & 1 & 0 & 0 \\
0 & 0 & 1 & 4 & 1 & 0 \\
0 & 0 & 0 & 1 & 4 & 1 \\
0 & 0 & 0 & 0 & 1 & 4
\end{bmatrix}
\begin{bmatrix}
a_1 \\ a_2 \\ a_3 \\ a_4 \\ a_5 \\ a_6
\end{bmatrix}
= (6/h^2)
\begin{bmatrix}
y_3 - 2y_2 + y_1 \\
y_4 - 2y_3 + y_2 \\
y_5 - 2y_4 + y_3 \\
y_6 - 2y_5 + y_4 \\
y_7 - 2y_6 + y_5 \\
y_8 - 2y_7 + y_6
\end{bmatrix}
$$

Cubic spline interpolation is presented in Chapter 8.

Numerical Solution of the Heat Equation

Numerical methods for solving partial differential equations often require the solution of a linear system of equations. The unknowns in the linear system are the approximate values of the unknown function, at discrete values of the independent variables. For the one-dimensional heat equation, the temperature of a thin rod is found (approximately) at several points along the rod. The solution is repeated at a sequence of different times. The right-hand side of the linear system depends on the solution at the previous time step; the coefficient matrix only depends on the solutions method. The size of the linear system depends on the number of points along the rod where the temperature must be approximated.

For the implicit method, the coefficient matrix is given by

$$\mathbf{d} = (3 \quad 3 \quad 3 \quad \ldots.3); \qquad \mathbf{a} = (-1 \quad -1 \quad \ldots -1 \ 0) \text{ and}$$
$$\mathbf{b} = (0 \quad -1 \quad -1 \quad \ldots -1)$$

For the Crank-Nicolson method, the coefficient matrix is given by

$$\mathbf{d} = (2 \quad 2 \quad 2 \quad \ldots.2); \quad \mathbf{a} = (-0.5 \quad -0.5 \quad \ldots -0.5 \ 0) \text{ and}$$
$$\mathbf{b} = (0 \quad -0.5 \quad 0.5 \quad \ldots -0.5)$$

These methods are discussed in Chapter 15.

LU factorization of a matrix A seeks to find a lower triangular matrix $\mathbf{L}$, and an upper triangular matrix $\mathbf{U}$, such that $\mathbf{A} = \mathbf{LU}$. In particular, for a three-by-three matrix $\mathbf{A}$, the problem is to find $\mathbf{L}$ and $\mathbf{U}$ so that $\mathbf{LU} = \mathbf{A}$:

$$\begin{bmatrix} \ell_{11} & 0 & 0 \\ \ell_{21} & \ell_{22} & 0 \\ \ell_{31} & \ell_{32} & \ell_{33} \end{bmatrix} \cdot \begin{bmatrix} u_{11} & u_{12} & u_{13} \\ 0 & u_{22} & u_{23} \\ 0 & 0 & u_{33} \end{bmatrix} = \begin{bmatrix} a_{11} & a_{12} & a_{13} \\ a_{21} & a_{22} & a_{23} \\ a_{31} & a_{32} & a_{33} \end{bmatrix}.$$

The process of Gaussian elimination forms the basis for finding a very useful representation of a matrix $\mathbf{A}$ known as an LU factorization. A lower triangular matrix $\mathbf{L}$, with 1's on the diagonal, can be constructed from the multipliers used in Gaussian elimination (see Chapter 3). The elimination process transforms the original matrix $\mathbf{A}$ into an upper triangular matrix $\mathbf{U}$. The lower triangular matrix $\mathbf{L}$ is formed by placing the negatives of the multipliers (as used in the multiply-and-add procedure) in the appropriate positions, as shown in the following examples. We first present the LU factorization process for basic Gaussian elimination (without row pivoting). We then consider the special form that results for a tridiagonal matrix, and the modifications that must be made to LU factorization when pivoting is used in the Gaussian elimination.

4.1.1 Using Basic Gaussian Elimination

The steps to find an LU factorization of an n-by-n matrix $\mathbf{A}$ using Gaussian elimination are summarized in the following algorithm.

LU Factorization from Basic Gaussian Elimination

Input	
A	*n-by-n matrix to be factored*
n	*dimension of A*
Initialize	
L = I	*n-by-n identity matrix*
U = A	
Compute	
For k = 1 to n-1	
For i = k + 1 to n	*each row of matrix U after the kth row*
m(i,k) = −U(i, k)/U(k,k)	
For j = k to n	*transform row i*
U(i, j) = U(i, j) + m(i,k)*U(k, j)	
End	
L(i,k) = −m(i,k)	*update L matrix*
End	
End	
Return	
L	*lower triangular matrix*
U	*upper triangular matrix*

Example 4.1 Using the Algorithm for LU Factorization

We now consider the LU factorization of a four-by-four matrix

$$A = \begin{bmatrix} 4 & 12 & 8 & 4 \\ 1 & 7 & 18 & 9 \\ 2 & 9 & 20 & 20 \\ 3 & 11 & 15 & 14 \end{bmatrix}.$$

Initialize

$$L = \begin{bmatrix} 1 & 0 & 0 & 0 \\ 0 & 1 & 0 & 0 \\ 0 & 0 & 1 & 0 \\ 0 & 0 & 0 & 1 \end{bmatrix} \quad U = \begin{bmatrix} 4 & 12 & 8 & 4 \\ 1 & 7 & 18 & 9 \\ 2 & 9 & 20 & 20 \\ 3 & 11 & 15 & 14 \end{bmatrix}$$

Step 1: $m(2,1) = -u(2,1)/u(1,1) = -1/4$; $m(3,1) = -u(3,1)/u(1,1) = -2/4$; $m(4,1) = -u(4,1)/u(1,1) = -3/4$;

Now

$$L = \begin{bmatrix} 1 & 0 & 0 & 0 \\ 1/4 & 1 & 0 & 0 \\ 1/2 & 0 & 1 & 0 \\ 3/4 & 0 & 0 & 1 \end{bmatrix} \quad U - \begin{bmatrix} 4 & 12 & 8 & 4 \\ 0 & 4 & 16 & 8 \\ 0 & 3 & 16 & 18 \\ 0 & 2 & 9 & 11 \end{bmatrix}$$

Step 2: $m(3,2) = -u(3,2)/u(2,2) = -3/4$; $m(4,2) = -u(4,2)/u(2,2) = -2/4$;

Now

$$L = \begin{bmatrix} 1 & 0 & 0 & 0 \\ 1/4 & 1 & 0 & 0 \\ 1/2 & 3/4 & 1 & 0 \\ 3/4 & 1/2 & 0 & 1 \end{bmatrix} \quad U = \begin{bmatrix} 4 & 12 & 8 & 4 \\ 0 & 4 & 16 & 8 \\ 0 & 0 & 4 & 12 \\ 0 & 2 & 1 & 7 \end{bmatrix}$$

Step 3: $m(4,3) = -u(4,3)/u(3,3) = -1/4$;

Now

$$L = \begin{bmatrix} 1 & 0 & 0 & 0 \\ 1/4 & 1 & 0 & 0 \\ 1/2 & 3/4 & 1 & 0 \\ 3/4 & 1/2 & 1/4 & 1 \end{bmatrix} \quad U = \begin{bmatrix} 4 & 12 & 8 & 4 \\ 0 & 4 & 16 & 8 \\ 0 & 0 & 4 & 12 \\ 0 & 2 & 0 & 4 \end{bmatrix}$$

Multiply **L** by **U** to verify the result:

$$\begin{bmatrix} 1 & 0 & 0 & 0 \\ 1/4 & 1 & 0 & 0 \\ 1/2 & 3/4 & 1 & 0 \\ 3/4 & 1/2 & 1/4 & 1 \end{bmatrix} \cdot \begin{bmatrix} 4 & 12 & 8 & 4 \\ 0 & 4 & 16 & 8 \\ 0 & 0 & 4 & 12 \\ 0 & 0 & 0 & 4 \end{bmatrix} = \begin{bmatrix} 4 & 12 & 8 & 4 \\ 1 & 7 & 18 & 9 \\ 2 & 9 & 20 & 20 \\ 3 & 11 & 15 & 14 \end{bmatrix}$$

4.1.2   Factorization of a Tridiagonal Matrix

As we found with Gaussian elimination, the LU factorization of a tridiagonal matrix **T** can be accomplished using much less computation (and less computer memory for the storage of the matrices) than for a full matrix **M** of the same size.

LU Factorization of a Tridiagonal Matrix

Input

a	*upper diagonal of M (matrix to be factored) with $a_n = 0$*
d	*diagonal of matrix M*
b	*lower diagonal of matrix M, with $b_1 = 0$*
n	*number of components in a, d, and b*

Initialize
$bb_1 = 0$
$dd_1 = d_1$

Compute
For i = 2 to n

$$bb_i = \frac{b_i}{dd_{i-1}}$$
$$dd_i = d_i - bb_i a_{i-1}$$

End

Return

bb	*lower diagonal of L (main diagonal is [1, 1, ..., 1])*
dd	*main diagonal of U (upper diagonal is a)*

If desired, the multipliers that are stored in vector **bb** and that form the lower diagonal of the matrix **L** could be written directly into the original vector **L**, and the modified main diagonal of the upper triangular matrix, **dd**, could be written over the original diagonal **d**. We have chosen to use more vectors than necessary to try to make the process as clear as possible and to allow verification of the result if necessary.

Note that this factorization follows the basic Gaussian elimination process and does not scale the diagonal elements to 1, as in the Thomas method. It is not, in general, possible to obtain an LU factorization with all of the diagonal elements of both **L** and **U** set equal to 1.

Example 4.2 LU Factorization of a Tridiagonal System

Consider the tridiagonal matrix

$$\mathbf{M} = \begin{bmatrix} 2 & -1 & 0 & 0 \\ -1 & 2 & -1 & 0 \\ 0 & -1 & 2 & -1 \\ 0 & 0 & -1 & 2 \end{bmatrix},$$

which can be represented by the vectors

$$\mathbf{d} = [2, 2, 2, 2]; \quad \mathbf{a} = [-1, -1, -1, 0]; \quad \mathbf{b} = [0, -1, -1, -1],$$

For this example, $n = 4$.

Begin computation

$$dd_1 = d_1 = 2$$

For $i = 2$

$$bb_2 = b_2/dd_1 \qquad\qquad\qquad = -1/2$$
$$dd_2 = d_2 - bb_2 a_1 = 2 - (-1/2)(-1) = 3/2$$

For $i = 3$

$$bb_3 = b_3/dd_2 = -1/(3/2) \qquad\qquad = -2/3$$
$$dd_3 = d_3 - bb_3 a_2 = 2 - (-2/3)(-1) = 4/3$$

For $i = 4$

$$bb_4 = b_4/dd_3 = -1/(4/3) \qquad\qquad = -3/4$$
$$dd_4 = d_4 - bb_4 a_3 = 2 - (-3/4)(-1) = 5/4$$

In general, the factorization is

$$\mathbf{L} = \begin{bmatrix} 1 & 0 & 0 & 0 \\ bb_2 & 1 & 0 & 0 \\ 0 & bb_3 & 1 & 0 \\ 0 & 0 & bb_4 & 1 \end{bmatrix}, \quad \mathbf{U} = \begin{bmatrix} dd_1 & a_1 & 0 & 0 \\ 0 & dd_2 & a_2 & 0 \\ 0 & 0 & dd_3 & a_3 \\ 0 & 0 & 0 & dd_4 \end{bmatrix},$$

which, for this example, is

$$\mathbf{L} = \begin{bmatrix} 1 & 0 & 0 & 0 \\ -1/2 & 1 & 0 & 0 \\ 0 & -2/3 & 1 & 0 \\ 0 & 0 & -3/4 & 1 \end{bmatrix}, \quad \mathbf{U} = \begin{bmatrix} 2 & -1 & 0 & 0 \\ 0 & 3/2 & -1 & 0 \\ 0 & 0 & 4/3 & -1 \\ 0 & 0 & 0 & 5/4 \end{bmatrix}.$$

4.1.3 Using Gaussian Elimination with Pivoting

For problems in which row pivoting must be performed on the coefficient matrix **A** during Gaussian elimination, we can obtain an LU factorization of the permuted matrix **PA**, where **P** is the permutation matrix that represents the row interchanges that occurred during the pivoting. We now give an algorithm for LU factorization using Gaussian elimination with row pivoting, an example, and an algebraic justification for the method.

LU Factorization with Row Pivoting ═══════════════════════════════════════

$$
\begin{array}{ll}
Input \\
\quad A & matrix\ to\ be\ factored\ (n\text{-}by\text{-}n) \\
Initialize \\
\quad U = A \\
\quad L = I & n\text{-}by\text{-}n\ identity\ matrix \\
\quad P = I \\
Compute \\
For\ k = 1\ to\ n\text{-}1 \\
\quad pivot = |\,U(k,k)\,| & pivot\ element \\
\quad p = k & pivot\ row \\
\quad For\ i = k + 1\ to\ n \\
\quad\quad If\ (|U(i,k)| > pivot) \\
\quad\quad\quad pivot = |\,U(i,k)\,| & update\ pivot\ element \\
\quad\quad\quad p = i & update\ pivot\ row \\
\quad\quad End \\
\quad End \\
\quad If\ (p > k) \\
\quad\quad t_1 = u(k,:) & interchange\ rows\ k\ and\ p\ of\ matrix\ U \\
\quad\quad U(k,:) = U(p,:) \\
\quad\quad U(p,:) = t_1 \\
\quad\quad t_2 = P(k,:) & interchange\ rows\ k\ and\ p\ of\ matrix\ P \\
\quad\quad P(k,:) = P(p,:) \\
\quad\quad P(p,:) = t_2 \\
\quad\quad For\ j = 1\ to\ k\text{-}1 & (if\ k > 1) \\
\quad\quad\quad t_3 = L(k,j) & interchange\ columns\ 1\ldots k-1\ of\ rows\ k\ and\ p \\
\quad\quad\quad L(k,j) = L(p,j) & in\ matrix\ L \\
\quad\quad\quad L(p,j) = t_3 \\
\quad\quad End \\
\quad End \\
\quad For\ i = k + 1\ to\ n \\
\quad\quad s = -U(i,k)/U(k,k) \\
\quad\quad U(i,:) = U(i,:) + s*U(k,:) & update\ row\ i\ in\ U \\
\quad\quad L(i,k) = -s \\
\quad End \\
End \\
Return \\
\quad L & lower\ triangular\ matrix \\
\quad U & upper\ triangular\ matrix \\
\end{array}
$$

Example 4.3 LU Factorization with Pivoting

Consider the matrix $\mathbf{A}$ introduced in Example 3.6

$$\mathbf{A} = \begin{bmatrix} 2 & 6 & 10 \\ 1 & 3 & 3 \\ 3 & 14 & 28 \end{bmatrix}$$

Initialize

$$\mathbf{L} = \begin{bmatrix} 1 & 0 & 0 \\ 0 & 1 & 0 \\ 0 & 0 & 1 \end{bmatrix} \quad \mathbf{U} = \begin{bmatrix} 2 & 6 & 10 \\ 1 & 3 & 3 \\ 3 & 14 & 28 \end{bmatrix} \quad \mathbf{P} = \begin{bmatrix} 1 & 0 & 0 \\ 0 & 1 & 0 \\ 0 & 0 & 1 \end{bmatrix}$$

$k = 1$

Interchange rows 1 and 3 in matrices $\mathbf{U}$ and $\mathbf{P}$

$$\mathbf{L} = \begin{bmatrix} 1 & 0 & 0 \\ 0 & 1 & 0 \\ 0 & 0 & 1 \end{bmatrix} \quad \mathbf{U} = \begin{bmatrix} 3 & 14 & 28 \\ 1 & 3 & 3 \\ 2 & 6 & 10 \end{bmatrix} \quad \mathbf{P} = \begin{bmatrix} 0 & 0 & 1 \\ 0 & 1 & 0 \\ 1 & 0 & 0 \end{bmatrix}$$

The first stage of elimination gives

$$\mathbf{L} = \begin{bmatrix} 1 & 0 & 0 \\ 1/3 & 1 & 0 \\ 2/3 & 0 & 1 \end{bmatrix} \quad \mathbf{U} = \begin{bmatrix} 3 & 14 & 28 \\ 0 & -5/3 & -19/3 \\ 0 & -10/3 & -26/3 \end{bmatrix} \quad \mathbf{P} = \begin{bmatrix} 0 & 0 & 1 \\ 0 & 1 & 0 \\ 1 & 0 & 0 \end{bmatrix}$$

$k = 2$

Interchange rows 2 and 3 in matrices $\mathbf{U}$ and $\mathbf{P}$, also rows 2 and 3, column 1 in $\mathbf{L}$

$$\mathbf{L} = \begin{bmatrix} 1 & 0 & 0 \\ 2/3 & 1 & 0 \\ 1/3 & 0 & 1 \end{bmatrix} \quad \mathbf{U} = \begin{bmatrix} 3 & 14 & 28 \\ 0 & -10/3 & -26/3 \\ 0 & -5/3 & -19/3 \end{bmatrix} \quad \mathbf{P} = \begin{bmatrix} 0 & 0 & 1 \\ 1 & 0 & 0 \\ 0 & 1 & 0 \end{bmatrix}$$

The second stage of elimination gives

$$\mathbf{L} = \begin{bmatrix} 1 & 0 & 0 \\ 2/3 & 1 & 0 \\ 1/3 & 1/2 & 1 \end{bmatrix} \quad \mathbf{U} = \begin{bmatrix} 3 & 14 & 28 \\ 0 & -10/3 & -26/3 \\ 0 & 0 & -2 \end{bmatrix} \quad \mathbf{P} = \begin{bmatrix} 0 & 0 & 1 \\ 1 & 0 & 0 \\ 0 & 1 & 0 \end{bmatrix}$$

Verify result:

$$\begin{bmatrix} 1 & 0 & 0 \\ 2/3 & 1 & 0 \\ 1/3 & 1/2 & 1 \end{bmatrix} \cdot \begin{bmatrix} 3 & 14 & 28 \\ 0 & -10/3 & -26/3 \\ 0 & 0 & -2 \end{bmatrix} = \begin{bmatrix} 3 & 14 & 28 \\ 2 & 6 & 10 \\ 1 & 3 & 3 \end{bmatrix}$$

4.1.4 Discussion

The operations of Gaussian elimination can be expressed as actions performed on matrix $\mathbf{A}$ by certain elementary matrices. We illustrate the process with three-by-three matrices for simplicity. For instance, the operations that perform the first stage of Gaussian elimination can be written as

$$\begin{bmatrix} 1 & 0 & 0 \\ m_{21} & 1 & 0 \\ m_{31} & 0 & 1 \end{bmatrix} \cdot \begin{bmatrix} a_{11} & a_{12} & a_{13} \\ a_{21} & a_{22} & a_{23} \\ a_{31} & a_{32} & a_{33} \end{bmatrix} = \begin{bmatrix} a_{11} & a_{12} & a_{13} \\ 0 & a'_{22} & a'_{23} \\ 0 & a'_{32} & a'_{33} \end{bmatrix}.$$

To show that we can obtain the LU factorization of $\mathbf{A}$ as previously illustrated, we define the matrices

$$\mathbf{M}_1 = \begin{bmatrix} 1 & 0 & 0 \\ m_{21} & 1 & 0 \\ m_{31} & 0 & 1 \end{bmatrix} \text{ and } \mathbf{M}_2 = \begin{bmatrix} 1 & 0 & 0 \\ 0 & 1 & 0 \\ 0 & m_{32} & 1 \end{bmatrix}$$

where m_{21} and m_{31} are determined to zero-out the subdiagonal elements in the first column of $\mathbf{A}$ and m_{32} is found in the manner required to reduce to zero the second column of the transformed matrix $\mathbf{A}$, below the diagonal. Thus, $\mathbf{U} = \mathbf{M}_2 \cdot (\mathbf{M}_1 \cdot \mathbf{A})$. The inverses of matrices $\mathbf{M}_1$ and $\mathbf{M}_2$ are

$$\mathbf{M}_1^{-1} = \begin{vmatrix} 1 & 0 & 0 \\ -m_{21} & 1 & 0 \\ -m_{31} & 0 & 1 \end{vmatrix} \text{ and } \mathbf{M}_2^{-1} = \begin{bmatrix} 1 & 0 & 0 \\ 0 & 1 & 0 \\ 0 & -m_{32} & 1 \end{bmatrix}$$

To see how Gaussian elimination produces an LU factorization, we let $\mathbf{I}$ be the identity matrix and gradually transform the identity $\mathbf{I} \cdot \mathbf{A} = \mathbf{A}$ into the product $\mathbf{L} \mathbf{U} = \mathbf{A}$ by inserting products of the form $\mathbf{M}^{-1} \mathbf{M}$ as indicated in the following sequence of identities.

$$\mathbf{I} \cdot \mathbf{A} = \mathbf{A}$$
$$\mathbf{I} \cdot \mathbf{M}_1^{-1} \cdot \mathbf{M}_1 \cdot \mathbf{A} = \mathbf{A}$$
$$\mathbf{I} \cdot \mathbf{M}_1^{-1} \cdot \mathbf{M}_2^{-1} \cdot \mathbf{M}_2 \cdot \mathbf{M}_1 \cdot \mathbf{A} = \mathbf{A}$$

The product $\mathbf{M}_2 \cdot \mathbf{M}_1 \cdot \mathbf{A}$ is the required upper triangular matrix $\mathbf{U}$, by construction. Direct computation shows that $\mathbf{I} \cdot \mathbf{M}_1^{-1} \cdot \mathbf{M}_2^{-1}$ is lower triangular, with 1's on the diagonal, as required for the matrix $\mathbf{L}$, i.e.,

$$\begin{bmatrix} 1 & 0 & 0 \\ -m_{21} & 1 & 0 \\ -m_{31} & 0 & 1 \end{bmatrix} \cdot \begin{bmatrix} 1 & 0 & 0 \\ 0 & 1 & 0 \\ 0 & -m_{32} & 1 \end{bmatrix} = \begin{bmatrix} 1 & 0 & 0 \\ -m_{21} & 1 & 0 \\ -m_{31} & -m_{32} & 1 \end{bmatrix}.$$

When row pivoting is used in Gaussian elimination, the matrices $\mathbf{L}$ and $\mathbf{U}$ that are obtained give a factorization of a *permutation* of $\mathbf{A}$, corresponding to the row interchanges performed during pivoting.

We now consider the role that permutation matrices play in Gaussian elimination with pivoting. Row interchanges on matrix $\mathbf{A}$ correspond to multiplying $\mathbf{A}$ on the left by a permutation matrix $\mathbf{P}$ (a permutation of the identity matrix). Column interchanges are accomplished by multiplying $\mathbf{A}$ on the right by a permutation matrix. The inverse of a permutation matrix is the matrix itself. For example, to interchange the second and third rows of $\mathbf{A}$, we perform the following multiplication:

$$\begin{bmatrix} 1 & 0 & 0 \\ 0 & 0 & 1 \\ 0 & 1 & 0 \end{bmatrix} \cdot \begin{bmatrix} a_{11} & a_{12} & a_{13} \\ a_{21} & a_{22} & a_{23} \\ a_{31} & a_{32} & a_{33} \end{bmatrix} = \begin{bmatrix} a_{11} & a_{12} & a_{13} \\ a_{31} & a_{32} & a_{33} \\ a_{21} & a_{22} & a_{23} \end{bmatrix}$$

Now, consider a simple three-by-three example in which no pivoting occurs at the first stage of Gaussian elimination, but pivoting does occur at the second stage. We begin with the identity

$$\mathbf{I} \cdot \mathbf{A} = \mathbf{A}$$

The first stage, with no pivoting gives

$$\mathbf{I} \cdot \mathbf{M}_1^{-1} \cdot \mathbf{M}_1 \cdot \mathbf{A} = \mathbf{A}$$

Pivoting at the beginning of the second stage gives (since $\mathbf{P} \cdot \mathbf{P} = \mathbf{I}$)

$$\mathbf{I} \cdot \mathbf{M}_1^{-1} \cdot \mathbf{P} \cdot \mathbf{P} \cdot \mathbf{M}_1 \cdot \mathbf{A} = \mathbf{A}$$

The elimination for the second stage gives

$$\mathbf{I} \cdot \mathbf{M}_1^{-1} \cdot \mathbf{P} \cdot \mathbf{M}_2^{-1} \cdot \mathbf{M}_2 \cdot \mathbf{P} \cdot \mathbf{M}_1 \cdot \mathbf{A} = \mathbf{A} \qquad (*)$$

The matrices $\mathbf{M}_2$ and $\mathbf{M}_2^{-1}$ are as defined previously, except that m_{32} is found to reduce the second column of $\mathbf{PM}_1\mathbf{A}$ to zero, below the diagonal.

The matrix $\mathbf{M}_2 \cdot \mathbf{P} \cdot \mathbf{M}_1 \cdot \mathbf{A}$ is the upper triangular matrix $\mathbf{U}$ formed by the Gaussian elimination. However, $\mathbf{I} \cdot \mathbf{M}_1^{-1} \cdot \mathbf{P} \cdot \mathbf{M}_2^{-1}$ is not lower triangular. The required lower triangular matrix is $\mathbf{P} \cdot \mathbf{M}_1^{-1} \cdot \mathbf{P} \cdot \mathbf{M}_2^{-1}$. Multiplying both sides of (*) on the left by $\mathbf{P}$ (and dropping the multiplication by $\mathbf{I}$) gives

$$\mathbf{P} \cdot \mathbf{M}_1^{-1} \cdot \mathbf{P} \cdot \mathbf{M}_2^{-1} \cdot \{\mathbf{M}_2 \cdot \mathbf{P} \cdot \mathbf{M}_1 \cdot \mathbf{A}\} = \mathbf{P}\,\mathbf{A}$$

To show that $\mathbf{P} \cdot \mathbf{M}_1^{-1} \cdot \mathbf{P} \cdot \mathbf{M}_2^{-1} = \mathbf{L}$, we first compute $\mathbf{P} \cdot \mathbf{M}_1^{-1} \cdot \mathbf{P} = \mathbf{B}$:

$$\begin{bmatrix} 1 & 0 & 0 \\ 0 & 0 & 1 \\ 0 & 1 & 0 \end{bmatrix} \begin{bmatrix} 1 & 0 & 0 \\ -m_{21} & 1 & 0 \\ -m_{31} & 0 & 1 \end{bmatrix} \begin{bmatrix} 1 & 0 & 0 \\ 0 & 0 & 1 \\ 0 & 1 & 0 \end{bmatrix} = \begin{bmatrix} 1 & 0 & 0 \\ -m_{31} & 1 & 0 \\ -m_{21} & 0 & 1 \end{bmatrix}$$

and then verify that $\mathbf{P} \cdot \mathbf{M}_1^{-1} \cdot \mathbf{P} \cdot \mathbf{M}_2^{-1} = \mathbf{B} \cdot \mathbf{M}_2^{-1} = \mathbf{L}$:

$$\begin{bmatrix} 1 & 0 & 0 \\ -m_{31} & 1 & 0 \\ -m_{21} & 0 & 1 \end{bmatrix} \cdot \begin{bmatrix} 1 & 0 & 0 \\ 0 & 1 & 0 \\ 0 & -m_{32} & 1 \end{bmatrix} = \begin{bmatrix} 1 & 0 & 0 \\ -m_{31} & 1 & 0 \\ -m_{21} & -m_{32} & 1 \end{bmatrix}$$

Thus, the positions of the elements of $\mathbf{L}$ reflect the interchanges that occurred during elimination; the matrix formed from the product of $\mathbf{L}$ and $\mathbf{U}$ is a permuted form of the original matrix $\mathbf{A}$.

If we store $\mathbf{L}$ as a separate matrix, then, whenever pivoting occurs, the elements of $\mathbf{L}$ that have already been computed must be permuted along with matrix $\mathbf{A}$. However, the diagonal elements of $\mathbf{L}$ are not permuted. If we store the elements of $\mathbf{L}$ below the diagonal in the positions of $\mathbf{A}$ that have been reduced to zero by the elimination process, the elements of $\mathbf{L}$ will appear in the correct positions, even when pivoting is used.

4.2 DIRECT LU FACTORIZATION

An alternative approach to Gaussian elimination for finding the LU factorization of matrix **A** is based on equating the elements of the product **LU** with the corresponding elements of **A** in a systematic manner. The three most common forms of LU factorization correspond to three different choices for the form of the diagonal elements in **L** and **U**: the diagonal elements of **L** are 1, the diagonal elements of **U** are 1, or the diagonal elements of **L** and **U** are equal.

4.2.1 Factorization of a General Matrix

The form of LU factorization that assumes that the diagonal elements of matrix **L** are 1's is known in the literature as Doolittle's method. For a three-by-three matrix **A**, the problem is to find matrices **L** and **U** so that **L U** = **A**:

$$
\begin{bmatrix} 1 & 0 & 0 \\ \ell_{21} & 1 & 0 \\ \ell_{31} & \ell_{32} & 1 \end{bmatrix} \cdot \begin{bmatrix} u_{11} & u_{12} & u_{13} \\ 0 & u_{22} & u_{23} \\ 0 & 0 & u_{33} \end{bmatrix} = \begin{bmatrix} a_{11} & a_{12} & a_{13} \\ a_{21} & a_{22} & a_{23} \\ a_{31} & a_{32} & a_{33} \end{bmatrix}.
$$

We begin by finding $u_{11} = a_{11}$ and then solving for the remaining elements in the first row of **U** and the first column of **L**. At the second stage, we find u_{22} and then the remainder of the second row of **U** and the second column of **L**. Continuing in this manner, we determine all of the elements of **U** and **L**. This process is described in the following algorithm and illustrated in Example 4.6.

A similar procedure can be carried out assuming that there are 1's on the diagonal of **U** rather than **L**. This variation is often called Crout's method. We limit our investigation to direct factorization with 1s on the diagonal of **L**.

Note that in the following algorithm,

$$
L(k, 1:k - 1)*U(1:k - 1, k) \text{ is equivalent to } \sum_{i=1}^{k-1} L_{k,i} U_{i,k}, \text{ etc.}
$$

Doolittle Form of LU Factorization

```
Input
    A               n-by-n matrix to be factored
    n               dimension of A
Initialize
    U = 0(n)        initialize U to n-by-n zero matrix
    L = I(n)        initialize L to identity matrix
Compute
For k = 1 to n
    U(k, k) = A(k, k) − L(k, 1:k − 1)*U(1:k − 1, k)
    For j = k + 1 to n
        U(k, j) = A(k, j) − L(k, 1:k − 1)*U(1:k − 1), j)
        L(j, k) = (A(j, k) − L(j, 1:k − 1)*U(1:k − 1, k))/U(k, k)
    End
End
```

Example 4.4 Doolittle Form of LU Factorization

To find the LU factorization for $\mathbf{A} = \begin{bmatrix} 1 & 4 & 5 \\ 4 & 20 & 32 \\ 5 & 32 & 64 \end{bmatrix}$

by Doolittle's method, we write the desired product as

$$\begin{bmatrix} 1 & 0 & 0 \\ \ell_{21} & 1 & 0 \\ \ell_{31} & \ell_{32} & 1 \end{bmatrix} \cdot \begin{bmatrix} u_{11} & u_{12} & u_{13} \\ 0 & u_{22} & u_{23} \\ 0 & 0 & u_{33} \end{bmatrix} = \begin{bmatrix} 1 & 4 & 5 \\ 4 & 20 & 32 \\ 5 & 32 & 64 \end{bmatrix}.$$

We begin by solving for the first row of $\mathbf{U}$ and the first column of $\mathbf{L}$:

$$(1)\, u_{11} = a_{11} = 1, \quad (1)\, u_{12} = a_{12} = 4, \quad (1)\, u_{13} = a_{13} = 5;$$
$$\ell_{21}\, u_{11} = a_{21} = 4, \quad \ell_{31}\, u_{11} = a_{31} = 5.$$

Next, using these values, we find the second row of $\mathbf{U}$ and the second column of $\mathbf{L}$:

$$\begin{bmatrix} 1 & 0 & 0 \\ 4 & 1 & 0 \\ 5 & \ell_{32} & 1 \end{bmatrix} \cdot \begin{bmatrix} 1 & 4 & 5 \\ 0 & u_{22} & u_{23} \\ 0 & 0 & u_{33} \end{bmatrix} = \begin{bmatrix} 1 & 4 & 5 \\ 4 & 20 & 32 \\ 5 & 32 & 64 \end{bmatrix},$$

$$(4)(4) + u_{22} = 20 \quad \Longrightarrow \quad u_{22} = 20 - 16 = 4;$$

$$(4)(5) + u_{23} = 32 \quad \Longrightarrow \quad u_{23} = 32 - 20 = 12;$$
$$(5)(4) + \ell_{32}\, u_{22} = 32 \Longrightarrow \quad \ell_{32} = (32 - 20)/4 = 3.$$

Finally, the only remaining unknown in matrix $\mathbf{U}$ is determined:

$$\begin{bmatrix} 1 & 0 & 0 \\ 4 & 1 & 0 \\ 5 & 3 & 1 \end{bmatrix} \cdot \begin{bmatrix} 1 & 4 & 5 \\ 0 & 4 & 12 \\ 0 & 0 & u_{33} \end{bmatrix} = \begin{bmatrix} 1 & 4 & 5 \\ 4 & 20 & 32 \\ 5 & 32 & 64 \end{bmatrix},$$

$$(5)(5) + (3)(12) + u_{33} = 64 \quad \Longrightarrow \quad u_{33} = 64 - 25 - 36 = 3.$$

The factorization is

$$\mathbf{L} = \begin{bmatrix} 1 & 0 & 0 \\ 4 & 1 & 0 \\ 5 & 3 & 1 \end{bmatrix}, \quad \mathbf{U} = \begin{bmatrix} 1 & 4 & 5 \\ 0 & 4 & 12 \\ 0 & 0 & 3 \end{bmatrix}.$$

4.2.2 Factorization of a Symmetric Matrix

If the matrix $\mathbf{A}$ is symmetric, there is a convenient form of LU factorization, called Cholesky factorization, for which the upper triangular matrix $\mathbf{U}$ is the transpose of the lower triangular matrix $\mathbf{L}$; that is, $\mathbf{A} = \mathbf{L}\mathbf{L}^T$. Furthermore, only $n(n+1)/2$ storage locations are required, rather than the usual n^2. For a three-by-three matrix $\mathbf{A}$, the problem is to find matrices $\mathbf{L}$ and $\mathbf{U}$ so that $\mathbf{L}\mathbf{U} = \mathbf{A}$; that is, we seek

$$
\begin{bmatrix} x_{11} & 0 & 0 \\ \ell_{21} & x_{22} & 0 \\ \ell_{31} & \ell_{32} & x_{33} \end{bmatrix} \cdot \begin{bmatrix} x_{11} & u_{12} & u_{13} \\ 0 & x_{22} & u_{23} \\ 0 & 0 & x_{33} \end{bmatrix} = \begin{bmatrix} a_{11} & a_{12} & a_{13} \\ a_{21} & a_{22} & a_{23} \\ a_{31} & a_{32} & a_{33} \end{bmatrix},
$$

where corresponding diagonal elements of $\mathbf{L}$ and $\mathbf{U}$ are equal ($u_{ii} = \ell_{ii} = x_{ii}$.)

If the matrix $\mathbf{A}$ is symmetric and positive definite, the Cholesky factorization can be carried out without pivoting or scaling (and the square roots that occur will be real). If $\mathbf{A}$ is not positive definite, the procedure may encounter the square root of a negative number at some stage of the computation. However, since all real symmetric matrices have real eigenvalues, and all eigenvalues may be shifted by the amount k, simply by adding k to each element on the principal diagonal, one can apply Cholesky factorization to $\mathbf{A} + k\mathbf{I}$ as long as $\mathbf{A}$ is symmetric. For further discussion, see Atkinson, 1989, or Acton, 1990.

Cholesky LU Factorization

Input	
A	*symmetric n-by-n matrix*
n	*number of rows or columns in A*
Initialize	
$L = I_n$	*n-by-n identity matrix*
If $(A \neq A^T)$ Error	*A must be symmetric*
Compute	
For k = 1 to n	
$\quad x = L(k, 1{:}k - 1)$	*columns 1 to k-1 of the kth row of L*
$\quad L(k,k) = \sqrt{A(k,k) - x \cdot x^T}$	
$\quad$ For j = k + 1 to n	
$\quad\quad y = L(j, 1{:}k - 1)$	*columns 1 to k-1 of the jth row of L*
$\quad\quad L(j,k) = \sqrt{A(j,k) - y \cdot y^T}$	
$\quad$ End	
End	
$U = L^T$	
Return	
L	*computed lower triangular matrix*
U	*u is defined to be L^T*

Example 4.5 Cholesky LU Factorization

The Cholesky form of LU factorization for $\mathbf{A} = \begin{bmatrix} 1 & 4 & 5 \\ 4 & 20 & 32 \\ 5 & 32 & 64 \end{bmatrix}$

requires the diagonal of the $\mathbf{L}$ and $\mathbf{U}$ matrices to be equal, so we write the desired product as

$$\begin{bmatrix} x_{11} & 0 & 0 \\ \ell_{21} & x_{22} & 0 \\ \ell_{31} & \ell_{32} & x_{33} \end{bmatrix} \cdot \begin{bmatrix} x_{11} & u_{12} & u_{13} \\ 0 & x_{22} & u_{23} \\ 0 & 0 & x_{33} \end{bmatrix} = \begin{bmatrix} 1 & 4 & 5 \\ 4 & 20 & 32 \\ 5 & 32 & 64 \end{bmatrix}$$

and proceed to solve for the unknowns in a systematic manner. The first stage of calculations gives

$$\begin{aligned}
x_{11} x_{11} = a_{11} = 1 &\quad\Rightarrow\quad x_{11} = 1; \\
x_{11} u_{12} = a_{12} = 4 &\quad\Rightarrow\quad u_{12} = 4/1 = 4; \\
x_{11} u_{13} = a_{13} = 5 &\quad\Rightarrow\quad u_{13} = 5/1 = 5; \\
\ell_{21} x_{11} = a_{21} = 4 &\quad\Rightarrow\quad \ell_{21} = 4/1 = 4; \\
\ell_{31} x_{11} = a_{31} = 5 &\quad\Rightarrow\quad \ell_{31} = 5/1 = 5.
\end{aligned}$$

Note that if $\mathbf{A}$ is symmetric, $a_{1j} = a_{j1}$, and it is automatic that $\ell_{j1} = u_{1j}$. Next, from the values computed in the first stage, the product is

$$\begin{bmatrix} 1 & 0 & 0 \\ 4 & x_{22} & 0 \\ 5 & \ell_{32} & x_{33} \end{bmatrix} \cdot \begin{bmatrix} 1 & 4 & 5 \\ 0 & x_{22} & u_{23} \\ 0 & 0 & x_{33} \end{bmatrix} = \begin{bmatrix} 1 & 4 & 5 \\ 4 & 20 & 32 \\ 5 & 32 & 64 \end{bmatrix}$$

we thus compute

$$\begin{aligned}
(4)(4) + x_{22} x_{22} = 20 &\quad\Rightarrow\quad x_{22} = (20 - 16)^{1/2} = 2 \\
(4)(5) + x_{22} u_{23} = 32 &\quad\Rightarrow\quad u_{23} = (32 - 20)/2 = 6 \\
(5)(4) + \ell_{32} x_{22} = 32 &\quad\Rightarrow\quad \ell_{32} = (32 - 20)/2 = 6
\end{aligned}$$

Finally, we find the last unknown:

$$\begin{bmatrix} 1 & 0 & 0 \\ 4 & 2 & 0 \\ 5 & 6 & x_{33} \end{bmatrix} \cdot \begin{bmatrix} 1 & 4 & 5 \\ 0 & 2 & 6 \\ 0 & 0 & x_{33} \end{bmatrix} = \begin{bmatrix} 1 & 4 & 5 \\ 4 & 20 & 32 \\ 5 & 32 & 64 \end{bmatrix}$$

$$(5)(5) + (6)(6) + x_{33} x_{33} = 64 \Rightarrow x_{33} = (64 - 25 - 36)^{1/2} = \sqrt{3}$$

The LU factorization, with $\mathbf{L}$ and $\mathbf{U}$ as follows, satisfies $\mathbf{L} = \mathbf{U}^{\mathrm{T}}$

$$\mathbf{L} = \begin{bmatrix} 1 & 0 & 0 \\ 4 & 2 & 0 \\ 5 & 6 & \sqrt{3} \end{bmatrix}, \quad \mathbf{U} = \begin{bmatrix} 1 & 4 & 5 \\ 0 & 2 & 6 \\ 0 & 0 & \sqrt{3} \end{bmatrix}.$$

4.3.1 Solving Systems of Linear Equations

One advantage of saving the multipliers so that the **L** matrix can be formed is evident from the situation in which the same system of equations must be solved again later, with a different right-hand side. If the coefficient matrix **A** of a linear system of equations is written as the product of a lower triangular matrix **L** and an upper triangular matrix **U,** the linear system can be solved easily in two steps.

The original matrix-vector equation, **A x** = **b**, is written in terms of the LU factorization of **A** as **L U x** = **b**. We introduce the unknown vector **y**, defined as **U x** = **y**. We first solve the system **L y** = **b** for **y** by "forward substitution"; that is, we solve for y_1 first, y_2 next, and so on. We then solve the system U **x** = **y** for **x** by "backward substitution," finding x_n first, then x_{n-1} next, etc. The process is described in the following algorithm, which allows for the possibility of multiple right-hand sides of the original linear system.

Solve L U x = B

> *Input*
>
> | | |
> |---|---|
> | L | *lower triangular matrix (with 1's on diagonal)* |
> | U | *upper triangular matrix* |
> | B | *right-hand side matrix (n-by-m)* |
> | n | *number of rows or columns in L or U, number of rows in B* |
> | m | *number of columns in B* |
>
> *Solve* L Z = B *using forward substitution*
> For j = 1 to m
>   Z(1,j) = B(1,j)
>   For i = 2 to n
>   Z(i, j) = B(i, j) − L(i, :)*Z(:, j) i^{th} *row of L dot j^{th} col of Z*
>   End
> End
>
> *Solve* U X = Z *using back substitution*
> For j = 1 to m
>   X(n, :) = Z(n, :)/U(i, i)
>   For i = n − 1 to 1
>   X(i, j) = (Z(i, j) − U(i, :)*X((:, j)))/U(i, i) i^{th} *row of U dot j^{th} col of Z*
>   End
> End
>
> *Return*
>
> | | |
> |---|---|
> | X | *matrix of solutions* |

Example 4.6 Solving an Electrical Circuit for Several Voltages

Consider again the electric circuit of Figure 3.1 with resistances as shown, but with $V_1 = 0$, $V_2 = 80$, and $V_3 = 0$. The system to be solved is $\mathbf{A}\,\mathbf{x} = \mathbf{b}$, where

$$\mathbf{A} = \begin{bmatrix} 30 & -20 & -10 \\ -20 & 55 & -10 \\ -10 & -10 & 50 \end{bmatrix}, \text{ and } \mathbf{b} = \begin{bmatrix} 0 \\ 80 \\ 0 \end{bmatrix}.$$

$\mathbf{A} = \mathbf{L}\,\mathbf{U}$, with

$$\mathbf{L} = \begin{bmatrix} 1 & 0 & 0 \\ -2/3 & 1 & 0 \\ -1/3 & -2/5 & 1 \end{bmatrix} \text{ and } \mathbf{U} = \begin{bmatrix} 30 & -20 & -10 \\ 0 & 125/3 & -50/3 \\ 0 & 0 & 40 \end{bmatrix}.$$

We first solve $\mathbf{L}\,\mathbf{y} = \mathbf{b}$, i.e.,

$$\begin{bmatrix} 1 & 0 & 0 \\ -2/3 & 1 & 0 \\ -1/3 & -2/5 & 1 \end{bmatrix} \begin{bmatrix} y_1 \\ y_2 \\ y_3 \end{bmatrix} = \begin{bmatrix} 0 \\ 80 \\ 0 \end{bmatrix},$$

and find, by forward substitution, that

$$y_1 = 0, \ y_2 = 80, \text{ and } y_3 = (2/5)(80) = 32.$$

Next, we solve $\mathbf{U}\,\mathbf{x} = \mathbf{y}$, or

$$\begin{bmatrix} 30 & -20 & -10 \\ 0 & 125/3 & -50/3 \\ 0 & 0 & 40 \end{bmatrix} \begin{bmatrix} x_1 \\ x_2 \\ x_3 \end{bmatrix} = \begin{bmatrix} 0 \\ 80 \\ 32 \end{bmatrix},$$

and find, by backward substitution, that

$$x_3 = 32/40 = 4/5,$$
$$x_2 = (80 + 40/3)(3/125) = 56/25,$$

and

$$x_1 = (1/30)[-20(56/25) - 10(4/5)] = 44/25.$$

The resulting electrical currents in each of the three loops are

$$i_1 = 1.76, \ i_2 = 2.24, \text{ and } i_3 = 0.80.$$

4.3.2　Solving a Tridiagonal System Using LU Factorization

We now consider the problem of solving a tridiagonal system $\mathbf{M}\mathbf{x} = \mathbf{r}$ in which the LU factorization of matrix $\mathbf{M}$ is given by the vectors $\mathbf{a}$, $\mathbf{d}$, and $\mathbf{b}$. The process for finding the solution is described in the following algorithm.

Solving a Tridiagonal System Using LU Factorization ═══════════════════════════

Input

$\mathbf{a}$	*above diagonal of matrix U; (with $\mathbf{a}_n = 0$)*
$\mathbf{d}$	*diagonal of matrix U*
$\mathbf{b}$	*below diagonal of matrix L (with $\mathbf{b}_1 = 0$)*
$\mathbf{r}$	*right-hand side of linear system*
n	*number of components in each vector*

Solve $\mathbf{L}\,\mathbf{z} = \mathbf{b}$ *using forward substitution*

$z(1) = r(1)$
For k = 2 to n
　　$z(k) = r(k) - b(k)\,z(k - 1)$
End

Solve $\mathbf{U}\mathbf{x} = \mathbf{z}$ *using back substitution*

$x(n) = z(n)/d(n)$
For k = n − 1 to 1
　　$x(k) = (z(k) - a(k)\,x(k + 1))/d(k)$
End

Return

$\mathbf{x}$	*vector of solution*

Example 4.7 Solving a Tridiagonal System Using LU Factorization

To illustrate the use of the preceding algorithm, we solve the linear system, $\mathbf{M}\mathbf{x} = \mathbf{r}$, with $\mathbf{r} = (4\ -3\ 9\ -10)$, and the LU factorization of $\mathbf{M}$ given by the vectors $\mathbf{a} = (-1\ -1\ -1\ 0)$, $\mathbf{d} = (2\ 3/2\ 4/3\ 5/4\ )$, $\mathbf{b} = (0\ -1/2\ -2/3\ -3/4)$ (see Example 4.2).

We begin by solving $\mathbf{L}\,\mathbf{z} = \mathbf{b}$ using forward substitution

$$
\begin{aligned}
z(1) &= r(1) & &= 4 \\
z(2) &= r(2) - b(2)\,z(1) = -3 - (-1/2)(4) & &= -1 \\
z(3) &= r(3) - b(3)\,z(2) = 9 - (-2/3)(-1) & &= 25/3 \\
z(4) &= r(4) - b(4)\,z(3) = -10 - (-3/4)(25/5) & &= -15/4
\end{aligned}
$$

We then solve $\mathbf{U}\mathbf{x} = \mathbf{z}$ using back substitution

$$
\begin{aligned}
x(1) &= z(4)/(4) & &= -3 \\
x(3) &= (z(3) - a(3)\,x(4))/d(3) = (25/3 - (-1)(-3))(3/4) &&= 4 \\
x(2) &= (z(2) - a(2)\,x(3))/d(2) = (-1 - (-1)(4))(2/3) & &= 2 \\
x(1) &= (z(1) - a(1)\,x(2))/d(1) = (4 - (-1)2))(1/2) & &= 3
\end{aligned}
$$

The solution vector is

$$\mathbf{x} = (3\ 2\ 4\ -3)$$

4.3.3   Inverse of a Matrix

The inverse of an n-by-n matrix $\mathbf{A}$ can be found by solving the system of equations, $\mathbf{A}\,\mathbf{x}_i = \mathbf{e}_i$ $(i = 1, \dots, n)$ for the vectors $\mathbf{e}_i = [0\ 0 \dots 1 \dots 0\ 0]^T$ where the 1 appears in the ith position. The matrix $\mathbf{X}$ whose columns are the solution vectors $\mathbf{x}_1, \dots, \mathbf{x}_n$ is $\mathbf{A}^{-1}$. The process is illustrated in the following example.

Example 4.8 Inverse of a Matrix

Using the LU factorization of $\mathbf{A}$ and the algorithm to solve $\mathbf{L}\,\mathbf{U}\,\mathbf{x} = \mathbf{B}$ given in section 4.3.1, we can construct $\mathbf{X} = \mathbf{A}^{-1}$ by taking $\mathbf{B}$ to be the identity matrix. To illustrate the process, we find the inverse of $\mathbf{A}$, using its L U factorization, where

$$\mathbf{A} = \begin{bmatrix} 1 & -1 & 2 \\ -2 & 1 & 1 \\ -1 & 2 & 1 \end{bmatrix}, \quad \mathbf{L} = \begin{bmatrix} 1 & 0 & 0 \\ -2 & 1 & 0 \\ -1 & -1 & 1 \end{bmatrix}, \quad \mathbf{U} = \begin{bmatrix} 1 & -1 & 2 \\ 0 & -1 & 5 \\ 0 & 0 & 8 \end{bmatrix}.$$

First we solve $\mathbf{L}\,\mathbf{Y} = \mathbf{I}$ for $\mathbf{Y}$, that is,

$$\begin{bmatrix} 1 & 0 & 0 \\ -2 & 1 & 0 \\ -1 & -1 & 1 \end{bmatrix} \begin{bmatrix} y_{11} & y_{12} & y_{13} \\ y_{21} & y_{22} & y_{23} \\ y_{31} & y_{32} & y_{33} \end{bmatrix} = \begin{bmatrix} 1 & 0 & 0 \\ 0 & 1 & 0 \\ 0 & 0 & 1 \end{bmatrix}.$$

The first column of $\mathbf{Y}$ is the solution vector for the system

$$\begin{bmatrix} 1 & 0 & 0 \\ -2 & 1 & 0 \\ -1 & -1 & 1 \end{bmatrix} \begin{bmatrix} y_{11} \\ y_{21} \\ y_{31} \end{bmatrix} = \begin{bmatrix} 1 \\ 0 \\ 0 \end{bmatrix}.$$

The second and third columns of $\mathbf{Y}$ are found in a similar manner, using the second and third columns of $\mathbf{I}$. Each column of $\mathbf{Y}$ is found by forward substitution, using the corresponding column of $\mathbf{I}$. The solution that is obtained is

$$\mathbf{Y} = \begin{bmatrix} 1 & 0 & 0 \\ 2 & 1 & 0 \\ 3 & 1 & 1 \end{bmatrix}.$$

Finally, we solve $\mathbf{U}\,\mathbf{X} = \mathbf{Y}$ for $\mathbf{X}$; then $\mathbf{A}^{-1} = \mathbf{X}$. We have

$$\begin{bmatrix} 1 & -1 & 2 \\ 0 & -1 & 5 \\ 0 & 0 & 8 \end{bmatrix} \begin{bmatrix} x_{11} & x_{12} & x_{13} \\ x_{21} & x_{22} & x_{23} \\ x_{31} & x_{32} & x_{33} \end{bmatrix} = \begin{bmatrix} 1 & 0 & 0 \\ 2 & 1 & 0 \\ 3 & 1 & 1 \end{bmatrix}.$$

The solution is easily found for each column of $\mathbf{X}$, using back substitution and the corresponding column of $\mathbf{Y}$. The solution is

$$\mathbf{X} = \mathbf{A}^{-1} = \begin{bmatrix} 1/8 & -5/8 & 3/8 \\ -1/8 & -3/8 & 5/8 \\ 3/8 & 1/8 & 1/8 \end{bmatrix}.$$

In the next section we consider the problem of factoring a square matrix $\mathbf{A}$ into the product of an orthogonal matrix $\mathbf{Q}$ and an upper (right) triangular matrix $\mathbf{R}$. Thus we seek to write $\mathbf{A} = \mathbf{QR}$, where $\mathbf{R}$ is right triangular, $\mathbf{Q}$ is orthogonal (so that $\mathbf{Q}^{-1} = \mathbf{Q}^T$), and both are real.

In this section we introduce two important transformations, the Householder and Givens transformations. Each is based on the creation of an orthogonal matrix with certain desirable properties, although in practice the equivalent operations are usually carried out more efficiently without explicitly forming the matrix or performing the matrix multiplication.

A Householder matrix is an orthogonal matrix $\mathbf{H}$ (n-by-n) with the property that for a given vector $\mathbf{x}$ and a specified index k ($1 \leq k \leq n - 1$), the vector $\mathbf{z}$, defined as $\mathbf{z} = \mathbf{Hx}$, has the form $[z_1, \ldots z_k, 0 \ldots \ldots 0]^T$. That is, the elements $x_{k+1}, \ldots x_n$ have been "zeroed-out." In applications it is often the case that vector $\mathbf{x}$ is a column of a given matrix and we need to zero-out all of the elements of the column below a certain point. The use of Householder transformations is illustrated for two important applications; transforming a matrix to upper triangular form (section 4.4.1) and transforming a matrix to upper Hessenberg form (section 4.4.2). Transformation to upper Hessenberg form can be achieved with a similarity transformation, but upper triangular form cannot. A matrix is upper Hessenberg if all entries below the subdiagonal are zero.

A Givens rotation is an orthogonal matrix with $g_{ii} = g_{jj} = c$, $g_{ij} = -s$, and $g_{ij} = s$ (with $i \leq j$), and all other elements as for the identity matrix, where $c^2 + s^2 = 1$. By selecting the appropriate values for c and s, a Givens rotation can be used to reduce a specific matrix element to zero. The use of Givens transformations is illustrated in section 4.4.4 for transforming an upper Hessenberg matrix to upper triangular form.

The QR factorization is more computationally intensive (about twice as many operations) to obtain than an LU factorization, but has superior stability properties. In the next chapter we present a method, based on QR factorization, for finding all of the eigenvalues of a matrix.

The process of finding the QR factorization of a matrix requires that we be able to transform a matrix $\mathbf{A}$ so that certain elements of the resulting matrix $\mathbf{B}$ are zero. Transformations of the form $\mathbf{B} = \mathbf{MA}$ and $\mathbf{B} = \mathbf{AM}$ are used in this process.

In applications of QR factorization for finding eigenvalues of a matrix $\mathbf{A}$ (discussed in Chapter 5), it is advantageous to perform a similarity transformation of $\mathbf{A}$ to Hessenberg form before beginning the QR-eigenvalue computations. If the matrix $\mathbf{M}$ is orthogonal, the transformation $\mathbf{B} = \mathbf{MAM}^{-1}$ is a similarity transformation, which preserves eigenvalues. The similarity transformation is usually based on Householder matrices.

4.4.1 Householder Transformation to Upper Triangular Form

Householder transformations are often described in terms of multiplication by a Householder matrix. A Householder matrix has the form $\mathbf{H} = \mathbf{I} - 2\,\mathbf{w}\,\mathbf{w}^T$, where $\mathbf{w}$ is a column vector with $\|\mathbf{w}\|_2 = 1$ and $\mathbf{I}$ is the n-by-n identity matrix.

The formation of the Householder matrix, which reduces to zero positions $k + 1$ through n of a vector $\mathbf{x}$, is summarized in the following algorithm. The algorithm sets the first k-1 components of $\mathbf{x}$ to 0; this simplifies the computation of the parameter g and the vector $\mathbf{w}$. Note that if $s = 0$, all of the required components are already zero, and vector $\mathbf{w}$ should be set to the zero vector, so that $\mathbf{H} = \mathbf{I}$.

Forming a Householder Matrix ────────────────────────────────────

Input
 k   *zero-out components $k + 1, \ldots n$*
 $\mathbf{x} = [x_1, \ldots, x_n]^T$ *vector to be transformed*
Initialize
 $\mathbf{x} = [0, \ldots, 0, x_k, \ldots, x_n]^T$ *computations apply to components $k \ldots n$*
Compute
 $g = \text{norm}(\mathbf{x})$
 $s = \sqrt{2g(g + |\mathbf{x}_k|)}$
 $\mathbf{w} = \mathbf{x}/s$
 $\mathbf{w}_k = \dfrac{1}{s}(\mathbf{x}_k + \text{sign}(\mathbf{x}_k)g)$
 $\mathbf{H} = \mathbf{I} - 2*\mathbf{w}*\mathbf{w}^T$

To find $\mathbf{H}\,\mathbf{A}$ efficiently, we do not actually construct the matrix $\mathbf{H}$. Instead we define $\mathbf{u} = \mathbf{A}^T\mathbf{w}$, so that $\mathbf{u}^T = \mathbf{w}^T\mathbf{A}$ and

$$\mathbf{H}\,\mathbf{A} = (\mathbf{I} - 2\mathbf{w}\mathbf{w}^T)\,\mathbf{A} = \mathbf{A} - 2\mathbf{w}\mathbf{w}^T\mathbf{A} = \mathbf{A} - 2\mathbf{w}\,\mathbf{u}^T$$

This provides the justification for the following algorithm to transform a matrix to upper triangular form.

To compute the product $\mathbf{A}\,\mathbf{H}$, we find

$$\mathbf{A}\,\mathbf{H} = \mathbf{A}(\mathbf{I} - 2\mathbf{w}\mathbf{w}^T) = \mathbf{A} - 2\mathbf{A}\mathbf{w}\mathbf{w}^T$$

To find $\mathbf{H}\,\mathbf{A}\,\mathbf{H}$ (for a similarity transformation) we define $\mathbf{C} = \mathbf{W}\mathbf{W}^T$ and $d = \mathbf{w}^T\mathbf{A}\,\mathbf{w}$ so that

$$
\begin{aligned}
\mathbf{H}\,\mathbf{A}\,\mathbf{H} &= (\mathbf{I} - 2\mathbf{w}\mathbf{w}^T)\mathbf{A}(\mathbf{I} - 2\mathbf{w}\mathbf{w}^T) \\
&= (\mathbf{I} - 2\mathbf{w}\mathbf{w}^T)\mathbf{A} - (\mathbf{I} - 2\mathbf{w}\mathbf{w}^T)\mathbf{A}\mathbf{w}\mathbf{w}^T \\
&= \mathbf{A} - 2\mathbf{w}\mathbf{w}^T\mathbf{A} - 2\mathbf{A}\mathbf{w}\mathbf{w}^T + 4\mathbf{w}\mathbf{w}^T\mathbf{A}\mathbf{w}\mathbf{w}^T \\
&= \mathbf{A} - 2\mathbf{C}\,\mathbf{A} - 2\mathbf{A}\,\mathbf{C} + 4d\,\mathbf{C}
\end{aligned}
$$

This provides the justification for the algorithm given in section 4.4.2.

The procedure for finding $\mathbf{B} = \mathbf{H}\,\mathbf{A}$ is used in the transformation of $\mathbf{A}$ to upper triangular form, described in section 4.5. As noted above, tridiagonal form cannot, in general, be achieved with a similarity transformation. This transformation is not a similarity transformation; it does not preserve eigenvalues.

The following algorithm converts the general matrix $\mathbf{A}$ to the upper triangular matrix $\mathbf{B}$ by computing $\mathbf{B} = \mathbf{H}\,\mathbf{A}$. Householder transformations are applied to columns 1 through $n-1$ of matrix $\mathbf{A}$. In the kth column, we zero-out positions $k+1$ through n.

The matrices are shown schematically below, with blanks indicating entries that are zero.

$$\mathbf{A} = \begin{bmatrix} x & x & x & x & x \\ x & x & x & x & x \\ x & x & x & x & x \\ x & x & x & x & x \\ x & x & x & x & x \end{bmatrix} \qquad \mathbf{B} = \begin{bmatrix} x & x & x & x & x \\ & x & x & x & x \\ & & x & x & x \\ & & & x & x \\ & & & & x \end{bmatrix}$$

Transformation of Matrix A to Upper Triangular Matrix B

Input
    A   *n-by-n matrix*
    n
Compute
For k = 1 to n
    $\mathbf{x} = \mathrm{A}(:, k)$ *vector to be transformed is k^{th} column of A*
    For j = 1 to k-1   *set elements above diagonal to zero*
        x(j) = 0
    End
    $g = \mathrm{norm}(\mathbf{x})$
    $s = \sqrt{2g(g + |\mathbf{x}_k|)}$
    If $(s \neq 0)$ *if s = 0, all required components are 0*
        $\mathbf{w} = \mathbf{x}/s$
        $\mathbf{w_k} = \dfrac{1}{s}(\mathbf{x}_k + \mathrm{sign}(\mathbf{x}_k)g)$
        $\mathbf{u} = \mathbf{A}^T \mathbf{w}$
        $\mathbf{B} = \mathbf{a} - 2\mathbf{w}\,\mathbf{u}^T$
    End
    A = **B**
End
Return
    B   *upper triangular matrix*

The next example illustrates the use of Householder transformations to convert a matrix to upper triangular form.

Example 4.9 Transformation to Upper Triangular Form

To transform the symmetric matrix **A** to upper triangular form, we use Householder transformations to zero-out the sub-diagonal elements, column by column.

$$
\mathbf{A} = \begin{bmatrix}
1.72 & 1.04 & 0.32 & 0.24 \\
1.04 & 3.28 & 0.24 & -0.32 \\
0.32 & 0.24 & 2.92 & -0.56 \\
0.24 & -0.32 & -0.56 & 2.08
\end{bmatrix}
$$

To introduce zeros below the diagonal in the first column of **A**:

$$
\begin{aligned}
\mathbf{x} &= [1.7200 \quad 1.0400 \quad 0.3200 \quad 0.2400]^T \\
g &= 2.0494 \\
s &= 3.9306 \\
\mathbf{w} &= [0.9590 \quad 0.2646 \quad 0.0814 \quad 0.0611]^T \\
\mathbf{u} &= [3.9306 \quad 3.7304 \quad 1.1478 \quad 0.4538]^T
\end{aligned}
$$

$$
\mathbf{B} = \begin{bmatrix}
-2.0494 & -2.5373 & -0.7807 & -0.1952 \\
0.0000 & 2.2930 & -0.0637 & -0.4401 \\
0.0000 & -0.0637 & 2.8266 & -0.5969 \\
0.0000 & -0.5478 & -0.6301 & 2.0523
\end{bmatrix}
$$

To introduce zeros below the diagonal in the second column of **B**:

$$
\begin{aligned}
\mathbf{x} &= [-2.5373 \quad 2.2930 \quad -0.0637 \quad -0.5478]^T \\
\mathbf{w} &= [\quad 0 \quad\quad 0.9930 \quad -0.0136 \quad -0.1169]^T \\
\mathbf{u} &= [\quad 0.0000 \quad 4.6839 \quad -0.0569 \quad -1.3378]^T
\end{aligned}
$$

$$
\mathbf{B} = \begin{bmatrix}
-2.0494 & -2.5373 & -0.7807 & -0.1952 \\
-0.0000 & -2.3584 & -0.0081 & 0.8884 \\
0.0000 & -0.0000 & 2.8258 & -0.6151 \\
0.0000 & -0.0000 & -0.6366 & 1.8958
\end{bmatrix}
$$

To introduce zeros below the diagonal in the third column of **B**:

$$
\begin{aligned}
\mathbf{x} &= [-0.7807 \quad -0.0081 \quad 2.8258 \quad -0.6366]^T \\
\mathbf{w} &= [\quad 0 \quad\quad\quad 0 \quad\quad 0.9939 \quad -0.1106]^T \\
\mathbf{u} &= [\quad 0.0000 \quad -0.0000 \quad 5.7577 \quad -1.6420]^T
\end{aligned}
$$

$$
\mathbf{B} = \begin{bmatrix}
-2.0494 & -2.5373 & -0.7807 & -0.1952 \\
-0.0000 & -2.3584 & -0.0081 & 0.8884 \\
-0.0000 & -0.0000 & -2.8966 & 1.0168 \\
0.0000 & -0.0000 & -0.0000 & 1.7143
\end{bmatrix}
$$

4.4.2 Householder Similarity Transformation to Upper Hessenberg Form

Because a Householder matrix $\mathbf{H}$ is orthogonal and symmetric, the transformation $\mathbf{B} = \mathbf{H}\,\mathbf{A}\,\mathbf{H}$ is a similarity transformation. The following algorithm converts the general matrix $\mathbf{A}$ to the upper Hessenberg matrix $\mathbf{B} = \mathbf{H}\,\mathbf{A}\,\mathbf{H}$. Householder transformations are applied to columns 1 through $n - 2$ of matrix $\mathbf{A}$. In the kth column, we zero-out positions $k + 2$ through n. The eigenvalues of $\mathbf{B}$ are the same as the eigenvalues of $\mathbf{A}$. Hessenberg form allows for nonzero elements on the first subdiagonal, as well as in the upper triangular portion of the matrix. The matrices are shown schematically below, with blanks indicating entries that are zero.

$$
\mathbf{A} = \begin{bmatrix} x & x & x & x & x \\ x & x & x & x & x \\ x & x & x & x & x \\ x & x & x & x & x \\ x & x & x & x & x \end{bmatrix} \qquad
\mathbf{B} = \begin{bmatrix} x & x & x & x & x \\ x & x & x & x & x \\ & x & x & x & x \\ & & x & x & x \\ & & & x & x \end{bmatrix}
$$

Similarity Transformation of Matrix A to Hessenberg Matrix B

```
Input
     A                            n-by-n matrix
     n
Compute
For k = 1 to n − 2
     x = A(:, k)                  vector to be transformed is kᵗʰ column of A
     For j = 1 to k               set elements above diagonal to zero
          x(j) = 0
     End
     g = norm(x)
     s = sqrt(2g (g + |x(k+1)|))
     w = x/s
     w(k+1) = x(k+1) + sign(x(k+1)g)/s
     C = xxᵀ
     d = wᵀ A w
     B = A − 2 C A − 2 A C + 4 d C
     A = B
End
Return
     B                           Hessenberg matrix
```

Householder and Givens transformations are used in finding the QR factorization of a matrix (section 4.5). In the next chapter we consider the application of QR factorization to the problem of finding the eigenvalues of a matrix. The solution to this problem requires forming a sequence of matrices, each of which must be factored. QR factorization is more efficient if the matrix is Hessenberg. If the original matrix is Hessenberg, each of the matrices formed is also Hessenberg.

The next example illustrates the use of Householder transformations to achieve a similarity transformation of a general matrix to a Hessenberg matrix. A similarity transformation is required to preserve the eigenvalues of the original matrix.

Example 4.10 Similarity Transformation to Upper Hessenberg Form

$$
\mathbf{A} = \begin{bmatrix} 11 & -26 & 3 & -12 \\ 3 & -12 & 3 & -16 \\ 31 & -99 & 15 & -44 \\ 9 & -10 & -3 & -4 \end{bmatrix}
$$

$k = 1$

$\mathbf{x} = \begin{bmatrix} 0 & 3 & 31 & 9 \end{bmatrix}^T$

$g = 32.4191$

$s = 47.9220$

$\mathbf{w} = \begin{bmatrix} 0 & 0.7391 & 0.6469 & 0.1878 \end{bmatrix}^T$

$$
\mathbf{C} = \begin{bmatrix} 0 & 0 & 0 & 0 \\ 0 & 0.5463 & 0.4781 & 0.1388 \\ 0 & 0.4781 & 0.4185 & 0.1215 \\ 0 & 0.1388 & 0.1215 & 0.0353 \end{bmatrix}
$$

$d = -54.2491$

$$
\mathbf{B} = \begin{bmatrix} 11.0000 & 2.8687 & 28.2668 & -4.6645 \\ -32.4191 & -8.0780 & -107.1151 & 16.6447 \\ 0.0000 & 0.0437 & 2.3056 & 0.1142 \\ 0.0000 & 2.8754 & -20.5835 & 4.7724 \end{bmatrix}
$$

$k = 2$

$\mathbf{x} = \begin{bmatrix} 0 & 0 & 0.0437 & 2.8754 \end{bmatrix}^T$

$g = 2.8757$

$s = 4.0977$

$\mathbf{w} = \begin{bmatrix} 0 & 0 & 0.7125 & 0.7017 \end{bmatrix}^T$

$$
\mathbf{C} = \begin{bmatrix} 0 & 0 & 0 & 0 \\ 0 & 0 & 0 & 0 \\ 0 & 0 & 0.5076 & 0.4999 \\ 0 & 0 & 0.4999 & 0.4924 \end{bmatrix}
$$

$d = -6.7132$

$$
\mathbf{B} = \begin{bmatrix} 11.0000 & 2.8687 & 4.2341 & -28.3345 \\ -32.4191 & -8.0780 & -15.0141 & 107.3558 \\ -0.0000 & -2.8757 & 4.4607 & -20.6163 \\ -0.0000 & 0.0000 & 0.0814 & 2.6174 \end{bmatrix}
$$

4.4.3   Analysis of the Householder Transformation

The basic ideas of how the Householder transformation works are as follows. Any matrix formed according to the equation $\mathbf{H} = \mathbf{I} - 2\,\mathbf{w}\,\mathbf{w}^T$ is symmetric. If $\mathbf{w}$ is a unit vector ($\|\mathbf{w}\|_2 = 1$), then $\mathbf{H}$ is orthogonal, since $\mathbf{H}^T\mathbf{H} = (\mathbf{I} - 2\mathbf{w}\mathbf{w}^T)(\mathbf{I} - 2\mathbf{w}\mathbf{w}^T) = \mathbf{I} - 4\mathbf{w}\mathbf{w}^T + 4\mathbf{w}\mathbf{w}^T\mathbf{w}\mathbf{w}^T = \mathbf{I}$. Because it is both symmetric and orthogonal, $\mathbf{H}$ is its own inverse! Any vector $\mathbf{v} \neq 0$ that is not a unit vector can be scaled to produce a unit vector $\mathbf{w}$ in the same direction by defining $\mathbf{w} = \dfrac{\mathbf{v}}{\|\mathbf{v}\|_2}$.

Now we outline how we can determine the vector $\mathbf{v}$ that will provide a Householder matrix of the form $\mathbf{H} = \mathbf{I} - \dfrac{2}{\mathbf{v}^T\mathbf{v}}\,\mathbf{v}\mathbf{v}^T$ such that multiplication of an n-dimensional vector $\mathbf{x}$ by $\mathbf{H}$ will reduce all the components of $\mathbf{x}$ to zero except for the kth component. Let $\mathbf{e}_k$ denote the n-dimensional vector with a 1 as its kth component and 0's for all other components. Then we want to determine $\mathbf{v}$ such that $\mathbf{H}\,\mathbf{x} = \alpha\,\mathbf{e}_k$, for some scalar α. Some matrix algebra tells us that $\mathbf{v}$ must be a linear combination of $\mathbf{x}$ and $\mathbf{e}_k$. We set $\mathbf{v} = \mathbf{x} + \alpha\,\mathbf{e}_k$ and find (after more algebra) that $\mathbf{v} = \mathbf{x} \pm \|\mathbf{x}\|_2\,\mathbf{e}_k$ and $\mathbf{H}\,\mathbf{x} \pm \|\mathbf{x}\|_2\,\mathbf{e}_k = 0$, as desired. We choose the sign of $\alpha = \pm\|\mathbf{x}\|_2$ to agree with the sign of x_k, in order to avoid cancellation in the kth component of $\mathbf{v}$. It is for this reason that we compute $w_k = (x_k + \text{sign}(x_k)\,g)/s$ in the algorithm for the Householder transformation (the norm of $\mathbf{v}$ is denoted as s).

To apply the Householder transformation to the first column of a matrix $\mathbf{A}$, we compute the vector $\mathbf{v}$ with $k = 1$, using the first column of $\mathbf{A}$ as the vector $\mathbf{x}$. For columns other than the first, we have $k > 1$, and we want to reduce to zero only elements after the kth component of column k. Therefore, we set the components of $\mathbf{v}$ before the kth component equal to zero; that is, $v_i = 0$ for $i = 1, \ldots k - 1$. We use only components k through n to compute the norm of the $\mathbf{x}$ term, denoted as g in the algorithm. We ignore the first k-1 components and treat the remaining components as an $(n - k + 1)$-dimensional vector.

Computational Effort

To see that the computation of $\mathbf{H}\,\mathbf{A}$ given in sect. 4.4.1 is preferable to actually forming $\mathbf{H}$ and performing the matrix multiplication, consider the computational effort of the two approaches. Computation of $\mathbf{u}$ requires the multiplication of a matrix and a vector, that of $\mathbf{w}\,\mathbf{u}^T$ requires the outer product of two vectors, and that of $\mathbf{A} - \mathbf{w}\,\mathbf{u}^T$ requires the subtraction of one matrix from another. Altogether these steps require $4n^2$ flops if $\mathbf{A}$ is an n-by-n matrix and $\mathbf{w}$ is n-by-1. On the other hand, explicit formation of the matrix $\mathbf{H} = \mathbf{I} - 2\,\mathbf{w}\,\mathbf{w}^T$ requires the outer product of a vector with itself and multiplication of the matrices $\mathbf{H}$ and $\mathbf{A}$, for a total of $2n^3$ flops. This is an order of magnitude more computational effort than it takes to compute $\mathbf{A} - \mathbf{w}\,\mathbf{u}^T$. For that reason, Householder matrices are rarely explicitly formed in practice. For further discussion, see Hager, 1988, or Press et al., 1992.

4.4.4   Givens Rotations

A Givens rotation is a matrix of the form

$$
\mathbf{G} = \begin{bmatrix}
1 & 0 & 0 & 0 & 0 \\
0 & c & 0 & -s & 0 \\
0 & 0 & 1 & 0 & 0 \\
0 & s & 0 & c & 0 \\
0 & 0 & 0 & 0 & 1
\end{bmatrix}
\begin{matrix}
\\
\leftarrow \text{ row } i \\
\\
\leftarrow \text{ row } j \\
\\
\end{matrix}
$$

where $c^2 + s^2 = 1$; the c's occur on the diagonal in row i and row j, where $i < j$.

By selecting the appropriate values for c and s, a Givens rotation can be used to reduce a specific matrix element to zero. In particular, if

$$
c = \frac{x_1}{\sqrt{x_1^2 + x_2^2}} \text{ and } s = \frac{-x_2}{\sqrt{x_1^2 + x_2^2}}
$$

then $c^2 + s^2 = 1$ and

$$
\begin{bmatrix} c & -s \\ s & c \end{bmatrix} \begin{bmatrix} x_1 \\ x_2 \end{bmatrix} = \begin{bmatrix} \sqrt{x_1^2 + x_2^2} \\ 0 \end{bmatrix}
$$

If $\mathbf{G}$ is a Givens matrix, then multiplication of a matrix $\mathbf{A}$ by $\mathbf{G}$ affects only rows i and j of matrix $\mathbf{A}$; that is, if $\mathbf{C} = \mathbf{G}\,\mathbf{A}$ then

$$
\mathbf{C}(i, 1{:}n) = c\,\mathbf{A}(i, 1{:}n) - s\,\mathbf{A}(j, 1{:}n),
$$
$$
\mathbf{C}(j, 1{:}n) = s\,\mathbf{A}(i, 1{:}n) + c\,\mathbf{A}(j, 1{:}n),
$$

and

$$
\mathbf{C}(k, 1{:}n) = \mathbf{A}(k, 1{:}n) \quad \text{ for } k \neq i, j.
$$

Similarly, multiplication on the right by $\mathbf{G}^{\mathbf{T}}$ affects only columns i and j, that is, if $\mathbf{D} = \mathbf{C}\,\mathbf{G}^{T}$, then

$$
\mathbf{D}(1{:}n, j) = c\,\mathbf{C}(1{:}n, i) - s\,\mathbf{C}(1{:}n, j),
$$
$$
\mathbf{D}(1{:}n, j) = s\,\mathbf{C}(1{:}n, i) + c\,\mathbf{C}(1{:}n, j),
$$

and

$$
\mathbf{D}(1{:}n, k) = \mathbf{C}(1{:}n, k) \quad \text{ for } k \neq i, j.
$$

Hence, the actions of multiplication on the left by $\mathbf{G}$ (or multiplication on the right by $\mathbf{G}^{T}$) can be accomplished without explicitly forming $\mathbf{G}$ or $\mathbf{G}^{T}$ and without performing the matrix multiplication.

A Givens rotation matrix is orthogonal, since $\mathbf{G}^{T}\,\mathbf{G} = \mathbf{I}$. This means that the product $\mathbf{B} = \mathbf{G}\,\mathbf{A}\,\mathbf{G}^{T}$ is a similarity transformation of matrix $\mathbf{A}$.

Our primary interest in Givens rotations is for the transformation of an upper Hessenberg matrix into an upper triangular matrix. In this case, when we are working on the kth column of the Hessenberg matrix $\mathbf{B}$, the only element that must be zeroed out is the element on the subdiagonal, namely $b_{k+1,k}$. It is the orthogonality of $\mathbf{G}$ that is most important in this application.

The following algorithm describes the computations to transform the Hessenberg matrix **B** to the (upper) triangular matrix **T**, by means of a sequence of Givens rotations to zero-out the subdiagonal elements of **B** (in columns 1 through *n*-1).

Givens Transformation of Hessenberg Matrix B to Triangular Matrix T

> *Input*
>   **B**   *Hessenberg matrix (n-by-n)*
>   n
> *Compute*
> For k = 1, ... n-1   *for each column of B except the last*
> $x_1 = $ **B**(k,k)   *diagonal element*
> $x_2 = $ **B**(k + 1,k)   *subdiagonal element, to be zeroed-out*
>
> $c = \dfrac{x_1}{\sqrt{x_1^2 + x_2^2}}$
>
> $s = \dfrac{-x_2}{\sqrt{x_1^2 + x_2^2}}$
>
>   **T = B**
>   For j = 1 to n
>   **T**(k, j) = c **B** (k, j) − s **B** (k + 1, j)   ***T = GB**, changes all columns of*
>   **T**(k + 1, j) = s **B** (k,j) + c **B** (k + 1, j)   *row k and row k + 1*
>   End
>   **B = T**
> End
> *Return*
> **T**   *triangular matrix*

If the parameters *c* and *s* that occur in a Givens matrix are interpreted as $\cos(\theta)$ and $\sin(\theta)$, then multiplication by the two-by-two Givens matrix

$$G = \begin{bmatrix} c & -s \\ s & c \end{bmatrix}$$

corresponds to rotation by the angle θ in R^2.

Givens rotations require approximately twice as many multiplications as Householder reflections. However, in the case of matrices with only a few elements that must be reduced to zero, Givens rotations are the method of choice. More efficient implementations of the Givens scheme are also available (see Hager, 1988, for further discussion).

Example 4.11 Givens Transformation of Hessenberg Matrix

We now consider the transformation of the Hessenberg matrix found in Example 4.10 to triangular form.

$$\mathbf{A} = \begin{bmatrix} 11.0000 & 2.8687 & 4.2341 & -28.3345 \\ -32.4191 & -8.0780 & -15.0141 & 107.3558 \\ 0 & -2.8757 & 4.4607 & -20.6163 \\ 0 & 0 & 0.0814 & 2.6174 \end{bmatrix}$$

$k = 1$

$x_1 = 11$
$x_2 = -32.4191$
$c = 0.3213$
$s = 0.9470$

$$\mathbf{A} = \begin{bmatrix} 34.2345 & 8.5714 & 15.5784 & -110.7673 \\ 0 & 0.1210 & -0.8147 & 7.6629 \\ 0 & -2.8757 & 4.4607 & -20.6163 \\ 0 & 0 & 0.0814 & 2.6174 \end{bmatrix}$$

$k = 2$

$x_1 = 0.1210$
$x_2 = -2.8757$
$c = 0.0420$
$s = 0.9991$

$$\mathbf{A} = \begin{bmatrix} 34.2345 & 8.5714 & 15.5784 & -110.7673 \\ 0 & 2.8782 & -4.4910 & 20.9202 \\ 0 & 0 & -0.6264 & 6.7894 \\ 0 & 0 & 0.0814 & 2.6174 \end{bmatrix}$$

$k = 3$

$x_1 = -0.6264$
$x_2 = 0.0814$
$c = -0.9917$
$s = -0.1289$

$$\mathbf{A} = \begin{bmatrix} 34.2345 & 8.5714 & 15.5784 & -110.7673 \\ 0 & 2.8782 & -4.4910 & 20.9202 \\ 0 & 0 & 0.6317 & -6.3954 \\ 0 & 0 & 0.0000 & -3.4705 \end{bmatrix}$$

A real matrix $\mathbf{A}$ (n-by-n) can be factored into the form $\mathbf{A} = \mathbf{Q}\,\mathbf{R}$, where $\mathbf{Q}$ is orthogonal, $\mathbf{R}$ is upper triangular, and both are real. The basic approach is that we form a sequence of matrices, which we call $\mathbf{Q}$ and $\mathbf{R}$, so that at each stage of the process, $\mathbf{A} = \mathbf{QR}$, and at the final stage, $\mathbf{Q}$ is orthogonal and $\mathbf{R}$ is upper triangular.

4.5.1   QR Factorization using Householder Transformations

We begin by letting $\mathbf{A} = \mathbf{I}\,\mathbf{A} = \mathbf{I}\,\mathbf{H}^{(1)}\,\mathbf{H}^{(1)}\,\mathbf{A}$, where $\mathbf{H}^{(1)}$ transforms the first column of $\mathbf{A}$ to zeros below the diagonal. We define $\mathbf{Q}^{(1)} = \mathbf{I}\,\mathbf{H}^{(1)}$ and $\mathbf{R}^{(1)} = \mathbf{H}^{(1)}\,\mathbf{A}$. Then $\mathbf{A} = \mathbf{Q}^{(1)}\,\mathbf{R}^{(1)} = \mathbf{Q}^{(1)}\,\mathbf{H}^{(2)}\,\mathbf{H}^{(2)}\,\mathbf{R}^{(1)}$, where $\mathbf{H}^{(2)}$ transforms the second column of A to zeros below the diagonal. We define $\mathbf{Q}^{(2)} = \mathbf{Q}^{(1)}\,\mathbf{H}^{(2)}$ and $\mathbf{R}^{(2)} = \mathbf{H}^{(2)}\,\mathbf{R}^{(1)}$. We continue in this manner until the final product, $\mathbf{A} = \mathbf{Q}\,\mathbf{R}$, is obtained. By construction, $\mathbf{R}$ is upper triangular. The following algorithm states the QR factorization process in terms of Householder transformations, without the formation of the Householder matrices.

QR Factorization Using Householder Transformations ━━━━━━━━━━━━━━━━━

Input
    A   *n-by-n matrix to be factored*
Initialize
R = A
Q = I
Compute
For k = 1 to n − 1
    For j = 1 to k − 1   *apply Householder transformation to*
        $\mathbf{x_j} = 0$ *k^{th} column of $\mathbf{R}$, to zero out elements*
    End   *in rows k + 1 ... n*
    For j = k to n
        $\mathbf{x_j} = \mathbf{R}_{j,k}$
    End
    $g = \text{norm}(\mathbf{x})$
    $s = \sqrt{2g(g + |\mathbf{x}_k|)}$
    If $s \neq 0$

        $\mathbf{w} = \dfrac{\mathbf{x}}{s}$

        $\mathbf{w}_k = \dfrac{1}{s}(\mathbf{x}_k + \text{sign}(\mathbf{x}_k)g)$

        $\mathbf{u} = 2\,\mathbf{R}^T\,\mathbf{w}$
        $\mathbf{R} = \mathbf{R} - \mathbf{w}\,\mathbf{u}^T$ *form $R_{\text{new}} = H\,R_{\text{old}}$*
        $\mathbf{Q} = \mathbf{Q} - 2\,\mathbf{Q}\,\mathbf{w}\,\mathbf{w}^T$ *form $Q_{\text{new}} = Q_{\text{old}}\,H$*
    End
End

Example 4.12 QR Factorization Using Householder Transformations

We now consider the QR factorization of the matrix introduced in Example 4.9.

$$
A = \begin{bmatrix}
1.7200 & 1.0400 & 0.3200 & 0.2400 \\
1.0400 & 3.2800 & 0.2400 & -0.3200 \\
0.3200 & 0.2400 & 2.9200 & -0.5600 \\
0.2400 & -0.3200 & -0.5600 & 2.0800
\end{bmatrix}
$$

First stage

$$
R = \begin{bmatrix}
-2.0494 & -2.5373 & -0.7807 & -0.1952 \\
0.0000 & 2.2930 & -0.0637 & -0.4401 \\
0.0000 & -0.0637 & 2.8266 & -0.5969 \\
0.0000 & -0.5478 & -0.6301 & 2.0523
\end{bmatrix}
$$

$$
Q = \begin{bmatrix}
-0.8393 & -0.5075 & -0.1561 & -0.1171 \\
-0.5075 & 0.8600 & -0.0431 & -0.0323 \\
-0.1561 & -0.0431 & 0.9867 & -0.0099 \\
-0.1171 & -0.0323 & -0.0099 & 0.9925
\end{bmatrix}
$$

Second stage

$$
R = \begin{bmatrix}
-2.0494 & -2.5373 & -0.7807 & -0.1952 \\
-0.0000 & -2.3584 & -0.0081 & 0.8884 \\
0.0000 & -0.0000 & 2.8258 & -0.6151 \\
0.0000 & -0.0000 & -0.6366 & 1.8958
\end{bmatrix}
$$

$$
Q = \begin{bmatrix}
-0.8393 & 0.4620 & -0.1694 & -0.2313 \\
-0.5075 & -0.8448 & -0.0197 & 0.1685 \\
-0.1561 & 0.0662 & 0.9852 & -0.0228 \\
-0.1171 & 0.2617 & -0.0140 & 0.9579
\end{bmatrix}
$$

Third stage

$$
R = \begin{bmatrix}
-2.0494 & -2.5373 & -0.7807 & -0.1952 \\
-0.0000 & -2.3584 & -0.0081 & 0.8884 \\
-0.0000 & -0.0000 & -2.8966 & 1.0168 \\
0.0000 & -0.0000 & -0.0000 & 1.7143
\end{bmatrix}
$$

$$
Q = \begin{bmatrix}
-0.8393 & 0.4620 & 0.1144 & -0.2629 \\
-0.5075 & -0.8448 & 0.0563 & 0.1600 \\
-0.1561 & 0.0662 & -0.9662 & 0.1943 \\
-0.1171 & 0.2617 & 0.2242 & 0.9314
\end{bmatrix}
$$

Note that the matrix **R** is the same as that found in Example 4.9.

4.5.2 QR Factorization of Hessenberg Matrix Using Givens Rotations

We now consider a computationally more efficient method for factoring an upper Hessenberg matrix, in which there is only one nonzero element below the diagonal in each column that must be zeroed out. Instead of using a product of Householder matrices at each stage (or the equivalent transformations), we use a product of a Givens rotation and its transpose. We let $\mathbf{A} = \mathbf{I}\,\mathbf{A} = \mathbf{I}\,\mathbf{G}^\mathbf{T}\,\mathbf{G}\,\mathbf{A}$, where $\mathbf{G}$ transforms the first column of $\mathbf{A}$ to zeros below the diagonal. We define $\mathbf{Q} = \mathbf{I}\,\mathbf{G}^\mathbf{T}$ and $\mathbf{R} = \mathbf{G}\,\mathbf{A}$. We continue in this manner until the final product, $\mathbf{A} = \mathbf{Q}\,\mathbf{R}$, is obtained. By construction, $\mathbf{R}$ is upper triangular.

The following algorithm carries out the computations for conversion to triangular form using Givens rotations (as given in the algorithm in section 4.4.2) together with the corresponding computations for multiplication of $\mathbf{Q}$, on the right, by the transpose of $\mathbf{G}$ at each stage.

QR Factorization of Upper Hessenberg Matrix ══════════════════════

Initialize
> $\mathbf{Q} = \mathbf{I}$
> $\mathbf{R} = \mathbf{A}$

Compute
For $k = 1$ to $n - 1$
> $x_1 = \mathbf{R}(k, k)$
> $x_2 = \mathbf{R}(k + 1, k)$
>
> $c = \dfrac{x_1}{\sqrt{x_1^2 + x_2^2}}$
>
> $s = \dfrac{-x_2}{\sqrt{x_1^2 + x_2^2}}$
>
> $\mathbf{R}_n = \mathbf{R}$
> $\mathbf{Q}_n = \mathbf{Q}$
>   For $j = 1$ to n
>> $\mathbf{R}_n(k, j) = c\,\mathbf{R}(k, j) - s\,\mathbf{R}(k+1, j)$
>> $\mathbf{R}_n(k+1, j) = s\,\mathbf{R}(k, j) + c\,\mathbf{R}(k+1, j)$
>> $\mathbf{Q}_n(j,k) = c\,\mathbf{Q}(j,k) - s\,\mathbf{Q}(j,k+1)$
>> $\mathbf{Q}_n(j,k+1) = s\,\mathbf{Q}(j,k) + c\,\mathbf{Q}(j,k+1)$
>   End
> $\mathbf{R} = \mathbf{R}_n$
> $\mathbf{Q} = \mathbf{Q}_n$
End
Return
> $\mathbf{Q}$ *orthogonal matrix*
> $\mathbf{R}$ *right triangular matrix*

Example 4.13 QR Factorization of a Hessenberg Matrix

We consider now the QR factorization of the Hessenberg matrix from Example 4.11.

$$A = \begin{bmatrix} 11.0000 & 2.8687 & 4.2341 & -28.3345 \\ -32.4191 & -8.0780 & -15.0141 & 107.3558 \\ 0 & -2.8757 & 4.4607 & -20.6163 \\ 0 & 0 & 0.0814 & 2.6174 \end{bmatrix}$$

Stage 1

$$x_1 = 11 \qquad x_2 = -32.4191 \qquad c = 0.3213 \qquad s = 0.9470$$

$$R = \begin{bmatrix} 34.2345 & 8.5714 & 15.5784 & -110.7673 \\ 0 & 0.1210 & -0.8147 & 7.6629 \\ 0 & -2.8757 & 4.4607 & -20.6163 \\ 0 & 0 & 0.0814 & 2.6174 \end{bmatrix}$$

$$Q = \begin{bmatrix} 0.3213 & 0.9470 & 0 & 0 \\ -0.9470 & 0.3213 & 0 & 0 \\ 0 & 0 & 1.0000 & 0 \\ 0 & 0 & 0 & 1.0000 \end{bmatrix}$$

Stage 2

$$x_1 = 0.1210 \qquad x_2 = -2.8757 \qquad c = 0.0420 \qquad s = 0.9991$$

$$R = \begin{bmatrix} 34.2345 & 8.5714 & 15.5784 & -110.7673 \\ 0 & 2.8782 & -4.4910 & 20.9202 \\ 0 & 0 & -0.6264 & 6.7894 \\ 0 & 0 & 0.0814 & 2.6174 \end{bmatrix}$$

$$Q = \begin{bmatrix} 0.3213 & 0.0398 & 0.9461 & 0 \\ -0.9470 & 0.0135 & 0.3210 & 0 \\ 0 & -0.9991 & 0.0420 & 0 \\ 0 & 0 & 0 & 1.0000 \end{bmatrix}$$

Stage 3

$$x_1 = -0.6264 \qquad x_2 = 0.0814 \qquad c = -0.9917 \qquad s = -0.1289$$

$$R = \begin{bmatrix} 34.2345 & 8.5714 & 15.5784 & -110.7673 \\ 0 & 2.8782 & -4.4910 & 20.9202 \\ 0 & 0 & 0.6317 & -6.3954 \\ 0 & 0 & 0.0000 & -3.4705 \end{bmatrix}$$

$$Q = \begin{bmatrix} 0.3213 & 0.0398 & -0.9382 & -0.1219 \\ -0.9470 & 0.0135 & -0.3184 & -0.0414 \\ 0 & -0.9991 & -0.0417 & -0.0054 \\ 0 & 0 & 0.1289 & -0.9917 \end{bmatrix}$$

The upper triangular matrix is the same as that found in Example 4.11.

4.5.3 Discussion

The key characteristic of these transformations is that they are orthogonal. That is, if $\mathbf{H}$ is a Householder matrix, then $\mathbf{H}\,\mathbf{H} = \mathbf{I}$. Similarly, if $\mathbf{G}$ is a Givens rotation, then $\mathbf{G}^T\,\mathbf{G} = \mathbf{I}$ (and $\mathbf{G}\,\mathbf{G}^T = \mathbf{I}$). The factorization process makes use of the fact that the product of orthogonal matrices is also orthogonal.

The basic approach is that we form a sequence of matrices, which we call $\mathbf{Q}$ and $\mathbf{R}$, so that at each stage of the process, $\mathbf{A} = \mathbf{Q}\,\mathbf{R}$, and at the final stage, $\mathbf{Q}$ is orthogonal and $\mathbf{R}$ is upper triangular. We begin by letting:

$$\mathbf{A} = \mathbf{A}\,\mathbf{H}^{(1)}\,\mathbf{H}^{(1)}\,\mathbf{A}$$

where $\mathbf{H}^{(1)}$ transforms the first column of $\mathbf{A}$ to zeros below the diagonal.

We define $\mathbf{Q}^{(1)} = \mathbf{H}^{(1)}$ and $\mathbf{R}^{(1)} = \mathbf{H}^{(1)}\,\mathbf{A}$. Then

$$\mathbf{A} = \mathbf{Q}^{(1)}\,\mathbf{R}^{(1)} = \mathbf{Q}^{(1)}\,\mathbf{H}^{(2)}\,\mathbf{H}^{(2)}\,\mathbf{R}^{(1)}$$

where $\mathbf{H}^{(2)}$ transforms the second column of $\mathbf{A}$ to zeros below the diagonal.

We define $\mathbf{Q}^{(2)} = \mathbf{Q}^{(1)}\,\mathbf{H}^{(2)}$ and $\mathbf{R}^{(2)} = \mathbf{H}^{(2)}\,\mathbf{R}^{(1)}$. We continue in this manner until the final product, $\mathbf{A} = \mathbf{Q}\,\mathbf{R}$, is obtained. By construction, $\mathbf{R}$ is upper triangular.

The process outlined above was phrased in terms of Householder matrices. Of course, it is computationally preferable to carry out the indicated computations without actually forming the matrices, as described in the algorithms in the previous sections. The same process is used for QR factorization of a Hessenberg matrix using Givens rotations, with the appropriate product $\mathbf{G}^T\,\mathbf{G}$ inserted at each stage.

For a single factorization of a matrix, Householder transformations are the more efficient method. An algorithm for QR factorization of a general matrix, based on Householder transformations, is given in section 4.5.1.

In the application of QR factorization to the problem of finding the eigenvalues of a matrix $\mathbf{A}$ (discussed in Chapter 5), a sequence of matrices must be factored. In this setting it is more efficient to perform a similarity transformation to matrix $\mathbf{A}$ to produce a matrix $\mathbf{B}$, which is in Hessenberg form and has the same eigenvalues as $\mathbf{A}$; the iterative procedure to find the eigenvalues is then carried out for matrix $\mathbf{B}$. Since the sequence of matrices that are produced (and must be factored) are all of Hessenberg form, it is preferable to use Givens rotations in the factorizations.

The built-in functions for LU and QR factorization that are included in software packages such as MATLAB and Mathcad generally use methods that are more refined versions of those discussed in this chapter.

4.6.1 Using Professionally Developed Software

MATLAB's Functions

MATLAB has four built-in functions that perform the numerical linear algebra operations discussed in this chapter. To find the LU decomposition of a square matrix **A**, the function lu can be used. The function call [L, U] = lu(A) returns an upper triangular matrix in **U**, and a product of lower triangular and permutation matrices in **L** such that **A** = **L U**. Calling the function with three output arguments, that is, [L, U, P] = lu(A), returns the upper triangular, lower triangular, and permutation matrices such that **P A** = **L U**. Additional options for the function lu allow the user to control the pivoting in sparse matrices. Calling lu(A) with one output argument (or with no output argument specifically defined) returns the output from LINPACK's ZGEFA routine.

For Cholesky factorization, the built-in MATLAB function is chol. This function uses only the diagonal and upper triangular part of **A**. The lower triangular part is assumed to be the (complex conjugate) transpose of the upper part. If **A** is positive definite, then R = chol(A) produces an upper triangular **R** so that $\mathbf{R}^T \mathbf{R} = \mathbf{A}$. If **A** is not positive definite, an error message is printed.

The functions det and inv find the determinant and the inverse of a matrix, respectively.

Mathcad's Functions

Mathcad also has two built-in functions for LU factorization, lu(M) and cholesky(M). The function lu(M) is described as using Crout's method with partial pivoting. This method places 1's on the diagonal of the lower triangular matrix, and thus will normally give the same results as the LU factorization with pivoting described in this chapter. Golub and Van Loan (1996, p. 104) observe that the Doolittle/Crout factorizations, which are based on inner products rather than the outer products that occur in Gaussian elimination, are popular because there are fewer intermediate results required than in Gaussian elimination. For discussion of many methods of implementing the computational loops for Gaussian elimination (and the corresponding LU factorization), see Golub and Van Loan, 1996, Ch. 3.

The function cholesky(M) assumes that **M** is symmetric, and only uses the upper triangular part of **M** in the computations.

Software in the NIST Index

The NIST Guide to Available Software has major headings for software to compute determinants, QR factorization, SVD, and matrix decompositions including LU and Cholesky.

4.6.2 LU Factorization with Implicit Row Pivoting

The routines for LU factorization that are included in software libraries (such as IMSL and NAG), and are implemented in software packages (such as MATLAB and Mathcad), do not actually perform the row interchanges indicated for partial pivoting. Instead, they utilize an index vector **v** in which the indicated interchanges are recorded. To avoid doing the row interchange, we define an index vector, whose entries are the row numbers. Initially **v** = [1 2 3]. If pivoting would require interchange of rows 1 and 3, we interchange the corresponding elements of **v**, so that **v** = [3 2 1]. Any actions that would have been performed on the first row would now be performed on row **v**(1). If the row interchanges indicated by the index vector are performed on the identity matrix, we obtain the permutation matrix **P**.

The following algorithm utilizes the index vector **v**, and also overwrites **A** with the elements of **L** and **U**.

LU Factorization with Implicit Pivoting ═══

$$
\begin{array}{ll}
\textit{Input} & \\
\quad \mathbf{A} & \textit{matrix to be factored (n-by-n)} \\
\textit{Initialize} & \\
\quad v = [1\ 2\ 3 \ldots . n] & \\
\text{For } k = 1 \text{ to } n-1 & \\
\quad \text{pivot} = |\, A(v(k),k)\, | & \textit{pivot element} \\
\quad p = k & \textit{pivot row} \\
\quad \text{For } j = k + 1 \text{ to } n & \\
\qquad \text{If } (|A(v(j),k)| > \text{pivot}) & \\
\qquad\qquad \text{pivot} = |\, U(v(j),k)\, | & \textit{update pivot element} \\
\qquad\qquad p = j & \textit{update pivot row} \\
\qquad \text{End} & \\
\quad \text{End} & \\
\quad \text{If } (p > k) & \\
\qquad\quad t = v(k) & \textit{update index vector} \\
\qquad\quad v(k) = v(j) & \\
\qquad\quad v(j) = t & \\
\quad \text{End} & \\
\quad \text{For } j = k + 1 \text{ to } n & \\
\qquad s = -A(v(j),\, k)/A(v(k),k) & \\
\qquad A(v(j),\, k + 1{:}n) = A(v(j),\, k + 1{:}n) + s*A(v(k),\, k + 1{:}n) & \\
& \textit{update appropriate columns of row v(j) in A} \\
\qquad A(v(j),\, k) = -s & \textit{store opposite of multiplier} \\
\quad \text{End} & \\
\text{End} & \\
\textit{Return} & \\
\quad \mathbf{A} & \textit{contains elements of U in upper triangular portion} \\
& \textit{element of L are in below diagonal portion}
\end{array}
$$

Example 4.14 LU Factorization with Implicit Pivoting

Consider again the LU factorization of the matrix that was found in Example 4.3. To avoid actually performing the row interchanges, we define an index vector, which is initially $\mathbf{v} = [1 \ 2 \ 3]$. It is not necessary to keep track of the permutation matrix at each stage, as it can be constructed at the end of the computations. Matrix $\mathbf{A}$ is overwritten by the elements of $\mathbf{L}$ and $\mathbf{U}$.

$$\mathbf{A} = \begin{bmatrix} 2 & 6 & 10 \\ 1 & 3 & 3 \\ 3 & 14 & 28 \end{bmatrix}$$
$$\mathbf{v} = [1 \ \ 2 \ \ 3]$$

First stage: pivoting yields

$$\mathbf{v} = [3 \ \ 2 \ \ 1]$$

first step of elimination

$$s = -1/3$$
$$\mathbf{A} = \begin{bmatrix} 2 & 6 & 10 \\ 1 & -5/3 & -19/3 \\ 3 & 14 & 28 \end{bmatrix}$$

second step of elimination

$$s = -2/3$$
$$\mathbf{A} = \begin{bmatrix} 2/3 & -10/3 & -26/3 \\ 1/3 & -5/3 & -19/3 \\ 3 & 14 & 28 \end{bmatrix}$$

Second stage: pivoting yields

$$\mathbf{v} = [3 \ \ 1 \ \ 2]$$

first step of elimination

$$s = -1/2$$
$$\mathbf{A} = \begin{bmatrix} 2/3 & -10/3 & -26/3 \\ 1/3 & 1/2 & -2 \\ 3 & 14 & 28 \end{bmatrix}$$

To find $\mathbf{L}$ and $\mathbf{U}$, we first form $\mathbf{P}$ from the information in vector $\mathbf{v}$

$$\mathbf{P} = \begin{bmatrix} 0 & 0 & 1 \\ 1 & 0 & 0 \\ 0 & 1 & 0 \end{bmatrix}$$

The elements of $\mathbf{U}$ are the diagonal upper triangular portion of $\mathbf{P}*\mathbf{A}$; the elements of $\mathbf{L}$ are the lower triangular portion of $\mathbf{P}*\mathbf{A}$ (1's on diagonal of $\mathbf{L}$)

$$\mathbf{P}*\mathbf{A} = \begin{bmatrix} 3 & 14 & 28 \\ 2/3 & -10/3 & -26/3 \\ 1/3 & 1/2 & -2 \end{bmatrix}$$

4.6.3 Efficient Conversion to Hessenberg Form

An alternative to the algorithm for conversion to Hessenberg form by Householder transformations is given in the following method based on Gaussian elimination; this description follows the presentation in Press et al., 1992, pp. 484–486. In general, elimination is more efficient (half the number of flops [Golub and Van Loan, 1989, p. 370]) than the Householder method. For some matrices the Householder method is stable and elimination is not, but such matrices are not common in actual practice. Pivoting is included in the following algorithm to improve stability.

Gaussian elimination must be modified to make the transformations into *similarity* transformations, by performing the indicated operations on columns to correspond to the operations on rows that are required to achieve the desired upper Hessenberg form. This process requires n-2 stages for an n-by-n matrix.

Input
>   A   matrix to be transformed

First stage:
>   Find element of maximum magnitude in first column, below the diagonal
>>   If this element is zero, this stage is finished.
>>   Otherwise, denote the element as $a_{p,1}$ (that is, the element is in the pth row)
>>>   If $p > 2$, interchange rows 2 and p; also interchange columns 2 and p.
>>>   For rows $i = 3, 4, \ldots n$
>>>>   compute multiplier
>>>> $$m_{i,2} = a_{i,1}/a_{2,1}$$
>>>>   subtract multiple of row 2 from row i
>>>>   add multiple of column i to column 2

Stage k:
>   Find element of max. magnitude in k^{th} column, rows $k + 1, \ldots n$.
>>   If this element is zero, this stage is finished.
>>   Otherwise, denote the element as $a_{p,k}$ (that is, the element is in the pth row)
>>>   If $p > k + 1$, interchange rows $k + 1$ and p;
>>>>   also interchange columns $k + 1$ and p
>>>   For rows $i = k + 2, \ldots n$
>>>>   compute multiplier
>>>> $$m_{i,k+1} = a_{i,k}/a_{k+1,k}$$
>>>>   subtract multiple of row $k + 1$ from row i
>>>>   add multiple of column i to column $k + 1$

LU Factorization

Factor $\mathbf{A} = \mathbf{L}\,\mathbf{U}$, where $\mathbf{U}$ is the upper triangular matrix obtained by Gaussian elimination (without pivoting) and

$$\mathbf{L} = \begin{bmatrix} 1 & 0 & 0 & 0 \\ -m_{21} & 1 & 0 & 0 \\ -m_{31} & -m_{32} & 1 & 0 \\ -m_{41} & -m_{42} & -m_{43} & 1 \end{bmatrix}$$

is the lower triangular matrix formed from the multipliers used in the elimination.

LU Factorization of Tridiagonal System

$$
\begin{aligned}
d_1 x_1 + a_1 x_2 \qquad\qquad\qquad &= r_1, \\
b_2 x_1 + d_2 x_2 + a_2 x_3 \qquad &= r_2, \\
b_3 x_2 + d_3 x_3 + a_3 x_4 &= r_3, \\
b_4 x_3 + d_4 x_4 &= r_4.
\end{aligned}
$$

Compute

$$dd_1 = d_1,$$
$$bb_2 = b_2/d_1, \quad dd_2 = d_2 - bb_2 a_1,$$
$$bb_3 = b_3/dd_2, \quad dd_3 = d_3 - bb_3 a_2,$$
$$bb_4 = b_4/dd_3, \quad dd_4 = d_4 - bb_4 a_3.$$

The factorization is

$$\mathbf{L} = \begin{bmatrix} 1 & 0 & 0 & 0 \\ bb_2 & 1 & 0 & 0 \\ 0 & bb_3 & 1 & 0 \\ 0 & 0 & bb_4 & 1 \end{bmatrix} \quad \mathbf{U} = \begin{bmatrix} dd_1 & a_1 & 0 & 0 \\ 0 & dd_2 & a_2 & 0 \\ 0 & 0 & dd_3 & a_3 \\ 0 & 0 & 0 & dd_4 \end{bmatrix}$$

Direct LU Factorization

1's on the diagonal of $\mathbf{L}$:

$$\begin{bmatrix} 1 & 0 & 0 \\ \ell_{21} & 1 & 0 \\ \ell_{31} & \ell_{32} & 1 \end{bmatrix} \cdot \begin{bmatrix} u_{11} & u_{12} & u_{13} \\ 0 & u_{22} & u_{23} \\ 0 & 0 & u_{33} \end{bmatrix} = \begin{bmatrix} a_{11} & a_{12} & a_{13} \\ a_{21} & a_{22} & a_{23} \\ a_{31} & a_{32} & a_{33} \end{bmatrix}.$$

1's on the diagonal of $\mathbf{U}$:

$$\begin{bmatrix} \ell_{11} & 0 & 0 \\ \ell_{21} & \ell_{22} & 0 \\ \ell_{31} & \ell_{32} & \ell_{33} \end{bmatrix} \cdot \begin{bmatrix} 1 & u_{12} & u_{13} \\ 0 & 1 & u_{23} \\ 0 & 0 & 1 \end{bmatrix} = \begin{bmatrix} a_{11} & a_{12} & a_{13} \\ a_{21} & a_{22} & a_{23} \\ a_{31} & a_{32} & a_{33} \end{bmatrix}.$$

Cholesky form makes the diagonals of $\mathbf{L}$ and $\mathbf{U}$ equal:

$$\begin{bmatrix} x_{11} & 0 & 0 \\ \ell_{21} & x_{22} & 0 \\ \ell_{31} & \ell_{32} & x_{33} \end{bmatrix} \cdot \begin{bmatrix} x_{11} & u_{12} & u_{13} \\ 0 & x_{22} & u_{23} \\ 0 & 0 & x_{33} \end{bmatrix} = \begin{bmatrix} a_{11} & a_{12} & a_{13} \\ a_{21} & a_{22} & a_{23} \\ a_{31} & a_{32} & a_{33} \end{bmatrix}.$$

QR factorization

Using transformations that correspond to Householder matrices, QR factorization of $\mathbf{A}$ is described in the following algorithm.

Define $\mathbf{R}^{(0)} = \mathbf{A}$
For $k = 1$ to $n-1$
    Find $\mathbf{H}^{(k)}$ to reduce positions $k + 1, \ldots n$ in the kth column of $\mathbf{R}^{(k-1)}$ to zero;
    Define $\mathbf{R}^{(k)} = \mathbf{H}^{(k)} \mathbf{R}^{(k-1)}$
End
Define $\mathbf{Q} = \mathbf{I}$
For $k = n - 1$ to 1
    $\mathbf{Q} = \mathbf{H}^{(k)} \mathbf{Q}$
End
Define $\mathbf{R} = \mathbf{R}^{(n-1)}$

For a matrix in Hessenberg form it is more efficient to perform the factorization using Givens rotations. The preprocessing to Hessenberg form and the use of Givens rotations for QR factorization are discussed in sections 4.4.2 and 4.5.2.

SUGGESTIONS FOR FURTHER READING

The following are a few of the many excellent undergraduate texts on linear algebra:

Kolman, B. *Introductory Linear Algebra with Applications*, 6th ed. Upper Saddle River, NJ; Prentice Hall, 1997.

Leon, S. J. *Linear Algebra with Applications*, 5th ed. Upper Saddle River, NJ; Prentice Hall, 1998.

Strang, G. *Linear Algebra and Its Applications* 3rd ed. San Diego, CA; Harcourt Brace Jovanovich, 1988.

Some references at a somewhat more advanced level include:

Dongarra, J. J., et al. *LINPACK User's Guide.* Philadelphia; SIAM, 1979.

Forsythe, G. E., M. A. Malcolm, and C. B. Moler. *Computer Methods for Mathematical Computations*, Englewood Cliffs; Prentice-Hall, 1977.

Fox, L. *An Introduction to Numerical Linear Algebra.* New York; Oxford University Press, 1965. This classic work also contains many bibliographic entries.

Golub, G. H., and C. F. Van Loan. *Matrix Computations*, 3rd ed. Baltimore; Johns Hopkins University Press, 1996.

Horn, R. A., and C. R. Johnson. *Matrix Analysis*, Cambridge; Cambridge University Press, 1985.

For problems P4.1 to P4.14 find the LU factorization of the matrix, using Gaussian elimination.

P4.1 $\quad \mathbf{A} = \begin{bmatrix} 1 & 2 & 3 \\ 2 & 8 & 11 \\ 3 & 22 & 35 \end{bmatrix}$

P4.2 $\quad \mathbf{A} = \begin{bmatrix} 3 & 6 & 12 \\ -1 & 0 & 2 \\ 3 & 2 & 1 \end{bmatrix}$

P4.3 $\quad \mathbf{A} = \begin{bmatrix} 2 & 1 & -2 \\ 4 & -1 & 2 \\ 2 & -1 & 1 \end{bmatrix}$

P4.4 $\quad \mathbf{A} = \begin{bmatrix} 3/2 & -1 & 1/2 \\ -1/2 & 1/2 & -1/4 \\ 1/2 & -1/2 & 1/2 \end{bmatrix}$

P4.5 $\quad \mathbf{A} = \begin{bmatrix} 1 & 1/2 & 1/3 \\ 1/2 & 1/3 & 1/4 \\ 1/3 & 1/4 & 1/5 \end{bmatrix}$

P4.6 $\quad \mathbf{A} = \begin{bmatrix} 1/5 & 0 & 0 & 0 \\ -26 & 13 & -4 & 2 \\ 12 & -6 & 2 & -1 \\ -3/2 & 3/4 & -1/4 & 1/4 \end{bmatrix}$

P4.7 $\quad \mathbf{A} = \begin{bmatrix} 1 & 1 & 0 & 3 \\ 2 & 1 & -1 & 1 \\ 3 & -1 & -1 & 2 \\ -1 & 2 & 3 & -1 \end{bmatrix}$

P4.8 $\quad \mathbf{A} = \begin{bmatrix} 1 & -2 & 6 & -12 \\ 0 & 1 & -3 & 6 \\ 0 & -5 & 16 & -32 \\ 0 & 15 & -48 & 97 \end{bmatrix}$

P4.9 $\quad \mathbf{A} = \begin{bmatrix} 3 & 7 & 4 & 0 \\ 0 & 3 & 13 & 3 \\ 0 & 0 & 1 & 4 \\ 1 & 2 & 0 & 0 \end{bmatrix}$

P4.10 $\quad \mathbf{A} = \begin{bmatrix} 1 & 2 & 3 & 1 & 0 & 0 \\ 2 & 6 & 10 & 2 & 1 & 0 \\ 3 & 14 & 28 & 3 & 4 & 1 \\ 1 & 2 & 3 & 4 & 6 & 12 \\ 0 & 2 & 4 & -1 & 1 & 2 \\ 0 & 0 & 3 & 3 & 2 & 2 \end{bmatrix}$

P4.11 $\quad \mathbf{A} = \begin{bmatrix} 1 & 2 & 1 & 1 & 0 & 0 \\ 2 & 6 & 4 & 2 & 1 & 0 \\ 3 & 14 & 12 & 3 & 4 & 1 \\ 1 & 2 & 1 & 2 & 6 & 12 \\ 0 & 2 & 2 & -1 & -3 & -6 \\ 2 & 4 & 3 & 3 & 2 & 2 \end{bmatrix}$

P4.12 $\quad \mathbf{A} = \begin{bmatrix} 2 & 1 & -2 & 1 & 0 & 0 \\ 4 & -1 & 2 & 2 & 1 & 0 \\ 2 & -1 & 1 & 1 & 2/3 & 1 \\ 2 & 1 & -2 & 5/2 & -1 & 1/2 \\ 0 & -3 & 6 & -1/2 & 10/3 & -7/6 \\ 0 & 0 & -1 & 1/2 & -7/3 & 29/12 \end{bmatrix}$

P4.13

$\mathbf{A} = \begin{bmatrix} 1 & 1 & 1 & 1 & 0 & 0 & 1 & 0 & -1 & 0 \\ 1 & 3 & 2 & 1 & 1 & 0 & 1 & 1 & 0 & 1 \\ 1 & 3 & 3 & 1 & 1 & 1 & 2 & 2 & 1 & 2 \\ 1 & 1 & 1 & 3 & 1 & 1 & 1 & 1 & 1 & 1 \\ 0 & 2 & 1 & -2 & 2 & 0 & 1 & -1 & 0 & 1 \\ 1 & 1 & 2 & 3 & -1 & 2 & 1 & 3 & 2 & 1 \\ 1 & 1 & 0 & 1 & 0 & 0 & 2 & 0 & -2 & 0 \\ 0 & 2 & 2 & 0 & -1 & 0 & 2 & 6 & 0 & 3 \\ 1 & -1 & -1 & 3 & 0 & 1 & 0 & -1 & 2 & -1 \\ 0 & 2 & 1 & 2 & 2 & 2 & 0 & 4 & 4 & 4 \end{bmatrix}$

P4.14

$\mathbf{A} = \begin{bmatrix} 1 & 2 & 1 & 1 & 0 & 0 & 1 & 0 & -1 & 0 \\ 2 & 6 & 4 & 2 & 1 & 0 & 2 & 2 & 0 & 1 \\ 3 & 14 & 12 & 3 & 4 & 1 & 4 & 9 & 6 & 5 \\ 1 & 2 & 1 & 2 & 2 & 3 & 1 & 1 & 1 & 3 \\ 0 & 2 & 2 & -1 & 1 & 3 & 2 & 0 & 1 & -1 \\ 2 & 4 & 3 & 3 & -2 & -7 & -1 & 4 & 0 & 2 \\ 1 & 2 & 0 & 1 & 0 & 1 & 1 & 0 & -1 & 0 \\ 0 & 2 & 4 & 0 & -1 & -4 & 3 & 9 & 0 & 7 \\ 1 & 0 & -3 & 2 & 1 & 2 & -1 & -3 & -1 & 0 \\ 0 & 2 & 2 & 1 & 3 & 4 & 0 & 4 & 5 & 7 \end{bmatrix}$

For Problems P4.15 to P4.25, find an LU factorization of the given matrix
a. Using the method for tridiagonal matrices.
b. Using Gaussian elimination.

P4.15 $\mathbf{A} = \begin{bmatrix} 4 & 2 & 0 \\ 16 & 12 & 1 \\ 0 & 8 & 5 \end{bmatrix}$

P4.16 $\mathbf{A} = \begin{bmatrix} 2 & 4 & 0 \\ 2 & 8 & 2 \\ 0 & 4 & 4 \end{bmatrix}$

P4.17 $\mathbf{A} = \begin{bmatrix} 5 & 1 & 0 \\ 15 & 6 & 3 \\ 0 & 9 & 11 \end{bmatrix}$

P4.18 $\mathbf{A} = \begin{bmatrix} 3 & 5 & 0 \\ 12 & 24 & 3 \\ 0 & 8 & 7 \end{bmatrix}$

P4.19 $\mathbf{A} = \begin{bmatrix} 1 & 3 & 0 & 0 \\ 2 & 7 & 2 & 0 \\ 0 & 2 & 5 & 5 \\ 0 & 0 & 1 & 6 \end{bmatrix}$

P4.20 $\mathbf{A} = \begin{bmatrix} 3 & 1 & 0 & 0 \\ 12 & 5 & 2 & 0 \\ 0 & 2 & 8 & 5 \\ 0 & 0 & 16 & 23 \end{bmatrix}$

P4.21 $\mathbf{A} = \begin{bmatrix} 1 & 4 & 0 & 0 \\ 1 & 6 & 2 & 0 \\ 0 & 6 & 10 & 3 \\ 0 & 0 & 12 & 13 \end{bmatrix}$

P4.22 $\mathbf{A} = \begin{bmatrix} 2 & 1 & 0 & 0 \\ 6 & 5 & 1 & 0 \\ 0 & 2 & 3 & 5 \\ 0 & 0 & 8 & 22 \end{bmatrix}$

P4.23 $\mathbf{A} = \begin{bmatrix} 5 & 0 & 0 & 0 \\ 10 & 1 & 2 & 0 \\ 0 & 3 & 7 & 4 \\ 0 & 0 & 1 & 8 \end{bmatrix}$

P4.24 $\mathbf{A} = \begin{bmatrix} 1 & 2 & 0 & 0 & 0 & 0 \\ 2 & 6 & 2 & 0 & 0 & 0 \\ 0 & 8 & 9 & 0 & 0 & 0 \\ 0 & 0 & 0 & 1 & 6 & 0 \\ 0 & 0 & 0 & -1 & -4 & 6 \\ 0 & 0 & 0 & 0 & -4 & -11 \end{bmatrix}$

P4.25 $\mathbf{A} = \begin{bmatrix} 1 & -5 & 0 & 0 & 0 & 0 \\ 2 & -8 & -4 & 0 & 0 & 0 \\ 0 & 6 & -9 & -3 & 0 & 0 \\ 0 & 0 & 12 & -8 & -2 & 0 \\ 0 & 0 & 0 & 20 & -5 & -1 \\ 0 & 0 & 0 & 0 & 30 & 0 \end{bmatrix}$

P4.26 $\mathbf{A} = \begin{bmatrix} 4 & 4 & 0 & 0 & 0 & 0 \\ 16 & 20 & 0 & 0 & 0 & 0 \\ 0 & 4 & 3 & 1 & 0 & 0 \\ 0 & 0 & 9 & 5 & 4 & 0 \\ 0 & 0 & 0 & 10 & 21 & 2 \\ 0 & 0 & 0 & 0 & 3 & 7 \end{bmatrix}$

P4.27 $\mathbf{A} = \begin{bmatrix} 5 & 2 & 0 & 0 & 0 & 0 \\ 15 & 10 & 0 & 0 & 0 & 0 \\ 0 & 8 & 2 & 2 & 0 & 0 \\ 0 & 0 & 2 & 5 & 4 & 0 \\ 0 & 0 & 0 & 9 & 16 & 4 \\ 0 & 0 & 0 & 0 & 16 & 17 \end{bmatrix}$

P4.28

$\mathbf{A} = \begin{bmatrix} 1 & 1 & 0 & 0 & 0 & 0 & 0 & 0 & 0 & 0 \\ 1 & 3 & 1 & 0 & 0 & 0 & 0 & 0 & 0 & 0 \\ 0 & 4 & 3 & 1 & 0 & 0 & 0 & 0 & 0 & 0 \\ 0 & 0 & 3 & 5 & 1 & 0 & 0 & 0 & 0 & 0 \\ 0 & 0 & 0 & -2 & 1 & 1 & 0 & 0 & 0 & 0 \\ 0 & 0 & 0 & 0 & -4 & -1 & 0 & 0 & 0 & 0 \\ 0 & 0 & 0 & 0 & 0 & -3 & 2 & 1 & 0 & 0 \\ 0 & 0 & 0 & 0 & 0 & 0 & 2 & 3 & 0 & 0 \\ 0 & 0 & 0 & 2 & 1 & 0 & 0 & 4 & 2 & 0 \\ 0 & 0 & 0 & 2 & 1 & 0 & 0 & 0 & 6 & 1 \end{bmatrix}$

For Problems P4.29 to P4.33 find an LU factorization of a permutation of Λ, using Gaussian elimination with row pivoting.

P4.29 $\mathbf{A} = \begin{bmatrix} 6 & 2 & 2 \\ 6 & 2 & 1 \\ 1 & 2 & -1 \end{bmatrix}$

P4.30 $\mathbf{A} = \begin{bmatrix} 1 & 2 & 3 \\ 2 & 4 & 10 \\ 3 & 14 & 28 \end{bmatrix}$

P4.31 $\mathbf{A} = \begin{bmatrix} -1 & 1 & 0 & 0 \\ 1 & -1 & 1 & 0 \\ 0 & 1 & -1 & 1 \\ 0 & 0 & 1 & -1 \end{bmatrix}$

P4.32 $\mathbf{A} = \begin{bmatrix} 2 & -1 & 0 & 0 & 0 & 0 \\ -1 & 2 & -1 & 0 & 0 & 0 \\ 0 & -1 & 2/3 & -1 & 0 & 0 \\ 0 & 0 & -1 & 2 & -1 & 0 \\ 0 & 0 & 0 & -1 & 2 & -1 \\ 0 & 0 & 0 & 0 & -1 & 2 \end{bmatrix}$

P4.33 $\mathbf{A} = \begin{bmatrix} 1 & -2 & 0 & 0 & 0 & 0 \\ -2 & 6 & 4 & 0 & 0 & 0 \\ 0 & 4 & 8 & -1/2 & 0 & 0 \\ 0 & 0 & -1/2 & 13/4 & 3/2 & 0 \\ 0 & 0 & 0 & 3/2 & 7/4 & -3 \\ 0 & 0 & 0 & 0 & -3 & 13 \end{bmatrix};$

For Problems P4.34 to P4.38 find the LU factorization of the given matrix
    a. Doolittle form
    b. Cholesky form
    c. use the LU factorization from part a or b to solve the linear system $\mathbf{A}\mathbf{x} = \mathbf{b}$

P4.34 $\mathbf{A} = \begin{bmatrix} 1 & 2 & 3 \\ 2 & 20 & 26 \\ 3 & 26 & 70 \end{bmatrix}$

  i. $\mathbf{b} = \begin{bmatrix} 14 & 120 & 265 \end{bmatrix}^T$

  ii. $\mathbf{b} = \begin{bmatrix} 7 & 38 & 123 \end{bmatrix}^T$

  iii. $\mathbf{b} = \begin{bmatrix} 10 & 48 & 173 \end{bmatrix}^T$

P4.35 $\mathbf{A} = \begin{bmatrix} 9 & 18 & 36 \\ 18 & 40 & 84 \\ 36 & 84 & 181 \end{bmatrix}$

  i. $\mathbf{b} = \begin{bmatrix} 63 & 146 & 313 \end{bmatrix}^T$

  ii. $\mathbf{b} = \begin{bmatrix} 0 & -8 & -25 \end{bmatrix}^T$

  iii. $\mathbf{b} = \begin{bmatrix} -18 & -32 & -59 \end{bmatrix}^T$

P4.36 $\mathbf{A} = \begin{bmatrix} 9 & 18 & 36 \\ 18 & 52 & 116 \\ 36 & 116 & 265.25 \end{bmatrix}$

  i. $\mathbf{b} = \begin{bmatrix} 63.00 & 186.00 & 417.25 \end{bmatrix}^T$

  ii. $\mathbf{b} = \begin{bmatrix} -9.00 & -46.00 & -113.25 \end{bmatrix}^T$

  iii. $\mathbf{b} = \begin{bmatrix} 81 & 306 & 721 \end{bmatrix}^T$

P4.37 $\mathbf{A} = \begin{bmatrix} 2 & -1 & 0 & 0 & 0 & 0 \\ -1 & 2 & -1 & 0 & 0 & 0 \\ 0 & -1 & 2/3 & -1 & 0 & 0 \\ 0 & 0 & -1 & 2 & -1 & 0 \\ 0 & 0 & 0 & -1 & 2 & -1 \\ 0 & 0 & 0 & 0 & -1 & 2 \end{bmatrix}$

  i. $\mathbf{b} = \begin{bmatrix} 3 & -3 & 2 & -2 & -3 & -1 \end{bmatrix}^T$

  ii. $\mathbf{b} = \begin{bmatrix} 0 & 0 & 1 & -2 & -3 & -1 \end{bmatrix}^T$

  iii. $\mathbf{b} = \begin{bmatrix} 3 & -5 & 13/3 & -9 & 11 & -9 \end{bmatrix}^T$

P4.38

$$\mathbf{A} = \begin{bmatrix} 1 & 1 & 1 & 1 & 0 & 0 & 1 & 0 & -1 & 0 \\ 1 & 5 & 3 & 1 & 2 & 0 & 1 & 2 & 1 & 2 \\ 1 & 3 & 3 & 1 & 1 & 1 & 2 & 2 & 1 & 2 \\ 1 & 1 & 1 & 5 & 2 & 2 & 1 & 2 & 3 & 2 \\ 0 & 2 & 1 & 2 & 6 & 3 & 2 & 0 & 5 & 4 \\ 0 & 0 & 1 & 2 & 3 & 4 & 2 & 1 & 5 & 3 \\ 1 & 1 & 2 & 1 & 2 & 2 & 7 & 2 & -1 & 4 \\ 0 & 2 & 2 & 2 & 0 & 1 & 2 & 9 & 2 & 5 \\ -1 & 1 & 1 & 3 & 5 & 5 & -1 & 2 & 14 & 4 \\ 0 & 2 & 2 & 2 & 4 & 3 & 4 & 5 & 4 & 7 \end{bmatrix}$$

  i. $\mathbf{b} = \begin{bmatrix} 0 & 8 & 3 & -14 & -39 & -32 & -1 & 45 & -56 & -1 \end{bmatrix}^T$

  ii. $\mathbf{b} = \begin{bmatrix} -15 & -43 & -43 & -27 & -12 & -14 & -59 & -79 & 2 & -63 \end{bmatrix}^T$

  iii. $\mathbf{b} = \begin{bmatrix} -6 & -10 & -8 & -12 & -7 & 0 & -29 & -19 & 24 & -21 \end{bmatrix}^T$

EXPLORE SOME APPLICATIONS

LU factorization is especially useful for solving linear systems that must be solved for several different right-hand sides which are not known in advance. One place that this occurs is in using the inverse power method, discussed in the next chapter.

For each of the following matrices, find the LU decomposition, and use it to solve the sequence of linear systems. Start with $\mathbf{b} = [\,1\ \ 1\ \ 1\,]^T$, and solve $\mathbf{A}\,\mathbf{x} = \mathbf{b}$. Then find $\mathbf{y}$ such that $\mathbf{A}\,\mathbf{y} = \mathbf{x}$.

A4.1 $\quad \mathbf{A} = \begin{bmatrix} 1 & 0 & 0 \\ 2 & -1 & 2 \\ 4 & -4 & 5 \end{bmatrix}$.

A4.2 $\quad \mathbf{A} = \begin{bmatrix} 5 & -2 & 1 \\ 3 & 0 & 1 \\ 0 & 0 & 2 \end{bmatrix}$

A4.3 $\quad \mathbf{A} = \begin{bmatrix} 2 & 2 & -1 \\ -5 & 9 & -3 \\ -4 & 4 & 1 \end{bmatrix}$.

A4.4 $\quad \mathbf{A} = \begin{bmatrix} -19 & 20 & -6 \\ -12 & 13 & -3 \\ 30 & -30 & 12 \end{bmatrix}$

The determinant of $A = LU$ is the product of the diagonal elements of L times the product of the diagonal elements of U. If pivoting is used, a factor of $(-1)^k$ is included in the product forming the determinant (k is the number of row interchanges that occured in the LU factorization).

A4.5 to A4.14 Find the inverse and the determinant of the matrices in P4.1 through 4.10

Problems A4.15 to A4.17 make use of a matrix formulation of quadratic equations. The quadratic form $a\,x^2 + b\,xy + c\,y^2 = F(x,y)$ can be written in matrix form as $[\,\mathbf{A}\,\mathbf{v}\,]\,\mathbf{v} = F(x,y)$, with $\mathbf{v} = [x,\ y]^T$ and

$$\mathbf{A} = \begin{bmatrix} a & b/2 \\ b/2 & c \end{bmatrix}$$

The form of the graph of the quadratic equation

$$a\,x^2 + b\,xy + c\,y^2 = d, \quad (d \neq 0)$$

is given by the sign of the determinant of the matrix $\mathbf{A}$:

> *If $det(\mathbf{A}) < 0$, the graph is a hyperbola;*
>
> *if $det(\mathbf{A}) > 0$, the graph is an ellipse, or a circle, (or is degenerate);*
>
> *if $det(\mathbf{A}) = 0$, the graph is a pair of straight lines (or is degenerate).*

(For further discussion of these ideas, see Grossman and Derrick, 1988, p. 490; Fraleigh and Beauregard, 1987, or Leon, 1998)

Write the following equations in matrix form, and determine whether the equation is a hyperbola, an ellipse, a circle, or a pair of straight lines.

A4.15 $\quad x^2 - \sqrt{3}\,x\,y + 2\,y^2 = 10$

A4.16 $\quad 4\,x^2 + 3\sqrt{3}\,xy + y^2 = 22$

A4.17 $\quad x^2 - \sqrt{3}\,xy = -2$

Eigenvalues and Eigenvectors

The factorization of a matrix $\mathbf{A}$ into the product of lower triangular and upper triangular matrices $\mathbf{L}$ and $\mathbf{U}$, discussed in Chapter 4, provides a method for finding several quantities associated with $\mathbf{A}$, including the determinant of $\mathbf{A}$, the inverse of $\mathbf{A}$, and the solution of the linear system $\mathbf{A}\mathbf{x} = \mathbf{b}$. In this chapter, we conclude our investigation into topics from numerical linear algebra by considering techniques for finding the eigenvalues and eigenvectors of a matrix.

A number λ is an eigenvalue of a matrix $\mathbf{A}$, and a nonzero vector $\mathbf{x}$ is a corresponding eigenvector of $\mathbf{A}$, if and only if $\mathbf{A}\mathbf{x} = \lambda\,\mathbf{x}$. A fundamental property is that λ is an eigenvalue of $\mathbf{A}$ if and only if it is a zero of the characteristic polynomial, $f(\lambda) = \det(\mathbf{A} - \lambda\mathbf{I})$. Except for very small matrices, direct calculation of the characteristic equation is not practical. Although in general an eigenvalue may be real or complex, the methods presented in this chapter are given in a form that assumes the eigenvalues are real.

We first consider a method, known as the power method, for finding a specific eigenvalue and its associated eigenvector for a given matrix $\mathbf{A}$. The basic power method finds the dominant eigenvalue, that is, the eigenvalue of largest magnitude. Variations of the power method can be used to find the eigenvalue of smallest magnitude or the eigenvalue closest to a specified value.

We next consider the use of QR factorization in finding the eigenvalues of $\mathbf{A}$. The QR eigenvalue method finds all of the eigenvalues of a matrix, but does not find the corresponding eigenvectors. If the eigenvalues of $\mathbf{A}$ are real, the QR method transforms matrix $\mathbf{A}$ into a product of an orthogonal matrix $\mathbf{Q}$ and an upper triangular matrix with the eigenvalues of $\mathbf{A}$ on the diagonal. If the eigenvalues of $\mathbf{A}$ are complex, $\mathbf{R}$ is not upper triangular, but has 2-by-2 blocks on the diagonal.

Eigenvalues are important in the analysis of the convergence characteristics of iterative methods for solving linear systems (Chapter 6). The estimation of eigenvalues based on the Gerschgorin theorem was presented in Chapter 1. The ratio of the largest to the smallest eigenvalue of a matrix is a useful measure of the "condition" of a matrix; a matrix with a large condition number is called *ill-conditioned*. The Hilbert matrix, introduced in Chapter 1, is a famous example of an ill-conditioned matrix.

Eigenvalues and eigenvectors are also important in many areas of science and engineering, including solving differential equations and finding physical characteristics of a structure, such as the principal stress, moments of inertia, and so on.

Example 5-A Inertial Matrix

The principal inertias and principal axes of a three-dimensional object can be found from the eigenvalues and eigenvectors, respectively, of its inertial matrix. For example, consider a body consisting of unit point masses at $(1, 0, 0)$, $(1, 2, 0)$ and $(0, 0, 1)$ (see Fig. 5.1). Its inertial matrix is

$$G = \begin{bmatrix} 5 & -2 & 0 \\ -2 & 3 & 0 \\ 0 & 0 & 6 \end{bmatrix}.$$

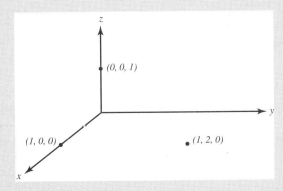

FIGURE 5.1   A body consisting of three unit point masses.

In general, the inertial matrix is

$$G = \begin{bmatrix} I_{xx} & -I_{xy} & -I_{xz} \\ -I_{yx} & I_{yy} & -I_{yz} \\ -I_{zx} & -I_{zy} & I_{zz} \end{bmatrix},$$

where the moments of inertia of the body around the x-, y-, and z-axes are, respectively,

$$I_{xx} = \int (y^2 + z^2)\, dm, \quad I_{yy} = \int (x^2 + z^2)\, dm, \quad I_{zz} = \int (x^2 + y^2)\, dm,$$

and the corresponding products of inertia are

$$I_{xy} = I_{yx} = \int xy\, dm, \quad I_{xz} = I_{zx} = \int xz\, dm, \quad I_{yz} = I_{zy} = \int yz\, dm.$$

(See Greenberg, 1998, p. 581, or Thomson, 1986, p. 103, for further discussion.)

Example 5-B Buckling and Breaking of a Beam

The bending moment of a simply supported beam (see Fig. 5.2) is described by the differential equation

$$-x'' = \lambda x \qquad 0 \leq x \leq 1$$

with boundary conditions

$$x(0) = x(1) = 0,$$

where λ is the applied load. When λ reaches a critical value, the beam buckles (and may break soon after the load exceeds that value). This smallest eigenvalue of the differential equation can be approximated by the smallest eigenvalue of the linear system obtained by the finite difference techniques we consider in Chapter 14. Thus, for large n, we are interested in the smallest eigenvalue of the n-by-n matrix

$$\mathbf{A} = (n+1)^2 \begin{bmatrix} 2 & -1 & & & & \\ -1 & 2 & -1 & & & \\ & -1 & 2 & -1 & & \\ & & \cdot & \cdot & \cdot & \\ & & & -1 & 2 & -1 \\ & & & & -1 & 2 \end{bmatrix},$$

FIGURE 5.2   Simply supported beam.

By implementing the inverse power method discussed in section 5.2, one can experiment to investigate how large n should be to achieve a reasonably accurate estimate of the smallest eigenvalue of the differential equation by using the eigenvalue of the discrete system. The smallest eigenvalue of the differential equations is $\mu_1 = \pi^2$. (See Hager, 1988, for further discussion.)

The power method is an iterative procedure for determining the dominant eigenvalue of a matrix $\mathbf{A}$. The basic idea behind the power method is that the defining relationship which is satisfied if $\mathbf{x}$ is an eigenvector of $\mathbf{A}$, namely,

$$\lambda\, \mathbf{x} = \mathbf{A}\, \mathbf{x},$$

can be converted into a sequence of approximations to λ and $\mathbf{x}$. We start with an initial guess $\mathbf{z}$ for the true eigenvector $\mathbf{x}$ and compute

$$\mathbf{w} = \mathbf{A}\, \mathbf{z}.$$

If $\mathbf{z}$ is an eigenvector, then for any component of $\mathbf{z}$ and $\mathbf{w}$, we would have $\lambda\, z_k = w_k$. If $\mathbf{z}$ is not an eigenvector, we would like to use $\mathbf{w}$ as the next approximation, and iterate until the process converges (if it does). However, because an eigenvector is determined only up to a scale factor, we normalize $\mathbf{w}$ before using it as the next approximation $\mathbf{z}$; the normalization is chosen so that the largest component of $\mathbf{z}$ is 1 at each stage of the iteration.

The method will converge if the initial estimate of the eigenvector has a (nonzero) component in the direction of the eigenvector corresponding to the dominant eigenvalue. For that reason, a starting vector with all components equal to 1 is used in the computations of the power method.

Briefly, the power method approach is based on the following observations. We iterate according to the equation $\mathbf{w} = \mathbf{A}\, \mathbf{z}$. From the basic definition of an eigenvalue, we also have the approximate relationship $\lambda \mathbf{z} \approx \mathbf{A}\mathbf{z}$; therefore, $\mathbf{w} \approx \lambda\, \mathbf{z}$.

Denoting the dominant component of $\mathbf{w}$ as w_k, we have

$$w_k \approx \lambda\, z_k \implies \lambda \approx \frac{w_k}{z_k}.$$

Since we scale the vector $\mathbf{z}$ at each stage so that $z_k = 1$, we have the approximation

$$\lambda \approx w_k.$$

Carrying out the iterations has the effect of multiplying the original estimate by successively higher powers of $\mathbf{A}$—hence the name of the method. The first two iterations, shown here, illustrate the basic pattern:

$$\mathbf{w}^{(1)} = \mathbf{A}\, \mathbf{z}^{(1)};$$

$$\mathbf{z}^{(2)} = \frac{1}{w^{(1)}{}_k}\, \mathbf{w}^{(1)} = \frac{1}{w^{(1)}{}_k}\, \mathbf{A}\, \mathbf{z}^{(1)};$$

$$\mathbf{w}^{(2)} = \mathbf{A}\, \mathbf{z}^{(2)} = \mathbf{A}\, \frac{1}{w^{(1)}{}_k}\, \mathbf{A}\, \mathbf{z}^{(1)} = \frac{1}{w^{(1)}{}_k}\, \mathbf{A}^2\, \mathbf{z}^{(1)};$$

$$\mathbf{z}^{(3)} = \frac{1}{w^{(2)}{}_k}\, \mathbf{w}^{(2)} = \frac{1}{w^{(2)}{}_k}\, \frac{1}{w^{(2)}{}_k}\, \mathbf{A}^2\, \mathbf{z}^{(1)}.$$

5.1.1 Basic Power Method

The following algorithm finds the dominant eigenvalue (the eigenvalue of largest magnitude), and the corresponding eigenvector, of matrix **M**.

Power Method

$$
\begin{aligned}
&\textit{Input} \\
&\quad \mathbf{M} \qquad\qquad\qquad\qquad \textit{n-by-n matrix} \\
&\quad \text{n} \qquad\qquad\qquad\qquad\; \textit{number of rows and columns in M} \\
&\quad \text{max} \qquad\qquad\qquad\; \textit{maximum number of iterations} \\
&\quad \text{tol} \qquad\qquad\qquad\quad\; \textit{tolerance for convergence} \\
&\textit{Initialize} \\
&\quad \mathbf{z} \qquad\qquad\qquad\qquad\; \textit{n-by-1 vector, all components are 1} \\
&\textit{Begin iterations} \\
&\text{For i = 1 to max} \\
&\quad \mathbf{w} = \mathbf{M}^{*}\mathbf{z} \\
&\quad \text{k = 1} \\
&\quad \text{b = | w(k) |} \\
&\quad \text{For j = 2 to n} \qquad\qquad \textit{find index of dominant component} \\
&\qquad \text{If | w(j) |} \geq \text{b} \\
&\qquad\qquad \text{k = j} \\
&\qquad\qquad \text{b = |w(j) |} \\
&\quad\;\; \text{End} \\
&\quad \text{End} \\
&\quad \text{m = w(k)} \qquad\qquad\; \textit{approx. eigenvalue} \\
&\quad \mathbf{z} = \dfrac{\text{w}}{\text{w}_k} \\
&\quad \text{If} \| \mathbf{M}^{*}\mathbf{z} - \text{m}\,\mathbf{z} \| < \text{tol, Break} \qquad\quad \textit{test for convergence} \\
&\text{End} \\
&\textit{Return} \\
&\quad \text{m} \qquad\qquad\qquad\qquad \textit{approximate eigenvalue} \\
&\quad \mathbf{z} \qquad\qquad\qquad\qquad\; \textit{approximate eigenvector}
\end{aligned}
$$

The basic power method is illustrated in the following example.

Example 5.1 Using the Basic Power Method

To find the eigenvalue λ of largest magnitude, and a corresponding eigenvector, of

$$\mathbf{A} = \begin{bmatrix} 21 & 7 & -1 \\ 5 & 7 & 7 \\ 4 & -4 & 20 \end{bmatrix},$$

we start with the initial vector $\mathbf{z} = [1, 1, 1]^T$.

Step 1: $\mathbf{w} = \mathbf{A}\,\mathbf{z} = [27, 19, 20]^T$.

Since the first component of $\mathbf{w}$ has the largest magnitude, the first estimate of λ is $w_1 = 27$. We use that component to scale the approximate eigenvector:

$$\mathbf{z} = \mathbf{w}/w_1 = [1.0000, 0.7037, 0.7407]^T$$

Step 2: $\mathbf{w} = \mathbf{A}\,\mathbf{z} = [25.1852, 15.1111, 16.0000]^T$.

Since the first component of $\mathbf{w}$ has the largest magnitude, the estimate of λ is $w_1 = 25.1852$, and

$$\mathbf{z} = \mathbf{w}/w_1 = [1.0000, 0.6000, 0.6353]^T$$

Step 3: $\mathbf{w} = \mathbf{A}\,\mathbf{z} = [24.5647, 13.6471, 14.3059]^T$.

The estimate of λ is $w_1 = 24.5647$, and

$$\mathbf{z} = \mathbf{w}/w_1 = [1.0000, 0.5556, 0.5824]^T$$

Step 4: $\mathbf{w} = \mathbf{A}\,\mathbf{z} = [24.3065, 12.9655, 13.4253]^T$.

The estimate of λ is $w_1 = 24.3065$, and

$$\mathbf{z} = \mathbf{w}/w_1 = [1.0000, 0.5334, 0.5523]^T$$

The final estimate of the dominant eigenvalue is $\lambda \approx w_1$.
The final estimate of the corresponding eigenvector is $\mathbf{z}$.
Checking the accuracy of our estimate, $\lambda = 24.3065$ and

$$\mathbf{z} = [1.0000, 0.5334, 0.5523]^T$$

we compute $A\,\mathbf{z} - \lambda\,\mathbf{z} = [-0.1249, -0.3653, -0.5123]^T$.

The maximum norm of this vector gives us a bound on the accuracy of the estimate after 4 steps, namely, $\|\mathbf{A}\,\mathbf{z} - \lambda\,\mathbf{z}\|_\infty = 0.5123$.

The actual eigenvalues of this matrix are 8, 16, and 24. The successive approximations of the power method are converging toward the largest eigenvalue, 24.

5.1.2   Accelerated Power Method

In some cases, it is possible to accelerate the convergence of the power method by using an estimate of λ that does not rely on a single component of the current vectors $\mathbf{w}$ and $\mathbf{z}$. The improved estimate of λ is called the *Rayleigh quotient*. It is given by:

$$\lambda = (\mathbf{z}^T \mathbf{w})/(\mathbf{z}^T \mathbf{z}).$$

When $\mathbf{A}$ is symmetric, the power method with the Rayleigh quotient converges more rapidly than the basic power method. The accelerated power method can be implemented by replacing the definition of λ in the algorithm for the basic power method.

Example 5.2 Dominant Eigenvalue for a Symmetric Matrix

To illustrate the acceleration in convergence of the dominant eigenvalue of a symmetric matrix that generally results when using the Rayleigh quotient, consider the following four-by-four matrix:

$$\mathbf{A} = \begin{bmatrix} 4 & 2/3 & -4/3 & 4/3 \\ 2/3 & 4 & 0 & 0 \\ -4/3 & 0 & 6 & 2 \\ 4/3 & 0 & 2 & 6 \end{bmatrix}.$$

The estimate of the dominant eigenvalue from the basic power method λ_b, the estimate from the Rayleigh quotient λ_r, and the eigenvector $\mathbf{z}$ are shown in the following table. After 10 iterations, the error from the basic method is 0.1328; that from the Rayleigh quotient approximation is 0.1036.

step	λ_b	λ_r	z(1)	z(2)	z(3)	z(4)
			Iterations of basic and accelerated power method.			
1	9.3333	6.3333	0.5000	0.5000	0.7143	1.0000
2	8.0952	7.2792	0.3353	0.2882	0.6941	1.0000
3	7.8353	7.6621	0.2477	0.1757	0.7297	1.0000
4	7.7898	7.8286	0.1885	0.1114	0.7764	1.0000
5	7.8042	7.9083	0.1443	0.0732	0.8210	1.0000
6	7.8344	7.9495	0.1104	0.0497	0.8595	1.0000
7	7.8661	7.9718	0.0842	0.0346	0.8911	1.0000
8	7.8945	7.9842	0.0640	0.0246	0.9164	1.0000
9	7.9181	7.9911	0.0485	0.0178	0.9362	1.0000
10	7.9371	7.9950	0.0366	0.0131	0.9516	1.0000

5.1.3   Shifted Power Method

We may need to find eigenvalues besides (or instead of) the eigenvalue of largest magnitude. Some simple properties of eigenvalues can help us do this. In particular, we can make use of the fact that if a matrix $\mathbf{A}$ has eigenvalues λ_1, λ_2, . . . , λ_n, with corresponding eigenvectors $\mathbf{v}_1$, $\mathbf{v}_2$, . . . $\mathbf{v}_n$, then the eigenvalues of $\mathbf{A} - b\,\mathbf{I}$ are $\mu_1 = \lambda_1 - b$, $\mu_2 = \lambda_2 - b$, . . . $\mu_2 = \lambda_n - b$; the eigenvectors are unchanged by the shift.

If we already know an eigenvalue λ of a matrix $\mathbf{A}$, we can find another eigenvalue of $\mathbf{A}$ by applying the power method to the matrix $\mathbf{b} = \mathbf{A} - \lambda\,\mathbf{I}$. We denote the dominant eigenvalue of the shifted matrix $\mathbf{B}$ as μ. No additional algorithm or function is required for the shifted power method, since it is simply the basic (or accelerated basic) power method applied to the shifted matrix.

Example 5.3 Dominant Eigenvalue of Shifted Matrix

Consider the inertial matrix introduced in Example 5-A. One eigenvalue of

$$\mathbf{G} = \begin{bmatrix} 5 & -2 & 0 \\ -2 & 3 & 0 \\ 0 & 0 & 6 \end{bmatrix}$$

is 6; to find another eigenvalue, we apply the power method to the shifted matrix

$$\mathbf{B} = \mathbf{G} - 6\,\mathbf{I} = \begin{bmatrix} -1 & -2 & 0 \\ -2 & -3 & 0 \\ 0 & 0 & 0 \end{bmatrix}$$

We start with $\mathbf{z} = [1, 1, 1]^T$ and use the Rayleigh quotient approximation.

Step 1: $\mathbf{w} = \mathbf{B}\,\mathbf{z} = [-3, -5, 0]^T$,

$$\mu = \frac{\mathbf{z}^T\mathbf{w}}{\mathbf{z}^T\mathbf{z}} = -\frac{8}{3}; \qquad \mathbf{z} = \frac{\mathbf{w}}{w_2} = [3/5, 1, 0]^T.$$

Step 2: $\mathbf{w} = B\,\mathbf{z} = [-13/5, -21/5, 0]^T$,

$$\mu = \frac{\mathbf{z}^T\mathbf{w}}{\mathbf{z}^T\mathbf{z}} = -\frac{72}{17}; \qquad \mathbf{z} = \frac{\mathbf{w}}{w_2} = [13/21, 1, 0]^T$$

The results of the first four iterations for the power method with Rayleigh quotient to estimate the eigenvalue are summarized in the following table. Using the basic power method requires one more iteration to achieve the stopping condition, namely, $\| \mathbf{A}\,\mathbf{z} - \mu\,\mathbf{z} \| < 0.0001$.

Iterations of shifted power method				
step	μ	z(1)	z(2)	z(3)
1	−2.6667	0.6000	1.0000	0
2	−4.2353	0.6190	1.0000	0
3	−4.2361	0.6180	1.0000	0
4	−4.2361	0.6180	1.0000	0

5.1.4   Discussion

The proof of the convergence of the basic power method assumes that the dominant eigenvalue is real and not a repeated eigenvalue, so that the eigenvalues can be ordered as $|\lambda_1| > |\lambda_2| \geq .. \geq |\lambda_n|$. Often, however, the method is applicable even if these assumptions are not met (see Ralston and Rabinowitz, 1978). The proof is based on the fact that if matrix $\mathbf{A}$ is diagonizable (i.e., if $\mathbf{A}$ has n linearly independent eigenvectors $\mathbf{v}^{(1)}, \ldots, \mathbf{v}^{(n)}$), then any vector $\mathbf{z}$ can be written as a unique linear combination of the eigenvectors:

$$\mathbf{z} = \sum_{i=1}^{n} c_i \mathbf{v}^{(i)} \quad \Rightarrow \quad \mathbf{A}^j \mathbf{z} = \sum_{i=1}^{n} c_i \mathbf{A}^j \mathbf{v}^{(i)}.$$

Since λ_i is the eigenvalue corresponding to eigenvector $\mathbf{v}^{(i)}$, it follows that

$$\mathbf{A}\,\mathbf{v}^{(i)} = \lambda_i \mathbf{v}^{(i)} \text{ and } \mathbf{A}^j \mathbf{v}^{(i)} = \lambda_i^j \mathbf{v}^{(i)}.$$

Therefore,

$$\mathbf{A}^j \mathbf{z} = \sum_{i=1}^{n} c_i \lambda_i^j \mathbf{v}^{(i)} = \lambda_1^j \left[c_1 \mathbf{v}^{(1)} + \sum_{i=2}^{n} c_i \frac{\lambda_i^j}{\lambda_1^j} \mathbf{v}^{(i)} \right]$$

If $\mathbf{A}$ has a single dominant eigenvalue (i.e., $|\lambda_1| > |\lambda_2| \geq |\lambda_3| \ldots \geq |\lambda_n|$), then $\dfrac{\lambda_i^j}{\lambda_1^j} \to 0$ as $j \to \infty$.

Without some control over the iterative process that this suggests, we cannot distinguish the unknown quantities λ_1^j, c_1, and $\mathbf{v}^{(1)}$ on the right-hand side of the equation for $\mathbf{A}^j \mathbf{z}$. It is also quite likely that all components of the limiting vector will grow without bound. However, by an appropriate scaling of the vectors produced during iteration, we can ensure that this limit is finite and nonzero.

The convergence of the estimate at the jth iteration depends on $|\lambda_2/\lambda_1|^j$, so the method will converge more rapidly when the dominant eigenvalue is much larger than the next most dominant eigenvalue.

Convergence may be improved for symmetric matrices by using the Rayleigh quotient to estimate the eigenvalue. In this case, the estimate at the jth iteration depends on $|\lambda_2/\lambda_1|^{2j}$ (because the eigenvectors can be taken to be orthonormal).

The trace of a square matrix $\mathbf{A}$, tr$(\mathbf{A})$, is defined as the sum of the diagonal elements of $\mathbf{A}$. The trace is also equal to the sum of the eigenvalues of $\mathbf{A}$ (cf. Golub and Van Loan, 1996, p. 310). This fact can be used to help determine values of the shift parameter b to use for finding other eigenvalues. It is especially useful when all diagonal elements are non-negative. In such a case, after the dominant eigenvalue λ_1 has been found, one might try a value of b given by $b = \dfrac{\text{tr}(\mathbf{A}) - \lambda_1}{n - 1}$.

The inverse power method provides an estimate of the eigenvalue of $\mathbf{A}$ that is of smallest magnitude. It is based on the fact that eigenvalues of $\mathbf{B} = \mathbf{A}^{-1}$ are the reciprocals of the eigenvalues of $\mathbf{A}$. Therefore, we apply the power method to $\mathbf{B} = \mathbf{A}^{-1}$ to find its dominant eigenvalue, μ. The reciprocal of μ will give the eigenvalue of $\mathbf{A}$ with the smallest magnitude; we denote this eigenvalue as λ. However, it is not desirable to actually compute $\mathbf{A}^{-1}$; instead, at the stage where the power method would compute $\mathbf{A}^{-1}\mathbf{z} = \mathbf{w}$ to find the next approximation to the eigenvector $\mathbf{w}$, we solve the system $\mathbf{A}\mathbf{w} = \mathbf{z}$ for $\mathbf{w}$. This is an example of a situation in which the LU factorization is useful, since we must solve a linear system with the same coefficient matrix, but different right-hand sides, at each stage.

The inverse power method can also be generalized to find the eigenvalue that is closest to a given number. This procedure is discussed in Section 5.2.2.

5.2.1   Basic Inverse Power Method

The computations of the inverse power method are described in the following algorithm. The use of the algorithm is illustrated in Example 5.4 and 5.5.

Inverse Power Method

> *Input*
>> $\mathbf{M}$ *n-by-n matrix*
>> n   *number of rows and columns in M*
>> max   *maximum number of iterations*
>> tol   *tolerance for convergence*
>> $\mathbf{z}$ *n-by-1 vector, all components are 1*
>
> *Begin iterations*
> For i = 1 to max
>> *Solve* $\mathbf{M}\mathbf{w} = \mathbf{z}$ *this corresponds to setting* $\mathbf{w} = \mathbf{M}^{-1}z$
>>
>> $m = \dfrac{\mathbf{z}^{T}\mathbf{z}}{\mathbf{z}^{T}\mathbf{w}}$ *approx. eigenvalue*
>>
>> k = 1
>> b = | w(k) |
>> For j = 2 to n   *find index of dominant component*
>>> If | w(j) | $\geq$ b
>>>> k = j
>>>> b = | w(j) |
>>>
>>> End
>>
>> End
>> m = w(k)   *approx. eigenvalue*
>>
>> $\mathbf{z} = \dfrac{\mathbf{w}}{\mathbf{w}(k)}$ *approx. eigenvector*
>>
>> If $\| \mathbf{M}*\mathbf{z} - m\,\mathbf{z} \| <$ tol, Break   *test for convergence*
> End
> *Return*
>> m   *approximate eigenvalue*
>> $\mathbf{z}$ *approximate eigenvector*

Example 5.4 Inverse Power Method

To find the smallest eigenvalue of a matrix, we apply the inverse power method with initial vector $\mathbf{z} = [1, 1, 1]^T$. The matrix $\mathbf{A}$ and its L U factorization are

$$\mathbf{A} = \begin{bmatrix} 21 & 7 & -1 \\ 5 & 7 & 7 \\ 4 & -4 & 20 \end{bmatrix} = \begin{bmatrix} 1 & 0 & 0 \\ 0.24 & 1 & 0 \\ 0.19 & -1 & 1 \end{bmatrix} \begin{bmatrix} 21 & 7 & -1 \\ 0 & 5.33 & 7.24 \\ 0 & -0 & 27.43 \end{bmatrix}.$$

Step 1: To solve $\mathbf{A}\mathbf{w} = \mathbf{z}$, we use $\mathbf{L}\mathbf{U}\mathbf{w} = \mathbf{z}$ to first find $\mathbf{y}$ such that $\mathbf{L}\mathbf{y} = \mathbf{z}$, and then solve $\mathbf{U}\mathbf{w} = \mathbf{y}$ to find $\mathbf{w}.$ This gives $\mathbf{w} = [0.0286, 0.0651, 0.0573]^T$. Since the largest component of $\mathbf{w}$ is w_2, the largest eigenvalue of $\mathbf{A}^{-1}$ is approximated by $\mu = \dfrac{w_2}{z_2} = 0.0651.$

The estimate of the smallest eigenvalue of $\mathbf{A}$ is $\lambda = 1/\mu = \dfrac{z_2}{w_2} = 15.3610$, and

$$\mathbf{z} = \frac{\mathbf{w}}{w_2} = [0.4400, 1.0000, 0.8800]^T.$$

Step 2: Solve $A\mathbf{w} = \mathbf{z} \implies \mathbf{w} = [-0.0042, 0.0842, 0.0617]^T$.
Since the largest component of $\mathbf{w}$ is w_2, we have

$$\mu = \frac{w_2}{z_2} = 0.0842, \quad \lambda = 1/\mu = \frac{z_2}{w_2} = 11.8777,$$

$$\mathbf{z} = \frac{\mathbf{w}}{w_2} = [-0.0495, 0.9997, 0.7324]^T.$$

The results for the first 10 iterations are summarized in the following table.

step	lambda	z(1)	z(2)	z(3)
1	15.3600	0.4400	1.0000	0.8800
2	11.8812	−0.0495	1.0000	0.7327
3	9.7154	−0.3267	1.0000	0.6212
4	8.7003	−0.4421	1.0000	0.5587
5	8.2823	−0.4825	1.0000	0.5279
6	8.1161	−0.4954	1.0000	0.5133
7	8.0493	−0.4991	1.0000	0.5064
8	8.0217	−0.5000	1.0000	0.5031
9	8.0098	−0.5002	1.0000	0.5015
10	8.0046	−0.5001	1.0000	0.5008

As indicated in Example 5.1, the eigenvalues of $\mathbf{A}$ are 24, 8, and 16.

The next example illustrates the results of using the inverse power method for the application introduced in Example 5-B.

Example 5.5 Eigenvalues for a Buckling Beam

The buckling and subsequent breaking of a simply supported beam is approximated by the smallest eigenvalue of the n-by-n matrix

$$
\mathbf{A} = (n + 1)^2
\begin{bmatrix}
2 & -1 & & & & \\
-1 & 2 & -1 & & & \\
 & -1 & 2 & -1 & & \\
 & & \cdot & \cdot & \cdot & \\
 & & & -1 & 2 & -1 \\
 & & & & -1 & 2
\end{bmatrix}.
$$

A better approximation is obtained for larger values of n. The smallest eigenvalue gives the first buckling mode (i.e., the value of the applied load that causes buckling to occur). As mentioned in Example 5-B, the smallest eigenvalue of the differential equation for which this matrix is the discrete approximation is π^2. To four decimal places, $\pi^2 = 9.8696$.

The results (to four decimal places) for several values of n are summarized in the following table.

n	first buckling mode	
	5 iterations	**10 iterations**
6	9.7045	9.7051
8	9.7693	9.7698
10	9.8022	9.8027
12	9.8212	9.8217
16	9.8411	9.8415
20	9.8508	9.8512

5.2.2 General Inverse Power Method

The ideas of the shifted power method and the simple inverse power method can be combined to enable us to find the eigenvalue of a matrix $\mathbf{A}$ that is closest to a given number b. This method is based on the fact that if the eigenvalues of a matrix $\mathbf{C}$ are $\lambda_1, \ldots, \lambda_n$, then the eigenvalues of $\mathbf{D} = \mathbf{C} - b\mathbf{I}$ are $\lambda_1 - b, \ldots, \lambda_n - b$. Furthermore, the eigenvalues of $\mathbf{D}^{-1}$ are $\dfrac{1}{\lambda_1 - b}, \ldots, \dfrac{1}{\lambda_n - b} = \mu_1, \ldots, \mu_n$. So μ_1, the dominant eigenvalue of $\mathbf{D}^{-1}$, corresponds to the eigenvalue of $\mathbf{C}$ that is closest to b, according to the relation $\mu_1 = \dfrac{1}{\lambda_1 - b}$. We illustrate the method in the next example. We do not include a separate algorithm, since the method is simply the inverse power method applied to a shifted matrix.

Example 5.6 Finding the Eigenvalue Closest to a Given Number

Let

$$\mathbf{A} = \begin{bmatrix} 21 & 7 & -1 \\ 5 & 7 & 7 \\ 4 & -4 & 20 \end{bmatrix}, \text{ and } \mathbf{B} = \mathbf{A} - 15\,\mathbf{I} = \begin{bmatrix} 6 & 7 & -1 \\ 5 & -8 & 7 \\ 4 & -4 & 5 \end{bmatrix}.$$

To find the eigenvalue of $\mathbf{A}$ that is closest to $b = 15$ by applying the inverse power method to $\mathbf{B} = \mathbf{A} - 15\,\mathbf{I}$, we start with $\mathbf{z} = [1, 1, 1]^T$.

Step 1: Solve $\mathbf{B}\,\mathbf{w} = \mathbf{z} \Rightarrow \mathbf{w} = [0.0317, 0.1587, 0.3016]^T$;

estimate of largest eigenvalue of $\mathbf{B}^{-1}$: $\mu = \dfrac{w_3}{z_3} = 0.3016$;

estimate of smallest eigenvalue of $\mathbf{B}$: $1/\mu = \dfrac{z_3}{w_3} = 3.3158$;

$$\mathbf{z} = \frac{\mathbf{w}}{w_3} = [0.1053, 0.5263, 1.000]^T.$$

Step 2: Solve $B\,\mathbf{w} = \mathbf{z} \Rightarrow \mathbf{w} = [0.3718, 0.4570, 0.8630]^T$;

estimate of largest eigenvalue of $\mathbf{B}^{-1}$: $\mu = \dfrac{w_3}{z_3} = 0.8630$;

estimate of smallest eigenvalue of $\mathbf{B}$: $1/\mu - \dfrac{z_3}{w_3} = 1.1588$;

$$\mathbf{z} = \frac{\mathbf{w}}{w_3} = [-0.4308, 0.5295, 1.0000]^T.$$

Step 3: Solve $B\,\mathbf{w} = \mathbf{z} \Rightarrow \mathbf{w} = [-0.4723, 0.4808, 0.9624]^T$;

estimate of smallest eigenvalue of $\mathbf{B}$: $1/\mu = \dfrac{z_3}{w_3} = 1.0390$.

The estimate of the desired eigenvalue of $\mathbf{A}$ is $b + 1/\mu$, where μ is the estimated largest eigenvalue of $\mathbf{B}^{-1}$ and $1/\mu$ is the estimated smallest eigenvalue of $\mathbf{B}$. Thus, the estimated eigenvalue of $\mathbf{A}$ that is closest to 15 is approximately 16.

To find the eigenvalues of a real matrix $\mathbf{A}$ using QR factorization, we generate a sequence of matrices $\mathbf{A}^{(m)}$ that are orthogonally similar to $\mathbf{A}$ (and thus have the same eigenvalues as $\mathbf{A}$). A similarity transformation is a transformation of the form $\mathbf{H}^{-1}\mathbf{A}\mathbf{H}$, where $\mathbf{H}$ is any nonsingular matrix. The sequence $\mathbf{A}^{(m)}$ converges to a matrix from which the eigenvalues can be found easily. If the eigenvalues of $\mathbf{A}$ satisfy $|\lambda_1| > |\lambda_2| > \ldots > |\lambda_n|$, the iterates converge to an upper triangular matrix with the eigenvalues on the diagonal.

We first consider the basic QR-eigenvalue algorithm. However, since the QR-eigenvalue method involves a sequence of factorizations, we conclude this section with a more efficient QR factorization method for finding eigenvalues. This better QR-eigenvalue algorithm is based on a preliminary transformation of $\mathbf{A}$ into Hessenberg form, that is, upper triangular, except for the first subdiagonal. The QR factorization of a matrix that is in Hessenberg form is computationally more efficient, since there is only one element that must be transformed to zero in each column. Furthermore, the upper Hessenberg form is preserved through the iterations of the algorithm. The QR factorization in this case is usually based on Givens rotations.

5.3.1 Basic QR Eigenvalue Method

The following algorithm describes the basic procedure for finding eigenvalues using QR factorization. The matrices formed at each iteration are indicated by superscripts. If $\mathbf{A}$ has n distinct real eigenvalues, the method will converge to a matrix $\mathbf{A}$ that is upper triangular matrix with the eigenvalues on the diagonal. In other cases, the final result may contain small blocks on the diagonal.

Basic QR Method for Finding Eigenvalues ══════════════════════════

Input
    $\mathbf{A}$ *a real n-by-n matrix*
Initialize
$\mathbf{A}^{(0)} = \mathbf{A}$
For k = 1 to k_max,
    Factor $\mathbf{A}^{(k-1)} = \mathbf{Q}^{(k)} \mathbf{R}^{(k)}$ $\mathbf{Q}^{(k)T} \mathbf{A}^{(k-1)} = \mathbf{R}^{(k)}$
    Define $\mathbf{A}^{(k)} = \mathbf{R}^{(k)} \mathbf{Q}^{(k)}$ $\mathbf{A}^{(k)} = \mathbf{Q}^{(k)T} \mathbf{A}^{(k)} \mathbf{Q}^{(k)}$
    For j = 1 to n − 1
        t(j) = max(abs($\mathbf{A}^{(k)}$ (j+1:n, j)))   *find max of each column*
                                                         (below diagonal)

    End
    t = max(abs(t))   *find max of column max*
    If t < 0.001 Break
End
Return
    $\mathbf{A}$ *upper triangular matrix, eigenvalues on diagonal*

Example 5.7 Finding Eigenvalues Using Basic QR Method

Consider again the problem of finding the eigenvalues of the matrix

$$\mathbf{A} = \begin{bmatrix} 21 & 7 & -1 \\ 5 & 7 & 7 \\ 4 & -4 & 2 \end{bmatrix},$$

which was introduced in Example 5.1, and explored further in Examples 5.4 and 5.6.

For the first iteration, the matrices $\mathbf{Q}$ and $\mathbf{R}$ are

$$\mathbf{Q} = \begin{bmatrix} -0.9565 & 0.0308 & -0.2900 \\ -0.2277 & -0.7001 & 0.6767 \\ -0.1822 & 0.7133 & 0.6767 \end{bmatrix} \quad \mathbf{R} = \begin{bmatrix} -21.9545 & -7.5611 & -4.2816 \\ -0.0000 & -7.5386 & 9.3351 \\ -0.0000 & 0.0000 & 18.5613 \end{bmatrix}$$

The matrix $\mathbf{A}$ is transformed to $\mathbf{A}^{(1)} = \mathbf{Q}^{(1)} \mathbf{R}^{(1)}$, so now

$$\mathbf{A} = \begin{bmatrix} 23.5021 & 1.5628 & -1.6469 \\ 0.0160 & 11.9372 & 1.2158 \\ -3.3818 & 13.2406 & 12.5607 \end{bmatrix}$$

We summarize the results by showing the transformed matrix $\mathbf{A}$ after 5, 10, 15, and 20 iterations. In practice there is no need to save the intermediate values of the matrices.

$$\mathbf{A}^{(5)} = \begin{bmatrix} 24.0461 & 0.9082 & 2.3198 \\ -0.3683 & 16.3816 & -11.6469 \\ -0.0257 & 0.3059 & 7.5723 \end{bmatrix} \quad \mathbf{A}^{(10)} = \begin{bmatrix} 24.0075 & 1.3035 & -2.7630 \\ -0.0458 & 16.0055 & 11.8464 \\ 0.0001 & -0.0088 & 7.9870 \end{bmatrix}$$

$$\mathbf{A}^{(15)} = \begin{bmatrix} 24.0010 & 1.3461 & 2.8204 \\ -0.0060 & 15.9994 & -11.8410 \\ -0.0000 & 0.0003 & 7.9996 \end{bmatrix} \quad \mathbf{A}^{(20)} = \begin{bmatrix} 24.0001 & 1.3515 & -2.8281 \\ -0.0008 & 15.9999 & 11.8395 \\ 0.0000 & -0.0000 & 8.0000 \end{bmatrix}$$

The QR method converged in 20 iterations, based on the criteria that the maximum of the absolute values of the subdiagonal elements of $\mathbf{A}$ be less than 0.001. The components of the vector $\mathbf{t}$ are the maximum of these values found at each iteration. As such, it gives an indication of the progress of the computations at each stage.

$$\begin{aligned} t = [13.2406 \quad & 5.3319 \quad 1.6978 \quad 0.6790 \quad 0.3683 \quad \ldots \\ & 0.2389 \quad 0.1568 \quad 0.1037 \quad 0.0688 \quad 0.0458 \quad \ldots \\ & 0.0305 \quad 0.0203 \quad 0.0135 \quad 0.0090 \quad 0.0060 \quad \ldots \\ & 0.0040 \quad 0.0027 \quad 0.0018 \quad 0.0012 \quad 0.0008] \end{aligned}$$

Example 5.8 Eigenvalues of a Non-symmetric Matrix Using Basic QR Method

We now investigate the eigenvalues of matrix $\mathbf{A}$ using the basic QR method.

$$\mathbf{A} = \begin{bmatrix} 11 & -26 & 3 & -12 \\ 3 & -12 & 3 & -6 \\ 31 & -99 & 15 & -44 \\ 9 & -10 & -3 & -4 \end{bmatrix}$$

The basic QR method converges in 22 iterations, based on the criteria that max(abs of subdiagonal elements) < 0.01. We summarize the results after 1, 5, 10, 15, 20, and 22 iterations.

$$\mathbf{A}^{(1)} = \begin{bmatrix} 2.8831 & 15.9684 & 10.7760 & 115.6638 \\ 2.5572 & 7.2316 & 8.1990 & 19.7750 \\ -0.9411 & -1.1453 & -0.0363 & -0.2867 \\ 0.0666 & -0.2168 & 0.0810 & -0.0784 \end{bmatrix}$$

$$\mathbf{A}^{(5)} = \begin{bmatrix} 8.7481 & 12.5340 & 27.8734 & 108.0829 \\ 0.2821 & -3.6037 & -2.5202 & -39.2580 \\ -0.0108 & 0.2004 & 2.9632 & 3.3934 \\ 0.0005 & -0.0300 & 0.0297 & 1.8924 \end{bmatrix}$$

$$\mathbf{A}^{(10)} = \begin{bmatrix} 9.0046 & 11.7358 & 33.1227 & -105.6830 \\ -0.0049 & -3.9874 & -5.3253 & 41.6113 \\ -0.0000 & -0.0322 & 22.9601 & -1.8888 \\ -0.0000 & -0.0011 & -0.0081 & 2.0228 \end{bmatrix}$$

$$\mathbf{A}^{(15)} = \begin{bmatrix} 8.9999 & 11.9093 & 33.7143 & 105.4936 \\ 0.0001 & -4.0053 & -5.5313 & -41.5267 \\ -0.0000 & 0.0071 & 3.0036 & 2.1194 \\ 0.0000 & -0.0000 & 0.0010 & 2.0018 \end{bmatrix}$$

$$\mathbf{A}^{(20)} = \begin{bmatrix} 9.0000 & 11.8675 & 33.8194 & -105.4643 \\ -0.0000 & -3.9987 & -5.5759 & 41.5252 \\ -0.0000 & -0.0017 & 2.9984 & -2.0664 \\ -0.0000 & -0.0000 & -0.0001 & 2.0003 \end{bmatrix}$$

$$\mathbf{A}^{(22)} = \begin{bmatrix} 9.0000 & 11.8710 & 33.8258 & -105.4619 \\ -0.0000 & -3.9993 & -5.5781 & 41.5246 \\ -0.0000 & -0.0009 & 2.9991 & -2.0706 \\ -0.0000 & -0.0000 & -0.0001 & 2.0001 \end{bmatrix}$$

The vector of the maximal subdiagonal element at each iteration is

$t = [2.5572 \quad 4.3537 \quad 1.2779 \quad 0.6743 \quad 0.2821 \quad 0.1414 \quad 0.0916 \quad 0.0636 \ldots$

$\quad 0.0451 \quad 0.0322 \quad 0.0236 \quad 0.0173 \quad 0.0128 \quad 0.0095 \quad 0.0071 \quad 0.0053 \ldots$

$\quad 0.0040 \quad 0.0030 \quad 0.0022 \quad 0.0017 \quad 0.0013 \quad 0.0009]$

Example 5.9 Eigenvalues of a Symmetric Matrix Using Basic QR Method

We now find the eigenvalues of the symmetric matrix **A**:

$$\mathbf{A} = \begin{bmatrix} 2.4400 & 0.6400 & -0.0800 & -0.4800 \\ 0.6400 & 1.8400 & -0.4800 & -0.8800 \\ -0.0800 & -0.4800 & 2.5600 & -0.6400 \\ -0.4800 & -0.8800 & -0.6400 & 3.1600 \end{bmatrix}$$

The QR method converges in 25 iterations, based on the criteria that the max(abs of subdiagonal elements) < 0.01. The total flops required is 19,825 (using a simple MATLAB program to implement the algorithm).

$$\mathbf{A}^{(1)} = \begin{bmatrix} 2.9879 & 0.7686 & 0.2575 & 0.3779 \\ 0.7686 & 2.2882 & 0.0211 & 0.7264 \\ 0.2575 & 0.0211 & 3.0330 & 0.7492 \\ 0.3779 & 0.7264 & 0.7492 & 1.6909 \end{bmatrix}$$

$$\mathbf{A}^{(5)} = \begin{bmatrix} 3.9395 & 0.1179 & 0.2242 & 0.0028 \\ 0.1179 & 2.0062 & 0.0136 & 0.0314 \\ 0.2242 & 0.0136 & 3.0533 & 0.0054 \\ 0.0028 & 0.0314 & 0.0054 & 1.0010 \end{bmatrix}$$

$$\mathbf{A}^{(10)} = \begin{bmatrix} 3.9968 & 0.0039 & 0.0561 & -0.0000 \\ 0.0039 & 2.0000 & 0.0001 & -0.0010 \\ 0.0561 & 0.0001 & 3.0032 & -0.0000 \\ -0.0000 & -0.0010 & -0.0000 & 1.0000 \end{bmatrix}$$

$$\mathbf{A}^{(15)} = \begin{bmatrix} 3.9998 & 0.0001 & 0.0134 & 0.0000 \\ 0.0001 & 2.0000 & 0.0000 & 0.0000 \\ 0.0134 & 0.0000 & 3.0002 & 0.0000 \\ 0.0000 & 0.0000 & 0.0000 & 1.0000 \end{bmatrix}$$

$$\mathbf{A}^{(20)} = \begin{bmatrix} 4.0000 & 0.0000 & 0.0032 & -0.0000 \\ 0.0000 & 2.0000 & 0.0000 & -0.0000 \\ 0.0032 & 0.0000 & 3.0000 & -0.0000 \\ -0.0000 & -0.0000 & -0.0000 & 1.0000 \end{bmatrix}$$

$$\mathbf{A}^{(25)} = \begin{bmatrix} 4.0000 & 0.0000 & 0.0008 & 0.0000 \\ 0.0000 & 2.0000 & 0.0000 & 0.0000 \\ 0.0008 & 0.0000 & 3.0000 & 0.0000 \\ 0.0000 & 0.0000 & 0.0000 & 1.0000 \end{bmatrix}$$

The vector of the maximal subdiagonal element at each iteration is

$t = [0.7686 \quad 0.6389 \quad 0.4036 \quad 0.2855 \quad 0.2242 \quad 0.1724 \quad 0.1311 \quad 0.0991 \ldots$
$\quad 0.0747 \quad 0.0561 \quad 0.0422 \quad 0.0316 \quad 0.0237 \quad 0.0178 \quad 0.0134 \quad 0.0100 \ldots$
$\quad 0.0075 \quad 0.0056 \quad 0.0042 \quad 0.0032 \quad 0.0024 \quad 0.0018 \quad 0.0013 \quad 0.0010 \ldots$
$\quad 0.0008]$

5.3.2 Better QR Eigenvalue Method

As mentioned in the previous section, in employing QR factorizations to find the eigenvalues of matrix **A,** it is preferable to first use a similarity transformation to convert **A** to Hessenberg form. As described earlier, the required computations can be performed more efficiently without explicitly forming the Householder matrices. The sequence of iterates (matrix A at each stage) converges to an upper triangular matrix with the eigenvalues on the diagonal. The algorithm for a similarity transformation of **A** to Hessenberg form is given in section 4.4.2.

QR Method for Eigenvalues of a Hessenberg Matrix

Input
    A   *similarity transformed to Hessenberg form*
    n   *number of rows or columns in A*
    k_max   *maximum number of iterations*
    tol   *tolerance for convergence*
Begin iterations
For i = 1 to k_max
    Q = I
    R = A
    For k = 1 to n-1
        $x1 = R(k, k)$
        $x2 = R(k + 1, k)$
        $c = x1/\sqrt{x1^2 + x2^2}$
        $s = -x2/\sqrt{x1^2 + x2^2}$
        Rn = R
        Qn = Q
        For j = 1 to n
            $Rn(k, j) = c*R*k, j) - s*R(k + 1, j)$
            $Rn(k + 1, j) = a*R(k, j) + c*R(k + 1, j)$
            $Qn(j, k) = c*Q(j, k) - s*Q*j, k + 1)$
            $Qn(j, k + 1) = s*Q(j, k) + c*Q(j, k + 1)$
        End
        R = Rn
        Q = Qn
    End
    A = R*Q
    For k = 1 to n-1 *test for convergence*
        $t(k) = \max(abs(A(k + 1{:}n, k)))$
    End
    $t = \max(abs(t))$
    tt(i) = t;
    If t < 0.001 Break
End
Return
    A   *upper triangular matrix with eigenvalues on diagonal*

Example 5.10 Finding Eigenvalues Using the Better QR Method

We illustrate the use of the better QR method to find the eigenvalues of the matrix **A**, which was introduced in Example 4.12. The similarity transformation applied in that example produces the Hessenberg matrix **B** given here. The algorithm for the better QR method is applied to matrix **B**.

$$
\mathbf{A} = \begin{bmatrix} 11 & -26 & 3 & -12 \\ 3 & -12 & 3 & -6 \\ 31 & -99 & 15 & -44 \\ 9 & -10 & -3 & -4 \end{bmatrix} \quad \mathbf{B} = \begin{bmatrix} 11.0000 & 2.8687 & 4.2341 & -28.3345 \\ -32.4191 & -8.0780 & -15.0141 & 107.3558 \\ -0.0000 & -2.8757 & 4.4607 & -20.6163 \\ -0.0000 & 0.0000 & 0.0814 & 2.6174 \end{bmatrix}
$$

We summarize the results by showing the transformed matrix **A** after 1, 7, and 13 iterations.

$$
\mathbf{A}^{(1)} = \begin{bmatrix} 2.8831 & -14.0862 & -49.7699 & 105.2320 \\ -2.7257 & 4.5259 & 1.9662 & -20.8405 \\ -0.0000 & -0.6311 & -0.8504 & 6.3390 \\ 0.0000 & 0.0000 & -0.4471 & 3.4414 \end{bmatrix}
$$

$$
\mathbf{A}^{(7)} = \begin{bmatrix} 8.9498 & -11.6727 & -46.9599 & -100.5349 \\ -0.0566 & -3.8861 & -10.5988 & -40.0570 \\ -0.0000 & -0.0381 & 3.1859 & 1.7037 \\ -0.0000 & 0.0000 & -0.1595 & 1.7505 \end{bmatrix}
$$

$$
\mathbf{A}^{(13)} = \begin{bmatrix} 8.9996 & -11.8338 & -34.7927 & -105.1526 \\ -0.0004 & -3.9923 & -5.9604 & -41.4710 \\ -0.0000 & -0.0085 & 3.0114 & 2.0710 \\ -0.0000 & 0.0000 & -0.0092 & 1.9813 \end{bmatrix}
$$

The better QR method converged in 13 iterations, based on the criteria that the maximum of the absolute values of the subdiagonal elements of **A** be less than 0.01. The components of the vector **t** are the maximum of these values found at each iteration. As such, it gives an indication of the progress of the computations at each stage.

$$
t = [2.7257 \quad 4.4100 \quad 2.0989 \quad 1.6194 \quad 0.6926 \quad 0.3020 \quad 0.1595 \quad \ldots
$$
$$
0.0896 \quad 0.0544 \quad 0.0338 \quad 0.0217 \quad 0.0140 \quad 0.0092]
$$

The basic QR method applied to this matrix (in Example 5.8) converged in 22 iterations. Not only does the better method take fewer iterations, but each iteration is also less computationally intensive. The effort involved in performing the initial similarity transformation to Hessenberg form is quite small in comparison to the savings in computational effort during the iterations.

Example 5.11 Finding Eigenvalues of a Symmetric Matrix

We consider again the problem of finding the eigenvalues of the symmetric matrix $\mathbf{A}$, introduced in Example 5.9.

$$\mathbf{A} = \begin{bmatrix} 2.4400 & 0.6400 & -0.0800 & -0.4800 \\ 0.6400 & 1.8400 & -0.4800 & -0.8800 \\ -0.0800 & -0.4800 & 2.5600 & -0.6400 \\ -0.4800 & -0.8800 & -0.6400 & 3.1600 \end{bmatrix}$$

After applying a similarity transformation to Hessenberg form, we have

$$\mathbf{A} = \begin{bmatrix} 2.4400 & -0.8040 & 0.0000 & 0.0000 \\ -0.8040 & 3.1541 & 0.7982 & -0.0000 \\ 0.0000 & 0.7982 & 1.9752 & -0.9277 \\ 0.0000 & -0.0000 & -0.9277 & 2.4308 \end{bmatrix}$$

We summarize the results after 1, 5, 10, 15, and 17 iterations. The better QR method converges in 17 iterations, based on the criteria that the max(abs of subdiagonal elements) < 0.01. The total flops required is 7,407, which includes the 913 flops required to convert the original matrix $\mathbf{A}$ to Hessenberg form.

$$\mathbf{A}^{(1)} = \begin{bmatrix} 2.9879 & -0.8943 & -0.0000 & 0.0000 \\ -0.8943 & 2.9636 & -0.5372 & -0.0000 \\ 0.0000 & 0.5372 & 2.5596 & -0.8198 \\ 0.0000 & -0.0000 & -0.8198 & 1.4889 \end{bmatrix}$$

$$\mathbf{A}^{(5)} = \begin{bmatrix} 3.9395 & -0.2534 & -0.0000 & -0.0000 \\ -0.2534 & 2.8378 & 0.4234 & -0.0000 \\ -0.0000 & 0.4234 & 2.2221 & -0.0265 \\ 0.0000 & -0.0000 & -0.0265 & 1.0006 \end{bmatrix}$$

$$\mathbf{A}^{(10)} = \begin{bmatrix} 3.9968 & -0.0563 & -0.0000 & -0.0000 \\ -0.0563 & 2.9984 & 0.0691 & -0.0000 \\ -0.0000 & 0.0691 & 2.0048 & -0.0007 \\ 0.0000 & -0.0000 & -0.0007 & 1.0000 \end{bmatrix}$$

$$\mathbf{A}^{(15)} = \begin{bmatrix} 3.9998 & -0.0134 & -0.0000 & -0.0000 \\ -0.0134 & 3.0001 & 0.0091 & -0.0000 \\ -0.0000 & 0.0091 & 2.0001 & -0.0000 \\ 0.0000 & 0.0000 & -0.0000 & 1.0000 \end{bmatrix}$$

$$\mathbf{A}^{(17)} = \begin{bmatrix} 3.9999 & -0.0075 & -0.0000 & -0.0000 \\ -0.0075 & 3.0000 & 0.0041 & -0.0000 \\ -0.0000 & 0.0041 & 2.0000 & -0.0000 \\ 0.0000 & 0.0000 & -0.0000 & 1.0000 \end{bmatrix}$$

max(absolute value of subdiagonal elements) for each iteration

$$t = [0.8943 \quad 0.7565 \quad 0.5375 \quad 0.5095 \quad 0.4234 \quad 0.3174 \quad 0.2239 \quad \ldots$$
$$0.1531 \quad 0.1032 \quad 0.0691 \quad 0.0462 \quad 0.0317 \quad 0.0237 \quad 0.0178 \quad \ldots$$
$$0.0134 \quad 0.0100 \quad 0.0075]$$

5.3.3   Discussion

Especially for a general matrix, which may have real or complex eigenvalues, setting good termination conditions is not an easy task. If the matrix has distinct, real eigenvalues, then the QR eigenvalue method will converge to an upper triangular matrix with the eigenvalues of the original matrix on the diagonal. In other cases the final form may have one or more 2-by-2 blocks on the diagonal. The eigenvalues of these submatrices are also eigenvalues of the original matrix. It is suggested (Press et al., p. 490) that the process terminate in the following manner

1. if $a_{n,n-1}$ is "negligible," then $a_{n,n}$ is an eigenvalue (delete n^{th} row, n^{th} col and continue)
2. if $a_{n-1,n-2}$ is "negligible," then the eigenvalues of the 2-by-2 submatrix in lower right corner are eigenvalues (delete n^{th} and $(n-1)^{st}$ rows and columns and continue).

For a proof of the fundamental theorem that sequence of iterates of QR method converges to an upper (or lower) triangular form with eigenvalues on the diagonal, see Stoer and Bulirsch, 1980.

5.4   METHODS OF MODERN COMPUTNG

Software packages such as MATLAB, Mathcad, and *Mathematica* have built-in functions to find eigenvalues and eigenvectors. Often there are different forms of the functions, depending on the information desired. For instance, there may be a different function, or a different form of calling the function, depending on whether one needs all eigenvalues of the matrix, or only the eigenvalue corresponding to a given eigenvector, or all eigenvalues and their corresponding eigenvectors. In some cases generalized eigenvectors may also be available (see Strang, 1988, for discussion of generalized eigenvectors).

These packages vary in the level of information that is readily available to the user about the methods implemented in the functions. In general, the methods are somewhat more general and robust forms of the basic approaches presented in this chapter. To illustrate the types of options that are often included in professionally developed software, we summarize the eigen-system functions from the NIST Index, MATLAB, Mathcad, and *Mathematica*.

5.4.1   Software in the NIST Index

The *NIST Guide to Available Software* (http://gams.nist.gov) lists software for finding eigenvalues and eigenvectors according to three subcategories of problems: ordinary eigenvalue problems, generalized eigenvalue problems, and associated problems. Software for ordinary eigenvalue problems is then listed according to whether the matrix is real symmetric, real nonsymmetric, complex Hermitian, complex non-Hermitian, tridiagonal, banded, or sparse.

5.4.2 MATLAB's Functions

MATLAB's built-in function for finding eigenvalues and eigenvectors is "eig". It can be called in several different ways, depending on the information desired. Using a single square matrix **A** as input, `eig(A)` returns a vector containing the eigenvalues of **A**. Alternatively, the output vector may be named, as in `m = eig(A)`. Using a single matrix as input and specifying two output variables, as in `[Z, D] = eig(A)` returns a matrix **Z** whose columns are the eigenvectors of **A**, and a diagonal matrix **D** with the eigenvalues of **A** on the diagonal. The matrices satisfy **A Z = Z D**. The eigenvectors are scaled to unit Euclidean length. Using two square matrices **A** and **B** as input, `eig(A, B)` returns a vector containing the generalized eigenvalues of **A** and **B**. Using two matrices as input and specifying two output variables, as in `[Z, D] = eig(A, B)` returns the generalized eigenvalues and corresponding eigenvectors such that **A Z = B Z D**.

5.4.3 Mathcad's Functions

Mathcad's function `eigenvals(M)` accepts as input a real or complex square matrix. The return from the function is a vector containing the eigenvalues of **M**.

The function `eigenvec(M,  z)` returns the normalized eigenvector associated with the eigenvalue z of the square matrix **M**. The matrix **M** is a real or complex square matrix; the eigenvalue may be real or complex.

Mathcad2000Pro has an additional function for finding all of the eigenvectors of a real or complex square matrix **M**. The function `eigenvecs(M)` returns a matrix whose columns contain the normalized eigenvectors corresponding to the eigenvalues returned by `eigenvals(M)`.

5.4.4 *Mathematica*'s Functions

Mathematica's built-in functions, `Eigenvalues[M]`, `Eigenvectors[M]`, and `Eigensystem[M]`, return lists of the {eigenvalues}, {eigenvectors}, and {eigenvalues, eigenvectors} respectively for matrix **M**. If the components of **M** are approximate real numbers, *Mathematica* will find the approximate numerical values for the eigenvalues and eigenvectors. For small matrices with exact (symbolic) entries, *Mathematica*'s functions will give the exact results of solving the characteristic equation for the matrix.

The function `Eigenvalues` returns a list of n eigenvalues for an n-by-n matrix; these values are not necessarily distinct. The function `Eigenvectors` returns a list of linearly independent eigenvectors; there may be fewer than n such eigenvectors.

Basic Power Method

This method finds the dominant (largest magnitude) eigenvalue of matrix $\mathbf{A}$:

$$\mathbf{z}^{(1)} = \begin{bmatrix} 1 & 1 & 1 & \ldots & 1 \end{bmatrix}^T$$

$$\mathbf{w}^{(1)} = \mathbf{A}\,\mathbf{z}^{(1)}; \mathbf{z}^{(2)} = \frac{1}{w^{(1)}_k}\,\mathbf{w}^{(1)},$$

$w^{(1)}_k$ is the component of $\mathbf{w}$ that is of largest magnitude;

$w^{(1)}_k$ is the first estimate of the dominant eigenvalue.

$\mathbf{z}^{(2)}$ is the corresponding (estimate of the) eigenvector.

$$\mathbf{w}^{(2)} = \mathbf{A}\,\mathbf{z}^{(2)}; \mathbf{z}^{(3)} = \frac{1}{w^{(2)}_k}\,\mathbf{w}^{(2)}.$$

Continue until the estimates have converged.

Accelerated Power Method

The Rayleigh quotient gives an improved estimate of the eigenvalue, especially for symmetric matrices.

$$\lambda = (\mathbf{z}^T\mathbf{w})/(\mathbf{z}^T\mathbf{z}).$$

Inverse Power Method

This method finds the eigenvalue of $\mathbf{A}$ that is of smallest magnitude.
Apply the power method to $\mathbf{B} = \mathbf{A}^{-1}$ to find its dominant eigenvalue, μ.
The reciprocal of μ gives the smallest magnitude eigenvalue λ of $\mathbf{A}$.
To avoid computing $\mathbf{A}^{-1}$; instead of finding $\mathbf{A}^{-1}\mathbf{z} = \mathbf{w}$
we solve the system $\mathbf{A}\mathbf{w} = \mathbf{z}$ for $\mathbf{w}$.

Shifted Inverse Power Method

Applying the inverse power method to a shifted matrix, $\mathbf{A} - b\,\mathbf{I}$, finds the eigenvalue closest to b.

QR Method for Eigenvalues

If $\mathbf{A}$ is a real matrix with simple eigenvalues, then the following sequence of similarity transformations of matrix $\mathbf{A}$ converges to a right-triangular matrix $\mathbf{R}$. The eigenvalues of $\mathbf{R}$ are on its diagonal, and are the same as the eigenvalues of $\mathbf{A}$.
Define $\mathbf{A}^{(1)} = \mathbf{A}$
For $k = 1$ to k_max,
    Factor $\mathbf{A}^{(k)} = \mathbf{Q}^{(k)}\mathbf{R}^{(k)}$
    Define $\mathbf{A}^{(k+1)} = \mathbf{R}^{(k)}\mathbf{Q}^{(k)}$
End

The following are a few of the many excellent undergraduate texts on linear algebra:

Kolman, B. *Introductory Linear Algebra with Applications* 6th ed. Prentice Hall, Upper Saddle River, NJ, 1997.

Leon, S. J. *Linear Algebra with Applications*, 5th ed. Prentice Hall, Upper Saddle River, NJ, 1998.

Strang, G. *Linear Algebra and Its Applications*, 3rd ed. Harcourt Brace Jovanovich, San Diego, CA, 1988.

Some references at a somewhat more advanced level include:

Golub, G. H., and C. F. Van Loan. *Matrix Computations*, 3rd ed. Johns Hopkins University Press, Baltimore, 1996.

Fox, L. *An Introduction to Numerical Linear Algebra.* Oxford University Press, New York, 1965. This classic work also contains many bibliographic entries.

Stoer, J., and R. Bulirsch *Introduction to Numerical Analysis.* Springer-Verlag, New York, 1980.

Wilkinson, J. H. and C. Reinsch. *Linear Algebra*, vol. II of *Handbook for Automatic Computation.* Springer-Verlag, New York, 1971.

For further discussion of the application of eigenvalues, see:

Thomson, W. T. *Introduction to Space Dynamics.* Dover, New York, 1986. (Originally published by Wiley & Sons, 1961.)

Greenberg, M. D. *Foundations of Applied Mathematics*, 2d ed. Prentice Hall, Englewood Cliffs, NJ, 1998.

For Problems P5.1 to P5.20 use the power method to find the specified eigenvalue, and a corresponding eigenvector, of the given matrix.

a.   *Use the basic power method to find the dominant eigenvalue.*

b.   *Use the inverse power method to find the eigenvalue of smallest magnitude.*

c.   *Use the shifted power method to find the eigenvalue that is closest to the average of the values found in parts a and b.*

P5.1 $A = \begin{bmatrix} 1 & 0 & 0 \\ 2 & -1 & 2 \\ 4 & -4 & 5 \end{bmatrix}$

P5.2 $A = \begin{bmatrix} -2 & 2 & -1 \\ -2 & 2 & 0 \\ 2 & -2 & 3 \end{bmatrix}$

P5.3 $A = \begin{bmatrix} 5 & -2 & 1 \\ 3 & 0 & 1 \\ 0 & 0 & 2 \end{bmatrix}$

P5.4 $A = \begin{bmatrix} 2 & 2 & -1 \\ -5 & 9 & -3 \\ -4 & 4 & 1 \end{bmatrix}$

P5.5 $A = \begin{bmatrix} -19 & 20 & -6 \\ -12 & 13 & -3 \\ 30 & -30 & 12 \end{bmatrix}$

P5.6 $A = \begin{bmatrix} 25 & -26 & 8 \\ 15 & -16 & 4 \\ -39 & 39 & -15 \end{bmatrix}$

P5.7 $A = \begin{bmatrix} 36 & 10 & -5 \\ -172 & 47 & -22 \\ -16 & 4 & 1 \end{bmatrix}$

P5.8 $A = \begin{bmatrix} 2 & 0 & 0 \\ -180 & 47 & -15 \\ -600 & 150 & -48 \end{bmatrix}$

P5.9 $A = \begin{bmatrix} 104 & -34 & 8 \\ 357 & -117 & 28 \\ 204 & -68 & 18 \end{bmatrix}$

P5.10 $A = \begin{bmatrix} 66 & -21 & 9 \\ 228 & -73 & 33 \\ 84 & -28 & 16 \end{bmatrix}$

P5.11 $A = \begin{bmatrix} 4 & 0 & 0 & 0 \\ -4 & 8 & -4 & 2 \\ -7 & 7 & -3 & 3 \\ -2 & 2 & -2 & 4 \end{bmatrix}$

P5.12 $A = \begin{bmatrix} 11 & -6 & 4 & -2 \\ 4 & 1 & 0 & 0 \\ -9 & 9 & -6 & 5 \\ -6 & 6 & -6 & 7 \end{bmatrix}$

P5.13 $A = \begin{bmatrix} 20 & -15 & 10 & -5 \\ 26 & -21 & 16 & -8 \\ 11 & -11 & 11 & -5 \\ 4 & -4 & 4 & -1 \end{bmatrix}$

P5.14 $A = \begin{bmatrix} -6 & 6 & -4 & 2 \\ -8 & 8 & -4 & 2 \\ 0 & 0 & 2 & 0 \\ 0 & 0 & 0 & 2 \end{bmatrix}$

P5.15 $A = \begin{bmatrix} -4 & 2 & -8 & 0 \\ -21 & 9 & -20 & 0 \\ 0 & 0 & 4 & 0 \\ 0 & 0 & 8 & 0 \end{bmatrix}$

P5.16 $A = \begin{bmatrix} 11 & -8 & 6 & -4 & 2 \\ 16 & -13 & 12 & -8 & 4 \\ 4 & -4 & 5 & 0 & 0 \\ -9 & 9 & -9 & 12 & -5 \\ -6 & 6 & -6 & 6 & -1 \end{bmatrix}$

P5.17 $\mathbf{A} = \begin{bmatrix} 2 & 0 & 0 & 0 & 0 \\ 3 & -1 & 3 & -2 & 1 \\ 2 & -2 & 4 & 0 & 0 \\ -5 & 5 & -5 & 8 & -3 \\ -4 & 4 & -4 & 4 & 0 \end{bmatrix}$

P5.18 $\mathbf{A} = \begin{bmatrix} -7 & 8 & -6 & 4 & -2 \\ -13 & 14 & -9 & 6 & -3 \\ -2 & 2 & 1 & 0 & 0 \\ 5 & -5 & 5 & -3 & 3 \\ 4 & -4 & 4 & -4 & 5 \end{bmatrix}$

P5.19 $\mathbf{A} = \begin{bmatrix} -8 & 8 & -6 & 4 & -2 \\ -7 & 7 & -3 & 2 & -1 \\ 8 & -8 & 10 & -6 & 3 \\ 8 & -8 & 8 & -5 & 4 \\ 4 & -4 & 4 & -4 & 5 \end{bmatrix}$

P5.20 $\mathbf{A} = \begin{bmatrix} -1 & 4 & -3 & 2 & -1 \\ -11 & 14 & -9 & 6 & -3 \\ -6 & 6 & -2 & 2 & -1 \\ 6 & -6 & 6 & -4 & 4 \\ 6 & -6 & 6 & -6 & 7 \end{bmatrix}$

*For the symmetric matrices in Problems P5.21 to
P5.40, find the dominant eigenvalue*

    a. using the power method.
    *b. using the accelerated power method
    (Rayleigh quotient).*

P5.21 $\mathbf{A} = \begin{bmatrix} 6 & -1 & -2 \\ -1 & 8 & 1 \\ -2 & 1 & 2 \end{bmatrix}$

P5.22 $\mathbf{A} = \begin{bmatrix} 1 & 0 & 1 \\ 0 & 9 & -2 \\ 1 & -2 & 11 \end{bmatrix}$

P5.23 $\mathbf{A} = \begin{bmatrix} 11 & -2 & -4 \\ -2 & 15 & 2 \\ -4 & 2 & 3 \end{bmatrix}$

P5.24 $\mathbf{A} = \begin{bmatrix} 10 & 3 & 6 \\ 3 & 4 & -3 \\ 6 & -3 & 22 \end{bmatrix}$

P5.25 $\mathbf{A} = \begin{bmatrix} 8 & -6 & -9 \\ -6 & 44 & 0 \\ -9 & 0 & 14 \end{bmatrix}$

P5.26 $\mathbf{A} = \begin{bmatrix} -9 & 0 & 1 \\ 0 & -1 & -2 \\ 1 & -2 & 1 \end{bmatrix}$

P5.27 $\mathbf{A} = \begin{bmatrix} 1 & -2 & -4 \\ -2 & 5 & 2 \\ -4 & 2 & -7 \end{bmatrix}$

P5.28 $\mathbf{A} = \begin{bmatrix} 5 & -3 & -9 & -7 \\ -3 & 33 & 3 & 10 \\ -9 & 3 & 9 & -3 \\ -7 & 10 & -3 & 37 \end{bmatrix}$

P5.29 $\mathbf{A} = \begin{bmatrix} 50 & 3 & 2 & -11 \\ 3 & 8 & 10 & 5 \\ 2 & 10 & 18 & -4 \\ -11 & 5 & -4 & 42 \end{bmatrix}$

P5.30 $\mathbf{A} = \begin{bmatrix} 51 & 5 & 11 & 1 \\ 5 & 5 & 3 & -8 \\ 11 & 3 & 37 & 1 \\ 1 & -8 & 1 & 21 \end{bmatrix}$

P5.31 $\mathbf{A} = \begin{bmatrix} 11 & -6 & -8 & 6 \\ -6 & 47 & -4 & 0 \\ -8 & -4 & 19 & 4 \\ 6 & 0 & 4 & 15 \end{bmatrix}$

P5.32 $\mathbf{A} = \begin{bmatrix} 4 & 2/3 & -4/3 & 4/3 \\ 2/3 & 4 & 0 & 0 \\ -4/3 & 0 & 12 & 8 \\ 4/3 & 0 & 8 & 12 \end{bmatrix}$

P5.33 $\mathbf{A} = \begin{bmatrix} 81/2 & 21/2 & -21 & 21 \\ 21/2 & 41/2 & -5 & 5 \\ -21 & -5 & 37 & -1 \\ 21 & 5 & -1 & 37 \end{bmatrix}$

P5.34 $\mathbf{A} = \begin{bmatrix} 32 & -2 & -5 & -8 & 1 \\ -2 & 20 & 8 & 6 & 0 \\ -5 & 8 & 6 & 0 & -3 \\ -8 & 6 & 0 & 32 & -2 \\ 1 & 0 & -3 & -2 & 24 \end{bmatrix}$

P5.35 $\mathbf{A} = \begin{bmatrix} 6 & 2 & -1 & -3 & -5 \\ 2 & 18 & -2 & 5 & 4 \\ -1 & -2 & 20 & -5 & -4 \\ -3 & 5 & -5 & 28 & 1 \\ -5 & 4 & -4 & 1 & 12 \end{bmatrix}$

P5.36 $\mathbf{A} = \begin{bmatrix} 35 & 5 & 9 & -1 & 4 & -3 \\ 5 & 5 & 3 & -8 & 2 & 0 \\ 9 & 3 & 33 & -1 & 4 & -3 \\ -1 & -8 & -1 & 21 & 0 & 1 \\ 4 & 2 & 4 & 0 & 29 & -2 \\ -3 & 0 & -3 & 1 & -2 & 31 \end{bmatrix}$

P5.37 $\mathbf{A} = \begin{bmatrix} 52 & 6 & 15 & 1 & 5 & 3 & 5 \\ 6 & 16 & 0 & -13 & 4 & -9 & -2 \\ 15 & 0 & 58 & -3 & 8 & 1 & 6 \\ 1 & -13 & -3 & 30 & 1 & -7 & -3 \\ 5 & 4 & 8 & 1 & 42 & 3 & 5 \\ 3 & -9 & 1 & -7 & 3 & 28 & -1 \\ 5 & -2 & 6 & -3 & 5 & -1 & 44 \end{bmatrix}$

P5.38

$\mathbf{A} = \begin{bmatrix} 46 & 0 & 5 & 14 & 10 & 2 & 5 & 4 \\ 0 & 46 & -5 & -14 & -10 & -2 & -5 & -4 \\ 5 & -5 & 56 & 9 & 14 & -1 & 7 & 3 \\ 14 & -14 & 9 & 18 & 2 & -11 & 1 & -7 \\ 10 & -10 & 14 & 2 & 64 & -4 & 9 & 2 \\ 2 & -2 & -1 & -11 & -4 & 44 & -3 & -5 \\ 5 & -5 & 7 & 1 & 9 & -3 & 58 & 1 \\ 4 & -4 & 3 & -7 & 2 & -5 & 1 & 42 \end{bmatrix}$

P5.39

$\mathbf{A} = \begin{bmatrix} 84 & -8 & -3 & 25 & -3 & -10 & -23 & -12 & -5 \\ -8 & 132 & -18 & -7 & -12 & 22 & 14 & 18 & 2 \\ -3 & -18 & 110 & 13 & 7 & -18 & -17 & -16 & -3 \\ 25 & -7 & 13 & 62 & 13 & 2 & 29 & 8 & 7 \\ -3 & -12 & 7 & 13 & 100 & -14 & -20 & -14 & -4 \\ -10 & 22 & -18 & 2 & -14 & 126 & 8 & 22 & 0 \\ -23 & 14 & -17 & 29 & -20 & 8 & 60 & 0 & -11 \\ -12 & 18 & -16 & 8 & -14 & 22 & 0 & 122 & -2 \\ -5 & 2 & -3 & 7 & -4 & 0 & -11 & -2 & 94 \end{bmatrix}$

P5.40

$\mathbf{A} = \begin{bmatrix} 84 & 1 & 1 & -9 & 23 & 7 & 1 & -7 & 1 & -3 \\ 1 & 46 & 15 & -5 & -11 & -17 & 7 & 1 & 3 & 1 \\ 1 & 15 & 50 & 5 & 11 & 17 & -7 & -1 & -3 & -1 \\ -9 & -5 & 5 & 68 & -17 & -12 & 3 & 4 & 1 & 2 \\ 23 & -11 & 11 & -17 & 100 & -3 & 9 & -13 & 5 & -5 \\ 7 & -17 & 17 & -12 & -3 & 44 & 11 & -2 & 5 & 0 \\ 1 & 7 & -7 & 3 & 9 & 11 & 58 & -1 & -3 & -1 \\ -7 & 1 & -1 & 4 & -13 & -2 & -1 & 72 & -1 & 3 \\ 1 & 3 & -3 & 1 & 5 & 5 & -3 & -1 & 64 & -1 \\ -3 & 1 & -1 & 2 & -5 & 0 & -1 & 3 & -1 & 70 \end{bmatrix}$

Problems P5.41 to P.580

For the matrices given in Problems P5.1 to P5.40:

 a. Find the eigenvalues using the basic QR method
 b. Find the eigenvalues using the better QR method

A5.1 Show that the quadratic equation in three variables

$$a\,x^2 + b\,y^2 + c\,z^2 + 2d\,xy + 2e\,xz + 2f\,yz = g$$

can be written as $[\,\mathbf{A}\,\mathbf{v}\,]\,\mathbf{v} = g$, with

$$\mathbf{A} = \begin{bmatrix} a & d & e \\ d & b & f \\ e & f & c \end{bmatrix}$$

The surfaces can be classified according to the signs of eigenvalues of $\mathbf{A}$, as indicated in the following table. (Degenerate cases may also occur.) (See Fraleigh and Beauregard, 1987, p. 381.)

Eigenvalues	Surface
$+++$ or $---$	Ellipsoid
$++-$ or $+--$	Elliptic cone, hyperboloid (1 or 2 sheets)
$++0$ or $--0$	Elliptic paraboloid or elliptic cylinder
$+-0$	Hyperbolic paraboloid or hyperbolic cylinder
$+00$ or -00	Parabolic cylinder or two parallel planes

For Problems A5.2 to A5.12, write the equation as a quadratic form, find the eigenvalues of $\mathbf{A}$, and classify the surface.

A5.2 $6\,x^2 + 8\,y^2 + 2\,z^2 - 2\,xy - 4\,xz + 2\,yz = 12$

A5.3 $x^2 + 9\,y^2 + 11\,z^2 + 2\,xz - 4\,yz = 24$

A5.4 $11\,x^2 + 15\,y^2 + 3\,z^2 - 4\,xy - 8\,xz + 4\,yz = 21$

A5.5 $10\,x^2 + 4\,y^2 + 22\,z^2 + 6\,xy + 12\,xz - 6\,yz = 48$

A5.6 $8\,x^2 + 44\,y^2 + 14\,z^2 - 12\,xy - 18\,xz = 36$

A5.7 $-x^2 + 7\,y^2 + 9\,z^2 + 2\,xz - 4\,yz = 24$

A5.8 $9\,x^2 + 13\,y^2 + z^2 - 4\,xy - 8\,xz + 4\,yz = 21$

A5.9 $7\,x^2 + 10\,y^2 + 19\,z^2 - 28\,xy - 8\,xz - 20\,yz = 18$

A5.10 $-4\,x^2 + 3\,y^2 + z^2 - 4\,xy + 12\,xz - 16\,yz = -36$

A5.11 $-16\,x^2 - 7\,y^2 - 13\,z^2 + 4\,xy + 20\,xz - 16\,yz = -28$

A5.12 $16\,x^2 - y^2 + 11\,z^2 - 20\,xy - 28\,xz + 8\,yz = 82$

For Problems A5.13 to A5.16, find the eigenvalues and eigenvectors of $\mathbf{A}$, the matrix of the quadratic form: $[\,x\ y\,]\,\mathbf{A}\,[\,x\ y\,]^T = g$ (See Problems A4.4 to A4.6.)

If $\mathbf{Q}$ *is the matrix whose columns are the eigenvectors of* $\mathbf{A}$ *(with each eigenvector of unit length), then the change of variables*

$$\begin{bmatrix} x \\ y \end{bmatrix} = \mathbf{Q}\begin{bmatrix} t \\ u \end{bmatrix}$$

performs the necessary rotation so that in the new coordinate system (t, u) the cross-product terms do not appear. Use the eigenvalues of $\mathbf{A}$ *to find the equation of the quadratic equation in terms of the rotated axes that eliminate the mixed-terms. (Ignore any linear terms, they can be eliminated by a translation of axes after the rotation.)*

A5.13 $x^2 - \sqrt{3}\,x\,y + 2\,y^2 = 10$

A5.14 $4\,x^2 + 3\sqrt{3}\,xy + y^2 = 22$

A5.15 $x^2 - \sqrt{3}\,xy = -2$

A5.16 $-x^2 + xy - y + 7\,x = 11$

In Problems A5.17 to A5.22, find the principal inertias and principal axes of the three-dimensional object consisting of point masses $m_1, \dots, m_k$ *located at* $(x_1, y_1, z_1), \dots, (x_k, y_k, z_k)$, *respectively. The inertial matrix is as given in Example 5-A, but for point masses the moment of inertia and products of inertia are*

$$I_{xx} = \sum_{i=1}^{k} (y_i^2 + z_i^2)\,m_i$$

$$I_{yy} = \sum_{i=1}^{k} (x_i^2 + z_i^2)\,m_i$$

$$I_{zz} = \sum_{i=1}^{k} (x_i^2 + y_i^2)\,m_i$$

$$I_{xy} = I_{yx} = \sum_{i=1}^{k} (x_i\,y_i)\,m_i$$

$$I_{xz} = I_{zx} = \sum_{i=1}^{k} (x_i\,z_i)\,m_i$$

$$I_{yz} = I_{zy} = \sum_{i=1}^{k} (y_i\,z_i)\,m_i$$

A5.17 Unit point masses ($m = 1$) at (1, 0, 0), (1, 1, 0), (1, 1, 1).

A5.18 Unit point masses at (1, 0, 0), (0, 1, 0), (1, 1, 0), (1, 0, 1), (1, 1, 1).

A5.19 Unit point masses at (0, 1, 0), (0, 0, 1), (1, 1, 0), (1, 0, 1), (1, 1, 1).

A5.20 Unit point masses at (1, 0, 0), (0, 2, 0), (0, 0, 1), (1, 1, 0), (1, 0, 1), (0, 1, 1), (1, 1, 2).

A5.21 Unit point masses at (1, 0, 0), (0, 1, 0), (0, 0, 1), (1, 1, 0), (1, 0, 1), (0, 1, 1); point mass with $m = 2$ at (1, 1, 1).

A5.22 Unit point masses at (1, 0, 0), (0, 1, 0), (1, 1, 0), (1, 0, 1), point masses with $m = 2$ at (0, 0, 1), (0, 1, 1), (1, 1, 1).

Problems A5.23 to A5.26 explore the eigenvalues and eigenvectors of matrices whose shapes resemble letters of the alphabet. (See Leon et al., 1996.)

A5.23 Find the eigenvalues and eigenvectors of the following matrices:

$$\mathbf{L3} = \begin{bmatrix} 1 & 0 & 0 \\ 1 & 0 & 0 \\ 1 & 1 & 1 \end{bmatrix}$$

$$\mathbf{L4} = \begin{bmatrix} 1 & 0 & 0 & 0 \\ 1 & 0 & 0 & 0 \\ 1 & 0 & 0 & 0 \\ 1 & 1 & 1 & 1 \end{bmatrix}$$

$$\mathbf{L5} = \begin{bmatrix} 1 & 0 & 0 & 0 & 0 \\ 1 & 0 & 0 & 0 & 0 \\ 1 & 0 & 0 & 0 & 0 \\ 1 & 0 & 0 & 0 & 0 \\ 1 & 1 & 1 & 1 & 1 \end{bmatrix}$$

Generate some larger **L** matrices and discuss any patterns you find in the eigenvalues and eigenvectors.

A5.24 Find the eigenvalues and eigenvectors of the following matrices:

$$\mathbf{H3} = \begin{bmatrix} 1 & 0 & 1 \\ 1 & 1 & 1 \\ 1 & 0 & 1 \end{bmatrix}$$

$$\mathbf{H5} = \begin{bmatrix} 1 & 0 & 0 & 0 & 1 \\ 1 & 0 & 0 & 0 & 1 \\ 1 & 1 & 1 & 1 & 1 \\ 1 & 0 & 0 & 0 & 1 \\ 1 & 0 & 0 & 0 & 1 \end{bmatrix}$$

$$\mathbf{H7} = \begin{bmatrix} 1 & 0 & 0 & 0 & 0 & 0 & 1 \\ 1 & 0 & 0 & 0 & 0 & 0 & 1 \\ 1 & 0 & 0 & 0 & 0 & 0 & 1 \\ 1 & 1 & 1 & 1 & 1 & 1 & 1 \\ 1 & 0 & 0 & 0 & 0 & 0 & 1 \\ 1 & 0 & 0 & 0 & 0 & 0 & 1 \\ 1 & 0 & 0 & 0 & 0 & 0 & 1 \end{bmatrix}$$

Generate some larger **H** matrices and discuss any patterns you find in the eigenvalues and eigenvectors.

A 5.25 Find the eigenvalues and eigenvectors of the following matrices:

$$\mathbf{T3} = \begin{bmatrix} 1 & 1 & 1 \\ 0 & 1 & 0 \\ 0 & 1 & 0 \end{bmatrix}$$

$$\mathbf{T5} = \begin{bmatrix} 1 & 1 & 1 & 1 & 1 \\ 0 & 0 & 1 & 0 & 0 \\ 0 & 0 & 1 & 0 & 0 \\ 0 & 0 & 1 & 0 & 0 \\ 0 & 0 & 1 & 0 & 0 \end{bmatrix}$$

$$\mathbf{T7} = \begin{bmatrix} 1 & 1 & 1 & 1 & 1 & 1 & 1 \\ 0 & 0 & 0 & 1 & 0 & 0 & 0 \\ 0 & 0 & 0 & 1 & 0 & 0 & 0 \\ 0 & 0 & 0 & 1 & 0 & 0 & 0 \\ 0 & 0 & 0 & 1 & 0 & 0 & 0 \\ 0 & 0 & 0 & 1 & 0 & 0 & 0 \\ 0 & 0 & 0 & 1 & 0 & 0 & 0 \end{bmatrix}$$

Generate some larger **T** matrices and discuss any patterns you find in the eigenvalues and eigenvectors.

A 5.26 Find the eigenvalues and eigenvectors of the following matrices:

$$N3 = \begin{bmatrix} 1 & 0 & 1 \\ 1 & 1 & 1 \\ 1 & 0 & 1 \end{bmatrix}$$

$$N4 = \begin{bmatrix} 1 & 0 & 0 & 1 \\ 1 & 1 & 0 & 1 \\ 1 & 0 & 1 & 1 \\ 1 & 0 & 0 & 1 \end{bmatrix}$$

$$N5 = \begin{bmatrix} 1 & 0 & 0 & 0 & 1 \\ 1 & 1 & 0 & 0 & 1 \\ 1 & 0 & 1 & 0 & 1 \\ 1 & 0 & 0 & 1 & 1 \\ 1 & 0 & 0 & 0 & 1 \end{bmatrix}$$

$$N6 = \begin{bmatrix} 1 & 0 & 0 & 0 & 0 & 1 \\ 1 & 1 & 0 & 0 & 0 & 1 \\ 1 & 0 & 1 & 0 & 0 & 1 \\ 1 & 0 & 0 & 1 & 0 & 1 \\ 1 & 0 & 0 & 0 & 1 & 1 \\ 1 & 0 & 0 & 0 & 0 & 1 \end{bmatrix}$$

Generate some larger **N** matrices and discuss any patterns you find in the eigenvalues and eigenvectors.

Problems A5.27 to A5.50 introduce the application of eigenvalues and eigenvectors to the solution of linear systems of first order ODE. (These problems are related to problems in Chapter 13.).

If the real matrix **A** has distinct, real eigenvalues, μ_1, and μ_2, with eigenvectors $\mathbf{v}_1$, $\mathbf{v}_2$ respectively, the general solution of the linear system of ODE, $\mathbf{x}' = \mathbf{A}\,\mathbf{x}$, is

$$\mathbf{x} = c_1\, e^{\mu_1 t}\, \mathbf{v}_1 + c_2\, e^{\mu_2 t}\, \mathbf{v}_2.$$

If the matrix **A** has a complex eigenvalue, $\mu = a + b\,i$, with eigenvector **v**, the general solution of the linear system of ODE, $\mathbf{x}' = \mathbf{A}\,\mathbf{x}$, is

$$\mathbf{x} = c_1\, e^{at}[\cos(b\,t)\,Re(\mathbf{v}) - \sin(b\,t)\,Im(\mathbf{v})]$$

$$+ c_2\, [\cos(b\,t)\,Im(\mathbf{v}) + \sin(b\,t)\,Re(\mathbf{v})].$$

Note that the complex conjugate of μ is also an eigenvalue, and its eigenvector is the complex conjugate of **v**. (See Leon, 1998 for a discussion of these basic ideas.) The extension to n-by-n systems follows in a similar manner as long as **A** has n linearly independent eigenvectors. (for discussion of the more general case, see e.g. Zill, 1986)

For Problems A5.27 to A5.50, find the general solution of $\mathbf{x}' = \mathbf{A}\,\mathbf{x}$.

$$\text{A5.27} \quad \mathbf{A} = \begin{bmatrix} 3 & -3 & 2 & -1 \\ 12 & -12 & 10 & -5 \\ 15 & -15 & 14 & -7 \\ 6 & -6 & 6 & -3 \end{bmatrix}$$

$$\text{A5.28} \quad \mathbf{A} = \begin{bmatrix} -26 & 21 & -14 & 7 \\ -34 & 29 & -20 & 10 \\ -13 & 13 & -11 & 7 \\ -8 & 8 & -8 & 7 \end{bmatrix}$$

$$\text{A5.29} \quad \mathbf{A} = \begin{bmatrix} 1 & -3 & 2 & -1 \\ 4 & -6 & 2 & -1 \\ -5 & 5 & -8 & 5 \\ -10 & 10 & -10 & 7 \end{bmatrix}$$

$$\text{A5.30} \quad \mathbf{A} = \begin{bmatrix} -6 & 6 & -4 & 2 \\ -16 & 16 & -12 & 6 \\ -17 & 17 & -15 & 9 \\ -10 & 10 & -10 & 8 \end{bmatrix}$$

$$\text{A5.31} \quad \mathbf{A} = \begin{bmatrix} 3 & -3 & 2 & -1 \\ 10 & -10 & 8 & -4 \\ 10 & -10 & 9 & -4 \\ 2 & -2 & 2 & 0 \end{bmatrix}$$

$$\text{A5.32} \quad \mathbf{A} = \begin{bmatrix} 29 & -24 & 16 & -8 \\ 52 & -46 & 34 & -17 \\ 35 & -34 & 30 & -16 \\ 14 & -14 & 14 & -9 \end{bmatrix}$$

$$\text{A5.33} \quad \mathbf{A} = \begin{bmatrix} 3 & -6 & 4 & -2 \\ 30 & -32 & 24 & -12 \\ 38 & -37 & 31 & -17 \\ 14 & -14 & 14 & -10 \end{bmatrix}$$

$$\text{A5.34} \quad \mathbf{A} = \begin{bmatrix} 16 & -15 & 10 & -5 \\ 42 & -40 & 30 & -15 \\ 35 & -34 & 29 & -14 \\ 8 & -8 & 8 & -3 \end{bmatrix}$$

A5.35 $\mathbf{A} = \begin{bmatrix} 9 & -9 & 6 & -3 \\ 24 & -23 & 16 & -8 \\ 14 & -13 & 9 & -3 \\ -4 & 4 & -4 & 5 \end{bmatrix}$

A5.36 $\mathbf{A} = \begin{bmatrix} -9 & 9 & -6 & 3 \\ -10 & 11 & -6 & 3 \\ 3 & -2 & 4 & -2 \\ 4 & -4 & 4 & -2 \end{bmatrix}$

A5.37 $\mathbf{A} = \begin{bmatrix} 20 & -18 & 12 & -6 \\ 34 & -31 & 20 & -10 \\ 14 & -13 & 8 & -5 \\ 2 & -2 & 2 & -3 \end{bmatrix}$

A5.38 $\mathbf{A} = \begin{bmatrix} -19 & 18 & -12 & 6 \\ -26 & 26 & -16 & 8 \\ -2 & 3 & 1 & -1 \\ 6 & -6 & 6 & -4 \end{bmatrix}$

A5.39 $\mathbf{A} = \begin{bmatrix} 14 & -9 & 6 & -3 \\ 3 & 34 & -4 & 2 \\ -23 & 24 & -21 & 12 \\ -15 & 15 & -14 & 10 \end{bmatrix}$

A5.40 $\mathbf{A} = \begin{bmatrix} 11 & -12 & 8 & -4 \\ 25 & -25 & 16 & -8 \\ 7 & -6 & 2 & 0 \\ -9 & 9 & -8 & 6 \end{bmatrix}$

A5.41 $\mathbf{A} = \begin{bmatrix} -2 & 3 & -2 & 1 \\ 1 & 1 & 2 & -1 \\ 10 & -9 & 12 & -7 \\ 9 & -9 & 10 & -7 \end{bmatrix}$

A5.42 $\mathbf{A} = \begin{bmatrix} -13 & 12 & -8 & 4 \\ -24 & 21 & -14 & 7 \\ -14 & 12 & -9 & 6 \\ -6 & 6 & -6 & 6 \end{bmatrix}$

A5.43 $\mathbf{A} = \begin{bmatrix} -16 & 18 & -12 & 6 \\ -39 & 38 & -24 & 12 \\ -19 & 16 & -8 & 4 \\ 4 & -4 & 4 & -2 \end{bmatrix}$

A5.44 $\mathbf{A} = \begin{bmatrix} -11 & 6 & -4 & 2 \\ 3 & -9 & 8 & -4 \\ 18 & -19 & 16 & -7 \\ 2 & -2 & 2 & 1 \end{bmatrix}$

A5.45 $\mathbf{A} = \begin{bmatrix} -16 & 18 & -12 & 6 \\ -39 & 38 & -24 & 12 \\ -18 & 15 & -7 & 3 \\ 6 & -6 & 6 & -4 \end{bmatrix}$

A5.46 $\mathbf{A} = \begin{bmatrix} -24 & 24 & -16 & 8 \\ -50 & 46 & -30 & 15 \\ -22 & 18 & -10 & 4 \\ 6 & -6 & 6 & -5 \end{bmatrix}$

A5.47 $\mathbf{A} = \begin{bmatrix} -36 & 30 & -20 & 10 \\ -61 & 50 & -36 & 18 \\ -34 & 29 & -25 & 13 \\ -10 & 10 & -10 & 6 \end{bmatrix}$

A5.48 $\mathbf{A} = \begin{bmatrix} 30 & -24 & 16 & -8 \\ 38 & -28 & 18 & -9 \\ 6 & -2 & 0 & 0 \\ -2 & 2 & -2 & 1 \end{bmatrix}$

A5.49 $\mathbf{A} = \begin{bmatrix} -9 & 6 & -4 & 2 \\ -7 & 3 & -2 & 1 \\ 6 & -7 & 6 & -5 \\ 8 & -8 & 8 & -8 \end{bmatrix}$

A5.50 $\mathbf{A} = \begin{bmatrix} -28 & 24 & -16 & 8 \\ -42 & 34 & -22 & 11 \\ -10 & 6 & -2 & 0 \\ 6 & -6 & 6 & -5 \end{bmatrix}$

U5.1 Compare the required number of iterations in using QR to find the eigenvalues of **F** with the number needed when **F** is preprocessed to Hessenberg form. Consider a reasonable test for convergence.

$$\mathbf{F} = \begin{bmatrix} -631 & 316 & -156 & 144 & -36 \\ -798 & 400 & -195 & 180 & -45 \\ 900 & -450 & 227 & -204 & 51 \\ -28 & 14 & -7 & 12 & -1 \\ 96 & -48 & 24 & -24 & 14 \end{bmatrix}$$

the exact eigenvalues are

$$\text{eig}(F) = 1 \quad 2 \quad 5 \quad 8 \quad 6$$

U5.2 The rate of convergence of the power method is influenced by the separation between the largest eigenvalue and the next largest. Compare the performance of the power method in finding the dominant eigenvalue for the following matrices. Use a reasonable test for convergence. The exact eigenvalues are given for comparison.

$$\mathbf{F} = \begin{bmatrix} -631 & 316 & -156 & 144 & -36 \\ -798 & 400 & -195 & 180 & -45 \\ 900 & -450 & 227 & -204 & 51 \\ -28 & 14 & -7 & 12 & -1 \\ 96 & -48 & 24 & -24 & 14 \end{bmatrix}$$

the exact eigenvalues are

$$\text{eig}(F) = 1 \quad 2 \quad 5 \quad 8 \quad 6$$

$$\mathbf{E} = \begin{bmatrix} -101 & 51 & -12 & 0 & 0 \\ -174 & 88 & -20 & 0 & 0 \\ 136 & -68 & 19 & 0 & 0 \\ 840 & -420 & 105 & -32 & 18 \\ 2016 & -1008 & 252 & -84 & 46 \end{bmatrix}$$

$$\text{eig}(E) = 10 \quad 1 \quad 2 \quad 3 \quad 4$$

U5.3 Compare QR for matrix **A** and for the preprocessed matrix **T**.

$$\mathbf{A} = \begin{bmatrix} 2 & 0 & 0 & 0 \\ -4 & 4 & 0 & 0 \\ 12 & -6 & 6 & 0 \\ -48 & 24 & -8 & 8 \end{bmatrix}$$

$$\mathbf{T} = \begin{bmatrix} 2 & 0 & 0 & 0 \\ 49.639 & 11.714 & -19.21 & -16.187 \\ -8.1096e-15 & 1.1265 & 3.3383 & -0.78038 \\ -1.2199e-14 & -3.1318e-16 & -1.425 & 2.9474 \end{bmatrix}$$

Note that because of rounding error, the elements that should be zero have small non-zero values. Consider how this could be remedied.

U5.4 Find the eigenvalues of the following matrices; each is the Jacobi iteration matrix for the indicated exercise.

$$\mathbf{T} = \begin{bmatrix} 0.0 & 0.2 & -0.1 \\ 0.2 & 0.0 & 0.2 \\ 0.2 & 0.5 & 0.0 \end{bmatrix} \quad (\text{exercise } 6.1)$$

$$\mathbf{T} = \begin{bmatrix} 0.0 & 0.2 & 0.0 \\ 0.2 & 0.0 & 0.2 \\ 0.2 & 0.0 & 0.2 \end{bmatrix} \quad (\text{exercise } 6.3)$$

$$\mathbf{T} = \begin{bmatrix} 0 & -1/4 & 0 \\ -1/3 & 0 & 1/3 \\ 0 & 1/4 & 0 \end{bmatrix} \quad (\text{exercise } 6.5)$$

$$\mathbf{T} = \begin{bmatrix} 0 & 1/2 & 0 & 0 \\ 1/2 & 0 & 1/2 & 0 \\ 0 & 1/2 & 0 & 1/2 \\ 0 & 0 & 1/2 & 0 \end{bmatrix} \quad (\text{exercise } 6.6)$$

$$\mathbf{T} = \begin{bmatrix} 0 & -1/5 & 0 & 0 \\ -1/5 & 0 & -1/5 & 0 \\ 0 & -1/5 & 0 & -1/5 \\ 0 & 0 & -1/5 & 0 \end{bmatrix} \quad (\text{exercise } 6.7)$$

Solving Systems of Linear Equations: Iterative Methods

Systems of linear equations for which numerical solutions are needed are often very large, making the computational effort of general, direct methods, such as Gaussian elimination, prohibitively expensive. For systems that have coefficient matrices with the appropriate structure—especially large, sparse systems (i.e., systems with many coefficients whose value is zero)—iterative techniques may be preferable.

We begin this chapter with an example of a linear system that occurs in the solution of Poisson's equation by a finite-difference method (see Chapter 15). For applications such as this, in which the elements of the coefficient matrix can be generated as needed from a simple formula, it is beneficial to use a method that does not require storing (and modifying) the entire coefficient matrix, as was the case with Gaussian elimination.

In this chapter we consider the three most common classical iterative techniques for linear systems: the Jacobi, Gauss-Seidel, and successive overrelaxation (SOR) methods. The performance of each technique is illustrated for several examples. For each method, an algorithm is given which can be used as the basis for computing the solution of a small linear system or writing a simple computer program to implement the method. Some theoretical results are presented to give guidance in determining when the method may be useful.

The convergence of each of the iterative techniques examined in this chapter depends on results from linear algebra. The eigenvalues of the iteration matrix play a crucial role in determining whether these methods will converge; numerical methods for finding eigenvalues were discussed in Chapter 5; software packages for numerical computation typically include one or more built-in functions for finding eigenvalues and eigenvectors. Such functions provide an efficient way of checking the conditions of the theorems given in this chapter.

Example 6-A Finite Difference Solution of a PDE

The two-dimensional potential equation can be solved numerically by defining a mesh of points in the region of interest and approximating the derivatives by finite differences. For example, to solve the partial differential equation (PDE)

$$u_{xx} + u_{yy} = 0, \quad 0 \le x \le 1, \quad 0 \le y \le 1,$$

with the values of the unknown function $u(x,y)$ given along the boundaries of the region (at $b_1 \ldots b_{12}$) and a mesh of $\Delta x = \Delta y = 0.25$ (so that there are 9 points interior to the region where the value of u must be computed), the grid looks like

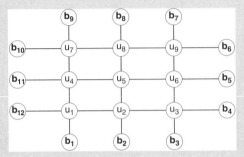

For each point there is an equation that states that 4 times the value at that point, minus the values of the unknowns at the 4 adjacent grid points (right, above, left, and below the point) is equal to 0. For some of the grid points, one or two of the adjacent points are on the boundary of the region, and the value of the solution of the PDE is given at those points. The linear system for the unknowns is:

$$
\begin{array}{llllllll}
4u_1 & -u_2 & & -u_4 & & & & = b_1 + b_{12} \\
-u_1 & +4u_2 & -u_3 & & -u_5 & & & = b_2 \\
& -u_2 & +4u_3 & & & -u_6 & & = b_3 + b_4 \\
-u_1 & & & +4u_4 & -u_5 & & -u_7 & = b_{11} \\
& -u_2 & & -u_4 & +4u_5 & -u_6 & & -u_8 & = 0 \\
& & -u_3 & & -u_5 & +4u_6 & & & -u_9 & = b_5 \\
& & & -u_4 & & & +4u_7 & -u_8 & & = b_9 + b_{10} \\
& & & & -u_5 & & -u_7 & +4u_8 & -u_9 & = b_8 \\
& & & & & -u_6 & & -u_8 & +4u_9 & = b_6 + b_7 \\
\end{array}
$$

This system is well suited for an iterative solution scheme, such as any of the methods that we consider in this chapter (since it is diagonally dominant and quite sparse). We solve this system in Examples 6.4, and 6.9.

In practice, the linear system would often be very large, and the coefficient matrix would not actually be generated. The finite-difference method used to form the linear system and the solution of the system by means of the iterative techniques introduced in the following sections, but without the explicit generation of the coefficient matrix, are discussed in Chapter 15.

Example 6-B Steady-State Concentrations

The modeling of an interconnected system of reservoirs, reactors, or any type of tank containing a chemical whose concentration may vary from one tank to another, may lead to a system of linear equations for which iterative solution techniques are appropriate. Each tank is characterized by known inflow and outflow rates. The contents of each tank are assumed to be well mixed, so that the concentration of the chemical is uniform throughout the tank.

The mass-balance equations for each tank state that the rate at which the chemical enters the tank must equal the rate at which it leaves. The rate or transfer of the chemical is the product of the concentration of the chemical in the flow stream (mass/volume) and the flow rate (volume/time). The diagram below illustrates an interconnected system of 9 tanks, labeled $T_1 \ldots T_9$. All tanks except 5 and 9 receive inflow from an external source, as well as from some other tanks. The concentration of the chemical in tank T_i is denoted c_i, and the flow rate from T_i to T_j is denoted r_{ij}. The concentration of chemical in flow into a tank from an external source is assumed known. The concentration into tank T_i is denoted c_{0i} and the corresponding flow rate is denoted r_{0i}. The rate of flow out from tank 9 is denoted r; for steady-state operation, r equals the total flow into the system. Furthermore, the total flow into each tank must equal the flow out.

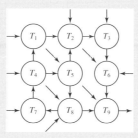

For the system illustrated in the diagram, the mass-balance equations are

$$r_{01}\, c_{01} + r_{41}\, c_4 \qquad\qquad = (r_{12} + r_{15})\, c_1$$
$$r_{02}\, c_{02} + r_{12}\, c_1 + r_{52}\, c_5 \qquad = (r_{23} + r_{26})\, c_2$$
$$r_{03}\, c_{03} + r_{23}\, c_2 \qquad\qquad = r_{36}\, c_3$$
$$r_{04}\, c_{04} + r_{74}\, c_7 \qquad\qquad = (r_{41} + r_{48} + r_{45})\, c_4$$
$$r_{15}\, c_1 + r_{45}\, c_4 \qquad\qquad = (r_{52} + r_{58} + r_{59})\, c_5$$
$$r_{06}\, c_{06} + r_{26}\, c_2 + r_{36}\, c_3 \qquad = r_{69}\, c_6$$
$$r_{07}\, c_{07} + r_{87}\, c_8 \qquad\qquad = r_{74}\, c_7$$
$$r_{08}\, c_{08} + r_{58}\, c_5 + r_{48}\, c_4 \qquad = (r_{87} + r_{89})\, c_8$$
$$r_{59}\, c_5 + r_{69}\, c_6 + r_{89}\, c_8 \qquad = r\, c_9$$

As an example, if we take the flow rates into the tanks as $r_{01} = r_{02} = r_{03} = r_{04} = r_{08} = 3$ and $r_{06} = r_{07} = 2$, then the flow rate out from tank 9 is $r = 19$. One set of internal flow rates that are compatible with these external values are $r_{12} = 6$; $r_{15} = 2$; $r_{23} = 5$; $r_{26} = 5$; $r_{36} = 8$; $r_{41} = 5$; $r_{45} = 1$; $r_{48} = 1$; $r_{52} = 1$; $r_{58} = 1$; $r_{59} = 1$; $r_{69} = 15$; $r_{74} = 4$; $r_{87} = 2$; $r_{89} = 3$. The distribution of concentrations of the chemical in the various tanks depends on the concentration in the different inflow streams. As would be expected, unit concentration in each inflow stream leads to unit concentration in each tank. Doubling the concentration in the inflow to tank 2 (while leaving all others at unit value) gives steady-state concentrations in tanks 1–9 as follows:

| 1 | 1.3 | 1.18 | 1 | 1 | 1.2 | 1 | 1 | 1.1579 |

An Overview of Iterative Methods for Linear Systems

Classical iterative methods for solving linear systems are based on converting the system $\mathbf{A}\mathbf{x} = \mathbf{b}$ into the equivalent system $\mathbf{x} = \mathbf{C}\mathbf{x} + \mathbf{d}$ and generating a sequence of approximations $\mathbf{x}^{(1)}, \mathbf{x}^{(2)}, \ldots$, where

$$\mathbf{x}^{(k)} = \mathbf{C}\mathbf{x}^{(k-1)} + \mathbf{d}.$$

This methodology is similar to the fixed-point iteration method introduced in Chapter 1 for nonlinear functions of a single variable.

In this chapter we consider three common iterative techniques for solving linear systems: the Jacobi, Gauss-Seidel, and SOR methods. The basic idea is to solve the ith equation in the system for the ith variable, in order to convert the given system (using a four-by-four system for illustration)

$$a_{11} x_1 + a_{12} x_2 + a_{13} x_3 + a_{14} x_4 = b_1$$

$$a_{21} x_1 + a_{22} x_2 + a_{23} x_3 + a_{24} x_4 = b_2$$

$$a_{31} x_1 + a_{32} x_2 + a_{33} x_3 + a_{34} x_4 = b_3$$

$$a_{41} x_1 + a_{42} x_2 + a_{43} x_3 + a_{44} x_4 = b_4$$

into the system

$$x_1 = \qquad -\frac{a_{12}}{a_{11}} x_2 - \frac{a_{13}}{a_{11}} x_3 - \frac{a_{14}}{a_{11}} x_4 + \frac{b_1}{a_{11}}$$

$$x_2 = -\frac{a_{21}}{a_{22}} x_1 \qquad - \frac{a_{23}}{a_{22}} x_3 - \frac{a_{24}}{a_{22}} x_4 + \frac{b_2}{a_{22}}$$

$$x_3 = -\frac{a_{31}}{a_{33}} x_1 - \frac{a_{32}}{a_{33}} x_2 \qquad - \frac{a_{34}}{a_{33}} x_4 + \frac{b_3}{a_{33}}$$

$$x_4 = -\frac{a_{41}}{a_{44}} x_1 - \frac{a_{42}}{a_{44}} x_2 - \frac{a_{43}}{a_{44}} x_3 \qquad + \frac{b_4}{a_{44}}$$

The Jacobi and Gauss-Seidel methods differ in the manner in which they update the values of the variables on the right-hand side of the equations. The SOR update is a convex combination of the previous solution vector and the Gauss-Seidel update.

Stopping conditions must be specified for any iterative process. Two possibilities are to stop the iterations when the norm of the change in the solution vector $\mathbf{x}$ from one iteration to the next is sufficiently small or to stop the iterations when the norm of the residual vector, $\| \mathbf{A}\mathbf{x} - \mathbf{b} \|$, is below a specified tolerance.

The Jacobi method is based on the transformation of the linear system $\mathbf{A}\mathbf{x} = \mathbf{b}$ into the system $\mathbf{x} = \mathbf{C}\mathbf{x} + \mathbf{d}$, in which the matrix $\mathbf{C}$ has zeros on the diagonal. The vector $\mathbf{x}$ is updated using the previous estimate for all components of $\mathbf{x}$ to evaluate the right-hand side of the equation.

Example 6.1 Illustrating the Jacobi Method Graphically

To visualize the Jacobi iterations, consider the two-by-two system

$$2x + y = 6,$$
$$x + 2y = 6.$$

For the Jacobi method, the equations are written as

$$x = -\frac{1}{2}y + 3$$

$$y = -\frac{1}{2}x + 3$$

Starting with $x^{(1)} = 1/2$ and $y^{(1)} = 1/2$, the first equation produces the next estimate for x (using $y^{(1)}$) and the second equation gives the next value of y (using $x^{(1)}$):

$$x^{(2)} = -\frac{1}{2}y^{(1)} + 3 = -\frac{1}{4} + 3 = \frac{11}{4}$$

$$y^{(2)} = -\frac{1}{2}x^{(1)} + 3 = -\frac{1}{4} + 3 = \frac{11}{4}$$

Notice that new values of the variables are not used until a new iteration step is begun. This is called *simultaneous updating*. The first iteration is illustrated in Fig. 6.1.

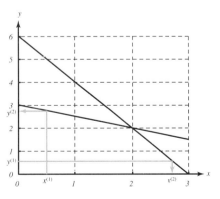

FIGURE 6.1   The first iteration for the Jacobi method.

Example 6.2 Matrix Form for Jacobi Iteration

Consider the three-by-three system of equations

$$
\begin{aligned}
2x_1 - x_2 + x_3 &= -1 \\
x_1 + 2x_2 - x_3 &= 6 \\
x_1 - x_2 + 2x_3 &= -3
\end{aligned}
$$

which are converted to

$$
\begin{aligned}
x_1 &= + 0.5x_2 - 0.5x_3 + -0.5 \\
x_2 &= -0.5x_1 + 0.5x_3 + 3.0 \\
x_3 &= -0.5x_1 + 0.5x_2 + -1.5
\end{aligned}
$$

In matrix notation, the original system, $\mathbf{A}\,\mathbf{x} = \mathbf{b}$, i.e.,

$$
\begin{bmatrix} 2 & -1 & 1 \\ 1 & 2 & -1 \\ 1 & -1 & 2 \end{bmatrix} \begin{bmatrix} x_1 \\ x_2 \\ x_3 \end{bmatrix} = \begin{bmatrix} -1 \\ 6 \\ -3 \end{bmatrix}
$$

has been transformed to

$$
\begin{bmatrix} x_1^{(k)} \\ x_2^{(k)} \\ x_3^{(k)} \end{bmatrix} = \begin{bmatrix} 0.0 & 0.5 & -0.5 \\ -0.5 & 0.0 & 0.5 \\ -0.5 & 0.5 & 0.0 \end{bmatrix} \begin{bmatrix} x_1^{(k-1)} \\ x_2^{(k-1)} \\ x_3^{(k-1)} \end{bmatrix} + \begin{bmatrix} -0.5 \\ 3.0 \\ -1.5 \end{bmatrix}
$$

(where the iteration counter is indicated by a superscript).
Starting with $\mathbf{x}^{(0)} = (0, 0, 0)$ we find

$$
\begin{bmatrix} x_1^{(1)} \\ x_2^{(1)} \\ x_3^{(1)} \end{bmatrix} = \begin{bmatrix} 0.0 & 0.5 & -0.5 \\ -0.5 & 0.0 & 0.5 \\ -0.5 & 0.5 & 0.0 \end{bmatrix} \begin{bmatrix} 0 \\ 0 \\ 0 \end{bmatrix} + \begin{bmatrix} -0.5 \\ 3.0 \\ -1.5 \end{bmatrix} = \begin{bmatrix} -0.5 \\ 3.0 \\ -1.5 \end{bmatrix}
$$

For the second iteration, we have

$$
\begin{bmatrix} x_1^{(2)} \\ x_2^{(2)} \\ x_3^{(2)} \end{bmatrix} = \begin{bmatrix} 0.0 & 0.5 & -0.5 \\ -0.5 & 0.0 & 0.5 \\ -0.5 & 0.5 & 0.0 \end{bmatrix} \begin{bmatrix} -0.5 \\ 3.0 \\ -1.5 \end{bmatrix} + \begin{bmatrix} -0.5 \\ 3.0 \\ -1.5 \end{bmatrix} = \begin{bmatrix} 1.75 \\ 2.50 \\ 0.25 \end{bmatrix}
$$

Continuing these iterations, we find that solution vector after 10 iterations is

$$
\mathbf{x} = [0.99854 \quad 2.00098 \quad -1.00049]^T
$$

The true solution is

$$
\mathbf{x}^* = [1 \quad 2 \quad -1]^T.
$$

6.1.1 Algorithm for the Jacobi Method

We summarize the steps in using the Jacobi Method to solve $\mathbf{M}\mathbf{x} = \mathbf{b}$ in the following algorithm.

Jacobi Iteration

Input
M	*coefficient matrix (n-by-n)*
b	*right-hand side vector (n-by-1)*
$\mathbf{x}_o$	*initial guess vector*
n	*number of rows and columns of M*
max	*maximum number of iterations*
tol	*tolerance for convergence*

Initialize
For i = 1 to n   *create iteration matrix* **C**
    C(i, :) = −M(i, :)/M(i,i)   *transform each row*
    C(i,i) = 0
    d(i) = b(i)/M(i,i)   *scale right-hand side vector*
End
Compute
For k = 1 to max
            Form new solution vector, $\mathbf{x}_n$ *from the old solution vector* $\mathbf{x}_o$
    $\mathbf{x}_n = \mathbf{C}\,\mathbf{x}_o + \mathbf{d}$
    If $(|\,\mathbf{M}\mathbf{x}_n − \mathbf{b}\,| < \text{tol})$ Break   *test for convergence*
    $\mathbf{x}_o = \mathbf{x}_n$
End
Return
    $\mathbf{x}_n$

Another possible test for convergence is to check the norm of the change in the solution vector, $|\,\mathbf{x}_n − \mathbf{x}_o\,|$,

If one is implementing this algorithm in a computing environment in which matrix-vector multiplication is not supported, then the single statement

$$\mathbf{x}_n = \mathbf{C}\,\mathbf{x}_o + \mathbf{d}$$

would be expanded into a loop, as

For $i = 1$ to n
    $\mathbf{x}_n(i) = \mathbf{C}(i, :)\,\mathbf{x}_o(:) + \mathbf{d}(i)$
End

The product of the ith row of matrix C and the column vector $\mathbf{x}_o$ (which is denoted as $\mathbf{C}(i, :)\,\mathbf{x}_o(i)$) could also be expanded into a loop, if necessary, as

dot − 0
For $j = 1$ to n
        dot = dot + $\mathbf{C}(i, j)\,\mathbf{x}_o(j)$
End

6.1.2　Application of the Jacobi Method

Example 6.3 A Linear System That Comes from a PDE

We illustrate the use of the Jacobi method for solving a system of linear equations that comes from a finite-difference approach to solving a partial differential equation (PDE). Consider the linear system introduced in Example 6-A. The finite difference method for solving Poisson's PDE is presented in Chapter 15. We take the values of the function on the boundary to be as shown on the grid below.

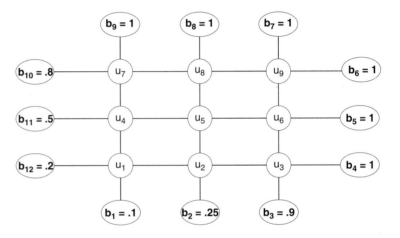

The 9 equations that state that 4 times the value at that point, minus the values of the unknowns at the 4 adjacent grid points (right, above, left, and below the point) is equal to 0 are as follows.

$$4u_1 \ -u_2 \ -u_4 \ -b_{12} \ -b_1 = 0$$
$$4u_2 \ -u_3 \ -u_5 \ -u_1 \ -b_2 = 0$$
$$4u_3 \ -b_4 \ -u_6 \ -u_2 \ -b_3 = 0$$
$$4u_4 \ -u_5 \ -u_7 \ -b_{11} \ -u_1 = 0$$
$$4u_5 \ -u_6 \ -u_8 \ -u_4 \ -u_2 = 0$$
$$4u_6 \ -b_5 \ -u_9 \ -u_5 \ -u_3 = 0$$
$$4u_7 \ -u_8 \ -b_9 \ -b_{10} \ -u_4 = 0$$
$$4u_8 \ -u_9 \ -b_8 \ -u_7 \ -u_5 = 0$$
$$4u_9 \ -b_6 \ -b_7 \ -u_8 \ -u_6 = 0$$

Putting the known values on the right, and writing the unknowns in order, we have

$$
\begin{array}{rrrrrrrrrr}
4u_1 & -u_2 & & -u_4 & & & & & & = \ .3 \\
-u_1 & +4u_2 & -u_3 & & -u_5 & & & & & = \ .25 \\
& -u_2 & +4u_3 & & & -u_6 & & & & = 1.9 \\
-u_1 & & & +4u_4 & -u_5 & & -u_7 & & & = \ .5 \\
& -u_2 & & -u_4 & +4u_5 & -u_6 & & -u_8 & & = 0 \\
& & -u_3 & & -u_5 & +4u_6 & & & -u_9 & = 1 \\
& & & -u_4 & & & +4u_7 & -u_8 & & = 1.8 \\
& & & & -u_5 & & -u_7 & +4u_8 & -u_9 & = 1 \\
& & & & & -u_6 & & -u_8 & +4u_9 & = 2
\end{array}
$$

Using a simple computer program to implement the Jacobi method (and starting with an initial solution vector that is identically $= 0$) we find that after 10 iterations the solution vector (elements shown to 4 decimal places) is

$$\mathbf{x}^T = [0.3481 \quad 0.5218 \quad 0.8160 \quad 0.5816 \quad 0.6963 \quad 0.8530 \quad 0.8053 \quad 0.8503 \quad 0.9231]$$

Displaying these values on the two-dimensional grid for the PDE makes the results easier to interpret (boundary values are shown in bold)

	1.0	**1.0**	**1.0**	
0.8	0.8053	0.8503	0.9231	**1.0**
0.5	0.5816	0.6963	0.8530	**1.0**
0.2	0.3481	0.5218	0.8160	**1.0**
	0.1	**0.25**	**0.9**	

As a measure of the error, we take the Euclidean norm of the residual vector $\mathbf{r} = \mathbf{Mx} - \mathbf{b}$; after 10 iterations $|\mathbf{r}| = 0.0558$.

After 20 iterations, the norm of the residual is 1.7456e-3; the solution is

$$\mathbf{x}^T = [0.3590 \quad 0.5383 \quad 0.8269 \quad 0.5981 \quad 0.7180 \quad 0.8696 \quad 0.8162 \quad 0.8669 \quad 0.9340]$$

After 30 iterations the solution agrees with the exact solution to 3 decimal places (and most components agree to 4 decimal places). After 40 iterations the solution agrees with the exact solution (to 4 decimal places). The exact solution (to 4 decimal places) is

$$\mathbf{y}^T = [0.3594 \quad 0.5388 \quad 0.8272 \quad 0.5987 \quad 0.7188 \quad 0.8701 \quad 0.8165 \quad 0.8674 \quad 0.9344]$$

The norm of the residual $\mathbf{My} - \mathbf{b}$ is 8.4734e-16.

	1.0	**1.0**	**1.0**	
0.8	0.8165	0.8674	0.9344	**1.0**
0.5	0.5987	0.7188	0.8701	**1.0**
0.2	0.3594	0.5388	0.8272	**1.0**
	0.1	**0.25**	**0.9**	

6.1.3   Discussion

The Jacobi method may be derived by converting the original system, $\mathbf{A}\,\mathbf{x} = \mathbf{b}$, into a decomposed form $(\mathbf{L} + \mathbf{D} + \mathbf{U})\,\mathbf{x} = \mathbf{b}$, where $\mathbf{D}$ is a diagonal matrix, $\mathbf{L}$ is a lower triangular matrix, and $\mathbf{U}$ is an upper triangular matrix. The decomposed form is expressed as $\mathbf{x} = \mathbf{C}\,\mathbf{x} + \mathbf{d}$ in the following way:

$$\mathbf{D}\,\mathbf{x} = (-\mathbf{L} \ -\mathbf{U})\,\mathbf{x} + \mathbf{b},$$

$$\mathbf{x} = \mathbf{D}^{-1}(-\mathbf{L} \ -\mathbf{U})\,\mathbf{x} + \mathbf{D}^{-1}\mathbf{b},$$

$$\mathbf{x} = \mathbf{C}\,\mathbf{x} + \mathbf{d}.$$

This formulation assumes that the diagonal of $\mathbf{A}$ contains no element that is zero. If $\mathbf{A}$ is nonsingular, but has a zero element on the diagonal, rows and columns may be permuted to obtain a form with nonsingular $\mathbf{D}$. It is desirable to have the diagonal elements large relative to the off-diagonal elements.

The primary considerations in determining when the Jacobi method (or some other iterative method) works well are convergence and computational effort.

Some Useful Theoretical Results on Convergence

There are several useful theoretical results concerning the relationships between the characteristics of the matrix $\mathbf{A}$ (or the iteration matrix $\mathbf{C}$) and the convergence of Jacobi iteration for the system $\mathbf{A}\,\mathbf{x} = \mathbf{b}$. Two such results are summarized next.

A *sufficient* condition for Jacobi iteration to converge to the solution of the system $\mathbf{A}\,\mathbf{x} = \mathbf{b}$ is that the original matrix $\mathbf{A}$ be strictly diagonally dominant. This means that, for each row, the magnitude of the diagonal element is greater than the sum of the magnitudes of the other elements in the row.

A *necessary and sufficient* condition for the convergence of the Jacobi method is that the magnitude of the largest eigenvalue of the iteration matrix $\mathbf{C}$ be less than 1. Eigenvalues and eigenvectors are discussed further in Chapter 5.

Using a built-in function to compute eigenvalues of the iteration matrix $\mathbf{C}$ in Example 6.4 (which follows), we find values of

$$3.4641 \qquad \text{and} \qquad -3.4641.$$

Clearly, Jacobi iteration is not suitable for this problem. The eigenvalues of the iteration matrix for the original ordering of the equations (in Example 6.1) are

$$0.28868 \qquad \text{and} \qquad -0.28868.$$

Of course, we would not normally use an iterative method on such a small system, but the point is that the method will not converge for this simple example. (For further discussion of these results, see Atkinson, 1989, pp. 546–54.)

Example 6.4 Jacobi Method is Sensitive to the Order of Equations

To illustrate the sensitivity of the Jacobi method to the form of the coefficient matrix $\mathbf{A}$ (or equivalently, to the form of the iteration matrix $\mathbf{C}$), consider the simple system from the beginning of this section, but with the order of the equations reversed, so that the system is no longer diagonally dominant:

$$x + 2y = 6,$$
$$2x + y = 6.$$

In the Jacobi iterative form, we have (see Fig. 6.2)

$$L_1: \quad x = -2y + 6,$$
$$L_2: \quad y = -2x + 6.$$

Starting with $x^{(1)} = 1/2$ and $y^{(1)} = 1/2$, we obtain

$$x^{(2)} = -2y^{(1)} + 6 = 5,$$
$$y^{(2)} = -2x^{(1)} + 6 = 5.$$

Further iterations show that the solution diverges, with x and y alternating between large positive and large negative values.

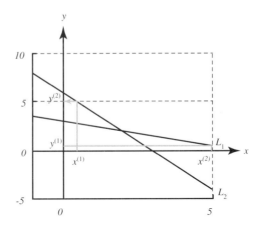

FIGURE 6.2   Divergent Jacobi iterations.

Computational Effort and Other Considerations

Each iteration of the Jacobi method requires one matrix-vector multiplication, or $(n - 1)^2$ scalar multiplications. Thus, if the method converges in a reasonable number of iterations, the computational effort could be significantly less than the $O(n^3)$ multiplications required for Gaussian elimination.

The Jacobi method is particularly convenient for parallel computation, because each component of the solution can be updated independently of the other components.

The Gauss-Seidel method of solving linear systems is a simple iterative technique obtained by transforming the linear system $\mathbf{A}\,\mathbf{x} = \mathbf{b}$ into the system $\mathbf{x} = \mathbf{C}\,\mathbf{x} + \mathbf{d}$, in which the matrix $\mathbf{C}$ has zeros on the diagonal. However, in contrast to the Jacobi method, each component of the vector $\mathbf{x}$ on the right-hand side of the transformed equation is updated immediately as each iteration progresses. This procedure is called *sequential updating*.

Example 6.5 Graphical Illustration of the Gauss-Seidel Method

To visualize the Gauss-Seidel iterations, consider the two-by-two system introduced in Example 6.1; the equations are written as

$$x = -\frac{1}{2}y + 3$$

$$y = -\frac{1}{2}x + 3$$

The first iteration is illustrated in Fig. 6.3 for the starting values of $x^{(1)} = 1/2$ and $y^{(1)} = 1/2$. The first equation then produces the next estimate for x (using $y^{(1)}$) and the second equation is used to find the next value of y (using the newly computed value, $x^{(2)}$). The result is

$$x^{(2)} = -\frac{1}{2}y^{(1)} + 3 = -\frac{1}{4} + 3 = \frac{11}{4},$$

$$y^{(2)} = -\frac{1}{2}x^{(2)} + 3 = -\frac{11}{8} + 3 = \frac{13}{8}.$$

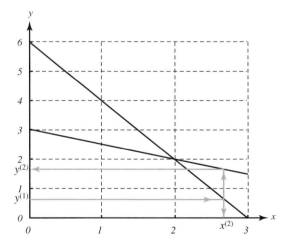

FIGURE 6.3 First step of Gauss-Seidel iteration.

6.2.1 Algorithm for the Gauss-Seidel Method

We summarize the steps in using the Gauss-Seidel method to solve $\mathbf{M x} = \mathbf{b}$ in the following algorithm. Since Gauss-Seidel iteration uses the updated value of each component of the solution vector as soon as it is computed, there is no need to maintain the old and the new forms of the solution vector separately. The product of the ith row of $\mathbf{C}$ with the column vector $\mathbf{x}$ is written out explicitly in the following algorithm.

Gauss-Seidel Iteration

Input
  $\mathbf{M}$ *coefficient matrix (n-by-n)*
  $\mathbf{b}$ *right-hand side vector (n-by-1)*
  $\mathbf{x}$ *initial guess vector*
  n   *number of rows or columns in* $\mathbf{M}$
  max   *maximum number of iterations*
  tol   *tolerance for convergence*

Initialize
  For i = 1 to n   *create iteration matrix* $\mathbf{C}$
          C(i, :) = −M(i, :)/M(i,i) *transform each row*
          C(i,i) = 0
          d(i) = b(i)/M(i,i)   *scale right-hand side vector*
  End

Compute
For k = 1 to max
          Form new solution vector $\mathbf{x}_n$ from the old solution vector $\mathbf{x}_o$
  For i = 1 to n
          dot = 0
          For j = 1 to n
              dot = dot + C(i, j)*x(j)
          End
          x(i) = dot + d(i)
  End
  If ($| \mathbf{M x} - \mathbf{b} | <$ tol) break   *Test for convergence*
End

Return
  $\mathbf{x}$

Another possible test for convergence is to check the norm of the change in the solution.

6.2.2 Application of the Gauss-Seidel Method

We illustrate the use of the Gauss-Seidel algorithm in the next example.

Example 6.6 Using the Gauss-Seidel Algorithm

Consider the three-by-three system of equations (as in Example 6.2)

$$
\begin{aligned}
2x_1 - x_2 + x_3 &= -1 \\
x_1 + 2x_2 - x_3 &= 6 \\
x_1 - x_2 + 2x_3 &= -3,
\end{aligned}
$$

which are converted to the iterative system

$$
\begin{aligned}
x_1^{(\text{new})} &= \qquad\qquad\quad + 0.5x_2^{(\text{old})} - 0.5x_3^{(\text{old})} + -0.5 \\
x_2^{(\text{new})} &= -0.5x_1^{(\text{new})} \qquad\qquad\quad + 0.5x_3^{(\text{old})} + \quad 3.0 \\
x_3^{(\text{new})} &= -0.5x_1^{(\text{new})} + 0.5x_2^{(\text{new})} \qquad\qquad + -1.5
\end{aligned}
$$

Note that the most recent estimate for each of the unknowns is used in evaluating the right-hand side of each equation.

Starting with $x^{(0)} = (0, 0, 0)$, we find

$$
\begin{aligned}
x_1 &= \qquad\qquad\qquad (0.5)(0) \quad + (-0.5)(0) + -0.5 = -0.5 \\
x_2 &= (-0.5)(-0.5) \qquad\qquad\quad + \quad (0.5)(0) + \quad 3.0 = \quad 3.25 \\
x_3 &= (-0.5)(-0.5) + (0.5)(3.25) + \qquad\qquad + -1.5 = \quad 0.375
\end{aligned}
$$

For the second iteration,

$$
\begin{aligned}
x_1 &= \qquad\qquad\qquad (0.5)(3.25) \quad + (-0.5)(0.375) + -0.5 = \quad 0.9375 \\
x_2 &= (-0.5)(0.9375) \qquad\qquad\quad + \quad (0.5)(0.375) + \quad 3.0 = \quad 2.7188 \\
x_3 &= (-0.5)(0.9375) + (0.5)(2.7188) \qquad\qquad + -1.5 = -0.6094
\end{aligned}
$$

The Gauss-Seidel method converges in 10 iterations to the vector

$$
\mathbf{x} = [1.0001 \quad 1.9999 \quad -1.0001]^T.
$$

The stopping condition is that the Euclidean norm of the difference of the solutions between two successive iterations be less than 0.001.

6.2.3 Discussion

The Gauss-Seidel method is usually derived by converting the original system, $\mathbf{A}\mathbf{x} = \mathbf{b}$, into a decomposed form $(\mathbf{L} + \mathbf{D} + \mathbf{U})\,\mathbf{x} = \mathbf{b}$ where $\mathbf{D}$ is a diagonal matrix, $\mathbf{L}$ is a lower triangular matrix, and $\mathbf{U}$ is an upper triangular matrix. The decomposed form is expressed as $\mathbf{x} = \mathbf{T}\mathbf{x} + \mathbf{c}$ in the following way:

$$
\begin{aligned}
(\mathbf{D} + \mathbf{L})\mathbf{x} &= -\mathbf{U}\mathbf{x} + \mathbf{b} \\
\mathbf{x} &= (\mathbf{D} + \mathbf{L})^{-1}(-\mathbf{U})\mathbf{x} + (\mathbf{D} + \mathbf{L})^{-1}\mathbf{b}. \\
\mathbf{x} &= \mathbf{T}\mathbf{x} + \mathbf{c}
\end{aligned}
$$

Like the Jacobi method, the Gauss-Seidel method is sensitive to the form of the coefficient matrix $\mathbf{A}$ (or equivalently, to the form of the iteration matrix $\mathbf{T}$); reversing the order of the equations in Example 6.6 shows a divergence similar to that for the Jacobi method.

Some Useful Theoretical Results on Convergence

There are several useful theoretical results concerning the relationships between the characteristics of the matrix $\mathbf{A}$ (or the iteration matrix $\mathbf{T}$) and the convergence of Gauss-Seidel iteration for the system $\mathbf{A}\,\mathbf{x} = \mathbf{b}$. The matrix form of the Gauss-Seidel method is used primarily for analyzing the convergence of the method; however, general theoretical results that guarantee convergence (which depend on the eigenvalues of the matrix $\mathbf{T}$) are not necessarily the most convenient for important applications.

The numerical solution of partial differential equations (see Chapter 15) leads to linear systems in which the matrix $\mathbf{A}$ is real and symmetric, with positive diagonal elements. For such matrices, the Gauss-Seidel method will converge (for any $x^{(0)}$) if and only if all of the eigenvalues of $\mathbf{A}$ are real and positive. (See Atkinson, 1989, pp. 499, 551; a proof is given in Isaacson and Keller, 1966, pp. 70–71.) For an example that does not satisfy the symmetry requirement, theoretical analysis is more difficult to carry out.

If $\mathbf{A}$ is positive definite, Gauss-Seidel iteration converges for any initial vector. (For a proof of this result, see Ralston and Rabinowitz, 1978, p. 445.) We discuss some tests for positive definite matrices in the next section.

If the iteration matrix $\mathbf{C}$ is non-negative (a situation that often occurs in the numerical solution of partial differential equations), then the Jacobi and Gauss-Seidel methods either both converge or both diverge. When they both converge, Gauss-Seidel iteration converges more rapidly (except in the trivial case when the largest eigenvalue of the iteration matrix for both methods is zero; see Ralston and Rabinowitz, 1978, p. 446).

Computational Effort and Other Considerations

The Gauss-Seidel method typically converges more rapidly than the Jacobi method, although it is more difficult to use for parallel computation. In particular, for a linear system arising in the finite-difference solution of Poisson's PDE, with a J-by-J grid (so there are J^2 equations), it can be shown that the number of iterations r required to reduce the error by a factor of 10^{-p} is $r \approx \dfrac{1}{4}\,p\,J^2$. The Jacobi method requires approximately twice as many iterations; $r \approx \dfrac{1}{2}\,p\,J^2$ Thus, although Gauss-Seidel converges more rapidly, it is still impractical for very large problems. Finite-difference problems often have $J = 100$ or more. In the next section, we consider a method of accelerating the convergence of Gauss-Seidel. See Press et al., 1992, for further discussion of these issues.

It is possible to modify the Gauss-Seidel method by introducing an additional para-meter, ω (omega), that may accelerate the convergence of the iterations. The idea is to take a combination of the previous value of $\mathbf{x}$ and the current update (from the Gauss-Seidel method). The parameter ω controls the proportion of the update that comes from the previous solution and the proportion that comes from the current calculation. For $0 < \omega < 1$, the method is called successive underrelaxation; for $1 < \omega < 2$, the method is called successive overrelaxation (SOR). For $\omega = 1$, SOR reduces to the Gauss-Seidel method.

Consider the three-by-three system

$$a_{11} x_1 + a_{12} x_2 + a_{13} x_3 = b_1,$$

$$a_{21} x_1 + a_{22} x_2 + a_{23} x_3 = b_2,$$

$$a_{31} x_1 + a_{32} x_2 + a_{33} x_3 = b_3.$$

The SOR equations are

$$x_1^{(new)} = (1 - \omega)x_1^{(old)} + \frac{\omega}{a_{11}} (b_1 \qquad\qquad - a_{12} x_2^{(old)} - a_{13} x_3^{(old)})$$

$$x_2^{(new)} = (1 - \omega)x_2^{(old)} + \frac{\omega}{a_{22}} (b_2 - a_{21} x_1^{(new)} \qquad - a_{23} x_3^{(old)})$$

$$x_3^{(new)} = (1 - \omega)x_3^{(old)} + \frac{\omega}{a_{33}} (b_3 - a_{31} x_1^{(new)} - a_{32} x_2^{(new)} \qquad)$$

Although underrelaxation can sometimes be used to convert a non-conver-gent problem into a convergent one, the primary use of relaxation methods is in applications where the coefficient matrix has a structure that allows overrelaxation to accelerate the convergence of an already convergent process. In particular, SOR is important for solving the linear systems that arise in the finite difference approach to solving certain partial differential equations (described in Chapter 15). Such problems often involve systems of $N = 10^4$ (or more) equations. The number of iterations required to achieve a specified accuracy using Jacobi or Gauss-Seidel is proportional to N^2. (The proportionality constant is smaller for Gauss-Seidel than for Jacobi.) With the proper choice of the relaxation parameter, the number of iterations for SOR is proportional to N rather than N^2. However, the proper choice of the relaxation parameter is a crucial consideration in the effective use of SOR; optimal values have been determined for some systems that occur in the solution of PDE. For systems for which the optimal value of ω has not already been determined, this can be a major difficulty in using the SOR method. We consider the choice of ω further after illustrating the use of SOR for some small problems.

6.3.1 Algorithm for SOR

The following algorithm for the SOR method assumes that matrix-vector multiplication, such as the product of a row of matrix **C** times the column vector **x,** (C(j, :) * x is defined.

SOR Method

Input
M	*coefficient matrix (n-by-n)*
b	*right-hand side vector (n-by-1)*
xo	*initial guess vector*
n	*number of rows or columns in **M***
max	*maximum number of iterations*
tol	*tolerance for convergence*
w	*relaxation parameter, $1 \leq w < 2$*

Initialize
For i = 1 to n   *create iteration matrix **C***
    $C(i, :) = -M(i, :)/M(i,i)$ *transform each row*
    $C(i,i) = 0$
    $d(i) = b(i)/M(i,i)$ *scale right-hand side vector*
    $xn(i) = xo(i)$ *set solution vector equal to initial estimate*
End

Compute
For k = 1 to max
    For i = 1 to n
        $xn(i) = (1 - w)*xo(i) + w*(C(i, :)*xn(:) + d(i))$
    End

    If ($|\mathbf{M\,xn} - \mathbf{b}| <$ tol) break   *test for convergence*
    For i = 1 to n
        $xo(i) = xn(i)$
    End

Return
xn

6.3.2 Applications of SOR

Example 6.7 Solving a Small System Using SOR

Consider the 3-by-3 system $\mathbf{A}\,\mathbf{x} = \mathbf{b}$, where

$$\mathbf{A} = \begin{bmatrix} 4 & -2 & 0 \\ -2 & 6 & -5 \\ 0 & -5 & 11 \end{bmatrix}$$

$$\mathbf{b} = [8 \quad -29 \quad 43]^T.$$

The system is converted to

$$x_1 = (1 - \omega)x_1^{(old)} + \omega\left(\qquad + \frac{1}{2}x_2^{(old)} + \qquad + 2 \right)$$

$$x_2 = (1 - \omega)x_2^{(old)} + \omega\left(\frac{1}{3}x_1^{(new)} \qquad + \frac{5}{6}x_3^{(old)} - \frac{29}{6} \right)$$

$$x_3 = (1 - \omega)x_3^{(old)} + \omega\left(\qquad + \frac{5}{11}x_2^{(new)} \qquad + \frac{43}{11} \right)$$

We illustrate the first iteration, using $\omega = 1.2$.

Starting with $x^{(0)} = (0, 0, 0)$, we find

$$x_1 = -0.8(0) + 1.2(\qquad + (1/2)(0) \qquad + 2 \quad) = \quad 2.4$$

$$x_2 = -0.8(0) + 1.2((1/3)(2.4) + \qquad + (5/6)(0) - 29/6) = -4.84$$

$$x_3 = -0.8(0) + 1.2(\qquad + (5/11)(-4.84) \qquad + 43/11 = \quad 2.05$$

Results from a simple computer program are shown in the following table.

Results for SOR iterations

i	x_1	x_2	x_3
1	2.4	−4.84	2.0509
2	−0.984	−3.1747	2.5491
3	0.69199	−2.3392	2.9052
4	0.85809	−2.0838	2.9733
5	0.97813	−2.0187	2.9951
6	0.99314	−2.0039	2.9989
7	0.99905	−2.0007	2.9998

The stopping condition is that the Euclidean norm of the difference of the solutions between two successive iterations be less than tol $= 0.001$.

> ### Example 6.8 A Linear System That Comes from a PDE
>
> We investigate the convergence of the boundary value problem discussed in Examples 6-A and 6.4, with $x^{(0)} = [0 \quad 0 \quad \ldots \quad 0]^T$ and tolerance $= 0.00001$ for several values of ω. Of course, for $\omega = 1$, the SOR method is the same as Gauss-Seidel iteration. The required number of iterations for selected values of ω are shown in the following table.
>
> **Number of iterations for different values of the relaxation parameter ω**
>
> | ω | 0.8 | 0.9 | 1.0 | 1.2 | 1.25 | 1.3 | 1.4 |
> |---|---|---|---|---|---|---|---|
> | No. of iterations | 44 | 36 | 29 | 18 | 15 | 13 | 16 |

6.3.3   Discussion

The SOR method can be derived by multiplying the decomposed system obtained from the Gauss-Seidel method by the relaxation parameter ω, i.e.,

$$\omega(\mathbf{D} + \mathbf{L})\mathbf{x} = -\omega\mathbf{U}\mathbf{x} + \omega\mathbf{b},$$

and adding $(1 - \omega)\,\mathbf{D}\mathbf{x}$ to each side of the equation. This gives

$$(\mathbf{D} - \omega\mathbf{L})\mathbf{x} = ((1 - \omega)\,\mathbf{D} - \omega\mathbf{U})\,\mathbf{x} + \omega\mathbf{b},$$

which can be solved for $\mathbf{x}$ (for purposes of analysis) to obtain

$$\mathbf{x} = (\mathbf{D} - \omega\mathbf{L})^{-1}((1 - \omega)\mathbf{D} + \omega\mathbf{U})\,\mathbf{x} + \omega(\mathbf{D} - \omega\mathbf{L})^{-1}\mathbf{b}.$$

The SOR iteration matrix is $\mathbf{C} = (\mathbf{D} - \omega\mathbf{L})^{-1}((1 - \omega)\mathbf{D} + \omega\mathbf{U})$. It can be shown that $\det \mathbf{C} = (1 - \omega)^n$. Since the determinant of a matrix is equal to the product of its eigenvalues, at least one eigenvalue of $\mathbf{C}$ must be greater than or equal to 1 in absolute value if either $\omega \leq 0$ or $\omega \geq 2$. Therefore, the iteration parameter ω should always be chosen such that $0 < \omega < 2$.

Given an approximate solution $\mathbf{x}^{(k)}$ to the linear system $\mathbf{A}\mathbf{x} = \mathbf{b}$, the residual vector $\mathbf{r}$ is defined to be $\mathbf{r} = \mathbf{b} - \mathbf{A}\mathbf{x}^{(k)}$. The SOR method is designed to reduce the residual vector more rapidly than the Gauss-Seidel method does (see Golub and Ortega, 1992, p. 299).

Some Useful Theoretical Results for Positive Definite Matrices

It is always important to consider whether an iterative process will converge to a solution. The Ostrowski theorem gives some information on the convergence of the SOR method for an important class of matrices, namely, positive definite matrices.

Ostrowski Theorem

If $\mathbf{A}$ is a positive definite matrix and $0 < \omega < 2$, then the SOR method will converge for any initial vector $\mathbf{x}$ (see Golub and Ortega, 1992, p. 298).

The matrix $\mathbf{A}$ is *positive definite* if $\mathbf{x}^T \mathbf{A} \mathbf{x} > \mathbf{0}$ for any vector $\mathbf{x}$ that is not the zero vector. Unfortunately, this definition does not provide a convenient way to check whether a particular matrix is positive definite. Since symmetric matrices occur in many applications for which SOR is important, we summarize a few useful results for testing whether a symmetric matrix is positive definite.

Necessary and Sufficient Tests for a Positive Definite Matrix

For a real, symmetric matrix $\mathbf{A}$, each of the following tests is a necessary and sufficient condition for $\mathbf{A}$ to be positive definite:

$\mathbf{x}^T \mathbf{A} \mathbf{x} > 0$
All eigenvalues of $\mathbf{A}$ are positive.
All upper left submatrices of $\mathbf{A}$ have positive determinants.
All pivots of $\mathbf{A}$ (without row interchanges) are positive.

(See Strang, 1988, p. 331.)

Another Test for a Positive Definite Matrix

A symmetric matrix is positive definite if it is diagonally dominant and each diagonal element is positive (Golub and Van Loan, 1996, p. 141).

Properties of a Symmetric Positive Definite Matrix

If $\mathbf{A}$ is symmetric and positive definite, then

1. $\mathbf{A}$ is nonsingular
2. $a_{ii} > 0$ for $i = 1, \dots n$
3. $a_{ii} a_{jj} > (a_{jj})^2$ for $i \neq j$

(See Faires and Burden, 1998, p. 276.)

Biconjugate Gradient Method

The biconjugate gradient method is a generalization of the conjugate gradient method for use in solving an n-by-n linear system that is not necessarily either symmetric or positive definite. This method does not have a direct connection with function minimization. The biconjugate gradient method works with four sequences of vectors, which we denote as $\mathbf{r}_k$, $\mathbf{s}_k$, $\mathbf{p}_k$ and $\mathbf{q}_k$. The sequence $\mathbf{r}_k$ is the sequence of residuals $\mathbf{r}_k = \mathbf{b} - \mathbf{A}\,\mathbf{x}_k$. The process is as follows.

Input
$\quad$ **A** $\qquad\qquad\qquad\qquad\qquad$ *coefficient matrix*
$\quad$ **b** $\qquad\qquad\qquad\qquad\qquad$ *right hand side vector*
$\quad$ $\mathbf{x}_1$ $\qquad\qquad\qquad\qquad\qquad$ *initial estimate of solution*

Initialize
$\qquad$ $\mathbf{r}_1 = \mathbf{b} - \mathbf{A}\,\mathbf{x}_1$ $\qquad\qquad\qquad$ *compute the residual*
$\qquad$ $\mathbf{s}_1 = \mathbf{r}_1$
$\qquad$ $\mathbf{p}_1 = \mathbf{r}_1$
$\qquad$ $\mathbf{q}_1 = \mathbf{s}_1$

Compute
For $k = 1, \ldots n$

$$\alpha_k = \frac{\mathbf{s}_k\,\mathbf{r}_k}{\mathbf{q}_k\,\mathbf{A}\,\mathbf{p}_k}$$

$\qquad$ $\mathbf{x}_{k+1} = \mathbf{x}_k + \alpha_k\,\mathbf{p}_k$ $\qquad\qquad$ *Compute new solution*

$\qquad$ $\mathbf{r}_{k+1} = \mathbf{r}_k - \alpha_k\mathbf{a}\,\mathbf{p}_k$
$\qquad$ $\mathbf{s}_{k+1} = \mathbf{r}_k - \alpha_k\mathbf{A}^{\mathrm{T}}\,\mathbf{q}_k$
$\qquad$ If $\mathbf{r}_{k+1} = \mathbf{s}_{k+1} = 0$, Break $\qquad$ *Check for termination*

$$\beta_k = \frac{\mathbf{s}_{k+1}\,\mathbf{r}_{k+1}}{\mathbf{s}_k\,\mathbf{r}_k}$$

$\qquad$ $\mathbf{p}_{k+1}\mathbf{r}_k + \beta_k\,\mathbf{p}_k$
$\qquad$ $\mathbf{q}_{k+1} = \mathbf{s}_k + \beta_k\,\mathbf{q}_k$
End

Return $\qquad$ $\mathbf{x}_{k+1}$

$\qquad$ It can be shown that the vector $\mathbf{r}_{k+1}$ is in fact the residual corresponding to the solution vector $\mathbf{x}_{k+1}$, and that the process will terminate in at most n steps. There are several important relationships that are satisfied by combinations of the vectors formed in this process; see Press et al., 1992, for more details on this and other conjugate gradient methods. A convergence condition on the relative residual `norm(b - A x)/norm(b)` may also be included.

6.4.2 Simplex Method

A linear programming problem is a problem in which we seek to find the maximum or minimum of a linear function, subject to linear constraints (equalities and inequalities). The standard solution method for such problems is known as the *simplex method*. We give a brief introduction to the basic simplex method here.

The problem of linear programming is to maximize a given linear function (called the *objective function*)

$$z = b_1 x_1 + b_2 x_2 + \ldots b_n x_n$$

subject to the constraints that each of the variables be non-negative, and also subject to m other linear inequality or equality constraints.

A vector that satisfies the constraints is called a *feasible solution*.

To illustrate the process, consider the following simple problem:

Maximize

$$z = x_1 + 3x_2$$

Subject to the constraints that

$$1 + x_1 - x_2 \geq 0$$
$$5 - x_1 - 2x_2 \geq 0$$
$$8 - 2x_1 - x_2 \geq 0$$

The foundation of the simplex method is that the region containing all of the feasible solutions is an n-dimensional convex polyhedron or simplex (since the boundaries are hyperplanes), and that the optimal feasible solution must occur at a vertex of this simplex. At a vertex of the feasible region some of the inequality constraints are satisfied as equalities. There are a total of $n + m$ constraints; n of these will be exactly satisfied by the optimal feasible solution. The simplex method gives us a systematic procedure in which the objective function increases at each step and the number of steps is (almost always) no more than the larger of m and n.

The simplest form of linear programming problem is one that is in "restricted normal form." Although this form may seem very limited in its usefulness, in fact general linear programming problems may be converted to this form by introducing additional variables. We limit our discussion of linear programming to problems in restricted normal form. The requirements for this form are that all constraints, other than the non-negativity of the variables, are equality constraints. Furthermore, we require that each constraint equation has at least one variable that appears only in that equation. We solve each constraint for one such variable. The variables that are thus selected are called *basic variables*; the other variables (which appear on the right-hand side of the equations) are *nonbasic variables*. The solution of the system is found by setting the nonbasic variables to zero. The method determines which of the variables should ultimately be basic, and which nonbasic, by investigating, in a systematic manner, the effect on the objective function of interchanging one basic and one nonbasic variable at each step.

Since the restricted normal form can only be achieved for $m \leq n$, we limit the discussion to that case. We write the objective function so that it depends only on nonbasic variables (substituting for any basic variables that may appear). A feasible solution can be found by setting all nonbasic variables to zero. A problem with inequality constraints can be transformed to the restricted normal form by the introduction of additional non-negative variables. The simplex method is usually presented in a tabular format (tableau). However, we only intend to sketch the general ideas of the method here, with as little special notation as is necessary for clarity.

To illustrate the process, consider the following simple problem, which is the problem introduced above, transformed to restricted normal form.

Maximize

$$z = x_1 + 3x_2$$

Subject to

$$x_3 = 1 + x_1 - x_2$$

$$x_4 = 5 - x_1 - 2x_2$$

$$x_5 = 8 - 2x_1 - x_2$$

The simplex method begins by considering the effect of setting all of the nonbasic variables to 0. The nonbasic variables in the example above are the variables x_1 and x_2. With that choice for x_1 and x_2, we would have $z = 0$ and $x_3 = 1$, $x_4 = 5$, and $x_5 = 8$. This is a feasible solution, in that all of the equations are satisfied, but is not a particularly good solution in terms of maximizing the objective function. We then consider the effect of increasing either x_1 or x_2, to improve the value of z. That is, we consider the effect of making either x_1 or x_2 into a basic variable. Increasing either x_1 or x_2 will increase (improve) z, since the coefficient of each of these variables in the z equation is positive; we now consider which one to increase. Whichever we choose, we would like to increase as much as possible, without causing any of the variables, x_3, x_4, or x_5 to become negative.

If we increase x_2, (and remember that x_1 is still 0), then

the first equation limits the increase to $x_2 \rightarrow 1$ (so that $x_3 \geq 0$);
the second equation limits the increase to $x_2 \rightarrow 5/2$ (so that $x_4 \geq 0$); and
the third equation limits the increase to $x_2 \rightarrow 8$ (so that $x_5 \geq 0$).

Since we require that *all* of the variables stay positive, we could only let x_2 increase to 1. This would change the value of z from 0 to 3, an increase of 3.

On the other hand, if we increase x_1 (with x_2 still equal to 0), then

the first equation places no limits on the increase (since the coefficient of x_1 is positive);
the second equation limits the increase to $x_1 \rightarrow 5$ (so that $x_4 > 0$); and
the third equation limits the increase to $x_1 \rightarrow 8/2 = 4$ (so that $x_5 \geq 0$).

Since we require that all of the variables stay positive, we can take $x_1 = 4$.

Since this would increase the value of z by 4, which is greater than the increase in z that we can achieve by increasing x_2, this is the preferred change.

To accomplish the change (to make x_1 into a basic variable), we solve the third equation for x_1, since it is the equation that limits the acceptable change in x_1

$$x_3 = 1 + x_1 - x_2$$

$$x_4 = 5 - x_1 - 2x_2$$

$$x_5 = 8 - 2x_1 - x_2 \rightarrow x_1 = 4 - \frac{1}{2}x_2 - \frac{1}{2}x_5$$

and substitute into the other equations

$$z = x_1 + 3x_2 \qquad \rightarrow \qquad z = \left(4 - \frac{1}{2}x_2 - \frac{1}{2}x_5\right) + 3x_2$$

$$= 4 + \frac{5}{2}x_2 - \frac{1}{2}x_5$$

$$x_3 = 1 + x_1 - x_2 \qquad \rightarrow \qquad x_3 = 1 + \left(4 - \frac{1}{2}x_2 - \frac{1}{2}x_5\right) - x_2$$

$$x_3 = 5 - \frac{3}{2}x_2 - \frac{1}{2}x_5$$

$$x_4 = 5 - x_1 - 2x_2 \qquad \rightarrow \qquad x_4 = 5 - \left(4 - \frac{1}{2}x_2 - \frac{1}{2}x_5\right) - 2x_2$$

$$x_4 = 1 - \frac{3}{2}x_2 + \frac{1}{2}x_5)$$

(already done) $x_5 = 8 - 2x_1 - x_2 \qquad \rightarrow \qquad x_1 = 4 - \frac{1}{2}x_2 - \frac{1}{2}x_5$

The basic variables are now x_1, x_3, and x_4. A couple of observations are in order before we proceed. The first is that only variables that appear in the z-equation with positive coefficients are candidates for selection as basic variables, as they are the only variables that are currently 0 that could increase the value of z if they were increased to a positive value. The second observation is that only equations (the constraint equations) in which the candidate variable appears with a negative coefficient place a restriction on how much the variable can be increased.

To proceed, we see that since

$$z = 4 + \frac{5}{2}x_2 - \frac{1}{2}x_5$$

the only one of the variables on the right-hand side of these equations that could be increased (from its present value of zero) to increase the value of z is x_2. To determine the maximum allowable increase, we see that

the first constraint equation limits the increase of x_2 to at most 10/3;

the second constraint equation limits the increase of x_2 to at most 2/3; and

the third equation limits the increase of x_2 to at most 8.

Thus, we will make x_2 into a basic variable by solving the second equation for x_2:

$$x_3 = 5 - \frac{3}{2}x_2 - \frac{1}{2}x_5$$

$$x_4 = 1 - \frac{3}{2}x_2 + \frac{1}{2}x_5 \qquad \longrightarrow \qquad x_2 = \frac{2}{3} - \frac{2}{3}x_4 + \frac{1}{3}x_5$$

$$x_1 = 4 - \frac{1}{2}x_2 - \frac{1}{2}x_5$$

and substituting into each of the other equations.

New equations

$$z = 4 + \frac{5}{2}x_2 - \frac{1}{2}x_5 \quad \longrightarrow \quad z = 4 + \frac{5}{2}\left(\frac{2}{3} - \frac{2}{3}x_4 + \frac{1}{3}x_5\right) - \frac{1}{2}x_5$$

$$z = \frac{17}{3} - \frac{5}{3}x_4 + \frac{1}{3}x_5$$

$$x_3 = 5 - \frac{3}{2}x_2 - \frac{1}{2}x_5 \quad \longrightarrow \quad x_3 = 5 - \frac{3}{2}\left(\frac{2}{3} - \frac{2}{3}x_4 + \frac{1}{3}x_5\right) - \frac{1}{2}x_5$$

$$x_3 = 4 + x_4 - x_5$$

(already transformed)

$$x_2 = \frac{2}{3} - \frac{2}{3}x_4 + \frac{1}{3}x_5$$

$$x_1 = 4 - \frac{1}{2}x_2 - \frac{1}{2}x_5 \quad \longrightarrow \quad x_1 = 4 - \frac{1}{2}\left(\frac{2}{3} - \frac{2}{3}x_4 + \frac{1}{3}x_5\right) - \frac{1}{2}x_5$$

$$x_1 = \frac{11}{3} + \frac{1}{3}x_4 - \frac{2}{3}x_5$$

Since the coefficient of x_5 in the objective function

$$z = \frac{17}{3} - \frac{5}{3}x_4 + \frac{1}{3}x_5$$

is positive, we consider making x_5 into a basic variable. The constraint equations are currently

$$x_3 = 4 + x_4 - x_5$$

$$x_2 = \frac{2}{3} - \frac{2}{3}x_4 + \frac{1}{3}x_5$$

$$x_1 = \frac{11}{3} + \frac{1}{3}x_4 - \frac{2}{3}x_5$$

Since the coefficient of x_5 is positive in the second constraint equation, only the first and third equations limit the amount by which x_5 could be increased. The first equation limits the increase to $x_5 \rightarrow 4$, whereas the third equation limits the increase to $x_5 \rightarrow 11/2$. Thus, we convert x_5 to a basic variable, by solving the first equation for x_5,

$$x_3 = 4 + x_4 - x_5 \qquad \rightarrow \qquad x_5 = 4 + x_4 - x_3$$

and substituting the resulting expression into the objective function and the other constraint equations.

$$z = \frac{17}{3} - \frac{5}{3} x_4 + \frac{1}{3} x_5 \qquad \rightarrow \qquad z = \frac{17}{3} - \frac{5}{3} x_4 + \frac{1}{3}(4 + x_4 - x_3)$$

$$z = 7 - \frac{4}{3} x_4 - \frac{1}{3} x_3$$

$$x_2 = \frac{2}{3} - \frac{2}{3} x_4 + \frac{1}{3} x_5 \qquad \rightarrow \qquad x_2 = \frac{2}{3} - \frac{2}{3} x_4 + \frac{1}{3}(4 + x_4 - x_3)$$

$$x_2 = 2 - \frac{1}{3} x_4 - \frac{1}{3} x_3$$

$$x_1 = \frac{11}{3} + \frac{1}{3} x_4 - \frac{2}{3} x_5 \qquad \rightarrow \qquad x_1 = \frac{11}{3} + \frac{1}{3} x_4 - \frac{2}{3}(4 + x_4 - x_3)$$

$$x_1 = 1 - \frac{1}{3} x_4 + \frac{2}{3} x_3$$

Since the objective function, $z = 7 - \frac{4}{3} x_4 - \frac{1}{3} x_3$ cannot be increased by increasing either of the nonbasic variables, the process is finished. The final solution is found by setting the nonbasic variables to 0, which gives

$$x_3 = x_4 = 0, \, x_1 = 1, \, x_2 = 2, \, x_5 = 4, \text{ and } z = 7.$$

To solve the linear system $\mathbf{A}\,\mathbf{x} = \mathbf{b}$ iteratively; convert it into an equivalent system $\mathbf{x} = \mathbf{C}\mathbf{x} + \mathbf{d}$ and generate a sequence of approximations $\mathbf{x}^{(1)}$, $\mathbf{x}^{(2)}$, ..., according to the formula $\mathbf{x}^{(k)} = \mathbf{C}\,\mathbf{x}^{(k-1)} + \mathbf{d}$. The ith equation is solved explicitly for the ith component of $\mathbf{x}$. The methods are illustrated for $n = 4$.

Jacobi Method

$$x_1^{(k)} = -\frac{a_{12}}{a_{11}} x_2^{(k-1)} - \frac{a_{13}}{a_{11}} x_3^{(k-1)} - \frac{a_{14}}{a_{11}} x_4^{(k-1)} + \frac{b_1}{a_{11}}$$

$$x_2^{(k)} = -\frac{a_{21}}{a_{22}} x_1^{(k-1)} - \frac{a_{23}}{a_{22}} x_3^{(k-1)} - \frac{a_{24}}{a_{22}} x_4^{(k-1)} + \frac{b_2}{a_{22}}$$

$$x_3^{(k)} = -\frac{a_{31}}{a_{33}} x_1^{(k-1)} - \frac{a_{32}}{a_{33}} x_2^{(k-1)} - \frac{a_{34}}{a_{33}} x_4^{(k-1)} + \frac{b_3}{a_{33}}$$

$$x_4^{(k)} = -\frac{a_{41}}{a_{44}} x_1^{(k-1)} - \frac{a_{42}}{a_{44}} x_2^{(k-1)} - \frac{a_{43}}{a_{44}} x_3^{(k-1)} + \frac{b_4}{a_{44}}$$

Gauss-Seidel Method

$$x_1^{(k)} = -\frac{a_{12}}{a_{11}} x_2^{(k-1)} - \frac{a_{13}}{a_{11}} x_3^{(k-1)} - \frac{a_{14}}{a_{11}} x_4^{(k-1)} + \frac{b_1}{a_{11}}$$

$$x_2^{(k)} = -\frac{a_{21}}{a_{22}} x_1^{(k)} - \frac{a_{23}}{a_{22}} x_3^{(k-1)} - \frac{a_{24}}{a_{22}} x_4^{(k-1)} + \frac{b_2}{a_{22}}$$

$$x_3^{(k)} = -\frac{a_{31}}{a_{33}} x_1^{(k)} - \frac{a_{32}}{a_{33}} x_2^{(k)} - \frac{a_{34}}{a_{33}} x_4^{(k-1)} + \frac{b_3}{a_{33}}$$

$$x_4^{(k)} = -\frac{a_{41}}{a_{44}} x_1^{(k)} - \frac{a_{42}}{a_{44}} x_2^{(k)} - \frac{a_{43}}{a_{44}} x_3^{(k)} + \frac{b_4}{a_{44}}$$

SOR Method

$$x_1^{(k)} = (1 - \omega)x_1^{(k-1)} + \frac{\omega}{a_{11}} \left(b_1 - a_{12}\, x_2^{(k-1)} - a_{13}\, x_3^{(k-1)} - a_{14}\, x_4^{(k-1)}\right)$$

$$x_2^{(k)} = (1 - \omega)x_2^{(k-1)} + \frac{\omega}{a_{22}} \left(b_2 - a_{21}\, x_1^{(k)} - a_{23}\, x_3^{(k-1)} - a_{24}\, x_4^{(k-1)}\right)$$

$$x_3^{(k)} = (1 - \omega)x_3^{(k-1)} + \frac{\omega}{a_{33}} \left(b_3 - a_{31}\, x_1^{(k)} - a_{32}\, x_2^{(k)} - a_{34}\, x_4^{(k-1)}\right)$$

$$x_4^{(k)} = (1 - \omega)x_4^{(k-1)} + \frac{\omega}{a_{44}} \left(b_4 - a_{41}\, x_1^{(k)} - a_{42}\, x_2^{(k)} - a_{43}\, x_3^{(k)}\right)$$

The discussion of the conjugate gradient and simplex methods presented in this chapter is based on material in:

Press, W. H., S. A. Teukolsky, W. T. Vetterling, and B. P. Flannery. *Numerical Recipes in C: The Art of Scientific Computing* 2^d ed. Cambridge Unversity Press, 1992.

For further discussion of conjugate gradient methods, see the following:

Freund, R. W, G. H. Golub, and N. M. Nachtigal. "Iterative Solution of Linear Systems." *Acta Numerica I*, 1992, pp. 57–100.

Golub, G. H., and J. M Ortega. *Scientific Computing and Differential Equations: An Introduction to Numerical Methods*. Academic Press, Boston, 1992.

Golub, G. H., and C. F. Van Loan. *Matrix Computations* 3rd ed. Johns Hopkins University Press, Baltimore, 1996.

Stoer, J., and R. Bulirsch. *Introduction to Numerical Analysis*. Springer-Verlag, New York, 1980.

For further discussion of linear programming and the simplex method, see the following texts:

Danzig, G. B. *Linear Programming and Extensions*, Princeton University Press, Princeton, NJ, 1963.

Taha, H. A. *Operations Research: An Introduction* 6th ed. Prentice Hall, Upper Saddle River, NJ, 1997.

Winston, W. L. *Operations Research: Applications and Algorithms* 3rd ed. Duxbury Press (Wadsworth), Belmont, CA, 1994.

The following are excellent references for applied linear algebra:

Strang, G. *Linear Algebra and Its Applications*, 3^d ed. Harcourt Brace Jovanovich, San Diego, CA, 1988.

Hager, W. W. *Applied Numerical Linear Algebra*. Prentice-Hall, Englewood Cliffs, NJ, 1988.

Datta, B. N. *Numerical Linear Algebra and Applications*. Brooks Cole, Pacific Grove, CA, 1995.

For more advanced discussion of iterative methods for linear systems, see the following texts:

Barrett, R., J. Donato, J. Dongarra, V. Eijkhout, R. Pozo, C. Romine, and H. van der Vorst. *Templates for the Solution of Linear Systems: Building Blocks for Iterative Methods*. SIAM, Philadelphia, 1993.

Greenbaum, A. *Iterative Methods for Solving Linear Systems*, SIAM, Philadelphia, 1997.

For Problems P6.1 to P6.5 approximate the solution of the system $A\ x = b$, *iteratively (if possible); use* $x^{(0)} = [\ 0,\ 0,\ 0\ ]^T.$
  a. *Use Jacobi iteration.*
  b. *Use Gauss-Seidel iteration.*

P6.1 $A = \begin{bmatrix} 10 & -2 & 1 \\ -2 & 10 & -2 \\ -2 & -5 & 10 \end{bmatrix}, \quad b = \begin{bmatrix} 9 \\ 12 \\ 18 \end{bmatrix}.$

P6.2 $A = \begin{bmatrix} 4 & 1 & 0 \\ 1 & 3 & -1 \\ 1 & 0 & 2 \end{bmatrix}, \quad b = \begin{bmatrix} 3 \\ -4 \\ 5 \end{bmatrix}.$

P6.3 $A = \begin{bmatrix} 5 & -1 & 0 \\ -1 & 5 & -1 \\ 0 & -1 & 5 \end{bmatrix}, \quad b = \begin{bmatrix} 9 \\ 4 \\ -6 \end{bmatrix}.$

P6.4 $A = \begin{bmatrix} 8 & 1 & -1 \\ -1 & 7 & -2 \\ 2 & 1 & 9 \end{bmatrix}, \quad b = \begin{bmatrix} 8 \\ 4 \\ 12 \end{bmatrix}.$

P6.5 $A = \begin{bmatrix} 4 & 1 & 0 \\ 1 & 3 & -1 \\ 0 & -1 & 4 \end{bmatrix}, \quad b = \begin{bmatrix} 3 \\ 4 \\ 5 \end{bmatrix}.$

For Problems P6.6 to P6.18 approximate the solution of the system $A\ x = b$, *iteratively; use* $x^{(0)} = [\ 0,\ 0,\ ...\ 0\ ]^T.$
  a. *Use Jacobi iteration.*
  b. *Use Gauss-Seidel iteration.*
  c. *Use SOR with* $\omega = 1.25$, $\omega = 1.5$, $\omega = 1.75$, $\omega = 1.9$.

P6.6 $A = \begin{bmatrix} -2 & 1 & 0 & 0 \\ 1 & -2 & 1 & 0 \\ 0 & 1 & -2 & 1 \\ 0 & 0 & 1 & -2 \end{bmatrix}, \quad b = \begin{bmatrix} -1 \\ 0 \\ 0 \\ 0 \end{bmatrix}.$

P6.7 $A = \begin{bmatrix} 5 & 1 & 0 & 0 \\ 1 & 5 & 1 & 0 \\ 0 & 1 & 5 & 1 \\ 0 & 0 & 1 & 5 \end{bmatrix}, \quad b = \begin{bmatrix} 33 \\ 26 \\ 30 \\ 15 \end{bmatrix}.$

P6.8 $A = \begin{bmatrix} 1 & 2 & 0 & 0 \\ 2 & 6 & 8 & 0 \\ 0 & 8 & 35 & 18 \\ 0 & 0 & 18 & 112 \end{bmatrix}, \quad b = \begin{bmatrix} 2 \\ 6 \\ -10 \\ -112 \end{bmatrix};$

(the optimal value is $\omega = 1.9387$.)

P6.9 $A = \begin{bmatrix} 4 & 8 & 0 & 0 \\ 8 & 18 & 2 & 0 \\ 0 & 2 & 5 & 1.5 \\ 0 & 0 & 1.5 & 1.75 \end{bmatrix},$

$b = \begin{bmatrix} 8 & 18 & 0.50 & -1.75 \end{bmatrix}^T;$

(the optimal value is $\omega = 1.634$.)

P6.10 $A \begin{bmatrix} 4 & -8 & 0 & 0 \\ -8 & 18 & -2 & 0 \\ 0 & -2 & 5 & -1.5 \\ 0 & 0 & -1.5 & 1.75 \end{bmatrix},$

$b = \begin{bmatrix} -12 & 22 & 5 & 2 \end{bmatrix}^T;$

(the optimal value is $\omega = 1.634$.)

P6.11 $A = \begin{bmatrix} 1 & -2 & 0 & 0 \\ -2 & 5 & -1 & 0 \\ 0 & -1 & 2 & -0.5 \\ 0 & 0 & -0.5 & 1.25 \end{bmatrix},$

$b = \begin{bmatrix} -3 & 5 & 2 & 3.5 \end{bmatrix}^T;$

(the optimal value is $\omega = 1.5431$.)

P6.12 $A = \begin{bmatrix} 1 & -2 & 0 & 0 & 0 \\ -2 & 5 & 1 & 0 & 0 \\ 0 & 1 & 2 & -2 & 0 \\ 0 & 0 & -2 & 5 & 1 \\ 0 & 0 & 0 & 1 & 2 \end{bmatrix},$

$b = \begin{bmatrix} 5 & -9 & 0 & 3 & 0 \end{bmatrix}^T;$

(the optimal value is $\omega = 1.7684$.)

P6.13 $\mathbf{A} = \begin{bmatrix} 1 & -2 & 0 & 0 & 0 \\ -2 & 6 & 4 & 0 & 0 \\ 0 & 4 & 9 & -0.5 & 0 \\ 0 & 0 & -0.5 & 1.25 & 0.5 \\ 0 & 0 & 0 & 0.5 & 3.25 \end{bmatrix}$,

$\mathbf{b} = \begin{bmatrix} 5 & -2 & 18 & 0.5 & -2.25 \end{bmatrix}^{T}$;

(the optimal value is $\omega = 1.7064$.)

P6.14

$\mathbf{A} = \begin{bmatrix} 1 & -2 & 0 & 0 & 0 & 0 \\ -2 & 6 & 4 & 0 & 0 & 0 \\ 0 & 4 & 9 & -0.5 & 0 & 0 \\ 0 & 0 & -0.5 & 3.25 & 1.5 & 0 \\ 0 & 0 & 0 & 1.5 & 1.75 & -3 \\ 0 & 0 & 0 & 0 & -3 & 13 \end{bmatrix}$

$\mathbf{b} = \begin{bmatrix} -3 & 22 & 35.5 & -7.75 & 4 & -33 \end{bmatrix}^{T}$;

(the optimal value is $\omega = 1.7113$.)

P6.15

$\mathbf{A} = \begin{bmatrix} 7.63 & 0.3 & 0.15 & 0.5 & 0.34 & 0.84 \\ 0.38 & 6.4 & 0.7 & 0.9 & 0.29 & 0.57 \\ 0.83 & 0.19 & 8.33 & 0.82 & 0.34 & 0.37 \\ 0.5 & 0.68 & 0.86 & 10.21 & 0.53 & 0.7 \\ 0.71 & 0.3 & 0.85 & 0.82 & 5.95 & 0.55 \\ 0.43 & 0.54 & 0.59 & 0.66 & 0.31 & 9.25 \end{bmatrix}$

$\mathbf{b} = \begin{bmatrix} -9.44 & 25.27 & -48.01 & 19.76 & -23.63 & 62.59 \end{bmatrix}^{T}$;

P6.16

$\mathbf{A} = \begin{bmatrix} 85.57 & 0.46 & 0.92 & 0.41 & 0.14 & 0.02 \\ 0.23 & 52.53 & 0.74 & 0.89 & 0.2 & 0.75 \\ 0.61 & 0.82 & 20.44 & 0.06 & 0.2 & 0.45 \\ 0.49 & 0.44 & 0.41 & 67.57 & 0.6 & 0.93 \\ 0.89 & 0.62 & 0.94 & 0.81 & 84.08 & 0.47 \\ 0.76 & 0.79 & 0.92 & 0.01 & 0.2 & 2.38 \end{bmatrix}$,

$\mathbf{b} = \begin{bmatrix} 85.61 & -267.18 & 54.91 & -140.66 & 331.55 & -18.69 \end{bmatrix}^{T}$

P6.17

$\mathbf{A} = \begin{bmatrix} 14.38 & 0.59 & 0.44 & 0.12 & 0.8 & 0.84 & 0.39 & 0.16 \\ 0.09 & 81.93 & 0.35 & 0.45 & 0.91 & 0.17 & 0.59 & 0.87 \\ 0.04 & 0.37 & 43.17 & 0.72 & 0.23 & 0.17 & 0.12 & 0.24 \\ 0.61 & 0.63 & 0.68 & 89.93 & 0.24 & 0.99 & 0.04 & 0.65 \\ 0.61 & 0.72 & 0.7 & 0.27 & 73.54 & 0.44 & 0.46 & 0.97 \\ 0.02 & 0.69 & 0.73 & 0.25 & 0.08 & 69.07 & 0.87 & 0.66 \\ 0.02 & 0.08 & 0.48 & 0.87 & 0.64 & 0.31 & 35.55 & 0.87 \\ 0.19 & 0.45 & 0.55 & 0.23 & 0.19 & 0.37 & 0.26 & 16.61 \end{bmatrix}$

$\mathbf{b} = \begin{bmatrix} -23.49 & 87.25 & 170.88 & -530.36 & 227.13 & 141.59 & -136.83 & 117.43 \end{bmatrix}^{T}$

P6.18

$\mathbf{A} = \begin{bmatrix} 10 & 0 & 1 & 0 & 0 & 0 & 0 & 0 \\ 0 & 10 & 0 & 0 & 0 & 0 & -1 & 0 \\ 0 & 0 & 10 & 0 & 0 & -2 & 0 & 0 \\ 2 & 0 & 0 & 10 & 0 & 0 & 0 & 0 \\ 0 & 0 & 1 & 0 & 10 & 0 & 0 & 0 \\ 0 & 0 & 0 & -3 & 0 & 10 & 0 & 0 \\ 0 & 3 & 0 & 0 & 0 & 0 & 10 & 0 \\ 0 & 0 & 0 & 0 & 1 & 0 & 0 & 10 \end{bmatrix}$

$\mathbf{b} = \begin{bmatrix} 13 & 13 & 18 & 42 & 53 & 48 & 76 & 85 \end{bmatrix}^{T}$

A6.1 To find the forces in the single triangle truss with angles a $= \pi/6$ and b $= \pi/3$, solve the linear system $\mathbf{T}\,\mathbf{x} = \mathbf{b}$, for $\mathbf{T}$ and $\mathbf{b}$ as given here.

$$\mathbf{T} = \begin{bmatrix} 1 & 0 & 0 & 0 & \sin(a) & 0 \\ 0 & 1 & 0 & 1 & \cos(a) & 0 \\ 0 & 0 & 1 & 0 & 0 & \sin(b) \\ 0 & 0 & 0 & -1 & 0 & -\cos(b) \\ 0 & 0 & 0 & 0 & -\cos(a) & \cos(b) \\ 0 & 0 & 0 & 0 & -\sin(a) & -\sin(b) \end{bmatrix}$$

$$\mathbf{b} = \begin{bmatrix} 0 & 0 & 0 & 0 & 0 & 10 \end{bmatrix}^T$$

A6.2 Iterative methods may be useful for systems that have a few small non-zero elements outside of a fairly pronounced banded structure (such elements prevent the application of the Thomas method and cause extensive fill in the lower triangular portion of the coefficient matrix if Gaussian elimination is used). For example, solve $\mathbf{A}\,\mathbf{x} = \mathbf{b}$:

$$\mathbf{A} = \begin{bmatrix} -2.9 & 0.9 & 0 & 0 & 0 & 0.01 & 0 & 0 & 0 & 0 \\ 1.0 & -2.9 & 0.9 & 0 & 0 & 0 & 0 & 0 & 0.01 & 0 \\ 0 & 1.0 & -2.9 & 0.9 & 0 & 0 & 0 & 0 & 0 & 0 \\ 0 & 0 & 1.0 & -2.9 & 0.9 & 0 & 0 & 0 & 0 & 0 \\ 0.01 & 0 & 0 & 1.0 & -2.9 & 0.9 & 0 & 0 & 0 & 0 \\ 0 & 0 & 0 & 0 & 1.0 & -2.9 & 0.9 & 0 & 0 & 0 \\ 0 & 0 & 0 & 0 & 0 & 1.0 & -2.9 & 0.9 & 0 & 0 \\ 0 & 0 & 0.01 & 0 & 0 & 0 & 1.0 & -2.9 & 0.9 & 0 \\ 0.01 & 0 & 0 & 0 & 0 & 0 & 0 & 1.0 & -2.9 & 0.9 \\ 0 & 0 & 0 & 0 & 0 & 0 & 0 & 0 & 1.0 & -2.9 \end{bmatrix}$$

$$\mathbf{b} = \begin{bmatrix} -0.1395 & -0.080 & -0.153 & -0.173 & -0.1842 & -0.255 & -0.296 & -0.3826 & -0.3492 & -1.05 \end{bmatrix}^T$$

A6.3 The following linear system corresponds to the finite difference solution to a PDE, with unequal spacing in the x and y directions.

$$\mathbf{A} = \begin{bmatrix} -68 & 9 & 25 & 0 & 0 & 0 & 0 & 0 \\ 9 & -68 & 0 & 25 & 0 & 0 & 0 & 0 \\ 25 & 0 & -68 & 9 & 25 & 0 & 0 & 0 \\ 0 & 25 & 9 & -68 & 0 & 25 & 0 & 0 \\ 0 & 0 & 25 & 0 & -68 & 9 & 25 & 0 \\ 0 & 0 & 0 & 25 & 9 & -68 & 0 & 25 \\ 0 & 0 & 0 & 0 & 25 & 0 & -68 & 9 \\ 0 & 0 & 0 & 0 & 0 & 25 & 9 & -68 \end{bmatrix}$$

$$\mathbf{b} = \begin{bmatrix} -25.6667 & -8.6933 & -8.0000 & -1.4400 & -9.0000 & -3.2400 & -34.0000 & -30.7600 \end{bmatrix}^T$$

U6.1 For each of the linear systems in problems P3.1 to P3.5, determine whether **A** is strictly diagonally dominant. Also solve (if possible) using the iterative methods presented in this chapter.

For problems U6.2 to U6. 6 write the linear system A x = b in the explicit iterative form for the Jacobi method, i.e. x = T x + c, where A = D − L − U, and T = D⁻¹(L + U); find the eigenvalues of T. For those problems for which the theorems apply, find the optimal SOR parameter.

U6.2 $\mathbf{A} = \begin{bmatrix} 10 & -2 & 1 \\ -2 & 10 & -2 \\ -2 & -5 & 10 \end{bmatrix}$ $\mathbf{b} = \begin{bmatrix} 9 \\ 12 \\ 18 \end{bmatrix}$

U6.3 $\mathbf{A} = \begin{bmatrix} 5 & -1 & 0 \\ -1 & 5 & -1 \\ 0 & -1 & 5 \end{bmatrix}$ $\mathbf{b} = \begin{bmatrix} 9 \\ 4 \\ -6 \end{bmatrix}$

U6.4 $\mathbf{A} = \begin{bmatrix} 4 & 1 & 0 \\ 1 & 3 & -1 \\ 0 & -1 & 4 \end{bmatrix}$ $\mathbf{b} = \begin{bmatrix} 3 \\ 4 \\ 5 \end{bmatrix}$

U6.5 $\mathbf{A} = \begin{bmatrix} -2 & 1 & 0 & 0 \\ 1 & -2 & 1 & 0 \\ 0 & 1 & -2 & 1 \\ 0 & 0 & 1 & -2 \end{bmatrix}$ $\mathbf{b} = \begin{bmatrix} -1 \\ 0 \\ 0 \\ 0 \end{bmatrix}$

U6.6 $\mathbf{A} = \begin{bmatrix} 5 & 1 & 0 & 0 \\ 1 & 5 & 1 & 0 \\ 0 & 1 & 5 & 1 \\ 0 & 0 & 1 & 5 \end{bmatrix}$ $\mathbf{b} = \begin{bmatrix} 33 \\ 26 \\ 30 \\ 15 \end{bmatrix}$

U6.7 Suppose Jacobi's method is used for the linear system **A x = b**, with

$$\mathbf{A} = \begin{bmatrix} 4 & 12 & 8 & 4 \\ 1 & 7 & 18 & 9 \\ 2 & 9 & 20 & 20 \\ 3 & 11 & 15 & 14 \end{bmatrix} \quad \mathbf{b} = \begin{bmatrix} -4 \\ -5 \\ -25 \\ -18 \end{bmatrix}$$

Perform 2 iterations and discuss the expected results.

U6.8 Other decompositions of the matrix **A** may be appropriate for solving the system **A x = b** iteratively when A has special structure. In particular, if **A = B + C**, where **B** is tridiagonal and the elements of C are small, consider the iterative scheme

$$\mathbf{A\,x = b}$$
$$\mathbf{(B + C)\,x = b}$$
$$\mathbf{B\,x = -\,C\,x + b}$$

The method will converge if the elements of **C** are sufficiently small so that $\| \mathbf{B}^{-1}\,\mathbf{C} \| < 1$. The usefulness of this method depends on the fact that the tridiagonal system **B x** is relatively easy to solve at each stage. See Hager, p. 334.

7

....

Nonlinear Functions of Several Variables

Several of the methods introduced in Chapter 2 for finding a zero of a nonlinear function of a single variable can be extended to nonlinear functions of several variables. However, the problem is much more difficult in several variables. For two nonlinear functions of two variables, $z = f(x, y)$ and $z = g(x, y)$, finding a zero of the system requires finding the intersection of the curves $f(x, y) = 0$ and $g(x, y) = 0$. It is very important to use any information available about the specific problem to identify the region where these curves may intersect, i.e., the possible location of a common root of the equations $f(x, y) = 0$ and $g(x, y) = 0$.

We begin this chapter by considering the extension of Newton's method to systems of nonlinear equations. Starting with an initial estimate of the solution, each nonlinear function is approximated by its tangent plane (at the current approximate solution); the common root of the resulting linear equations provides the next approximation to the desired zero. Forming the linear system requires either the computation of the Jacobian matrix (the matrix of partial derivatives) for the nonlinear system or approximation of the Jacobian numerically.

Fixed-point iteration, introduced for functions of a single variable in Chapter 1, provides an approach to solving a system of nonlinear equations that does not require the computation of partial derivatives. However, the transformation of the original problem into fixed-point form is more straightforward for some problems than for others.

We also consider the problem of finding the minimum of a scalar function of several variables. In addition to many other applications of minimization, root-finding problems may be solved by constructing a function whose minimum corresponds to the desired root. A basic gradient-descent minimization function is presented in section 7.3. More powerful approaches, implemented in various software packages, are discussed briefly in section 7.4.

Nonlinear systems of equations occur in many settings, including the solution of nonlinear partial differential equations by means of finite differences.

Example 7-A Nonlinear System from Geometry

The problem of finding the points of intersection of two curves in the xy-plane may require solving a nonlinear system of equations. For example, suppose we would like to know where the ellipse of eccentricity 0.5 (which described the orbit in an example in Chapter 2) would intersect a circle with the same area and the same center (see Fig. 7.1). The area of an ellipse is $\pi\, a\, b$; for this example, with an eccentricity of 0.5, we take

$a = 1$ and $b = \sqrt{3}/2$, so the equation of the ellipse is

$$x^2 + 4y^2/3 = 1.$$

Since the area of a circle is $\pi\, r^2$, the equation of a circle with the same area as the ellipse is

$$x^2 + y^2 = r^2 = \sqrt{3}/2.$$

The points of intersection are solutions of the nonlinear system

$$3x^2 + 4y^2 - 3 = 0,$$
$$x^2 + y^2 - \sqrt{3}/2 = 0.$$

We solve this system in Example 7.2.

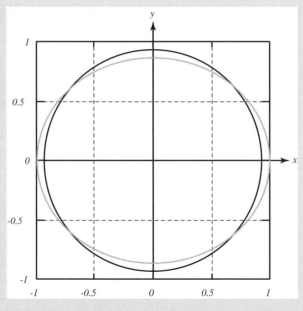

FIGURE 7.1   Intersections of a circle and an ellipse with the same area.

Example 7-B Position of a Two-Link Robot Arm

The position of a two-link robot arm can be described in terms of the angle that the first link makes with the horizontal axis and the angle that the second link makes with the first link. In this example, we assume that the lengths of the two links are d_1 and d_2; the first link makes an angle α with the horizontal axis, and the second link makes an angle β with the direction defined by the first link. Our problem is to find the angles α and β that allow the end of the second link to be at a specified point, with coordinates (p_1, p_2). The arrangement is illustrated in Fig. 7.2. The equations for these requirements are as follows:

Location of the end of the first link (x_1, y_1)

$$x_1 = d_1 \cos(\alpha),$$
$$y_1 = d_1 \sin(\alpha);$$

Location of the end of the second link (x_2, y_2)

$$x_2 = x_1 + d_2 \cos(\alpha + \beta),$$
$$y_2 = y_1 + d_2 \sin(\alpha + \beta).$$

Thus, we need to solve

$$p_1 = d_1 \cos(\alpha) + d_2 \cos(\alpha + \beta),$$
$$p_2 = d_1 \sin(\alpha) + d_2 \sin(\alpha + \beta),$$

for the unknown angles α and β.

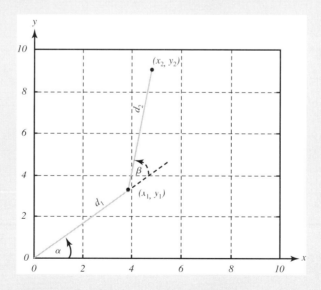

FIGURE 7.2 Two-link robot arm, initial position.

We solve a problem of this type in Example 7.4.

Newton's method for finding the root of a nonlinear function, discussed in Chapter 2, can be extended to solving a system of nonlinear equations. In the following examples, we show iterations as superscripts (in parentheses), since we often use vector notation, denoting components of the unknown vector by subscripts. In cases where we do not wish to retain all iterates, we denote the current estimate as x_old, and the next estimate as x_new.

Example 7.1 Intersection of a Circle and a Parabola

We first consider a system of two equations describing the intersection of the unit circle (centered at the origin) and a given parabola (with vertex at the origin). The curves are illustrated in Fig. 7.3. We are looking for the common zeros of the functions

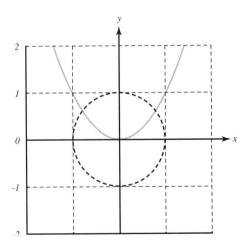

FIGURE 7.3   Intersections of a circle and a parabola.

$$f(x, y) = x^2 + y^2 - 1 \quad \text{and} \quad g(x, y) = x^2 - y.$$

We start with an initial estimate of a common solution (x_0, y_0). The plane that is tangent to the function $z = f(x, y)$ at $(x_0, y_0, f(x_0, y_0))$ has the equation:

$$z - f(x_0, y_0) = f_x(x_0, y_0)(x - x_0) + f_y(x_{0, y_0})(y - y_0),$$

where $f_x(x_0, y_0)$ is the partial derivative of $f(x, y)$ with respect to x, evaluated at (x_0, y_0) and $f_y(x_0, y_0)$ is the partial derivative of $f(x, y)$ with respect to y, evaluated at (x_0, y_0).

Similarly, the plane tangent to $z = g(x, y)$ at $(x_0, y_0, g(x_0, y_0))$ is

$$z - g(x_0, y_0) = g_x(x_0, y_0)(x - x_0) + g_y(x_0, y_0)(y - y_0).$$

To find the next approximation to the desired solution, we find the intersection of these two tangent planes with the xy-plane (i.e., with $z = 0$). We define $r = (x - x_0)$ and $s = (y - y_0)$ and solve the linear system

$$f_x(x_0, y_0)\, r + f_y(x_0, y_0)\, s = -f(x_0, y_0),$$
$$g_x(x_0, y_0)\, r + g_y(x_0, y_0)\, s = -g(x_0, y_0).$$

Note that r and s give the location of the intersection point in terms of its displacement from the point (x_0, y_0); i.e., $(x, y) = (r + x_0, s + y_0)$.

For this example, $f_x = 2x$, $f_y = 2y$, $g_x = 2x$, and $g_y = -1$.

Choosing the initial estimate as $(x_0, y_0) = (1/2, 1/2)$, we have

$$f_x = 1, f_y = 1, g_x = 1, g_y = -1, f(1/2, 1/2) = -1/2, \text{ and } g(1/2, 1/2) = -1/4$$

The resulting linear system to be solved is

$$r + s = 1/2,$$
$$r - s = 1/4.$$

Its solution is $r = 3/8$, $s = 1/8$.

The second approximate solution (x_1, y_1) is the intersection point in terms of its (x, y) coordinates:

$$x_1 = x_0 + r = 1/2 + 3/8 = 7/8,$$
$$y_1 = y_0 + s = 1/2 + 1/8 = 5/8.$$

The process is repeated, using the new approximate solution to evaluate the partial derivatives f_x, f_y, g_x, and g_y, and the functions, f and g. The true solution is $(x, y) = (0.78615, 0.61803)$ (see Fig. 7.4).

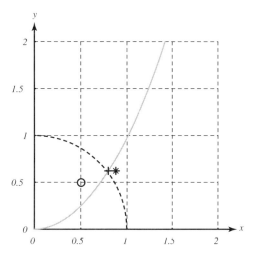

FIGURE 7.4   Initial estimate and two iterations of Newton's method.

7.1.1 Matrix-Vector Notation

The general nonlinear system

$$f_1(x_1, x_2, x_3, \ldots, x_n) = 0$$
$$f_2(x_1, x_2, x_3, \ldots, x_n) = 0$$
$$f_3(x_1, x_2, x_3, \ldots, x_n) = 0$$

$$\ldots$$

$$f_n(x_1, x_2, x_3, \ldots, x_n) = 0$$

can be written in a more compact vector form as $F(\mathbf{x}) = \mathbf{0}$, where

$$\mathbf{x} = [x_1, x_2, x_3, \ldots, x_n],$$

$$F(\mathbf{x}) = \begin{bmatrix} f_1(\mathbf{x}) \\ f_2(\mathbf{x}) \\ \cdot \\ \cdot \\ \cdot \\ f_n(\mathbf{x}) \end{bmatrix}, \quad \text{and } \mathbf{0} = \begin{bmatrix} 0 \\ 0 \\ \cdot \\ \cdot \\ \cdot \\ 0 \end{bmatrix}.$$

Newton's method uses the Jacobian (matrix of partial derivatives) of the system:

$$\mathbf{J}(x_1, \ldots x_n) = \begin{bmatrix} \partial f_1/\partial x_1 & \cdots & \partial f_1/\partial x_n \\ \cdot & \cdots & \cdot \\ \cdot & \cdots & \cdot \\ \cdot & \cdots & \cdot \\ \partial f_n/\partial x_1 & \cdots & \partial f_n/\partial x_n \end{bmatrix}.$$

At each stage of the iterative process, an updated approximate solution vector **x_new** is found from the current approximate solution **x** according to the equation

$$\mathbf{x\_new} = \mathbf{x} - \mathbf{J}^{-1}(\mathbf{x})\, \mathbf{F}(\mathbf{x}).$$

In the case of a single equation and a single variable, this reduces to the Newton iteration introduced in section 2.3:

$$x_{k+1} = x_k - \frac{y_k}{y'_k}, \quad \text{or} \quad x_{(new)} = x_{(old)} - \frac{f(x_{(old)})}{f'(x_{(old)})}.$$

However, evaluating the inverse of the Jacobian matrix is an expensive computation, so in practice the equivalent system of linear equations

$$\mathbf{J}(\mathbf{x})\, \mathbf{y} = -\mathbf{F}(\mathbf{x}), \text{ where } \mathbf{y} = \mathbf{x\_new} - \mathbf{x}$$

is solved for the vector **y**, which is used to update **x**. That is,

$$\mathbf{x\_new} = \mathbf{x} + \mathbf{y}$$

7.1.2   Algorithm for Newton's Method

The following algorithm requires user-supplied functions defining $\mathbf{F(x)}$ (which returns a column vector of values) and its Jacobian matrix, $\mathbf{J(x)}$.

$$
\mathbf{F(x)} = \begin{bmatrix} f_1(\mathbf{x}) \\ \cdot \\ \cdot \\ \cdot \\ f_n(\mathbf{x}) \end{bmatrix}
\qquad
J(\mathbf{x}) = \begin{bmatrix} \partial f_1/\partial x_1 & \cdots & \partial f_1/\partial x_n \\ \cdot & \cdots & \cdot \\ \cdot & \cdots & \cdot \\ \cdot & \cdots & \cdot \\ \partial f_n/\partial x_1 & \cdots & \partial f_n/\partial x_n \end{bmatrix}
$$

The algorithm also assumes a function or subroutine to solve a linear system, which for convenience we denote as Solve(M, b). Many software packages have such routines, or a user-written routing for Gaussian elimination (see Chapter 2) could be used.

Newton's Method

Input
  F(x)   *function whose zero is desired*
  J(x)   *Jacobian matrix of F(x)*
  xo   *initial estimate of solution vector*
  max   *maximum number of iterations*
  tol   *tolerance for convergence*

Compute
For i = 1 to max
    b = −F(xo)
    M = J(xo)
    u = Solve(M, b)   *Solve the linear system M u = $\mathbf{b}$*
    xn = xo + u   *Update solution*
    if (| F(xn)| < tol) break   *Test for convergence*
    xo = xn
End

Return
xn

Another common test for convergence is to check the norm of the change in the solution vector.

7.1.3 Applications of Newton's Method

Example 7.2 Intersection of a Circle and an Ellipse

Consider now the problem of finding the points of intersection of two curves. The first equation represents an ellipse of eccentricity 0.5. The second equation represents a circle with the same area as the ellipse. Both curves are centered at the origin. The equations are, respectively,

$$3x^2 + 4y^2 - 3 = 0,$$
$$x^2 + y^2 - \sqrt{3}/2 = 0.$$

The Jacobian of this system is the matrix

$$\mathbf{J}(x, y) = \begin{bmatrix} 6x & 8y \\ 2x & 2y \end{bmatrix}$$

The following table gives a summary of the computations using a simple computer program to implement Newton's method, with a starting estimate of $x_0 = [0.5 \ 0.5]^T$. The last column, denoted $\| \mathbf{d} \|$, gives the Euclidean norm of the vector denoting the change in the solution. At iteration k, the change vector is $\mathbf{d} = [x(k) - x(k-1), y(k) - y(k-1)]$. The curves are illustrated in Fig. 7.1.

Intersection of circle and ellipse using Newton's method

iteration	x	y	$\| \mathbf{d} \|$
0	0.5000	0.5000	
1	0.7141	0.6519	0.2625
2	0.6820	0.6342	0.0367
3	0.6813	0.6340	0.0008
4	0.6813	0.6340	0.0000

Example 7.3 Newton's Method for a System of Three Equations

To illustrate the use of Newton's method, we seek a common solution of the following three equations, which represent the unit sphere centered at the origin, a cylinder with radius 1/2 and axis along the x_2-axis, and a paraboloid of revolution around the x_3-axis.

$$f_1(x_1, x_2, x_3) = x_1^2 + x_2^2 + x_3^2 - 1 = 0,$$
$$f_2(x_1, x_2, x_3) = x_1^2 + x_3^2 - 1/4 = 0,$$
$$f_3(x_1, x_2, x_3) = x_1^2 + x_2^2 - 4x_3 = 0.$$

In vector form,

$$\mathbf{F}(\mathbf{x}) = \begin{bmatrix} x_1^2 + x_2^2 + x_3^2 - 1 \\ x_1^2 + x_3^2 - 1/4 \\ x_1^2 + x_2^2 - 4x_3 \end{bmatrix}$$

The Jacobian is

$$\mathbf{J}(\mathbf{x}) = \begin{bmatrix} 2x_1 & 2x_2 & 2x_3 \\ 2x_1 & 0 & 2x_3 \\ 2x_1 & 2x_2 & -4 \end{bmatrix}$$

Using an initial estimate of $\mathbf{x}^{(0)} = [1 \quad 1 \quad 1]$, a tolerance of 0.00001 to test for the stopping condition, and a simple computer program to implement Newton's method, we obtain the results summarized in the following table. Here we represent the change in the components of the approximate solution vector at each stage of iteration as $\Delta x = x\_new - x\_old$. With this notation, the stopping conditions can be written as $\| \Delta x \| < 0.00001$. Newton's method has converged in seven iterations.

Newton iterations for a system of three equations.

step	x(1)	x(2)	x(3)	$\| \Delta x \|$
0	1	1	1	
1	0.79167	0.875	0.33333	0.70956
2	0.44345	0.86607	0.42857	0.36111
3	0.28027	0.86603	0.44538	0.16405
4	0.2296	0.86603	0.44705	0.0507
5	0.22371	0.86603	0.4472	0.0058853
6	0.22361	0.86603	0.44721	0.00010352
7	0.22361	0.86603	0.44721	2.4665e-06

Example 7.4 Positioning a Robot Arm

Consider a two-link robot arm, as introduced in Example 7-B. Let the length of the first link be 5 and the second link of length 6. We wish to find the angles so that the arm will move to the point (10, 4), starting from initial angles of $\alpha = 0.7$ and $\beta = 0.7$.

The system of equations in this case is

$$5\cos(\alpha) + 6\cos(\alpha + \beta) - 10 = 0,$$

$$5\sin(\alpha) + 6\sin(\alpha + \beta) - 4 = 0.$$

The following table gives the results of six iterations. The initial position and final position of the arm are illustrated in Fig. 7.5.

step	α	β	$\|\Delta x\|$
0	0.7	0.7	
1	−0.59855	1.8339	1.724
2	−0.10782	0.89987	1.0551
3	0.086882	0.53893	0.4101
4	0.14791	0.426	0.12837
5	0.15585	0.41139	0.016621
6	0.15598	0.41114	0.00029053

Iterations to find position of robot arm using Newton's method.

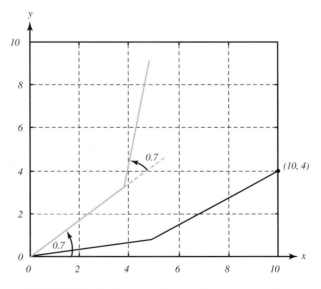

FIGURE 7.5   Initial and final positions of two-link robot arm.

It is sometimes convenient to solve a system of nonlinear equations by an iterative process that does not require the computation of partial derivatives. An example of the use of fixed-point iteration for finding a zero of a nonlinear function of a single variable appears in Chapter 1. The extension of this idea to systems is straightforward.

Example 7.5 Fixed-Point Iteration for a System of Two Equations

To introduce the use of fixed-point iteration for nonlinear systems, consider the problem of finding a zero of the system

$$f_1(x_1, x_2) = x_1^3 + 10x_1 - x_2 - 5 = 0,$$
$$f_2(x_1, x_2) = x_1 + x_2^3 - 10x_2 + 1 = 0,$$

by converting these equations to the form $x_1 = g_1(x_1, x_2)$, $x_2 = g_2(x_1, x_2)$ in the following manner:

$$x_1 = -0.1x_1^3 + 0.1x_2 + 0.5,$$
$$x_2 = 0.1x_1 + 0.1x_2^3 + 0.1.$$

The graphs of the equations $f_1 = 0$ and $f_2 = 0$ are shown in Fig. 7.6.

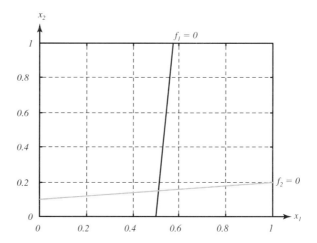

FIGURE 7.6   System of two nonlinear equations.

Approximate solutions at each stage of iteration.

iter	x1	x2	$\|\Delta x\|$
0	0.6	0.6	
1	0.5384	0.1816	0.42291
2	0.50255	0.15444	0.044975
3	0.50275	0.15062	0.0038204

7.2.1 Algorithm for Fixed-Point Iteration

The steps needed to solve a fixed-point iteration problem, $\mathbf{x} = \mathbf{G}(\mathbf{x})$, are described in the following algorithm. Vector quantities are shown in bold.

Fixed-Point Iteration for a Nonlinear System

Input

$$\mathbf{G}(\mathbf{x}) = \begin{bmatrix} g_1(\mathbf{x}) \\ \cdot \\ \cdot \\ \cdot \\ g_n(\mathbf{x}) \end{bmatrix}$$

$\mathbf{x}_0$ *initial solution vector*
kmax   *maximum number of iterations allowed*
tol   *tolerance for convergence*

Initialize
$\mathbf{x}(0) = \mathbf{x}_0$

Begin iterations
For i = 0 to kmax
     $\mathbf{y} = \mathbf{G}(\mathbf{x}(i))$
     $\mathbf{x}(i + 1) = \mathbf{y}$
     If $|\mathbf{y} - \mathbf{x}(i)| < $ tol   *iterations have converged*
           Break
     End   *(otherwise, continue)*
End
Return
     $\mathbf{x}$

The algorithm above tests for convergence by measuring the error as the difference between $\mathbf{x}(i)$ and $\mathbf{G}(\mathbf{x}(i))$. Another common test for convergence is to test the norm of change in solution vector, $\mathbf{x}_{i+1} - \mathbf{x}_i$.

One may wish to add a message indicating whether the iterations terminated with convergence, or by reaching the maximum allowed number of iterations.

In this section, we turn our attention to the problem of finding a minimum of a scalar function of several variables. Minimization problems are important in many applications. Also, the problem of finding the common zeros of several nonlinear functions can be converted into a minimization problem, as illustrated in Example 7.7. An interesting geometric problem is presented in Example 7.8.

7.3.1 Algorithm for Gradient Descent

The gradient of a function of several variables is a vector in the direction of most rapid increase, and the negative of the gradient gives the direction of most rapid decrease. A simple gradient search technique starts with an initial estimate of the location of a minimum and determines the direction in which the function is decreasing most rapidly. A new approximate solution is found by moving a specified distance in the direction of the negative gradient. If the function value is lower at the new point, it is accepted as the new solution; if not, a smaller step in the direction of the negative gradient is taken. The step size is reduced until the new point is an improvement (i.e., the function value is smaller at the new point than at the previous point) or until the step size is less than a given tolerance, in which case convergence has been achieved.

Minimization by Gradient Descent

$$
\begin{aligned}
&Input \\
&\quad f \qquad\qquad\qquad\qquad\quad function\ whose\ minimum\ is\ sought \\
&\quad g \qquad\qquad\qquad\qquad\quad gradient\ of\ f \\
&\quad x0 \qquad\qquad\qquad\qquad initial\ estimate\ of\ solution \\
&\quad max \qquad\qquad\qquad\quad maximum\ number\ of\ iterations \\
&\quad tol \qquad\qquad\qquad\qquad tolerance\ for\ convergence \\
&For\ i = 1\ to\ max \\
&\quad xo = x0 \\
&\quad dx = -g(xo) \\
&\quad xn = xo + dx \\
&\quad z0 = f(xo) \\
&\quad z1 = f(xn) \\
&\quad ch = z1 - z0 \\
&\quad While\ (ch\ >\ =\ 0) \\
&\qquad\qquad dx = dx/2 \\
&\qquad\qquad If\ (norm(dx) < 0.00001)\ Break \\
&\qquad\qquad xn = xo + dx/2 \\
&\qquad\qquad z1 = f(xn) \\
&\qquad\qquad ch = z1 - z0 \\
&\quad End \\
&\quad If\ (abs(ch) < tol)\ Break \qquad iterations\ have\ converged \\
&\quad xo = xn \\
&End \\
&Return \\
&\quad xn
\end{aligned}
$$

7.3.2 Applications of Gradient Descent

Example 7.7 Finding a Zero by Gradient Descent

To use minimization techniques to find a zero of a system of nonlinear functions, we define a new function that is the sum of the squares of the functions whose common zero is desired. For example, if we want a zero of the functions

$$f(x, y) = x^2 + y^2 - 1$$

and

$$g(x, y) = x^2 - y,$$

we define

$$h(x, y) = (x^2 + y^2 - 1)^2 + (x^2 - y)^2.$$

The minimum value of $h(x, y)$ is 0, which occurs when $f(x, y) = 0$ and $g(x, y) = 0$. The derivatives for the gradient are

$$h_x(x, y) = 2(x^2 + y^2 - 1)2x + 2(x^2 - y)2x,$$
$$h_y(x, y) = 2(x^2 + y^2 - 1)2y + 2(x^2 - y)(-1).$$

A summary of the results using a simple computer program to implement gradient descent are given in the following table. Example 7.1 solved the same problem by Newton's method.

	Approximate zeros at each iteration.		
step	x	y	change
0	0.5	0.5	
1	0.875	0.625	−0.26831
2	0.74512	0.61133	−0.035987
3	0.79251	0.61902	−0.0079939
4	0.78446	0.6178	−0.00019414
5	0.78657	0.6181	−1.3631e-05

We now consider an example in which finding the minimum of a function is the primary objective.

Example 7.8 Optimal Location of a Point in the Plane

Given three points in the plane, we wish to find the location of the point $P = (x, y)$ so that the sum of the squares of the distances from P to the three given points, (x_1, y_1), (x_2, y_2) and (x_3, y_3), is as small as possible. In other words, we need to find the minimum of

$$f(x, y) = (x - x_1)^2 + (y - y_1)^2 + (x - x_2)^2 + (y - y_2)^2 + (x - x_3)^2 + (y - y_3)^2.$$

The necessary derivatives are

$$f_x(x, y) = 2(x - x_1) + 2(x - x_2) + 2(x - x_3) = 6x - 2x_1 - 2x_2 - 2x_3$$
$$f_y(x, y) = 2(y - y_1) + 2(y - y_2) + 2(y - y_3) = 6y - 2y_1 - 2y_2 - 2y_3$$

The initial estimate of $(0.2, 0.2)$ and the results of the first two updates are shown in Fig. 7.6, together with the three given points, $(0, 0)$, $(0, 1)$, and $(1/2, 1)$.

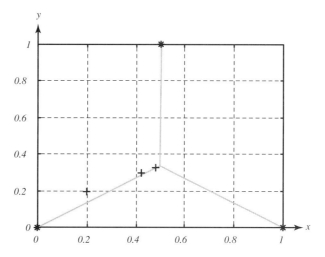

FIGURE 7.7   First three iterations to find optimal location of P.

We begin this section by summarizing briefly the built-in functions in MATLAB, Mathcad, and *Mathematica* for finding the minimum of a function of several variables. We then introduce three methods that are used in various software packages and libraries for minimization of a function of several variables. These are the Levenberg-Marquardt method, the quasi-Newton methods (Davidon-Fletcher-Powell [DFP] method [sometimes called just Fletcher-Powell] and the Broyden-Fletcher-Goldfarb-Shanno [BFGS] method) and the downhill simplex method (not to be confused with the simplex method for linear programming discussed in Chapter 6).

7.4.1 Using Professionally Developed Software

MATLAB provides an implementation of the simplex search method in the function fmins. The basic function call is x = fmins('F', x0), where 'F' is a string containing the name of the function to be minimized, $F(x)$ is a scalar-valued function of a vector variable, and x0 is the initial estimate of location of the (local) minimum. As is typically the case with built-in Matlab functions, the user can supply values for optional parameters that control the printout of intermediate steps, the termination tolerance for x, the termination tolerance for $F(x)$, and the maximum number of evaluations of $F(x)$.

The problems discussed in this chapter may be solved using Mathcad's Solve Block structure. In addition, problems discussed in previous chapters such as finding the root of a single nonlinear equation and solving linear systems may be solved by the same methods. The use of the functions Find, Maximize, and Minimize is essentially the same for nonlinear systems as for linear systems. The function Minerr seeks an approximate solution to a system that may not have an exact solution. The Solve Block structure requires: 1) providing an initial guess for each of the unknowns in the problem and defining the function to be maximized or minimized; 2) typing the word "Given"; 3) typing the equations and inequalities to be solved; and 4) calling the desired function.

The Mathematica function FindMinimum[f, {x, x0}, {y, y0}, ...] uses steepest descent to find the minimum of a function of several variables. Starting estimates are required for each variable.

The NIST Index lists functions for multivariate optimization, according to whether the function is smooth (and if so, how many derivatives are supplied by the user) or nonsmooth.

7.4.2 Levenberg-Marquardt Method

The Levenberg-Marquardt algorithm is a method for solving nonlinear least-squares problems. It is also the basis for some globally convergent methods for minimization and zero finding. These methods are known collectively as the model-trust region approach; individual algorithms include the hook-step and dogleg-step methods. For a discussion of these methods, see Dennis and Schnabel, 1983.

The general setting for the Levenberg-Marquardt (L-M) algorithm is the problem of fitting a model (which depends on some parameters) to a set of data. To find the best-fit values for the parameters, we minimize a function that measures the agreement of the data and the model for any particular choice of parameter values. This function, often called a merit function, is designed so that its value is small for parameter values that give good agreement between the model and the data. Since the most widely used merit function is the sum of the squares of the differences between the data values and the corresponding model value, these problems are generally known as least-squares problems. We consider the basics of least-squares problems in Chapter 9. The following description of the L-M algorithm is based on the discussion in Press et al., 1992, pp. 683–685.

The L-M method provides a smooth transition between two approaches to the minimization of the merit function: the steepest descent method (used when the approximate solution is far from the desired value) and the inverse-Hessian method (used when the solution is close to the value that minimizes the merit function).

The Hessian matrix of a function is the matrix of the second partial derivatives, i.e., $\mathbf{H}(f) = [h_{ij}]$ where $h_{ij} = \dfrac{\partial^2 f}{\partial x_i \partial x_j}$. The L-M method uses a modification of the Hessian matrix, which we denote as $\mathbf{M} = [m_{ij}]$, where

$$m_{ij} = \frac{1}{2} \frac{\partial^2 f}{\partial x_i \partial x_j} \qquad \text{for } i \neq j$$

$$\frac{1}{2} \frac{\partial^2 f}{\partial x_i \partial x_j} (1 + \lambda) \qquad \text{for } i = j$$

We also define the vector $\mathbf{b}$, with $b_i = \dfrac{-1}{2} \dfrac{\partial f}{\partial x_i}$.

The basic idea is to start with an initial estimate of the vector $\mathbf{x}$, compute a correction vector $\mathbf{d}$ by solving the linear system $\mathbf{M}\mathbf{d} = \mathbf{b}$, and then increase or decrease λ depending on whether $f(\mathbf{x} + \mathbf{d})$ is larger or smaller than $f(\mathbf{x})$. We continue iterating in this manner until the value of f decreases by an amount that is significantly less than 1.

7.4.3 Simplex Search

MATLAB's built-in function to find the minimum of a function of several variables uses a Nelder-Mead type of simplex search. We sketch the method briefly here.

In two dimensions, a *simplex* is a geometrical figure consisting of three points (vertices), together with all line segments connecting them—in other words, a triangle. In three dimensions, a simplex is a tetrahedron, i.e, four points and the polygonal faces connecting them. In R^n, a simplex consists of $n + 1$ points and the hyperplane segments connecting them. For simplicity, we limit our description of the simplex method to two dimensions. The method starts with an initial simplex (triangle) and identifies the vertex (call it "bad") where the function to be minimized is largest. Each iteration of the simplex method transforms the simplex by a combination of reflections, expansions, and contractions. A reflection takes the vertex "bad" and projects it through the center of the opposite face of the simplex. If the new point is better (i.e., if the function evaluated at "new" is smaller), the method continues expanding the simplex by moving "new" further along the same ray, until the improvement stops. Other possible moves include contraction along the ray from the vertex "bad" to the center of the opposite face and contraction of all vertices (except the best) toward the best. (For a more detailed description, see Press et al., 1986.)

7.4.4 Quasi-Newton Methods

The goal of the quasi-Newton methods, which are also known as variable metric methods, is the same as the goal of a conjugate gradient method, namely, to minimize a function of several variables by performing a sequence of minimizations along various well-chosen lines. Both conjugate gradient and quasi-Newton method require that the gradient of the function being minimized can be computed. The two main quasi-Newton methods are the Davidon-Fletcher-Powell (DFP) method (sometimes called just Fletcher-Powell) and the Broyden-Fletcher-Goldfarb-Shanno (BFGS) method. The methods differ only in some details; the following discussion is based on the presentation in Press et al. (1992), pp. 425–428 and Acton (1990), pp. 467–469. The assumption is that the function $f(\mathbf{x})$ whose minimum is desired can be approximated by a quadratic form, i.e., $f(\mathbf{x}) \approx c - \mathbf{b}\,\mathbf{x} + \frac{1}{2}\mathbf{x}\,\mathbf{A}\,\mathbf{x}$.

However, we do not know the matrix $\mathbf{A}$. The plan is to construct a sequence of approximations $\mathbf{H}_i \rightarrow \mathbf{A}^{-1}$, the inverse Hessian matrix.

If $\mathbf{x}_i$ is the approximation at step i to the vector $\mathbf{x}$ that minimizes f, and $\mathbf{g}(\mathbf{x})$ is the gradient of f, then we can write (to second order)

$$f(\mathbf{x}) = f(\mathbf{x}_i) + (\mathbf{x} + \mathbf{x}_i)\,g(\mathbf{x}_i) + \frac{1}{2}(\mathbf{x} - \mathbf{x}_i)\,\mathbf{A}\,(\mathbf{x} - \mathbf{x}_i)$$

which gives

$$g(\mathbf{x}) = g(\mathbf{x}_i) + \mathbf{A}\,(\mathbf{x} - \mathbf{x}_i)$$

If we knew $\mathbf{A}^{-1}$, we could set $g(\mathbf{x}) = 0$ and solve for $(\mathbf{x} - \mathbf{x}_i)$, as in standard Newton's method. Instead, we use our current approximation to $\mathbf{A}^{-1}$, which remarkably is often better than using the true Hessian. This paradox is a result of the fact that if we are far from a minimum there is no guarantee that the Hessian is positive definite, as it must be to be assured that Newton's method takes us in a direction where the function is decreasing. The sequence of approximations $\mathbf{H}_i$ are constructed so that they are always positive definite.

In the following algorithm, subscripts denote iteration, not a component of a vector. The vectors are column vectors, so the transpose of a vector is a row vector.

Quasi-Newton Method

Initialize
> $\mathbf{H}_1$ *Identity matrix*
> $\mathbf{x}_1$ *initial estimate of minimum point*

Define the required functions
> $f(\mathbf{x})$ *function to be minimized*
> $\mathbf{g}(\mathbf{x})$ *gradient of f(x)*

Compute
> $f_1 = f(\mathbf{x}_1)$
> $\mathbf{g}_1 = \mathbf{g}(\mathbf{x}_1)$

For $i = 1, \ldots n$
> $\mathbf{s}_i = -\mathbf{H}_i \mathbf{g}_i$ *downhill direction for search*
> Find α_i so that $f(\mathbf{x}_i + \alpha_i \mathbf{s}_i)$ is minimal (along the direction $\mathbf{s}_i$)
> $\mathbf{d}_i = \alpha_i \mathbf{s}_i$
> $\mathbf{x}_{i+1} = \mathbf{x}_i + \mathbf{d}_i$
> $f_{i+1} = f(\mathbf{x}_{i+1})$
> $\mathbf{g}_{i+1} = \mathbf{g}(\mathbf{x}_{i+1})$
> $\mathbf{y}_i = \mathbf{g}_{i+1} - \mathbf{g}_i$
> $\mathbf{A}_i = \dfrac{\mathbf{d}_i \mathbf{d}_i^T}{\mathbf{d}_i^T \mathbf{y}_i}$ *numerator is matrix, denominator is scalar*
> $\mathbf{B}_i = \dfrac{(\mathbf{H}_i \mathbf{y}_i)(\mathbf{H}_i \mathbf{y}_i)^T}{\mathbf{y}_i^T \mathbf{H}_i \mathbf{y}_i}$ *numerator is matrix, denominator is scalar*
> $\mathbf{H}_{i+1} = \mathbf{H}_i + \mathbf{A}_i - \mathbf{B}_i$

Stop if either $i > n$ (too many iterations)
> or if $\mathbf{d}_i$ and $\mathbf{s}_i$ are sufficiently small

Otherwise
> Increment index i and continue

Efficient line search procedures (minimization along a ray) are discussed extensively in the literature. See Acton (1990) and Press et al. (1992).

The general nonlinear system

$$f_1(x_1, x_2, x_3, \ldots, x_n) = 0$$
$$f_2(x_1, x_2, x_3, \ldots, x_n) = 0$$
$$f_3(x_1, x_2, x_3, \ldots, x_n) = 0$$
$$f_n(x_1, x_2, x_3, \ldots, x_n) = 0$$

is written in vector form as $F(\mathbf{x}) = \mathbf{0}$.

Newton's Method

The update for Newton's method is given by

$$\mathbf{x\_new} = \mathbf{x} - J^{-1}(\mathbf{x})\, F(\mathbf{x})$$

To avoid computing the inverse of the Jacobian, the equivalent system of linear equations

$$J(\mathbf{x})\, \mathbf{y} = -F(\mathbf{x}), \text{ where } \mathbf{y} = \mathbf{x\_new} - \mathbf{x},$$

is solved for the vector $\mathbf{y}$, which is used to update $\mathbf{x}$. That is,

$$\mathbf{x\_new} = \mathbf{x} + \mathbf{y}$$

Fixed-Point Iteration

The system $F(\mathbf{x}) = \mathbf{0}$ may be converted to fixed-point form $\mathbf{x} = \mathbf{g}(\mathbf{x})$ in many different ways.

The fixed-point iteration $\mathbf{x}^{(k+1)} = \mathbf{g}(\mathbf{x}^{(k)})$ will converge if
there is a region $\mathbf{D}$, such that $\mathbf{g}(\mathbf{D})$ is in $\mathbf{D}$, and
the Jacobian of g satisfies $\| \mathbf{G}(\mathbf{p}) \|_\infty < 1$.

Minimization of a Scalar Function of Several Variables

The problem of solving the nonlinear system $F(\mathbf{x}) = \mathbf{0}$ may be converted to a minimization problem by defining

$$h(\mathbf{x}) = (F_1(\mathbf{x}))^2 + (F_2(\mathbf{x}))^2 + \ldots + (F_n(\mathbf{x}))^2$$

The minimum value of $h(\mathbf{x})$ is 0, which occurs when each of the component functions of $F(\mathbf{x})$ is zero. Minimization problems occur in many areas of application.

Gradient Search

A simple gradient search for the minimum of $h(\mathbf{x})$ begins with an initial estimate $\mathbf{x}^{(0)}$; at each iteration the approximate solution is moved a small distance in the direction of the negative gradient of h. Care must be taken in determining the distance the solution should be moved.

The following texts examine numerical methods applied to nonlinear functions of several variables:

Acton, F. S. *Numerical Methods That (usually) Work.* Harper and Row, New York, 1970.

Ortega, J. M. *Numerical Analysis—A Second Course.* Academic Press, New York, 1972.

Press, W. H., S. A. Teukolsky, W. T. Vetterling, and B. P. Flannery. *Numerical Recipes in C; The Art of Scientific Computing* 2^d ed. Cambridge University Press, Cambridge, 1992.

Reinboldt, W. C. *Methods for Solving Systems of Nonlinear Equations.* SIAM, Philadelphia, 1974.

For further reading on the Levenberg-Marquardt method, see:

Dennis, J. E., and Schnabel, R. B. *Numerical Methods for Unconstrained Optimization and Nonlinear Equations.* Prentice-Hall, Englewood Cliffs, NJ, 1983.

Marquardt, D. W. "An algorithm for least-squares estimation of nonlinear parameters." *Journal of the Society for Industrial and Applied Mathematics,* vol. 11, pp. 431-441, 1963.

For discussion of quasi-Newton methods, see (in addition to Press, et al. p. 425, 430):

Jacobs, D. A. H. (ed.). *The State of the Art in Numerical Analysis.* Academic Press, London, 1977, Chapter 3.1.7 (by K. W. Brodie)

Polak, E. *Computational Methods in Optimization.* Academic Press, New York, 1971, section 2.3.

The following are among the well-respected texts that provide a more in-depth treatment of multivariable analysis:

Dillon, W. R., and M. Goldstein. *Multivariate Analysis: Methods and Applications.* Wiley and Sons, New York, 1984.

Hair, J. F., R. E. Anderson, R. L. Tatham, and W. Black. *Multivariate Data Analysis,* 5th ed. Prentice Hall, Englewood Cliffs, NJ, 1998.

Johnson, R. A., and D. W. Wichern. *Applied Multivariate Statistical Analysis,* 4th ed. Prentice Hall, Englewood Cliffs, NJ, 1998.

Kachigan, S. K. *Multivariate Statistical Analysis: A Conceptual Introduction,* 2^d ed. Radius Press, New York, 1991.

Mardia, K. V. *Multivariate Analysis.* Academic Press, London, 1980.

Morrison, D. F. *Multivariate Statistical Methods,* 3rd ed. McGraw-Hill, New York, 1990.

For Problems P7.1 to P7.10, solve the nonlinear system

    a. *using Newton's method*
    b. *by finding the minimum of the function $f^2 + g^2$ (or $f^2 + g^2 + h^2$)*

P7.1 $f(x, y) = x^2 - \sqrt{3}\,x\,y + 2\,y^2 - 10 = 0$
      $g(x, y) = 4\,x^2 + 3\,\sqrt{3}\,xy + y^2 - 22 = 0$

P7.2 $f(x, y) = x^2 - \sqrt{3}x\,y + 2\,y^2 - 10 = 0$
      $g(x, y) = x^2 - \sqrt{3}\,xy + 2 = 0$

P7.3 $f(x,y) = 4\,x^2 + 3\,\sqrt{3}\,xy + y^2 - 22 = 0$
      $g(x,y) = x^2 - \sqrt{3}\,xy + 2 = 0$

P7.4 $f(x,y) = -x^2 + xy - y + 7\,x - 11 = 0$
      $g(x,y) = x^2 + y^2 - 9 = 0$

P7.5 $f(x,y) - x^2 + 4\,y^2 - 16 = 0$
      $g(x,y) = x\,y^2 - 4 = 0$

P7.6 $f(x,y) = x^3\,y = y = 2\,x^3 + 16 = 0$
      $g(x,y) = x - y^2 + 1 = 0$

P7.7 $f(x,y,z) = x\,y\,z - 1 = 0$
      $g(x, y, z) = x^2 + y^2 + z^2 - 4 = 0$
      $h(x,y,z) = x^2 + 2\,y^2 - 3 = 0$

P7.8 $f(x,y,z) = x^2 + 4\,y^2 + 9\,z^2 - 36 = 0$
      $g(x,y,z) = x^2 + 9\,y^2 \qquad - 47 = 0$
      $h(x,y,z) = x^2z - 11 \qquad\qquad = 0$

P7.9 $f(x,y,z) = x^2 + 2\,y^2 + 4\,z^2 - 7 = 0$
      $g(x,y,z) = 2x^2 + y^3 + 6\,z - 10 = 0$
      $h(x,y,z) = x\,y\,z + 1 = 0$

P7.10 $f(x,y,z) = x^2 + y^2 + z^2 - 14 = 0$
        $g(x,y,z) = x^2 + 2\,y^2 \qquad - 9 = 0$
        $h(x,y,z) = x - 3\,y^2 + z^2 \qquad = 0$

For Problems P7.11 to P7.15, solve the nonlinear system

    a. *using Newton's method*
    b. *by finding the minimum of the function $f^2 + g^2$ (or $f^2 + g^2 + h^2$)*
    c. *using fixed point iteration*

P7.11 $f(x,y,z) = x^3 - 10x + y - x + 3 = 0$
        $g(x,y,z) = y^3 + 10\,y - 2\,x - 2\,z - 5 = 0$
        $h(x,y,z) = x + y - 10\,z + 2\sin(z) + 5 = 0$

P7.12 $f(x,y,z) = x^2 + 20\,x + y^2 + z^2 - 20 = 0$
        $g(x,y,z) = x^2 + 20\,y + z^2 - 20 = 0$
        $h(x,y,z) = x^2 + y^2 - 40\,z = 0$

P7.13 $f(x,y,z) = x^2 + y^2 + z^2 + 10\,x - 4 = 0$
        $g(x,y,z) = x^2 - y^2 + z^2 + 10\,y - 5 = 0$
        $h(x,y,z) = x^2 + y^2 - z^2 + 10\,z - 6 = 0$

P7.14 $f(x,y,z) = 10\,x - x^2 - y - z^2 - 4 = 0$
        $g(x,y,z) = 10\,y - x^2 - y^2 - z - 5 = 0$
        $h(x,y,z) = 10\,z - x - y^2 - z^2 - 6 = 0$

P7.15 $f(x,y,z) = 10\,x - x^3 + y^2 - z - 5 = 0$
        $g(x,y,z) = 10\,y + 0.5\,x^2 - y^2 - z - 3 = 0$
        $h(x,y,z) = 10\,z - x - y^2 - z^3 - 6 = 0$

A7.1 Find the minimum of the following function:

$$f(x,y) = -y + x^{-1} + \frac{y^2 - y + 1}{(y - y^2)(1 - x)}$$

Find the minimum by setting the partial derivatives, f_x and f_y equal to zero and solving the resulting nonlinear system using Newton's method. Investigate the effect of different starting estimates; $x = y = 0.5$ is one suitable choice.

A7.2 The equations for the optimal two-stage finite-difference scheme for parabolic PDE are

$$12\,r\,q = 6\,r - 1$$

$$60\,r^2 - 180\,r^2\,q - 30\,r\,q = 1.$$

Compare your result to the exact solution, which is $r = \dfrac{\sqrt{5}}{10}$ and $q = \dfrac{3 - \sqrt{5}}{6}$. (See Ames, 1992, p. 65.)

A7.3 Solve the following nonlinear system using Newton's method (this gives the coefficients and evaluation points for Gauss-Legendre quadrature, $n = 2$, which are discussed in Chapter 11).

$$2 = a_1 + a_2 \qquad 0 = a_1 x_1 + a_2 x_2$$

$$\frac{2}{3} = a_1 x_1^2 + a_2 x_2^2 \qquad 0 = a_1 x_1^3 + a_2 x_2^3$$

A7.4 Find the roots of the steady-state of the Lorenz equations.

$$y - x = 0$$

$$5x - y - xz = 0$$

$$xy - 16z = 0$$

(See Garcia, 1994, p. 109 for discussion of a similar problem.)

A7.5 The steady-state of the concentration of two chemical species in an oscillatory chemical system described by the Brusselator model is given by the nonlinear system:

$$0 = A + x^2 y - (B + 1)\,x$$

$$0 = B\,x - x^2 y$$

Find the solution for the following values of the parameters, A and B:
  a) $B = 1$, $A = 1$
  b) $B = 3$, $A = 1$
  c) $B = 2$, $A = 1$.
(See Garcia, 1994, p. 111 for discussion of a similar problem.)

A7.6 Find the angles of a two-link robot arm that enable it to reach the point (3, 4); (the lengths of the two links are $d_1 = 5$, $d_2 = 6$). Use the starting values for the angles of $a = 1$, $b = 1$.

A7.7 Find the location of two points, (x_1, x_2) and (x_3, x_4) so that the sum of the distances squared required to link the 4 given points by paths as shown in the figure is minimal.

$$p1 = [0\ \ 0]; \quad p2 = [1.8\ \ 0];$$

$$p3 = [1.5\ \ 1]; \quad p4 = [0.3\ \ 1.6];$$

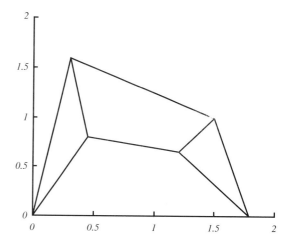

A7.8 Find the location of two points, (x_1, x_2) and (x_3, x_4) so that the sum of the distances (not squared) required to link the 4 given points by paths as shown in the figure is minimal.

$$p1 = [0\ \ 0]; \quad p2 = [1.8\ \ 0];$$

$$p3 = [1.5\ \ 1]; \quad p4 = [0.3\ \ 1.6];$$

EXTEND YOUR UNDERSTANDING

U7.1 to U7.5 For each of the problems P7.11 to P7.15, determine whether the conditions of the fixed point convergence theorem or the corollary are satisfied.

U7.6 Compare the sum of the distances found in A7.8 for the optimal placement of the two points with the sum of the distances if only one interior point is used.

U7.7 Repeat A7.7 and A7.8 using the four given points (0, 0), (1, 0), (1, 1) and (0, 1). Compare your results with those found using only one interior point.

8

∙ ∙

Interpolation

In this chapter, we study methods for representing a function based on knowledge of its behavior at certain discrete points. From this information, we may wish to obtain estimates of function values at other points, or we may need to use the closed-form representation of the function as the basis for other numerical techniques, such as numerical differentiation or integration, which we consider in Chapter 11.

Interpolation produces a function that matches the given data exactly; we seek a function that also provides a good approximation to the (unknown) data values at intermediate points. The data may come from measured experimental values or computed values from other numerical methods, such as the solution of differential equations (Chapters 12–15). Our first interpolation methods provide a polynomial of an appropriate degree to exactly match a given set of data. The two standard forms for the polynomial (Lagrange and Newton) are presented with algorithms and examples. It is also possible to interpolate not only function values, but derivative values. Hermite interpolation is included as the simplest example of "osculatory interpolation" for function and first-derivative values.

For some functions that are not well approximated by polynomial interpolation, rational function interpolation gives better results. In this chapter, we consider the problem of interpolating a set of data values with a rational function. In the next chapter, we present a method for finding a rational function to match the function and derivative values at a single point.

Finally, we investigate piecewise polynomial interpolation. This technique allows us to produce a smooth curve without too many "wiggles" through a large number of data points. After a brief presentation of piecewise linear and piecewise quadratic interpolation, we focus on one of the most important piecewise polynomial interpolation techniques, that of cubic splines.

Interpolation may be needed in any field in which measured data are important; the technique may be used to generate function values at points intermediate between those for which measurements are available. Interpolation may also be used to produce a smooth graph of a function for which values are known only at discrete points, either from measurements or calculations.

Example 8-A Chemical Reaction Product

Consider the observed concentration of the product of a simple chemical reaction as a function of time:

Time: 0.0   0.5   1.0   1.5   2.0

Product: 0.0   0.19   0.26   0.29   0.31

In this chapter, we discuss several techniques for approximating the concentration of the product at other times. The data are illustrated in Fig. 8.1.

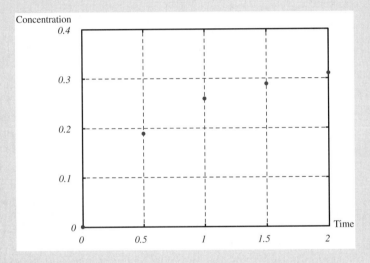

FIGURE 8.1   Chemical reaction product data.

Besides interpolating the data shown above, we also consider the effect of utilizing a more extensive set of data.

Time:
| 0.00 | 0.10 | 0.40 | 0.50 | 0.60 | 0.90 | 1.00 | 1.10 | 1.40 | 1.50 | 1.60 | 1.90 | 2.00 |

Product:
| 0.00 | 0.06 | 0.17 | 0.19 | 0.21 | 0.25 | 0.26 | 0.27 | 0.29 | 0.29 | 0.30 | 0.31 | 0.31 |

One possibility is to use these data directly in the interpolation. Another approach is to use the data to estimate the first derivative of the desired interpolation function by means of the techniques discussed in Chapter 11.

Example 8-B Spline Interpolation for Parametric Functions

Spline interpolation is used in computer graphics to represent smooth curves (in parametric form). Several points are chosen along the curve and are indexed in terms of a parameter, t. Interpolation is performed on the x and y coordinates separately (each as a function of t). The resulting parametric plot, $(x(t), y(t))$ gives the interpolated curve. For example, we take the points shown in Fig. 8.2 as the data, which gives

$$t = [1 \quad 2 \quad 3 \quad 4 \quad 5 \quad 6 \quad 7 \quad 8 \quad 9 \quad 10 \quad 11 \quad 12]$$

$$x = [0 \quad 1 \quad 2 \quad 2 \quad 1 \quad 1 \quad 2 \quad 3 \quad 3 \quad 3 \quad 4 \quad 5]$$

$$y = [0 \quad 0 \quad 0 \quad 1 \quad 1 \quad 2 \quad 2 \quad 2 \quad 1 \quad 0 \quad 0 \quad 0]$$

Data for several other curves are given in the exercises.

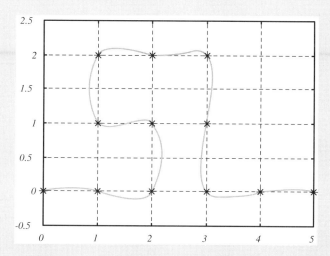

FIGURE 8.2   Spline interpolation for a parametric curve.

Although the uniform spacing used for the parameter values in this example is probably appropriate, it is not required. For figures in which consecutive pairs of points are not all the same Euclidean distance apart, the parameter values are sometimes adjusted to reflect the distance between the points. Some experimentation with the effect of different choices of the parameter t may be necessary to produce the most pleasing results. For a discussion of the use of splines in computer graphics, see Bartels, Beatty, and Barsky (1987).

The two most common forms of polynomial interpolation are Lagrangian interpolation and Newton interpolation. Of course, since the polynomial determined by a set of points is unique, the differences in these forms occur in the process of finding the polynomial (and the form in which it is expressed), not in the resulting function. Each approach has its advantages in different circumstances.

8.1.1   Lagrange Interpolation Polynomials

The Lagrange form of the equation of the straight line passing through two points (x_1, y_1) and (x_2, y_2) is

$$p(x) = \frac{(x - x_2)}{(x_1 - x_2)} y_1 + \frac{(x - x_1)}{(x_2 - x_1)} y_2.$$

It is easy to verify that this equation represents a line and that the given points are on the line.

The Lagrange form of the equation of the parabola passing through three points (x_1, y_1), (x_2, y_2), and (x_3, y_3) is

$$p(x) = \frac{(x - x_2)(x - x_3)}{(x_1 - x_2)(x_1 - x_3)} y_1 + \frac{(x - x_1)(x - x_3)}{(x_2 - x_1)(x_2 - x_3)} y_2 + \frac{(x - x_1)(x - x_2)}{(x_3 - x_1)(x_3 - x_2)} y_3,$$

which can also be checked directly.

The general form of the polynomial passing through the n data points (x_1, y_1), $\ldots$, (x_n, y_n) has n terms on the right-hand side, one corresponding to each data point:

$$p(x) = L_1 y_1 + L_2 y_2 + \ldots + L_n y_n.$$

The kth term is the product of the kth data value and the $(n - 1)^{\text{st}}$ degree polynomial

$$L_k(x) = \frac{(x - x_1) \ldots (x - x_{k-1})(x - x_{k+1}) \ldots (x - x_n)}{(x_k - x_1) \ldots (x_k - x_{k-1})(x_k - x_{k+1}) \ldots (x_k - x_n)}.$$

The numerator is the product

$$N_k(x) = (x - x_1) \ldots (x - x_{k-1})(x - x_{k+1}) \ldots (x_k - x_n).$$

and the denominator is of the same form, but with the variable x replaced by the given value x_k:

$$D_k = N_k(x_k) = (x_k - x_1) \ldots (x_k - x_{k-1})(x_k - x_{k+1}) \ldots (x_k - x_n).$$

Thus $L_k(x_k)$ is 1 and $L_k(x)$ is 0 when x is one of the other specified values of the independent variable, i.e., when $x = x_j$ for $j \neq k$.

Lagrange Interpolation Polynomial: Compute Coefficients

$$P(x) = c_1(x - x_2)\ldots(x - x_n) + c_2(x - x_1)(x - x_3)\ldots(x - x_n) +$$

$$c_3(x - x_1)(x - x_2)(x - x_4)\ldots(x - x_n) + \ldots + c_n(x - x_1)\ldots(x - x_{n-1})$$

Input

  x   *data vector for independent variable*
  y   *data vector for dependent variable*
  n   *number of components in vectors x and y*
For k = 1 to n
  d(k) = 1
  For j = 1 to n
   If (j ≠ k)
    d(k) = d(k) (x(k) − x(j))
   End
   c(k) = y(k)/d(k)
  End
End

Return

  c   *vector of coefficients*

Lagrange Interpolation: Evaluate Polynomial

Input

  x   *data vector*
  c   *coefficient vector*
  n   *number of components in vector x*
  t   *vector of points for interpolation $t_1, \ldots t_m$*
  m   *number of components in vector t*

For i = 1 to m
  P(i) = 0
  For j = 1 to n
   d(j) = 1
   For k = 1 to n
    If (j ≠ k)
     d(j) = d(j) (t(i) − x(k))
    End
   End
   P(i) = P(i) + c(j) d(j)
  End
End

Return

  P   *vector of interpolated values*

Example 8.1 Lagrange Interpolation Parabola

We can find a quadratic polynomial using the three given points

$$(x_1, y_1) = (-2, 4).$$
$$(x_2, y_2) = (0, 2),$$
$$(x_3, y_3) = (2, 8),$$

by substituting into the general formula, which gives

$$p(x) = \frac{(x-0)(x-2)}{(-2-0)(-2-2)}\, 4 + \frac{(x-(-2))(x-2)}{(0-(-2))(0-2)}\, 2 + \frac{(x-(-2))(x-0)}{(2-(-2))(2-0)}\, 8.$$

This simplifies to

$$p(x) = \frac{x(x-2)}{8}\, 4 + \frac{(x+2)(x-2)}{-4}\, 2 + \frac{x(x+2)}{8}\, 8$$
$$= x^2 + x + 2.$$

The data points and the interpolation polynomial are illustrated in Fig. 8.3.

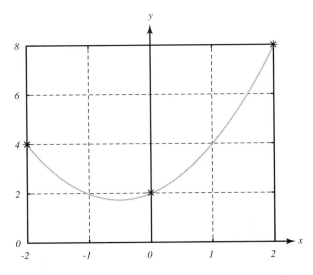

FIGURE 8.3   Parabolic interpolation polynomial.

Example 8.2 Additional Data Points

If we add two more data points to those that we previously interpolated in Example 8.1, we must rework the problem. Suppose that the new data vectors are

$$\mathbf{x} = [-2 \quad 0 \quad -1 \quad 1 \quad 2],$$
$$\mathbf{y} = [\ 4 \quad 2 \quad -1 \quad 1 \quad 8].$$

The coefficients computed by following the algorithm presented previously are

$$c_1 = y_1/[(x_1 - x_2)(x_1 - x_3)(x_1 - x_4)(x_1 - x_5)] \quad = 4/[(-2)(-1)(-3)(-4)] = 1/6$$

$$c_2 = y_2/[(x_2 - x_1)(x_2 - x_3)(x_2 - x_4)(x_2 - x_5)] \quad = 2/[(2)(1)(-1)(-2)] \quad = 1/2$$

$$c_3 = y_3/[(x_3 - x_1)(x_3 - x_2)(x_3 - x_4)(x_3 - x_5)] \quad = -1/[(1)(-1)(-2)(-3)] = 1/6$$

$$c_4 = y_4/[x_4 - x_1)(x_4 - x_2)(x_4 - x_3)(x_4 - x_5)] = 1/[(3)(1)(2)(-1)] \quad = -1/6$$

$$c_5 = y_5/[x_5 - x_1)(x_5 - x_2)(x_5 - x_3)(x_5 - x_4)] = 8/[(4)(2)(3)(1)] \quad = 1/3$$

The resulting Lagrange interpolation polynomial is

$$p(x) = \frac{1}{6}(x)(x + 1)(x - 1)(x - 2) + \frac{1}{2}(x + 2)(x + 1)(x - 1)(x - 2)$$

$$+ \frac{1}{6}(x + 2)(x)(x - 1)(x - 2) - \frac{1}{6}(x + 2)(x)(x + 1)(x - 2) + \frac{1}{3}(x + 2)(x)(x + 1)(x - 1)$$

The polynomial and the data points are illustrated in Fig. 8.4.

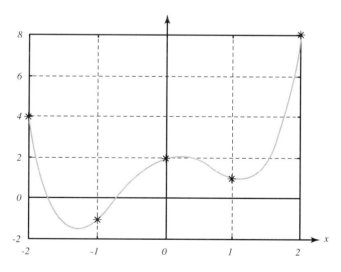

FIGURE 8.4 Quartic interpolation polynomial.

The next example investigates the effect of interpolating using a few data points, as compared to using more data points.

Example 8.3 Chemical Reaction Product Data

The interpolation polynomial and the data points for the observed product concentration data given in Example 8.A are shown in Fig. 8.5.

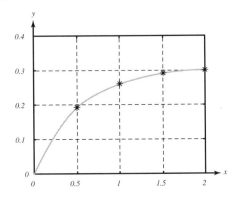

FIGURE 8.5   Quartic interpolation polynomial.

Suppose now that we use the additional data given in Example 8-A to attempt to improve the nice-looking production curve. The graph of the new interpolation polynomial, shown in Fig. 8.6, demonstrates the difficulties resulting from using a polynomial of very high degree for interpolation.

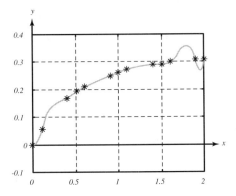

FIGURE 8.6   Polynomial for interpolating additional data.

We note that, in addition to not improving the appearance of the curve, it is necessary to completely rework the problem with the new, expanded data set when one uses the Lagrange form of interpolation.

The next example shows that the (apparent) degree of the Lagrange interpolation polynomial is determined by the number of data points. In fact, the data points all fall on a cubic polynomial, which would be evident if the Lagrange polynomial were simplified.

Example 8.4 Higher Order Interpolation Polynomials

Consider the following data:

$$\mathbf{x} = [\ -2 \quad -1 \quad 0 \quad 1 \quad 2 \quad 3 \quad 4]$$
$$\mathbf{y} = [-15 \quad 0 \quad 3 \quad 0 \quad -3 \quad 0 \quad 15]$$

We find the coefficients for the interpolation polynomial, which appears to be of sixth degree (as is expected for seven data points), by using the algorithm given previously. The data and the polynomial are shown in Fig. 8.7. This example will be revisited in the next section in Example 8.7.

The equation of the polynomial is

$$p(x) = -0.0208(x + 1)(x)(x - 1)(x - 2)(x - 3)(x - 4)$$
$$+0.0625(x + 2)(x + 1)(x - 1)(x - 2)(x - 3)(x - 4)$$
$$-0.0625(x + 2)(x + 1)(x)(x - 1)(x - 3)(x - 4)$$
$$+0.0208(x + 2)(x + 1)(x)(x - 1)(x - 2)(x - 3).$$

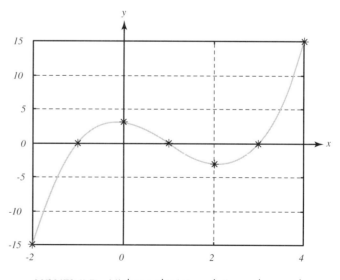

FIGURE 8.7 Higher order interpolation polynomial.

Discussion

Consider first of all the problem of writing the equation of a line that goes through two points (x_1, y_1) and (x_2, y_2). It is easy to see that

$$p(x) = \frac{(x - x_2)}{(x_1 - x_2)} y_1 + \frac{(x - x_1)}{(x_2 - x_1)} y_2$$

has the desired properties:

1. It is the equation of a straight line.
2. If $x = x_1$, then the coefficient of y_1 is 1, and the coefficient of y_2 is 0, so $y = y_1$.
3. If $x = x_2$, then the coefficient of y_1 is 0, and the coefficient of y_2 is 1, so $y = y_2$.
4. Geometrically this corresponds to determining two straight lines, one of which (call it L_0) is 1 at x_0 and 0 at x_1; the other (call it L_1) is 1 at x_1 and 0 at x_0. These lines are determined by the abscissas of the data points. The final interpolating polynomial is a linear combination of the two lines. Thus, we have

$$L_1\colon y = \frac{x - x_2}{x_1 - x_2}, \quad L_2\colon y = \frac{x - x_1}{x_2 - x_1}; \quad L(x) = L_1\, y_1 + L_2\, y_2.$$

The lines L_1 and L_2 are illustrated in Fig. 8.8 for $x_1 = 0$ and $x_2 = 1$. For these particular values of x_1 and x_2, the basis lines are

$$L_1\colon y = -x + 1, \quad L_2\colon y = x.$$

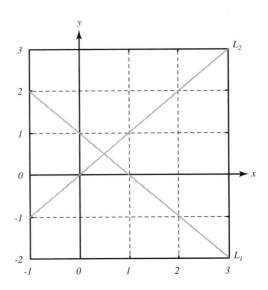

FIGURE 8.8   Lagrange basis functions for linear interpolation polynomial.

Chapter 8 Interpolation

Now let us use the same idea on the problem of writing the equation of a quadratic polynomial through three points: $(x_1, y_1), (x_2, y_2)$ and (x_3, y_3). We see that

$$p(x) = \frac{(x - x_2)(x - x_3)}{(x_1 - x_2)(x_1 - x_3)} y_1 + \frac{(x - x_1)(x - x_3)}{(x_2 - x_1)(x_2 - x_3)} y_2 + \frac{(x - x_1)(x - x_2)}{(x_3 - x_1)(x_3 - x_2)} y_3$$

has the desired properties:

1. It is the equation of a parabola.
2. If $x = x_1$, then $y = y_1$.
3. If $x = x_2$, then $y = y_2$.
4. If $x = x_3$, then $y = y_3$.

The basis polynomials (for $x_1 = 0$, $x_2 = 1$, and $x_3 = 2$) are $P_1 = (x - 1)(x - 2)/2$, $P_2 = x(2 - x)$, and $P_3 = x(x - 1)/2$; they are are illustrated in Fig. 8.9.

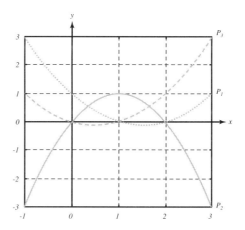

FIGURE 8.9   Lagrange basis polynomials for quadratic interpolation polynomial.

In general, there are as many terms on the right-hand side as there are data points. The coefficient of the kth term is a fraction whose numerator is the product $(x - x_1) \ldots (x - x_{k-1})(x - x_{k+1}) \ldots (x - x_n)$ and whose denominator is of the same form with x replaced by x_k. This gives a fraction that is 1 when $x = x_k$ and is 0 when x equals any of the other specified values of the independent variable.

The Lagrange form of polynomial interpolation is particularly convenient when the same abscissas may occur in different applications (with only the corresponding y values changed). This form is less convenient than the Newton form (discussed in the next section) when additional data points may be added to the problem or when the appropriate degree of the interpolating polynomial is unknown.

Let I be the smallest interval containing $x_1, \ldots, x_n$, and t. Then if $f(x)$ has n continuous derivatives, the error in computing $f(x)$ at $x = t$ using the polynomial that interpolates $f(x)$ at $x_1, \ldots, x_n$, is $\dfrac{(t - x_1)\ldots(t - x_n)}{n!} f^{(n)}(\eta)$, for some η in I (see Atkinson, 1989, pp. 134–135).

8.1.2 Newton Interpolation Polynomials

The Newton form of the equation of a straight line passing through two points (x_1, y_1) and (x_2, y_2) is

$$p(x) = a_1 + a_2(x - x_1).$$

The Newton form of the equation of a parabola passing through three points (x_1, y_1), (x_2, y_2), and (x_3, y_3) is

$$p(x) = a_1 + a_2(x - x_1) + a_3(x - x_1)(x - x_2),$$

and the general form of the polynomial passing through n points (x_1, y_1), $\ldots$, (x_n, y_n) is

$$p(x) = a_1 + a_2(x - x_1) + a_3(x - x_1)(x - x_2) + \ldots + a_n(x - x_1)\ldots(x - x_{n-1}).$$

To illustrate the method for finding the coefficients, consider the problem of finding the values of a_1, a_2, and a_3 for the parabola passing through the points (x_1, y_1), (x_2, y_2) and (x_3, y_3).

Substituting (x_1, y_1) into $y = a_1 + a_2(x - x_1) + a_3(x - x_1)(x - x_2)$ gives

$$a_1 = y_1.$$

Substituting (x_2, y_2) into $y = a_1 + a_2(x - x_1) + a_3(x - x_1)(x - x_2)$ gives $y_2 = a_1 + a_2(x_2 - x_1)$, or

$$a_2 = \frac{y_2 - y_1}{x_2 - x_1}.$$

Substituting (x_3, y_3) into $y = a_1 + a_2(x - x_1) + a_3(x - x_1)(x - x_2)$ gives $y_3 = a_1 + a_2(x_3 - x_1) + a_3(x_3 - x_1)(x_3 - x_2)$, or (after a little algebra)

$$a_3 = \frac{\dfrac{y_3 - y_2}{x_3 - x_2} - \dfrac{y_2 - y_1}{x_2 - x_1}}{x_3 - x_1}.$$

The calculations can be performed in a systematic manner by using the "divided differences" of the function values, as illustrated in Examples 8.5–8.7.

Example 8.5 Newton Interpolation Parabola

Consider again the data from Example 8.1. We can find a quadratic polynomial passing through the points $(x_1, y_1) = (-2, 4)$, $(x_2, y_2) = (0, 2)$, and $(x_3, y_3) = (2, 8)$. The Newton form of the equation is

$$p(x) = a_1 + a_2(x - (-2)) + a_3(x - (-2))(x - 0),$$

where the coefficients are

$$a_1 = y_1 = 4,$$

$$a_2 = \frac{y_2 - y_1}{x_2 - x_1} = \frac{2 - 4}{0 - (-2)} = -1,$$

and

$$a_3 = \frac{\dfrac{y_3 - y_2}{x_3 - x_2} - \dfrac{y_2 - y_1}{x_2 - x_1}}{x_3 - x_0} = \frac{\dfrac{8 - 2}{2 - 0} - \dfrac{2 - 4}{0 - (-2)}}{2 - (-2)} = 1.$$

Thus,

$$p(x) = 4 - (x + 2) + x(x + 2) = x^2 + x + 2,$$

as before.

The calculations can be performed in a systematic manner, using a "divided-difference table":

x_i	y_i	$d_i = \dfrac{y_{i+1} - y_i}{x_{i+1} - x_i}$	$dd_i = \dfrac{d_{i+1} - d_i}{x_{i+2} - x_i}$
-2	$\boxed{4}$		
		$\dfrac{y_2 - y_1}{x_2 - x_1} = \dfrac{2 - 4}{0 - (-2)} = \boxed{-1}$	
0	2		$\dfrac{d_2 - d_1}{x_3 - x_1} = \dfrac{3 - (-1)}{2 - (-2)} = \boxed{1}$
		$\dfrac{y_3 - y_2}{x_3 - x_2} = \dfrac{8 - 2}{2 - 0} = 3$	
2	8		

The coefficients of the Newton polynomial are the top entries in this table. The graph of the interpolation polynomial is shown in Fig. 8.3.

The following algorithms compute the Newton interpolating polynomial

$$N(x) = a_1 + a_2(x - x_1) + a_3(x - x_1)(x - x_2) + \ldots + a_n(x - x_1)(x - x_2)\ldots(x - x_{n-1})$$

Newton Interpolation Polynomial: Compute Coefficients

Input

x	*data vector for independent variable*
y	*data vector for dependent variable*
n	*number of components in vectors x and y*

Compute
a(1) = y(1)
For k = 1 to n − 1   *form first divided difference*
    d(k, 1) = (y(k + 1) − y(k))/(x(k + 1) − x(k))
End
For j = 2 to n − 1   *form j^th divided difference*
    For k = 1 to n − j
        d(k, j) = (d(k + 1, j − 1) − d(k, j − 1))/(x(k + j) − x(k))
    End
End
For j = 2 to n
    a(j) = d(1, j − 1)
End
Return

a	*vector of coefficients*

Newton Interpolation: Evaluate Polynomial

Input

x	*data vector*
a	*coefficient vector*
n	*number of components in vector x*
t	*vector of points for interpolation $t_1, \ldots t_m$*
m	*number of components in vector t*

Compute
For k = 1 to m
    d(1) = 1
    N(k) = a(1)
    For j = 2 to n
        d(j) = (t(k) − x(j − 1))d(j − 1)
        N(k) = N(k) + a(j) d(j)
    End
End

Return

N	*vector of interpolated values*

One of the advantages of the Newton form of polynomial interpolation is that it is easy to add more data points and try a higher order polynomial. This is illustrated in the next example.

Example 8.6 Additional Data Points

If we extend the previous example, adding the points $(x_4, y_4) = (-1, -1)$ and $(x_5, y_5) = (1, 1)$, the polynomial has the form

$$p(x) = a_1 + a_2(x - x_1) + a_3(x - x_1)(x - x_2)$$
$$+ a_4(x - x_1)(x - x_2)(x - x_3)$$
$$+ a_5(x - x_1)(x - x_2)(x - x_3)(x - x_4).$$

The divided-difference table becomes (with new entries shown in bold)

x_i	y_i				

-2 $\boxed{4}$

$$\frac{(2-4)}{(0+2)} = \boxed{-1}$$

0 2

$$\frac{(3+1)}{(2+2)} = \boxed{1}$$

$$\frac{(8-2)}{(2-0)} = 3$$

$$\frac{(0-1)}{(-1+2)} = \boxed{-1}$$

2 8

$$\frac{(3-3)}{(-1-0)} = 0$$

$$\frac{(2+1)}{(1+2)} = \boxed{1}$$

$$\frac{(-1-8)}{(-1-2)} = 3$$

$$\frac{(2-0)}{(1-0)} = 2$$

-1 -1

$$\frac{(1-3)}{(1-2)} = 2$$

$$\frac{(1+1)}{(1+1)} = 1$$

1 1

The Newton interpolation polynomial is

$$p(x) = 4 - (x + 2) + (x + 2)(x) - (x + 2)(x)(x - 2) + (x + 2)(x)(x - 2)(x + 1).$$

This expression looks quite different from that obtained for the Lagrange interpolation polynomial in Example 8.2; however, the two polynomials are equivalent. The graph of the interpolation polynomial is shown in Fig. 8.4.

Another advantage of the Newton form of the interpolation polynomial is that the degree of the interpolating polynomial may be more evident than from the Lagrange form. This is the case for the next example.

Example 8.7 Higher Order Interpolation Polynomials

Consider again the data from Example 8.4, shown in the first two columns of the following divided-difference table:

x	f						
−2	−15						
		15					
−1	0		−6				
		3		1			
0	3		−3		0		
		−3		1		0	
1	0		0		0		0
		−3		1		0	
2	−3		3		0		
		3		1			
3	0		6				
		15					
4	15						

The fact that the last three columns are zeros means that the degree of the interpolation polynomial is three less than it could have been based on the number of data points. The entry at the top of each column is the coefficient of the corresponding term in the Newton interpolation polynomial:

$$N(x) = -15 + 15(x + 2) - 6(x + 2)(x + 1) + (x + 2)(x + 1)x.$$

In this form it is clear that the polynomial is cubic. The interpolation polynomial and the data are shown in Fig. 8.7.

If the y values are modified slightly, the divided difference table shows the small contribution from the higher degree terms:

x	f						
−2	−14						
		14.5					
−1	0.5		−5.95				
		2.6		1.0333			
0	3.1		−2.85		−0.0167		
		−3.1		0.9667		0.0042	
1	0		0.05		0.0042		0.0007
		−3.0		0.9833		0.0083	
2	−3		3.00		0.0458		
		3.0		1.1667			
3	0		6.50				
		16.0					
4	16						

The Newton interpolation polynomial is

$$N(x) = -14 + 14.5(x + 2) - 5.95(x + 2)(x + 1) + 1.0333(x + 2)(x + 1)x - 0.0167(x + 2)(x + 1)x(x - 1)$$
$$+ 0.0042(x + 2)(x + 1)x(x - 1)(x - 2) + 0.0007(x + 2)(x + 1)x(x - 1)(x - 2)(x - 3).$$

Discussion

The Newton form of polynomial interpolation is especially convenient when the spacing between the x values of the data is constant. The spacing would have been constant in Example 8.6 if we had taken the points in order. However, instead we placed the additional points at the bottom of the table to emphasize the primary advantage of Newton interpolation, which is that more data points can be incorporated and a higher degree polynomial generated without repeating the calculations used for the lower order polynomial. This is in contrast to Lagrange interpolation, where the work to generate a higher degree polynomial does not make use of calculations to form lower order functions.

Geometrically, Newton's form of the interpolating polynomial starts with a constant function that has the correct value at $x = x_1$. The next term is a linear function that is 0 at x_1 and has the desired value at x_2, i.e., the value such that the sum of the linear and constant parts is y_2. The three terms in the Newton form of the quadratic passing through the points $(0, 1)$, $(1, 3)$, and $(2, 6)$ are illustrated in Fig. 8.10. These points are

$$P_1(x) = 1,$$

$$P_2(x) = x,$$

and

$$P_3(x) = x(x - 1).$$

The interpolation polynomial is $N(x) = 1 + 2(x - 0) + 0.5x(x - 1)$.

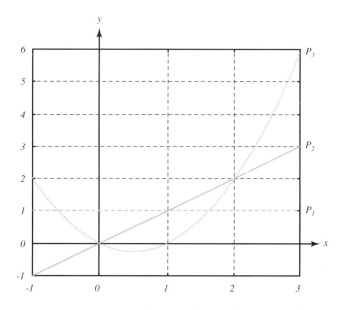

FIGURE 8.10 Newton-basis polynomials to interpolate $(0,1)$, $(1,3)$, and $(2,6)$.

Explaining the Divided Difference Table

We now consider in a little more detail how the divided difference table can be justified. The first few coefficients can be computed directly, as indicated in the introduction to the Newton form of polynomial interpolation. We repeat the computations here, calling the interpolating polynomial for one data point $N_1(x)$, the polynomial for two data points $N_2(x)$, and so on.

The polynomial to interpolate the single point (x_1, y_1) is the constant function

$$N_1(x) = a_1,$$

where $a_1 = y_1$.

The polynomial to interpolate the points (x_1, y_1) and (x_2, y_2) is of the form

$$N_2(x) = a_1 + a_2(x - x_1) = N_1(x) + a_1(x - x_1).$$

We require that $N_2(x_2) = y_2 = a_1 + a_2(x_2 - x_1)$; solving for a_2 yields

$$a_2 = \frac{y_2 - y_1}{x_2 - x_1}.$$

The polynomial to interpolate the points (x_1, y_1), (x_2, y_2), and (x_3, y_3) is of the form

$$N_3(x) = a_1 + a_2(x - x_1) + a_3(x - x_1)(x - x_2) = N_2(x) + a_3(x - x_1)(x - x_2),$$

where we determine a_3 so that

$$N_3(x_3) = y_3 = a_1 + a_2(x_3 - x_1) + a_3(x_3 - x_1)(x_3 - x_2).$$

After some algebra, we obtain

$$a_3 = \frac{\dfrac{y_3 - y_2}{x_3 - x_2} - \dfrac{y_2 - y_1}{x_2 - x_1}}{x_3 - x_1}.$$

Rather than continuing in this direct computation manner, we wish to find a more general iterative approach. Writing the polynomial to interpolate the points (x_1, y_1), (x_2, y_2), and (x_3, y_3) in the form

$$N_3(x) = a_1 + a_2(x - x_1) + a_3(x - x_1)(x - x_2) = N_2(x) + a_3(x - x_1)(x - x_2)$$

suggests that $N_3(x)$ is formed as an extension of the polynomial (call it $N_2(x)$) that interpolates the points (x_1, y_1) and (x_2, y_2) by adding the point (x_3, y_3). On the other hand, we could just as well have supposed that we already had a polynomial (call it $M_2(x)$) that interpolates the points (x_2, y_2) and (x_3, y_3) that we extended by adding the point (x_1, y_1). From this point of view, we would write

$$M_3(x) = b_1 + b_2(x - x_2) + b_3(x - x_2)(x - x_3) = M_2(x) + b_3(x - x_2)(x - x_3).$$

However, these polynomials are simply different expressions for the same function. Comparing them, we see that the coefficient of the highest power of x must be the same, so $a_3 = b_3$. We now proceed to find an expression for a_3. Setting $N_3(x) = M_3(x)$, we have

$$N_2(x) + a_3(x - x_1)(x - x_2) = M_2(x) + a_3(x - x_2)(x - x_3),$$

so rearranging terms and factoring out the common factor of a_3 yields

$$M_2(x) - N_2(x) = a_3[(x - x_1)(x - x_2) - (x - x_2)(x - x_3)]$$
$$= a_3(x - x_2)(x_3 - x_1).$$

The coefficient of x on the left-hand side of the equation is $b_2 - a_2$; the coefficient of x on the right-hand side is $a_3(x_3 - x_1)$. Solving $b_2 - a_2 = a_3(x_3 - x_1)$ for a_3 gives

$$a_3 = \frac{b_2 - a_2}{x_3 - x_1},$$

where $b_2 = \dfrac{y_3 - y_2}{x_3 - x_2}$, and $a_2 = \dfrac{y_2 - y_1}{x_2 - x_1}$.

For the general case, assume that $P_{k-1}(x)$ interpolates $f(x)$ at $x_1, \ldots, x_{k-1}$ and $Q_{k-1}(x)$ interpolates $f(x)$ at $x_2, \ldots, x_k$. Denote the leading coefficient of $P_{k-1}(x)$ as p; this coefficient is the $(k\text{-}1)^{\text{st}}$ divided difference formed using the points (x_1, y_1), $\ldots, (x_{k-1}, y_{k-1})$. Similarly, let q be the leading coefficient of $Q_{k-1}(x)$; then q is the $(k\text{-}1)^{\text{st}}$ divided difference formed using the points $(x_2, y_2), \ldots, (x_k, y_k)$. We can write the polynomial interpolating $f(x)$ at $x_1, \ldots x_k$ in two ways:

Viewed as $P_{k-1}(x)$ with the addition of x_k, the polynomial is written

$$N(x) = P_{k-1}(x) + a(x - x_1) \ldots (x - x_{k-1});$$

viewed as $Q_{k-1}(x)$ with the addition of x_1, the polynomial is written

$$N(x) = Q_{k-1}(x) + a(x - x_2) \ldots (x - x_k).$$

As before, the coefficient a that we seek to find must be the same in each of these expressions, because it is the coefficient of the highest power of x and the interpolation polynomial is unique.

Equating the two expressions for $N(x)$ and rearranging terms, we have

$$Q_{k-1}(x) + a(x - x_2) \ldots (x - x_k) = P_{k-1}(x) + a(x - x_1) \ldots (x - x_{k-1}),$$
$$Q_{k-1}(x) - P_{k-1}(x) = a(x - x_1) \ldots (x - x_{k-1}) - a(x - x_2) \ldots (x - x_k)$$
$$= a(x - x_2) \ldots (x - x_{k-1})[(x - x_1) - (x - x_k)]$$
$$= a(x - x_2) \ldots (x - x_{k-1})(x_k - x_1)$$

Equating the coefficients of x^{k-1} gives $q - p = a(x_k - x_1)$, so

$$a = \frac{q - p}{x_k - x_1}$$

The standard notation for the divided differences is illustrated in the following table, but it is not particularly convenient for computation:

$x_1 \ f[x_1]$

$$f[x_1; x_2] = \frac{f[x_2] - f[x_1]}{x_2 - x_1}$$

$x_2 \ f[x_2]$
$$f[x_1; x_2; x_3] = \frac{f[x_2; x_3] - f[x_1; x_2]}{x_3 - x_1}$$

$$f[x_2; x_3] = \frac{f[x_3] - f[x_2]}{x_3 - x_2}$$

$x_3 \ f[x_3]$

8.1.3 Difficulties with Polynomial Interpolation

There are many types of problems in which polynomial interpolation through a moderate number of data points works very poorly. We illustrate three well-known cases in Examples 8.8–8.10. The first is an example of a function that varies over part of its domain, but is essentially constant over other portions of the domain. The second example is a function that is essentially a straight line. The third is a classic example due to Runge.

Example 8.8 Humped and Flat Data

The data

$$x = [-2 \quad -1.5 \quad -1 \quad -0.5 \quad 0 \quad 0.5 \quad 1 \quad 1.5 \quad 2]$$
$$y = [\,0 \quad\quad 0 \quad\quad 0 \quad 0.87 \quad 1 \quad 0.87 \quad 0 \quad 0 \quad\quad 0]$$

illustrate the difficulty with using higher order polynomials to interpolate a moderately large number of points, especially when the curve changes shape significantly over the interval (being flat in some regions and not in others). (See Fig. 8.11.)

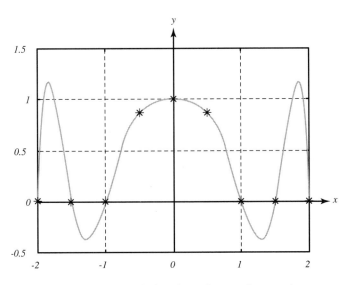

FIGURE 8.11   Difficult data for polynomial interpolation.

The next example illustrates the fact that since polynomial interpolation must go through every data point, noisy data can cause extreme oscillations in the interpolating function.

Example 8.9 Noisy Straight Line

Another example of data to which polynomial interpolation is not well suited is a noisy straight line, with y values given at unevenly spaced x values, like the following data:

$$\mathbf{x} = [0.00 \quad 0.20 \quad 0.80 \quad 1.00 \quad 1.20 \quad 1.90 \quad 2.00 \quad 2.10 \quad 2.95 \quad 3.00]$$
$$\mathbf{y} = [0.01 \quad 0.22 \quad 0.76 \quad 1.03 \quad 1.18 \quad 1.94 \quad 2.01 \quad 2.08 \quad 2.90 \quad 2.95]$$

The following divided-difference table is in the form produced by a simple computer program for Newton interpolation; the data are not shown. The top row of the array gives the coefficients of the interpolation polynomial, which is shown in Fig. 8.12.

```
1.0500  -0.1875   0.7500  -2.3438   2.3993  -2.4070   2.4061  -1.3332 0.7254
0.9000   0.5625  -2.0625   2.2148  -2.4147   2.6458  -1.5270   0.8429
1.3500  -1.5000   1.7027  -2.1316   2.6123  -1.5535   0.8331
0.7500   0.3730  -0.8552   1.2644  -0.7276   0.2793
1.0857  -0.4821   0.5357  -0.1545  -0.1691
0.7000   0.0000   0.2654  -0.4589
0.7000   0.2786  -0.2394
0.9647   0.0392
1.0000
```

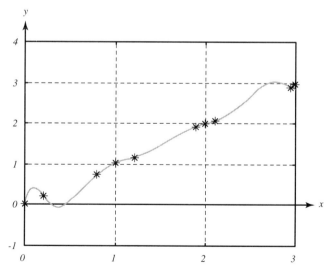

FIGURE 8.12   Noisy data for a straight line.

The third example of a function that is difficult to interpolate with a polynomial is a classic example due to Carl Runge.

Example 8.10 Runge Function

The function

$$f(x) = \frac{1}{1 + 25x^2}$$

is a famous example of the fact that polynomial interpolation does not produce a good approximation for some functions and that using more function values (at evenly spaced x values) does not necessarily improve the situation. This example is widely known in the literature as *Runge's example*, or the *Runge function*.

First, we interpolate using five equally spaced points in the interval $[-1, 1]$:

$$\mathbf{x} = [-1 \quad\quad -0.5 \quad\quad 0.0 \quad\quad 0.5 \quad\quad 1.0 \quad],$$
$$\mathbf{y} = [\ \ 0.0385 \quad 0.1379 \quad 1.0000 \quad 0.1379 \quad 0.0385].$$

The divided-difference table, with data values, is as follows.

x	y				
−1	0.0385				
		0.1989			
−0.5	0.1379		1.5252		
		1.7241		−3.3156	
0.0	1.0000		−3.4483		3.3156
		−1.7241		3.3156	
0.5	0.1379		1.5252		
		−0.1989			
1	0.0385				

The interpolation polynomial (solid line) and the original function (dashed line) are shown in Fig. 8.13.

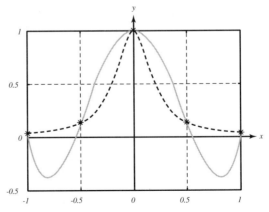

FIGURE 8.13 Runge function and interpolation polynomial.

If we use nine equally spaced data points for the interpolation, that is,

$$\mathbf{x} = [\,-1.000 \quad -0.750 \quad -0.500 \quad -0.250 \quad 0.00 \quad 0.250 \quad 0.500 \ 0.750 \quad 1.000\ ],$$
$$\mathbf{y} = [\ 0.0385 \quad 0.0664 \quad 0.138 \quad 0.3902 \ 1.000 \ 0.3902 \ 0.138 \ 0.0664 \ 0.0385],$$

then the divided-difference table (without the data) is as follows:

```
0.1117
        0.3489
0.2862                1.4630
        1.4462                0.4215
1.0093                1.8845                -15.3015
        2.8595                -18.7054                38.1194
2.4390                -16.8209                41.8777                -53.6893
        -9.7561                33.6417                -55.8369                53.6893
-2.4390                16.8209                -41.8777                53.6893
        2.8595                -18.7054                38.1194
-1.0093                -1.8845                15.3015
        1.4462                0.4215
-0.2862                -1.4630
        0.3489
-0.1117
```

The interpolation polynomial overshoots the true polynomial much more severely than the polynomial formed by using only five points; note the change of vertical scale in Fig. 8.14, compared with Fig. 8.13.

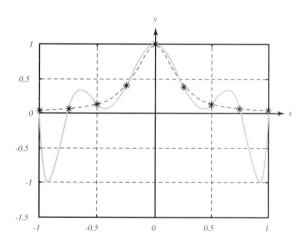

FIGURE 8.14   Interpolating the Runge function with more data points is worse!

Hermite interpolation allows us to find a polynomial that matches both function values and some of the derivative values at specified values of the independent variable; it includes both Taylor polynomials and Lagrange and Newton interpolation as special cases. In this section we consider the simplest case of Hermite interpolation, that in which function values and first-derivative values are given at each point. A classic example would be data for the position and velocity of a vehicle at several different times; instead, we use the data from two of our previous examples to estimate the desired derivative value at several data points.

Suppose we have data measurements representing the values of a function and its first derivative at several values of the independent variable. The computationally most efficient form of Hermite interpolation is based on the Newton divided-difference tables. However, we require the interpolating polynomial to match each data point twice. For two data points, we obtain a cubic polynomial. The divided-difference table is of the same format as for Newton, except that each data point is entered twice, with values supplied for the first derivative at points where the denominators of the difference quotients would be zero, i.e., between repeated data points:

z_i	x_i	w_i	y_i	$d_i = \dfrac{w_{i+1} - w_i}{z_{i+1} - z_i}$	$dd_i = \dfrac{d_{i+1} - d_i}{z_{i+2} - z_i}$	$ddd_i = \dfrac{dd_{i+1} - dd_i}{z_{i+3} - z_i}$
$z_1 = x_1$		$w_1 = y_1$				
				$d_1 = y'_1$		
$z_2 = x_1$		$w_2 = y_1$			$dd_1 = \dfrac{d_2 - d_1}{z_3 - z_1}$	
				$d_2 = \dfrac{w_3 - w_2}{z_3 - z_2}$		$\dfrac{dd_2 - dd_1}{z_4 - z_1}$
$z_3 = x_2$		$w_3 = y_2$			$dd_2 = \dfrac{d_3 - d_2}{z_4 - z_2}$	
				$d_3 = y'_2$		
$z_4 = x_2$		$w_4 = y_2$				

The interpolating polynomial is

$$H(x) = a_1 + a_2(x - z_1) + a_3(x - z_1)(x - z_2) + \ldots + a_n(x - z_1)(x - z_2) \ldots (x - z_{n-1})$$

where the coefficients are found from the table as for Newton's form, i.e.,

$$a_1 = y_1, a_2 = d_1, a_3 = dd_1, \text{etc.}$$

Example 8.11 More Data for Product Concentration

Consider again the product concentration data introduced in Example 8.3. This time, instead of using all the data as separate points, we estimate the values for the derivative (using techniques from Chapter 11). The divided-difference table is as follows, with the data shown in bold:

x_i	y_i	dy								
0	**0**									
		0.6								
0	**0**		−0.44							
		0.38		0.16						
0.5	**0.19**		−0.36		0.08					
		0.2		0.24		−0.24				
0.5	**0.19**		−0.12		−0.16		0.1956			
		0.14		0.08		0.0533		−0.0652		
1.00	**0.26**		−0.08		−0.08		0.0978		−0.0519	
		0.1		0.00		0.20		−0.1689		0.1259
1.00	**0.26**		−0.08		0.12		0.20		0.2000	
		0.06		0.12		−0.16		0.2311		
1.50	**0.29**		−0.02		−0.12		0.1067			
		0.05		0.00		0.00				
1.50	**0.29**		−0.02		−0.12					
		0.04		−0.12						
2.00	**0.31**		−0.08							
		0.00								
2.00	**0.31**									

The resulting polynomial is illustrated in Fig. 8.15.

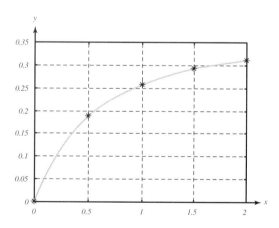

FIGURE 8.15   Hermite interpolation for product concentration data.

Hermite Interpolation Polynomial: Compute Coefficients

$$H(x) = a_1 + a_2(x - u_1) + a_3(x - u_1)(x - u_2) + \ldots + a_n(x - u_1)(x - u_2)\ldots(x - u_{n-1})$$

Input

    x, **y**, and **dy**   *data vectors*

For k = 1 to n   *duplicate data entries*

    u(2k − 1) = x(k)

    v(2k − 1) = y(k)

    u(2k) = x(k)

    v(2k) = y(k)

End

For k = 1 to n − 1   *form 1st divided difference*

    d(2k − 1, 1) = dy(k)

    d(2k, 1) = (v(2k + 1) − v(2k))/(u(2k + 1) − u(2k))

End

d(2n − 1, 1) = dy(n)

For j = 2 to 2n − 2   *form jth divided difference*

    For k = 1 to 2n − j

        d(k, j) = (d(k + 1, j − 1) − d(k, j − 1))/(u(k + j) − u(k))

    End

End

d(1, 2n − 1) = (d(2, 2n − 2) − d(1, 2n − 2))/(u(2n) − u(1))   *form last divided difference*

                                                     compute coefficients

a(1) = y(1)

For j = 2 to 2n

    a(j) = d(1, j − 1)

End

Return

    a   *vector of coefficients*

Hermite Interpolation: Evaluate Polynomial

Input

    x   *data vector*

    a   *vector of coefficients*

    t = $(t_1, \ldots t_m)$ *vector of points where interpolated values are needed*

For k = 1 to n   *duplicate data entries*

    u(2k − 1) = x(k)

    u(2k) = x(k)

End

For k = 1 to m

    d(1) = 1

    H(k) = a(1)

    For j = 2 to 2n

        d(j) = (t(k) − u(j − 1)) d(j − 1)

        H(k) = H(k) + a(j) d(j)

    End

End

Return

    H   *vector of interpolated values*

Example 8.12 Difficult Data

If we use the data from Example 8.8 to estimate both the function values and first derivative values at seven points, we have

$$x = [-2 \quad -1 \quad -0.5 \quad 0 \quad 0.5 \quad 1 \quad 2]$$
$$y = [\ 0 \quad 0 \quad 0.87 \quad 1 \quad 0.87 \quad 0 \quad 0]$$
$$dy = [\ 0 \quad 0 \quad 0.5 \quad 0 \quad -0.5 \quad 0 \quad 0]$$

As with lower order polynomial interpolation, trying to interpolate in humped and flat regions (see Fig. 8.16) causes overshoots.

The difference table, without the data values for x and y, is shown here. The results are rounded to 2 decimal places (except that the 3rd decimal is shown when it is 5).

```
 0      0      0     1.55  -7.36    9.53 -11.69   8.75 -6.475   3.45 -1.58 0.395 0
 0      0      2.32 -9.49  11.71  -13.85  10.19  -7.43   3.88  -1.29   0    0.395
 0      3.48 -11.92 13.92 -16.00   11.63  -8.39   4.20   0     -1.29  1.58
 1.74  -2.48   2.00 -2.08   1.44   -0.96   0      4.20  -3.88   3.45
 0.50  -0.48  -0.08  0.08   0      -0.96   8.39  -7.43   6.475
 0.26  -0.52   0     0.08  -1.44   11.63 -10.19   8.75
 0     -0.52   0.08 -2.08  16.00  -13.85  11.69
-0.26  -0.48  -2.00 13.92 -11.71    9.53
-0.5   -2.48  11.92 -9.49   7.36
-1.74   3.48  -2.32  1.55
 0      0      0
 0      0
 0
```

The coefficients of the interpolating polynomial are found from the first row of the difference table (including the value of y). They are (to 4 decimal places) as follows:

$$a = 0 \ 0 \ 0 \ 0 \ 1.5467 \ -7.36 \ 9.5333 \ -11.6933 \ 8.7541 \ -6.4750 \ 3.4504 \ -1.5808 \ 0.3952 \ 0$$

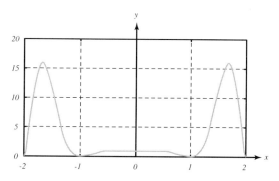

FIGURE 8.16   Hermite interpolation of humped and flat function.

Polynomials are not always the most effective form of representation of a function or a set of data. A *rational function* (a ratio of two polynomials) may be a better choice, especially if the function to be approximated has a *pole* (zero of the denominator) in the region of interest. Difficulties occur with polynomial interpolation even if the pole occurs in the complex plane, unless it is far removed from the data being interpolated. The Runge function introduced in Example 8.10, when viewed as a function of the complex variable $z = x + yi$, becomes $f(z) = 1/(1 + 25z^2)$; its poles at $z = \pm 0.2$ i are too close to the region of interest, namely, the real interval $[-1, 1]$.

In this section, we present a brief description of rational-function interpolation. The Bulirsch-Stoer algorithm produces a "diagonal" rational function, i.e., a rational function in which the degree of the numerator is either the same as, or one less than, the degree of the denominator. The approach is recursive, based on tabulated data (in a manner similar to that for the Newton form of polynomial interpolation). In the next chapter we consider *Pade approximation*, which seeks to find a rational function to fit the function value and derivative values at a given point x_0, in a manner more reminiscent of Taylor polynomials.

Given a set of k data points $(x_1, y_1), \ldots, (x_k, y_k)$, we seek an interpolation function of the form

$$r(x) = \frac{p_m(x)}{q_n(x)} = \frac{a_m x^m + \ldots + a_0}{b_n x^n + \ldots + b_0}.$$

In general, we would need to specify the degree of the numerator and the degree of the denominator. However, for the Bulirsch-Stoer method, $r(x)$ will have either $m = n$ or $m = n - 1$ (depending on whether the number of data points, k, is even or odd). The algorithm can be described recursively; we begin by showing the steps for $k = 3$ in some detail.

The following table shows the Bulirsch-Stoer method for three data points:

Data	First stage	Second stage	Third stage
$x_1\ y_1$	$R_1 = y_1$		
		$R_{12} = R_2 + \dfrac{R_2 - R_1}{\dfrac{x - x_1}{x - x_2}\left[1 - \dfrac{R_2 - R_1}{R_2}\right] - 1}$	
$x_2\ y_2$	$R_2 = y_2$		$R_{123} = R_{23} + \dfrac{R_{23} - R_{12}}{\dfrac{x - x_1}{x - x_3}\left[1 - \dfrac{R_{23} - R_{12}}{R_{23} - R_2}\right] - 1}$
		$R_{23} = R_3 + \dfrac{R_3 - R_2}{\dfrac{x - x_2}{x - x_3}\left[1 - \dfrac{R_3 - R_2}{R_3}\right] - 1}$	
$x_3\ y_3$	$R_3 = y_3$		

The general pattern is established by the third stage. The rational function $R_{123\ldots k}$ to interpolate k points $(x_1, y_1), \ldots, (x_k, y_k)$ is formed from the function $R_{23\ldots k}$ to interpolate the $(k\text{-}1)$ points $(x_2, y_2), \ldots, (x_k, y_k)$, the function $R_{123\ldots(k-1)}$ to interpolate the $(k\text{-}1)$ points $(x_1, y_1), \ldots, (x_{k-1}, y_{k-1})$, and the function $R_{23\ldots(k-1)}$ to interpolate the $(k\text{-}2)$ points $(x_2, y_2), \ldots, (x_{k-1}, y_{k-1})$, as follows:

$$R_{123\ldots k} = R_{23\ldots k-1} + \cfrac{R_{23\ldots k} - R_{123\ldots(k-1)}}{\cfrac{x - x_1}{x - x_k}\left[1 - \cfrac{R_{23\ldots k} - R_{12\ldots(k-1)}}{R_{23\ldots k} - R_{23\ldots(k-1)}}\right] - 1}$$

The computation at the second stage follows this form also, with the understanding that the rational function to interpolate the $k - 2$ points is zero at that stage.

It is fairly easy to verify that the expressions at the second stage, i.e., the result of interpolating two data points, have the expected form. However, the algorithm does not yield a simple algebraic expression for the rational function to interpolate several points; rather, it provides a systematic method of computing the interpolated value at specified points. (See Press et al. (1986) and Stoer and Bulirsch (1980) for further discussion.)

The results of rational function interpolation are illustrated in Example 8.13, which is followed by an algorithm for the method.

Example 8.13 Rational-Function Interpolation

We illustrate the use of a simple computer program for Bulirsch-Stoer rational-function interpolation by considering the data for the Runge function introduced in Example 8.10. The interpolated results and the actual function values are shown in Fig. 8.17.

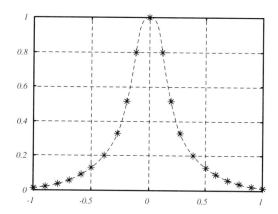

FIGURE 8.17   Data and interpolated values for Runge function.

The following algorithm for Bulirsch-Stoer interpolation treats interpolation at the data points separately, to save computational effort and to avoid many possible divisions by zero. The general expression for the computation of R at the jth stage has been written in a form that reduces the number of divisions that could lead to the indeterminant form of 0/0. Note that unlike the previous interpolation algorithms, this algorithm interpolates the data at specified values of the independent variable, rather than computing the coefficients of the interpolation function.

Bulirsch-Stoer Rational Function Interpolation

Input
  x   *data vector for independent variable ($x_1, \ldots x_n$)*
  y   *data vector for dependent variable ($y_1, \ldots y_n$)*
  t   *find interpolated values at ($t_1, \ldots t_m$)*
  n   *number of data values*
  m   *number of values to interpolate*
Begin computation
For h = 1 to m
    If t(h) = x(j) for some j
        z(h) = y(j)   *no need to interpolate, go to next value of t*
    Else
        R(:, 1) = y(:)   *form first column of R = y*
        For i = 1 to n − 1   *form second column of R*
            D = R(i + 1, 1) − R(i, 1)
            r = (t(h) − x(i))/(t(h) − x(i + 1))
            d = r(1 − D/R(i + 1, 1)) − 1
            R(i, 2) = R(i + 1, 1) + D/d
        End
        For j = 3 to n   *form remaining columns of R*
            For i = 1 to n − j + 1
                D_1 = R(i + 1, j − 1) − R(i, j − 1)
                D_2 = R(i + 1, j − 1) − R(i + 1, j − 2)
                r = (t(h) − x(i))/(t(h) − x(i + j + 1))
                If D_1 = 0
                    R(i, j) = R(i + 1, j − 1)
                Else if D_2 = 0
                    R(i, j) = R(i + 1, j − 1)
                Else
                    d = r(1 − D_1/D_2) − 1
                    R(i, j) = R(i + 1, j − 1) + D_1/d
                Endif
            End
        End
        z(h) = R(1, n)   *interpolated value*
    Endif
End
Return
  z   *vector of interpolated values*

The disadvantage of using a single polynomial (of high degree) to interpolate a large number of data points is illustrated in Example 8.10. To avoid these problems, we can use piecewise polynomials. Historically, the design and construction of a ship or aircraft involved the use of full-sized models. One method of forming a smooth curve passing through specified points was to take a thin, flexible metal or wooden lath and bend it around pegs set at the required points. The resulting curve was traced out and used in the design process. Curves generated in this manner were known as *splines* (as were the thin laths used in their construction). Spline curves represent the curve of minimum strain energy; they are also aesthetically pleasing. These physical splines assume the shape of a piecewise cubic polynomial. After a brief discussion of piecewise linear and quadratic interpolation, we consider cubic spline interpolation.

8.4.1 Piecewise Linear Interpolation

To illustrate the simplest form of piecewise polynomial interpolation, namely, piecewise linear interpolation, consider a set of four data points $(x_1, y_1), (x_2, y_2), (x_3, y_3), (x_4, y_4)$, with $x_1 < x_2 < x_3 < x_4$. These points define three subintervals of the x axis: $I_1 = [x_1, x_2]$, $I_2 = [x_2, x_3]$, $I_3 = [x_3, x_4]$.

If we use a straight line on each subinterval, we can interpolate the data with a piecewise linear function, where

$$P_i(x) = \frac{(x - x_{i+1})}{x_i - x_{i+1})} y_i + \frac{(x - x_i)}{(x_{i+1} - x_i)} y_{i+1}$$

Example 8.14 Piecewise Linear Interpolation

Using $\mathbf{x} = [0 \quad 1 \quad 2 \quad 3]$ and $\mathbf{y} = [0 \quad 1 \quad 4 \quad 3]$, we find the piecewise linear function illustrated in Fig. 8.18. The function is continuous, but not smooth.

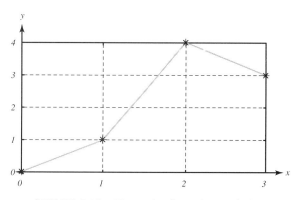

FIGURE 8.18   Piecewise linear interpolation.

8.4.2 Piecewise Quadratic Interpolation

We could use quadratic functions on each subinterval and try to make the first derivatives, as well as the function values agree at the data points. For $n + 1$ data points, there are n intervals. Also, there are three unknowns to determine for each quadratic polynomial, so we have $3n$ unknowns. Furthermore, there are two equations for each interval, corresponding to specified values for the quadratic function at the interval endpoints. (That is, (x_1, y_1) and (x_2, y_2) must satisfy the quadratic equation on the first interval, etc.) In addition, there are $n - 1$ points at which the intervals meet; we require that the first derivatives of the parabolas on the adjacent intervals be continuous. This gives $2n + n - 1$ equations for the $3n$ unknowns. We have one free parameter; it is not clear how to best define one additional condition.

In order to have a more useful interpolation scheme based on piecewise quadratics, we define the "knots" where the intervals meet to be the midpoints between the data points where the function values are given. We illustrate the process for four data points (x_1, y_1), (x_2, y_2), (x_3, y_3), and (x_4, y_4), with $x_1 < x_2 < x_3 < x_4$. We define the node points

$$z_1 = x_1; \quad z_2 = (x_1 + x_2)/2; \quad z_3 = (x_2 + x_3)/2; \quad z_4 = (x_3 + x_4)/2; \quad z_5 = x_4;$$

The spacings between consecutive data points are $h_1 = x_2 - x_1$, $h_2 = x_3 - x_2$, and $h_3 = x_4 - x_3$. Then $z_2 - x_1 = h_1/2$, $z_3 - x_2 = h_2/2$, $z_4 - x_3 = h_3/2$, and $z_2 - x_2 = -h_1/2$, $z_3 - x_3 = -h_2/2$, $z_4 - x_4 = -h_3/2$.

We define

$$
\begin{array}{lll}
P_1 \text{ on } [z_1, z_2]: & P_1(x) = a_1(x - x_1)^2 + b_1(x - x_1) + c_1; \\
P_2 \text{ on } [z_2, z_3]: & P_2(x) = a_2(x - x_2)^2 + b_2(x - x_2) + c_2; \\
P_3 \text{ on } [z_3, z_4]: & P_3(x) = a_3(x - x_3)^2 + b_3(x - x_3) + c_3; \\
P_4 \text{ on } [z_4, z_5]: & P_4(x) = a_4(x - x_4)^2 + b_4(x - x_4) + c_4.
\end{array}
$$

Since $P_k(x_k) = c_k$, imposing the interpolation condition that $P_k(x_k) = y_k$ immediately yields $c_k = y_k$ for $k = 1, 2, 3, 4$. Now if we impose continuity conditions on the polynomials at the interior nodes, we obtain the following:

$$
\begin{array}{lll}
P_1(z_2) = P_2(z_2): & h_1^2 a_1 - h_1^2 a_2 + 2h_1 b_1 + 2h_1 b_2 = 4(y_2 - y_1); \\
P_2(z_3) = P_3(z_3): & h_2^2 a_2 - h_2^2 a_3 + 2h_2 b_2 + 2h_2 b_3 = 4(y_3 - y_2); \\
P_3(z_4) = P_4(z_4): & h_3^2 a_3 - h_3^2 a_4 + 2h_3 b_3 + 2h_3 b_4 = 4(y_4 - y_3).
\end{array}
$$

Similarly, if we impose continuity conditions on the first derivatives of the polynomials at the interior nodes, we obtain another three equations:

$$
\begin{array}{lll}
P_1{}'(z_2) = P_2{}'(z_2): & h_1 a_1 + h_1 a_2 + b_1 - b_2 = 0; \\
P_2{}'(z_3) = P_3{}'(z_3): & h_2 a_2 + h_2 a_3 + b_2 - b_3 = 0; \\
P_3{}'(z_4) = P_4{}'(z_4): & h_3 a_3 + h_3 a_4 + b_3 - b_4 = 0.
\end{array}
$$

At this stage, we have a system of six equations for the eight unknown coefficients ($a_1, a_2, a_3, a_4, b_1, b_2, b_3$, and b_4). Since $P_k{}'(x) = 2a_k(x - x_k) + b_k$, we can determine b_1 and b_4 by imposing conditions on the derivative values at the interval endpoints, x_1 and x_4. Setting $P_1{}'(x_1) = 0$ gives $b_1 = 0$, and setting $P_4{}'(x_4) = 0$ gives $b_4 = 0$. With these zero-slope conditions at the endpoints of the interval, the equations for the coefficients become

$$\begin{aligned}
a_1 h_1^2 \quad -a_2 h_1^2 \qquad\qquad\qquad +2b_2 h_1 \qquad\qquad &= 4(y_2 - y_1) \\
+a_2 h_2^2 \quad -a_3 h_2^2 \qquad\qquad +2b_2 h_2 \quad +2b_3 h_2 &= 4(y_3 - y_2) \\
+a_3 h_3^2 \quad -a_4 h_3^2 \qquad\qquad +2b_3 h_3 &= 4(y_4 - y_3) \\
a_1 h_1 \quad +a_2 h_1 \qquad\qquad\qquad\qquad -b_2 \qquad\qquad &= 0 \\
+a_2 h_2 \quad +a_3 h_2 \qquad\qquad +b_2 \quad -b_3 &= 0 \\
+a_3 h_3 \quad +a_4 h_3 \qquad\qquad +b_3 &= 0
\end{aligned}$$

Although there are circumstances in which piecewise quadratic interpolation has some theoretical advantages, compared with cubic spline interpolation, we illustrate the former in a simple example and then proceed to the more popular cubic spline interpolation in the next section.

Example 8.15 Piecewise Quadratic Interpolation

For the data points $(0, 0)$, $(1, 1)$, $(2, 4)$, and $(3, 3)$, the linear system of equations for the coefficients is defined by the matrix $\mathbf{A}$ and right-hand side $\mathbf{r}$:

$$\mathbf{A} = \begin{bmatrix} 1 & -1 & 0 & 0 & 2 & 0 \\ 0 & 1 & -1 & 0 & 2 & 2 \\ 0 & 0 & 1 & -1 & 0 & 2 \\ 1 & 1 & 0 & 0 & -1 & 0 \\ 0 & 1 & 1 & 0 & 1 & 1 \\ 0 & 0 & 1 & 1 & 0 & 1 \end{bmatrix}, \quad \mathbf{r} = \begin{bmatrix} 4 \\ 12 \\ -4 \\ 0 \\ 0 \\ 0 \end{bmatrix}.$$

The solution vector gives the coefficients a_1, a_2, a_3, a_4, b_2, and b_3:

$$x = [0.7429 \quad 1.7714 \quad -3.3714 \quad 2.4571 \quad 2.5143 \quad 0.9143]^T$$

The piecewise interpolating polynomial is illustrated in Fig. 8.19 and is given by

$$\begin{aligned}
P_1(x) &= 0.7429(x - 0)^2 & &\text{on } [0.0, 0.5], \\
P_2(x) &= 1.7714(x - 1)^2 + 2.5143(x - 1) + 1 & &\text{on } [0.5, 1.5], \\
P_3(x) &= -3.3714(x - 2)^2 + 0.9143(x - 2) + 4 & &\text{on } [1.5, 2.5], \\
P_4(x) &= 2.4571(x - 3)^2 + 3 & &\text{on } [2.5, 3.0].
\end{aligned}$$

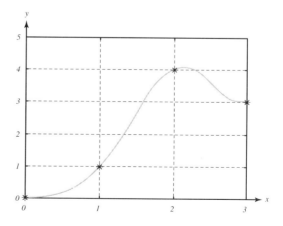

FIGURE 8.19   Piecewise quadratic interpolation.

8.4.3   Piecewise Cubic Interpolation

We can do better, without much more work, if we use cubic splines (i.e., a piecewise cubic polynomial). A simple calculation shows that we have enough information to require continuity of the function and its first and second derivatives at each of the "node points," i.e., the boundaries of the subintervals.

The calculation of the coefficients of the cubic polynomials on each subinterval is simplified by a suitable choice of the algebraic representation of the equations. The n given points $(x_1, y_1), (x_2, y_2), \ldots, (x_i, y_i), \ldots, (x_n, y_n)$ define n-1 subintervals. Since the spacing between the x values is not required to be uniform, let $h_i = x_{i+1} - x_i$. We are looking for a spline function

$$S(x) = \begin{cases} P_1(x), & x_1 \le x \le x_2, \\ P_i(x), & x_i \le x \le x_{i+1}, \\ P_{n-1}(x) & x_{n-1} \le x \le x_n, \end{cases}$$

that is a piecewise cubic with continuous derivatives up to order 2.

For $i = 1, \ldots, n - 1$, we write

$$P_i(x) = a_{i-1} \frac{(x_{i+1} - x)^3}{6h_i} + a_i \frac{(x - x_i)^3}{6h_i} + b_i(x_{i+1} - x) + c_i(x - x_i).$$

The motivation for this form of the cubic and the derivation of the equations for the coefficients a_i, b_i, and c_i are given in the discussion at the end of this section. First we illustrate the method with several examples and an algorithm for generating cubic splines. The n-2 equations ($i = 1, \ldots n - 2$) for the n unknowns $a_0, \ldots, a_{n-1}$ have the form

$$\frac{h_i}{6} a_{i-1} + \frac{h_i + h_{i+1}}{3} a_i + \frac{h_{i+1}}{6} a_{i+1} = \frac{y_{i+1} - y_{i+1}}{h_{i+1}} - \frac{y_{i+1} - y_i}{h_i}$$

There are several possible choices for the conditions on the second derivatives at the endpoints, which provide the additional conditions to determine all of the unknowns. The simplest choice, the natural cubic spline, assigns values of zero to the second derivatives at x_1 and x_n. The values of b_i and c_i ($i = 1, \ldots, n - 1$) are expressed in terms of the a_i coefficients as follows:

$$b_i = \frac{y_i}{h_i} - \frac{a_{i-1} h_i}{6},$$

$$c_i = \frac{y_{i+1}}{h_i} - \frac{a_i h_i}{6}.$$

Example 8.16 Natural Cubic Spline Interpolation

Consider the data points $(-2, 4)$, $(-1, -1)$, $(0, 2)$, $(1, 1)$, and $(2, 8)$. We have $h_i = 1$ for all intervals, and $a_0 = a_4 = 0$ for a natural cubic spline. The equations for a_1, a_2, and a_3 are as follows

$$i = 1 \quad \frac{1}{6}a_0 + \frac{2}{3}a_1 + \frac{1}{6}a_2 \qquad = (y_3 - y_2) - (y_2 - y_1);$$

$$i = 2 \qquad \frac{1}{6}a_1 + \frac{2}{3}a_2 + \frac{1}{6}a_3 \quad = (y_4 - y_3) - (y_3 - y_2);$$

$$i = 3 \qquad \frac{1}{6}a_2 + \frac{2}{3}a_3 + \frac{1}{6}a_4 = (y_5 - y_4) - (y_4 - y_3).$$

Substituting in the values for a_0, a_4, and $y_1. \ldots, y_5$ and simplifying, gives

$$
\begin{aligned}
4a_1 + a_2 &= 48 \\
a_1 + 4a_2 + a_3 &= -24 \\
a_2 + 4a_3 &= 48
\end{aligned}
$$

This gives a tridiagonal system that can be solved as in Chapter 3. We find that

$$a_1 = 15.4286, \quad a_2 = -13.7143, \quad a_3 = 15.4286.$$

Solving for the b_i gives

$$b_1 = y_1 - a_0/6 = 4, \qquad b_2 = y_2 - a_1/6 = -3.5714,$$
$$b_3 = y_3 - a_2/6 = 4.2857, \qquad b_4 = y_4 \quad a_3/6 = 1.5714,$$

and for the c_i gives

$$c_1 = y_2 - a_1/6 = -3.5714, \quad c_2 = y_3 - a_2/6 = 4.2857,$$
$$c_3 = y_4 - a_3/6 = -1.5714, \quad c_4 = y_5 - a_4/6 = 8.$$

The cubic spline is illustrated in Fig. 8.20; it simplifies to

$$S(x) =
\begin{cases}
2.57(x + 2)^3 - 4(x + 1) - 3.57(x + 2) & -2 \leq x \leq -1 \\
-2.57x^3 \quad\quad - 2.29(x + 1)^3 + 3.57x + 4.29(x + 1) & -1 \leq x \leq 0 \\
-2.29(1 - x)^3 + 2.57x^3 \quad\quad + 4.29(1 - x) - 1.57x & 0 \leq x \leq 1 \\
2.57(2 - x)^3 - 1.57(2 - x) + 8(x - 1) & 1 \leq x \leq 2
\end{cases}$$

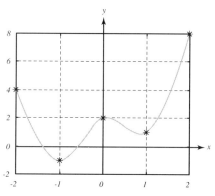

FIGURE 8.20 Cubic spline interpolant.

Given data vectors $\mathbf{x} = [x_1 \dots x_n]$ and $\mathbf{y} = [y_1 \dots y_n]$, the following algorithm computes the coefficients for a natural cubic spline function. The natural cubic spline assumes that $a_0 = a_{n-1} = 0$. The algorithm makes use of previous algorithms for solving a tridiagonal system.

Natural Cubic Spline Interpolation: Compute Coefficients

Input

x	*vector of values of independent variable*
y	*vector of values of dependent variable*
n	*number of data points*

Begin computation
For k = 1 to n − 1   *parameters used to form tridiagonal system*
   h(k) = x(k + 1) − x(k)
   T(k) = (y(k + 1) − y(k))/h(k)
End
For k = 1 to n − 2   *tridiagonal system (n-2) by (n-2)*
   R(k) = T(k + 1) − T(k)   *right-hand side*
   D(k) = (h(k) + h(k + 1))/3   *diagonal*
End
For k = 1 to n − 3
   U(k) = h(k + 1)/6
   L(k + 1) = U(k)
End
U(n − 2) = 0
L(1) = 0

a   *solution of $\mathbf{M}\,\mathbf{a} = \mathbf{R}$*
        $\mathbf{M}$ is tridiagonal, given by $\mathbf{U}$, $\mathbf{D}$, and $\mathbf{L}$

b(1) = y(1)/h(1)   *Define $\mathbf{b}$ and $\mathbf{c}$ coefficients of spline function*
c(1) = y(2)/h(1) − a(1) h(1)/6
For k = 2 to n − 2
   b(k) = y(k)/h(k) − a(k − 1) h(k)/6
   c(k) = y(k + 1)/h(k) − a(k) h(k)/6
End
b(n − 1) = y(n − 1)/h(n − 1) − a(n − 2) h(n − 1)/6
c(n − 1) = y(n)/h(n − 1)

Return
   a
   b
   c   *vectors of coefficients*

The following algorithm computes the interpolated values based on the spline function coefficients computed in the previous algorithm.

The spline is given by the piecewise cubic function

$$S(x) = \begin{cases} \dfrac{a_1(x - x_1)^3}{6h_1} + b_1(x_2 - x) + c_1(x - x_1) & \text{(if } x_1 < x < x_2) \\ \quad \cdots \\ \dfrac{a_{i-1}(x_{i+1} - x)^3}{6h_i} + \dfrac{a_i(x - x_i)^3}{6h_i} + b_i(x_{i+1} - x) + c_i(x - x_i) & \text{(if } x_i < x < x_{i+1}) \\ \quad \cdots \\ \dfrac{a_{n-2}(x_n - x)^3}{6h_{n-1}} + b_{n-1}(x_n - x) + c_{n-1}(x - x_{n-1}) & \text{(if } x_{n-1} < x < x_n) \end{cases}$$

Natural Cubic Spline Interpolation: Evaluate Spline

Input

t		*vector of values to be interpolated ($t(1)$ .... $t(m)$)*
m		*number of values to be interpolated*
a		*vector of coefficients*
b		*vector of coefficients*
c		*vector of coefficients*
x		*vector of values of independent variable*
n		*number of components of vector **x***

Begin computation

```
For k = 1 to m
    For j = 1 to n − 1              determine appropriate interval
        If t(k) >= x(j)
            d = j
        End
    End

    h = x(d + 1) − x(d)
    If d == 1
        s(k) = a(1) (t(k) − x(1))^3/(6 h) + b(1) (x(2) − t(k)) + c(1) (t(k) − x(1))
    Elseif d == n − 1
        s(k) = a(n − 2) (x(n) − t(k))^3/(6 h) + b(n − 1) (x(n) − t(k)) + c(n − 1) (t(k)
            − x(n − 1))
    Else
        s(k) = (a(d − 1)(x(d + 1) − t(k))^3 + a(d)(t(k) − x(d))^3/(6h)
            + b(d)(x(d + 1) − t(k)) + c(d)(t(k) − x(d))
    End
End
```

Return

s	*vector of interpolated values*

Example 8.17 Runge Function

Consider again the Runge function introduced in Example 8.10:

$$f(x) = \frac{1}{1 + 25x^2}.$$

The cubic spline interpolation polynomial based on five equally spaced points in the interval $[-1, 1]$ has the following data values:

$$x = [-1.0 \qquad -0.5 \qquad 0.0 \qquad 0.5 \qquad 1.0 \quad]$$
$$y = [\ 0.0385 \qquad 0.1379 \quad 1.0000 \quad 0.1379 \quad 0.0385]$$

The data are shown in Fig. 8.21, together with the spline function (solid) and the actual Runge function (dashed). The agreement is much better than that found previously using polynomial interpolation, but is not as good as that with rational function interpolation.

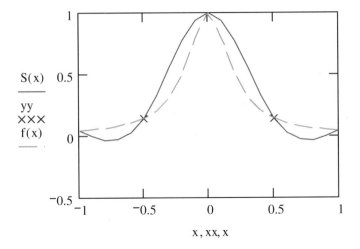

FIGURE 8.21   Runge function and spline interpolation curve.

Example 8.18 Difficult Data

Consider again the data presented in Example 8.8 for the humped and flat function:

$$\mathbf{x} = [-2 \quad -1.5 \quad -1 \quad -0.5 \quad 0 \quad 0.5 \quad 1 \quad 1.5 \quad 2]$$
$$\mathbf{y} = [\ \ 0 \qquad 0 \qquad 0 \quad 0.87 \quad 1 \quad 0.87 \quad 0 \quad 0 \qquad 0]$$

The resulting piecewise function is made up of the following polynomials given over each subinterval:

$$P_1 = -0.61(x + 2)^3 + 0.15(x + 2), \qquad\qquad\qquad -2 \le x \le -1.5,$$

$$P_2 = -0.61(-1 - x)^3 + 2.45(x + 1.5)^3 + 0.15(-1 - x) - 0.61(x + 1.5),$$
$$-1.5 \le x \le -1,$$

$$P_3 = \ \ 2.45(-0.5 - x)^3 - 2.24(x + 1)^3 - 0.61(-0.5 - x) + 2.30(x + 1),$$
$$-1 \le x \le -0.5,$$

$$P_4 = -2.24(-x)^3 + 0.60(x + 0.5)^3 + 2.30(-x) + 1.85(x + 0.5), \quad -0.5 \le x \le 0,$$

$$P_5 = \ \ 0.60(0.5 - x)^3 - 2.24(x)^3 + (1.85)(0.5 - x) + 2.30x, \qquad 0 \le x \le 0.5,$$

$$P_6 = -2.24(1 - x)^3 + 7.36(x - 0.5)^3/3 + 2.30(1 - x) - 0.61(x - 0.5),$$
$$0.5 \le x \le 1,$$

$$P_7 = \ \ 7.36(1.5 - x)^3/3 - 1.84(x - 1)^3/3 - 0.61(1.5 - x) + 0.15(x - 1),$$
$$1 \le x \le 1.5,$$

$$P_8 = -1.84(2 - x)^3/3 + 0.15(2 - x) + 0(x - 1.5), \qquad\qquad 1.5 \le x \le 2.$$

Figure 8.22 shows that the curve is still oscillating in the flat region, as well as near the peak of the hump. It is likely that setting the first derivative, instead of the second, equal to zero at the endpoints of the interval would improve the results obtained.

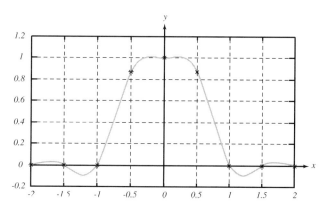

FIGURE 8.22 Cubic spline interpolation of humped and flat data.

Discussion

To see that we can require continuity of the cubic polynomials and their first and second derivatives at the node points, assume that we have n data points $(x_1, y_1), \ldots,$ (x_n, y_n). In other words, the node points coincide with the data points in this case. We have $n - 1$ intervals and four unknowns to determine a cubic polynomial on each interval; thus, we have $4(n - 1)$ unknowns. Now, two data points must lie on the curve of each cubic polynomial, so there are $2(n - 1)$ equations for the given data. In addition, there are $n - 2$ values of x at which we must have continuity of the first and second derivatives. This gives $2(n - 2)$ more equations, so altogether we have $4n - 6$ equations for $4n - 4$ unknowns. We can obtain two more equations by specifying the value of either the first or the second derivative at each of the two endpoints of the interval (i.e., at x_1 and x_n).

The actual derivation of the spline interpolation formulas is simplified by a suitable choice of the algebraic representation of the equations. Since the spacing between the x values of the data is not required to be uniform, we let $h_i = x_{i+1} - x_i$. We are looking for a piecewise polynomial function of the form

$$P_i(x) = a_{i-1}\frac{(x_{i+1} - x)^3}{6h_i} + a_i\frac{(x - x_i)^3}{6h_i} + b_i(x_{i+1} - x) + c_i(x - x_i) \text{ (for } x_i \leq x \leq x_{i+1}).$$

This form of the cubic is motivated by the fact that the second derivatives of the polynomials on adjacent subintervals must be equal at the common node between the two subintervals. Using the definition of h_i, we easily see that $P_i''(x_{i+1}) = a_i$ and that $P_{i+1}''(x_{i+1}) = a_i$ also. Thus, the form of the expression for $P_i(x)$ ensures that the second derivatives are continuous at the interior nodes. By integrating

$$P_i''(x) = a_{i-1}\frac{(x_{i+1} - x)}{h_i} + a_i\frac{(x - x_i)}{h_i} \text{ twice and using the facts that } P_i(x_i) = y_i$$

and $P_i(x_{i+1}) = y_{i+1}$, we find the coefficients b_i and c_i, so that

$$P_i(x) = a_{i-1}\frac{(x_{i+1} - x)^3}{6h_i} + a_i\frac{(x - x_i)^3}{6h_i}$$
$$+ \left[y_i - \frac{a_{i-1}h_i^2}{6}\right]\frac{(x_{i+1} - x)}{h_i} + \left[y_{i+1} - \frac{a_i h_i^2}{6}\right]\frac{(x - x_i)}{h_i}.$$

We now apply the requirement that the first derivatives of P_i and P_{i+1} must agree at x_{i+1}. After some algebra, we find that

$$\frac{h_i}{6}a_{i-1} + \frac{h_i + h_{i+1}}{3}a_i + \frac{h_{i+1}}{6}a_{i+1} = \frac{y_{i+1} - y_{i+1}}{h_{i+1}} - \frac{y_{i+1} - y_i}{h_i} \quad (i = 1, 2, \ldots, n - 2).$$

We thus have $n - 2$ equations, but n unknowns ($a_0, \ldots a_{n-1}$). The natural cubic spline assigns values of zero for both a_0 and a_{n-1}; thus, the second derivative is zero at the endpoints. A clamped spline specifies the value of the first derivative at the endpoints.

The error in using natural or clamped cubic spline interpolation is $|S(x) - g(x)|$, where $S(x)$ is the spline interpolation function and $g(x)$ is the function that generated the data. If h is the maximum spacing between node points, and $G = \max |g^{(4)}(x)|$, then

$$|S(x) - g(x)| < k h^4 G = O(h^4). \text{ (See Kahaner et al., 1989).}$$

Software packages such as Mathcad and MATLAB have several built-in functions for data interpolation. Software libraries, such as the NAG library and the NIST Index, also include routines for interpolation. The routines are distinguished according to whether the problem involves univariate data (curve fitting) or multivariate data (surface fitting). The routines for curve fitting use more refined versions of the method presented in this chapter.

The general interpolation problem for two (or more) independent variables is much more difficult than for a single variable. One reason is that, unless the function values are known on a rectangular grid of points, it is not easy either to order the data points or to determine which of them should be used to find the interpolated value at any particular point in the region.

We begin by illustrating the use of professionally developed software for interpolating data given on a rectangular grid. The usual approach is to have one function or routine to compute the coefficients, and another to find the interpolated values at specified points. Linear and cubic spline interpolation are the standard methods. We then consider briefly the problem of interpolating scattered data.

8.5.1 Using Mathcad for Interpolation on a Rectangular Grid

Mathcad's built-in functions, `cspline`, `lspline`, or `pspline`, may be used for either univariate or multivariate interpolation. Multivariate data must be given on an n-by-n grid. The array is specified by an n-by-2 matrix, **Mxy**, whose elements are the x-y coordinates of the diagonal of the grid. The data values are given in the n-by-n matrix, **Mz**. As for the one-dimensional case, the function `cspline`(**Mxy**, **Mz**) returns the vector of coefficients **vs** for cubic spline interpolation with cubic ends; the return vector is the first input to the function `interp`. Similarly, `lspline`(**Mxy**, **Mz**) returns the vector of coefficients for cubic spline interpolation with linear ends, and `pspline`(**Mxy**, **Mz**) returns the vector of coefficients for cubic spline interpolation with parabolic ends.

The function `interp`(**vs**, **Mxy**, **Mz**, **v**) interpolates the value from spline coefficients or regression coefficients, where $\mathbf{v} = (x, y)$ is the point where the interpolated value is desired.

8.5.2   Using MATLAB for Interpolation on a Rectangular Grid

MATLAB's built-in function `interp2` interpolates data defined on a rectangular grid:

$$
\begin{matrix}
(x_1, y_1) & (x_1, y_2) & (x_1, y_3) & \cdots & (x_1, y_m) \\
(x_2, y_1) & (x_2, y_2) & (x_2, y_3) & \cdots & (x_2, y_m) \\
\vdots & \vdots & \vdots & & \vdots \\
(x_n, y_1) & (x_n, y_2) & (x_n, y_3) & \cdots & (x_n, y_m)
\end{matrix}
$$

The data is given on a rectangular grid specified by the vectors **x** and **y.** The interpolated values are found on a grid defined by the user-specified vectors **xx** and **yy.** The default form of interpolation is "linear," which is more precisely called bilinear. Additional options for using `interp2` allow the user to specify other forms of the interpolation, including "cubic" (bicubic interpolation) and "nearest" (nearest neighbor interpolation).

The linear interpolation in two dimensions used in MATLAB's `interp2` functions is more properly known as bilinear interpolation. On each rectangular subregion, the interpolation is based on a bilinear function (linear in either **x** or **y**) of the form

$$z = a + bx + cy + dxy,$$

using the data values at the four corners of the region. Thus, for region R_{ij}, with data values (x_i, y_j), (x_i, y_{j+1}), (x_{i+1}, y_j), and (x_{i+1}, y_{j+1}), there are four equations for the four unknowns, a_{ij}, b_{ij}, c_{ij}, and d_{ij}:

$$
\begin{aligned}
z(i, j) &= a_{ij} + b_{ij}\,x(i) + c_{ij}\,y(j) + d_{ij}\,x(i)\,y(j) \\
z(i, j+1) &= a_{ij} + b_{ij}\,x(i) + c_{ij}\,y(j+1) + d_{ij}\,x(i)\,y(j+1) \\
z(i+1, j) &= a_{ij} + b_{ij}\,x(i+1) + c_{ij}\,y(j) + d_{ij}\,x(i+1)\,y(j) \\
z(i+1, j+1) &= a_{ij} + b_{ij}\,x(i+1) + c_{ij}\,y(j+1) + d_{ij}\,x(i+1)\,y(j+1)
\end{aligned}
$$

Example 8.19 Interpolation on a Rectangular Grid

Let $\mathbf{x} = [2, 4]$ and $\mathbf{y} = [3, 5, 7]$; define $\mathbf{z} = \mathbf{x}^T * \mathbf{y}$, so that

$$\mathbf{z} = \begin{bmatrix} 6 & 10 & 14 \\ 12 & 20 & 28 \end{bmatrix}$$

We now wish to interpolate $\mathbf{z}$ on the grid defined by the vectors

$$\mathbf{xx} = [2, \quad 2.4, \quad 2.6, \quad 2.8, \quad 3, \quad 3.5, \quad 4]$$

and

$$\mathbf{yy} = [3, \quad 3.5, \quad 5, \quad 7].$$

The input to the function `interp2` consists of:

the original data vectors ($\mathbf{x}$ as a row vector, $\mathbf{y}$ as a column vector),

the matrix of data values (the transpose of the matrix $\mathbf{z}$ defined above), and

vectors defining the points to be interpolated

(again $\mathbf{xx}$ as a row vector, $\mathbf{yy}$ as a column vector).

The transpose of a vector or matrix in MATLAB is denoted by a single prime.

```
zz = interp2 (x, y', z', xx, yy')
zz =
   6.00    7.20    7.80    8.40    9.00   10.50   12.00
   7.00    8.40    9.10    9.80   10.50   12.25   14.00
  10.00   12.00   13.00   14.00   15.00   17.50   20.00
  14.00   16.80   18.20   19.60   21.00   24.50   28.00
```

The interpolated function, plotted using `mesh(xx, yy, zz)`, is shown in Fig. 8.23.

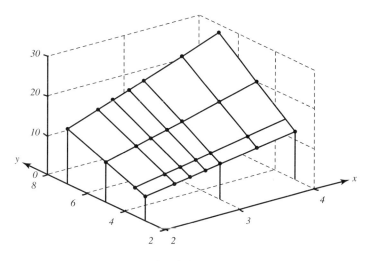

FIGURE 8.23   Interpolated data on a more general mesh.

8.5.3   Smoother Interpolation on a Rectangular Grid

The routines for achieving more smooth interpolation are beyond the scope of this text. We mention a few common approaches to this problem, along with appropriate references.

Bicubic Interpolation

MATLAB includes a bicubic interpolation option. A description of bicubic interpolation, and software routines for its implementation, are found in *Numerical Recipes* (Press et al., 1992). In this approach, the user specifies not only the data value, but also the gradients in the x and y directions, and the mixed second derivative at each of the grid points.

Bicubic Spline Interpolation

A second approach to improving the smoothness of interpolation on a rectangular grid is to use a two-dimensional variant of cubic spline interpolation. The basic idea is to first perform one-dimensional spline interpolation across each row of the table of data values. The second step is to perform a one-dimensional interpolation down the appropriate column of the newly interpolated data. See Press et al. (1992) for further details, and subroutines implementing the method.

8.5.4   Interpolation of Scattered Data

Another important and challenging area of two-dimensional interpolation deals with data that is not given on a rectangular grid. There are several routines for such interpolation included in the NAG software library. The basic idea is to define a triangular subdivision of the region of the plane described by the data. Linear interpolation can then be used on each triangular region.

MATLAB includes a routine (`inpolygon`) for determining whether a given point is inside a polygon specified by the vectors for the x and y coordinates of the vertices of the polygon. There are also routines for plotting surfaces defined by a triangular mesh. These are used in finite element solutions of partial differential equations, discussed in Chapter 15.

Polynomial Interpolation

Lagrange form of polynomial through the points (x_1, y_1), (x_2, y_2), and (x_3, y_3):

$$p(x) = \frac{(x - x_2)(x - x_3)}{(x_1 - x_2)(x_1 - x_3)} y_1 + \frac{(x - x_1)(x - x_3)}{(x_2 - x_1)(x_2 - x_3)} y_2 + \frac{(x - x_1)(x - x_2)}{(x_3 - x_1)(x_3 - x_2)} y_3$$

Newton form of polynomial through the points (x_1, y_1), (x_2, y_2), and (x_3, y_3):

$$p(x) = a_1 + a_2(x - x_1) + a_3(x - x_1)(x - x_2),$$

where coefficients

$$a_1 = y_1, \quad a_2 = \frac{y_2 - y_1}{x_2 - x_1}, \quad a_3 = \frac{\dfrac{y_3 - y_2}{x_3 - x_2} - \dfrac{y_2 - y_1}{x_2 - x_1}}{x_3 - x_1}.$$

The coefficients are the top entries in the divided-difference table:

$x_i \ y_i$	$d_i = \dfrac{y_{i+1} - y_i}{x_{i+1} - x_i}$	$dd_i = \dfrac{d_{i+1} - d_i}{x_{i+2} - x_i}$
$x_1 \ y_1$		
	$\dfrac{y_2 - y_1}{x_2 - x_1}$	
$x_2 \ y_2$		$\dfrac{d_2 - d_1}{x_3 - x_1}$
	$\dfrac{y_3 - y_2}{x_3 - x_2}$	
$x_3 \ y_3$		

Hermite Interpolation

Find a polynomial that agrees with function values and first derivative values

z_i	x_i	w_i	y_i	$d_i = \dfrac{w_{i+1} - w_i}{z_{i+1} - z_i}$	$dd_i = \dfrac{d_{i+1} - d_i}{z_{i+2} - z_i}$	$ddd_i = \dfrac{dd_{i+2} - dd_i}{z_{i+3} - z_i}$
$z_1 = x_1$		$w_1 = y_1$				
				$d_1 = y'_1$		
$z_2 = x_1$		$w_2 = y_1$			$dd_1 = \dfrac{d_2 - d_1}{z_3 - z_1}$	
				$d_2 = \dfrac{w_3 - w_2}{z_3 - z_2}$		$\dfrac{dd_2 - dd_1}{z_4 - z_1}$
$z_3 = x_2$		$w_3 = y_2$			$dd_2 = \dfrac{d_3 - d_2}{z_4 - z_2}$	
$z_4 = x_2$		$w_4 = y_2$		$d_3 = y'_2$		

Rational Function Interpolation

See equations in section 8.3.

Quadratic Spline Interpolation

Given four data points (x_1, y_1), (x_2, y_2), (x_3, y_3), and (x_4, y_4), with node points $z_1 = x_1$; $z_2 = (x_1 + x_2)/2$; $z_3 = (x_2 + x_3)/2$; $z_4 = (x_3 + x_4)/2$; $z_5 = x_4$; and $h_1 = x_2 - x_1$, $h_2 = x_3 - x_2$, $h_3 = x_4 - x_3$, the spline is

$$P_1 \text{ on } [z_1, z_2]: \qquad P_1(x) = a_1(x - x_1)^2 + b_1(x - x_1) + c_1;$$

$$P_2 \text{ on } [z_2, z_3]: \qquad P_2(x) = a_2(x - x_2)^2 + b_2(x - x_2) + c_2;$$

$$P_3 \text{ on } [z_3, z_4]: \qquad P_3(x) = a_3(x - x_3)^2 + b_3(x - x_3) + c_3;$$

$$P_4 \text{ on } [z_4, z_5]: \qquad P_4(x) = a_4(x - x_4)^2 + b_4(x - x_4) + c_4.$$

The coefficients are found by solving the following system:

$$
\begin{array}{llllll}
a_1 h_1^2 & -a_2 h_1^2 & & +2b_2 h_1 & & = 4(y_2 - y_1) \\
 & +a_2 h_2^2 & -a_3 h_2^2 & +2b_2 h_2 & +2b_3 h_2 & = 4(y_3 - y_2) \\
 & & +a_3 h_3^2 & -a_4 h_3^2 & +2b_3 h_3 & = 4(y_4 - y_3) \\
a_1 h_1 & +a_2 h_1 & & -b_2 & & = 0 \\
 & +a_2 h_2 & +a_3 h_2 & +b_2 & -b_3 & = 0 \\
 & & +a_3 h_3 & +a_4 h_3 & +b_3 & = 0
\end{array}
$$

Cubic Spline Interpolation

Given the data points $(x_1, y_1), \ldots (x_n, y_n)$; define $h_i = x_{i+1} - x_i$. The spline is $P_i(x)$, for $x_i \le x \le x_{i+1}$; for $i = 1, \ldots, n - 1$, we have

$$P_i(x) = a_{i-1}\frac{(x_{i+1} - x)^3}{6h_i} + a_i\frac{(x - x_i)^3}{6h_i} + b_i(x_{i+1} - x) + c_i(x - x_i).$$

The natural cubic spline sets $a_0 = a_{n-1} = 0$.

The $n - 2$ equations $(i = 1, \ldots n - 2)$ for the unknowns $a_1, \ldots, a_{n-2}$ have the form

$$\frac{h_i}{6}a_{i-1} + \frac{h_i + h_{i+1}}{3}a_i + \frac{h_{i+1}}{6}a_{i+1} = \frac{y_{i+2} - y_{i+1}}{h_{i+1}} - \frac{y_{i+1} - y_i}{h_i}$$

The remaining coefficients are found from

$$b_i = \frac{y_i}{h_i} - \frac{a_{i-1} h_i}{6}$$

$$c_i = \frac{y_{i+1}}{h_i} - \frac{a_i h_i}{6}$$

For a more extensive discussion of interpolation, see:

Kahaner, D., C. Moler, and S. Nash. *Numerical Methods and Software.* Prentice Hall, Englewood Cliffs, NJ, 1989.

Press, W. H., S. A. Teukolsky, W. T. Vetterling, and B. P. Flannery. *Numerical Recipes in C: The Art of Scientific Computing* 2^d ed. Cambridge Unversity Press, Cambridge, 1992. See especially sections 3.2 and 3.3.

Stoer, J., and R. Bulirsch. *Introduction to Numerical Analysis.* Springer Verlag, New York, 1980. (Especially for rational function interpolation.)

An excellent description of spline interpolation is given in:

deBoor, C. *A Practical Guide to Splines.* Springer-Verlag, New York, 1978.

Applications of spline interpolation for computer graphics are presented in:

Bartels, R. H., J. C. Beatty, and B. A. Barsky. *An Introduction to Splines for Use in Computer Graphics and Geometric Modeling.* Morgan Kaufmann, Los Altos, CA, 1987.

Farin, G. *Curves and Surfaces for Computer Aided Geometric Design: A Practical Guide,* 2^d ed. Academic Press, Boston, 1990.

Quadratic spline interpolation is discussed in:

Kammer, W. J., G. W. Reddien, and R. S. Varga. "Quadratic Splines." *Numerische Mathematik,* vol. 22, pp. 241–259, 1974.

For further discussion of interpolation in two dimensions, see:

Lancaster, P., and K. Salkauskas. *Curve and Surface Fitting: An Introduction,* Academic Press, Boston, 1986.

For a more mathematically advanced treatment of interpolation and approximation, see:

Davis, P. J. *Interpolation and Approximation.* Dover, New York, 1975. (Originally published by Blaisdell Publishing in 1963.)

For Problems P8.1 to P8.10 find the

   a. *interpolating polynomial in Lagrange form;*
   b. *interpolating polynomial in Newton form;*
   c. *piecewise linear interpolating function.*

P8.1 $x = [1 \quad 2 \quad 3]$,
        $y = [1 \quad 4 \quad 8]$.

P8.2 $x = [1 \quad 4 \quad 9]$,
        $y = [1 \quad 2 \quad 3]$.

P8.3 $x = [4 \quad 9 \quad 16]$,
        $y = [2 \quad 3 \quad 4]$.

P8.4 $x = [-1 \quad 0 \quad 1]$,
        $y = [-2 \quad 3 \quad -2]$.

P8.5 $x = [0 \quad 1 \quad 2]$,
        $y = [1 \quad 2 \quad 4]$.

P8.6 $x = [0 \quad 1 \quad 2 \quad 4]$,
        $y = [1 \quad 1 \quad 2 \quad 5]$.

P8.7 $x = [-1 \quad 0 \quad 1 \quad 2]$,
        $y = [1/3 \quad 1 \quad 3 \quad 9]$.

P8.8 $x = [0 \quad 1 \quad 2 \quad 3]$,
        $y = [1 \quad 2 \quad 4 \quad 8]$.

P8.9 $x = [0 \quad 1 \quad 2 \quad 3]$,
        $y = [0 \quad 1 \quad 0 \quad -1]$.

P8.10 $x = [-1 \quad 0 \quad 1 \quad 2]$,
        $y = [0 \quad 1 \quad 2 \quad 9]$.

For Problems P8.11 to P8.15 find the:

   a. *interpolating polynomial in Lagrange form;*
   b. *interpolating polynomial in Newton form;*
   c. *piecewise linear interpolating function;*
   d. *piecewise quadratic interpolating function (knots midway between data points);*
   e. *cubic spline interpolating function.*

P8.11 $x = [0 \quad 2/3 \quad 1 \quad 2]$,
        $y = [2 \quad -2 \quad -1 \quad -1/2]$.

P8.12 $x = [0 \quad 2/3 \quad 1 \quad 2]$,
        $y = [4 \quad -4 \quad -2 \quad -1/2]$.

P8.13 $x = [0 \quad 2/3 \quad 1 \quad 2]$,
        $y = [4 \quad -4 \quad -7/2 \quad -1/2]$.

P8.14 $x = [1 \quad 2 \quad 3 \quad 4]$,
        $y = [2 \quad 4 \quad 8 \quad 16]$.

P8.15 $x = [0 \quad 1/2 \quad 1 \quad 3/2]$,
        $y = [1 \quad 2 \quad 1 \quad 0]$.

For Problems P8.16 to P8.20:

   a. *Find the interpolation polynomial (either form).*
   b. *Find the cubic spline interpolation function.*
   c. *Compare the interpolated values to the given function.*

P8.16 $x = [0 \quad 1 \quad 8 \quad 27]$,
        $y = [0 \quad 1 \quad 2 \quad 3]$.

Compare interpolated values at $x = 0.5, 3.5,$ and 18 to $f(x) = \sqrt[3]{x}$.

P8.17 $x = [0 \quad 1 \quad 4 \quad 9]$,
        $y = [0 \quad 1 \quad 2 \quad 3]$.

Compare interpolated values at $x = 0.5, 2.5,$ and 6.5 to $f(x) = \sqrt{x}$.

P8.18 $x = [-1 \quad -0.75 \quad -0.25 \quad 0.25 \quad 0.75 \quad 1]$
        $y = [0 \quad -0.7 \quad -0.7 \quad 0.7 \quad 0.7 \quad 0]$

Compare interpolated values $x = -0.5, 0,$ and 0.5 to $f(x) = \sin(\pi x)$.

P8.19 $x = [-2 \quad -1 \quad 0 \quad 1 \quad 2 \quad 3 \quad 4]$
        $y = [-14 \quad 0.5 \quad 3.1 \quad 0 \quad -3 \quad 0 \quad 16]$

Compare to Example 8.4 and 8.7.

P8. 20 $x = [0 \quad 0.5 \quad 1.0 \quad 1.5 \quad 2.0 \quad 2.5 \quad 3.0]$
        $y = [4.0 \quad 0 \quad -2.0 \quad 0 \quad 1.0 \quad 0 \quad -0.5]$

Compare the interpolated values to those of the function $y = 2^{(2-x)} \cos(\pi x)$.

For Problems P8.21 to P8.30 find the
   a.   interpolation polynomial (either form);
   b.   cubic spline interpolation function;
   c.   Bulirsch-Stoer rational interpolation function.

P8.21 $x = [0 \quad 1 \quad 2 \quad\quad 3 \quad 4 \quad\quad 5 \quad 6 \quad\quad 7 \quad 8 \quad\quad 9 \quad 10 \quad\quad]$
$y = [2.0 \quad 0 \quad 0.6667 \quad 0 \quad 0.40 \quad 0 \quad 0.2857 \quad 0 \quad 0.2222 \quad 0 \quad 0.1818]$

Compare the interpolated values to $y = \dfrac{1 + \cos(\pi x)}{1 + x}$.

P8.22 $x = [0 \quad\quad 1 \quad\quad\quad 2 \quad\quad\quad 3 \quad\quad\quad 4 \quad\quad\quad 5 \quad\quad\quad 6 \quad\quad\quad 7 \quad\quad\quad 8 \quad\quad\quad 9 \quad\quad\quad 10 \quad\quad]$
$z = [2.0 \quad 0.7702 \quad 0.1946 \quad 0.0025 \quad 0.0693 \quad 0.2139 \quad 0.280 \quad 0.2192 \quad 0.0949 \quad 0.0089 \quad 0.0146]$

Compare the interpolated values to $z = \dfrac{1 + \cos(x)}{1 + x}$.

P8.23 $x = [0 \quad 1 \quad\quad 2 \quad\quad 3 \quad\quad 4 \quad\quad 5 \quad\quad\quad 6 \quad\quad\quad 7 \quad\quad\quad 8 \quad\quad\quad 9 \quad\quad\quad 10 \quad\quad]$
$w = [0 \quad 0.5 \quad 0.5 \quad 0.375 \quad 0.25 \quad 0.1562 \quad 0.0938 \quad 0.0547 \quad 0.0312 \quad 0.0176 \quad 0.0098]$

Compare the interpolated values to $w = x\, 2^{-x}$.

P8.24 $x = [1 \quad 2 \quad\quad\quad 3 \quad\quad\quad 4 \quad\quad\quad 5 \quad\quad\quad 6 \quad\quad\quad 7 \quad\quad\quad 8 \quad\quad\quad 9 \quad\quad\quad 10 \quad\quad]$
$y = [0 \quad 0.3466 \quad 0.3662 \quad 0.3466 \quad 0.3219 \quad 0.2986 \quad 0.2780 \quad 0.2599 \quad 0.2441 \quad 0.2303]$

Compare the interpolated values to $y = \dfrac{\ln(x)}{x}$.

P8.25 $x = [0 \quad\quad\quad 0.50 \quad\quad 1.00 \quad\quad\quad 1.50 \quad\quad 2.00 \quad\quad 2.50 \quad\quad 3.00]$
$y = [-0.3333 \quad -0.2703 \quad -0.2000 \quad -0.1333 \quad -0.0769 \quad -0.0328 \quad 0 \quad]$

Compare the interpolated values to $y = \dfrac{x - 3}{x^2 + 9}$.

P8.26 $x = [0.0 \quad\quad 1.00 \quad\quad 2.00 \quad\quad 3.00 \quad 4.00 \quad 5.00 \quad 6.00]$
$y = [-0.33 \quad -0.20 \quad -0.08 \quad 0.00 \quad 0.04 \quad 0.06 \quad 0.07]$

Compare the interpolated values to $y = \dfrac{x - 3}{x^2 + 9}$.

P8.27 $x = [0 \quad\quad\quad\quad 5 \quad\quad\quad 10 \quad\quad\quad 15 \quad\quad 20 \quad\quad 25 \quad\quad 30 \quad\quad 35 \quad\quad 40 \quad\quad]$
$y = [-0.3333 \quad 0.0588 \quad 0.0642 \quad 0.0513 \quad 0.0416 \quad 0.0347 \quad 0.0297 \quad 0.0259 \quad 0.0230]$

Compare the interpolated values to $y = \dfrac{x - 3}{x^2 + 9}$.

P8.28   Interpolate
$x = [-5 \quad\quad -4 \quad\quad -3 \quad\quad -2 \quad\quad -1 \quad\quad 0 \quad\quad 1 \quad\quad 2 \quad\quad 3 \quad\quad 4 \quad\quad 5 \quad\quad]$
$y = [-0.1923 \quad -0.2353 \quad -0.30 \quad -0.40 \quad -0.50 \quad 0.00 \quad 0.50 \quad 0.40 \quad 0.30 \quad 0.2353 \quad 0.1923]$

Compare the interpolated values at $x = -4.5, -3.5, \ldots, 3.5, 4.5$ to $y = \dfrac{x}{x^2 + 1}$.

P8.29 $x = [0 \quad 1 \quad 2 \quad 3 \quad 4 \quad 5 \quad 6 \quad 7 \quad 8 \quad 9 \quad 10 \quad]$
$y = [1.0 \quad 1.0 \quad 0.5556 \quad 0.3571 \quad 0.2615 \quad 0.2063 \quad 0.1705 \quad 0.1453 \quad 0.1267 \quad 0.1123 \quad 0.1009]$

Compare the interpolated values to $y = \dfrac{x^2 + 1}{x^3 + 1}$.

P8.30 $x = [0 \quad 1 \quad 2 \quad 3 \quad 4 \quad 5 \quad 6 \quad 7 \quad 8 \quad 9 \quad 10 \quad]$
$y = [0.5 \quad 1.0 \quad 1.7 \quad 1.8966 \quad 1.9545 \quad 1.9764 \quad 1.9862 \quad 1.9913 \quad 1.9942 \quad 1.9959 \quad 1.9970]$

Compare the interpolated values to $y = \dfrac{2\,x^2 + 1}{x^3 + 2}$.

Problems P8.31 to P8.35 provide practice in the use of Hermite interpolation.
  a. Find the interpolation polynomial using the given data.
  b. Find the Hermite interpolation polynomial using the given function and derivative values.
  c. Compare the interpolated values (at some intermediate values of x) from Parts a and b to those of the specified function

P8.31 Interpolate

$x = [-5 \quad -4 \quad -3 \quad -2 \quad -1 \quad 0 \quad 1 \quad 2 \quad 3 \quad 4 \quad 5]$
$w = [0.0385 \quad 0.0588 \quad 0.10 \quad 0.20 \quad 0.50 \quad 1.00 \quad 0.50 \quad 0.20 \quad 0.10 \quad 0.0588 \quad 0.0385]$

for Hermite interpolation use

$x = [-5 \quad -3 \quad -1 \quad 1 \quad 3 \quad 5 \quad]$
$w = [0.0385 \quad 0.10 \quad 0.50 \quad 0.50 \quad 0.10 \quad 0.0385 \quad]$
$dw = [0.0148 \quad 0.06 \quad 0.50 \quad -0.50 \quad -0.06 \quad -0.0148]$

or

$x = [-4 \quad -2 \quad 0 \quad 2 \quad 4 \quad]$
$w = [0.0588 \quad 0.20 \quad 1.00 \quad 0.20 \quad 0.0588 \quad]$
$dw = [0.0277 \quad 0.1600 \quad 0 \quad -0.1600 \quad -0.0277]$

Compare the interpolated values to those from the function $w = \dfrac{1}{x^2 + 1}$.

P8.32 Interpolate

$x = [1 \quad 2 \quad 3 \quad 4 \quad 5 \quad 6 \quad 7 \quad 8 \quad 9 \quad 10 \quad]$
$y = [0 \quad 0.6931 \quad 1.0986 \quad 1.3863 \quad 1.6094 \quad 1.7918 \quad 1.9459 \quad 2.0794 \quad 2.1972 \quad 2.3026]$

For Hermite interpolation use

$x = [1 \quad 3 \quad 5 \quad 7 \quad 9 \quad]$
$y = [0 \quad 1.0986 \quad 1.6094 \quad 1.9459 \quad 2.1972]$
$dy = [1.0 \quad 0.3333 \quad 0.20 \quad 0.1429 \quad 0.1111]$

Compare the interpolated values to those of $\ln(x)$.

P8.33 $x = [0 \quad 1 \quad 2 \quad 3 \quad 4 \quad 5 \quad 6 \quad 7 \quad 8 \quad]$
$y - [0.50 \quad 0.731 \quad 0.881 \quad 0.953 \quad 0.982 \quad 0.993 \quad 0.997 \quad 0.999 \quad 0.9997]$

For Hermite interpolation, use half of the data above, with the corresponding derivative values.

$dy = [0.25 \quad 0.197 \quad 0.105 \quad 0.045 \quad 0.018 \quad 0.0066 \quad 0.0025 \quad 0.0009 \quad 0.0003]$

Compare the interpolated values to $y = \dfrac{1}{1 + \exp(-x)}$.

P8.34 $x = [0 \quad 1 \quad 2 \quad 3 \quad 4 \quad 5 \quad 6 \quad 7 \quad 8 \quad]$
$y = [0 \quad 0.5000 \quad 0.6667 \quad 0.7500 \quad 0.8000 \quad 0.8333 \quad 0.8571 \quad 0.8750 \quad 0.8889]$

For Hermite interpolation, use half of the data above, with the corresponding derivative values.

$dy = [1 \quad 0.2500 \quad 0.1111 \quad 0.0625 \quad 0.0400 \quad 0.0278 \quad 0.0204 \quad 0.0156 \quad 0.0123]$

Compare the interpolated values to $y = \dfrac{x}{1 + x}$.

P8.35 $x = [0.0100 \quad 1.0000 \quad 4.0000 \quad 9.0000 \quad 16.0000 \quad 25.0000 \quad 36.0000]$
$y = [0.1000 \quad 1.0000 \quad 2.0000 \quad 3.0000 \quad 4.0000 \quad 5.0000 \quad 6.0000 \quad]$
$dy = [5.0000 \quad 0.5000 \quad 0.2500 \quad 0.1667 \quad 0.1250 \quad 0.1000 \quad 0.0833 \quad]$

Compare the interpolated values to $y = \sqrt{x}$.

Problems P8.36 to P8.40 give practice using a built-in interpolation function for data in two dimensions in the software package of your choice.

Interpolate the data given in matrix Z. $Z(i, j)$ is the value at the grid point $x(i)$, $y(j)$ where x and y are given as column vector.

P8.36

$$
x = \begin{bmatrix} 0.0 \\ 0.2 \\ 0.4 \\ 0.6 \\ 0.8 \\ 1.0 \end{bmatrix} \quad
y = \begin{bmatrix} 0.0 \\ 0.2 \\ 0.4 \\ 0.6 \\ 0.8 \\ 1.0 \end{bmatrix} \quad
Z = \begin{bmatrix}
0 & 0 & 0 & 0 & 0 & 0 \\
0 & 0.0047 & 0.0374 & 0.1263 & 0.2994 & 0.5848 \\
0 & 0.0059 & 0.0472 & 0.1592 & 0.3772 & 0.7368 \\
0 & 0.0067 & 0.0540 & 0.1822 & 0.4318 & 0.8434 \\
0 & 0.0074 & 0.0594 & 0.2005 & 0.4753 & 0.9283 \\
0 & 0.0080 & 0.0640 & 0.2160 & 0.5120 & 1.0000
\end{bmatrix}
$$

Find the interpolated values at the points $v = [0.1\ 0.1]$, $[0.3\ 0.3\ ]$, etc. Compare the interpolated results to those found from the function that generated the data, namely $z = x^{1/3}y^3$.

P8.37

$$
x = \begin{bmatrix} 0.0 \\ 0.1 \\ 0.2 \\ 0.4 \\ 0.7 \\ 1.0 \end{bmatrix} \quad
y = \begin{bmatrix} 0.0 \\ 0.1 \\ 0.2 \\ 0.4 \\ 0.7 \\ 1.0 \end{bmatrix} \quad
Z = \begin{bmatrix}
0 & 0 & 0 & 0 & 0 & 0 \\
0 & 0.0005 & 0.0037 & 0.0297 & 0.1592 & 0.4642 \\
0 & 0.0006 & 0.0047 & 0.0374 & 0.2006 & 0.5848 \\
0 & 0.0007 & 0.0059 & 0.0472 & 0.2527 & 0.7368 \\
0 & 0.0009 & 0.0071 & 0.0568 & 0.3046 & 0.8879 \\
0 & 0.0010 & 0.0080 & 0.0640 & 0.3430 & 1.0000
\end{bmatrix}
$$

Find the interpolated values at the points $v = [0.3\ 0.3]$, $[0.5\ 0.5\ ]$, etc. Compare interpolated results to those found from the function that generated the data, namely $z = x^{1/3}y^3$.

P8.38

$$x = \begin{bmatrix} 0.0 \\ 0.2 \\ 0.4 \\ 0.6 \\ 0.8 \\ 1.0 \end{bmatrix} \quad y = \begin{bmatrix} 0.0 \\ 0.2 \\ 0.4 \\ 0.6 \\ 0.8 \\ 1.0 \end{bmatrix} \quad Z = \begin{bmatrix} 0 & 0.0400 & 0.1600 & 0.3600 & 0.6400 & 1.0000 \\ 0.4472 & 0.4872 & 0.6072 & 0.8072 & 1.0872 & 1.4472 \\ 0.6325 & 0.6725 & 0.7925 & 0.9925 & 1.2725 & 1.6325 \\ 0.7746 & 0.8146 & 0.9346 & 1.1346 & 1.4146 & 1.7746 \\ 0.8944 & 0.9344 & 1.0544 & 1.2544 & 1.5344 & 1.8944 \\ 1.0000 & 1.0400 & 1.1600 & 1.3600 & 1.6400 & 2.0000 \end{bmatrix}$$

P 8.39

$$x = \begin{bmatrix} 0.0 \\ 0.2 \\ 0.4 \\ 0.6 \\ 0.8 \\ 1.0 \end{bmatrix} \quad y = \begin{bmatrix} 0.0 \\ 0.2 \\ 0.4 \\ 0.6 \\ 0.8 \\ 1.0 \end{bmatrix} \quad Z = \begin{bmatrix} 1.0000 & 1.2214 & 1.4918 & 1.8221 & 2.2255 & 2.7183 \\ 1.7878 & 2.0092 & 2.2796 & 2.6099 & 3.0133 & 3.5061 \\ 2.3511 & 2.5725 & 2.8429 & 3.1732 & 3.5766 & 4.0693 \\ 2.5511 & 2.7725 & 3.0429 & 3.3732 & 3.7766 & 4.2693 \\ 2.3878 & 2.6092 & 2.8796 & 3.2099 & 3.6133 & 4.1061 \\ 2.0000 & 2.2214 & 2.4918 & 2.8221 & 3.2255 & 3.7183 \end{bmatrix}$$

P8.40

$$x = \begin{bmatrix} 0.0 \\ 0.2 \\ 0.4 \\ 0.6 \\ 0.8 \\ 1.0 \end{bmatrix} \quad y = \begin{bmatrix} 0.0 \\ 0.2 \\ 0.4 \\ 0.6 \\ 0.8 \\ 1.0 \end{bmatrix} \quad Z = \begin{bmatrix} 0 & 0 & 0 & 0 & 0 & 0 \\ 0.7878 & 0.9622 & 1.1752 & 1.4354 & 1.7532 & 2.1414 \\ 1.3511 & 1.6502 & 2.0155 & 2.4618 & 3.0068 & 3.6726 \\ 1.5511 & 1.8945 & 2.3139 & 2.8262 & 3.4519 & 4.2162 \\ 1.3878 & 1.6950 & 2.0703 & 2.5287 & 3.0886 & 3.7724 \\ 1.0000 & 1.2214 & 1.4918 & 1.8221 & 2.2255 & 2.7183 \end{bmatrix}$$

Compare interpolated values to $z = (x + \sin(\pi x)) \exp(y)$.

Problems P8.41 to P8.50 give practice using spline interpolation for parametric curves. Use a function Spline for cubic interpolation to find xs(t) (that interpolates the data t and x) and also ys(t) (that interpolates t and y). Generate values for these functions for a suitable range of values of t, and then plot ys versus xs. Also plot the data points (x, y).

    a. Use spline interpolation to find xx = spline(t, x) *and* yy = spline(t, y).
    b. Plot the curve using plot (xx, yy) *and the data using* plot (x, y, '*').

P8.41 $t = \begin{bmatrix} 1 & 2 & 3 & 4 & 5 & 6 & 7 & 8 & 9 & 10 & 11 & 12 & 13 \end{bmatrix}$
        $x = \begin{bmatrix} 7 & 4 & 3 & 0 & -3 & -4 & -7 & -4 & -3 & 0 & 3 & 4 & 7 \end{bmatrix}$
        $y = \begin{bmatrix} 0 & 2 & 5 & 8 & 5 & 2 & 0 & -2 & -5 & -8 & -5 & -2 & 0 \end{bmatrix}$

P8.42 $t = \begin{bmatrix} 1 & 2 & 3 & 4 & 5 & 6 & 7 & 8 & 9 & 10 & 11 & 12 & 13 & 14 & 15 & 16 & 17 & 18 & 19 & 20 & 21 \end{bmatrix}$
        $x = \begin{bmatrix} 3 & 4 & 3 & 2 & 1 & 0 & -1 & -2 & -3 & -4 & -3 & -4 & -3 & -2 & -1 & 0 & 1 & 2 & 3 & 4 & 3 \end{bmatrix}$
        $y = \begin{bmatrix} 0 & 1 & 2 & 3 & 4 & 4 & 3 & 2 & 1 & 0 & -1 & -2 & -3 & -4 & -4 & -4 & -3 & -2 & -1 & 0 \end{bmatrix}$

P8.43 $t = \begin{bmatrix} 1 & 2 & 3 & 4 & 5 & 6 & 7 & 8 & 9 & 10 & 11 \end{bmatrix}$
        $x = \begin{bmatrix} 0 & 2 & 5 & 2 & 4 & 0 & -4 & -2 & -5 & -2 & 0 \end{bmatrix}$
        $y = \begin{bmatrix} 5 & 3 & 3 & 1 & -2 & -1 & -2 & 1 & 3 & 3 & 5 \end{bmatrix}$

P8.44 $t = [1 \quad 2 \quad 3 \quad 4 \quad 5 \quad 6 \quad 7 \quad 8 \quad 9]$
$x = [5 \quad 1 \quad 0 \quad -1 \quad -5 \quad -1 \quad 0 \quad 1 \quad 5]$
$y = [0 \quad 2 \quad 5 \quad 2 \quad 0 \quad -1 \quad -5 \quad -1 \quad 0]$

P8.45 $t = [\,1 \quad 2 \quad 3 \quad 4 \quad 5 \quad 6 \quad 7 \quad 8 \quad 9 \quad 10 \quad 11 \quad 12]$
$x = [-2 \quad -1 \quad 0 \quad 1 \quad 1 \quad 0 \quad -1 \quad -1 \quad 0 \quad 1 \quad 2 \quad 3]$
$y = [\,0 \quad 0 \quad 0 \quad 1 \quad 2 \quad 3 \quad 2 \quad 1 \quad 0 \quad 0 \quad 0 \quad 0]$

P8.46 $t = [1 \quad 2 \quad 3 \quad 4 \quad 5 \quad 6 \quad 7 \quad 8 \quad 9\,]$
$x = [0.9 \quad 0.25 \quad 0 \quad -0.25 \quad -0.9 \quad -0.25 \quad 0 \quad 0.25 \quad 0.9]$
$y = [0 \quad 0.25 \quad 0.9 \quad 0.25 \quad 0 \quad -0.25 \quad -0.9 \quad -0.25 \quad 0\,]$

P8.47 $t = [1 \quad 2 \quad 3 \quad 4 \quad 5 \quad 6 \quad 7 \quad 8 \quad 9\,]$
$x = [0.9 \quad 0.25 \quad 0 \quad -0.25 \quad -0.9 \quad -0.25 \quad 0 \quad 0.25 \quad 0.9]$
$y = [0 \quad 0.25 \quad 0.9 \quad -0.25 \quad 0 \quad -0.25 \quad -0.9 \quad 0.25 \quad 0\,]$

P8.48 $t = [\,1 \quad 2 \quad 3 \quad 4 \quad 5 \quad 6 \quad 7 \quad 8 \quad 9 \quad 10 \quad 11 \quad 12\,]$
$x = [\,1 \quad 1 \quad 1/4 \quad 1/4 \quad -1/4 \quad -1/4 \quad -1 \quad -1 \quad -1/4 \quad 0 \quad 1/4 \quad 1\,]$
$y = [-1/4 \quad 1/4 \quad 1/4 \quad 1 \quad 1 \quad 1/4 \quad 1/4 \quad -1/4 \quad -1/4 \quad -1 \quad -1/4 \quad -1/4]$

Investigate the effect of taking the same points, in a different order.

EXPLORE SOME APPLICATIONS

A8.1 Using the following data for the heat capacity C_p (kJ/kg °K) of methylcyclohexane C_7H_{14} as a function of temperature (°K), interpolate to estimate the heat capacity at $T = 175, 225$, and 275.

$T = [150 \quad 200 \quad 250 \quad 300]$
$C_p = [1.43 \quad 1.54 \quad 1.70 \quad 1.89]$

(These data are adapted from Vargaftik, 1975.)

A8.2 The drag coefficient C_d for a baseball is a function of velocity (mph)

$v = [\,0 \quad 50 \quad 75 \quad 100 \quad 125]$
$C_d = [0.5 \quad 0.5 \quad 0.4 \quad 0.28 \quad 0.23]$

Approximate the drag coefficient for a baseball at 90 mph.
(These data are adapted from Garcia, 1994, p. 42.)

A8.3 Use interpolation on data for Bessel functions J_0, and J_1.
Data for Bessel function (J_0)

$x = [0 \quad 1 \quad 2 \quad 3 \quad 4 \quad 5 \quad 6 \quad 7 \quad 8 \quad 9 \quad 10 \quad]$
$y = [1.00 \quad 0.77 \quad 0.22 \quad -0.26 \quad -0.40 \quad -0.18 \quad 0.15 \quad 0.30 \quad 0.17 \quad -0.09 \quad -0.25]$

    a. Find interpolated values at $x = 0.5, 1.5, \ldots 9.5$;
    b. Compare your interpolation polynomial to the function $P(x) = 1 - x^2/4 + x^4/64 - x^6/2304$, the first four terms of the series expansion for J_0.

Data for Bessel function (J_1)

$x = [0 \quad 1 \quad 2 \quad 3 \quad 4 \quad 5 \quad 6 \quad 7 \quad 8 \quad 9 \quad 10 \quad]$
$y = [0 \quad 0.44 \quad 0.58 \quad 0.34 \quad -0.07 \quad -0.33 \quad -0.28 \quad -0.0047 \quad 0.23 \quad 0.25 \quad 0.0435]$

Find interpolated values at $x = 0.5, 1.5, \ldots 9.5$;

A8.4 The following data give viscosity N-sec/m^2 at several different temperatures (C°):

$T = [5 \quad 20 \quad 30 \quad 50 \quad 55]$
$\mu = [0.08 \quad 0.15 \quad 0.009 \quad 0.006 \quad 0.0055]$

Use interpolation for find an estimate for the viscosity at $T = 25$ and $T = 40$.
(These data are adapted from Ayyub and McCuen, 1996, p. 174)

A8.5 Using the tabulated data for the specific enthalpy (h) of superheated steam as a function of temperature (at constant pressure of 2500 lb/in.^{2}), find an interpolating polynomial and estimate the enthalpy at 1100°F. The dimensions on h are (Btu/lb)

$T = [800 \quad 1000 \quad 1200 \quad 1400 \quad 1600]$
$h = [1303.6 \quad 1458.4 \quad 1585.3 \quad 1706.1 \quad 1826.2]$

(These data are adapted from Ayyub and McCuen, 1996, p. 176)

A8.6 Using the tabulated data for the short-wave radiation flux (in gram-calories per cm^2 per day for September) at the outer limit of the atmosphere, estimate the flux at a latitutde of 35° (°N)

Latitude $= [0 \quad 20 \quad 40 \quad 60 \quad 80]$
flux $\quad = [891 \quad 856 \quad 719 \quad 494 \quad 219]$

(These data are adapted from Ayyub and McCuen, 1996, p. 176)

A8.7 Using the tabulated data for the vapor pressure (mm Hg) of water as a function of temperature (°C), find an interpolating polynomial and estimate the pressure at T = 50.

$T = [40 \quad 48 \quad 56 \quad 64 \quad 72]$
$P = [55.3 \quad 83.7 \quad 123.8 \quad 179.2 \quad 254.5]$

(These data are adapted from Ayyub and McCuen, p. 151)

A8.8 Using the tabulated data for the saturation values of dissolved oxygen concentration (mg/L) as a function of temperature (°C) , find an interpolating polynomial.

$T = [0 \quad 5 \quad 10 \quad 15 \quad 20 \quad 25]$
$D = [14.6 \quad 12.8 \quad 11.3 \quad 10.2 \quad 9.2 \quad 8.4]$

(These data are adapted from Ayyub and McCuen, p. 159)

A8.9 Given the following tabulated values (truncated to 2 decimal places) for the elliptic integrals of the first and second kinds, use interpolation to find values for m = 0.1, 0.3, 0.5, 0.7, 0.9.

$$K(m) = \int_0^{\pi/2} \frac{dt}{\sqrt{1 - m \sin^2 t}} \qquad\qquad E(m) = \int_0^{\pi/2} \sqrt{1 - m \sin^2 t} \; dt$$

$m = [0.00 \quad 0.20 \quad 0.40 \quad 0.60 \quad 0.80 \quad 1.00]$
$K = [1.57 \quad 1.66 \quad 1.78 \quad 1.95 \quad 2.26 \quad \infty \;]$
$E = [1.57 \quad 1.49 \quad 1.40 \quad 1.30 \quad 1.18 \quad 1.00]$
(These data are adapted from Abramowitz and Stegun, pp. 608-609.)

A8.10 Given the following tabulated values (truncated to 3 decimal places) for the Fresnel integrals, use interpolation to find the values for $m - 0.5, 1.5, 2.5, 3.5$, and 4.5.

$$C(x) = \int_0^x \cos\left(\frac{\pi}{2}t^2\right) dt \qquad\qquad S(x) = \int_0^x \sin\left(\frac{\pi}{2}t^2\right) dt$$

$x = [0.00 \quad 1.00 \quad 2.00 \quad 3.00 \quad 4.00 \quad 5.00]$
$C = [0.000 \quad 0.780 \quad 0.488 \quad 0.606 \quad 0.498 \quad 0.564]$
$S = [0.000 \quad 0.438 \quad 0.343 \quad 0.496 \quad 0.421 \quad 0.499]$
(These data are adapted from Abramowitz and Stegun, pp. 321–322.)

A8.11 In modeling a combustion process it is required to find enthalpy as a function of temperature. Find an interpolation polynomial, spline, or rational function interpolation for the following data, and compare the interpolated values to the tabulated values given below.

$T = [60 \quad 80 \quad 100 \quad 120 \quad 140 \quad 160 \quad 180 \quad 200 \quad]$
$E = [0.0 \quad 17.2 \quad 45.2 \quad 92.9 \quad 178.8 \quad 349.4 \quad 764.3 \quad 2648.4]$

Data adapted from the *Handbook of Hazardous Waste Incineration*, Tab Professional and Reference books, 1989.

A8.12 Use the data on annual building permits issued (in millions of permits), to estimate the number of permits issued in 1982, 1988, 1993, and 1996.

$Y = [1980 \quad 1985 \quad 1990 \quad 1995]$
$P = [1.19 \quad 1.73 \quad 1.11 \quad 1.33]$
(These data are adapted from the U.S. Census web page.)

A8.13 Use the following data to estimate the average (mean) annual earnings for workers in 1993, 1988, 1983, and 1978.

$y = [1975 \quad 1980 \quad 1985 \quad 1990 \quad 1995]$
salary for high school graduates $S = [7,843 \quad 11,314 \quad 14,457 \quad 17,820 \quad 21,431]$
salary for workers with AA degree $S = [8,388 \quad 12,409 \quad 16,349 \quad 20,694 \quad 23,862]$
salary for workers with BA/BS degree $S = [12,332 \quad 18,075 \quad 24,877 \quad 31,112 \quad 36,980]$
salary for workers with advanced degree $S = 16,725 \quad 23,308 \quad 32,909 \quad 41,458 \quad 56,667]$
(These data are adapted from the U. S. Census web page.)

A8.14 Use the following data (with enrollments given in millions) to estimate the school enrollments in 1993, 1988, 1983, and 1978. (K $\Rightarrow$ Kindergarten, E $\Rightarrow$ elementary school, etc.)

$y = [1955 \quad 1960 \quad 1965 \quad 1970 \quad 1975 \quad 1980 \quad 1985 \quad 1990 \quad 1995]$
$K = [1.6 \quad 2.1 \quad 3.1 \quad 3.2 \quad 3.4 \quad 3.2 \quad 3.8 \quad 4.0 \quad .9]$
$E = [25.5 \quad 30.3 \quad 32.5 \quad 33.9 \quad 30.5 \quad 27.5 \quad 26.9 \quad 29.2 \quad 31.8]$
$H = [8.0 \quad 10.2 \quad 13.0 \quad 14.7 \quad 15.7 \quad 14.6 \quad 14.0 \quad 12.7 \quad 14.8]$
$C = [2.4 \quad 3.6 \quad 5.7 \quad 7.4 \quad 9.7 \quad 10.2 \quad 10.9 \quad 11.3 \quad 12.0]$

These data are adapted from the U. S. Census Web page, which cites the source as the U.S. Bureau of the Census, Current Population Survey.

U8.2 Investigate the difficulties in interpolating a "noisy line" by generating some data:

$x = [0 \quad 1 \quad 2 \quad 3 \quad 4 \quad 5 \quad 6]$

$y = x + 0.1*\text{rand}(1,7) - 0.05$

where rand (1,7) denotes a function that generates a vector of 7 random numbers uniformly distributed between 0 and 1.

Show that even if the interpolating polynomial appears to fit the data well, extrapolating beyond the data is not a good idea.

U8.3 Show that the difficulties in interpolating a "noisy line" are much more severe when the data is not evenly spaced; e.g., generate some data of the form:

$x = [0 \quad 0.2 \quad 0.4 \quad 2 \quad 4 \quad 4.2 \quad 4.4]$

$y = x + 0.1*\text{rand}(1,7) - 0.05$

or

$x = [0 \quad 0.1 \quad 0.2 \quad 2 \quad 4.1 \quad 4.2 \quad 4.3]$

$y = x + 0.1*\text{rand}(1,7) - 0.05$

U8.4 Show that for a cubic spline, specifying the value of $P_1'(x_1)$ gives the following equation relating a_0 and a_1:

$$\frac{a_0 h_1}{3} + \frac{a_1 h_1}{6} = \frac{y_2 - y_1}{h_1} - P_1'(x_1).$$

U8.5 Modify the algorithm for the natural cubic spline by adding the equation from U8.4 to the system of equations for $a_0, \ldots, a_{n-1}$ given in Section 8.4.3, to form a function for a spline that is clamped at x_1.

U8.6 Use the function from U8.5 to repeat some of the exercises P8.16 to P8.25.

U8.7 Show that the equation describing a clamped boundary at x_n (see U8.4) is

$$\frac{a_{n-2} h_{n-1}}{6} + \frac{a_{n-1} h_{n-1}}{3} = P_{n-1}'(x_n) - \frac{y_n - y_{n-1}}{h_{n-1}}.$$

U8.8 Use Hermite cubic polynomials for piecewise cubic interpolation by specifying the function value and derivative value at each node point. Use the data from Example 8.12.

U8.9 Use Hermite cubic polynomials for piecewise cubic interpolation by specifying the function value and derivative value at each node point. Compare your results using the following dat to the results of Example 8.10.

$x = [-1 \quad -0.5 \quad 0 \quad 0.5 \quad 1 \quad]$,

$y = [0.0385 \quad 0.1379 \quad 1.00 \quad 0.1379 \quad 0.0385]$,

$dy = [0.074 \quad 0.4756 \quad 0.00 \quad -0.4756 \quad -0.074]$.

U8.10 The error bound formula for cubic spline interpolation given in the discussion at the end of Section 8.4.3 does not state the proportionality constant, since it depends on the choice of endpoint conditions. With clamped boundary conditions, it is

$$|S(x) - g(x)| < (5/384) h^4 G.$$

(See deBoor, 1978.)

Use $g(x) = \cos(x)$ to generate evenly spaced data on $[0, \pi]$ for different values of h. Find the cubic spline interpolation function $S(x)$, the actual error $|S(x) - g(x)|$, and error bound $(5/384) h^4 G$.

9

··

Approximation

Approximation is closely related to the idea of interpolation, discussed in the previous chapter. In approximation, we do not require the approximating function to match the given data exactly. This avoids some of the difficulties demonstrated previously in regard to trying to match a moderate-to-large amount of data, especially if noise (such as errors in measurement) is present. There are also many applications in which a theoretical functional form is known and the "best" function of that form is required.

The most common approach to "best fit" approximation is to minimize the sum of the squares of the differences between the data values and the values of the approximating function; this is the *method of least squares.* We first investigate *linear* least-squares approximation, also known as linear regression (especially in statistics). The same approach is used to find the *quadratic* least squares function or a polynomial of some other (specified) degree. For data that appear to follow an exponential function, the standard approach is to find a linear function that fits the natural logarithm of the data. This gives a close approximation to the "best fit" exponential (but with much less effort).

It may also be desirable in some applications to approximate a given function by the best function of a specified form on a given interval. This leads to the topic of *continuous* least squares approximation.

In certain situations, a function may be better represented by a rational function than by a polynomial. *Padé approximation* is the rational-function analog of Taylor polynomial approximation. In these cases, knowledge of the function and its derivatives at a single point is used to construct the best local representation of the function.

In the next chapter, we consider fitting periodic data with trigonometric polynomials. In that case, the appropriate function for approximation or interpolation of a given set of data can be found by the least squares approach.

Example 9-A Oil Reservoir Modeling

In modeling an oil reservoir, it may be necessary to find a relationship between the equilibrium constant of a reaction and the pressure at constant temperature. The data shown in the following table relate equilibrium constants (K-values) to pressure (expressed in terms of 1,000 PSIA) and were obtained from an experimental PVT analysis. Figure 9.1 is a plot of these data.

Oil reservoir data	
Pressure	K-value
0.635	7.5
1.035	5.58
1.435	4.35
1.835	3.55
2.235	2.97
2.635	2.53
3.035	2.2
3.435	1.93
3.835	1.7
4.235	1.46
4.635	1.28
5.035	1.11
5.435	1.0

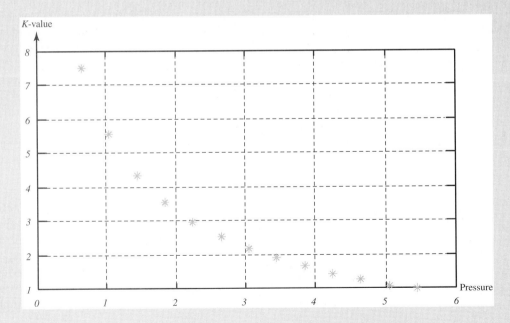

FIGURE 9.1 Equilibrium constant as a function of pressure.

Example 9-B Logistic Population Growth

The data in Fig. 9.2 describe the growth of a population following a logistic model. The plot would also represent a uniform sampling from a cumulative distribution. Several kinds of functions can be used to fit data that display this "s-shaped" form; the appropriate choice depends on the particular application.

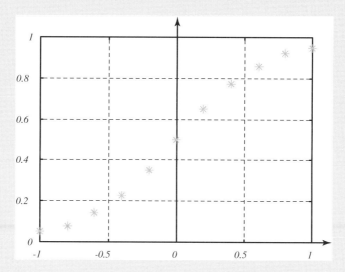

FIGURE 9.2   Logistic population growth.

We see in Example 9.7 that a cubic polynomial provides a reasonable fit to the given data.

On the other hand, if we wish to obtain an approximating function of the appropriate form for the solution of a logistic differential equation, we may look for a function of the form $y = 1/(1 + \exp(ax + b))$.

We transform the given data:

$$x = [-1.0 \quad -0.8 \quad -0.6 \quad -0.4 \quad -0.2 \quad 0.0 \quad 0.2 \quad 0.4 \quad 0.6 \quad 0.8 \quad 1.0 \;]$$
$$y = [\;\; 0.05 \quad 0.08 \quad 0.14 \quad 0.23 \quad 0.35 \quad 0.50 \quad 0.65 \quad 0.77 \quad 0.86 \quad 0.92 \quad 0.95]$$

to form $z = 1/y - 1$

$$z = [19.0 \quad 11.50 \quad 6.143 \quad 3.348 \quad 1.857 \quad 1.00 \quad 0.539 \quad 0.299 \quad 0.163 \quad 0.087 \quad 0.053]$$

We then find the coefficients a and b for the exponential function to fit z, by finding a linear fit to $zz = \ln(z)$.

$$zz = [2.94 \quad 2.44 \quad 1.82 \quad 1.21 \quad 0.62 \quad 0 \quad -0.62 \quad -1.21 \quad -1.82 \quad -2.44 \quad -2.94]$$

The resulting approximation function is $y - 1/(1 + \exp(-3x))$.

9.1 LEAST SQUARES APPROXIMATION

Some of the most common methods of approximating data are based on the desire to minimize some measure of the difference between the approximating function and the given data points. The method of least squares seeks to minimize the sum (over all data points) of the squares of the differences between the function value and the data value. The method is based on results from calculus demonstrating that a function, in this case the total squared error, attains a minimum value when its partial derivatives are zero.

There are several advantages to using the square of the differences at each point, rather than the difference, the absolute value of the difference, or some other measure of the error. By squaring the difference,

1. positive differences do not cancel negative differences;
2. differentiation is not difficult; and
3. small differences become smaller and large differences are magnified.

We begin with an example in which the data can be approximated nicely by a straight line. We then consider several variations, in which the appropriate choice of approximating function is a higher degree polynomial, an exponential function, or the reciprocal of a polynomial. The choice depends to a large extent on the general characteristics of the data.

For data to be approximated by a straight line, we wish to find the best function $f(x) = a x + b$ that approximates the data. In order to find the coefficients a and b, we must define what we mean by the "best fit" of a function to some data. Of course, we want to minimize the difference between the data points and the points on our approximating function, in some sense. The most common method is to minimize the sum of the squares of the differences between the given data values y_i and the computed function values $f_i = a x_i + b$. Another approach, known as total least squares, minimizes the distance from each data point to the straight line, where distance is measured perpendicular to the line, not in the vertical direction. This leads to a much more difficult mathematical problem, which is beyond the scope of our discussion.

9.1.1 Linear Least-Squares Approximation

To introduce the ideas of linear least-square approximation, we consider the error involved in approximating four data points by a straight line, determined by visual inspection of the graph of the points.

Example 9.1 Linear Approximation to Four Points

Consider the data $(1, 2.1)$, $(2, 2.9)$, $(5, 6.1)$, and $(7, 8.3)$, as shown in Fig. 9.3.

If we approximate the data by the straight line $f(x) = 0.9 x + 1.4$, as shown in Fig. 9.4, the squared errors are as follows:

at $x_1 = 1$	$f(1) = 2.3$	$y_1 = 2.1$	$e_1 = (2.3 - 2.1)^2$	$= 0.04;$
at $x_2 = 2$	$f(2) = 3.2$	$y_2 = 2.9$	$e_2 = (3.2 - 2.9)^2$	$= 0.09;$
at $x_3 = 5$	$f(5) = 5.9$	$y_3 = 6.1$	$e_3 = (5.9 - 6.1)^2$	$= 0.04;$
at $x_4 = 7$	$f(7) = 7.7$	$y_4 = 8.3$	$e_4 = (7.7 - 8.3)^2$	$= 0.36.$

The total squared error is $0.04 + 0.09 + 0.04 + 0.36 = 0.53$. By finding better values for the coefficients of the straight line, we can make this number smaller.

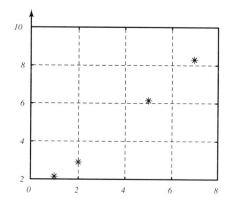

FIGURE 9.3 Data for linear least squares example.

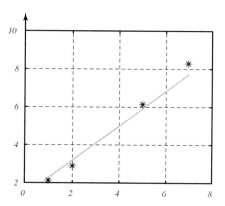

FIGURE 9.4 Approximating data by a straight line.

Let us consider a systematic way of finding the coefficients of the "best fit" straight line to approximate data; we illustrate the process for four data points.

The best coefficients for the straight line are those that minimize the total-squared-error function:

$$E = [f(x_1) - y_1]^2 + [f(x_2) - y_2]^2 + [f(x_3) - y_3]^2 + [f(x_4) - y_4]^2$$

$$= [ax_1 + b - y_1]^2 + [ax_2 + b - y_2]^2 + [ax_3 + b - y_3]^2 + [ax_4 + b - y_4]^2$$

The minimum of a function of several variables (two in this case, the coefficients a and b) occurs when the partial derivatives of the function with respect to each of the variables are equal to zero. Here, we have the system of equations

$$\frac{\partial E}{\partial a} = 0 \quad \text{and} \quad \frac{\partial E}{\partial b} = 0.$$

The solution depends on several quantities that can be computed from the data. The required four summations can be denoted as

$$S_{xx} = \sum_{i=1}^{4} x_i^2, \qquad S_x = \sum_{i=1}^{4} x_i,$$

$$S_{xy} = \sum_{i=1}^{4} x_i y_i, \qquad S_y = \sum_{i=1}^{4} y_i.$$

The unknowns (a and b) can be found from the following system of equations, known as the *normal equations*:

$$a\,S_{xx} + b\,S_x = S_{xy}$$

$$a\,S_x + b\,4 = S_y$$

For a small linear system, Cramer's rule provides a convenient way of writing the solution of the system in terms of the ratio of the determinants of the appropriate matrices. We let **A** be the coefficient matrix, **A1** be the coefficient matrix with the first column replaced by the right-hand side of the system, and **A2** be the coefficient matrix with the second column replaced by the right-hand side; we continue in this manner if the system is larger than 2-by-2. Then (if the determinant of the coefficient matrix is not zero),

$$a = \det(\mathbf{A1})/\det(\mathbf{A}) \quad \text{and} \quad b = \det(\mathbf{A2})/\det(\mathbf{A})$$

Thus, the solution to the normal equations is

$$a = \frac{4\,S_{xy} - S_x\,S_y}{4\,S_{xx} - S_x\,S_x} \qquad\qquad b = \frac{S_{xx}\,S_y - S_{xy}\,S_x}{4\,S_{xx} - S_x\,S_x}.$$

Input
    x   *vector of values of independent variable*
    y   *vector of values of dependent variable*
    n   *number of components in vectors x and y*
Initialize
    Sx = 0
    Sy = 0
    Sxx = 0
    Sxy = 0
Compute
For i = 1 to n
    Sx = Sx + x(i)
    Sy = Sy + y(i)
    Sxx = Sxx + x(i)*x(i)
    Sxy = Sxy + x(i)*y(i)
End
Solve the linear system (results from Cramer's rule)

$$a = \frac{n\,Sxy - Sx\,Sy}{n\,Sxx - Sx\,Sx}$$

$$b = \frac{Sxx\,Sy - Sxy\,Sx}{n\,Sxx - Sx\,Sx}$$

Return
    a
    b

It is quite easy to expand the basic algorithm above to include computation of the total squared error.

Define a vector of the approximated values:

$$\mathbf{z} = a\,\mathbf{x} + b$$

Define a vector of the difference between the data and approximated values:

$$\mathbf{d} = \mathbf{y} - \mathbf{z}$$

Compute the total squared error as the dot product:

$$TSE = \mathbf{d}*\mathbf{d}$$

Example 9.2 Linear Least-Squares Fit with Four Data Points

For our previous example with the data points $(1, 2.1)$, $(2, 2.9)$, $(5, 6.1)$, and $(7, 8.3)$, the system of equations for a and b is

$$79\,a + 15\,b = 96.5,$$

$$15\,a + 4\,b = 19.4.$$

The solution is $a = 1.0440$, $b = 0.9352$.

Using the preceding algorithm, the following table gives the difference between the data and the computed values. The total squared error is

$$d_1^2 + d_2^2 + d_3^2 + d_4^2 = 0.0360.$$

Figure 9.5 plots the linear least-squares line with the data.

		Linear least squares straight line	
x_i	y_i	$a\,x_i + b$	$d_i = y_i - a\,x_i - b$
1	2.1	1.9791	0.1209
2	2.9	3.0231	−0.1231
5	6.1	6.1549	−0.0549
7	8.3	8.2429	0.0571

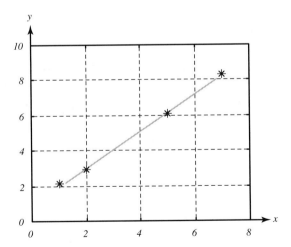

FIGURE 9.5   Linear least squares line
$f(x) = 1.044\,x + 0.9352$.

Example 9.3 Noisy Straight-Line Data

Let us revisit the data introduced in Example 8.9

$$\mathbf{x} = [0.00 \quad 0.20 \quad 0.80 \quad 1.00 \quad 1.20 \quad 1.90 \quad 2.00 \quad 2.10 \quad 2.95 \quad 3.00]$$
$$\mathbf{y} = [0.01 \quad 0.22 \quad 0.76 \quad 1.03 \quad 1.18 \quad 1.94 \quad 2.01 \quad 2.08 \quad 2.90 \quad 2.95]$$

Using the algorithm, we find that the coefficients for the linear least-squares approximation are

$$a = 0.9839, \quad b = 0.0174$$

In other words, the linear function that best fits the data (in the least-squares sense) is

$$y(x) = 0.9839\,x + 0.0174$$

The data values (x_i and y_i), computed function values $y(x_i)$, and the actual difference at each x_i are shown in the following table. The line is plotted in Fig. 9.6.

Data and linear fit for noisy straight line			
x_i	y_i	$a\,x_i + b$	$d_i = y_i - a\,x_i - b$
0.00	0.01	0.0174	−0.0074
0.20	0.22	0.2142	0.0058
0.80	0.76	0.8045	−0.0445
1.00	1.03	1.0013	0.0287
1.20	1.18	1.1981	−0.0181
1.90	1.94	1.8868	0.0532
2.00	2.01	1.9852	0.0248
2.10	2.08	2.0836	−0.0036
2.95	2.90	2.9199	−0.0199
3.00	2.95	2.9691	−0.0191

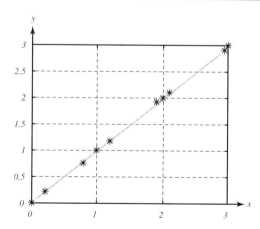

FIGURE 9.6   Linear least squares line and data for noisy straight line.

Discussion

We now consider in a little more detail how the normal equations for linear least squares approximation arise, illustrating the derivation for four arbitrary data points, namely,

$$(x_1, y_1), (x_2, y_2), (x_3, y_3), (x_4, y_4),$$

that we wish to approximate by the linear function $f(x) = a x + b$.

We want to find those values of a and b that minimize the total squared error E over the data points; that is, we have

$$E = [f(x_1) - y_1]^2 + [f(x_2) - y_2]^2 + [f(x_3) - y_3]^2 + [f(x_4) - y_4]^2$$

$$= [ax_1 + b - y_1]^2 + [ax_2 + b - y_2]^2 + [ax_3 + b - y_3]^2 + [ax_4 + b - y_4]^2.$$

Setting $\dfrac{\partial E}{\partial a} = 0$ and $\dfrac{\partial E}{\partial b} = 0$ gives

$$[ax_1 + b - y_1]x_1 + [ax_2 + b - y_2]x_2 + [ax_3 + b - y_3]x_3 + [ax_4 + b - y_4]x_4 = 0,$$

and

$$[ax_1 + b - y_1] + [ax_2 + b - y_2] + [ax_3 + b - y_3] + [ax_4 + b - y_4] = 0.$$

Simplifying gives

$$a[x_1^2 + x_2^2 + x_3^2 + x_4^2] + b[x_1 + x_2 + x_3 + x_4] = x_1y_1 + x_2y_2 + x_3y_3 + x_4y_4,$$

and

$$a[x_1 + x_2 + x_3 + x_4] + b[1 + 1 + 1 + 1] = y_1 + y_2 + y_3 + y_4.$$

We see that no matter how many data points we have, if we want a straight line to minimize the error in the y-coordinate, we get two equations in two unknowns. In general form, the equations are

$$a \sum_{i=1}^{n} x_i^2 + b \sum_{i=1}^{n} x_i = \sum_{i=1}^{n} x_i y_i,$$

$$a \sum_{i=1}^{n} x_i + b \sum_{i=1}^{n} 1 = \sum_{i=1}^{n} y_i.$$

Of course, $\sum_{i=1}^{n} 1 = n$, so there are only four summations that must be calculated. For simplicity, they can be denoted as

$$S_{xx} = \sum_{i=1}^{n} x_i^2, \quad S_x = \sum_{i=1}^{n} x_i, \quad S_{xy} = \sum_{i=1}^{n} x_i y_i, \quad S_y = \sum_{i=1}^{n} y_i.$$

The solution to the system of equations (the normal equations) is

$$a = \frac{n S_{xy} - S_x S_y}{n S_{xx} - S_x S_x}, \quad b = \frac{S_{xx} S_y - S_{xy} S_x}{n S_{xx} - S_x S_x}.$$

9.1.2 Quadratic Least-Squares Approximation

Using the same approach as before, let us now approximate our data with a quadratic function $f(x) = a x^2 + b x + c$. The error function is

$$E = \sum_{i=1}^{n} [f(x_i) - y_i]^2.$$

in other words, for n data points, $(x_1, y_1) \ldots (x_n, y_n)$ we wish to minimize

$$E = [a(x_1)^2 + b(x_1) + c - y_1]^2 + \ldots + [a(x_n)^2 + b(x_n) + c - y_n]^2.$$

We find the minimum by equating the partial derivatives of E with respect to a, b, and c to zero.

Setting $\dfrac{\partial E}{\partial a} = 0$ gives

$$[a(x_1)^2 + b(x_1) + c - y_1](x_1)^2 + \ldots + [a(x_n)^2 + b(x_n) + c - y_n](x_n)^2 = 0,$$

and similarly setting $\dfrac{\partial E}{\partial b} = 0$ yields

$$[a(x_1)^2 + b(x_1) + c - y_1](x_1) + \ldots + [a(x_n)^2 + b(x_n) + c - y_n](x_n) = 0,$$

while setting $\dfrac{\partial E}{\partial c} = 0$ gives

$$[a(x_1)^2 + b(x_1) + c - y_1] + \ldots + [a(x_n)^2 + b(x_n) + c - y_n] = 0$$

These equations simplify to give us the normal equations for a, b, and c:

$$a\sum_{i=1}^{n} x_i^4 + b\sum_{i=1}^{n} x_i^3 + c\sum_{i=1}^{n} x_i^2 = \sum_{i=1}^{n} x_i^2 y_i$$

$$a\sum_{i=1}^{n} x_i^3 + b\sum_{i=1}^{n} x_i^2 + c\sum_{i=1}^{n} x_i = \sum_{i=1}^{n} x_i y_i$$

$$a\sum_{i=1}^{n} x_i^2 + b\sum_{i=1}^{n} x_i + c[n] = \sum_{i=1}^{n} y_i$$

The following algorithm finds the coefficients for the quadratic approximation function, $y = a x^2 + b x + c$

Quadratic Least-Squares Approximation

Input
- x   *vector of values of independent variable*
- y   *vector of values of dependent variable*
- n   *number of components in vectors x and y*

Initialize
- Sx = 0
- Sy = 0
- Sx2 = 0
- Sxy = 0
- Sx3 = 0
- Sx4 = 0
- Syx2 = 0

Compute

For i = 1 to n
- Sx = Sx + x(i)
- Sy = Sy + y(i)
- Sx2 = Sx2 + x(i)^2
- Sx3 = Sx3 + x(i)^3
- Sx4 = Sx4 + x(i)^4
- Sxy = Sxy + x(i)*y(i)
- Syx2 = S yx2 + y(i)*x(i)^2

End

Define

$$A = \begin{bmatrix} Sx4 & Sx3 & Sx2 \\ Sx3 & Sx2 & Sx \\ Sx2 & Sx & n \end{bmatrix} \qquad r = \begin{bmatrix} Syx2 \\ Syx \\ Sy \end{bmatrix}$$

Solve linear system $\mathbf{A}\,\mathbf{z} = \mathbf{r}$

- a = z_1
- b = z_2
- c = z_3

Return
- a
- b
- c

Example 9.4 Chemical Reaction Data

Consider again the product data from a simple chemical reaction (see Chapter 8):

$$\mathbf{x} = [0.00 \quad 0.50 \quad 1.00 \quad 1.50 \quad 2.00],$$
$$\mathbf{y} = [0.00 \quad 0.19 \quad 0.26 \quad 0.29 \quad 0.31].$$

The normal equations to find the quadratic least squares polynomial can be written as $\mathbf{A}\,\mathbf{x} = \mathbf{b}$, with

$$\mathbf{A} = \begin{bmatrix} 22.125 & 12.500 & 7.500 \\ 12.500 & 7.500 & 5.000 \\ 7.500 & 5.000 & 5.000 \end{bmatrix},$$

and

$$\mathbf{b} = [2.2000 \quad 1.4100 \quad 1.0500]^T$$

The least squares quadratic function for these points is

$$p(x) = -0.1086\, x^2 + 0.3611\, x + 0.0117.$$

The data points, corresponding approximations from $p(x)$, and differences are presented in the following table. The data and the least squares parabola are shown in Fig. 9.7. The total squared error is 0.0012.

Data and least squares quadratic approximation for chemical reaction data.

x_i	y_i	p_i	$d_i = y_i - p_i$
0.0000	0.0000	0.0117	−0.0117
0.5000	0.1900	0.1651	0.0249
1.0000	0.2600	0.2643	−0.0043
1.5000	0.2900	0.3091	−0.0191
2.0000	0.3100	0.2997	0.0103

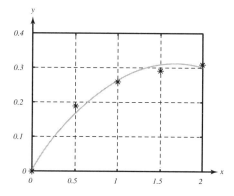

FIGURE 9.7   Least squares quadratic and data for chemical reaction.

Example 9.5 Gompertz Growth Curve

Consider the problem of fitting a quadratic function to data generated from the Gompertz growth curve, $y = \exp(-2\exp(-x))$. The data vectors

$$x = [0 \quad 1 \quad 2 \quad 3 \quad 4 \quad 5 \quad 6 \quad],$$
$$y = [0.135 \quad 0.479 \quad 0.763 \quad 0.905 \quad 0.964 \quad 0.987 \quad 0.995],$$

result in the following linear system for the coefficients

$$\begin{bmatrix} 2275 & 441 & 91 \\ 441 & 91 & 21 \\ 91 & 21 & 7 \end{bmatrix} \begin{bmatrix} z_1 \\ z_2 \\ x_3 \end{bmatrix} \begin{bmatrix} 87.5895 \\ 19.4801 \\ 5.2283 \end{bmatrix}$$

The data, approximations, and errors are listed in the following table. The total squared error is 0.0047.

The least square parabola

$$p(x) = -0.0375\, x^2 + 0.3605\, x + 0.1528$$

is shown together with the data in Fig. 9.8.

Least squares parabola and data for Gompertz growth curve.

x_i	y_i	p_i	d_i
0.0000	0.1353	0.1528	−0.0174
1.0000	0.4791	0.4758	0.0033
2.0000	0.7629	0.7238	0.0390
3.0000	0.9052	0.8969	0.0083
4.0000	0.9640	0.9949	−0.0309
5.0000	0.9866	1.0180	−0.0314
6.0000	0.9951	0.9661	0.0290

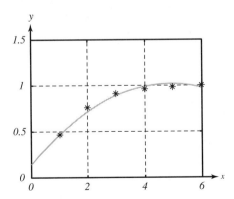

FIGURE 9.8 Least squares parabola and data for Gompertz growth curve.

Example 9.6 Oil Reservoir Data

Let us consider the problem of finding the least squares quadratic function to approximate a subset of the experimental data introduced in Example 9-A. The data represent the relationship between pressure x and reaction rate y for an oil reservoir modeling problem:

$$\mathbf{x} = [5.435 \quad 4.635 \quad 3.835 \quad 3.035 \quad 2.325 \quad 1.435 \quad 0.635]$$
$$\mathbf{y} = [1.00 \quad 1.28 \quad 1.70 \quad 2.20 \quad 2.97 \quad 4.35 \quad 7.50 \ ].$$

The normal equations are $\mathbf{A}\,\mathbf{z} = \mathbf{b}$, with

$$\mathbf{A} = \begin{bmatrix} 1668.9 & 360.3 & 82.8 \\ 360.3 & 82.8 & 21.3 \\ 82.8 & 21.3 & 7.0 \end{bmatrix}$$

and $\mathbf{b} = [130.3413 \quad 42.4743 \quad 21.0000]^T$.

The solution is $\mathbf{z} = [9.0748, \ -3.3833, \ 0.3582]^T$, so the desired quadratic function is $p(x) = 0.3582\, x^2 - 3.3833\, x + 9.0748$.

The total squared error is $E = \sum_{i=1}^{n} [d_i]^2 = 0.8110$.

The following table lists the data, approximations, and errors for this problem. The data and the least squares parabola are plotted in Fig. 9.9.

Data and least squares parabola for oil reservoir example

x_i	y_i	p_i	d_i
5.4350	1.0000	1.2664	−0.2664
4.6350	1.2800	1.0877	0.1923
3.8350	1.7000	1.3674	0.3326
3.0350	2.2000	2.1056	0.0944
2.3250	2.9700	3.1447	−0.1747
1.4350	4.3500	4.9573	−0.6073
0.6350	7.5000	7.0708	0.4292

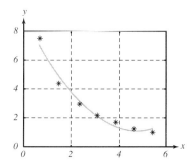

FIGURE 9.9 Data and least squares parabola for oil reservoir.

9.1.3   General Least-Squares Approximation

Proceeding in a manner analogous to that of quadratic least squares approximation, we find the following system of linear equations to determine the coefficients for the "best-fit" cubic function $f(x) = a x^3 + b x^2 + c x + d$,

$$a\sum_{i=1}^{n} x_i^6 + b\sum_{i=1}^{n} x_i^5 + c\sum_{i=1}^{n} x_i^4 + d\sum_{i=1}^{n} x_i^3 = \sum_{i=1}^{n} x_i^3 y_i$$

$$a\sum_{i=1}^{n} x_i^5 + b\sum_{i=1}^{n} x_i^4 + c\sum_{i=1}^{n} x_i^3 + d\sum_{i=1}^{n} x_i^2 = \sum_{i=1}^{n} x_i^2 y_i$$

$$a\sum_{i=1}^{n} x_i^4 + b\sum_{i=1}^{n} x_i^3 + c\sum_{i=1}^{n} x_i^2 + d\sum_{i=1}^{n} x_i = \sum_{i=1}^{n} x_i y_i$$

$$a\sum_{i=1}^{n} x_i^3 + b\sum_{i=1}^{n} x_i^2 + c\sum_{i=1}^{n} x_i + d\sum_{i=1}^{n} 1 = \sum_{i=1}^{n} y_i$$

In more general terms, we may seek to approximate a set of data by a function which is a linear combination of a fixed set of functions, $g_1(x)$, $g_2(x)$, ... $g_m(x)$; these functions are called basis functions. In section 9.1.1, the basis functions were $g_1(x) = 1$ and $g_2(x) = x$. In section 9.1.2, the basis functions were $g_1(x) = 1$, $g_2(x) = x$, and $g_3(x) = x^2$. The "best-fit" cubic function above uses as its basis function the powers of x up through x^3. All of these approximations are "linear" in the sense that the dependence of the problem on the parameters (the coefficients) is linear, even though the basis functions themselves are nonlinear.

In terms of four arbitrary basis functions, we now approximate our data with a function $f(x) = a_1 g_1(x) + a_2 g_2(x) + a_3 g_3(x) + a_4 g_4(x)$. The error function is

$$E = \sum_{i=1}^{n} [f(x_i) - y_i]^2.$$

In other words, for n data points, $(x_1, y_1) \ldots (x_n, y_n)$ we wish to minimize

$$E = [a_1 g_1(x_1) + a_2 g_2(x_1) + a_3 g_3(x_1) + a_4 g_4(x_1) - y_1]^2 + \ldots$$

$$+ [a_1 g_1(x_n) + a_2 g_2(x_n) + a_3 g_3(x_n) + a_4 g_4(x_n) - y_n]^2.$$

Setting the partial derivatives of E with respect to each of the 4 unknowns, $a_1 \ldots a_4$, equal to zero gives the normal equations. For example, the first equation (setting $\dfrac{\partial E}{\partial a_1} = 0$) simplifies to

$$a_1 \sum_{i=1}^{4} g_1(x_i)\, g_1(x_i) + a_2 \sum_{i=1}^{4} g_1(x_i) g_2(x_i)$$

$$+ a_3 \sum_{i=1}^{4} g_1(x_i) g_3(x_i) + a_4 \sum_{i=1}^{4} g_1(x_i)\, g_4(x_i) = \sum_{i=1}^{4} g_1(x_i)\, y_i$$

The following algorithm is written for basis functions $g_1 = x^3$, $g_2 = x^2$, $g_3 = x$, $g_4 = 1$. It uses a function (sum) that sums the components of a vector; it also uses component by component products and powers (denoted as $y.*x$ or $x.^2$, etc.).

The algorithm can be generalized for arbitrary basis functions. The entries in matrix $\mathbf{A}$ are sums of products of the basis functions evaluated at the data points. More specifically, the element in row k, column j is

$$a_{kj} = g_j(x_1)\, g_k(x_1) + g_j(x_2)\, g_k(x_2) + \ldots + g_j(x_n)\, g_k(x_n)$$

The kth element of the right hand side vector is

$$r_k = y_1\, g_k(x_1) + y_2\, g_k(x_2) + \ldots + y_n\, g_k(x_n)$$

Cubic Least-squares Approximation

Input
  $\mathbf{x}$ *data vector for independent variable*
  $\mathbf{y}$ *data vector for dependent variable*
  n   *number of components in vector $\mathbf{x}$ or $\mathbf{y}$*
Begin computation
sx = sum(x)
sx2 = sum(x.^2)
sx3 = sum(x.^3)
sx4 = sum(x.^4)
sx5 = sum(x.^5)
sx6 = sum(x.^6)
sy = sum(y)
syx = sum(y.* x)
syx2 = sum(y.*x.^2)
syx3 = sum(y.*x.^3)

$$\mathbf{A} = \begin{bmatrix} sx6 & sx5 & sx4 & sx3 \\ sx5 & sx4 & sx3 & sx2 \\ sx4 & sx3 & sx2 & sx \\ sx3 & sx2 & sx & n \end{bmatrix}$$

$\mathbf{r} = \begin{bmatrix} syx3 & syx2 & syx & sy \end{bmatrix}^T$
Solve
    $\mathbf{A\,z} = \mathbf{r}$
Return
    $\mathbf{z}$ $a = z(1);\ b = z(2);\ c = z(3);\ d = z(4)$

Example 9.7 Cubic Least-squares Problem, Data on $[-1, 1]$

The data introduced in Example 9-B looks like it might be approximated reasonably by a cubic equation. The linear system for the coefficients is $\mathbf{A}\,\mathbf{z} = \mathbf{r}$, with

$$
\mathbf{A} =
\begin{bmatrix}
2.6259 & 0.0000 & 3.1328 & 0.0000 \\
0.0000 & 3.1328 & 0.0000 & 4.4 \\
3.1328 & 0.0000 & 4.4 & 0 \\
0.0000 & 4.4 & 0 & 11
\end{bmatrix}
\quad\text{and}\quad
\mathbf{r} =
\begin{bmatrix}
1.5226 \\
2.2000 \\
2.2800 \\
5.5
\end{bmatrix}.
$$

Using a simple computer program based on the preceding algorithm, we find that the least squares cubic function is $p(x) = a\,x^3 + b\,x^2 + c\,x + d$, with the computed coefficients

$$a = -0.2550, \quad b = 0.0000, \quad c = 0.6997, \quad d = 0.5.$$

The data, approximated function values, and differences are shown in the following table. The data and the cubic function are plotted in Figure 9.10. The total squared error is 0.000646.

Cubic least squares data and approximated values			
x	y	$p(x)$	$y - p(x)$
−1	0.05	0.0552	−0.0052
−0.8	0.08	0.0708	0.0092
−0.6	0.14	0.1352	0.0048
−0.4	0.23	0.2364	−0.0064
−0.2	0.35	0.3621	−0.0121
0	0.5	0.5000	−0.0000
0.2	0.65	0.6379	0.0121
0.4	0.77	0.7636	0.0064
0.6	0.86	0.8648	−0.0048
0.8	0.92	0.9292	−0.0092
1	0.95	0.9448	0.0052

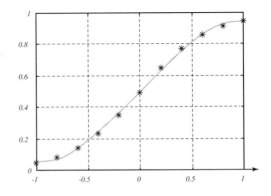

FIGURE 9.10   Data and cubic least-squares function.

Example 9.8 Cubic Least-squares Problem, Data on [0, 1]

We now consider the cubic approximation function found by using only a portion of the data in Example 9-B—specifically, the data on the interval [0, 1]. The linear system of equations for the coefficients is $\mathbf{A}\,\mathbf{z} = \mathbf{r}$, with

$$\mathbf{A} = \begin{bmatrix} 1.3130 & 1.4160 & 1.5664 & 1.8 \\ 1.4160 & 1.5664 & 1.8000 & 2.2 \\ 1.5664 & 1.8000 & 2.2000 & 3.0 \\ 1.8000 & 2.2000 & 3.000 & 6.0 \end{bmatrix}$$

and

$$\mathbf{r} = \begin{bmatrix} 1.6613 \\ 1.9976 \\ 2.6400 \\ 4.6500 \end{bmatrix}$$

The cubic approximation function is $p(x) = ax^3 + bx^2 + cx + d$, with

$$a = 0.00, \quad b = -0.375, \quad c = 0.825, \quad d = 0.500$$

The resulting function is actually a quadratic for this data, which is quite different than what we found in Example 9.7. The total squared error is computed by MATLAB to be 6.8902e-30, so we have essentially a perfect fit, on [0, 1].

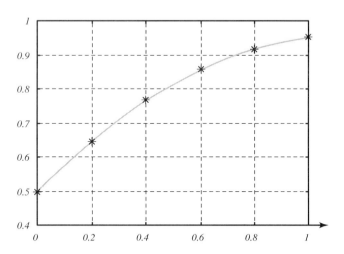

FIGURE 9.11   Cubic least-squares approximation on [0, 1].

The coefficient matrix for this example has a condition number of 8358, which indicates that the problem is very ill conditioned.

9.1.4   Other Forms of Approximation

If the data are best fit by an exponential function, it is convenient instead to fit the logarithm of the data by a straight line. This gives a very close approximation to the best fit exponential. The following example illustrates the process.

Example 9.9 Oil Reservoir Data.

Consider the data introduced in Example 9-A. We find an approximating function of the form $y = \exp(ax+b)$ by finding the linear least squares fit to $\ln(y)$. The transformed function values are

$$\mathbf{yy} = \ln(y) = [0\quad 0.2469\quad 0.5306\quad 0.7885\quad 1.0886\quad 1.4702\quad 2.0149]^T.$$

The computed coefficients are $a = -0.406$, and $b = 2.115$. The results are summarized in the following table and illustrated in Figures 9.12 and 9.13. The total squared error for the linear approximation and the logarithm of the data is 0.0538; the total squared error for the exponential function and the original data is 71.4017.

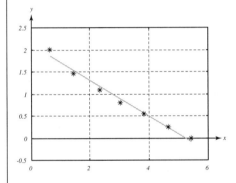

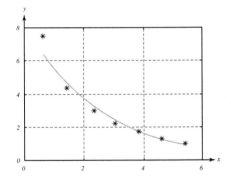

FIGURE 9.12 Logarithm of data and straight-line fit, $y = ax + b$.

FIGURE 9.13 Data and exponential fit, $y = \exp(ax + b)$.

Data and best fit exponential for oil reservoir

x_i	$\ln y_i$	$a\,x_i + b$	d_i	y_i	$\exp(a\,x_i + b)$	e_i
5.435	0.0000	−0.0922	0.0922	1.00	0.9120	0.0880
4.635	0.2469	0.2327	0.0142	1.28	1.2619	0.0181
3.835	0.5306	0.5575	0.0269	1.70	1.7463	−0.0463
3.035	0.7885	0.8823	−0.0938	2.20	2.4165	−0.2165
2.325	1.0886	1.1706	−0.0820	2.97	3.2239	−0.2539
1.435	1.4702	1.5320	−0.0618	4.35	4.6272	−0.2772
0.635	2.0149	1.8568	0.1581	7.50	6.4030	1.0970

Transformations of the original data may be helpful in other settings also. For example, if the data seem to describe an inverse relation, it may be appropriate to perform a least-squares approximation to the reciprocal of the original data.

Example 9.10 Least-Squares Approximation of a Reciprocal Relation

The plot (see Fig. 9.14) of the following data suggests that they could be fit by a function of the form $y = 1/(ax + b)$

$$\mathbf{x} = [0 \quad 0.5 \quad 1 \quad 1.5 \quad 2 \quad],$$

$$\mathbf{y} = [1.00 \quad 0.50 \quad 0.30 \quad 0.20 \quad 0.20].$$

To find such a function, we consider the reciprocal of the original data and perform a linear least-squares approximation to the data given by $\mathbf{x}$ and

$$\mathbf{z} = 1/y = [1.00 \quad 2.00 \quad 3.3333 \quad 5.00 \quad 5.00].$$

The computed coefficients are $a = 2.2$ and $b = 1.0667$. Figure 9.14 shows the data and the linear least squares fit to the reciprocal of the data.

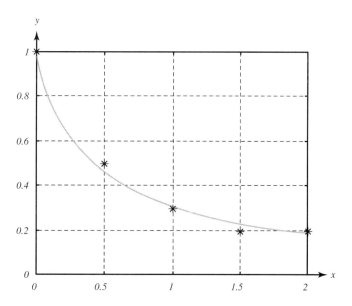

FIGURE 9.14   Linear least squares fit to reciprocal of data.

Example 9.11 Light Intensity Data

The following data describe the intensity of light as a function of the distance from the light source; they were measured in a classroom experiment.

$\mathbf{d} = [30.0 \quad 35.0 \quad 40.0 \quad 45.0 \quad 50.0 \quad 55.0 \quad 60.0 \quad 65.0 \quad 70.0 \quad 75.0 \ ];$

$\mathbf{i} = [\ 0.85 \quad 0.67 \quad 0.52 \quad 0.42 \quad 0.34 \quad 0.28 \quad 0.24 \quad 0.21 \quad 0.18 \quad 0.15];$

The inverse nature of the relationship is evident from a plot of the data (see Fig. 9.15). We consider several least-squares approximations to the reciprocal of the data. Figure 9.15 illustrates the linear least squares fit (dashed line) and the quadratic least squares fit (solid line) to the reciprocal of the data. The agreement between the data and the computed function,

$$z = \frac{1}{0.0013\, d^2 - 0.0208\, d + 0.6161},$$

is quite good.

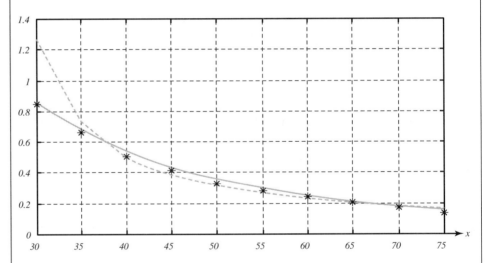

FIGURE 9.15 Linear and quadratic least squares fit to reciprocal of light-intensity data.

Suppose that instead of just knowing the value of the function we wish to approximate at some specific points, we know the exact value of the function for all points in an interval—say, for all x in $[0, 1]$. We can then find the best fit linear, quadratic, or other given form of function by minimizing the error over the entire interval. The summations are replaced by the corresponding integrals. In this section we consider several forms of continuous least-squares approximation.

9.2.1 Approximation Using Powers of x

To approximate a given function $s(x)$ with a quadratic function $p(x) = a\,x^2 + b\,x + c$ on the interval $[0, 1]$, we wish to minimize

$$E = \int_0^1 [a\,x^2 + b\,x + c - s(x)]^2\,dx.$$

The resulting equations for $a, b,$ and c are

$$\frac{a}{5} + \frac{b}{4} + \frac{c}{3} = \int_0^1 x^2\,s(x)\,dx,$$

$$\frac{a}{4} + \frac{b}{3} + \frac{c}{2} = \int_0^1 x\,s(x)\,dx,$$

$$\frac{a}{3} + \frac{b}{2} + c = \int_0^1 s(x)\,dx.$$

To approximate a given function $s(x)$ with a quadratic function $p(x) = a\,x^2 + b\,x + c$, on the interval $[-1, 1]$, we wish to minimize

$$E = \int_{-1}^1 [a\,x^2 + b\,x + c - s(x)]^2\,dx.$$

The resulting equations for $a, b,$ and c are

$$\frac{2}{5}a + 0 + \frac{2}{3}c = \int_{-1}^1 x^2\,s(x)\,dx,$$

$$0 + \frac{2}{3}b + 0 = \int_{-1}^1 x\,s(x)\,dx,$$

$$\frac{2}{3}a + 0 + 2c = \int_{-1}^1 s(x)\,dx.$$

Example 9.12 Continuous Least-Squares Approximation

To find the continuous least-squares quadratic approximation to the exponential function on $[-1, 1]$, we have the coefficient matrix

$$A = \begin{bmatrix} 2/5 & 0 & 2/3 \\ 0 & 2/3 & 0 \\ 2/3 & 0 & 2 \end{bmatrix}.$$

To find the right-hand side of the linear system, we use the following results:

$$\int x^2 e^x \, dx = x^2 e^x - 2 \int x e^x \, dx = x^2 e^x - 2(x e^x - e^x) = e^x (x^2 - 2x + 2);$$

$$\int x e^x \, dx = x^2 e^x - e^x; \qquad \text{and} \quad \int e^x \, dx = e^x.$$

Then

$$\int_{-1}^{1} x^2 e^x \, dx = e - \frac{5}{e} \approx 0.8789,$$

$$\int_{-1}^{1} x e^x \, dx = \frac{2}{e} \approx 0.7358,$$

and

$$\int_{-1}^{1} e^x \, dx = e - \frac{1}{e} \approx 2.3504.$$

Thus, the right-hand side of the system is $\mathbf{r} = [0.8789 \quad 0.7358 \quad 2.3504]^T$, and solving the linear system gives $\mathbf{z} = [0.5367 \quad 1.1036 \quad 1.1036]^T$.

Figure 9.16 shows the exponential function (solid), the quadratic approximation $p = 0.5367x^2 + 1.1036x + 1.1036$ (dashed), and the Taylor polynomial for the exponential function, $t(x) = 0.5 x^2 + x + 1$ (dash-dotted).

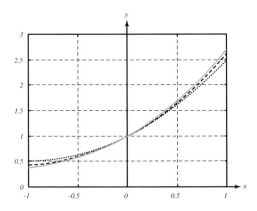

FIGURE 9.16   Exponential function, least squares, and Taylor approximations.

Discussion

We wish to minimize $E = \int_0^1 [a\,x^2 + b\,x + c - s(x)]^2\,dx$.

Setting $\dfrac{\partial E}{\partial a} = 0$ gives

$$\int_0^1 x^2\,[a\,x^2 + b\,x + c - s(x)]\,dx = 0$$

$$a\int_0^1 x^4\,dx + b\int_0^1 x^3\,dx + c\int_0^1 x^2\,dx = \int_0^1 x^2\,s(x)\,dx$$

$$\frac{1}{5}a + \frac{1}{4}b + \frac{1}{3}c = \int_0^1 x^2\,s(x)\,dx$$

Setting $\dfrac{\partial E}{\partial b} = 0$ gives

$$\int_0^1 x\,[a\,x^2 + b\,x + c - s(x)]\,dx = 0$$

$$a\int_0^1 x^3\,dx + b\int_0^1 x^2\,dx + c\int_0^1 x\,dx = \int_0^1 x\,s(x)\,dx$$

$$\frac{1}{4}a + \frac{1}{3}b + \frac{1}{2} = \int_0^1 x\,s(x)\,dx$$

And setting $\dfrac{\partial E}{\partial c} = 0$ gives

$$\int_0^1 [a\,x^2 + b\,x + c - s(x)]\,dx = 0$$

$$a\int_0^1 x^2\,dx + b\int_0^1 x\,dx + c\int_0^1 dx = \int_0^1 s(x)\,dx$$

$$\frac{1}{3}a + \frac{1}{2}b + c = \int_0^1 s(x)\,dx$$

The coefficient matrix is the 3-by-3 Hilbert matrix, which is notoriously ill-conditioned. If we continue this approach with higher degree polynomial approximations, we find that the coefficient matrix is the correspondingly larger Hilbert matrix. The larger the Hilbert matrix, the worse is the conditioning. The computations for continuous least-squares approximation on $[-1, 1]$ are completely analogous. Here, the coefficient matrix is not as ill-conditioned as the Hilbert matrix, but its conditioning does become increasingly worse for higher order polynomials.

To utilize continuous least squares for higher degree polynomials, it is better to use a basis of polynomials that are orthogonal on the interval over which the approximation is desired. In addition to reducing the computational difficulties encountered in solving a linear system with an ill-conditioned coefficient matrix, the use of orthogonal polynomials allows us to progress easily from a lower degree approximation to the next higher degree polynomial.

9.2.2 Orthogonal Polynomials

We say that a set of functions $\{f_0, f_1, f_2, \ldots, f_n\}$ is linearly independent on the interval $[a, b]$ if a linear combination of the functions is the zero function only if all of the coefficients are zero. In other words, if $c_0 f_0(x) + c_1 f_1(x) + c_2 f_2(x) + \ldots + c_n f_n(x) = 0$ for all x in $[a, b]$, then $c_0 = c_1 = c_2 = \ldots = c_n = 0$. The functions $f_0 = 1, f_1 = x, f_2 = x^2, \ldots, f_n = x^n$, are linearly independent on any interval $[a, b]$, but in fact, any set of functions $\{p_0, p_1, p_2, \ldots p_n\}$ where p_j is a polynomial of degree j is linearly independent ($p_0 \neq 0$). Another important set of linearly independent functions, which we will use in the next chapter, is the set of trigonometric functions $\{1, \sin(x), \cos(x), \sin(2x), \cos(2x), \ldots \sin(nx), \cos(nx)\}$.

The set of functions $\{f_0, f_1, f_2, \ldots f_n\}$ is said to be orthogonal on $[a, b]$ if

$$\int_a^b f_i(x)\, f_j(x)\, dx = \begin{cases} 0 & \text{if } i \neq j \\ d_j > 0 & \text{if } i = j \end{cases}$$

A more general concept of orthogonality includes a weighting function w in the integral, but we restrict our investigations to the case where $w = 1$. If the functions are orthogonal and $d_j = 1$ for all j, the functions are called *orthonormal*.

Construction by Gram-Schmidt

We now show how we can construct a sequence of polynomials that are orthogonal on the interval $[a, b]$. For $n = 0, 1, 2, \ldots$, we require that

1. p_n be a polynomial of degree n, with the coefficient of x^n positive.

2. $\displaystyle\int_a^b p_n(x)\, p_m(x)\, dx = 0 \quad \text{if } n \neq m.$

3. $\displaystyle\int_a^b p_n(x)\, p_n(x)\, dx = 1.$

We start by taking $p_0(x) = c > 0$.

To satisfy condition 3, we must have

$$\int_a^b c^2\, dx = 1 \Rightarrow (b - a)c^2 = 1, \text{ so } c = \frac{1}{\sqrt{b - a}}.$$

To construct $p_1(x)$, we begin by letting $q_1(x) = x + c_{1,0}\, p_0$.

We first require that $q_1(x)$ be orthogonal to p_0:

$$\int_a^b p_0\, (x + c_{1,0}\, p_0)\, dx = 0 \Rightarrow \int_a^b x\, p_0\, dx + c_{1,0} \int_a^b p_0\, p_0\, dx = 0$$

Since $\displaystyle\int_a^b p_0\, p_0\, dx = 1$, we have, by construction, $c_{1,0} = -\displaystyle\int_a^b x\, p_0\, dx.$

With this choice of $c_{1,0}$, $q_1(x) = x + c_{1,0}\, p_0$ is orthogonal to p_0.

To satisfy condition 3, we normalize $q_1(x)$ to get

$$p_1(x) = \frac{q_1(x)}{\left[\displaystyle\int_a^b q_1 \, q_1 \, dx\right]^{1/2}}$$

To construct $p_2(x)$, we begin by letting $q_2(x) = x^2 + c_{2,1} \, p_1(x) + c_{2,0} \, p_0(x)$.
We first require that $q_2(x)$ be orthogonal to $p_1(x)$:

$$\int_a^b p_1(x) \, (x^2 + c_{2,1} \, p_1(x) + c_{2,0} \, p_0(x)) \, dx = 0 \Rightarrow$$

$$\int_a^b x^2 \, p_1(x) \, dx + c_{2,1} \int_a^b p_1(x) \, p_1(x) \, dx + c_{2,0} \int_a^b p_1(x) \, p_0(x) \, dx = 0.$$

Because p_1 is orthogonal to p_0, the third integral is zero; the second integral evaluates to one, so we have

$$c_{2,1} = -\int_a^b x^2 \, p_1(x) \, dx.$$

Similarly, we require that $q_2(x)$ be orthogonal to $p_0(x)$:

$$\int_a^b p_0(x) \, (x^2 + c_{2,1} \, p_1(x) + c_{2,0} \, p_0(x)) \, dx = 0 \Rightarrow$$

$$\int_a^b x^2 p_0(x) \, dx + c_{2,1} \int_a^b p_0(x) p_1(x) \, dx + c_{2,0} \int_a^b p_0(x) p_0(x) \, dx = 0.$$

As before, since p_1 is orthogonal to p_0, the second integral is zero and the third integral is one, so we have

$$c_{2,0} = -\int_a^b x^2 p_0(x) \, dx.$$

We complete this step by normalizing $q_2(x)$ to form $p_2(x)$:

$$p_2(x) = \frac{q_2(x)}{\left[\displaystyle\int_a^b q_2(x) \, q_2(x) \, dx\right]^{1/2}}$$

The process continues in the same manner, as we construct each higher degree polynomial in turn. The polynomial $p_n(x)$ is formed from

$$q_n(x) = x^n + c_{n,0} \, p_0(x) + c_{n,1} \, p_1(x) + \ldots + c_{n,n-1} \, p_{n-1}(x),$$

by normalization. (The coefficients $c_{n,0} \ldots c_{n,n-1}$ are found so that $q_n(x)$ is orthogonal to each of the previously generated polynomials.)

9.2.3 Legendre Polynomials

Although the difficulties with forming and solving a linear system of equations for the coefficients of the continuous least-squares approximation problem are most severe on $[0, 1]$, the situation is not good on any other finite interval. The most convenient interval for finding a continuous least-squares approximating function using orthogonal polynomials is $[-1, 1]$. A function of x defined on any finite interval $a \leq x \leq b$ can be transformed to a function of t defined for $-1 \leq t \leq 1$ by the change of variables $x = \dfrac{b-a}{2} t + \dfrac{b+a}{2}$.

The functions known as *Legendre polynomials* form an orthogonal set on $[-1, 1]$; they are useful for continuous least-squares function approximation on a finite interval (transformed, if necessary, to $[-1, 1]$). We will encounter them again in Chapter 11 when we discuss Gaussian quadrature. We list the first few Legendre polynomials here, normalized so that the coefficient of the leading term is unity.

$$P_0(x) = 1, \qquad\qquad P_1(x) = x,$$

$$P_2(x) = x^2 - \frac{1}{3}, \qquad\qquad P_3(x) = x^3 - \frac{3}{5} x,$$

$$P_4(x) = x^4 - \frac{6}{7} x^2 - \frac{3}{35}, \quad P_5(x) = x^5 - \frac{10}{9} x^3 - \frac{5}{21}.$$

For this normalization, we have

$$\int_{-1}^{1} P_0(x)\, P_0(x)\, dx = 2,$$

$$\int_{-1}^{1} P_1(x)\, P_1(x)\, dx = \int_{-1}^{1} x^2\, dx = \frac{2}{3},$$

$$\int_{-1}^{1} P_2(x)\, P_2(x)\, dx = \int_{-1}^{1} x^4 - \frac{2}{3} x^2 + \frac{1}{9}\, dx = \frac{8}{45}.$$

An alternative definition of the Legendre polynomials gives

$$p_0(x) = 1 \text{ and } p_n(x) = \frac{(-1)^n}{2^n\, n!} \frac{d^n}{dx^n} [(1 - x^2)^n], \text{ for } n \geq 1.$$

The polynomials defined in this way are normalized so that $p_n(1) = 1$ and

$$\int_{-1}^{1} p_n(x) p_n(x)\, dx = \frac{2}{2n + 1}.$$

We turn our attention next to illustrating how the property of orthogonality can be used for finding a continuous least-squares approximation function.

Approximation Using Legendre Polynomials

To find the quadratic least-squares approximation to $f(x)$ on the interval $[-1, 1]$ in terms of the Legendre polynomials, we need to determine the coefficients c_0, c_1, c_2 that minimize

$$E = \int_{-1}^{1} [c_0 P_0(x) + c_1 P_1(x) + c_2 P_2(x) - f(x)]^2 \, dx.$$

The normal equations are found as before, by setting the partial derivatives of E equal to zero. Setting $\dfrac{\partial E}{\partial c_0} = 0$ yields

$$\int_{-1}^{1} 2[c_0 P_0(x) + c_1 P_1(x) + c_2 P_2(x) - f(x)]P_0(x) \, dx = 0,$$

which, after dividing out the common factor of 2, expands to give

$$\int_{-1}^{1} c_0 P_0(x)P_0(x) \, dx + \int_{-1}^{1} c_1 P_1(x)P_0(x) \, dx + \int_{-1}^{1} c_2 P_2(x)P_0(x) \, dx = \int_{-1}^{1} f(x) P_0(x) \, dx.$$

Now, because the Legendre polynomials are orthogonal, the second and third integrals on the left side of the equations are zero, so we have

$$c_0 \int_{-1}^{1} P_0(x) P_0(x) \, dx = \int_{-1}^{1} f(x) P_0(x) \, dx.$$

In a similar manner, the equations formed by setting $\dfrac{\partial E}{\partial c_1} = 0$ and $\dfrac{\partial E}{\partial c_2} = 0$ give

$$c_1 \int_{-1}^{1} P_1(x) P_1(x) \, dx = \int_{-1}^{1} f(x) P_1(x) \, dx,$$

and

$$c_2 \int_{-1}^{1} P_2(x) P_2(x) \, dx = \int_{-1}^{1} f(x) P_2(x) \, dx.$$

The integrations on the left were performed earlier; the result is

$$c_0 = \frac{1}{2} \int_{-1}^{1} f(x)P_0(x) \, dx; \quad c_1 = \frac{3}{2} \int_{-1}^{1} f(x)P_1(x) \, dx; \quad c_2 = \frac{45}{8} \int_{-1}^{1} f(x) P_2(x) \, dx$$

If we wish a higher order approximation, we have only to compute the additional integrals; this is in contrast to the system of linear equations approach, in which the entire problem must be reworked if the order of the approximating polynomial is to be increased.

Example 9.13 Approximation Using Legendre Polynomials

To find the quadratic least-squares approximation to $f(x) = e^x$ on the interval $[-1, 1]$ in terms of the Legendre polynomials, we write

$$g(x) = c_0 P_0(x) + c_1 P_1(x) + c_2 P_2(x),$$

where $P_0(x) = 1$, $P_1(x) = x$, and $P_2(x) = x^2 - \dfrac{1}{3}$. We determine the coefficients c_0, c_1, and c_2 as described previously. We will need the values of the following integrals, found in Example 9.12.

$$\int_{-1}^{1} x^2 e^x \, dx = e - \frac{5}{e} \approx 0.8789, \quad \int_{-1}^{1} x e^x \, dx = \frac{2}{e} \approx 0.7358, \quad \int_{-1}^{1} e^x \, dx = e - \frac{1}{e} \approx 2.3504;$$

$$c_0 = \frac{1}{2} \int_{-1}^{1} f(x) P_0(x) \, dx = \frac{1}{2} \int_{-1}^{1} e^x \, dx \approx \frac{1}{2}(2.3504) \approx 1.1752;$$

$$c_1 = \frac{3}{2} \int_{-1}^{1} f(x) P_1(x) \, dx = \frac{3}{2} \int_{-1}^{1} e^x x \, dx \approx \frac{3}{2}(0.7358) \approx 1.1037;$$

$$c_2 = \frac{45}{8} \int_{-1}^{1} f(x) P_2(x) \, dx = \frac{45}{8} \int_{-1}^{1} e^x \left(x^2 - \frac{1}{3} \right) dx \approx 0.5368.$$

We thus have $g(x) = c_0 P_0(x) + c_1 P_1(x) + c_2 P_2(x) = c_0 + c_1 x + c_2 \left(x^2 - \dfrac{1}{3} \right)$; the plot of $g(x)$ and $f(x)$ shown in Fig. 9.17 strongly suggests what we could verify algebraically if we desire, namely, that this is the same quadratic approximation function as that found in Example 9.12.

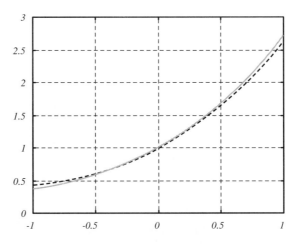

FIGURE 9.17   Exponential and least-squares approximation function.

In this section we consider two important methods of approximating a function $f(x)$ at a specific value of x: Taylor polynomial approximation and Padé rational function approximation. Each of these approximations agrees with the given function and its derivatives at a given point.

9.3.1 Taylor Approximation

For a polynomial approximation, the Taylor polynomial (of degree n) gives the highest possible order of contact between the function and the polynomial. That is, the Taylor polynomial agrees with the function and its first n derivatives at $x = a$; the formula is

$$p(x) = f(a) + f'(a)(x - a) + \frac{f''(a)}{2!}(x - a)^2 + \frac{f'''(a)}{3!}(x - a)^{-3} + \ldots + \frac{f^{(n)}(a)}{n!}(x - a)^n.$$

The Taylor polynomial is widely used in the analysis of numerical techniques. (It was introduced in Chapter 1 in the discussion of truncation error.) The error incurred in using $p(x)$ to approximate the actual value of the function $f(x)$ is given by $\frac{f^{(n+1)}(\eta)}{(n + 1)!}(x - a)^{n+1}$, for some η between x and a. Taylor's formula is derived in most standard calculus texts.

The Taylor polynomial was included in Example 9.12 for comparison with the exponential function and its least-squares approximation. Figure 9.18 shows the Taylor polynomial $g(x) = x - x^3/3! + x^5/5! - x^7/7!$, and interpolating polynomial (degree 8, based on 9 evenly spaced data values between $-\pi$ and π) for $y = \sin(x)$.

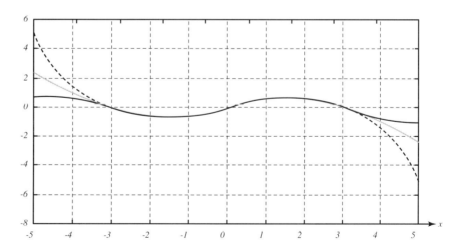

FIGURE 9.18   Graph of $y = \sin(x)$ (black), Taylor polynomial (dashed) and the interpolating polynomial (grey).

9.3.2 Padé Approximation

Padé approximation seeks to approximate a function $f(x)$ by finding a rational function that fits the values of the function and its derivatives at a given point x_0. The desired rational function has the form

$$r(x) = \frac{p_m(x)}{q_n(x)} = \frac{a_m x^m + \ldots + a_0}{b_n x^n + \ldots + b_0}.$$

We assume that $f(x_0), f'(x_0), \ldots, f^{(k)}(x_0)$ are given for $k = m + n$, and, in the discussion that follows, we assume, for simplicity, that $x_0 = 0$.

Let $t(x)$ be the Taylor polynomial for the given function $f(x)$. We write

$$t(x) = c_k x^k + \ldots + c_2 x^2 + c_1 x + c_0.$$

In terms of information about the derivatives of $f(x)$, we have $c_k = \dfrac{f^{(k)}(0)}{k!}$.

We want $r(x)$ to be the same as $t(x)$, i.e., to have the same value at $x = 0$ and the same derivatives of all orders up to, and including, $k = m + n$. Our basic approach is to use the equivalence of the expressions

$$t(x) = r(x) = \frac{p_m(x)}{q_n(x)} \quad \text{and} \quad q_n(x)\, t(x) = p_m(x).$$

Thus, we work with the relationship

$$(b_n x^n + \ldots + b_0)(c_k x^k + \ldots + c_2 x^2 + c_1 x + c_0) = a_m x^m + \ldots + a_0 \quad (9.1)$$

We begin by considering the requirement that $q_n(0)\, t(0) = p_m(0)$; this gives

$$b_0 c_0 = a_0.$$

The preceding rational function $r(x)$ is determined only up to a scale factor. We choose $b_0 = 1$. With this convention, we have an equation for determining a_0.

Taking the first derivative of eq. (9.1), we find that

$$(b_n x^n + \ldots + b_0)(c_1 + 2c_2 x + \ldots + k\, c_k x^{k-1})$$
$$+ (n\, b_n x^{n-1} + \ldots + b_1)(c_0 + c_1 x + c_2 x^2 + \ldots + c_k x^k)$$
$$= m\, a_m x^{m-1} + \ldots + a_1.$$

We require that this equation be satisfied when $x = 0$, so we have

$$b_0 c_1 + b_1 c_0 = a_1.$$

This gives us an equation relating the unknown coefficients a_1 and b_1 to the known quantities c_0, c_1, and b_0. We rewrite the equation as

$$a_1 - b_1 c_0 = c_1.$$

To continue the process of finding higher derivatives of the product $g(x) = q(x)t(x)$ efficiently, we note the following formulae, which can be found by repeated applications of the product rule:

$$g'(x) = q(x)t'(x) + q'(x)t(x),$$

$$g''(x) = q(x)t''(x) + 2\,q'(x)t'(x) + q''(x)t(x),$$

$$\cdot$$
$$\cdot$$
$$\cdot$$

$$g^{(n)}(x) = \sum_{j=0}^{n} \frac{n!}{j!(n-j)!}\, q^{(j)}(x)t^{(n-j)}(x).$$

We are interested in the values of the derivative at $x = 0$, so we have

$$g^{(n)}(0) = \sum_{j=0}^{n} \frac{n!}{j!(n-j)!}\, q^{(j)}(0)t^{(n-j)}(0).$$

Taking the second derivative of eq. (9.1) at $x = 0$, we find that

$$q(0)t''(0) + 2\,q'(0)t'(0) + q''(0)t(0) = p''(0).$$

Substituting in the values of these derivatives (in terms of the coefficients), we have

$$b_0\, 2\, c_2 + 2\, b_1\, c_1 + 2\, b_2\, c_0 = 2\, a_2,$$

or, after simplifying,

$$a_2 - b_1\, c_1 - b_2\, c_0 = c_2.$$

We continue in this manner until all required equations are specified (depending on the degrees of the polynomials p_m and q_n).

If we define $a_j = 0$ for $j > m$ and $b_j = 0$ for $j > n$, then the unknowns a_k and b_k can be found from the general relationship

$$a_k - \sum_{i=0}^{k-1} c_i\, b_{k-i} = c_k \qquad k = 0, 1, \ldots, m + n.$$

In general, errors for Padé approximates are less when the degree of the numerator and the degree of the denominator are the same or when the degree of the numerator is one larger than the denominator (see Ralston and Rabinowitz, 1978, p. 295). It is desired to have the polynomial in the denominator of sufficiently high degree to account for any poles that the original function may have in the complex plane (since such poles are often the cause of the difficulties that arise with polynomial interpolation, even when our interest is restricted to real variables only).

Example 9.14 Padé Approximation of the Runge Function

The values of the Runge function

$$f(x) = \frac{1}{1 + 25\,x^2}$$

and its first three derivatives at $x = 0$ are

$$f(0) = 1,\ f'(0) = 0,\ f''(0) = -50,\ f'''(0) = 0.$$

The Taylor polynomial of the function (at $x = 0$) is

$$t(x) = 1 + 0\,x - 25\,x^2 + 0\,x^3.$$

We seek a rational-function representation, using $k = 3$, $m = 1$, and $n = 2$. That is, we want

$$r(x) = \frac{a_1 x + a_0}{b_2\,x^2 + b_1\,x + 1}.$$

For $k = 3$, the linear system of equations is

$$a_0 \qquad\qquad\qquad\qquad = c_0$$
$$a_1 - c_0\,b_1 \qquad\qquad\quad = c_1$$
$$a_2 - c_0\,b_2 - c_1\,b_1 \qquad = c_2$$
$$a_3 - c_0\,b_3 - c_1\,b_2 - c_2\,b_1 = c_3$$

In this particular problem, we have

$$c_0 = 1, \qquad c_1 = 0, \qquad c_2 = -25, \qquad \text{and } c_3 = 1.$$

The solution of the linear system is found to be

$$a_0 = 1, \qquad a_1 = b_1 = 0, \qquad b_2 = 25,$$

so

$$r(x) = \frac{1}{1 + 25\,x^2}.$$

Thus, the Padé approximation has given us the exact representation of the Runge function in this example.

Built-in functions for least-squares approximation (regression) are included in software packages such as MATLAB, Mathcad, and *Mathematica*; routines are also found in software libraries such as NAG and the NIST Index. We begin this section by summarizing the software routines for least-squares approximation in the NIST Index and NAG Libraries. We then illustrate the use of the built-in functions in *Mathematica*, MATLAB, and Mathcad.

9.4.1 Some Software Library Routines

The *NIST Guide to Available Mathematical Software* lists software for least-squares approximation in several sections of the index; the main headings and the relevant subheadings are summarized here.

> K1 Least-square approximation
> > Linear least squares; Nonlinear least squares
> L8 Regression
> > Simple linear; Polynomial;
> > Multiple linear; Polynomial in several variables

The routines in the NAG (Numerical Algorithms Group Ltd.) Library that are related to the topics discussed in this chapter are listed in two sections in the index of software. The sections and the relevant routines are summarized here (there are also many other routines in each of these sections).

> E02 Curve and Surface Fitting
> > Least-squares curve fit, by polynomials
> > Least-squares curve cubic spline fit (including interpolation)
> > Least-squares surface fit, bicubic splines
> G02 Correlation and Regression Analysis
> > Simple linear regression with constant term
> > Multiple linear regression models

9.4.2 Mathematica's Functions

Mathematica's function FIT[data, funs, vars] provides for a very general least-squares fit to a list of data. As a simple example, a quadratic fit to a set of function values $\{f1, f2, f3, \ldots fn\}$ given at $x = \{1, 2, 3, \ldots n\}$ can be found by using

FIT[{f1, f2, f3, . . . fn}, {1, x, x^2}, x]

If the function values are given at more general values of the independent variable, then the data takes the form $\{\{x1, f1\}, \{x2, f2\}, \ldots, \{xn, fn\}\}$ and the quadratic fit is found from

FIT[{ {x1, f1}, {x2, f2}, . . . ,{xn, fn}}, {1,x,x^2}, x]

Multivariate least-squares follows a similar pattern; for a function of two variables, funs is a list of the functions to be used in fitting the data. For example

FIT[{{x1,y1,f1}, {x2,y1,f2},. . . ,{xn,yn,fn}}, {1,x,y}, {x,y}]

9.4.3 MATLAB's Functions

The MATLAB function `polyfit` finds the coefficients of the polynomial of specified degree that best fits a set of data, in a least-squares sense. The function is called as `[p,S] = polyfit(x,y,n)`, where **x** and **y** are vectors containing the data, and n is the degree of the polynomial desired. The function returns the coefficients of the polynomial in the vector **p**. The returned structure S can be used with the function `polyval` to obtain error bounds on the predictions. As described in the comments at the beginning of the function `polyfit`, if the errors in **y** are independent random variables, normally distributed with constant variance, `polyval` will produce error bounds that contain at least 50% of the predictions.

The polynomial coefficients are a row vector by convention, with the coefficient of the highest power of the independent variable given first.

Example 9.15 Higher Order Least-Squares Approximation

Let us illustrate the use of higher degree polynomials for a leasts-quares fit to data. The data are illustrated in Figs. 9.19–9.21, together with the fourth-degree, fifth-degree and sixth-degree polynomials found by MATLAB's built-in function `polyfit`. The polynomial is evaluated using the function `polyval`.

The data used in this example consists of 61 data points. A subset of that data (10 points rather than 61) is shown here.

$$x = [-3 \quad -2.33 \quad -1.67 \quad -1 \quad -0.33 \quad 0.33 \quad 1 \quad 1.67 \quad 2.33 \quad 3 \ ]$$
$$y = [0.82 \quad -0.77 \quad -1.98 \quad -1.26 \quad 0.46 \quad 1.11 \quad 0.43 \quad 0.01 \quad 0.68 \quad 1.1]$$

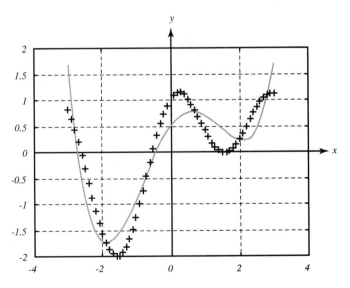

FIGURE 9.19 Data and fourth-degree polynomial approximation.

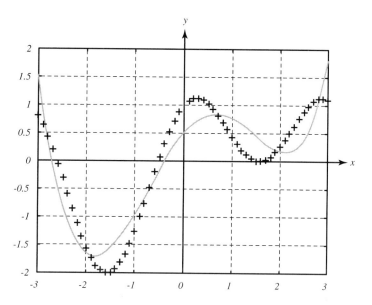

FIGURE 9.20   Data and fifth-degree polynomial approximation.

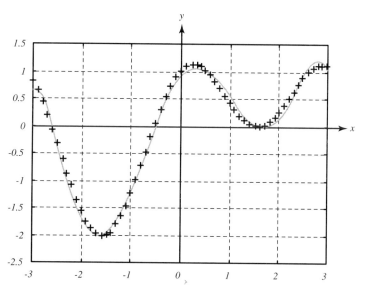

FIGURE 9.21   Data and sixth-degree polynomial approximation.

The coefficients for the sixth-degree polynomial are computed as

$$\mathbf{z} = \begin{bmatrix} -0.02412 & 0.0057 & 0.398 & -0.156 & -1.627 & 0.991 & 0.9199 \end{bmatrix},$$

so the approximation polynomial is

$$p(x) = -0.02412x^6 + 0.0057x^5 + 0.398x^4 - 0.156x^3 - 1.627x^2 + 0.991x + 0.9199.$$

9.4.4 Mathcad's Functions

The Mathcad functions for regression follow the same basic form as the functions for interpolation. However, the returned vector gives the parameters of the regression function, rather than input to another function (such as the function `interp` in Chapter 8). The functions for linear regression, general polynomial regression, and general least-squares approximation using a user-specified functional form are summarized here.

The input to each of the following functions includes the vectors **vx** and **vy** which contain the data to be approximated.

Linear Regression

intercept(**vx**,**vy**)

This function returns the y-intercept of the least-squares regression line.

slope(**vx**,**vy**)

This function returns the slope of the least-squares regression line.

line(**vx**,**vy**)

This function returns a vector containing the y-intercept and the slope of the least-squares regression line.

stderr(**vx**,**vy**)

This function returns the standard error of the linear regression.

medfit(**vx**,**vy**)

This function returns the y-intercept and slope of the median–median regression line. This linear fit is less sensitive to outliers than the standard regression line produced by the function `line(`**vx**,**vy**`)`. To generate the median–median line, the data is divided into three sets, the median of first and last subsets is calculated, and the result is the line connecting these medians.

Polynomial Regression

regress(**vx**, **vy**, n)

This function retruns the parameters for the nth degree polynomial least squares fit to the data.

General Approximation

Mathcad has a function `genfit` for general least-squares approximation, using a user-defined functional form, as well as several special cases for fitting the data with specified functional forms. Most of these functions require as input, in addition to the data vectors described previously, a vector **vg,** which contains the initial guess of the parameters that are to be determined.

genfit(**vx**, **vy**, **vg**, F)

    This function returns the parameters that make $f(x)$ approximate (fit) data The user-supplied function, F, returns an $n + 1$ element vector, containing the definition of the approximating function f and its partial derivatives with respect to the parameters that are to be determined by genfit.

    Special cases of genfit

expfit(**vx**, **vy**, **vg**)

    This function returns a vector containing the parameters (a, b, c) so that $f(x) = a \exp\wedge(b\ x) + c$ fits (approximates in the least-squares sense) the data.

lgsfit(**vx**, **vy**, **vg**)

    This function returns a vector containing the parameters (a, b, c) so that $f(x) = a\ (1 + b \exp\wedge(-c\ x))$ ' fits the data.

linfit(**vx**, **vy**, F)

    The input function F is a function of a single variable, which returns a vector of functions. The function linfit returns a vector containing the coefficients so that a linear combination of the functions in F approximates the data. This function is not as general as genfit, but does not require an initial guess of the parameters, since it is doing a linear fit.

logfit(**vx**, **vy**, **vg**)

    This function returns a vector containing the parameters (a, b, c) so that $f(x) = a \ln(x + b) + c$ fits the data.

pwrfit(**vx**, **vy**, **vg**)

    This function returns a vector containing the parameters (a, b, c) so that $f(x) = a\ x^b + c$ fits the data.

sinfit(**vx**, **vy**, **vg**)

    This function returns a vector containing the parameters (a, b, c) so that $f(x) = a \sin(x + b) + c$ fits the data.

    The regression function regress solves the normal equations by Gauss-Jordan elimination.

    The approximation function linfit finds the required parameters by solving the linear system using singular value decomposition (SVD). SVD is the method of choice for any linear system that is numerically close to singular. Since the coefficient matrix for the normal equations is ill-conditioned, SVD is also the method of choice for linear least-squares problems. See Press et al. (1992), pp. 59–70, 416, for a discussion of the method.

    The general approximation function genfit finds the required parameters using the Levenberg-Marquardt method, described in section 7.4.2.

Linear Least-Squares Approximation

The coefficients a and b for the straight line $y = a x + b$, to approximate the data $x = [x_1, x_2, \ldots, x_n], y = [y_1, y_2, \ldots, y_n]$ can be found from the following system of equations:

$$a S_{xx} + b S_x = S_{xy}$$

$$a S_x + b 4 = S_y$$

where $S_{xx} = \sum_{i=1}^{n} x_i^2$, $S_x = \sum_{i=1}^{n} x_i$, $S_{xy} = \sum_{i=1}^{n} x_i y_i$, $S_y = \sum_{i=1}^{n} y_i$.
The solution to the system of equations is

$$a = \frac{n S_{xy} - S_x S_y}{n S_{xx} - S_x S_x}, \qquad b = \frac{S_{xx} S_y - S_{xy} S_x}{n S_{xx} - S_x S_x}.$$

Quadratic Least-Squares Approximation

The coefficients for the quadratic function $f(x) = a x^2 + b x + c$ that best fits the data are found by solving the system of equations:

$$a \sum_{i=1}^{n} x_i^4 + b \sum_{i=1}^{n} x_i^3 + c \sum_{i=1}^{n} x_i^2 = \sum_{i=1}^{n} x_i^2 y_i,$$

$$a \sum_{i=1}^{n} x_i^3 + b \sum_{i=1}^{n} x_i^2 + c \sum_{i=1}^{n} x_i = \sum_{i=1}^{n} x_i y_i.$$

$$a \sum_{i=1}^{n} x_i^2 + b \sum_{i=1}^{n} x_i + c[n] = \sum_{i=1}^{n} y_i.$$

Exponential Approximation

To find an exponential function of the form $y = \exp(a x + b)$ to fit a set of data, we first find a linear fit to the logarithm of the data.

Continuous Least-Squares Approximation

To approximate a given function $s(x)$ with a quadratic function $p(x) = a x^2 + b x + c$ on the interval $[-1, 1]$, the resulting equations for a, b, and c are

$$\frac{2}{5} a + 0 \quad + \frac{2}{3} c = \int_{-1}^{1} x^2 s(x)\, dx,$$

$$0 \quad + \frac{2}{3} b + 0 \quad = \int_{-1}^{1} x s(x)\, dx,$$

$$\frac{2}{3} a + 0 \quad + 2 c = \int_{-1}^{1} s(x)\, dx.$$

Quadratic Approximation with Legendre Polynomials

The quadratic least-squares approximation to $f(x)$ in terms of the Legendre polynomials (on $[-1, 1]$) is $c_0 P_0(x) + c_1 P_1(x) + c_2 P_2(x)$; the coefficients are

$$c_0 = \frac{1}{2} \int_{-1}^{1} f(x) P_0(x)\, dx; \quad c_i = \frac{3}{2} \int_{-1}^{1} f(x) P_1(x)\, dx; \quad c_2 = \frac{45}{8} \int_{-1}^{1} f(x) P_2(x)\, dx.$$

Padé Approximation

The desired rational function has the form

$$r(x) = \frac{p_m(x)}{q_n(x)} = \frac{a_m x^m + \ldots + a_0}{b_n x^n + \ldots + b_0}.$$

Given $f(0), f'(0), \ldots, f^{(k)}(0)$ for $k = m + n$; the Taylor polynomial for $f(x)$ is

$$t(x) = c_k x^k + \ldots + c_2 x^2 + c_1 x + c_0, \text{ where } c_k = \frac{f^{(k)}(0)}{k!}.$$

We choose $b_0 = 1$, then the coefficients are determined as:

$$b_0 c_0 = a_0.$$

$$a_1 - b_1 c_0 = c_1.$$

$$a_2 - b_1 c_1 - b_2 c_0 = c_2.$$

If we define $a_j = 0$ for $j > m$ and $b_j = 0$ for $j > n$, then the unknowns a_k and b_k can be found from the general relationship

$$a_k - \sum_{i=0}^{k-1} c_i b_{k-i} = c_k \qquad k = 0, 1, \ldots, m + n.$$

SUGGESTIONS FOR FURTHER READING

The standard texts on approximation of functions include:

Achieser, N. I. *Theory of Approximation.* Dover, New York, 1993.

Cheney, E. W. *Introduction to Approximation Theory.* McGraw-Hill, New York, 1966.

Rivlin, T. J. *An Introduction to the Approximation of Functions.* Dover, New York, 1981. (Originally published by Blaisdell Publishing, 1969.)

Timan, A. F., C. J. Hyman, and N. I. Achieser. *Theory of Approximation.* Dover, New York, 1993.

For further discussion of Padé approximation, see:

Brezinski, C. *History of Continued Fractions and Padé Approximants.* Springer-Verlag, Berlin, 1991.

Jensen, J. A., and J. H. Rowland. *Methods of Computation.* Scott, Foresman and Company, Glenview, IL, 1975.

For Problems P9.1 to P 9.5, find the linear least-squares approximation to the data.

P9.1 $x = [1 \ 2 \ 3]$,
$y = [1 \ 4 \ 8]$.

P9.2 $x = [1 \ 4 \ 9]$,
$y = [1 \ 2 \ 3]$.

P9.3 $x = [4 \ 9 \ 16]$,
$y = [2 \ 3 \ 4]$.

P9.4 $x = [-1 \ 0 \ 1]$,
$y = [-2 \ 3 \ -2]$.

P9.5 $x = [0 \ 1 \ 2]$,
$y = [1 \ 2 \ 4]$.

For Problems P9.6 to P 9.15:
   a. *Find the linear least-squares approximation to the data.*
   b. *Find the quadratic least-squares approximation to the data.*

P9.6 $x = [0 \ 1 \ 2 \ 4]$,
$y = [1 \ 1 \ 2 \ 5]$.

P9.7 $x = [-1 \ 0 \ 1 \ 2]$,
$y = [1/3 \ 1 \ 3 \ 9]$.

P9.8 $x = [0 \ 1 \ 2 \ 3]$,
$y = [1 \ 2 \ 4 \ 8]$.

P9.9 $x = [0 \ 1 \ 2 \ 3]$,
$y = [1 \ 2 \ 4 \ 8]$.

P9.10 $x = [-1 \ 0 \ 1 \ 2]$,
$y = [0 \ 1 \ 2 \ 9]$.

P9.11 $x = [0 \ 2/3 \ 1 \ 2]$,
$y = [2 \ -2 \ -1 \ -1/2]$.

P9.12 $x = [0 \ 2/3 \ 1 \ 2]$,
$y = [4 \ -4 \ -2 \ -1/2]$.

P9.13 $x = [0 \ 2/3 \ 1 \ 2]$,
$y = [4 \ -4 \ -3.5 \ -0.5]$.

P9.14 $x = [1 \ 2 \ 3 \ 4]$,
$y = [2 \ 4 \ 8 \ 16]$.

P9.15 $x = [0 \ 1/2 \ 1 \ 3/2]$,
$y = [1 \ 2 \ 1 \ 0]$.

For Problems P9.16 to P9.20:
   a. *Find the linear least-squares approximation to the data.*
   b. *Find the quadratic least-squares approximation to the data.*
   b. *Find the cubic least-squares approximation to the data.*

P9.16 $x = [0 \ 1 \ 2 \ 3 \ 4]$,
$y = [0 \ 1 \ 4 \ 8 \ 16]$.

P9.17 $x = [0 \ 1 \ 4 \ 9 \ 16]$,
$y = [0 \ 1 \ 2 \ 3 \ 4]$.

P9.18 $x = [-1 \ -0.75 \ -0.25 \ 0.25 \ 0.75 \ 1]$,
$y = [0 \ -0.7 \ -0.7 \ 0.7 \ 0.7 \ 0]$.

P9.19 $x = [-1 \ -0.5 \ 0.0 \ 0.5 \ 0.75 \ 1]$,
$y = [0.4 \ 0.6 \ 1.0 \ 1.6 \ 2.1 \ 2.7]$.

P9.20 $x = [0.5 \ 0.75 \ 1.0 \ 1.25 \ 1.5 \ 1.75]$,
$y = [-0.7 \ -0.3 \ 0.0 \ 0.2 \ 0.4 \ 0.6]$.

For Problems P9.21 to P9.25, find the linear least-squares approximation to the data.

P9.21 $x = [1 \ 2 \ 3 \ 4 \ 5 \ 6 \ 7 \ 8 \ 9 \ 10]$
$y = [6.0 \ 9.2 \ 13.0 \ 14.7 \ 19.7 \ 21.8 \ 22.8 \ 29.1 \ 30.2 \ 32.2]$

P9.22 $x = [1 \ 2 \ 3 \ 4 \ 5 \ 6 \ 7 \ 8 \ 9 \ 10]$
$y = [5.7 \ 8.9 \ 15.2 \ 16.6 \ 20.9 \ 26.7 \ 28.6 \ 34.0 \ 34.1 \ 47.0]$

P9.23 $x = [1 \ 2 \ 3 \ 4 \ 5 \ 6 \ 7 \ 8 \ 9 \ 10]$
$y = [-3.3 \ -7.1 \ -9.8 \ -12.3 \ -14.0 \ -21.4 \ -21.3 \ -28.6 \ -29.0 \ -32.8]$

P9.24 $x = [1 \ 2 \ 3 \ 4 \ 5 \ 6 \ 7 \ 8 \ 9 \ 10]$
$y = [2.9 \ 0.5 \ -0.2 \ -3.8 \ -5.4 \ -4.3 \ -7.8 \ -13.8 \ -10.4 \ -13.9]$

P9.25 $x = [\ 4.6 \quad 8.7 \quad 9.3 \ 2.6 \ 1.6 \quad 8.7 \ 2.4 \quad 6.5 \quad 9.7 \quad 6.6]$
$y = [16.5 \ 35.8 \ 31.6 \ 6.6 \ 2.5 \ 28.0 \ 6.8 \ 21.1 \ 38.8 \ 20.8]$

For Problems P9.26 to P9.30, find the quadratic least-squares approximation to the data.

P9.26 $x = [1 \quad 2 \quad 3 \quad 4 \quad 5 \quad 6 \quad 7 \quad 8 \quad 9 \quad 10 \ ]$
$y = [2.9 \ \ 4.8 \ \ 6.0 \ 18.9 \ 8.7 \ 30.7 \ 25.7 \ 77.7 \ 55.8 \ 104.8]$

P9.27 $x = [\ 1 \quad 2 \quad 3 \quad 4 \quad 5 \quad 6 \quad 7 \quad 8 \quad 9 \quad 10 \ ]$
$y = [-0.4 \ -4.1 \ -7.4 \ -21.5 \ -21.3 \ -45.2 \ -44.7 \ -62.8 \ -80.6 \ -96.5]$

P9.28 $x = [-4 \quad -3 \quad -2 \quad -1 \quad 0 \quad 1 \quad 2 \quad 3 \quad 4 \quad 5 \ ]$
$y = [\ 8.0 \quad 9.9 \quad 1.8 \quad 1.4 \ 1.7 \ 3.6 \ 7.5 \ 16.8 \ 14.1 \ 27.2]$

P9.29 $x = [-3.2 \ 0.0 \ -0.8 \quad 1.6 \quad 1.7 \quad 4.6 \ -3.1 \ -3.9 \ 0.7 \quad 4.7 \ ]$
$y = [57.7 \ \ 4.4 \quad 6.4 \quad 17.6 \ 19.6 \ 101.6 \ 49.8 \ 86.2 \ 6.7 \ 117.1]$

P9.30 $x = [\ -3.8 \quad -4.3 \quad 3.5 \quad -3.2 \quad -4.7 \quad 2.3 \quad 0.4 \quad -2.2 \quad -1.3 \quad -4.9]$
$y = [-91.8 \ -120.5 \ -50.4 \ -70.2 \ -125.1 \ -23.5 \ -4.1 \ -36.1 \ -18.1 \ -150.7]$

For Problems P9.31 to P9.45, plot the data, choose an appropriate form for the least-squares approximation function (linear, quadratic, cubic, exponential, reciprocal of linear, or reciprocal of quadratic) and then determine the best fit function of the chosen form.

P9.31 $x = [3.0 \quad 0.5 \quad 6.9 \quad 6.5 \quad 9.8 \quad 5.5 \quad 4.0 \ 2.0 \quad 6.3 \quad 7.3]$
$y = [5.8 \ -2.5 \ 22.1 \ 23.9 \ 36.5 \ 18.0 \ 10.3 \ 2.2 \ 18.4 \ 21.5]$

P9.32 $x = [\ 5.80 \ 1.40 \quad 8.70 \ 3.30 \quad 4.90 \ 4.30 \ 2.60 \quad 9.80 \quad 9.70 \quad 9.50]$
$y = [10.90 \ 1.40 \ 15.30 \ 5.90 \ 11.10 \ 9.20 \ 3.30 \ 14.50 \ 17.00 \ 14.00]$

P9.33 $x = [-3.5 \ -1.2 \ -1.9 \ -3.3 \quad 4.0 \ -1.8 \quad 2.3 \ -0.9 \ -1.0 \quad 0.1]$
$y = [32.2 \ -0.9 \quad 4.9 \ 25.7 \ 81.2 \quad 4.8 \ 28.5 \ -2.0 \ -2.3 \ -1.2]$

P9.34 $x = [\ -2.5 \quad 3.0 \quad 1.7 \quad -4.9 \ 0.6 \quad -0.5 \quad 4.0 \quad -2.2 \quad -4.3 \ -0.2]$
$y = [-20.1 \ -21.8 \ -6.0 \ -65.4 \ 0.2 \quad 0.6 \ -41.3 \ -15.4 \ -56.1 \quad 0.5]$

P9.35 $x = [3.00 \ 1.80 \ 6.90 \ 2.60 \ 4.60 \ 8.40 \ 8.80 \ 7.00 \ 7.60 \ 9.70]$
$y = [0.08 \ 0.14 \ 0.03 \ 0.10 \ 0.05 \ 0.03 \ 0.02 \ 0.03 \ 0.03 \ 0.02]$

P9.36 $x = [4.70 \ 2.30 \ 3.20 \ 7.90 \ 6.30 \ 6.60 \ 5.40 \ 9.20 \ 7.80 \ 3.30]$
$y = [0.13 \ 0.33 \ 0.18 \ 0.10 \ 0.13 \ 0.07 \ 0.13 \ 0.08 \ 0.08 \ 0.17]$

P9.37 $x = [0.70 \ 3.10 \ 9.40 \ 9.80 \ 5.60 \ 9.90 \ 6.90 \ 2.40 \ 8.10 \ 9.30]$
$y = [0.36 \ 0.07 \ 0.02 \ 0.02 \ 0.04 \ 0.02 \ 0.03 \ 0.09 \ 0.03 \ 0.02]$

P9.38 $x = [\ 8.80 \quad 4.90 \quad 8.90 \quad 7.60 \quad 6.60 \quad 9.70 \quad 1.70 \quad 1.40 \quad 7.60 \quad 3.10]$
$y = [-0.02 \ -0.04 \ -0.02 \ -0.02 \ -0.03 \ -0.02 \ -0.11 \ -0.13 \ -0.03 \ -0.06]$

P9.39 $x = [-0.20 \ 0.00 \ -2.10 \ -4.40 \ -2.40 \ -3.10 \quad 4.20 \ -3.80 \ -4.90 \ -1.30]$
$y = [\ 0.42 \ 0.63 \quad 0.05 \quad 0.01 \quad 0.04 \quad 0.02 \ 0.02 \quad 0.01 \quad 0.01 \quad 0.10]$

P9.40 $x = [4.40 \ -0.10 \ -4.10 \ 1.70 \ 0.10 \ -2.80 \ 2.30 \ -4.30 \ 4.60 \ -2.90]$
$y = [0.02 \quad 1.23 \quad 0.07 \ 0.08 \ 0.70 \quad 0.18 \ 0.05 \quad 0.04 \ 0.01 \quad 0.14]$

P9.41 $x = [4.20\ \ 0.20\ \ -4.10\ \ 2.40\ \ -5.00\ \ 1.00\ \ 4.60\ \ -1.00\ \ 2.30\ \ 1.80]$
$y = [0.01\ \ 0.20\ \ \ 0.01\ \ \ 0.04\ \ \ \ 0.01\ \ 0.11\ \ 0.01\ \ \ 0.11\ \ 0.04\ \ 0.05]$

P9.42 $x = [-0.90\ \ 0.30\ \ 4.20\ \ -1.20\ \ 1.40\ \ -3.30\ \ 2.90\ \ -1.30\ \ 2.80\ \ \ -1.60]$
$y = [\ 1.10\ \ 1.70\ \ 6.40\ \ \ 0.90\ \ 2.60\ \ \ 0.50\ \ 4.80\ \ \ 0.90\ \ 4.80\ \ \ \ 0.80]$

P9.43 $x = [0.30\ \ 0.00\ \ -0.20\ \ -1.20\ \ 0.20\ \ 3.20\ \ -2.90\ \ -1.10\ \ -4.50\ \ -2.00]$
$y = [0.80\ \ 0.70\ \ \ 0.70\ \ \ 0.50\ \ 0.70\ \ 1.60\ \ \ 0.30\ \ \ \ 0.50\ \ \ \ 0.30\ \ \ \ 0.40]$

P9.44 $x = [-4.90\ \ 1.40\ \ -3.90\ \ -2.80\ \ 4.10\ \ -3.60\ \ -2.90\ \ 3.50\ \ 2.10\ \ -4.20]$
$y = [\ 0.20\ \ 1.70\ \ \ 0.30\ \ \ 0.50\ \ 3.90\ \ \ 0.30\ \ \ 0.50\ \ 3.40\ \ 2.60\ \ \ 0.40]$

P9.45 $x = [-2.00\ \ 1.00\ \ -3.20\ \ 2.30\ \ 0.50\ \ -3.40\ \ 4.30\ \ -3.00\ \ -4.90\ \ 1.90]$
$y = [\ 0.50\ \ 1.20\ \ \ 0.30\ \ 1.80\ \ 1.00\ \ \ 0.30\ \ 2.80\ \ \ 0.30\ \ \ 0.10\ \ 1.40]$

P9.46 $x = [\ -2.60\ \ \ \ \ 4.40\ \ \ \ \ -4.10\ \ \ 0.40\ \ \ \ \ \ 4.00\ \ \ \ \ \ 3.60\ \ \ \ \ 1.30\ \ \ \ \ -2.40\ \ -1.20\ \ \ -1.60]$
$y = [-11.70\ \ \ 380.40\ \ -119.20\ \ 2.80\ \ \ 260.70\ \ \ 188.90\ \ 14.00\ \ \ -15.40\ \ \ \ \ 5.10\ \ \ \ \ \ 4.60]$

P9.47 $x = [-0.40\ \ \ \ \ 3.30\ \ -2.00\ \ \ \ \ 2.10\ \ \ \ \ \ -4.30\ \ \ \ \ \ 2.50\ \ -0.30\ \ \ \ \ \ 4.40\ \ \ \ \ -4.90\ \ \ \ \ \ -4.50]$
$y = [-1.20\ \ \ 145.10\ \ -1.90\ \ \ 32.10\ \ \ -144.10\ \ \ 54.50\ \ -1.60\ \ \ 307.70\ \ -236.30\ \ -146.10]$

P9.48 $x = [\ \ 4.80\ \ \ \ \ \ 4.00\ \ \ \ \ \ -4.70\ \ \ \ \ \ -2.20\ \ \ \ \ \ -3.10\ \ \ 1.10\ \ \ \ \ -2.90\ \ \ \ \ \ 5.00\ \ \ \ \ \ \ -4.80\ \ \ -0.60]$
$y = [262.00\ \ \ 156.10\ \ -200.60\ \ \ -27.00\ \ \ -75.20\ \ 9.10\ \ \ -62.40\ \ \ 331.30\ \ -262.70\ \ \ -2.60]$

P9.49 $x = [\ \ 3.10\ \ \ \ \ \ \ 2.60\ \ \ \ \ \ 3.10\ \ \ \ \ \ \ 1.80\ \ \ \ \ \ 1.20\ \ \ -1.30\ \ \ \ \ -3.00\ \ \ \ \ \ -2.20\ \ \ -0.20\ \ -1.00\ ]$
$y = [-33.90\ \ -20.00\ \ -33.70\ \ \ -9.70\ \ \ -0.40\ \ \ -4.90\ \ \ -34.50\ \ -20.80\ \ \ \ 2.20\ \ -1.60\ ]$

P9.50 $x = [\ \ 1.10\ \ -1.30\ \ -3.00\ \ \ \ \ 4.00\ \ \ \ \ 4.90\ \ \ \ \ 4.20\ \ -1.10\ \ \ \ \ \ 1.60\ \ \ \ \ \ 0.40\ \ -2.90]$
$y = [-4.60\ \ \ \ \ 0.70\ \ \ 14.60\ \ \ 20.50\ \ \ 40.80\ \ \ 22.00\ \ -0.40\ \ \ -2.20\ \ \ -6.10\ \ \ 23.00]$

EXPLORE SOME APPLICATIONS

A9.1

The following data describe the product of a chemical reaction as a function of time:

$t = [0.00\ \ \ 0.10\ \ \ 0.40\ \ \ 0.50\ \ \ 0.60\ \ \ 0.90\ \ \ 1.00\ \ \ 1.10\ \ \ \ 1.40\ \ \ \ 1.50\ \ \ 1.60\ \ \ 1.90\ \ \ 2.00]$
$y = [0.00\ \ \ 0.06\ \ \ 0.17\ \ \ 0.19\ \ \ 0.21\ \ \ 0.25\ \ \ 0.26\ \ \ 0.27\ \ \ 0.29\ \ \ 0.29\ \ \ 0.30\ \ \ 0.31\ \ \ 0.31]$

Find a least squares approximating function for the data. Compare your function with the functions found in Examples 8.3 and 8.11, in which interpolation was used on a subset of these data.

A9.2

Use the following rounded data to find the linear relationship between C and F:

$C = [\ 50\ \ \ \ 45\ \ \ \ 40\ \ \ 35\ \ \ 30\ \ \ 25\ \ \ 20\ \ \ 15\ \ \ 10\ \ \ \ 5\ \ \ \ \ 0\ \ \ -5\ \ \ -10]$
$F = [122\ \ \ 113\ \ \ 104\ \ \ 95\ \ \ 86\ \ \ 77\ \ \ 68\ \ \ 59\ \ \ 50\ \ \ 41\ \ \ 32\ \ \ 23\ \ \ \ \ 14]$

A9.3

A laboratory experiment measured the height of a bouncing ball; the following data give the time and height of the peak of each bounce:

$t = [0.43\ \ \ \ 0.989\ \ \ 1.462\ \ \ 1.892\ \ \ 2.279\ \ \ 2.623\ \ \ 2.924\ \ \ 3.182]$
$h = [0.428\ \ \ 0.308\ \ \ 0.239\ \ \ 0.19\ \ \ \ 0.153\ \ \ 0.121\ \ \ 0.097\ \ \ 0.079]$

Find the best fit function of the form suggested by a plot of the data.

A9.4

According to Newton's law of cooling, the rate of change of the temperature of a cup of hot liquid (such as coffee) is proportional to the difference between the temperature and the surrounding air. The following data were obtained from a simple classroom laboratory experiment.

$$t = [0 \quad 5 \quad 10 \quad 15 \quad 20 \quad 25 \quad 30 \quad \ldots$$
$$35 \quad 40 \quad 45 \quad 50 \quad 55 \quad 60 \quad \ldots ;$$
$$65 \quad 70 \quad 75 \quad 80 \quad 85 \quad 90 \quad 95]$$

$$d = T - A \; (A = \text{room temperature} = 74 \, \text{F})$$

$$d = [88.266 \quad 75.072 \quad 66.144 \quad 60.204 \quad 54.912 \quad 50.43 \quad 46.398 \quad \ldots$$
$$42.51 \quad 38.748 \quad 35.562 \quad 32.646 \quad 29.802 \quad 27.228 \quad \ldots ;$$
$$24.906 \quad 22.602 \quad 20.514 \quad 18.678 \quad 16.626 \quad 15.006 \quad 13.584]$$

Find the coefficients in the "best fit" exponential function.

A9.5

An experiment was conducted to measure the weight of the water in a cylindrical can. The water drained out through a small hole in the bottom of the can. Find the quadratic best fit to the following data obtained from the experiment:

time (in seconds)
1.00   6.06   11.12   16.18   21.23   26.29   31.35   36.41   41.47   46.53   51.59   56.64
weight of water (in Newtons).
2.85   2.74   2.63   2.46   2.35   2.24   2.14   2.03   1.97   1.92   1.81   1.81

A9.6

An experiment that involved rolling a can up an inclined plane produced the following data for the distance of the can from the measuring device as a function of time:

$$t = [0.00 \; 0.27 \; 0.54 \; 0.81 \; 1.08 \; 1.34 \; 1.61 \; 1.88 \; 2.15 \; 2.42 \; 2.69 \; 2.96 \; 3.23 \; 3.49 \; 3.76 \; 4.03 \; 4.30 \; 4.57 \; 4.84]$$

$$d = [1.91 \; 1.82 \; 1.61 \; 1.43 \; 1.28 \; 1.18 \; 1.10 \; 1.04 \; 1.00 \; 0.99 \; 1.00 \; 1.03 \; 1.08 \; 1.15 \; 1.24 \; 1.34 \; 1.48 \; 1.66 \; 1.86]$$

Find the best fit quadratic function.

A9.7

An experiment to measure the intensity of light as a function of the distance from source of the light produced the following data:

$$d = [30 \quad 35 \quad 40 \quad 45 \quad 50 \quad 55 \quad 60 \quad 65 \quad 70 \quad 75 \quad];$$
$$i = [0.85 \quad 0.67 \quad 0.52 \quad 0.42 \quad 0.34 \quad 0.28 \quad 0.24 \quad 0.21 \quad 0.18 \quad 0.15];$$

Find the best fit exponential function and the best–fit quadratic function.

EXTEND YOUR UNDERSTANDING

U9.1 Show that the functions $P_2 = x^2 - 1/3$ and $P_3 = x^3 - 3/5\, x$ are orthogonal on $[-1, 1]$ with respect to the weight function $w(x) = 1$. Are the two functions orthonormal? Why or why not?

U9.2 Use the Gram–Schmidt process to construct the first four Legendre polynomials.

U9.3 Use the Gram–Schmidt process to construct the first four polynomials that are orthonomal on the interval $[0, 4]$.

For Problems U9.4 to U9.8, find the Padé approximation function with $k = 6$.

   a. Take $m = 2$, and $n = 4$; that is, find the best approximation function of the form

   $$\frac{a_2\, x^2 + a_1\, x + a_0}{b_4\, x^4 + b_3\, x^3 + b_2\, x^2 + b_1\, x + 1}$$

   b. Take $m = 3$, and $n = 3$; that is, find the best approximation function of the form

   $$\frac{a_3\, x^3 + a_2\, x^2 + a_1\, x + a_0}{b_3\, x^3 + b_2\, x^2 + b_1\, x + 1}$$

   c. Take $m = 4$, $n = 2$; i.e., find the best approximation function of the form

   $$\frac{a_4\, x^4 + a_3\, x^3 + a_2\, x^2 + a_1\, x + a_0}{b_2\, x^2 + b_1\, x + 1}$$

   d. Compare the errors incurred in using the approximations from Parts a, b, and c on the interval $[-1, 1]$.

U9.4 $f(x) = \sin(x)$.

U9.5 $f(x) = \cos(x)$.

U9.6 $f(x) = \tan(x)$.

U9.7 $f(x) = e^x$.

U9.8 $f(x) = \ln(x + 1)$

10

Fourier Methods

In the previous two chapters, we interpolated data by polynomials and approximated data by polynomials, exponential functions, or rational functions, depending on the general characteristics of the data. However, for periodic data, it is more appropriate to use sine and cosine functions for the approximation or interpolation.

We begin this chapter with an investigation into data approximation and interpolation using trigonometric polynomials, also known as (finite) Fourier series. The approach is the same as that discussed previously, namely, we seek to minimize the total squared error by setting the partial derivatives of the error equal to zero. The formulas for the coefficients are found by using the appropriate orthogonality results for the sine and cosine functions. The coefficients are given by sums of the form

$$a_j = \frac{2}{n} \sum_{k=0}^{n-1} x_k \cos(j \ t_k)$$

or

$$b_j = \frac{2}{n} \sum_{k=0}^{n-1} x_k \sin(j \ t_k).$$

If we form a single complex quantity, $c_j = a_j + i \ b_j$, these summations can be combined to give one example of the discrete Fourier transform, which maps the data x_k to the transformed data c_j.

The *fast Fourier transform* (FFT), a computationally efficient method of computing the discrete Fourier transform, has greatly increased the feasibility of using this transform for large sets of data. In Section 10.2, we introduce the FFT in its most common setting, the case in which n is a power of 2; this is called a *radix-2* FFT. The method is presented in both matrix and algebraic forms for $n = 4$. An algorithm is also given for this simple case.

In Section 10.3, we describe the general FFT for the case when n is not a power of 2. The process is a generalization of the algebraic approach for the radix-2 transform. An algorithm is given for the case in which the number of data points is the product of two primes.

We illustrate several cases where the number of data points is a power of 2 that is larger than 4, or the number of data points is not a power of 2, using built-in functions from MATLAB and Mathcad.

Example 10-A Waveforms for Several Instruments

The characteristic sound of different instruments playing the same pitch can be shown by the vibrational waveform of the sound (see Figure 10.1). Such periodic vibrations are often analyzed by Fourier transform methods.

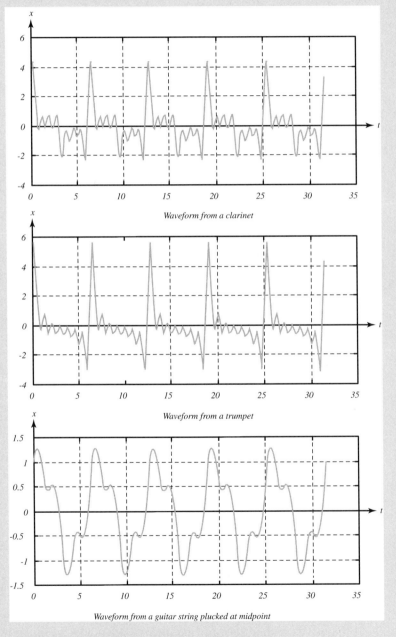

Waveform from a clarinet

Waveform from a trumpet

Waveform from a guitar string plucked at midpoint

FIGURE 10.1 Waveforms from musical instruments.

Example 10-B Geometric Figures

Fourier transforms may be used to remove angular dependence in data. Consider, for example, describing various geometric figures, centered at the origin, by measuring the distance from the origin to the boundary of the figure at certain (evenly spaced) angles. In different rotations, a square is distinguishable from a triangle or a cross (see Fig. 10.2).

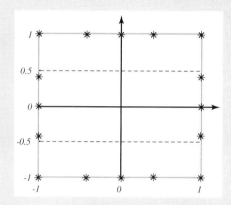

FIGURE 10.2A Square

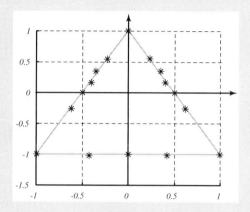

FIGURE 10.2B Triangle

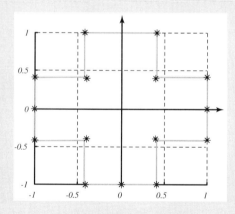

FIGURE 10.2C Cross

The distances from the origin, measured at angular intervals of $\pi/8$, of these three figures are as follows:

Square
[1.00 1.08 1.40 1.08 1.00 1.08 1.40 1.08 1.00 1.08 1.40 1.08 1.00 1.08 1.40 1.08]

Triangle
[0.50 0.43 0.50 0.60 1.00 0.60 0.50 0.43 0.50 0.67 1.40 1.10 1.00 1.10 1.40 0.67]

Cross
[1.00 1.08 0.56 1.08 1.00 1.08 0.56 1.08 1.00 1.08 0.56 1.08 1.00 1.08 0.56 1.08]

10.1 FOURIER APPROXIMATION AND INTERPOLATION

In order to approximate or interpolate a set of data using a trigonometric polynomial, i.e., a function of the form

$$f(t) = \frac{a_0}{2} + a_1\cos t + a_2\cos 2t + \ldots + a_m\cos mt$$

$$+ b_1\sin t + b_2\sin 2t + \ldots + b_m\sin mt,$$

we must find the coefficients $a_0, a_1, \ldots, a_m$, and $b_1, \ldots, b_m$. The function $f(t)$ is a trigonometric polynomial of degree m if a_m and b_m are not both zero.

We assume that the interval $[0, 2\pi)$ is divided into n equal subintervals and that we have the data values given at the points

$$t_0 = 0, \quad t_1 = \frac{2\pi}{n}, \quad t_2 = 2\frac{2\pi}{n}, \ldots, \quad t_k = k\frac{2\pi}{n}, \ldots, \quad t_{n-1} = (n-1)\frac{2\pi}{n}.$$

We denote the corresponding data values as $x_0, x_1, \ldots, x_{n-1}$.

The functional form for $f(t)$ is appropriate for a least-squares approximation problem when $2m + 1 < n$, i.e., when we have more data points than there are coefficients to be determined.

For exact interpolation, the appropriate form of the trigonometric polynomial depends on whether the number of data points is even or odd. If n is odd, the polynomial for exact interpolation has the same form as that for approximation (except that $n = 2m + 1$). However, if n is even ($n = 2m$), the polynomial for interpolation is

$$f(t) = \frac{a_0}{2} + a_1\cos t + a_2\cos 2t + \ldots + \frac{a_m}{2}\cos mt$$

$$+ b_1\sin t + b_2\sin 2t + \ldots + b_m\sin mt.$$

The reason for the difference in functional form will be made clear when we consider the derivation of the formulas for the coefficients.

The formulas for the coefficients ($j = 0, 1, \ldots, m$) are

$$a_j = \frac{2}{n}\sum_{k=0}^{n-1} x_k\cos(j\ t_k), \quad b_j = \frac{2}{n}\sum_{k=0}^{n-1} x_k\sin(j\ t_k).$$

We do not have to solve a linear system, since the set of functions

$$\{1, \cos(t), \cos(2t), \ldots \cos(mt), \sin(t), \ldots \sin(mt)\}$$

are orthogonal as long as the data are evenly spaced on an interval of length 2π; we assume that the data are given on $[0, 2\pi)$. The formulas are found in a manner analogous to that for continuous least squares with orthogonal polynomials in Chapter 9.

The following algorithm describes the process for computing the coefficients of the trigonometric approximation or interpolation function

Approximation ($n > 2m + 1$)

$$x = \frac{a_0}{2} + a_1 \cos(t) + a_2 \cos(2t) + \ldots + a_m \cos(m\ t)$$

$$+ b_1 \sin(t) + b_2 \sin(2t) + \ldots + b_m \sin(m\ t).$$

Interpolation (if $n = 2m + 1$):

$$x = \frac{a_0}{2} + a_1 \cos(t) + a_2 \cos(2t) + \ldots + a_m \cos(m\ t)$$

$$+ b_1 \sin(t) + b_2 \sin(2t) + \ldots + b_m \sin(m\ t).$$

Interpolation (if $n = 2m$):

$$x = \frac{a_0}{2} + a_1 \cos(t) + a_2 \cos(2t) + \ldots + \frac{a_m}{2} \cos(m\ t)$$

$$+ b_1 \sin(t) + b_2 \sin(2t) + \ldots + b_m \sin(m\ t).$$

The data values for $x(t)$ are given at

$$\mathbf{t} = \left[0, \frac{2\pi}{n}, \ldots, \frac{2k\pi}{2}, \ldots, \frac{2(n-1)\pi}{n} \right]$$

Fourier Approximation or Interpolation

Input
    x   *data values for the dependent variable*
    n   *number of data points*
    m   *degree of desired trig polynomial, $2m \leq n - 1$, or $2m \leq n$*
Find coefficients
    For j = 0 to m

$$a_j = \frac{2}{n} \sum_{k=1}^{n} x_k \cos(j\ t_k)$$

$$b_j = \frac{2}{n} \sum_{k=1}^{n} x_k \sin(j\ t_k) \qquad note\ that\ b(0) = 0$$

    End
Return
    a   *vector of coefficients on cosine terms; constant term is $a_0/2$*
          if $2m = n$, coefficient on m^{th} term is $a_m/2$
    b   *vector of coefficients for sine terms*

Example 10.1 Trigonometric Approximation

We seek the least-squares trigonometric polynomial, with $m = 1$, for the five data points shown in the following table:

$k =$	0	1	2	3	4t
t_k	0	$\dfrac{2\pi}{5}$	$\dfrac{4\pi}{5}$	$\dfrac{6\pi}{5}$	$\dfrac{8\pi}{5}$
x_k	1	3	2	0	-1

The formulas for the coefficients,

$$a_0 = \frac{2}{5} \sum_{k=0}^{4} x_k, \quad a_1 = \frac{2}{5} \sum_{k=0}^{4} x_k \cos(t_k), \quad b_1 = \frac{2}{5} \sum_{k=0}^{4} x_k \sin(t_k),$$

make use of the sine and cosine values given in the following table:

t_k	0	$\dfrac{2\pi}{5}$	$\dfrac{4\pi}{5}$	$\dfrac{6\pi}{5}$	$\dfrac{8\pi}{5}$
$\cos(t_k)$	1	0.3090	-0.8090	-0.8090	0.3090
$\sin(t_k)$	0	0.9511	0.5878	-0.5878	-0.9511

The coefficients are:

$$a_0 = \frac{2}{5} [x_0 + x_1 + x_2 + x_3 + x_4] = \frac{2}{5} [5] = 2$$

$$a_1 = \frac{2}{5} \left[\cos(0) + 3 \cos\left(\frac{2\pi}{5}\right) + 2 \cos\left(\frac{4\pi}{5}\right) + 0 \cos\left(\frac{6\pi}{5}\right) - 1 \cos\left(\frac{8\pi}{5}\right) \right] = 0$$

$$b_1 = \frac{2}{5} \left[\sin(0) + 3 \sin\left(\frac{2\pi}{5}\right) + 2 \sin\left(\frac{4\pi}{5}\right) + 0 \sin\left(\frac{6\pi}{5}\right) - 1 \sin\left(\frac{8\pi}{5}\right) \right] = 1.992$$

Figure 10.3 shows the approximating function,

$$x = \frac{a_0}{2} + a_1 \cos(t) + b_1 \sin(t) = 1 + 1.922 \sin t$$

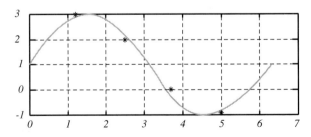

FIGURE 10.3 Data points and trigonometric approximating function.

Example 10.2 Trigonometric Interpolation

Continuing Example 10.1, for interpolation we take $m = 2$:

$$x = \frac{a_0}{2} + a_1 \cos(t) + a_2 \cos(2t) + b_1 \sin(t) + b_2 \sin(2t)$$

where
a_0, a_1, and b_1 are as computed previously, and

$$a_2 = \frac{2}{5} \sum_{k=0}^{4} x_k \cos(2t_k), \quad b_2 = \frac{2}{5} \sum_{k=0}^{4} x_k \sin(2t_k)$$

$$a_2 = \frac{2}{5} \left[\cos(0) + 3 \cos\left(\frac{4\pi}{5}\right) + 2 \cos\left(\frac{8\pi}{5}\right) + 0 \cos\left(\frac{12\pi}{5}\right) - 1 \cos\left(\frac{16\pi}{5}\right) \right]$$

$$= \frac{2}{5} \left[\cos(0) + 3 \cos\left(\frac{4\pi}{5}\right) + 2 \cos\left(\frac{8\pi}{5}\right) + 0 \cos\left(\frac{2\pi}{5}\right) - 1 \cos\left(\frac{6\pi}{5}\right) \right]$$

$$= \frac{2}{5} [1 + 3(-0.8090) + 2(0.3090) + 0(0.3090) - 1(-0.8090)] = 0$$

$$b_2 = \frac{2}{5} \left[\sin(0) + 3 \sin\left(\frac{4\pi}{5}\right) + 2 \sin\left(\frac{8\pi}{5}\right) + 0 \sin\left(\frac{2\pi}{5}\right) - 1 \sin\left(\frac{6\pi}{5}\right) \right]$$

$$= \frac{2}{5} [0 + 3(0.5878) + 2(-0.9511) + 0(0.9511) - 1(-0.5878)] = 0.1796$$

The trigonometric interpolating function, shown in Figure 10.4, is

$$x = 1 + 1.992 \sin t + 0.1796 \sin(2t)$$

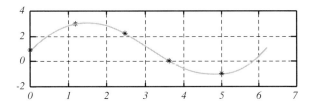

FIGURE 10.4 Trigonometric interpolating function and data points.

The previous examples show that for more data points, we have more terms in each summation. For exact-fit trigonometric polynomials, we have as many coefficients to be determined as there are data points.

Example 10.3 Interpolating or Approximating a Step Function

We now illustrate the use of the algorithm for Fourier approximation and interpolation for a step function with $n = 8$ data points. The data values are

$$z = [1 \quad 1 \quad 1 \quad 1 \quad 0 \quad 0 \quad 0 \quad 0]$$

For interpolation we have $n = 2m$, so $m = 4$. The coefficients (including a_0 and b_0 as the respective first elements of the vectors **a** and **b**) are found to be

$$\mathbf{a} = [0.5 \quad 0.25 \quad 0 \quad 0.25 \quad 0]$$
$$\mathbf{b} = [0 \quad 0.6036 \quad 0 \quad 0.1036 \quad 0]$$

The coefficients b_0 and b_4 are included for completeness, even though they are always zero for $n = 8$. In fact, b_0 is always zero; b_m is zero for m even.

With $m = 3$, the approximation function is identical to the interpolation function. This should not be surprising since a_4 and b_4 are both 0.

For $m = 2$, the approximation function is

$$f(t) = \frac{a_0}{2} + a_1\cos t + \frac{a_2}{2}\cos 2t + b_1 \sin t,$$

with $a_0 = 0.5$, $a_1 = 0.25$, $a_2 = 0$, and $b_1 = 0.6036$.

A plot of the data and the interpolation and approximation functions is given in Fig. 10.5.

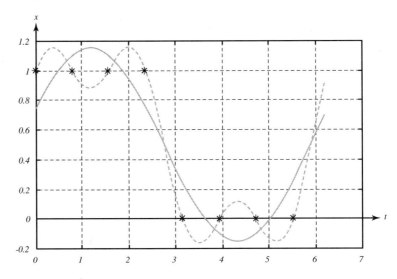

FIGURE 10.5 Trigonometric polynomial interpolation and approximation.

Example 10.4 Geometric Figures

The following data represent the distance from the origin to the perimeter of a square (shown in Figure 10.2a), measured at evenly spaced angular intervals t_k:

$$\mathbf{t} = [0 \quad \pi/4 \quad \pi/2 \quad 3\pi/4 \quad \pi \quad 5\pi/4 \quad 3\pi/2 \quad 7\pi/4],$$
$$\mathbf{x} = [1.0 \quad 1.4 \quad 1.0 \quad 1.4 \quad 1.0 \quad 1.4 \quad 1.0 \quad 1.4 \ ].$$

The coefficients are found to be

$$\mathbf{a} = [1.2 \quad 0 \quad 0 \quad 0 \quad -0.2],$$
$$\mathbf{b} = [0 \quad 0 \quad 0 \quad 0 \quad 0 \ ].$$

We denote the interpolation function as $r(t)$ because it represents radial distance from the origin:

$$r(t) = 1.2 - 0.2\cos(4t).$$

We can reconstruct a rough approximation of the original figure by plotting $x = r\cos(t)$, $y = r\sin(t)$, as shown in Fig. 10.6.

For the triangle shown in Figure 10.2b (sampled at angular intervals of $\pi/4$), the data are $\mathbf{d} = [0.5 \quad 0.5 \quad 1.0 \quad 0.5 \quad 0.5 \quad 1.4 \quad 1.0 \quad 1.4]$.

The coefficients are

$$\mathbf{a} = [0.85 \quad 0.00 \quad -0.25 \quad 0.00 \quad -0.1],$$
$$\mathbf{b} = [0.00 \quad -0.3182 \quad 0.00 \quad -0.3182 \quad 0.0].$$

so the interpolation function for the radial distance is

$$r(t) = 0.85 - 0.25\cos(2t) - 0.1\cos(4t) - 0.3182\sin(t) - 0.3182\sin(3t).$$

The reconstructed triangle is shown in Fig. 10.7. Using more data points improves the figures, as we shall see later.

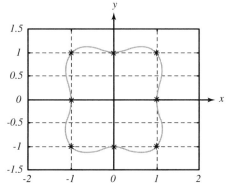

FIGURE 10.6   Reconstructed square

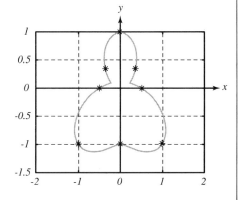

FIGURE 10.7   Reconstructed triangle

Discussion

Derivation of Fourier Approximation and Interpolation Formulas

Fourier approximation and interpolation formulas can be derived in the same manner as polynomial and other least-squares approximation formulas were in the previous chapter. However, the special properties of the sine and cosine functions at evenly spaced data points lead to simplifications that make the calculation of the coefficients more manageable.

Given n data at evenly spaced points in $[0, 2\pi)$, viz.,

$$\mathbf{t} = \left[0, \quad \frac{2\pi}{n}, \quad 2\frac{2\pi}{n}, \quad \ldots, \quad k\frac{2\pi}{n}, \quad \ldots, \quad (n-1)\frac{2\pi}{n} \right],$$

$$\mathbf{x} = [x_0, \quad x_1, \quad x_2, \quad \ldots, \quad x_k, \quad \ldots, \quad x_{n-1}].$$

we consider the trigonometric polynomial

$$p(t) = \frac{a_0}{2} + a_1\cos t + a_2\cos 2t + \ldots + a_m\cos mt + b_1\sin t + b_2\sin 2t + \ldots + b_m\sin mt$$

$$= \frac{a_0}{2} + \sum_{j=1}^{m} a_j \cos(j\ t_k) + \sum_{j=1}^{m} b_j \sin(j\ t_k).$$

where $2m + 1 \le n$.

We wish to minimize

$$E = \sum_{k=0}^{n-1} \left[\frac{a_0}{2} + \sum_{j=1}^{m} a_j \cos(j\ t_k) + \sum_{j=1}^{m} b_j \sin(j\ t_k) - x_k \right]^2.$$

We proceed by setting the partial derivatives of E with respect to each of the unknown coefficients to zero. We use the index J to denote the generic coefficient a_J or b_J during this derivation, to distinguish it from the index of summation. We will return to the more common lowercase later. Because of the restriction that $2m + 1 \le n$, we only need to consider $J \le n/2$.

Setting $\partial E/\partial a_0 = 0$ results in

$$\sum_{k=0}^{n-1} \left[\frac{a_0}{2} + \sum_{j=1}^{m} a_j \cos(j\ t_k) + \sum_{j=1}^{m} b_j \sin(j\ t_k) - x_k \right] = 0. \tag{10.1}$$

Setting $\partial E/\partial a_J = 0$ yields

$$\sum_{k=0}^{n-1} \left[\frac{a_0}{2} + \sum_{j=1}^{m} a_j \cos(j\ t_k) + \sum_{j=1}^{m} b_j \sin(j\ t_k) - x_k \right]\cos(J\ t_k) = 0. \tag{10.2}$$

And setting $\partial E/\partial b_J = 0$ gives

$$\sum_{k=0}^{n-1} \left[\frac{a_0}{2} + \sum_{j=1}^{m} a_j \cos(j\ t_k) + \sum_{j=1}^{m} b_j \sin(j\ t_k) - x_k \right]\sin(J\ t_k) = 0. \tag{10.3}$$

Equation (10.1) can be written as

$$\frac{n}{2} a_0 + \sum_{k=0}^{n-1} \sum_{j=1}^{m} a_j \cos(j \ t_k) + \sum_{k=0}^{n-1} \sum_{j=1}^{m} b_j \sin(j \ t_k) = \sum_{k=0}^{n-1} x_k,$$

which, after interchanging the order of the summations, becomes

$$\frac{n}{2} a_0 + \sum_{j=1}^{m} a_j \sum_{k=0}^{n-1} \cos(j \ t_k) + \sum_{j=1}^{m} b_j \sum_{k=0}^{n-1} \sin(j \ t_k) = \sum_{k=0}^{n-1} x_k.$$

However, since the data are evenly spaced, we have, for each j

$$\sum_{k=0}^{n-1} \cos(j \ t_k) = 0 \quad \text{and} \quad \sum_{k=0}^{n-1} \sin(j \ t_k) = 0,$$

so that

$$\frac{n}{2} a_0 = \sum_{k=0}^{n-1} x_k$$

which gives

$$a_0 = \frac{2}{n} \sum_{k=0}^{n-1} x_k$$

The analysis of eqs. (10.2) and (10.3) makes use of the fact that the functions

$$a, \cos t, \cos 2t, \ldots \cos (n - 1)t, \sin t, \ldots \sin (n - 1)t$$

are orthogonal with respect to n evenly spaced data points in $[0, 2\pi)$, which gives the following results:

$$\sum_{k=0}^{n-1} \cos(J \ t_k) \cos(j \ t_k) = \begin{cases} 0, & \text{for } j \neq J, \\ n/2 & \text{for } j = J < n/2, \\ n, & \text{for } j = J = n/2, \end{cases}$$

$$\sum_{k=0}^{n-1} \cos(J \ t_k) \sin(j \ t_k) = 0,$$

$$\sum_{k=0}^{n-1} \sin(J \ t_k) \sin(j \ t_k) = \begin{cases} 0, & \text{for } j \neq J, \\ n/2 & \text{for } j = J < n/2, \\ 0, & \text{for } j = J = n/2, \end{cases}$$

The summations that are equal to zero for $j \neq J$ may be verified using the following basic trigonometric identities:

$$\cos j \cos J = (\cos(j - J) + \cos(j + J))/2;$$

$$\cos j \sin J = (\sin(j + J) - \sin(j - J))/2;$$

$$\sin j \sin J = (\cos(j - J) - \cos(j + J))/2.$$

When $j = J < n/2$, we use the half angle formulas

$$(\sin j)^2 = (1 - \cos 2j)/2 \quad \text{and} \quad (\cos j)^2 = (1 + \cos 2j)/2$$

Finally, in the case of $j = J = n/2$ (which occurs only for the exact interpolation of an even number of data points),

$$\sum_{k=0}^{n-1} \cos(j\ t_k)^2 = \sum_{k=0}^{n-1} \cos\left(\frac{n}{2} k \frac{2\pi}{n}\right)^2 = \sum_{k=0}^{n-1} \cos^2(k\ \pi) = n.$$

On the other hand,

$$\sum_{k=0}^{n-1} \sin(J\ t_k) \sin(j\ t_k) = 0,$$

since all terms in the summation involve $\sin(k\pi)$, which is zero.

We now consider eq. (10.2) in some detail; the simplification of (10.3) follows in a similar manner. Rearranging the terms in eq. (10.2) yields

$$\sum_{k=0}^{n-1} \frac{a_0}{2} \cos(J\ t_k) + \sum_{k=0}^{n-1} \cos(J\ t_k) \sum_{j=0}^{m} a_j \cos(j\ t_k) + \sum_{k=0}^{n-1} \cos(J\ t_k) \sum_{j=0}^{m} b_j \sin(j\ t_k)$$

$$= \sum_{k=0}^{n-1} \cos(J\ t_k)\ x_k.$$

We simplify each summation on the left-hand side of the equation separately:

$$\sum_{k=0}^{n-1} \frac{a_0}{2} \cos(J\ t_k) = \frac{a_0}{2} \sum_{k=0}^{n-1} \cos(J\ t_k) = 0,$$

$$\sum_{k=0}^{n-1} \cos(J\ t_k) \sum_{j=0}^{m} a_j \cos(j\ t_k) = \sum_{j=0}^{m} a_j \sum_{k=0}^{n-1} \cos(j\ t_k) \cos(J\ t_k))$$

$$= \begin{cases} 0 & \text{for } j \neq J, \\ \dfrac{a_J\ n}{2} & \text{for } j = J < n/2, \\ a_J n & \text{for } j = J = n/2, \end{cases}$$

$$\sum_{k=0}^{n-1} \cos(J\ t_k) \sum_{j=0}^{m} b_j \sin(j\ t_k) = \sum_{j=0}^{m} b_j \sum_{k=0}^{n-1} \sin(j\ t_k) \cos(J\ t_k)) = 0.$$

Thus, for $J < n/2$, the second equation gives us

$$a_J = \frac{2}{n} \sum_{k=0}^{n-1} \cos(J\ t_k) x_k.$$

For exact interpolation with an even number of data points, we have $n = 2m$. Rather than using a different formula for a_m in this case (which would be required by the difference in the value of the summation of $\cos(J\ t_k)^2$ when $J = n/2$), we choose, for $n = 2m$, to define the interpolating polynomial as

$$p(t) = \frac{a_0}{2} + a_1 \cos t + a_2 \cos 2t + \ldots + \frac{a_m}{2} \cos mt$$

$$+ b_1 \sin t + b_2 \sin 2t + \ldots + b_{m-1} \sin (m - 1)t$$

$$= \frac{a_0}{2} + \sum_{j=1}^{m-1} a_j \cos(j\ t_k) + \frac{a_m}{2} \cos m\ t + \sum_{j=1}^{m-1} b_j \sin(j\ t_k)$$

Using this form, we find that for $j = 0, \ldots, m$, all of the coefficients follow the same formulas:

$$a_j = \frac{2}{n} \sum_{k=0}^{n-1} \cos(j\ t_k)\ x_k$$

$$b_j = \frac{2}{n} \sum_{k=0}^{n-1} \sin(j\ t_k)\ x_k$$

Note that the formula for b_j can be included for $j = 0$; however, b_0 is always zero, so it is not necessary to compute it. Similarly, for $n = 2m$ (interpolation of an even number of data points), we always have $b_m = 0$, since all terms in the summation are of the form $\sin(k\ \pi)$.

Data on Other Intervals

If the given data are evenly spaced on $[-\pi, \pi]$, the formulas for a_j and b_j in terms of t_k remain the same; however, the t_k change. Although the form of the polynomial and the formulas for the coefficients are the same, the values of the coefficients will be different because the t_k are different.

Data on any other interval may be transformed to $[0, 2\pi)$ or $[-\pi, \pi)$ by a linear transformation;

The relationship between the variable s (with s in the interval $[a, b)$) and t (with t in the interval $[0, 2\pi)$) is given by

$$s = t(b - a)/(2\pi - 0) + a = a + t(b - a)/2\pi$$

or

$$t = (s - a)(2\pi - 0)/(b - a) = (s - a)2\pi/(b - a)$$

Example 10.5 Trigonometric Interpolation

We consider the trigonometric polynomial that interpolates the following data (given at points evenly spaced in the interval $[0, 1)$)

$$k = [0 \quad 1 \quad 2 \quad 3 \ ]$$
$$s = [0 \quad 1/4 \quad 1/2 \quad 3/4]$$
$$x = [1 \quad 1 \quad 0 \quad 0 \ ]$$

Transforming to $[0, 2\pi)$ using the transformation $t = 2\pi s$, we have

$$t = [0 \quad \pi/2 \quad \pi \quad 3\pi/2]$$
$$x = [1 \quad 1 \quad 0 \quad 0 \ ]$$

For interpolation, we have $n = 4$, $m = 2$,

$$x(t) = \frac{a_0}{2} + a_1 \cos(t) + \frac{a_2}{2} \cos(2t) + b_1 \sin(t) + b_2 \sin(2t)$$

The coefficients are a

$$a_0 = \frac{1}{2} [x_0 + x_1 + x_2 + x_3] = 1$$

$$a_1 = \frac{1}{2} [x_0 \cos(t_0) + x_1 \cos(t_1) + x_2 \cos(t_2) + x_3 \cos(t_3)]$$
$$= \frac{1}{2} [1 \cos(0) + 1 \cos(\pi/2) + 0 \cos(\pi) + 0 \cos(3\pi/2)] = \frac{1}{2}$$

$$a_2 = \frac{1}{2} [x_0 \cos(2 t_0) + x_1 \cos(2 t_1) + x_2 \cos(2 t_2) + x_3 \cos(2 t_3)]$$
$$= \frac{1}{2} [1 \cos(0) + 1 \cos(\pi) + 0 + 0 \cos(2\pi) + 0 \cos(3\pi)] = 0$$

$$b_1 = \frac{1}{2} [x_0 \sin(t_0) + x_1 \sin(t_1) + x_2 \sin(t_2) + x_3 \sin(t_3)]$$
$$= \frac{1}{2} [1 \sin(0) + 1 \sin(\pi/2) + 0 \sin(\pi) + 0 \sin(3\pi2)] = \frac{1}{2}$$

$$b_2 = \frac{1}{2} [x_0 \sin(2 t_0) + x_1 \sin(2 t_1) + x_2 \sin(2 t_2) + x_3 \sin(2 t_3)]$$
$$= \frac{1}{2} [1 \sin(0) + 1 \sin(\pi) + 0 \sin(2\pi) + 0 \sin(3\pi)] = 0$$

The interpolating polynomial is

$$x(t) = \frac{1}{2} + \frac{1}{2} \cos(t) + \frac{1}{2} \sin(t),$$

or, in terms of the original independent variable

$$x(s) = \frac{1}{2} + \frac{1}{2} \cos(2\pi s) + \frac{1}{2} \sin(2\pi s)$$

Finding the coefficients of a Fourier polynomial leads to the problem of computing, for $j = 0, \ldots, m$,

$$a_j = \frac{2}{n} \sum_{k=0}^{n-1} x_k \cos(j\ t_k), \qquad b_j = \frac{2}{n} \sum_{k=0}^{n-1} x_k \sin(j\ t_k).$$

The a_j and b_j can be combined into a single complex quantity

$$c_j = a_j + i\,b_j = \frac{2}{n} \sum_{k=0}^{n-1} x_k \left[\cos(j\ t_k) + i \sin(j\ t_k)\right], \text{ where } i = \sqrt{-1}.$$

These computations can be carried our more conveniently by working in the complex domain. Using Euler's formula relating the trigonometric and exponential functions for complex variables, we may write

$$c_j = \frac{2}{n} \sum_{k=0}^{n-1} x_k \exp(i\ j\ t_k)].$$

Recalling that the points t_k are evenly spaced on $[0,\ 2\pi)$, we define $\omega = \dfrac{2\pi}{n}$ and write t_k as $k\,\omega$ to obtain

$$c_j = \frac{2}{n} \sum_{k=0}^{n-1} x_k \exp(i\ j\ k\ \omega)].$$

The coefficients of the Fourier polynomial are the scaled real and imaginary parts of the discrete Fourier transform of the data, which we consider in the remainder of this section.

10.2.1   Discrete Fourier Transform

The discrete Fourier transform of a set of n complex data values z_k evenly spaced on $[0,\ 2\pi)$ is the set of complex numbers $(j = 0, \ldots n - 1)$

$$g_j = \sum_{k=0}^{n-1} z_k \exp(i\ j\ k\ \omega)],$$

or a constant multiple of this set of numbers.

This transformation has a wide range of applications beyond just the computation of interpolating coefficients discussed in the previous section. Since $e^{i\theta} = \cos\theta + i \sin\theta$, the periodicity of $\cos\theta$ and $\sin\theta$ cause the complex exponential to be periodic also. Direct computation of the g_j requires $O(n^2)$ operations. However, by exploiting the efficiencies of the fast Fourier transform, this can be reduced to $O(n \log n)$ operations.

10.2.2 Fast Fourier Transform

We begin by considering the FFT when n is a power of 2, i.e., $n = 2^r$; this is the case to which the FFT is most often applied. The basic idea in the FFT is to make use of the periodic nature of the complex exponential function and clever reordering of the computations, in order to reduce the total effort required to find the transform.

We define $w = \exp(i\ \omega)$ (with $\omega = \dfrac{2\pi}{n}$, as before). With this notation, we write

$$g_j = \sum_{k=0}^{n-1} z_k\, w^{jk}, \qquad \text{for } j = 0, \ldots, n-1. \tag{10.4}$$

Note that $w^n = 1$, so that some simplifications can be achieved in some of the equations for the g_j.

The cleverness in the computations results from the fact that the index on the components of the transform and the index on the summation both run from 0 to $n-1$. Each value of j ($0 \le j \le n-1$) can be written in binary form as $j = 2^{r-1}j_r + \ldots + 2^2 j_3 + 2 j_2 + j_1$, where each of the numbers $j_1, j_2, \ldots, j_r$ is either 0 or 1.

For example, if $n = 4$, we express the numbers $0, 1, \ldots, 3$ as $j = 2j_2 + j_1$:

j	j_2	j_1
0	0	0
1	0	1
2	1	0
3	1	1

We also write the numbers $k = 0, 1, \ldots, 3$ in binary form, but as $k = 2k_1 + k_2$. If we keep the values of k_1 and k_2 in the same order as for j_1 and j_2, the values of k appear in a scrambled form, which is useful for the FFT. Combining the representations of j and k in a single table, clarifies the relationship between the binary coefficients. This reordering of the k values relative to the j values is called *bit reversal*.

Binary Coefficients in Natural and Scrambled Order

j	j_2	j_1	k_2	k_1	k
0	0	0	0	0	0
1	0	1	0	1	2
2	1	0	1	0	1
3	1	1	1	1	3

There are several equivalent methods of presenting the FFT method. We first consider the matrix form, which we illustrate for $n = 4$. The resulting computations are shown schematically. Finally, the FFT method for $n = 4$ is developed from a more algebraic point of view, which allows generalization to the case when n has prime factors other than 2.

The following algorithm finds the FFT for 4 data points, $\mathbf{z} = [z_0, z_1, z_2, z_3]$, given at $\mathbf{t} = \left[0, \dfrac{\pi}{2}, \pi, \dfrac{3\pi}{2} \right]$ and then forms the trigonometric interpolating polynomial.

FFT with $n = 4$ ══

Input
    $\mathbf{z} = [z_0, z_1, z_2, z_3]$
Begin computation
For h = 0 to 3
    $w(h) = \exp(i\,\pi\,h/2)$
End

For $k_2 = 0$ to 1   *perform bit reversal*
    For $k_1 = 0$ to 1
        $zz(2\,k_2 + k_1) = z(2\,k_1 + k_2)$
    End
End

For $k_2 = 0$ to 1
    For $j_1 = 0$ to 1
        $s(2\,k_2 + j_1) = zz(2\,k_2)\,w(0) + zz(2\,k_2 + 1)\,w(2\,j_1)$
    End
End

For $j_2 = 0$ to 1
    For $j_1 = 0$ to 1
        $g(2\,j_2 + j_1) = s(j_1)\,w(0) + s(2 + j_1)\,w(j_1 + 2\,j_2)$
    End
End

Form trigonometric polynomial from transform of z

$a_0 = 2\,\mathrm{Re}(g_0)/4$
$a_1 = 2\,\mathrm{Re}(g_1)/4$
$a_2 = 2\,\mathrm{Rc}(g_2)/4$
$b_1 = 2\,\mathrm{Im}(g_1)/4$
$y = \dfrac{a_0}{2} + a_1 \cos(t) + \dfrac{a_2}{2} \cos(2t) + b_1 \sin(t)$

Matrix Form of FFT

We begin by writing out the linear system of equations for the Fourier transform components, for the case $n = 4$:

$$w^0 z_0 + w^0 z_1 + w^0 z_2 + w^0 z_3 = g_0,$$

$$w^0 z_0 + w^1 z_1 + w^2 z_2 + w^3 z_3 = g_1,$$

$$w^0 z_0 + w^2 z_1 + w^4 z_2 + w^6 z_3 = g_2,$$

$$w^0 z_0 + w^3 z_1 + w^6 z_2 + w^9 z_3 = g_3.$$

Making use of the fact that $w^4 = w^0 = 1$ to simplify the equations and interchanging the order of the second and third equations (which corresponds to the previous interchange in the order of the j and k indices) gives the system

$$1 z_0 + 1 z_1 + 1 z_2 + 1 z_3 = g_0,$$

$$1 z_0 + w^2 z_1 + 1 z_2 + w^2 z_3 = g_2,$$

$$1 z_0 + w_1 z_1 + w^2 z_2 + w^3 z_3 = g_1,$$

$$1 z_0 + w^3 z_1 + w^2 z_2 + w^1 z_3 = g_3.$$

Writing these equations in matrix form, we have

$$
\begin{bmatrix}
1 & 1 & 1 & 1 \\
1 & w^2 & 1 & w^2 \\
1 & w & w^2 & w^3 \\
1 & w^3 & w^2 & w
\end{bmatrix}
\begin{bmatrix}
z_0 \\
z_1 \\
z_2 \\
z_3
\end{bmatrix}
=
\begin{bmatrix}
g_0 \\
g_2 \\
g_1 \\
g_3
\end{bmatrix}
\tag{10.5}
$$

We now factor the coefficient matrix:

$$
\begin{bmatrix}
1 & 1 & 0 & 0 \\
1 & w^2 & 0 & 0 \\
0 & 0 & 1 & w \\
0 & 0 & 1 & w^3
\end{bmatrix}
\begin{bmatrix}
1 & 0 & 1 & 0 \\
0 & 1 & 0 & 1 \\
1 & 0 & w^2 & 0 \\
0 & 1 & 0 & w^2
\end{bmatrix}
=
\begin{bmatrix}
1 & 1 & 1 & 1 \\
1 & w^2 & 1 & w^2 \\
1 & w & w^2 & w^3 \\
1 & w^3 & w^2 & w
\end{bmatrix}.
$$

Next, we carry out the computation of the g's in two steps. Substituting the factored form of the coefficient matrix into eq. (10.5), we obtain

$$\begin{bmatrix} 1 & 1 & 0 & 0 \\ 1 & w^2 & 0 & 0 \\ 0 & 0 & 1 & w \\ 0 & 0 & 1 & w^3 \end{bmatrix} \begin{bmatrix} 1 & 0 & 1 & 0 \\ 0 & 1 & 0 & 1 \\ 1 & 0 & w^2 & 0 \\ 0 & 1 & 0 & w^2 \end{bmatrix} \begin{bmatrix} z_0 \\ z_1 \\ z_2 \\ z_3 \end{bmatrix} = \begin{bmatrix} g_0 \\ g_2 \\ g_1 \\ g_3 \end{bmatrix}. \tag{10.6}$$

First we find the product

$$\begin{bmatrix} 1 & 0 & 1 & 0 \\ 0 & 1 & 0 & 1 \\ 1 & 0 & w^2 & 0 \\ 0 & 1 & 0 & w^2 \end{bmatrix} \begin{bmatrix} z_0 \\ z_1 \\ z_2 \\ z_3 \end{bmatrix} = \begin{bmatrix} z_0 + z_2 \\ z_1 + z_3 \\ z_0 + w^2 z_2 \\ z_1 + w^2 z_3 \end{bmatrix} = \begin{bmatrix} s_0 \\ s_1 \\ s_2 \\ s_3 \end{bmatrix}.$$

Then we form the second product

$$\begin{bmatrix} 1 & 1 & 0 & 0 \\ 1 & w^2 & 0 & 0 \\ 0 & 0 & 1 & w \\ 0 & 0 & 1 & w^3 \end{bmatrix} \begin{bmatrix} s_0 \\ s_1 \\ s_2 \\ s_3 \end{bmatrix} = \begin{bmatrix} s_0 + s_1 \\ s_0 + w^2 s_1 \\ s_2 + w s_3 \\ s_2 + w^3 s_3 \end{bmatrix} = \begin{bmatrix} g_0 \\ g_2 \\ g_1 \\ g_3 \end{bmatrix}.$$

The efficiencies in this computation result from the structure of the matrices that are employed in the two stages. The method is implemented not by using general matrix multiplication, but by performing only the necessary mutiplications and additions.

The computations are shown schematically in Figure 10.8. Pathways with powers of w on them indicate that the quantity on the left is multiplied by that amount.

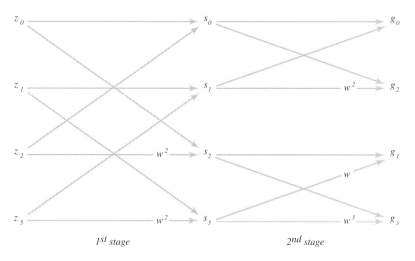

FIGURE 10.8 Two-stage computational procedure.

Algebraic Form of FFT

We now consider an alternative approach to the FFT for $n = 2^r$. As before, each value of j ($0 \le j \le n - 1$) is written in binary form, and each value of k is written in binary form with the bits reversed. For example, if $n = 4$, the binary coefficients are given in the table on p. 384.

To calculate the discrete Fourier transform of the data z_k, i.e.,

$$g_j = \sum_{k=0}^{3} z_k \exp(i \ j \ k \ \omega)] \qquad \text{for } j = 0, \ldots 3;$$

we write $w = \exp(i \ \omega) = \exp\left(i \dfrac{\pi}{2}\right)$. Then the sum is given (as in eq. 10.4) by

$$g_j = \sum_{k=0}^{3} z_k \, w^{j \, k}.$$

Note that $w^4 = 1$, and therefore, $w^{4a} = 1$ for any integer a. Using the binary factorizations of j and k, we have

$$g_j = g(j_1 + 2j_2) = \sum_{k=0}^{3} z(k_2 + 2k_1) \, w^{(j_1 + 2 j_2)(k_2 + 2 k_1)}$$

$$= \sum_{k=0}^{3} z(k_2 + 2 \, k_1) \, w^{(j_1 + 2 j_2) \, k_2} \, w^{(j_1 + 2 j_2) \, k_1}$$

$$= \sum_{k_2=0}^{1} \sum_{k_1=0}^{1} z(k_2 + 2k_1) \, w^{(j_1 + 2 j_2) \, 2 \, k_1} \, w^{(j_1 + 2 j_2) \, k_2}$$

$$= \sum_{k_2=0}^{1} \left[\sum_{k_1=0}^{1} z(k_2 + 2k_1) w^{(j_1)(2)(k_1)} \right] w^{(j_1 + 2 j_2) \, k_2}.$$

Since $w = \exp\left(i \dfrac{2\pi}{4}\right) = \exp\left(i \dfrac{\pi}{2}\right) = \cos \dfrac{\pi}{2} + i \sin \dfrac{\pi}{2}$, we have

$$w^0 = 1; \quad w = 0 + i(1/2); \quad w^2 = -1; \quad w^3 = 0 - i(1/2).$$

We can use these results to simplify our final calculations, but first we observe that the way in which the original summation over all data points has been decomposed into two nested summations forms the basis for the FFT.

We first compute the inner summation, $\left[\sum_{k_1=0}^{1} z(k_2 + 2k_1)\, w^{(j_1)(2)(k_1)} \right]$, for each value of j, but we do so by using each possible value of j_1 (0 or 1) and each possible value of j_2 (0 or 1).

Writing the digits so that j is in natural order, we have $k = k_2 + 2k_1$ and $j = j_1 + 2j_2$; the first stage produces the values of $s(j_1 + 2\,k_2)$:

$$s(j_1 + 2\,k_2) = \sum_{k_1=0}^{1} z(k_2 + 2k_1)\, w^{(j_1)(2)(k_1)}$$

$$= z(k_2 + 0)w^{(j_1)(2)(0)} + z(k_2 + 2)w^{(j_1)(2)(1)}.$$

These values are summarized in the following table:

$z(j_2 + 2k_1)$	k_1	k_2	j_1	j_2	$s(j_1 + 2\,k_2)$
z_0	0	0	0	0	$z_0 w^{(0)(2)(0)} + z_2 w^{(0)(2)(1)} = s_0$
z_3	1	0	1	0	$z_0 w^{(1)(2)(0)} + z_2 w^{(1)(2)(1)} = s_1$
z_1	0	1	0	1	$z_1 w^{(0)(2)(0)} + z_3 w^{(0)(2)(1)} = s_2$
z_4	1	1	1	1	$z_1 w^{(1)(2)(0)} + z_3 w^{(1)(2)(1)} = s_3$

The results of this first summation are expressed in terms of the digits j_1 and k_2, since the summation over the possible values of k_1 has been performed, but the second summation, over k_2, remains to be done.

We now compute the outer summation,

$$g(j_1 + 2j_2) = \sum_{k_2=0}^{1} s(j_1 + 2\,k_2)\, w^{(j_1 + 2\,j_2)\,k_2}$$

$$= s(j_1 + 2(0))w^{(j_1 + 2\,j_2)(0)} + s(j_1 + 2(1))w^{(j_1 + 2\,j_2)(1)},$$

and its corresponding table of values:

s	k_1	k_2	j_1	j_2	g
s_0	0	0	0	0	$s_0 w^{(0+2(0))0} + s_2\, w^{(0+2(0))1} = s_0\, w^0 + s_2\, w^0$
s_1	1	0	1	0	$s_1 w^{(1+2(0))0} + s_3\, w^{(1+2(0))1} = s_1\, w^0 + s_3\, w^1$
s_2	0	1	0	1	$s_0 w^{(0+2(1))0} + s_2\, w^{(0+2(1))1} = s_0\, w^0 + s_2\, w^2$
s_3	1	1	1	1	$s_1 w^{(1+2(1))0} + s_3\, w^{(1+2(1))1} = s_1\, w^0 + s_3\, w^3$

Although the FFT is most often applied for $n = 2^r$, the general FFT does not require the factorization of n to have any specific form. We designate the prime factorization of n as $n = r_1 r_2 \ldots r_t$, where we assume that $r_1 \leq r_2 \leq \ldots \leq r_t$. In a generalization of the binary representation of a number, each value of j ($0 \leq j \leq n - 1$) can be written in terms of the prime factors of n as $j = r_1 \ldots r_{t-1} j_t + \ldots + r_1 r_2 j_3 + r_1 j_2 + j_1$. The possible values for j_1 are $0, 1, \ldots, r_1 - 1$; for j_2 are $0, 1, \ldots, r_2 - 1$; and for j_t are $0, 1, \ldots, r_t - 1$.

We also write the numbers $k = 0, 1, \ldots n - 1$ in terms of the factors of n, but as $k = r_t \ldots r_2 k_1 + \ldots + r_t r_{t-1} k_{t-2} + r_t k_{t-1} + k_t$. The coefficient k_s can take on values $0, 1, \ldots, r_s - 1$.

For example, if $n = 6$ we have $r_1 = 2$ and $r_2 = 3$. We express the numbers $0, 1, \ldots, 5$ as $j = r_1 j_2 + j_1 = 2 j_2 + j_1$; j_1 is 0 or 1, and j_2 is 0, 1, or 2. The following table gives j in terms of j_2 and j_1:

j	j_2	j_1
0	0	0
1	0	1
2	1	0
3	1	1
4	2	0
5	2	1

For this example, $k = r_2 k_1 + k_2 = 3 k_1 + k_2$; k_1 is 0 or 1, k_2 is 0, 1, or 2, and the table is as follows:

k	k_1	k_2
0	0	0
1	0	1
2	0	2
3	1	0
4	1	1
5	1	2

Note that the possible values for k_1 and j_1 are the same, for k_2 and j_2 are the same, and so on. However, k_2 is the *lowest* order digit in the representation of k, whereas j_2 is the *highest* order digit in the representation of j. In what follows, we perform the operations in each computation by letting j_1 and j_2 run through all possible values. We also let k_1 and k_2 run through their range of values, in the same order as j_1 and j_2; this generates all possible values of k also, but in a scrambled order, as shown in the following table.

$j = 2 j_2 + j_1$	j_2	j_1	k_1	k_2	$k = 3 k_1 + k_2$
0	0	0	0	0	0
1	0	1	1	0	3
2	1	0	0	1	1
3	1	1	1	1	4
4	2	0	0	2	2
5	2	1	1	2	5

Now let us consider the calculation of the discrete Fourier transform of the data z_k, where $w = \exp(i\ \omega) = \exp\left(i\ \dfrac{2\pi}{n}\right)$, in which $n = r_1\, r_2$. We have

$$g_j = \sum_{k=0}^{n-1} z_k \exp(i\ j\ k\omega) = \sum_{k=0}^{n-1} z_k\, w^{jk} \qquad \text{for } j = 0, \ldots, n - 1.$$

Since $w^n = 1$, any term of the form $w^{r_1\, r_2\, a}$ is equal to unity, and can be dropped from the calculations in the formulas that follow. Using the preceding factorization of j and k, we have

$$g_j = g(r_1\ j_2 + j_1) = \sum_{k=0}^{n-1} z(r_2\, k_1 + k_2)\, w^{(j_1 + r_1 j_2)(k_2 + r_2 k_1)}$$

$$= \sum_{k=0}^{n-1} z(r_2\, k_1 + k_2)\, w^{(j_1 + r_1 j_2)\, k_2}\, w^{(j_1 + r_1 j_2)\, r_2 k_1}$$

$$= \sum_{k_2=0}^{r_2-1} \sum_{k_1=0}^{r_1-1} z(r_2\, k_1 + k_2)\, w^{(j_1 + r_1 j_2)\, r_2 k_1}\, w^{(j_1 + r_1 j_2)\, k_2}$$

$$= \sum_{k_2=0}^{r_2-1} \left[\sum_{k_1=0}^{r_1-1} z(r_2\, k_1 + k_2)\, w^{j_1 r_2 k_1} \right] w^{(j_1 + r_1 j_2)\, k_2}$$

The result of the first stage is

$$s(2k_2 + j_1) = \sum_{k_1=0}^{1} z(3k_1 + k_2)\, w^{3\, j_1 k_1} = z(3(0) + k_2)\, w^{3\, j_1(0)} + z(3(1) + k_2) w^{3\, j_1\,(1)}$$

so that we have the following table:

$z(k_2 + 3k_1)$	k_1	k_2	j_1	j_2	$s(2k_2 + j_1)$
z_0	0	0	0	0	$z_0\, w^{(0)(3)(0)} + z_3\, w^{(0)(3)(1)} = s_0$
z_3	1	0	1	0	$z_0\, w^{(1)(3)(0)} + z_3\, w^{(1)(3)(1)} = s_1$
z_1	0	1	0	1	$z_1\, w^{(0)(3)(0)} + z_4\, w^{(0)(3)(1)} = s_2$
z_4	1	1	1	1	$z_1\, w^{(1)(3)(0)} + z_4\, w^{(1)(3)(1)} = s_3$
z_2	0	2	0	2	$z_2\, w^{(0)(3)(0)} + z_5\, w^{(0)(3)(1)} = s_4$
z_5	1	2	1	2	$z_2\, w^{(1)(3)(0)} + z_5\, w^{(1)(3)(1)} = s_5$

We next compute the outer summation,

$$g(2j_2 + j_1) = \sum_{k_2=0}^{3-1} s(2k_2 + j_1)\, w^{(j_1 + 2j_2)k_2}$$

$$= s(2(0) + j_1)w^{(j_1 + 2j_2)0} + s(2(1) + j_1)w^{(j_1 + 2j_2)1} + s(2(2) + j_1)w^{(j_1 + 2j_2)2},$$

yielding the following table:

j	k_1	k_2	j_1	j_2	s	g
0	0	0	0	0	s_0	$s_0 w^{(0+2(0))0} + s_2\, w^{(0+2(0))1} + s_4\, w^{(0+2(0))2}$
1	1	0	1	0	s_3	$s_1 w^{(1+2(0))0} + s_3\, w^{(1+2(0))1} + s_5\, w^{(1+2(0))2}$
2	0	1	0	1	s_1	$s_0 w^{(0+2(1))0} + s_2\, w^{(0+2(1))1} + s_4\, w^{(0+2(1))2}$
3	1	1	1	1	s_4	$s_1 w^{(1+2(1))0} + s_3\, w^{(1+2(1))1} + s_5\, w^{(1+2(1))2}$
4	0	2	0	2	s_2	$s_0 w^{(0+2(2))0} + s_2\, w^{(0+2(2))1} + s_4\, w^{(0+2(2))2}$
5	1	2	1	2	s_5	$s_1 w^{(1+2(2))0} + s_3\, w^{(1+2(2))1} + s_5\, w^{(1+2(2))2}$

Simplifying, we obtain the final table:

j	k_1	k_2	j_1	j_2	s	g
0	0	0	0	0	s_0	$s_0\, w^0 + s_2\, w^0 + s_4\, w^0$
1	1	0	1	0	s_3	$s_1\, w^0 + s_3\, w^1 + s_5\, w^2$
2	0	1	0	1	s_1	$s_0\, w^0 + s_2\, w^2 + s_4\, w^4$
3	1	1	1	1	s_4	$s_1\, w^0 + s_3\, w^3 + s_5\, w^6$
4	0	2	0	2	s_2	$s_0\, w^0 + s_2\, w^4 + s_4\, w^8$
5	1	2	1	2	s_5	$s_1\, w^0 + s_3\, w^5 + s_5\, w^{10}$

Since

$$w = \exp\left(1\frac{2\pi}{n}\right) = \exp\left(1\frac{\pi}{3}\right),$$

we have

$$w^0 = 1 = w^6 = \exp\left(i\frac{6\pi}{3}\right) = 1$$

$$w = \exp\left(i\frac{\pi}{3}\right) = \cos\frac{2\pi}{3} + i\sin\frac{\pi}{3} = 1/2 + i\sqrt{3}/2$$

$$w^2 = \exp\left(i\frac{2\pi}{3}\right) = \cos\frac{2\pi}{3} + i\sin\frac{2\pi}{3} = -1/2 + i\sqrt{3}/2 = w^8$$

$$w^3 = \exp(i\pi) = -1$$

$$w^4 = \exp\left(i\frac{4\pi}{3}\right) = \cos\frac{4\pi}{3} + i\sin\frac{4\pi}{3} = -1/2 - i\sqrt{3}/2 = w^{10}$$

$$w^5 = \exp\left(i\frac{5\pi}{3}\right) = \cos\frac{5\pi}{3} + i\sin\frac{5\pi}{3} = 1/2 - i\sqrt{3}/2.$$

Example 10.6 FFT for Six Data Points

We illustrate the previous computations by finding the interpolation function for the data $\mathbf{z} = \begin{bmatrix} 0 & 1 & 2 & 3 & 2 & 1 \end{bmatrix}$. With $n = 6$, we have $k = 3k_1 + k_2$ and $j = 3j_2 + j_1$. The data are listed in scrambled order so that the final results (the g's) are in natural order.

First, we compute the inner sum for each pair of values of j_1 and k_2:

$$s(2k_2 + j_1) = \sum_{k_1=0}^{2-1} z(3k_1 + k_2) \, w^{j_1 \, (3) \, k_1}$$

$$= z(0 + k_2) \, w^{j_1 \, (3)(0)} + z(3 + k_2) w^{j_1 \, (3)(1)}.$$

This yields the following table:

z	k	j	k_1	k_2	j_1	j_2	$s(2k_2 + j_1)$
0	0	0	0	0	0	0	$0\,w^0 + 3\,w^0 = 3 = s_0$
3	3	1	1	0	1	0	$0\,w^0 + 3\,w^3 = -3 = s_1$
1	1	2	0	1	0	1	$1\,w^0 + 2\,w^0 = 3 = s_2$
2	4	3	1	1	1	1	$1\,w^0 + 2\,w^3 = -1 = s_3$
2	2	4	0	2	0	2	$2\,w^0 + 1\,w^0 = 3 = s_4$
1	5	5	1	2	1	2	$2\,w^0 + 1\,w^3 = 1 = s_5$

Next, we compute the outer sum

$$g_j = \sum_{k_2=0}^{3-1} s(2k_2 + j_1) \, w^{(j_1 + 2j_2)(k_2)}$$

$$= s(0 + j_1)(w^{(j_1 + 2j_2)(0)} + s(2 + j_1) \, w^{(j_1 + 2j_2)(1)} + s(4 + j_1) \, w^{(j_1 + 2j_2)(2)}.$$

The associated table is as follows:

j	k_1	k_2	j_1	j_2	$g(2j_2 + j_1)$	
0	0	0	0	0	$s_0\,w^0 + s_2\,w^0 + s_4\,w^0$	$g_0 = 9$
1	1	0	1	0	$s_1\,w^0 + s_3\,w^1 + s_5\,w^2$	$g_1 = -4$
2	0	1	0	1	$s_0\,w^0 + s_2\,w^2 + s_4\,w^4$	$g_2 = 0$
3	1	1	1	1	$s_1\,w^0 + s_3\,w^3 + s_5\,w^6$	$g_3 = -1$
4	0	2	0	2	$s_0\,w^0 + s_2\,w^4 + s_4\,w^8$	$g_4 = 0$
5	1	2	1	2	$s_1\,w^0 + s_3\,w^5 + s_5\,w^{10}$	$g_5 = -4$

To use these results to find the interpolating trigonometric polynomial, we note that, in general, $a = 2\text{Re}(g)/n$, $b = 2\text{Im}(g)/n$, and the function (for $n = 6$, $m = 3$) is

$$x = \frac{a_0}{2} + a_1 \cos(t) + a_2 \cos(2t) + \frac{a_3}{2} \cos(3t) + b_1 \sin(t) + b_2 \sin(2t) + b_3 \sin(3t)$$

In this example, all g's are real, so all b's are zero. We have

$$a_0 = g_0/3 = 3; \quad a_1 = g_1/3 = -4/3; \quad a_2 = g_2/3 = 0; \quad a_3 = g_3/3 = -1/3$$

so we have

$$x = \frac{3}{2} - \frac{4}{3} \cos(t) - \frac{1}{6} \cos(3t)$$

The following algorithm finds the FFT for $\mathbf{z} = [z_1, z_2, z_3, \ldots z_n]$ where n has 2 prime factors.

The data values $\mathbf{z}$ are given at $\mathbf{t} = \left[0, \dfrac{2\pi}{n}, \ldots \dfrac{2(n-1)\pi}{n} \right]$.

FFT with $n = r\,s$

Input
$z = [z_0, z_1, z_2, z_3, \ldots z_{n-1}]$,
n   *where $n = r\,s$, r and s prime, $r \leq s$.*
r
s

Begin computation
For h = 0 to 2n
    $w(h) = \exp(2\pi\, i\, h/n)$
End

For $k_2 = 0$ to s − 1   *perform bit reversal*
    For $k_1 = 0$ to r − 1
        $zz(r\, k_2 + k_1) = z(s\, k_1 + k_2)$
    End
End

For $k_2 = 0$ to s − 1
    For $j_1 = 0$ to r − 1
        $ss(r\, k_2 + j_1) = \sum_{k_1=0}^{r-1} zz(r\, k_2 + k_1)\, w(s\, j_1\, k_1)$
    End
End

For $j_2 = 0$ to s − 1
    For $j_1 = 0$ to r − 1
        $g(r\, j_2 + j_1) = \sum_{k_2=0}^{s-1} ss(r\, k_2 + j_1)\, w(k_2(j_1 + r\, j_2))$
    End
End

Example 10.7 FFT for Step Function With 6 Data Points

We illustrate the use of the algorithm for the FFT with $n = (2)(3)$ by finding the interpolating trigonometric polynomial for the data

$$\mathbf{z} = [1 \quad 1 \quad 1 \quad 0 \quad 0 \quad 0]$$

For this example, we have $r = 2$, $s = 3$, $n = 6$. Although it is not necessary to display the intermediate results of the computations, we list them here for the sake of completeness. Subsequent computations use the powers of $\exp(2 \pi i / n)$ given as $w(h)$, for $h = 0, \ldots 11$

$w =$

$$
\begin{aligned}
[\quad & 1.0000 & 0.5000 + 0.8660i & \quad -0.5000 + 0.8660i & \quad -1.0000 + 0.0000i \\
& -0.5000 - 0.8660i & 0.5000 - 0.8660i & \quad 1.0000 - 0.0000i & \quad 0.5000 + 0.8660i \\
& -0.5000 + 0.8660i & -1.0000 + 0.0000i & \quad -0.5000 - 0.8660i & \quad 0.5000 - 0.8660i]
\end{aligned}
$$

The data after bit reversal are

$$zz = [1 \quad 0 \quad 1 \quad 0 \quad 1 \quad 0]$$

The first stage of the computations gives

$$ss = [1 \quad 1 \quad 1 \quad 1 \quad 1 \quad 1]$$

Finally, the Fourier transform is given by $g(0), \ldots g(5)$

$$
\begin{aligned}
g = [\quad & 3.0000 & 1.0000 + 1.7321i & \quad -0.0000 + 0.0000i \\
& 1.0000 - 0.0000i & 0.0000 + 0.0000i & \quad 1.0000 - 1.7321i]
\end{aligned}
$$

The coefficients of the trigonometric polynomial are

$$
\begin{aligned}
a(0) &= 2 \, \mathrm{Re}(g(0))/n = 1 \\
a(1) &= 2 \, \mathrm{Re}(g(1))/n = 1/3 \\
a(2) &= 2 \, \mathrm{Re}(g(2))/n = 0 \\
a(3) &= 2 \, \mathrm{Re}(g(3))/n = 1/3 \\
\\
b(1) &= 2 \, \mathrm{Im}(g(1))/n = 2 \, (1.7321)/6 = 0.57735 \\
b(2) &= 2 \, \mathrm{Im}(g(2))/n = 2 \, (0) = 0
\end{aligned}
$$

$$
\begin{aligned}
f(x) &= 0.5 \, a(0) + a(1) \cos(x) + b(1) \sin(x) + a(2) \cos(2 x) \\
&\quad + b(2) \sin(2 x) + 0.5 \, a(3) \cos(3 x) \\
&= 0.5 \quad + 0.3333 \cos(x) + 0.57735 \sin(x) + \quad + 0.16667 \cos(3 x)
\end{aligned}
$$

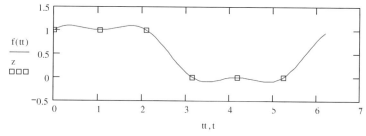

FIGURE 10.9 Data and interpolating trigonometric polynomial.

There are a number of different forms of the Fourier transform of a set of data, depending on the convention adopted concerning the sign of the exponent in the transform, and the normalization of the transformed data.

10.4.1 Definitions

We begin this section by summarizing the forms used in this chapter, and the forms used by the built-in functions in MATLAB, Mathcad, and *Mathematica*. Recall from section 10.2.1 that we have used the following definition of the transform of the data $z(k)$:

$$g_j = \sum_{k=0}^{n-1} z_k \exp(i \; j \; k \; \omega), \qquad \text{for } j = 0, \ldots, n-1.$$

where $\omega = 2\pi/n$. Using this form, the coefficients of the Fourier polynomials are found from the real and imaginary parts of $c_j = (2/n) \, g_j$. The trigonometric interpolation polynomial (for n even, $m = n/2$) is

$$f(x) = 0.5\text{Re}(c_0) + \sum_{j=1}^{m-1} [\text{Re}(c_j) \cos(j\,x) + \text{Im}(c_j) \sin(j\,x)]$$
$$+ 0.5\,\text{Re}(c_m) \cos(m\,x)$$

MATLAB

The MATLAB function `fft` uses the following definition of the discrete Fourier transform

$$g_j = \sum_{k=0}^{n-1} x_k \exp(-i \; j \; k \; \omega), \qquad j = 0, \ldots, n-1.$$

Using this form, the coefficients of the Fourier polynomials are found from the real and imaginary parts of $c_j = (2/n) \, g_j$, but with j replaced by $(-j)$ in the construction of the trigonometric polynomial (however, $\cos(j\,x) = \cos(-j\,x)$). The trigonometric interpolation polynomial (for n even, $m = n/2$) is

$$f(x) = 0.5\,\text{Re}(c_0) + \sum_{j=1}^{m-1} [\text{Re}(c_j) \cos(j\,x) + \text{Im}(c_j) \sin(-j\,x)]$$
$$+ 0.5\,\text{Re}(c_m) \cos(m\,x)$$

Mathematica

The *Mathematica* function `Fourier` uses the following definition of the discrete Fourier transform

$$g_j = 1/\sqrt{n} \sum_{k=0}^{n-1} z_k \exp(i \; j \; k \; \omega), \qquad \text{for } j = 0, \ldots, n-1.$$

Using this form, the coefficients of the Fourier polynomials are found from the real and imaginary parts of $c_j = 2/\sqrt{n} \, g_j$ The trigonometric interpolation polynomial (for n even, $m = n/2$) is the same as that given above.

Mathcad

Mathcad has several functions for performing Fast Fourier Transforms and the corresponding Inverse Fast Fourier Transform. The functions fft(**v**) and FFT(**v**) are the same except for the convention used for the initial factor of the transform, and whether the results of the transform are conjugated.

The function fft(**v**) returns the vector **g**

$$g_j = 1/\sqrt{n} \sum_{k=0}^{n-1} z_k \exp(i\ j\ k\ \omega), \qquad \text{for } j = 0, \ldots, n-1.$$

This is the same as the FFT formula used in *Mathematica*.

The function FFT(**v**) differs from fft(**v**) in the normalization of the transform, and the choice of sign on the exponent. FFT(**v**) uses a negative exponent in going from the time domain to the frequency domain (and a positive exponent for the inverse transform).

The function FFT(**v**) returns the vector **g**

$$g_j = (1/n) \sum_{k=0}^{n-1} x_k \exp(-i\ j\ k\ \omega), \qquad j = 0, \ldots, n-1.$$

This is the same as the form used by the MATLAB function fft except for the scaling by the factor of $(1/n)$. Using this form, the coefficients of the Fourier polynomials are found from the real and imaginary parts of $c_j - 2\ g_j$, but with j replaced by $(-j)$ in the construction of the trigonometric polynomial (however, $\cos(j\ x) = \cos(-j\ x)$). The trigonometric interpolation polynomial (for n even, $m = n/2$) is

$$f(x) = 0.5\ \mathrm{Re}(c_0) + \sum_{j=1}^{m-1} [\mathrm{Re}(c_j)\cos(j\ x) + \mathrm{Im}(c_j)\sin(-j\ x)]$$

$$+ 0.5\ \mathrm{Re}(c_m)\cos(m\ x)$$

Power Spectrum

The power spectrum of a set of data is obtained from the absolute value of z (the Fourier transform of the data). The absolute value of a complex number z is the real number defined as the product of z and its complex conjugate. The power spectrum of a waveform is a common method of describing a musical sound. The power spectrum of the data describing a geometric figure (such as those given in Example 10-B) remains invariant when the figure is rotated. As with the reconstruction of the waveform (or the geometric figure) itself, only the first $n/2$ terms are relevant. Computing the power spectrum from the absolute value of z may involve a scale factor, depending on the choice of normalization used in the computation of the Fourier transform.

10.4.2 MATLAB's Functions

MATLAB has built-in functions for computing both continuous and discrete Fourier transforms. We limit our description to the use of the function `fft`, which finds the discrete Fourier transform of a vector **x**. If the length (number of components) of **x** is a power of two, a fast radix-2 FFT algorithm is used. If the length of **x** is not a power of two, a slower, non-power-of-two algorithm is employed.

Example 10.8 Waveform of a Clarinet

We sample the waveform of a clarinet over one period, at 16 evenly spaced points (from 0 to $2\pi - \pi/8$), and use the data together with the MATLAB function `fft` to find the interpolation function as shown in Figure 10.10.

    We apply the function `fft` to the data representing the amplitude of the wave; i.e., $yy =$

```
[ 3.304   2.5535  −0.22396   0.56711   0.067979   0.69711  −0.14572   0.70309...
 −1.635  −1.1464  −0.55064  −0.70925  −0.18781   −0.55497  −0.62887  −2.1101]
```

and obtain the transformed data $z =$

```
[−1.1102e-15         5.6569 − 5.6569i   1.7889 − 1.7889i   5.3666 − 5.3666i ...
    3.0984 − 3.0984i  4.7329 − 4.7329i   1.7889 − 1.7889i   4       − 4i      ...
    1.6653e-14        4      + 4i        1.7889 + 1.7889i   4.7329 + 4.7329i ...
    3.0984 + 3.0984i  5.3666 + 5.3666i   1.7889 + 1.7889i   5.6569 + 5.6569i]
```

The power spectrum is `2*z*conj(z)/n` $=$

```
[1.3878e-16   1          0.31623   0.94868...
 0.54772      0.83666    0.31623   0.70711...
 2.0817e-15   0.70711    0.31623   0.83666...
 0.54772      0.94868    0.31623   1          ]
```

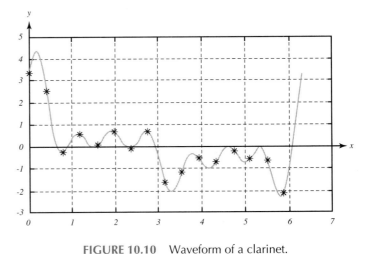

FIGURE 10.10 Waveform of a clarinet.

10.4.1 Mathcad's Functions

Mathcad has several functions for performing Fast Fourier Transforms and the corresponding Inverse Fast Fourier Transform. The appropriate form of FFT depends on whether or not the number of data points is a power of 2, whether the data is real or complex valued, and on the desired scaling of the transform.

Radix-2 FFT Functions

The functions $fft(\mathbf{v})$ and $FFT(\mathbf{v})$ return the fast discrete Fourier transform of real data. The input vector has 2^n elements, representing measurements at equally spaced points in the time domain. The function returns a vector with $2^{n-1} + 1$ elements, giving the Fourier transform of the input data. The functions $fft(\mathbf{v})$ and $FFT(\mathbf{v})$ are the same except for the convention used for the initial factor of the transform, and whether the results of the transform are conjugated.

We illustrate the use of fft for a two-dimensional interpolation problem in the next example. FFT are useful in pattern recognition because the spectral radius of the transform $\mathbf{z}$ (the spectral radius is a scaled form of $\mathbf{z}^*\mathrm{conj}(\mathbf{z})$) remains the same when a figure is rotated. Note that in using the function fft to construct an interpolating polynomial, the result must be scaled by $2/\sqrt{n}$ before forming the coefficients of the polynomial, to compensate for the difference in the normalizations used in section 10.2 and in fft.

The function $FFT(\mathbf{v})$ differs from $fft(\mathbf{v})$ in the normalization of the transform, and the choice of sign on the exponent. $FFT(\mathbf{v})$ uses a negative exponent in going from the time domain to the frequency domain (and a positive exponent for the inverse transform).

The formulas for these functions are based on Bracewell (1986). The functions $fft(\mathbf{v})$ and $FFT(\mathbf{v})$ are based on the Cooley-Tukey algorithm, in which the data is stored in bit-reversed order before the transform is computed.

If the sampling frequency is f_s, the frequency corresponding to c_k is $f_k = \dfrac{k}{m} f_s$. For further discussion of issues of sampling frequency, see a text on digital signal processing.

General FFT Functions

The FFT functions $cfft(A)$ and $CFFT(A)$, and the corresponding inverse FFT functions, $icfft(B)$ and $ICFFT(B)$, are more general than the functions $fft(\mathbf{v})$, $FFT(\mathbf{v})$, $ifft(\mathbf{v})$, and $IFFT(\mathbf{v})$. In particular, the functions $cfft(A)$ and $CFFT(A)$ do not require that the data to be transformed are real, and they do not require that the number of data points is a power of 2. These methods work more efficiently when the number of data points can be factored into many small factors. These functions are based on Singleton (1986). The normalization and sign of exponent conventions for $cfft(A)$ are the same as for $fft(\mathbf{v})$. The conventions for $CFFT(A)$ are the same as for $FFT(\mathbf{v})$.

Example 10.9 Rotation-Invariant Figures

We conclude our investigation of FFT by illustrating its use in pattern recognition, where the figures we wish to identify may appear in different orientations. Using the data from Example 10-B, we can reconstruct a reasonable approximation to the original figures (see Figure 10.11).

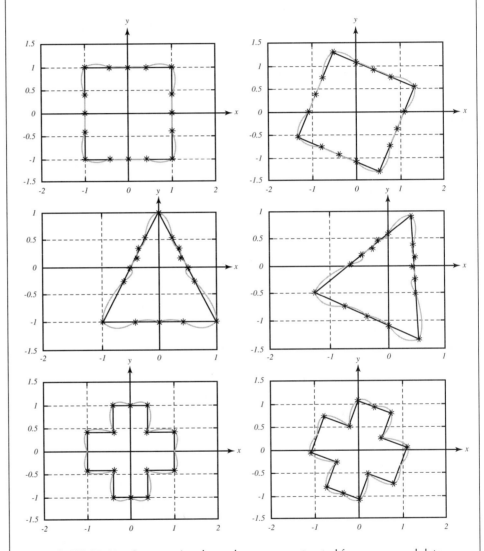

FIGURE 10.11   Square, triangle, and cross reconstructed from measured data.

The power spectrum for the square does not change when it is rotated:

$$ps = [332.7 \quad 0 \quad 0 \quad 0 \quad 2.56 \quad 0 \quad 0 \quad 0].$$

Not only does the power spectrum for the triangle not change when the figure is rotated, but it is significantly different from that of the square:

$$ps = [153.76 \quad 5.6661 \quad 3.4171 \quad 1.7784 \quad 0.64 \quad 1.469 \quad 0.022944 \quad 0.027299].$$

The power spectrum for the cross does not change when the figure is rotated; it is much more similar to that of the square than that of the triangle:

$$ps = [221.41 \quad 0 \quad 0 \quad 0 \quad 3.0976 \quad 0 \quad 0 \quad 0].$$

10.4.4 Cooley-Tukey FFT

The standard presentation of the Cooley-Tukey FFT (also called decimation in time) is based on the Danielson-Lanczos Lemma, which shows that a discrete Fourier transform of length N can be expressed as the sum of two transforms of length $N/2$. Applied recursively, this provides an efficient method of computing the transform when the number of data points is a power of 2. The Fourier transform of a single element is just the identity operation.

The basic recursion is given in the following, in which the number of data points, $n = 2^r$; we write (for $j = 0, \ldots, n - 1$)

$$g_j = \sum_{k=0}^{n-1} z_k \exp(2\pi i j k/n)$$

$$= \sum_{k=0}^{n/2-1} z_{2k} \exp(2\pi i j 2k/n) + \sum_{k=0}^{n/2-1} z_{2k+1} \exp(2\pi i j (2k + 1)/n)$$

$$= \sum_{k=0}^{n/2-1} z_{2k} \exp(2\pi i j k/(n/2)) + w^j \sum_{k=0}^{n/2-1} z_{2k+1} \exp(2\pi i j k/(n/2))$$

$$= g_j^e + W^j g_j^o$$

where $w^j = \exp(2\pi i j/n)$, and g_j^e and g_j^o denote the jth component of the transform of the vectors of length $n/2$ formed by the even components of z_k and the odd components of z_k, respectively.

Data values $x_0, x_1, \ldots, x_{n-1}$ are given at points evenly spaced on $[0, 2\pi)$; i.e., at

$$t_0 = 0, \quad t_1 = \frac{2\pi}{n}, \ldots, \quad t_k = k\frac{2\pi}{n}, \ldots, \quad t_{n-1} = (n-1)\frac{2\pi}{n}.$$

The coefficients for the trigonometric polynomial that approximates or interpolates the data are given by

$$a_j = \frac{2}{n}\sum_{k=0}^{n-1} x_k \cos(j\, t_k) \qquad b_j = \frac{2}{n}\sum_{k=0}^{n-1} x_k \sin(j\, t_k)$$

The trigonometric polynomial approximates the data if $n > 2m + 1$.
The trigonometric polynomial interpolates the data if $n = 2m + 1$ or $n = 2m$.
The appropriate form of the polynomial for each of these cases is given below.

Least-Squares Approximation ($n > 2m + 1$)

If $n > 2m + 1$, the trigonometric polynomial

$$f(t) = \frac{a_0}{2} + a_1\cos t + a_2\cos 2t + \ldots + a_m\cos mt + b_1\sin t + b_2\sin 2t + \ldots + b_m\sin mt,$$

gives the least squares approximation to the data.

Interpolation ($n = 2m + 1$)

If $n = 2m + 1$, the trigonometric polynomial

$$f(t) = \frac{a_0}{2} + a_1\cos t + a_2\cos 2t + \ldots + a_m\cos mt + b_1\sin t + b_2\sin 2t + \ldots + b_m\sin mt,$$

interpolates the data.

Interpolation ($n = 2m$)

If $n = 2m$, the trigonometric polynomial

$$f(t) = \frac{a_0}{2} + a_1\cos t + a_2\cos 2t + \ldots + \frac{a_m}{2}\cos mt$$
$$+ b_1\sin t + b_2\sin 2t + \ldots + b_{m-1}\sin(m-1)t.$$

interpolates the data.

Fourier Transform

$$c_j = a_j + i\,b_j = \frac{2}{n}\sum_{k=0}^{n-1} x_k\,[\cos(j\ t_k) + i\,\sin(j\ t_k)]$$

$$= \frac{2}{n}\sum_{k=0}^{n-1} x_k\,\exp(i\ j\ k\ \omega)$$

Thus, the coefficients of the trigonometric polynomials are the real and imaginary parts of the Fourier transform (or a scaled form of the transform) of the data.

Chapter 10 Fourier Methods

The following books are recommended for additional discussion of trigonometric interpolation, approximation, and FFT:

Bloomfield, P. *Fourier Analysis of Time Series—An Introduction,* Wiley, New York, 1976.

Bracewell, R. *The Fourier Transform and Its Applications.* New York: McGraw Hill, 1986.

Briggs, W. L., and V. E. Henson. *The DFT: An Owner's Manual for the Discrete Fourier Transform.* SIAM, Philadelphia, 1995.

Bringham, E. O. *The Fast Fourier Transform.* Prentice-Hall, Englewood Cliffs, 1974.

Elliott, D. F., and K. R. Rao. *Fast Transforms: Algorithms, Analyses, Applications.* Academic Press, New York, 1982.

Golub, G. H., and C. F. Van Loan. *Matrix Computations,* 3^d ed. Johns Hopkins University Press, Baltimore, 1996.

Nussbaumer, H. J. *Fast Fourier Transform and Convolution Algorithms.* Springer-Verlag, New York, 1982.

Ralston, A., and P. Rabinowitz. *A First Course in Numerical Analysis,* 2^d ed. McGraw-Hill, New York, 1978.

Singleton, R. C. "An Algorithm for Computing the Mixed Radix Fast Fourier Transform," *IEEE Transactions on Audio and Electroacoustics*, vol. AU-17, pp. 93–103, 1969.

Singleton, R. C. "A Method for Computing the Fast Fourier Transform with Auxiliary Memory and Limited High-Speed Storage," *IEEE Transactions on Audio and Electroacoustics,* vol. AU-15, pp. 91–98, 1967.

Van Loan, C. *Computational Frameworks for the Fast Fourier Transform,* SIAM, New York, 1992.

In Problems P10.1 to P10.5, assume that the data are evenly distributed on [0, 2π).

    a. *Find the best-fit trigonometric polynomial of degree m = 1.*

    b. *Find the trigonometric interpolating polynomial.*

P10.1 $x = [1\ 1\ 0\ 0]$

P10.2 $x = [0\ 1\ 0\ -1]$

P10.3 $x = [0\ 1\ 1\ 0]$

P10.4 $x = [0\ 1/2\ 1\ 1/2]$

P10.5 $x = [0\ 1/3\ 2/3\ 1]$

In Problems P10.6 to P10.10, assume that the data are evenly distributed on [0, 2π).

    a. *Find the best fit trigonometric polynomial of degrees m = 1, and m = 2.*

    b. *Find the trigonometric interpolating polynomial.*

P10.6 $x = [1\ 1\ 1\ 0\ 0\ 0]$

P10.7 $x = [0\ 1/3\ 2/3\ 1\ 2/3\ 1/3]$

P10.8 $x = [0\ 1/2\ 1\ 0\ -1\ -1/2]$

P10.9 $x = [1\ 1\ 1\ 1\ 0\ 0\ 0\ 0]$

P10.10 $x = [0\ 1/2\ 1\ 1/2\ 0\ -1/2\ -1\ -1/2]$

Problems P10.11 to P10.20: Use the data values from Problems P10.1 to P10.10, but assume that the data are evenly distributed on [−π, π).

Problems P10.21 to P10.30: Find the FFT of the data in Problems P10.1 to P10.10, evenly distributed on the interval [0, 2π).

A10.1 Find the waveform and power spectrum for the following sounds:

    a. *A guitar string plucked at the midpoint;*

y = [2.2118 2.1734 1.1321 1.2247 0.8702 0.9085 0.6849 0.5923 2.2118 2.1734 1.1321 1.2247 0.8702 0.9085 0.6849 0.5923]

    b. *A guitar string plucked one-fourth of the way from one end of the string;*

y = [3.0572 3.2011 2.0739 2.3860 1.7887 0.9738 0.7410 0.5787 1.1081 0.9605 0.4487 0.1454 −0.1605 0.6580 0.7410 0.8945]

    c. *A guitar string plucked fairly close to one end;*

y = [4.6101 5.3621 2.6796 1.3951 1.4639 0.9843 0.9115 1.0058 0.4658 0.4313 0.6075 0.1599 0.1480 − 0.0899 −1.0885 0.5493]

    d. *A trumpet;*

y = [3.9408 3.8613 1.1210 1.0305 0.5567 0.7601 0.4008 0.6906 0.0800 0.2362 0.2165 0.1217 0.0398 −0.2403 −0.6988 −0.8033]

A 10.2 Find the best fit trigonometric polynomial of degree $m = 1$ for the following data, which give the monthly (average daily) high temperature at various locations (such data are available from the Internet, travel brochures, and a variety of other sources):

	Jan	Feb	Mar	Apr	May	Jun	Jul	Aug	Sep	Oct	Nov	Dec
Paris	43	45	54	60	68	73	76	75	70	60	50	44
Amsterdam	40	42	49	56	64	70	72	71	67	57	48	42
Prague	31	34	44	54	64	70	73	72	65	53	42	34
St. Petersburg, Russia												
	19	22	32	46	59	68	70	69	60	48	35	26
Rome	52	55	59	66	74	82	87	86	79	71	61	55
Madrid	47	52	59	65	70	80	87	85	77	65	55	48
Marrakesh, Morocco												
	65	68	74	79	84	92	101	100	92	83	73	66
Palermo, Sicily	60	62	63	68	74	81	85	86	83	77	71	64
Ankara, Turkey	39	42	51	63	73	78	86	87	78	69	57	43
Shanghai, China	46	47	55	66	77	82	90	90	82	74	63	53
Reykjavik, Iceland												
	35	37	39	43	50	54	57	56	52	45	39	36
Edinburgh, Scotland												
	42	43	46	51	56	62	65	64	60	54	48	44
London, England												
	43	44	50	56	62	69	71	71	65	58	50	45
Toronto, Canada												
	30	30	37	50	63	73	79	77	69	56	43	33
Santa Fe, New Mexico												
	40	43	51	59	68	78	80	79	73	62	50	40
Melbourne, Florida												
	73	73	75	79	83	86	89	90	89	86	80	74
Aiken, South Carolina												
	58	61	65	74	82	88	92	91	89	81	72	62

The data in Problems A10.3 to A10.20 give the radial distance from the origin to the perimeter of a geometric figure. For each problem

    a.   Find the Fourier transform of the data.
    b.   Find the power spectrum of the data (z*conj(z)).
    c.   Reconstruct the figure represented by each set of data.

A10.3
y = [1.40 1.08 1.00 1.08 1.40 1.08 1.00 1.08 1.401.08 1.00 1.08 1.40 1.08 1.00 1.08]
A10.4
y = [1.00 1.08 1.40 1.08 1.00 1.08 1.40 1.08 1.001.08 1.40 1.08 1.00 1.08 1.40 1.08]
A10.5
y = [0.5 0.6 1.0 0.6 0.5 0.43 0.5 0.67 1.4 1.1 1.0 1.1 1.4 0.67 0.5 0.43]
A10.6
y = [1.0 0.6 0.5 0.43 0.5 0.67 1.4 1.1 1.0 1.1 1.4 0.67 0.5 0.43 0.5 0.6]
A10.7
y = [0.56 1.08 1.00 1.08 0.56 1.08 1.00 1.08 0.56 1.08 1.00 1.08 0.56 1.08 1.00 1.08]
A10.8
y = [1.00 1.08 0.56 1.08 1.00 1.08 0.56 1.08 1.00 1.08 0.56 1.08 1.00 1.08 0.56 1.08]

A10.9

y = [2.83 2.16 2.00 1.18 0.94 0.90 1.00 1.36 2.83 2.16 2.00 1.18 0.94 0.90 1.00 1.36]

A10.10

y = [1.26 1.06 1.00 1.06 1.26 1.67 2.00 1.67 1.26 1.06 1.00 1.06 1.26 1.67 2.00 1.67]

A10.11

y = [2.00 0.81 0.57 0.81 2.00 0.81 0.57 0.81 2.00 0.81 0.57 0.81 2.00 0.81 0.57 0.81]

A10.12

y = [0.57 0.81 2.00 0.81 0.57 0.81 2.00 0.81 0.57 0.81 2.00 0.81 0.57 0.81 2.00 0.81]

A10.13

y = [1.08 1.00 1.08 1.40 1.08 1.00 1.08 1.40 1.08 1.00 1.08 1.40 1.08 1.00 1.08 1.40]

A10.14

y = [1.08 1.00 1.08 0.56 1.08 1.00 1.08 0.56 1.08 1.00 1.08 0.56 1.08 1.00 1.08 0.56]

A10.15

y = [1.67 1.26 1.06 1.00 1.06 1.26 1.67 2.00 1.67 1.26 1.06 1.00 1.06 1.26 1.67 2.00]

A10.16

y = [1.36 2.83 2.16 2.00 1.18 0.94 0.90 1.00 1.36 2.83 2.16 2.00 1.18 0.94 0.90 1.00]

A10.17

y = [0.81 0.57 0.81 2.00 0.81 0.57 0.81 2.00 0.81 0.57 0.81 2.00 0.81 0.57 0.81 2.00]

A10.18

y = [2.00 1.67 1.26 1.06 1.00 1.06 1.26 1.67 2.00 1.67 1.26 1.06 1.00 1.06 1.26 1.67]

A10.19

y = [1.00 1.36 2.83 2.16 2.00 1.18 0.94 0.90 1.00 1.36 2.83 2.16 2.00 1.18 0.94 0.90]

A10.20

y = [0.6 1.0 0.6 0.5 0.43 0.5 0.67 1.4 1.1 1.0 1.1 1.4 0.67 0.5 0.43 0.5]

A10.21 Using your results from Part a of Problems A10.3 to A10.20, determine which data represent the same figure (in different rotations).

EXTEND YOUR UNDERSTANDING

U10.1 Modify the algorithm for n data points evenly spaced on an arbitrary interval of length 2π (i.e., on $[t_0, t_0 + 2\pi)$).

U10.2 Transform (evenly spaced) data on $[a, b]$ to the interval $[0, 2\pi)$; find the coefficients for the best fit trigonometric polynomial, and display the plot in terms of the original independent variable.

U10.3 Write an algorithm for the FFT for $n = 8$.

U10.4 Construct the table showing the bit-reversal scheme for $n = 8$.

U10.5 Write an algorithm for the case in which $n = r_1 r_2 r_3$.

In Problems U10.6 to U10.9, find the interpolative trigonometric polynomial for the given data.

U10.6 **z** = [0 0.5 1 0.5 0 −0.5 −1 −0.5]

U10.7 **z** = $\left[1 \ \dfrac{\sqrt{2}}{2} \ \dfrac{\sqrt{2}}{2} \ 1 \ \sqrt{2} \ 1 \ \sqrt{2} \right]$

U10.8 **z** = $\left[0 \ \dfrac{1}{4} \ \dfrac{1}{2} \ \dfrac{3}{4} \ 1 \ \dfrac{3}{4} \ \dfrac{1}{2} \ \dfrac{1}{4} \right]$

U10.9 **z** = [0 0 1 1 1 1 0 0]

U10.10 Show that the matrix form of the FFT can be applied with the order of the data shuffled, so that the transform components appear in natural order. Use the factorization of the coefficient matrix to create a schematic diagram for the two-stage computations.

11

Numerical Differentiation and Integration

We now turn our attention to the use of numerical methods for solving problems from calculus and differential equations. In this chapter, we investigate numerical techniques for finding derivatives and definite integrals. Several formulas for approximating a first or second derivative by a difference quotient are given. These formulas can be found with the use of Taylor polynomials or Lagrange interpolation polynomials.

Numerical methods of integration approximate the definite integral of a given function by a weighted sum of function values at specified points. We first consider several methods, known as Newton-Cotes formulas, that use evenly spaced data points. These methods are based on the integral of a simple interpolating polynomial. The trapezoid rule uses the function values at the ends of the interval of integration; Simpson's rule is based on a parabola through the ends of the interval and the midpoint of the interval. Improved accuracy can be obtained by subdividing the interval of integration and applying one of these simple techniques on each subinterval. Finally, we present a powerful integration technique, Gaussian quadrature, in which the points used in evaluting a function are chosen to provide the best possible result for a certain class of functions.

Applications of numerical differentiation are especially common in converting differential equations into difference equations for numerical solution. One must be very careful when using numerical techniques to estimate the rate of change of measured data, since small errors are exaggerated by differentiation. Integration, on the other hand, tends to smooth out errors. Numerical integration is widely used in applications, because some simple functions are difficult or impossible to integrate exactly. We present a few representative problems and use them, together with other examples, to illustrate the techniques of the chapter. We consider techniques for ordinary differential equations in Chapters 12–14 and for partial differential equations in Chapter 15.

Example 11-A Simple Functions That Do Not Have Simple Antiderivatives

The normal distribution is a very important function in statistics. Gaussian noise is one of many ways in which this function is used in engineering and science. The normal distribution function (Fig. 11.1) is a scaled form of the function

$$f(x) = e^{-x^2}$$

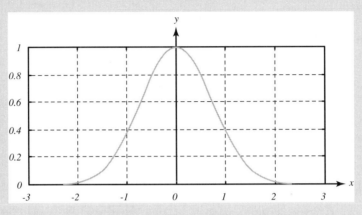

FIGURE 11.1 $f(x) = e^{-x^2}$

The indefinite integral of this function cannot be represented as a simple function. Instead, we find numerical approximations to the area under the graph of the function between any two finite values of x ($x = a$ and $x = b$), that is,

$$A = \int_a^b e^{-x^2} \, dx.$$

Another function that is important in optics and other applications, but does not have a simple antiderivative, is $f(x) = \sin(x)/x$; its graph is illustrated in Fig. 11.2.

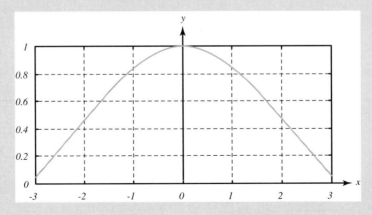

FIGURE 11.2 $f(x) = \sin(x)/x$

Example 11-B Length of an Elliptical Orbit

The simplest form of planetary orbit is an ellipse. Example 2-B describes the motion of a planet in an elliptical orbit with an eccentricity of 0.5 according to Kepler's law. If, instead of wishing to find the position of the planet at certain times, we desire to find the length of the orbit or the distance traveled between certain positions (measured by the central angle), we are faced with an example of the difficulty of calculating arc length, even for fairly simple functions. The well-known formula for the arc length of a curve described parametrically as $x(r)$, $y(r)$ is

$$L = \int_a^b \sqrt{(x')^2 + (y')^2} \, dr.$$

If $x(r) = \cos(r)$ and $y(r) = \dfrac{3}{4} \sin(r)$, the function to be integrated is

$$f(r) = 0.25 \sqrt{16 \sin^2(r) + 9 \cos^2(r)}.$$

We will find approximate values for the length of this ellipse using several different techniques.

For example, we may wish to compare the length of the arc traversed from $t = 0$ to $t = 10$ with the arc from $t = 60$ to $t = 70$ (see Fig. 11.3). The central angles at 10-day intervals were found in Chapter 2 to be

$$r = [0.00 \quad 1.07 \quad 1.75 \quad 2.27 \quad 2.72 \quad 3.14 \quad 3.56 \quad 4.01 \quad 4.53 \quad 5.22 \quad 6.28],$$

so we are interested in the arc length from $r = 0.00$ to $r = 1.07$ and the length from $r = 3.56$ to $r = 4.01$.

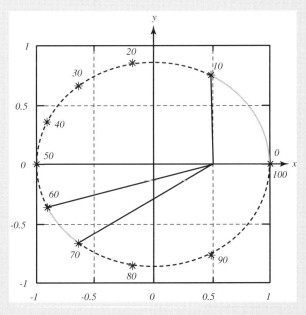

FIGURE 11.3   Length of arc from day 0 to day 10 and day 60 to day 70.

Numerical differentiation requires us to find estimates for the derivative or slope of a function by using the function values at only a set of discrete points. We begin by considering methods of approximating a first derivative. We then present formulas for second and higher derivatives. The final topic in our treatment of numerical differentiation is the use of acceleration (introduced in Chapter 1) to improve an approximate derivative value.

11.1.1   First Derivatives

The simplest difference formulas are based on using a straight line to interpolate the given data; they use two data points to estimate the derivative. We assume that we have function values at x_{i-1}, x_i, and x_{i+1}; we let $f(x_{i-1}) = y_{i-1}$, $f(x_i) = y_i$, and $f(x_{i+1}) = y_{i+1}$. The spacing between the values of x is constant, so that $x_{i+1} - x_i = x_i - x_{i-1} = h$. The standard two-point formulas are:

Forward Difference Formula

$$f'(x_i) \approx \frac{f(x_{i+1}) - f(x_i)}{x_{i+1} - x_i} = \frac{y_{i+1} - y_i}{x_{i+1} - x_i} = \frac{y_{i+1} - y_i}{h}$$

Backward Difference Formula

$$f'(x_i) \approx \frac{f(x_{i-1}) - f(x_i)}{x_{i-1} - x_i} = \frac{y_i - y_{i-1}}{x_i - x_{i-1}} = \frac{y_i - y_{i-1}}{h}$$

A more balanced approach gives an approximation to the derivative at x_i using function values $f(x_{i-1})$ and $f(x_{i+1})$. The central difference formula is the average of the forward and backward approximations.

Central Difference Formula

$$f'(x_i) \approx \frac{f(x_{i+1}) - f(x_{i-1})}{x_{i+1} - x_{i-1}} = \frac{y_{i+1} - y_{i-1}}{x_{i+1} - x_{i-1}} = \frac{y_{i+1} - y_{i-1}}{2h}$$

Interpolating the data by a polynomial rather than a straight line gives a difference formula that makes use of more than two data points. The forward and backward three-point formulas for evenly spaced data are given next.

Three-Point Forward Difference Formula

$$f'(x_i) \approx \frac{-f(x_{i+2}) + 4 f(x_{i+1}) - 3 f(x_i)}{x_{i+2} - x_i}$$

Three-Point Backward Difference Formula

$$f'(x_i) \approx \frac{3 f(x_i) - 4 f(x_{i-1}) + f(x_{i-2})}{x_i - x_{i-2}}.$$

Example 11.1 Forward, Backward, and Central Differences

To illustrate the three kinds of difference formula, consider the data points $(x_0, y_0) = (1, 2)$, $(x_1, y_1) = (2, 4)$, $(x_2, y_2) = (3, 8)$, $(x_3, y_3) = (4, 16)$, and $(x_4, y_4) = (5, 32)$. Using the forward difference formula, we estimate $f'(x_2) = f'(3)$, with $h = x_3 - x_2 = 1$, as

$$f'(x_2) \approx \frac{f(x_3) - f(x_2)}{x_3 - x_2} = \frac{y_3 - y_2}{1} = 16 - 8 = 8.$$

Using the backward difference formula, we find that

$$f'(x_2) \approx \frac{f(x_2) - f(x_1)}{x_2 - x_1} = \frac{y_2 - y_1}{1} = 8 - 4 = 4.$$

With the central difference formula, the estimate for $f'(x_2)$, with $h = 1$, is

$$f'(x_2) \approx \frac{f(x_3) - f(x_1)}{x_3 - x_1} = \frac{y_3 - y_1}{2} = \frac{16 - 4}{2} = 6.$$

We also observe that we can use any of these formulas with the given data and $h = 2$. For example, the central difference formula estimate for $f'(x_2)$ with $h = 2$ is

$$f'(x_2) \approx \frac{f(x_4) - f(x_0)}{x_4 - x_0} = \frac{y_4 - y_0}{4} = \frac{32 - 2}{4} = 7.5.$$

Although it may seem surprising that we would want to use a larger step size (like $h = 2$), we will use this result in Example 11.4.

The data are taken from the function $y = f(x) = 2^x$, so we can compare estimates of the derivative with the true value, found by evaluating $f'(x) = 2^x (\ln 2)$ at $x = 3$. The result is $f'(3) \approx 2^3 (0.693) = 5.544$.

Example 11.2 Three-Point Difference Formulas

We illustrate these difference formulas by using the data from Example 11.1. Using the three-point forward difference formula, we find that

$$f'(x_2) \approx \frac{-f(x_4) + 4f(x_3) - 3f(x_2)}{x_4 - x_2} = \frac{-y_4 + 4y_3 - 3y_2}{2} = \frac{-3(8) + 4(16) - 32}{2} = 4$$

Using the three-point backward difference formula, we find that

$$f'(x_2) \approx \frac{3f(x_2) - 4f(x_1) + f(x_0)}{x_2 \quad x_0} = \frac{3y_2 - 4y_1 + y_0}{2} = \frac{3(8) - 4(4) + 2}{2} = 5$$

Discussion

The forward difference formula can be found from the Taylor polynomial with remainder:

$$f(x + h) = f(x) + h f'(x) + \frac{h^2}{2} f''(\eta).$$ (11.1)

For $h = x_{i+1} - x_i$, this gives

$$f'(x_i) = \frac{f(x_{i+1}) - f(x_i)}{h} - \frac{h}{2} f''(\eta),$$

for some $x_i \leq \eta \leq x_{i+1}$.

Thus, the truncation error for the forward difference formula is $O(h)$. The formula can also be obtained by considering the Lagrange interpolating polynomial for the points (x_i, y_i) and (x_{i+1}, y_{i+1}).

Similarly, the backward difference formula can be found from eq. (11.1) by letting $h = x_{i-1} - x_i$. This gives $f(x_{i-1}) = f(x_i) + h f'(x_i) + \frac{h^2}{2} f''(\eta)$, or

$$f'(x_i) = \frac{f(x_{i-1}) - f(x_i)}{h} - \frac{h}{2} f''(\eta), \qquad \text{for some } x_{i-1} \leq \eta \leq x_i.$$

The central difference formula for the first derivative of f at the point x can be found from the next higher order Taylor polynomial, with $h = x_{i+1} - x_i = x_i - x_{i-1}$.

$$f(x_{i+1}) = f(x_i + h) = f(x_i) + h f'(x_i) + \frac{h^2}{2!} f''(x_i) + \frac{h^3}{3!} f'''(\eta_1),$$

$$f(x_{i-1}) = f(x_i - h) = f(x_i) - h f'(x_i) + \frac{h^2}{2!} f''(x_i) - \frac{h^3}{3!} f'''(\eta_2),$$

where $x \leq \eta_1 \leq x + h$ and $x - h \leq \eta_2 \leq x$. Although the error term involves the third derivative at two unknown points in two different intervals, if we assume that the third derivative is continuous on $[x-h, x+h]$ we can write the central difference formula with the error term as

$$f'(x_i) = \frac{f(x_{i+1}) - f(x_{i-1})}{2h} + \frac{h^2}{6} f'''(\eta) \quad \text{for some point } x_{i-1} \leq \eta \leq x_{i+1}.$$

The central difference formula can also be found from the three-point Lagrange interpolating polynomial and is therefore known as a three-point formula (although $f(x_i)$ does not appear in it).

General Three-Point Formulas

Three-point approximation formulas for the first derivative, based on the Lagrange interpolation polynomial, do not require that the data points be equally spaced. Given the three points, (x_1, y_1), (x_2, y_2), and (x_3, y_3), with $x_1 < x_2 < x_3$, the formula that follows can be used to approximate the derivative at any point in the interval $[x_1, x_3]$. The first derivative at each of the data points is given by

$$f'(x_1) \approx \frac{2x_1 - x_2 - x_3}{(x_1 - x_2)(x_1 - x_3)} y_1 + \frac{x_1 - x_3}{(x_2 - x_1)(x_2 - x_3)} y_2 + \frac{x_1 - x_2}{(x_3 - x_1)(x_3 - x_2)} y_3,$$

$$f'(x_2) \approx \frac{x_2 - x_3}{(x_1 - x_2)(x_1 - x_3)} y_1 + \frac{2x_2 - x_1 - x_3}{(x_2 - x_1)(x_2 - x_3)} y_2 + \frac{x_2 - x_1}{(x_3 - x_1)(x_3 - x_2)} y_3,$$

$$f'(x_3) \approx \frac{x_3 - x_2}{(x_1 - x_2)(x_1 - x_3)} y_1 + \frac{x_3 - x_1}{(x_2 - x_1)(x_2 - x_3)} y_2 + \frac{2x_3 - x_1 - x_2}{(x_3 - x_1)(x_3 - x_2)} y_3.$$

For evenly spaced data, the formula for $f'(x_2)$ reduces to the central difference formula presented earlier.

As discussed in Chapter 8, the Lagrange interpolation polynomial for the points (x_1, y_1), (x_2, y_2), and (x_3, y_3) can be written as

$$L(x) = L_1(x) \, y_1 + L_2(x) \, y_2 + L_3(x) \, y_3,$$

where

$$L_1(x) = \frac{(x - x_2)(x - x_3)}{(x_1 - x_2)(x_1 - x_3)}, \quad L_2(x) = \frac{(x - x_1)(x - x_3)}{(x_2 - x_1)(x_2 - x_3)}, \quad L_3(x) = \frac{(x - x_1)(x - x_2)}{(x_3 - x_1)(x_3 - x_2)}.$$

The approximation to the first derivative of f comes from $f'(x) \approx L'(x)$, which can be written as

$$L'(x) = L_1'(x) \, y_1 + L_2'(x) \, y_2 + L_3'(x) \, y_3,$$

where

$$L_1'(x) = \frac{2x - x_2 - x_3}{(x_1 - x_2)(x_1 - x_3)}, \quad L_2'(x) = \frac{2x - x_1 - x_3}{(x_2 - x_1)(x_2 - x_3)}, \quad L_3'(x) = \frac{2x - x_1 - x_2}{(x_3 - x_1)(x_3 - x_2)},$$

Thus,

$$f'(x) \approx \frac{2x - x_2 - x_3}{(x_1 - x_2)(x_1 - x_3)} y_1 + \frac{2x - x_1 - x_3}{(x_2 - x_1)(x_2 - x_3)} y_2 + \frac{2x - x_1 - x_2}{(x_3 - x_1)(x_3 - x_2)} y_3.$$

11.1.2 Higher Derivatives

Formulas for higher derivatives can be found by differentiating the interpolating polynomial repeatedly or by using Taylor expansions. For example, given data at three equally spaced abscissas, x_{i-1}, x_i, and x_{i+1}, the formula for the second derivative is

$$f''(x_i) \approx \frac{1}{h^2} [f(x_{i+1}) - 2f(x_i) + f(x_{i-1})], \quad \text{with truncation error } O(h^2).$$

Example 11.3 Second Derivative

Using the data given in Example 11.1, we estimate the second derivative at $x_2 = 3$, using the points $(x_1, y_1) = (2, 4)$, $(x_2, y_2) = (3, 8)$, and $(x_3, y_3) = (4, 16)$; for this example, $h = 1$, so we have

$$f''(3) \approx [f(4) - 2f(3) + f(2)] = [16 - 2(8) + 4] = 4.$$

Derivation of Second Derivative Formula

From the Taylor polynomial with remainder, we find that

$$f(x + h) = f(x) + h f'(x) + \frac{h^2}{2!} f''(x) + \frac{h^3}{3!} f'''(x) + \frac{h^4}{4!} f^{(4)}(\eta_1),$$

$$f(x - h) = f(x) - h f'(x) + \frac{h^2}{2!} f''(x) - \frac{h^3}{3!} f'''(x) + \frac{h^4}{4!} f^{(4)}(\eta_2),$$

where $x \leq \eta_1 \leq x + h$ and $x - h \leq \eta_2 \leq x$. Adding gives

$$f(x + h) + f(x - h) = 2f(x) + f''(x) h^2 + \frac{h^4}{4!} [f^{(4)}(\eta_1) + f^{(4)}(\eta_2)],$$

or $f''(x) \approx \dfrac{1}{h^2} [f(x + h) - 2f(x) + f(x - h)]$,

with truncation error $O(h^4)$. The error depends on even powers of h. If we assume that the fourth derivative is continuous on $[x - h, x + h]$, we can write the error term as $-\dfrac{h^2}{12} f^{(4)}(\eta)$ for some point $x - h \leq \eta \leq x + h$.

To find formulas for the third and fourth derivatives, we seek a linear combination of the Taylor expansions for $f(x+2h)$, $f(x+h)$, $f(x-h)$, and $f(x-2h)$ so that all derivatives below the desired derivative cancel.

Centered Difference Formulas, All $O(h^2)$.

$$f'(x_i) \approx \frac{1}{2h} [f(x_{i+1}) - f(x_{i-1})]$$

$$f''(x_i) \approx \frac{1}{h^2} [f(x_{i+1}) - 2f(x_i) + f(x_{i-1})]$$

$$f'''(x_i) \approx \frac{1}{2h^3} [f(x_{i+2}) - 2f(x_{i+1}) + 2f(x_{i-1}) - f(x_{i-2})]$$

$$f''''(x_i) \approx \frac{1}{h^4} [f(x_{i+2}) - 4f(x_{i+1}) + 6f(x_i) - 4f(x_{i-1}) + f(x_{i-2})]$$

11.1.3 Partial Derivatives

Finite-difference approximations for partial derivatives of a function of two variables are based on a discrete mesh of points for both variables. We denote a general point as (x_i, y_j), and the value of the function $u(x,y)$ at that point as $u_{i,j}$; the spacing in the x and y directions is the same, h. The simplest partial-derivative formulas are direct analogs of the preceding ordinary-derivative formulas; we use subscripts to indicate partial differentiation. Also, each formula is given in a schematic form, indicating only the coefficients on each function value. All of the following formulas are $O(h^2)$; the approximation to each partial derivative is given at (x_i, y_j):

$$u_x(x_i, y_j) \approx \frac{1}{2h}\left[-u_{i-1,j} + u_{i+1,j}\right] \qquad u_x \approx \frac{1}{2h}\;\{\;\boxed{-1}\!-\!\boxed{0}\!-\!\boxed{1}\;\}\quad j;$$
$$i-1 \quad i \quad i+1$$

$$u_{xx}(x_i, y_j) \approx \frac{1}{h^2}\left[u_{i-1,j} - 2u_{i,j} + u_{i+1,j}\right] \qquad u_{xx} \approx \frac{1}{h^2}\;\{\;\boxed{1}\!-\!\boxed{-2}\!-\!\boxed{1}\;\}\quad j;$$
$$i-1 \quad i \quad i+1$$

For the mixed second partial derivative and higher derivatives, the schematic form is especially convenient. The Laplacian operator is $\nabla^2 u = u_{xx} + u_{yy}$, and the biharmonic operator is $\nabla^4 u = u_{xxxx} + u_{xxyy} + u_{yyyy}$. We thus have

$$u_{xy} \approx \frac{1}{4h^2}\left\{\begin{array}{ccc} \boxed{-1}\!-\!\boxed{0}\!-\!\boxed{1} & \quad j+1 \\ \boxed{0}\!-\!\boxed{0}\!-\!\boxed{0} & \quad j, \\ \boxed{1}\!-\!\boxed{0}\!-\!\boxed{-1} & \quad j-1 \end{array}\right.$$
$$i-1 \quad i \quad i+1$$

$$\nabla^2 u \approx \frac{1}{h^2}\left\{\begin{array}{ccc} \boxed{1} & \quad j+1 \\ \boxed{1}\!-\!\boxed{-4}\!-\!\boxed{1} & \quad j, \\ \boxed{1} & \quad j-1 \end{array}\right.$$
$$i-1 \quad i \quad i+1$$

$$\nabla^4 u \approx \frac{1}{h^4}\left\{\begin{array}{c} \boxed{1} \\ \boxed{2}\!-\!\boxed{-8}\!-\!\boxed{2} \\ \boxed{1}\!-\!\boxed{-8}\!-\!\boxed{20}\!-\!\boxed{-8}\!-\!\boxed{1} \\ \boxed{2}\!-\!\boxed{-8}\!-\!\boxed{2} \\ \boxed{1} \end{array}\right\}.$$

(See Ames, 1992, for a discussion of these and other formulas.)

11.1.4 Richardson Extrapolation

The technique known as Richardson extrapolation, introduced in Chapter 1, provides a method of improving the accuracy of a low-order approximation formula $A(h)$ whose error can be expressed as

$$A - A(h) = a_2 h^2 + a_4 h^4 + \ldots,$$

where A is the true (unknown) value of the quantity being approximated by $A(h)$ and the coefficients of the error terms do not depend on the step size h. To apply Richardson extrapolation, we form approximations to A separately using the step sizes h and $h/2$. These are combined to give an $O(h^4)$ approximation to A by means of two applications of an $O(h^2)$ formula:

$$A = \frac{4A(h/2) - A(h)}{3}.$$

To continue the extrapolation process, consider

$$A = B(h) + b_4 h^4 + b_6 h^6 + b_8 h^8 + \ldots,$$

where $B(h)$ is simply the extrapolated approximation to A, using step sizes h and $h/2$. If we can also find an approximation to A using step sizes $h/2$ and $h/4$, this would correspond to $B(h/2)$. If we extrapolate using $B(h)$ and $B(h/2)$, we get

$$C(h) \approx \frac{16B(h/2) - B(h)}{15},$$

which has error $O(h^6)$.

The central difference formula can be written as

$$D(h) = f'(x) = \frac{1}{2h}[f(x + h) - f(x - h)] - \frac{h^2}{6}f''(x) + O(h^4).$$

We can also find $f'(x)$ using one-half the previous value of h (whatever it may have been):

$$D(h/2) = f'(x) = \frac{1}{h}[f(x + h/2) - f(x - h/2)] - \frac{h^2}{24}f'''(x) + O(h^4).$$

Since the coefficient of the h^2 term does not change (although we do not, in general, know its value), the two estimates can be combined to give

$$D = \frac{4D(h/2) - D(h)}{3}.$$

Example 11.4 Improved Estimate of the Derivative

We illustrate the use of Richardson extrapolation with the values from Example 11.1. The value of h is 2, and the approximation to $f'(x_2)$ is based on $D(h) = 7.5$ and $D\left(\dfrac{h}{2}\right) = 6$. We have

$$D = \frac{4(6) - 7.5}{3} = \frac{16.5}{3} \approx 5.5.$$

The data in the example are points on the curve $f(x) = 2^x$. The actual value of $f'(x)$ is $(\ln 2)2^x$, which gives $f'(3) \approx 5.54$.

Discussion

Richardson extrapolation forms a linear combination of approximations $A(h)$ and $A(h/2)$, the first using a step size h, the second based on half the original step size; the combination is chosen so that the dominant error term, which depends on h^2, cancels. Representing A in terms of the approximation and the error terms, we have

$$A = A(h) + a_2 h^2 + a_4 h^4 + \dots . \qquad (11.2)$$

If the same approximation formula is used with step size $h/2$ in place of h, the true value can be expressed as

$$A = A\left(\frac{h}{2}\right) + a_2 \frac{h^2}{4} + a_4 \frac{h^4}{16} + \dots ,$$

or

$$4A = 4A\left(\frac{h}{2}\right) + a_2 h^2 + a_4 \frac{h^4}{4} + \dots . \qquad (11.3)$$

Subtracting (11.2) from (11.3) gives

$$3A = 4A\left(\frac{h}{2}\right) - A(h) + O(h^4),$$

or

$$A = \frac{1}{3}\left[4A\left(\frac{h}{2}\right) - A(h)\right] + O(h^4)$$

The h^2 error terms cancel, although the higher order terms do not. However, we now have an $O(h^4)$ approximation to A derived by using two applications of an $O(h^2)$ formula.

To continue the extrapolation, we write

$$A = B(h) + b_4 h^4 + b_6 h^6 + b_8 h^8 + \dots , \qquad (11.4)$$

where $B(h)$ is simply the extrapolated approximation to A, using step sizes h and $h/2$. If we can also find an approximation to A using step sizes $h/2$ and $h/4$, this would correspond to $B\left(\frac{h}{2}\right)$. We begin with

$$A = B\left(\frac{h}{2}\right) + b_4 \frac{h^4}{16} + b_6 \left(\frac{h^6}{64}\right) + b_8 \left(\frac{h^8}{2^8}\right) + \dots . \qquad (11.5)$$

Multiplying eq. (11.5) by 16 and subtracting eq. (11.4) from the result, so that the h^4 terms cancel, yields

$$15A = 16B\left(\frac{h}{2}\right) - B(h) + c_6 h^6 + c_8 h^8 + \dots .$$

Now we define the second level extrapolated approximation to A as

$$C(h) \approx \frac{16}{15} B\left(\frac{h}{2}\right) - \frac{1}{15} B(h).$$

Numerical integration (quadrature) rules are very important because even simple functions may not have exact formulas for their antiderivatives (indefinite integrals). Even when an exact formula for the antiderivative does exist, it may be difficult to find.

In general, a numerical integration formula approximates a definite integral by a weighted sum of function values at points within the interval of integration. A numerical integration rule has the form

$$\int_a^b f(x)\, dx \approx \sum_{i=0}^n c_i\, f(x_i)$$

where the coefficients c_i and the points where the function is evaluated x_i depend on the particular method.

In this section, we investigate several basic quadrature formulas that use function values at equally spaced points; these methods are known as Newton-Cotes formulas. There are two types of Newton-Cotes formulas, depending on whether or not the function values at the ends of the interval of integration are used. The trapezoid and Simpson rules are examples of "closed" formulas, in which the endpoint values *are* used. The midpoint rule is the simplest example of an "open" formula, in which the endpoints are not used.

The formulas for each of these Newton-Cotes methods can be derived by approximating the function to be integrated by its Lagrange interpolating polynomial (different methods use polynomials of different degree) and then integrating the polynomial exactly. Since the interpolation polynomials also have an explicit formula for the error bound, error bounds can be obtained for the numerical integration formulas.

Although it might seem that one could achieve greater accuracy in numerical integration by using a method based on a higher order interpolating polynomial, in fact interpolation with higher degree polynomials is not generally a good idea. In the next section, more accurate methods based on subdivision of the original interval of integration are presented. In section 11.4, we present Gaussian quadrature, which is an effective method of obtaining more accurate results (for a given number of function evaluations) if the function to be integrated may be evaluated at any desired points.

11.2.1 Newton-Cotes Closed Formulas

Trapezoid Rule

One of the simplest ways to approximate the area under a curve is to approximate the curve by a straight line. The trapezoid rule approximates the curve by the straight line that passes through the points $(a, f(a))$ and $(b, f(b))$, the two ends of the interval of interest. We have $x_0 = a$, $x_1 = b$, and $h = b - a$, and then

$$\int_a^b f(x)\, dx \approx \frac{h}{2}[f(x_0) + f(x_1)].$$

Example 11.5 Integral of e^{-x^2} Using the Basic Trapezoid Rule

Consider now a very important function for which the exact value of the integral is not known:

$$f(x) = \exp(-x^2), \quad x_0 = a = 0, \quad x_1 = b = 2.$$

Using the trapezoid rule, we find (since $(b - a)/2 = 1$ for this example) that

$$\int_0^2 \exp(-x^2)\, dx \approx [\exp(-0^2) + \exp(-2^2)] = 1 + \exp(-4) = 1.0183.$$

The function and the straight-line approximation are shown in Fig. 11.4.

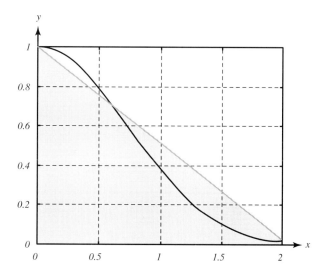

FIGURE 11.4 $f(x) = e^{-x^2}$ and area given by the trapezoid rule.

The trapezoid rule can be derived from the foregoing geometric reasoning, or, more formally, from the Lagrange form of linear interpolation of $f(x)$ using the endpoints of the interval of integration. To demonstrate the latter method, define $h = b - a = x_1 - x_0$ and let

$$L(x) = L_0(x) y_0 + L_1(x) y_1 = \frac{(x - x_1)}{(x_0 - x_1)} f(x_0) + \frac{(x - x_0)}{(x_1 - x_0)} f(x_1).$$

Then

$$\int_a^b f(x) \, dx \approx \int_a^b \frac{(x - x_1)}{(x_0 - x_1)} f(x_0) + \frac{(x - x_0)}{(x_1 - x_0)} f(x_1) \, dx$$

$$= \int_a^b \frac{(x_1 - x)}{h} f(x_0) + \frac{(x - x_0)}{h} f(x_1) \, dx$$

$$= \frac{1}{h} \int_a^b x_1 f(x_0) - x_0 f(x_1) + x[f(x_1) - f(x_0)] \, dx$$

$$= x_1 f(x_0) - x_0 f(x_1) + \frac{1}{h} \int_a^b x \, [f(x_1) - f(x_0)] \, dx$$

$$= x_1 f(x_0) - x_0 f(x_1) + \frac{b^2 - a^2}{2h} [f(x_1) - f(x_0)]$$

$$= bf(x_0) - af(x_1) + \frac{b + a}{2} [f(x_1) - f(x_0)]$$

$$= \frac{b - a}{2} f(x_0) + \frac{b - a}{2} f(x_1)$$

$$= \frac{h}{2} [f(x_0) + f(x_1)].$$

The degree of precision r of an integration formula is the (highest) degree of polynomial for which the method gives an exact result. Error analysis (see, e.g., Atkinson, 1989) shows that the trapezoid rule gives exact results for polynomials of degree ≤ 1, that is, linear functions for which the interpolating polynomial is exact. Thus, the trapezoid rule has a degree of precision, $r = 1$. In general, if we assume that $f(x)$ is twice continuously differentiable on $[a, b]$, then

$$\int_a^b f(x) \, dx = \frac{b - a}{2} [f(a) + f(b)] - \frac{(b-a)^3}{12} f''(\eta), \text{ for some } \eta \in [a, b] \quad (11.6)$$

Simpson's Rule

Approximating the function to be integrated by a quadratic polynomial leads to the basic Simpson's rule:

$$h = \frac{b - a}{2}, \qquad x_0 = a, \qquad x_1 = x_0 + h = \frac{b + a}{2}, \qquad x_2 = b.$$

The approximate integral is given by

$$\int_a^b f(x)\, dx \approx \frac{h}{3}[f(x_0) + 4f(x_1) + f(x_2)] = \frac{b - a}{6}\left[f(a) + 4f\left(\frac{b + a}{2}\right) + f(b)\right].$$

Example 11.6 Approximating $\pi/4$ Using the Basic Simpson's Rule

Since the exact value of the integral $\displaystyle\int_0^1 \frac{1}{1 + x^2}\, dx$ is $\arctan(1) = \pi/4 \approx 0.7853\ldots$, we can approximate $\pi/4$ by approximating the integral numerically. Using Simpson's rule with $f(x) = 1/(1+x^2)$, $a = 0$, and $b = 1$ gives $h = 1/2$, and

$$\int_0^1 \frac{1}{1 + x^2}\, dx \approx \frac{1}{6}[f(0) + 4f(1/2) + f(1)] = \frac{1}{6}\left[\frac{1}{1} + (4)\frac{4}{5} + \frac{1}{2}\right] = \frac{47}{60} \approx 0.78333.$$

The graphs of $f(x) = 1/(1+x^2)$ and the quadratic polynomial that passes through the points $(0,1)$, $(1/2, 4/5)$, and $(1,1/2)$ are shown in Fig. 11.5. It is not surprising that the approximate value of the integral from Simpson's rule is quite good, because the two functions are very similar.

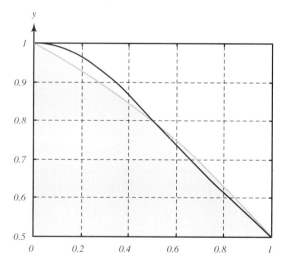

FIGURE 11.5 $f(x) = \dfrac{1}{1 + x^2}$ and area given by Simpson's rule.

Example 11.7 Integral of e^{-x^2} Using the Basic Simpson's Rule

Consider again the integral of the function $f(x) = \exp(-x^2)$, on $[0, 2]$.
The required values for applying Simpson's rule are

$$h = \frac{b - a}{2} = 1, \qquad x_0 = a = 0, \qquad x_1 = (2 + 0)/2 = 1, \qquad x_2 = b = 2,$$

which gives

$$\int_0^2 \exp(-x^2)\, dx \approx \frac{1}{3} [\exp(-0^2) + 4 \exp(-1^2) + \exp(-2^2)] = .8299.$$

The graphs of $f(x) = \exp(-x^2)$ and the quadratic polynomial passing through the points $(0, 1)$, $(1, \exp(-1))$, and $(2, \exp(-4))$ are shown in Fig. 11.6.

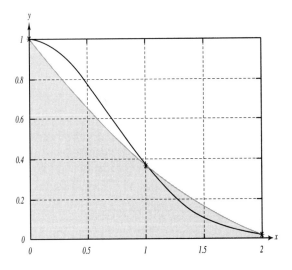

FIGURE 11.6 $f(x) = e^{-x^2}$ and area given by Simpson's rule.

To simplify the derivation of Simpson's rule, we assume that the function values are given at $x_0 = -h$, $x_1 = 0$, and $x_2 = h$; there is no loss of generality in this assumption, since it is a simple matter to shift any other interval of length $2h$ to $[-h, h]$. We write the polynomial that interpolates these points as $p(x) = a\, x^2 + b\, x + c$, so that

$$p(-h) = a(-h)^2 + b(-h) + c \qquad \text{or} \qquad y_0 = a\, h^2 - b\, h + c$$

$$p(0) = a(0)^2 + b(0) + c \qquad \text{or} \qquad y_1 = c$$

$$p(h) = a(h)^2 + b(h) + c \qquad \text{or} \qquad y_2 = a\, h^2 + b\, h + c$$

The second equation gives

$$c = y_1$$

Adding the first and third equations yields

$$2\, a\, h^2 + 2c = y_0 + y_2$$

or

$$2\, a = (y_0 + y_2 - 2y_1)/h^2$$

Integrating $p(x)$, we find

$$\int_{-h}^{h} ax^2 + b\, x + c\, dx = (2/3)\, a\, h^3 + 2\, c\, h$$

Substituting for a and c (in terms of y_0, y_1, and y_2) and simplifying gives

$$\int_{-h}^{h} a\, x^2 + b\, x + c\, dx = (h/3)\, (y_0 + 4y_1 + y_2)$$

Error analysis shows that Simpson's rule gives the exact value of the integral for polynomials of degree ≤ 3, even though quadratic interpolation is exact only if $f(x)$ is a polynomial of degree ≤ 2. This surprising result indicates that Simpson's rule is significantly more accurate than the trapezoid rule. The degree of precision for Simpson's rule is $r = 3$. If $f(x)$ is four times continuously differentiable on $[a, b]$, then

$$\int_{a}^{b} f(x)\, dx = \frac{h}{3} [f(a) + 4f\left(\frac{a + b}{2}\right) + f(b)] - \frac{h^5}{90} f^{(4)}(\eta)$$

$$\text{for some } \eta \in [a, b]. \qquad (11.7)$$

(See Atkinson, 1989 for details.)

11.2.2 Newton-Cotes Open Formulas

Midpoint Rule

The trapezoid and Simpson rules are the simplest examples of Newton-Cotes closed formulas; closed formulas use function evaluations at the endpoints of the interval of integration. If we use only function evaluations at points within the interval, the simplest formula (a Newton-Cotes *open* formula) is the midpoint rule. This formula uses only one function evaluation (so $n = 1$) at the midpoint of the interval, $x_m = (a + b)/2$. Interpolating the function by the constant value $f(x_m)$, we get the midpoint rule:

$$\int_a^b f(x)\, dx \approx (b - a)\, f\!\left(\frac{a + b}{2}\right).$$

Assuming that f is twice continuously differentiable yields

$$\int_a^b f(x)\, dx = (b - a)\, f\!\left(\frac{a + b}{2}\right) + \frac{(b - a)^3}{24}\, f''(\eta), \quad \text{for some } \eta \in [a, b].$$

Example 11.8 Integrating sin(*x*)/*x* Using the Midpoint Rule

Using the midpoint rule to approximate the integral

$$S = \int_0^\pi \frac{\sin(x)}{x}\, dx,$$

we find that

$$\int_0^\pi \frac{\sin(x)}{x}\, dx \approx \pi\, \frac{\sin(\pi/2)}{\pi/2} = \pi\, \frac{1}{\pi/2} = 2$$

Figure 11.7 compares the actual value of the area with that found by using the midpoint rule.

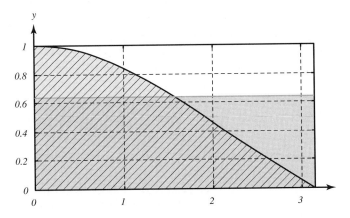

FIGURE 11.7   The area given by the integral S (shaded) and the approximation using the midpoint rule (hatched).

Two-Point Formula

The Newton-Cotes open formula that uses two function evaluations is given by

$$x_0 = a, \quad x_1 = \frac{2a + b}{3}, \quad x_2 = \frac{a + 2b}{3}, \quad f_1 = f(x_1), \quad f_2 = f(x_2).$$

$$\int_a^b f(x)\, dx = \frac{b - a}{2}[f_1 + f_2] + \frac{(b - a)^3}{108} f''(\eta), \quad \text{for some } \eta \in [a, b]. \quad (11.8)$$

The coefficient of the error term is smaller than that in the trapezoid rule (eq. (11.6)), which uses the same number of function evaluations. (See Isaacson and Keller, 1994, p. 316.)

Three-Point Formula

For the Newton-Cotes open formula using three functions evaluations, we define $f_1 = f(x_1), f_2 = f(x_2)$, and $f_3 = f(x_3)$, where

$$x_0 = a, \quad x_1 = \frac{3a + b}{4}, \quad x_2 = \frac{2a + 2b}{4}, \quad x_3 = \frac{a + 3b}{4}.$$

Then, taking $h = \dfrac{b - a}{4}$, we have

$$\int_a^b f(x)\, dx = \frac{4h}{3}[2f_1 - f_2 + 2f_3] + \frac{14h^5}{45} f^{(4)}(\eta), \text{ for some } \eta \in [a, b]. \quad (11.9)$$

The coefficient of the error term is smaller than that in Simpson's rule (eq. (11.7)), which uses the same number of function evaluations. (Note the difference in definition of h in eqs. (11.7) and (11.9)); see Isaacson and Keller (1994), p. 316).

11.2.3   Discussion

Care must be taken in comparing open and closed formulas, since a comparison can be made on the number of nodes or on the number of function evaluations. Issacson and Keller define the number of nodes to be the number of subintervals used, so that closed formulas use $n + 1$ function evaluations and open formulas use $n - 1$ evaluations, for a given number of subintervals.

Improving the Results

Rather than continuing to use quadrature formulas based on interpolating polynomials of ever higher order, we now consider three more effective methods of improving the accuracy of integration. The first two of these improvements are based (as are all our formulas so far) on function evaluations at evenly spaced points. Composite integration formulas, which we examine in the next section, are based on subdividing the interval of integration into subintervals and applying the basic integration rule in each subinterval. An algorithm is presented for the more general, composite form of the method.

The easiest method of improving the accuracy of numerical integration is to apply one of the lower order methods presented in the previous section repeatedly on several subintervals. This is known as *composite integration*.

11.3.1   Trapezoid Rule

If we divide the interval of integration, [a,b], into two or more subintervals and use the trapezoid rule on each subinterval, we obtain the composite trapezoid rule. For the simplest case, which uses the same function evaluations as the Simpson rule, consider two subintervals $[a, x_1]$ and $[x_1, b]$, where $x_1 = (b + a)/2$. For each subinterval $h = (b - a)/2$. Then

$$\int_a^b f(x)\, dx = \int_a^{x_1} f(x)\, dx + \int_{x_1}^b f(x)\, dx \approx \frac{h}{2}[f(a) + f(x_1)] + \frac{h}{2}[f(x_1) + f(b)],$$

or

$$\int_a^b f(x)\, dx \approx \frac{h}{2}[f(a) + 2f(x_1) + f(b)] = \frac{b - a}{4}[f(a) + 2f(x_1) + f(b)].$$

If we divide the interval into n subintervals, we get $h = \dfrac{b - a}{n}$, so that

$$\int_a^b f(x)\, dx = \int_a^{x_1} f(x)\, dx + \ldots + \int_{x_{n-1}}^b f(x)\, dx$$

$$\approx \frac{h}{2}[f(a) + f(x_1)] + \ldots + \frac{h}{2}[f(x_{n-1}) + f(b)]$$

$$\approx \frac{b - a}{2n}[f(a) + 2f(x_1) + \ldots + 2f(x_{n-1}) + f(b)].$$

Trapezoid Rule

$$
\begin{array}{ll}
\textit{Input} & \\
\quad \text{f(x)} & \textit{function to be integrated} \\
\quad \text{a} & \textit{lower limit of integral} \\
\quad \text{b} & \textit{upper limit of integral} \\
\quad \text{n} & \textit{number of subintervals} \\
\end{array}
$$

Begin computations
h = (b−a)/n
S = 0
For i = 1 to n−1
    x_i = a + h i
    S = S + f(x_i)
End
I = (h/2) (f(a) + f(b) + 2 S)
Return
    I

Example 11.9 Integral of $1/x$ Using the Trapezoid Rule

Consider the problem of finding

$$\int_1^2 \frac{dx}{x} \approx \frac{h}{2}[f(a) + 2f(x_1) + \ldots + 2f(x_{n-1}) + f(b)].$$

For $n = 2$ subintervals, $h = (2 - 1)/2 = 1/2$, and the composite trapezoid rule gives

$$I_1 = \frac{1}{4}[f(1) + 2f(1.5) + f(2)] = \frac{1}{4}\left[\frac{1}{1} + \frac{2}{1.5} + \frac{1}{2}\right] = \frac{17}{24} \approx 0.7083.$$

The function and the two straight-line approximations are shown in Fig. 11.8.

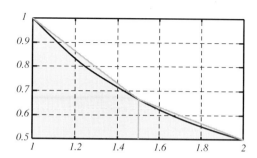

FIGURE 11.8 $y = 1/x$ and trapezoid rule approximations on $[1,1.5]$ and $[1.5,2]$.

For $n = 2^2 = 4$ subintervals, $h = 1/4$, and the composite trapezoid rule gives

$$I_2 = \frac{1}{8}[f(1) + 2f(5/4) + 2f(3/2) + 2f(7/4) + f(2)] = \frac{1}{8}\left[1 + \frac{8}{5} + \frac{4}{3} + \frac{8}{7} + \frac{1}{2}\right]$$

$$= 0.6970 \ldots.$$

For $n = 2^3 = 8$ subintervals, $h = 1/8$, and the composite trapezoid rule yields

$$I_3 = \frac{1}{16}[f(1) + 2f(9/8) + 2f(5/4) + 2f(11/8) + 2f(3/2) + 2f(13/8) + 2f(7/4) + 2f(15/8) + f(2)]$$

$$= 0.6941 \ldots.$$

The exact value of the integral is $\ln(2) \approx 0.693147 \ldots.$

11.3.2 Simpson's Rule

Applying the same idea of subdivision of intervals to Simpson's rule and requiring that n be even gives the composite Simpson rule. If we divide the interval of integration $[a, b]$ into two subintervals, we have $n = 4$, and we can apply Simpson's rule twice. Accordingly, consider the two subintervals $[a, x_2]$ and $[x_2, b]$, where $x_2 = (b+a)/2$ and $h = (b-a)/4$. Then

$$\int_a^b f(x)\, dx = \int_a^{x_2} f(x)\, dx + \int_{x_2}^b f(x)\, dx$$

$$\approx \frac{h}{3}[f(a) + 4f(x_1) + f(x_2)] + \frac{h}{3}[f(x_2) + 4f(x_3) + f(b)],$$

$$\approx \frac{h}{3}[f(a) + 4f(x_1) + 2f(x_2) + 4f(x_3) + f(b)].$$

In general, for n even, we have $h = (b - a)/n$ and Simpson's rule is

$$\int_a^b f(x)\, dx \approx \frac{h}{3}[f(a) + 4f(x_1) + 2f(x_2) + 4f(x_3)$$

$$+ 2f(x_4) + \ldots + 2f(x_{n-2}) + 4f(x_{n-1}) + f(b)]$$

Simpson's Rule

Input
    f(x)   *function to be integrated*
    a   *lower limit of integral*
    b   *upper limit of integral*
    n   *number of subintervals (must be even)*
Begin computations
h = (b−a)/n
m = n/2
S1 = 0
S2 = 0
For k = 0 to m−1
    x(2k+1) = a + h (2k+1)
    S1 = S1 + f(x(2k+1))
End
For k = 1 to m−1
    x(2k) = a + h (2k)
    S2 = S2 + f(x(2k))
End
I = (h/3) (f(a) + f(b) + 2 S1 + 4 S2)
Return
    I

Example 11.10 Integral of e^{-x^2} Using Simpson's Rule

For $n = 4$ and $f(x) = e^{-x^2}$, the integral of f is approximately 0.84232. The function and the two quadratic approximations are shown in Fig. 11.9.

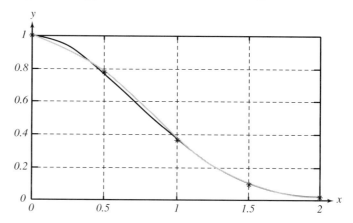

FIGURE 11.9 $y = e^{-x^2}$ and Simpson's rule approximations for $n = 4$.

Example 11.11 Length of an Elliptical Orbit

Consider the problem of finding the length of an elliptical orbit, where the ellipse is described parametrically as $x(r) = \cos(r)$ and $y(r) = \dfrac{3}{4} \sin(r)$. The length of the orbit is

$$L = \int_a^b \sqrt{(x')^2 + (y')^2}\, dr = 0.25 \int_a^b \sqrt{16\sin^2(r) + 9\cos^2(r)}\, dr.$$

We can approximate the length of the orbit by using Simpson's rule, with $a = 0$ and $b = 2\pi$.

With $n = 4$, we find that $L \approx 5.759587$.

With a finer subdivision of the interval of integration, $n = 20$, we find $L \approx 5.525879$

As described in Example 11-B, we can estimate the difference in the speed of the orbiting object when it is close to the planet (say, between day 0 and day 10) and the speed when it is further away (say, between day 60 and day 70). The arc length covered from day 0 to day 10 is approximately $I = 0.8556$; the arc length covered from day 60 to day 70 is approximately $I = 0.3702$. Thus, during the 10 days that the orbiting object is closest to the object it is revolving around, it is traveling more than twice as fast as it travels during days 60 to 70 (not quite the time it is farthest away).

11.3.3   Extrapolation Methods

As we saw earlier, an approximation formula whose error can be expressed as even powers of the step size may be extrapolated by using results from two step sizes (h and $h/2$) to obtain an estimate that is more accurate than either of the original results. The extrapolated form of the trapezoid rule is known as *Romberg integration*. The midpoint rule is also suitable for extrapolation.

The composite trapezoid rule can be expressed as

$$\int_a^b f(x)\, dx = \frac{h}{2}[f(a) + 2f(x_1) + \ldots + 2f(x_{n-1}) + f(b)] + \sum_{j=1}^{\infty} c_j\, h^{2j},$$

which indicates that we can apply Richardson extrapolation. We start with a simple example.

Example 11.12 Integrating f(x) = 1/x Using Romberg Integration

Consider the problem of finding $\int_1^2 \frac{dx}{x}$ using the trapezoid rule.

We start with one subinterval, so $h = 1$, and the trapezoid rule gives

$$\int_1^2 \frac{dx}{x} \approx I_0 = \frac{1}{2}[f(1) + f(2)] = \frac{1}{2}\left[\frac{1}{1} + \frac{1}{2}\right] = \frac{3}{4} = 0.75.$$

For Romberg integration, we next apply the trapezoid rule with two subintervals, $h = 1/2$, which gives

$$I_1 = \frac{1}{4}[f(1) + 2f(1.5) + f(2)] = \frac{1}{4}\left[\frac{1}{1} + \frac{2}{1.5} + \frac{1}{2}\right] = \frac{17}{24} \approx 0.708333.$$

We then apply Richardson extrapolation, using $A \approx \frac{1}{3}\left[4A\left(\frac{h}{2}\right) - A(h)\right]$, with $A(h) = I_0$ and $A\left(\frac{h}{2}\right) = I_1$, to give the extrapolated value

$$I \approx \frac{1}{3}[aI_1 - I_0] = [4(0.708333) - 0.7500]/3 = 0.694444.$$

In the following table of approximations, Column I gives the result from the trapezoid rule, and column II gives the extrapolated approximation:

	I	II
$h = 1$	0.750000	
		0.694444
$h = 1/2$	0.708333	

Since the exact value of the integral is known to be $\ln(2) \approx 0.693147$, it is clear that the extrapolated value is more accurate than the most accurate of the trapezoid rule approximations.

We can extend this process by applying the trapezoid rule again, using twice as many subintervals. We denote the approximation formed using $n = 2^k$

---

subintervals as I_k. Each time we increase k by 1, we double the number of points at which the function is evaluated and halve the value of h (as is required for Richardson extrapolation). Before giving the general formulas, we continue the problem of finding the integral of $f(x) = 1/x$.

1. For $k = 0$, we found that $I_0 = 0.7500$.
2. For $k = 1$, we found that $I_1 = 0.708333$.
3. For $k = 2$, we have $n = 2^2 = 4$ subintervals; so $h = 1/4$ and $I_2 \approx 0.697024$.

To apply Richardson extrapolation we can now use I_1 as $A(h)$ and I_2 as $A(h/2)$, yielding $I \approx \frac{1}{3}[4\,I_2 - I_1] = 0.693254$. Extending the previous table of the approximations, with the first column giving the values computed by the composite trapezoid rule and the second column giving the extrapolated approximation, results in the following new table:

	I	II
$h = 1$	0.7500	
		0.694444
$h = 1/2$	0.708333	
		0.693254
$h = 1/4$	0.697024	

Since the error term in the composite trapezoid rule can be represented as a series with only even powers of h (see, e.g., Ralston and Rabinowitz, 1978), the extrapolation can be extended using the first level extrapolated values, I_2 and I_1. For the second level of extrapolation, we have

$$C(h) \approx \frac{16}{15} B\left(\frac{h}{2}\right) - \frac{1}{15} B(h)$$

and the following table:

	I	II	III
$h = 1$	0.7500		
		0.694444	
$h = 1/2$	0.708333		0.693175
		0.693254	
$h = 1/4$	0.697024		

As a measure of convergence for the iterations, we consider the relative change in the solution. At this stage we have $|(0.693175 - 0.694444)/0.693175| = 0.00183$.

If further iterations are desired, the next stage would consist of computing

1. an approximation using the trapezoid rule ($k = 3$, $n = 2^3$, $h = 1/8$)
2. an additional extrapolated value, for levels I, II, and III
3. the fourth-level extrapolated value

Romberg Integration

The following algorithm calls a function or subroutine `trap(f,a,b,n)`, which implements the trapezoid rule with n subintervals.

Input
f(x)	*function to be integrated*
a	*lower limit of integral*
b	*upper limit of integral*
kmax	*(maximum) number of levels of extrapolation*
tol	*convergence criteria, tolerance on relative change in solution*

Begin computations

$h = (b-a)/n$

$Q(1,1) = \text{trap}(f, a, b, 1)$

For k = 1 to kmax

    $n = 2\text{^}k$

    $Q(k+1, 1) = \text{trap}(f,a,b,n)$ *another entry in col 1*

    For j = 2 to k+1

        $c = 4\text{^}(j-1)$

        $Q(k-j+2, j) = \dfrac{c\,Q(k-j+3, j-1) - Q(k-j+2, j-1)}{c-1}$ *entry in column j*

    End

    $m = k$ *save value of index*

    If (| (Q(1,k+1)-Q(1,k))/ Q(1,k+1) | < tol) break   *test for convergence*

End

Return

    Q(1, m+1)

In general, for the kth level of extrapolation, the appropriate formula is

$$D(h) \approx \frac{4^k C(h/2) - C(h)}{4^k - 1}.$$

A more efficient algorithm for Romberg integration would make use of the fact that the same function evaluations that were used in the previous approximation are needed (along with some additional ones) in the current approximation; the preceding algorithm uses calls to the function `trap` for simplicity.

Example 11.13 Completing the Romberg Integration of $f(x) = 1/x$

A simple program for Romberg integration yields the following table of values for $f(x) = 1/x$. The first column gives results from the trapezoid rule.

0.7500	0.694444	0.693175	0.693147	0.693147
0.708333	0.693254	0.693148	0.693147	
0.697024	0.693155	0.693147		
0.694122	0.693148			
0.693391				

The Newton-Cotes formulas are based on evaluations of a function at equally spaced values of the independent variable. Gaussian integration formulas evaluate functions at points that are chosen so that the formula is exact for polynomials of as high a degree as possible. Gaussian integration formulas are usually expressed in terms of the interval of integration $[-1, 1]$. For other intervals, a change of variable is used to transform the problem to the interval $[-1, 1]$.

11.4.1 Gaussian Quadrature on $[-1, 1\,]$

The general form of a Gaussian quadrature formula is

$$\int_{-1}^{1} f(x)\, dx \approx \sum_{i=1}^{n} c_i\, f(x_i),$$

where the appropriate values of the points x_i and the coefficients c_i depend on the choice of n. By choosing the quadrature points $x_1, \ldots, x_n$ as the n zeros of the nth-degree Legendre polynomial, and by using the appropriate coefficients, the integration formula is exact for polynomials of degree up to $2n - 1$.

For example, the Gauss-Legendre quadrature rule for two evaluation points, which is exact for polynomials up to and including degree 3, has the form

$$\int_{-1}^{1} f(x)\, dx \approx c_1\, f(x_1) + c_2\, f(x_2) = f(-1/\sqrt{3}) + f(1/\sqrt{3})$$

Similarly, the Gauss-Legendre quadrature rule for $n = 3$ evaluation points, which is exact for polynomials up to and including degree 5, has the form

$$\int_{-1}^{1} f(x)\, dx \approx c_1\, f(x_1) + c_2\, f(x_2) + c_3\, f(x_3) = \frac{5}{9} f(-\sqrt{3/5}) + \frac{8}{9} f(0) + \frac{5}{9} f(\sqrt{3/5})$$

The values of the Gaussian quadrature parameters x_i and c_i for $n = 2, \ldots, 4$ are given in the following table.

Parameters for Gaussian quadrature

n	x_i	c_i
2	$\pm 1/\sqrt{3} \approx \pm 0.57735$	1
3	0	8/9
	$\pm \sqrt{3/5} \approx \pm 0.77459$	5/9
4	$\approx \pm 0.861136$	0.34785
	$\approx \pm 0.339981$	0.652145

Example 11.14 Integral of exp($-x^2$) on [-1, 1] Using Gaussian Quadrature

To find the integral of exp($-x^2$) on [-1, 1] using Gaussian quadrature with two quadrature points, we compute

$$\int_{-1}^{1} \exp(-x^2)dx \approx c_1 f(x_1) + c_2 f(x_2) = f(-1/\sqrt{3}) + f(1/\sqrt{3})$$

$$= \exp[-(-1/\sqrt{3})^2] + \exp[-(1/\sqrt{3})^2]$$

$$= \exp[-(1/3)] + \exp[-(1/3)] \approx 2(0.7165) \approx 1.433.$$

The following algorithm for Gaussian quadrature to approximate the integral of $f(x)$ on [-1, 1], with $k = 2, \ldots 5$ quadrature points, uses the matrix of evaluation points

$$t = \begin{bmatrix} -0.5773502692 & -0.7745966692 & -0.8611363116 & -0.9061798459 \\ 0.5773502692 & 0.0000000000 & -0.3399810436 & -0.5384693101 \\ 0.0 & 0.7745966692 & 0.3399810436 & 0.0000000000 \\ 0.0 & 0.0 & 0.8611363116 & 0.538469310 \\ 0.0 & 0.0 & 0.0 & 0.9061798459 \end{bmatrix}$$

and the matrix of coefficients

$$c = \begin{bmatrix} 1.0 & 0.5555555556 & 0.3478548451 & 0.2369268850 \\ 1.0 & 0.8888888889 & 0.6521451549 & 0.4786286705 \\ 0.0 & 0.5555555556 & 0.6521451549 & 0.5688888889 \\ 0.0 & 0.0 & 0.3478548451 & 0.4786286705 \\ 0.0 & 0.0 & 0.0 & 0.2369268850 \end{bmatrix}$$

Gaussian Quadrature on [-1, 1]

Input
- f(x)   *function to be integrated*
- k   *number of quadrature points*
- t   *matrix of quadrature points (only column k-1 is used)*
- c   *matrix of coefficients (only column k-1 is used)*

Form sum to approximate the integral
S = 0
For j = 1 to k
  S = S + c(j,k−1) f(x(j))
End

Return
 S

To illustrate the use of the algorithm for Gaussian quadrature, we compute the integral of $\exp(-x^2)$ on $[-1, 1]$ using 2, 3, 4, and 5 quadrature points.

Example 11.15 Gaussian Quadrature Using More Quadrature Points

We apply the algorithm for Gaussian quadrature to find the integral of $\exp(-x^2)$ on $[-1, 1]$.

Using 3 quadrature points, we find (with exact values shown for the coefficients and evaluation points)

$$\int_{-1}^{1} \exp(-x^2)\, dx \approx c_1 f(x_1) + c_2 f(x_2) + c_3 f(x_3)$$

$$\approx (5/9)\exp(-(-\sqrt{3/5})^2) + (8/9)\exp(-0^2) + 5/9)\exp(-(\sqrt{3/5})^2)$$

$$\approx (5/9)\exp(-3/5) + (8/9)\exp(-0^2) + (5/9)\exp(-3/5)$$

$$\approx 1.49868$$

Using 4 quadrature points:

$$\int_{-1}^{1} \exp(-x^2)\, dx \approx c_1 f(x_1) + c_2 f(x_2) \quad + c_3 f(x_3) + c_4 f(x_4)$$

$$\approx 0.3479 f(-0.86114) + 0.6521 f(-0.33998)$$

$$+ 0.6521 f(0.33998) + 0.3479 f(0.86114)$$

$$\approx 1.49333$$

Using 5 quadrature points:

$$\int_{-1}^{1} \exp(-x^2)\, dx \approx c_1 f(x_1) + c_2 f(x_2) + c_3 f(x_3) + c_4 f(x_4) + c_5 f(x_5)$$

$$\approx 0.2369 f(-0.90618) + 0.47863 f(-0.53847)$$

$$+ 0.56889 f(0) + 0.47863 f(0.53847) + 0.2369 f(0.90618)$$

$$\approx 1.493643$$

11.4.2   Gaussian Quadrature on [*a, b*]

If we have an integral on an interval $[a, b]$ that is not $[-1, 1]$, we must make a change of variable to transform the integral to the required interval. We start by writing the desired integral in terms of some variable other than t, say, x:

$$\int_a^b f(x)\, dx.$$

The change of variable that is required to convert an integral on the interval $x \in [a, b]$ to the required interval $t \in [-1, 1]$ for Gaussian quadrature is simply the linear transformation

$$x = \frac{(b - a)\, t + b + a}{2}, \quad \text{or} \quad \frac{2x - b - a}{b - a} = t.$$

Thus, the integral from a to b of the function $f(x)$ is changed into the integral from -1 to 1 of the function

$$f\left[\frac{(b - a)\, t + b + a}{2}\right] \frac{b - a}{2},$$

where the factor $\dfrac{b - a}{2}$ comes from the conversion from dx to dt. Accordingly, we now apply Gaussian quadrature to the integral

$$\int_{-1}^1 f\left[\frac{(b - a)\, t + b + a}{2}\right] \frac{b - a}{2}\, dt.$$

This change of variable is included in the following algorithm for Gaussian quadrature on $[a,b]$; the matrices are as defined for the basic algorithm above.

Gaussian Quadrature on [a, b]

> *Input*
>   f(x), k, t, c *as defined in basic algorithm for Gaussian quadrature*
>   [a, b]   *interval for integration*
> *Find points x(j) in [a, b] that corresponds to the quadrature points t(j, k−1).*
> For j = 1 to k
>   x(j) = 0.5 ((b − a) t(j,k−1) + b + a)
> End
> S = 0   *Form sum to approximate the integral*
> For j = 1 to k
>   S = S + c(j,k−1) f(x(j))
> End
> S = S (b−a)/2   *factor of (b-a)/2 from change of variable for interval [a,b]*
>
> *Return*
>   S

Example 11.16 Integral of exp(−x²) on [0, 2] Using Gaussian Quadrature

Consider again the integral from $a = 0$ to $b = 2$ of

$$f(x) = \exp(-x^2).$$

The required change of variable gives

$$x = \frac{(b - a)t + b + a}{2} = \frac{(2 - 0)t + 2 + 0}{2} = t + 1,$$

Thus, the integral from a to b of the function $f(x)$ is changed into the integral from -1 to 1 of the function $\exp[-(t + 1)^2]$. For this example $dt = dx$.

We now apply Gaussian quadrature to the integral $\displaystyle\int_{-1}^{1} \exp[-(t + 1)^2]\, dt$:

$$\int_{-1}^{1} f(t)\, dt \approx c_1 f(t_1) + c_2 f(t_2) = \exp[-(1.5774)^2] + \exp[-(0.4226)^2]$$

$$\approx 0.9195.$$

Example 11.17 Integral of 1/x on [1,2] Using Gaussian Quadrature

Consider again the integral from $a = 1$ to $b = 2$ of $f(x) = 1/x$.

The required change of variable gives

$$x = (t + 3)/2,$$

Thus, the integral from a to b of the function $f(x)$ is changed into the integral from -1 to 1 of the function $[2/(t + 3)](1/2) = 1/(t + 3)$. The factor of $1/2$ comes from the fact that for this example, $dx = (1/2)\, dt$.

We now apply Gaussian quadrature to the integral $\displaystyle\int_{-1}^{1} \frac{1}{t + 3}\, dt$

$$\int_{-1}^{1} f(t)\, dx \approx c_1 f(t_1) + c_2 f(t_2) = 1/(-0.57735 + 3) + 1/(0.57735 + 3)$$

$$\approx .41277 + .27954 = 0.69231$$

The exact value of the integral is $\ln(2) \approx 0.693147\ldots$.

The approximate value found with $n - 2$ and Gaussian quadrature compares favorably to that found with the trapezoid rule (Example 11.9) using $n = 8$.

11.4.3 Discussion

It is fairly simple to directly derive the coefficients for the case of $n = 2$ by requiring that the integration formula give the exact result for the polynomials $f_0 = 1$, $f_1 = x$, $f_2 = x^2$ and $f_3 = x^3$. For $f_0 = 1$, we require that

$$\int_{-1}^{1} 1 \, dx = 2 = c_1 + c_1;$$

for $f_1 = x$, we require that

$$\int_{-1}^{1} x \, dx = 0 = c_1 x_1 + c_1 x_2;$$

for $f_2 = x^2$, we require that

$$\int_{-1}^{1} x^2 \, dx = \frac{2}{3} = c_1 x_1^2 + c_1 x_2^2;$$

and for $f_3 = x^3$, we require that

$$\int_{-1}^{1} x^3 \, dx = 0 = c_1 x_1^3 + c_1 x_2^3.$$

These four equations must be solved for the points x_1 and x_2 and the coefficients c_1 and c_2. First, we observe that none of the unknowns can be zero. Then, solving the second equation for c_1 and substituting into the fourth equation gives $x_1^2 = x_2^2$. Since we assume that $x_1 \neq x_2$, we must have $x_1 = -x_2$. Substituting the expressions for c_1 and x_1 into the first equation gives $c_2 = c_1 = 1$. Finally, using the third equation gives $x_1 = -1/\sqrt{3}$ and $x_2 = +1/\sqrt{3}$.

Using a direct algebraic approach to derive higher degree Gaussian quadrature is not practical. Instead, the analysis utilizes the orthogonality of the Legendre polynomials (introduced in Chapter 9). The best approximation to the integral is obtained when the function is evaluated at the zeros of the appropriate Legendre polynomial. (See Atkinson, 1989, for details.)

The n-point Gauss-Legendre quadrature rule evaluates a function at the n zeros of the nth-degree Legendre polynomial; the quadrature rule has a degree of precision of at least $2n-1$ (i.e., it is exact for polynomials of degree at least $2n-1$).

The coefficients are

$$c_i = \frac{-2}{(n + 1)P_n'(x_i)P_{n+1}(x_i)}.$$

(See Atkinson, 1989, p. 276; Ralston and Rabinowitz, 1978, p. 105.)

The error in Gaussian quadrature goes to zero more rapidly for integrands that are smoother, whereas the composite trapezoid rule converges as h^2, regardless of the smoothness of $f(x)$ (see Atkinson, 1989).

11.5 METHODS OF MODERN COMPUTING

We illustrate some of the methods used for differentiation and integration in professionally developed software by summarizing the built-in functions for these operations from MATLAB and Mathcad. We then describe briefly the algorithms used in some of these methods.

11.5.1 MATLAB's Functions

Differentiation

Since small changes in a function can create large changes in its slope, numerical differentiation is much more difficult than numerical integration. Especially if the data to be differentiated are obtained experimentally, the best approach may be to find a least-squares fit to the data and then differentiate the approximating function. MATLAB's function $p = polyfit(x, y, n)$ will find the coefficients of the polynomial of degree n that best fits the data in the least-squares sense. The resulting polynomial (with coefficients given in the vector **p**) can be evaluated using $polyfit(p, x)$ and differentiated with $polyder(p)$.

MATLAB can also provide the forward or backward difference approximation to dy/dx by using the function diff. For $\mathbf{x} = [x(1), x(2), \ldots x(n)]$, $diff(x)$ gives a vector, of length $n-1$, consisting of the differences between successive elements of x; that is, $diff(x) = [x(2)-x(1), x(3)-x(2), \ldots x(n)-x(n-1)]$. Thus, the ith element of $dy = diff(y)./diff(x)$ is the forward difference approximation to dy/dx at $x(i)$ and is also the backward difference approximation to dy/dx at $x(i+1)$.

Integration

MATLAB has three built-in functions for numerically computing a definite integral (over a finite range). The function $traps(x, y)$ uses the composite trapezoid rule for the data points given in the vectors **x** and **y**. Vector y gives the function values at **x**.

The functions $Q=quad('f', xmin, xmax)$ and $Q=quad8('f', xmin, xmax)$ evaluate the function f at whatever points are necessary to achieve accurate results; 'f' is a string containing the name of the function. The function f must return a vector of output values if given a vector of input values. $Q = quad('f', xmin, xmax)$ approximates the integral of $f(x)$ from xmin to xmax to within a relative error of 0.001 using an adaptive recursive Simpson's rule. $Q = quad8('f', xmin, xmax)$ approximates the integral of $f(x)$ from xmin to xmax to within a relative error of 0.001, using an adaptive recursive Newton Cotes eight-panel rule.

For both quad and quad8, $Q = $ Inf is returned if an excessive recursion level is reached, indicating a possibly singular integral. Additional optional parameters may be passed to the quad function, allowing the user to specify the desired tolerance (either relative or a combination of relative and absolute). A trace of the function evaluations with a point plot of the integrand as well as coefficients to be passed to the function f, may also be specified. The documentation for implementing these options is included in the comments at the beginning of the function.

11.5.2 Mathcad's Functions and Operators

Derivative Operator

To use the derivative operator on the Calculus Toolbar, one must first define the function whose derivative is desired. The function is a scalar (not vector) valued function of a scalar variable.

The value of the first derivative computed by Mathcad is usually accurate to 7 or 8 significant digits, unless the point where the derivative is being approximated is close to a singularity of the function. The accuracy of higher derivatives decreases by one significant digit for each higher order of derivative.

Definite Integral

To use the definite integral operator on the Calculus Toolbar, first define the function $f(t)$ to be integrated. All variables in the expression $f(t)$, except the variable of integration t, must be defined. The limits of integration (real scalars, or positive or negative infinity) must also be defined. The numerical integration algorithm makes successive estimates of the integral and returns a value when the two most recent estimates differ by less than the tolerance.

To evaluate a double, or multiple, integral, press the ampersand key [&] twice, and fill in the integrand and limits on the integrals. In general, multiple integrals take much longer to compute than single integrals.

Mathcad has several methods of numerical integration, and selects the appropriate method according to the characteristics of the integrand. In Mathcad2000Pro, the user may specify the desired method.

11.5.3 Understanding the Algorithms

Numerical Differentiation

Although the intuitive idea of a finite difference approximation for computing a numerical derivative is attractive, there are severe difficulties in choosing an appropriate step size to minimize both truncation and round-off error. See Press et al. (1992, pp. 186–189) for a discussion of the difficulties involved in using a simple finite difference approximation for computing a numerical derivative, as well as a presentation of Ridders' method for derivatives (which is the method implemented by Mathcad). The basic idea of Ridders' method is to apply extrapolation to a sequence of finite difference approximations to the derivative.

Numerical Integration

The most basic method used in Mathcad is Romberg integration with Richardson extrapolation. The method is essentially as described in section 11.2.3.

If the integrand varies rapidly on the interval, an adaptive integration routine is used, with unequal subintervals. This corresponds to rewriting the problem

$$I = \int_a^b f(x)\, dx \qquad \text{as} \qquad \frac{dy}{dx} = f(x); \qquad y(a) = 0$$

and solving for $I = y(b)$. See Press et al. (1992, Ch. 16) for discussion of adaptive step-size ODE solution techniques.

If one or both of the limits of the integration are infinite, we need an integration formula that does not require a function evaluation at the end of the interval. Such formulas are known as open formulas, and were discussed briefly in section 11.2. The preferred open method (Press et al., 1992, p. 142) is the Second Euler-Maclaurin summation formula, namely

$$\int_{x1}^{xN} f(x)\, dx = h[f_{3/2} + f_{5/2} + \ldots f_{N-3/2} + f_{N-1/2}]$$

where the function evaluations are at the midpoints of the subintervals.

The first Euler-Maclaurin summation formula is the extended or composite trapezoid rule

$$\int_{x1}^{xN} f(x)\, dx = h\left[\frac{1}{2}f_1 + f_2 + \ldots f_{N-1} + \frac{1}{2}f_N\right]$$

The importance of these formulas comes from the fact (not at all trivial) that the error for each of these formulas can be expressed as a power series in h, with only even powers of h. The second Euler-Maclaurin formula can be found by taking the first with step size h, and again with step size $h/2$, and subtracting the first from twice the second.

In order to extrapolate the second Euler-Maclaurin formula (and reuse the function evaluations from one stage to the next), we triple the number of subintervals in the second stage. If the result of the first stage is A and the result of the second stage is B, then the extrapolated integral is $I = (9B - A)/8$ since tripling the number of subintervals reduces the error by a factor of 1/9 rather than the 1/4 that occurs when the number of subintervals is doubled.

To use an open integration formula, such as this, for an integral on an infinite interval, the integration routine includes a change of variable, $t = e^{-x}$ or $x = -\ln t$, so that an integral from $x = a$ to $x = \inf$ becomes an integral from $t = 0$ to $t = e^{-a}$. See Press et al. (1992, pp. 141–147).

Mathcad also implements the Gauss-Kronod method, which is an extension of Gaussian quadrature in which each higher order method uses the abscissas of the previous lower order method, thus allowing the reuse of previous function evaluations. The original paper by Kronod was published in 1964, in Russian. An automatic integration routine in the popular subroutine package QUADPACK (Piessens et al., 1983])uses a sequence of Gauss-Kronod integration methods with $N = 10, 21, 43, 87, \ldots$ points.

Other integration methods are based on ideas from function approximation; in particular, Mathcad incorporates Clenshaw-Curtis quadrature. The basic idea is that for a smooth function, the coefficients c_j, which represent the function in terms of Chebyshev polynomials, decrease very rapidly as j increases. Furthermore, if the coefficients are known, the coefficients of the antiderivative function (or the derivative function) can be found directly from the c_j. For an adaptive method, one can compute the coefficients as a sum of products of cosine functions; the sum can be computed efficiently using fast cosine transforms. See Press et al. (1992, p. 196) for further discussion.

First derivative:

Forward difference formula

$$f'(x_i) \approx \frac{y_{i+1} - y_i}{x_{i+1} - x_i}.$$

Backward difference formula

$$f'(x_i) \approx \frac{y_i - y_{i-1}}{x_i - x_{i-1}}.$$

Central difference formula

$$f'(x_i) \approx \frac{f(x_{i+1}) - f(x_{i-1})}{x_{i+1} - x_{i-1}}.$$

Three-point forward formula

$$h = x_{i+1} - x_i = x_{i+2} - x_{i+1},$$

$$f'(x_i) \approx \frac{1}{2h}\left[-3 f(x_i) + 4 f(x_{i+1}) - f(x_{i+2})\right].$$

Second derivative:

$$f''(x_i) \approx \frac{1}{h^2}\left[f(x_{i+1}) - 2 f(x_i) + f(x_{i-1})\right].$$

Integration: $h = (b - a)/n$

Trapezoid rule

$$\int_a^b f(x)\, dx \approx (h/2)\left[f(a) + 2f(x_1) + \cdots + 2f(x_{n-1}) + f(b)\right]$$

Simpson's rule (n must be even)

$$\int_a^b f(x)\, dx \approx (h/3)\left[f(a) + 4f(x_1) + 2f(x_2) + 4f(x_3)\right.$$

$$\left. + 2f(x_4) + \cdots + 2f(x_{n-2}) + 4f(x_{n-1}) + f(b)\right]$$

Midpoint rule

$$\int_a^b f(x)\, dx \approx h \sum_{j=1}^{n} f(x_j); \qquad x_j = a + \left(j - \frac{1}{2}\right)h$$

Gaussian quadrature

$$\int_{-1}^{1} f(x)\, dx \approx \sum_{i=1}^{n} c_i\, f(x_i)$$

n	x_i	c_i
2	$\pm 1/\sqrt{3} \approx \pm 0.57735$	1
3	0	8/9
	$\pm\sqrt{3/5} \approx \pm 0.77459$	5/9
4	$\approx \pm 0.861136$	0.34785
	$\approx \pm 0.339981$	0.652145

SUGGESTIONS FOR FURTHER READING

Basic formulas

Ames, W. F. *Numerical Methods for Partial Differential Equations*, 3rd ed. Academic Press, Boston, 1992.

Atkinson, K. E. *An Introduction to Numerical Analysis*, 2d ed. John Wiley & Sons, New York, 1989.

Isaacson, E., and H. B. Keller. *Analysis of Numerical Methods*. Dover, New York, 1994 (Originally published by Wiley, 1966).

Ralston, A., and P. Rabinowitz. *A First Course in Numerical Analysis*, 2d ed. McGraw-Hill, New York, 1978.

Applications

Abramowitz, M., and I. A. Stegun (eds.). *Handbook of Mathematical Functions, with Formulas, Graphs, and Mathematical Tables*. Dover, New York, 1965.

Ayyub, B. M., and R. H. McCuen. *Numerical Methods for Engineers*. Prentice Hall, Upper Saddle River, NJ, 1996.

Jensen, J. A., and J. H. Rowland. *Methods of Computation*. Scott, Foresman and Company, Glenview, IL, 1975.

Ritger, P. D., and N. J. Rose. *Differential Equations with Applications*. McGraw-Hill, New York, 1968.

More advanced method:

Clenshaw, C. W., and A. R. Curtis. *Numerische Mathematik*, vol. 2, pp. 197–205, 1960.

Piessens, R., E. de Doncker, C. W. Uberhuber, and D. K. Kahaner. *QUAD-PACK: A Subroutine Package for Automatic Integration*. Springer-Verlag, New York, 1983.

Ridders, C. J. F. *Advances in Engineering Solftware*, vol. 4, no. 2, 1982, pp. 75–76.

PRACTICE THE TECHNIQUES

For problems P11.1 to P11.5, approximate the specified derivative

a. *Using the forward-difference formula.*
b. *Using the backward-difference formula.*
c. *Using the central-difference formula.*
d. *Using Richardson extrapolation to improve your answer to Part c.*

P11.1 Approximate $y'(1.0)$ if

$$\mathbf{x} = [0.8 \quad 0.9 \quad 1.0 \quad 1.1 \quad 1.2]$$

$$\mathbf{y} = [0.992 \quad 0.999 \quad 1.000 \quad 1.001 \quad 1.008]$$

P11.2 Approximate $y'(2)$ if

$$\mathbf{x} = [0 \quad 1 \quad 2 \quad 3 \quad 4]$$

$$\mathbf{y} = [0 \quad 1 \quad 4 \quad 9 \quad 16]$$

P11.3 Approximate $y'(1)$ if

$$\mathbf{x} = [-1 \quad 0 \quad 1 \quad 2 \quad 3]$$

$$\mathbf{y} = [1/3 \quad 1 \quad 3 \quad 9 \quad 27]$$

P11.4 Approximate $y'(1)$ if

$$\mathbf{x} = [-1 \quad 0 \quad 1 \quad 2 \quad 3]$$

$$\mathbf{y} = [1/2 \quad 1 \quad 2 \quad 4 \quad 8]$$

P11.5 Approximate $y'(4)$ if

$$\mathbf{x} = [0 \quad 1 \quad 4 \quad 9 \quad 16]$$

$$\mathbf{y} = [0 \quad 1 \quad 2 \quad 3 \quad 4]$$

For Problems P11.6 to P11.15, approximate the specified integral

a. *Using the trapezoid rule with 2 subintervals.*
b. *Using the trapezoid rule with 10 subintervals.*
c. *Using Simpson's rule with 2 subintervals.*
d. *Using Simpson's rule with 10 subintervals.*
e. *Using Gaussian quadrature with $n = 2$.*
f. *Using Romberg integration.*

P11.6 $\int_0^1 x \sin(\pi x)\, dx.$

P11.7 $\int_0^4 2^x\, dx.$

P11.8 $\int_0^2 \sqrt{x}\, dx.$

P11.9 $\int_1^2 \dfrac{dx}{1 + x}.$

P11.10 $\int_1^2 \dfrac{dx}{x}.$

P11.11 $\int_{-1}^1 \dfrac{dx}{1 + x^2}.$

P11.12 $\int_0^2 e^x\, dx.$

P11.13 $\int_0^1 \dfrac{1 + x}{1 + x^3}\, dx.$

P11.14 $\int_1^2 \sqrt{x^3 - 1}\, dx.$

P11.15 $\int_2^3 \sqrt{x^2 - 4}\, dx.$

P11.16 $\int_0^\pi x^2 \sin(2x)\, dx.$

P11.17 $\int_0^3 \dfrac{1}{\sqrt{x^3 + 1}}\, dx.$

P11.18 $\int_0^\pi x^3 \sin(x^2)\, dx.$

P11.19 $\int_0^3 \sqrt{x^3 + 1}\, dx.$

P11.20 $\int_0^2 \ln(x^3 + 1)\, dx.$

EXPLORE SOME APPLICATIONS

A11.1 The flow rate of an incompressible fluid in a pipe of radius 1 is given by

$$Q = \int_0^1 2 \pi r V \, dr$$

where r is the distance from the center of the pipe and V is the velocity of the fluid. Find Q if only the following tabulated velocity measurements V are available:

$\mathbf{r} = [0.0 \quad 0.1 \quad 0.2 \quad 0.3 \quad 0.4 \quad 0.5 \quad 0.6 \quad 0.7$
$\quad\quad 0.8 \quad 0.9 \quad 1.0]$

$\mathbf{V} = [1.0 \quad 0.99 \quad 0.96 \quad 0.91 \quad 0.84 \quad 0.75 \quad 0.64 \quad 0.51$
$\quad\quad 0.36 \quad 0.19 \quad 0.0]$

Compare your result with the value obtained by using $V = 1 - r^2$. (See Ayyub and McCuen, 1996, for a discussion of similar problems.)

Problems A11.2 to A11.7 investigate some important nonelementary functions that are defined by integrals. Tabulated values are available for these functions in many reference books.

A11.2 The error function is defined as

$$\text{Erf}(x) = \frac{2}{\sqrt{\pi}} \int_0^x e^{-t^2} \, dt.$$

Find Erf(2).

A11.3 The sine-integral is defined as

$$Si(x) = \int_0^x \frac{\sin t}{t} \, dt.$$

Find $Si(2)$.

A11.4 The cosine-integral is defined as

$$Ci(x) = \int_1^x \frac{\cos t}{t} \, dt.$$

Find $Ci(2)$.

A11.5 The exponential-integral is defined as

$$Ei(x) = \int_1^x \frac{e^{-t}}{t} \, dt.$$

Find $Ei(2)$.

A11.6 The Fresnel integrals are defined as

$$C(x) = \int_0^x \cos\left(\frac{\pi}{2} t^2\right) dt$$

$$S(x) = \int_0^x \sin\left(\frac{\pi}{2} t^2\right) dt.$$

Find $C(2)$ and $S(2)$.

A11.7 There are several forms of elliptic integrals.

a. The complete elliptic integral of the first kind is defined as

$$K(m) = \int_0^{\pi/2} \frac{dt}{\sqrt{1 - m \sin^2 t}}.$$

Find $K(1)$ and $K(4)$.

b. The complete elliptic integral of the second kind is defined as

$$E(m) = \int_0^{\pi/2} \sqrt{1 - m \sin^2 t} \, dt.$$

Find $E(1)$ and $E(4)$.

c. The elliptic integral of the first kind is

$$K(k, x) = \int_0^x \frac{dt}{\sqrt{1 - k^2 \sin^2 t}}.$$

Find $K(1,1)$ and $K(2,1)$.

d. The elliptic integral of the second kind is

$$E(k, x) = \int_0^x \sqrt{1 - k^2 \sin^2 t} \, dt.$$

Find $E(1,1)$ and $E(2,1)$. (See Ritger and Rose, 1968, or Abramowitz and Stegun, 1965, for tabulated values.)

Problems A11.8 to A11.15 illustrate some integrals that arise in the measurement of arc length. For many functions, the integral that measures its arc length cannot be evaluated exactly.

A11.8 Find the arc length of the curve described by the function $y = x^2$, $0 < x < 2$; the length is given by the integral

$$\int_0^2 \sqrt{1 + 4x^2}\ dx.$$

A11.9 Find the arc length of the curve described by the function $y = x^3$, $0 < x < 2$; the length is given by the integral

$$\int_0^2 \sqrt{1 + 9x^4}\ dx.$$

A11.10 Find the arc length of the curve described by the function $y = x^{-1}$, $1 < x < 2$; the length is given by the integral

$$\int_1^2 \sqrt{1 + x^{-4}}\ dx.$$

A11.11 Find the arc length of the curve described by the function $y = 1/x$, $1 < x < 2$; the length is given by the integral

$$\int_1^2 \sqrt{1 + (1/4)x^{-1}}\ dx.$$

A11.12 Find the arc length of the curve described by the function $y = \sin(x)$, $0 < x < \pi$; the length is given by the integral

$$\int_0^\pi \sqrt{1 + \cos^2(x)}\ dx.$$

A11.13 Find the arc length of the curve described by the function $y = \tan(x)$, $0 < x < \pi/4$; the length is given by the integral

$$\int_0^{\pi/4} \sqrt{1 + \sec^4(x)}\ dx.$$

A11.14 Find the arc length of the curve described by the function $y = e^x$, $0 < x < 2$; the length is given by the integral

$$\int_0^2 \sqrt{1 + (e^x)^2}\ dx = \int_0^2 \sqrt{1 + e^{2x}}\ dx.$$

A11.15 Find the arc length of the curve described by the function $y = \ln(x)$, $1 < x < 2$; the length is given by the integral

$$\int_1^2 \sqrt{1 + x^{-2}}\ dx.$$

EXTEND YOUR UNDERSTANDING

U11.1 Use the definition of the Legendre polynomial

$$P_n(x) = \frac{(-1)^n}{2^n n!} \frac{d^n}{dx^n}[(1 - x^2)^n], n \geq 1,$$

to find a relationship between $P_n'(x)$ and $P_{n+1}(x)$, and then show the equivalence of the following expressions for the coefficients for Gaussian quadrature:

$$c_i = \frac{-2}{(n + 1)\, P_n'(x_i)P_{n+1}(x_i)} \quad \text{and}$$

$$c_i = \frac{2\,(1 - x_i^2)}{(n + 1)^2 P_{n+1}^2(x_i)}.$$

U11.2 The coefficients for Gauss-Legendre quadrature can be given by the integral of the Lagrange interpolating polynomial (Jensen and Rowland, 1975, p. 225) as follows:

$$c_j = \int_{-1}^1 \frac{(x - x_1)\ldots(x - x_{j-1})(x - x_{j+1})\ldots(x - x_n)}{(x_j - x_1)\ldots(x_j - x_{j-1})(x_j - x_{j+1})\ldots(x_j - x_n)}\, dx.$$

Use this form to compute the c_j for $n = 1, 2$, and 3.

U11.3 Use Gaussian quadrature with $n = 3$ and exact arithmetic to approximate $\int_{-1}^1 x^4\, dx$.

Compare your results to the exact value of the integral and discuss the two.

U11.4 Consider again the computations for I_0, I_1, and I_2 in Romberg integration, but now pay special attention to the function evaluations that can be reused at each stage. Since the value of h changes at each stage, it may be helpful to denote the value at stage i as h_i.

$$\int_a^b f(x)\,dx \approx \frac{h}{2}[f(a) + 2f(x_1) + \ldots + 2f(x_{n-1}) + f(b)]$$

$$h = \frac{b - a}{n}, \; n \text{ subinternvals}$$

First take 1 subinterval, i.e., $n = 1$, $h_0 = b - a$:

$$I_0 \approx \frac{b - a}{2}[f(a) + f(b)]$$

Next, 2 subintervals, $n = 2$, $h_1 = \dfrac{b - a}{2}$

$$I_1 \approx \frac{b - a}{4}\left[f(a) + 2f\left(\frac{a + b}{2}\right) + f(b)\right]$$

$$= \frac{b - a}{4}[f(a) + f(b)] + \frac{b - a}{4}2f\left(\frac{a + b}{2}\right)$$

$$= \frac{1}{2}I_0 + h_1 f\left(\frac{a + b}{2}\right)$$

Subdividing again, 4 subintervals, $n = 4$, $h_2 = \dfrac{b - a}{4}$

$$I_2 \approx \frac{b - a}{8}\left[f(a) + 2f\left(\frac{3a + b}{4}\right) + 2f\left(\frac{a + b}{2}\right)\right.$$

$$\left. + 2f\left(\frac{a + 3b}{4}\right) + f(b)\right]$$

$$= \frac{b - a}{8}\left[f(a) + 2f\left(\frac{a + b}{2}\right) + f(b)\right]$$

$$+ \frac{b - a}{8}\left[2f\left(\frac{3a + b}{4}\right) + 2f\left(\frac{a + 3b}{4}\right)\right]$$

$$= \frac{1}{2}I_1 + h_2\left[f\left(\frac{3a + b}{4}\right) + f\left(\frac{a + 3b}{4}\right)\right]$$

Expand the algorithm for Romberg integration to minimize the number of function evaluations required by replacing the calls to the trapezoid function by the computation shown here. Compare the computational effort and the clarity of the process for the two forms.

U11.5 Show that the first extrapolated value obtained in Romberg integration is identical to that found by Simpson's rule.

U11.6 The error incurred in using the composite trapezoid rule to integrate $f(x)$ for $a \le x \le b$, with n subdivisions and $h = (b - a)/n$ is

$$E_T = \frac{-1}{12}(b - a)\,h^2\,f''(\eta) \quad \text{for some } \eta \quad \varepsilon\,[a, b].$$

Use this formula to find a bound on the error in the results obtained for Problems P11.6, P11.8, P11.10, P11.12, P11.15

Now, find the actual error for each of the preceding integrals—i.e., the difference between the exact value and the approximate value of the given integral. Compare the actual error with the error bound.

U11.7 The error incurred in using the composite Simpson rule to integrate $f(x)$ for $a \le x \le b$, with n subdivisions and $h = (b - a)/n$ is

$$E_S = \frac{-1}{180}(b - a)\,h^4\,f^{(4)}(\eta), \quad \text{for some } \eta \quad \varepsilon\,[a, b].$$

Use this formula to find a bound on the error in the results obtained for Problems P11.6, P11.8, P11.10, P11.12, P11.15

Now, find the actual error for each of the preceding integrals—i.e., the difference between the exact value and the approximate value of the given integral. Compare the actual error with the error bound.

U11.8 The error incurred in using the composite midpoint rule to integrate $f(x)$ for $a \le x \le b$, with n subdivisions and $h = (b - a)/n$ is

$$E_M = \frac{1}{24}(b - a)\,h^2\,f''(\eta), \quad \text{for some } \eta \quad \varepsilon \quad [a, b].$$

Use this formula to find a bound on the error in the results obtained for Problems P11.6, P11.8, P11.10, P11.12, P11.15

Now, find the actual error for each of the preceding integrals—i.e., the difference between the exact value and the approximate value of the given integral. Compare the actual error with the error bound.

12

. . . .

Ordinary Differential Equations: Initial-Value Problems

The numerical differentiation formulas presented in the previous chapter are used extensively in the numerical solution of ordinary and partial differential equations; techniques for solving first-order ordinary differential equations are the subject of this chapter. We assume that the differential equation is written in the form $y' = f(x, y)$ with the value of the function $y(x)$ given at x_0; that is, $y(x_0) = y_0$. The basic idea is to divide the interval of interest into discrete steps (of fixed width h) and find approximations to the function y at those values of x. In other words, we find solutions at $x_1, x_2, x_3, \ldots, x_n$.

The first methods we consider are based on the Taylor polynomial representation of the unknown function $y(x)$. The simplest method, Euler's, retains only the first-derivative term in the Taylor expansion. In order to use higher order Taylor polynomials, it is necessary to find higher derivatives of the function $f(x, y)$ that defines the slope of the unknown function $y(x)$.

The Runge-Kutta method achieves a more accurate solution than Euler's method does, without computing higher derivatives of f. Each step of a Runge-Kutta method involves evaluating $f(x, y)$ at several different values of x and y and combining the results to form the approximation to y at the next x.

The third group of techniques that we study are the "multistep methods," which include both explicit and implicit forms. The term "multistep" refers to the fact that these methods make use of the computed value of the solution at several previous points. Implicit methods have superior stability characteristics, but are more difficult to solve than the explicit methods. An implicit and an explicit method are often combined to form a predictor-corrector formula.

In the next chapter, we investigate techniques for solving higher order ordinary differential equation initial-value problems (ODE-IVPs) and systems of first order ODE-IVPs. In Chapter 14, we consider techniques for solving ODE boundary-value problems (BVPs). Finally, Chapter 15 presents an introduction to methods for numerically solving partial differential equations.

Example 12-A Motion of a Falling Body

The motion of a falling body is described by Newton's second law, $F = m\,a$. The acceleration a is the rate of change of the velocity of the body with respect to time. The forces acting on the body may include, in addition to gravity, air resistance that is proportional to a power of the velocity. Empirical studies suggest that air resistance can be modeled as

$$F = k\,v^p$$

where $1 \le p \le 2$ and the value of the proportionality constant k depends on the size and shape of the body, as well as the density and viscosity of the air; typically, $p = 1$ for relatively slow velocities and $p = 2$ for high velocities. For intermediate velocities (with $0 < p < 1$), numerical methods may be especially appropriate.

For $p = 1$, the differential equation takes the form

$$m\frac{dv}{dt} = -k\,v - m\,g,$$

with the positive y-direction upward and $y = 0$ at ground level. Thus, when the body is falling ($v < 0$), the resistance force is positive (upward); when the body is rising ($v > 0$), the resistance acts in the downward direction.

The ratio k/m is known as the drag coefficient; for a parachutist, a typical value is $k/m \approx 1.5$; the terminal velocity is on the order of 21 ft/s. (See Edwards and Penney, 1996.)

For resistance proportional to the square of the velocity, we must distinguish between upward and downward motion, to be sure that the resistance force is acting opposite to the motion of the object. If we leave our coordinate axis as before (with up positive), we have

$$m\frac{dv}{dt} = -k\,v^2 - m\,g \qquad \text{(for a body moving upward)}$$

or

$$m\frac{dv}{dt} = k\,v^2 - m\,g \qquad \text{(for a body moving downward)}.$$

The velocity for downward motion with air resistance proportional to velocity squared is

$$v(t) = b\frac{1 + C\,e^{pt}}{1 - C\,e^{pt}}$$

where $p = 2\sqrt{g\,k/m}$ and $b = \sqrt{g\,m/k}$. The terminal velocity is $v_f = -b$.

In this section, we consider two methods that are based on the Taylor series representation of the unknown function $y(x)$. We first discuss Euler's method, which uses only the first term in the Taylor series; we then present a higher order Taylor method.

12.1.1 Euler's Method

The simplest method of approximating the solution of the differential equation

$$y' = f(x, y)$$

is to treat the function as a constant, $f(x_0, y_0)$ and to replace the derivative y' by the forward difference quotient. This gives

$$y_1 - y_0 = f(x_0, y_0) (x_1 - x_0)$$

or

$$y_1 = y_0 + h f(x_0, y_0)$$

where $h = (b - a) / n$, and n is the number of values of the independent variable where we wish to calculate the approximate solution. Geometrically, this corresponds to using the line tangent to the true solution curve $y(x)$ to find the value of y_1, the approximation to the value of y at x_1.

In general, Euler's method gives

$$y_i = y_{i-1} + h f(x_{i-1}, y_{i-1}) \qquad \text{for } i = 1, \ldots, n.$$

If we take $f(x, y) = x + y$, $x_0 = 0$, $y_0 = 2$, and $h = 1/2$, the first step of Euler's method proceeds along the straight line shown in Fig. 12.1.

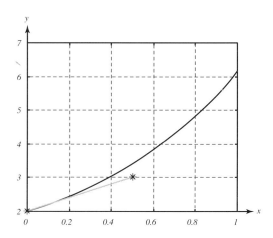

FIGURE 12.1 Exact solution and first step of Euler's method for $y' = x+y$.

Input
  f(x,y)   *right-hand side of ODE y' = f(x, y)*
  y0   *initial condition y(a) = y0*
  a   *initial value of x*
  b   *final value of x*
  n   *number of steps*
Begin computations
$$h = \frac{b - a}{n}$$ *step size*

y(0) = y0
For i = 0 to n−1   *compute next approximate value*
   x(i) = a + h i
   y(i+1) = y(i) + h f(x(i), y(i))
End
Return
y   *vector of approximate values*

The use of the algorithm for Euler's method is illustrated in the next examples.

Example 12.1 Solving a Simple ODE with Euler's Method

Consider the differential equation $y' = f(x, y)$ on $a \le x \le b$. Let

$$y' = x + y; \quad 0 \le x \le 1 \quad \text{(i.e., } a = 0, b = 1), \ y(0) = 2.$$

First, we find the approximate solution for $h = 0.5$ ($n = 2$), a very large step size. The approximation at $x_1 = 0.5$ is

$$y_1 = y_0 + h(x_0 + y_0) = 2.0 + 0.5(0.0 + 2.0) = 3.0.$$

Next, we find the approximate solution y_2 at $x_2 = 0.0 + 2h = 1.0$

$$y_2 = y_1 + h(x_1 + y_1) = 3.0 + 0.5(0.5 + 3.0) = 4.75.$$

To find a better approximate solution, we use $n = 20$ intervals, so that $h = 0.05$. Figure 12.2 shows the solution, along with the exact solution, $y = 3e^x - x - 1$.

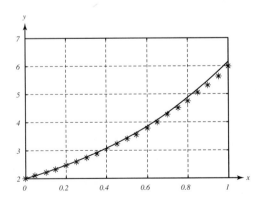

FIGURE 12.2   Exact solution and solution by
Euler's method with $n = 20$.

Example 12.2 Using Euler's Method on a More Challenging Example

Consider the differential equation

$$y' = f(x, y) = \begin{cases} y\left(-2x + \dfrac{1}{x}\right) & x \neq 0 \\ 1 & x = 0 \end{cases}$$

on the interval $0 \leq x \leq 2$ with initial value $y(0) = 0.0$. With $n = 10$ intervals, the step size $h = (b - a) / n = 0.2$. The solution is illustrated in Figure 12.3. The approximate values, z, and the values of the exact solution, $y = x \exp(-x^2)$, are listed below.

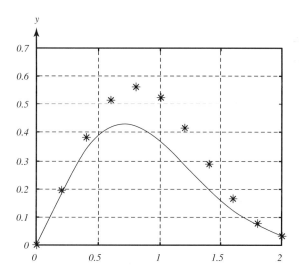

FIGURE 12.3   Euler solution with $n = 10$, and exact solution.

grid points

$x = [0 \quad 0.2 \quad 0.4 \quad 0.6 \quad 0.8 \quad 1.0 \quad 1.2 \quad 1.4 \quad 1.6 \quad 1.8 \quad 2.0 \quad]$

approximate solution

$z = [0 \quad 0.2 \quad 0.384 \quad 0.515 \quad 0.563 \quad 0.523 \quad 0.419 \quad 0.287 \quad 0.168 \quad 0.081 \quad .0317 \quad]$

exact solution (three significant digits)

$y = [0.1 \quad 0.192 \quad 0.341 \quad 0.419 \quad 0.422 \quad 0.368 \quad 0.284 \quad 0.197 \quad 0.124 \quad 0.0705 \quad 0.0366]$

Discussion

The question of how well a numerical technique for solving an initial-value ordinary differential equation works is closely related to the truncation error of the method. This is a measure of the error introduced by the approximation to the first derivative of y that is used in deriving the method. Euler's method employs only the first term in the Taylor expansion of the unknown function $y(x)$; that is,

$$y(x + h) = y(x) + h\, y'(x) + \frac{h^2}{2}\, y''(\eta)$$

with $y(x+h) = y_{i+1}$, $y(x) = y_i$, $y'(x) = f(x_i, y_i)$, $x < \eta < x + h$. Thus the *local truncation error* is $O(h^2)$. Of course, the actual error also depends on the higher derivatives of y, so if, in fact, y is linear, there will be no error. However, since the actual form of y is, in general, unknown, the dependence of the error on the step size is the most direct way to compare methods.

The total truncation error ε_n in going from x_0 to $x_0 + nh$ is bounded by an expression that depends on the Lipschitz constant for f, the bound for f', and the step size h. If f satisfies the Lipschitz condition $|f(x, y_2) - f(x, y_1)| < L\, |y_2 - y_1|$ and the second derivative of y is bounded ($|y''(\eta)| \le N$), then

$$|\varepsilon_n| \le \frac{h}{2}\, N\, \frac{\exp(L(x - x_0)) - 1}{L}.$$

Thus, the total truncation error for Euler's method is $O(h)$ and Euler's method is a first order method.

The usefulness of Euler's method is primarily a result of its simplicity, which makes it convenient for hand calculations. It may be used to provide a very few starting values for a multistep method (Section 12.3), although the Runge-Kutta methods presented in Section 12.2 give more accurate results for only slightly more computational effort.

The results of the basic Euler's method can be improved by using it with Richardson extrapolation (Froberg, 1985, p. 323). We sketch the process here, following the discussion in Jain (1979, pp. 57–58). For a given value of h, the value of y at x_{i+1} is

$$y_{i+1} = y_i + \sum_{j=1}^{\infty} c_i\, h^i.$$

If we denote the computed value as $Y(h)$, we can also find y_{i+1} by taking two steps with $h/2$ or by taking four steps with $h/4$, etc. Because the error expansion includes all powers of h, rather than only even powers, as we saw before, the extrapolation formula is

$$Y_m(k) = \frac{2^m\, Y_{m-1}(k + 1) - Y_{m-1}(k)}{2^m - 1},$$

where k designates the step size. ($k = 0, 1, \ldots$ correspond to step sizes of $h/2^0$, $h/2$, $h/2^2, \ldots, h/2^k$). The parameter m gives the extrapolation level, with Y_0 ($m = 1$) being the values computed directly from Euler's method.

12.1.2 Higher Order Taylor Methods

The discussion in the previous section suggests that one way to obtain a better solution technique is to use more terms in the Taylor series for y in order to obtain higher order truncation error. For example, a second-order Taylor method uses

$$y(x + h) = y(x) + h\,y'(x) + \frac{h^2}{2}\,y''(x) + O(h^3).$$

The local truncation error is $O(h^3)$ and the total (or global) truncation error is $O(h^2)$. However, we do not have a formula for $y''(x)$. If $y'(x) = f(x, y)$ is not too complicated, it may be practical to differentiate f with respect to x (using the chain rule, since y is a function of x) to find a representation for $y''(x)$.

Example 12.3 Solving a Simple ODE with Taylor's Method

Consider again the differential equation

$$y' = x + y;\ 0 \le x \le 1,$$

with initial condition

$$y(0) = 2.$$

To apply the second order Taylor method to the equation, we find

$$y'' = \frac{d}{dx}(x + y) = 1 + y' = 1 + x + y$$

This gives the approximation formula

$$y(x + h) = y(x) + h\,y'(x) + \frac{h^2}{h}\,y''(x),$$

or

$$y_{i+1} = y_i + h\,(x_i + y_i) + \frac{h^2}{2}\,(1 + x_i + y_i)$$

For $n = 2$ ($h = 0.5$), we find

$$y_1 = y_0 + h(x_0 + y_0) + \frac{h^2}{2}(1 + x_0 + y_0) = 2 + \frac{0 + 2}{2} + \frac{1 + 0 + 2}{8} = \frac{27}{8}$$

$$y_2 = y_1 + h(x_1 + y_1) + \frac{h^2}{2}(1 + x_1 + y_1)$$

$$= \frac{27}{8} + \frac{1}{2}\left(\frac{1}{2} + \frac{27}{8}\right) + \frac{1}{8}\left(1 + \frac{1}{2} + \frac{27}{8}\right) = 5.9219$$

A minor modification to the algorithm given for Euler's method produces the algorithm for the second order Taylor approximation; in addition to the function $f(x, y)$, the function for y'' must be provided.

Second-Order Taylor's Method

Input
  f(x,y)   *right-hand side of ODE* $y' = f(x, y)$
  g(x,y) = $f_x + f_y$ y' = $f_x + f_y$ f
  y0   *initial condition* $y(a) = y0$
  a   *initial value of x*
  b   *final value of x*
  n   *number of steps*
Begin computations

$$h = \frac{b-a}{n} \qquad \text{\textit{step size}}$$

$$k = \frac{h^2}{2}$$

For i = 0 to n   *define grid points*
    x(i) = a + h i
End

For i = 1 to n   *compute next approximate value*
    y(i) = y(i−1) + h f(x(i−1), y(i−1)) + k g(x(i−1), y(i−1))
End

Return
  y   *vector of approximate values*

In the previous section, we saw that using more terms in the Taylor series representation for the unknown function y gives more accurate results, but the necessity of computing derivatives of $f(x,y)$ is often too difficult to make the higher order Taylor methods attractive.

In this section, we consider several forms of a method of obtaining estimates for the slope of our unknown function y that do not require differentiating $f(x, y)$ in order to use higher order Taylor series expansions, but that still improve on the accuracy we can obtain from Euler's method. For example, if we could use the slope of y (i.e., the value of f) at the midpoint of the interval, it would seem to be a more balanced approximation than relying only on information at the left end of the interval. We do not know the value of y at the midpoint, but we can estimate it, as we shall see.

12.2.1   Midpoint Method

One of the simplest Runge-Kutta methods is based on approximating the value of y at $x_i + h/2$ by taking one-half of the change in y that is given by Euler's method and adding that on to the current value y_i. This method is known as the *midpoint method*. The formulas are

$$k_1 = h f(x_i, y_i) \qquad \text{(change in } y \text{ given by Euler's method),}$$

$$k_2 = h f\left(x_i + \frac{1}{2}h, y_i + \frac{1}{2}k_1\right) \quad \text{(change in } y \text{ using slope estimate at midpoint),}$$

$$y_{i+1} = y_i + k_2.$$

Although the geometric interpretation helps the method seem more intuitively plausible, the derivation of a Runge-Kutta method depends on finding ways of approximating the slope of y, using the function f evaluated at various points in the interval, so that the accuracy agrees with that obtained from Taylor series approximations. Not too surprisingly, using more involved approximations gives higher order (more accurate) methods.

The point (x_e, y_e) would be the next estimate from Euler's method; the slope at (x_m, y_m) is used to find (x_2, y_2).

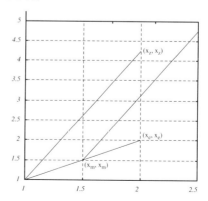

FIGURE 12.4   Geometric interpretation of midpoint method.   **457**

Midpoint Method

The use of this algorithm is illustrated in the next examples.

Example 12.4 Solving a Simple ODE with the Midpoint Method

Consider the differential equation $y' = f(x,y)$ on $a \le x \le b$.

$$y' = x + y, \qquad 0 \le x \le 1 \text{ (i.e., } a = 0, b = 1), y(0) = 2.$$

First, we find the approximate solution for $h = 0.5$ ($n = 2$), a very large step size. The approximation at $x_1 = 0.5$ is

$$k_1 = h f(x_0, y_0) \qquad\qquad = 0.5\,(x_0 + y_0) \qquad\qquad = 1.0,$$

$$k_2 = h f\left(x_0 + \frac{h}{2}, y_0 + \frac{k_1}{2} \right) = 0.5\,(x_0 + 0.25 + y_0 + 0.5) \quad = 1.375,$$

$$y_1 = y_0 + k_2 \qquad\qquad\qquad\qquad\qquad\qquad\qquad\qquad\qquad = 3.375.$$

Next, we find the approximate solution y_2 at point $x_2 = 0.0 + 2h = 1.0$:

$$k_1 = h f(x_1, y_1) \qquad\qquad = 0.5\,(x_1 + y_1) = 0.5\,(0.5 + 3.375) = 1.9375,$$

$$k_2 = h f\left(x_1 + \frac{h}{2}, y_1 + \frac{k_1}{2} \right) = 0.5\,(0.5 + 0.25 + 3.375 + 0.97) \quad = 2.547,$$

$$y_2 = y_1 + k_2 \qquad\qquad\qquad = 3.375 + 2.5469 \qquad\qquad\qquad = 5.922.$$

The computed points and the exact solution, $y = 3\,e^x - x - 1$, are shown in Fig. 12.5.

With $n = 10$, the computed values appear to fall directly on the graph of the exact solution. For comparison, the midpoint method with $n = 10$ requires approximately the same number of function evaluations as does Euler's method with $n = 20$ (Fig. 12.2) and the fourth-order Runge-Kutta method presented in the next section, with $n = 5$.

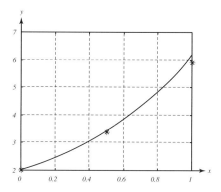

FIGURE 12.5   Solution of $y' = x + y$ using midpoint method, $n = 2$, and exact solution.

Example 12.5 ODE for Dawson's Integral

Let

$$y' = 1 - 2\,x\,y,\ y(0) = 0, \qquad a = 0, b = 1, n = 10.$$

The computed points, shown in Fig. 12.6, are as follows:

$x =$ 0.00 0.10 0.20 0.30 0.40 0.50 0.60 0.70 0.80 0.90 1.000,
$y =$ 0.00 0.099 0.19 0.28 0.36 0.42 0.47 0.51 0.53 0.54 0.54.

The exact solution is $y = \exp(-x^2) \int_0^x \exp(t^2)\, dt$ which is known as Dawson's integral.

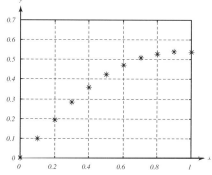

FIGURE 12.6   Solution of $y' = 1 - 2xy$ using midpoint method, $n = 10$.

12.2.2   Other Second-Order Runge-Kutta Methods

The general form for a second-order Runge-Kutta method is

$$k_1 = h\,f(x_n, y_n), \qquad k_2 = h\,f(x_n + c_2 h, y_n + a_{21} k_1)$$

$$y_{n+1} = y_n + w_1 k_1 + w_2 k_2.$$

We can summarize any such method by listing its parameters in an array whose standard form is as follows:

$$
\begin{array}{c|c}
c_2 & a_{21} \\
\hline
 & w_1 \quad w_2
\end{array}
$$

A parameter array is even more useful for higher order methods, which we consider shortly.

The **improved Euler's** (or Euler-Cauchy) method is given by the formulas

$$k_1 = h\,f(x_n, y_n), \qquad k_2 = h\,f(x_n + h, y_n + k_1),$$

$$y_{n+1} = y_n + \frac{1}{2} k_1 + \frac{1}{2} k_2.$$

The parameter array for the improved Euler method is as follows:

$$
\begin{array}{c|c}
1 & 1 \\
\hline
 & 1/2 \quad 1/2
\end{array}
$$

Heun's method, with

$$k_1 = h\,f(x_n, y_n), \qquad k_2 = h\,f\left(x_n + \frac{2}{3} h, y_n + \frac{2}{3} k_1\right),$$

$$y_{n+1} = y_n + \frac{1}{4} k_1 + \frac{3}{4} k_2,$$

has the following parameter array:

$$
\begin{array}{c|c}
2/3 & 2/3 \\
\hline
 & 1/4 \quad 3/4
\end{array}
$$

For comparison, the formulas for the **midpoint method** are:

$$k_1 = h\,f(x_{n=y_i}),\ k_2 = h\,f\left(x_n + \frac{1}{2} h, y_n + \frac{1}{2} k_1\right),\ y_{n+1} = y_n + k_2.$$

The parameters for the midpoint method are as follows:

$$
\begin{array}{c|c}
1/2 & 1/2 \\
\hline
 & 0 \quad 1
\end{array}
$$

Example 12.6 Improved Euler and Midpoint Methods

Consider the differential equation $y' = x\,y$ on $1 \le x \le 2$, $y(1) = 1$.
First we find the approximate solution for $h = 0.5$ $(n = 2)$, a very large step size.

Using the Improved Euler's Method:
The approximation at $x_1 = 1.5$ is

$$
\begin{aligned}
k_1 &= h\,f(x_0,\, y_0) & &= 0.5 \\
k_2 &= h\,f(x_0 + h,\, y_0 + k_1) & &= 1.125 \\
y_1 &= y_0 + 0.5\,k_1 + 0.5\,k_2 & &= 1.8125
\end{aligned}
$$

Next, we find the approximate solution y_2 at $x_2 = 2.0$:

$$
\begin{aligned}
k_1 &= h\,f(x_1,\, y_1) & &= 3.171875 \\
y_2 &= y_1 + 0.5\,k_1 + 0.5\,k_2 & &= 4.078125
\end{aligned}
$$

Using the Midpoint Method:
The approximation at $x_1 = 1.5$ is

$$
\begin{aligned}
k_1 &= h\,f(x_0,\, y_0) & &= 0.5 \\
k_2 &= h\,f(x_0 + 0.5\,h,\, y_0 + 0.5\,k_1) & &= 0.7812 \\
y_1 &= y_0 + k_2 & &= 1.7812
\end{aligned}
$$

Next, we find the approximate solution y_2 at $x_2 = 2.0$:

$$
\begin{aligned}
k_1 &= h\,f(x_1,\, y_1) & &= 0.8906 \\
k_2 &= h\,f(x_1 + 0.5\,h,\, y_1 + 0.5\,k_1) & &= 1.9482 \\
y_2 &= y_1 + k_2 & &= 3.7295
\end{aligned}
$$

For comparison, we note that the exact solution to this problem is

$$
y = e^{-1/2}\,\exp(0.5\,x^2)
$$

To four decimal places, $y(1.5) = 1.8682$ and $y(2.0) = 4.4817$, so for this problem the improved Euler method gives better results.

Discussion of Improved Euler and Midpoint Methods

It is not easy to obtain error bounds for Runge-Kutta methods because the error depends on both the behavior of the function that defines the ODE and its partial derivatives. However, to give an indication of the relationship between the error bounds for the most common second-order Runge-Kutta methods, we can summarize the results of the error analysis in Ralston and Rabinowitz (1978, p. 216) by letting K denote the appropriate combination of bounds on f and its partial derivatives. Then the error bounds are summarized in the following table. These bounds are quite conservative, and the actual error is often much less.

Method	bound on error
midpoint	$K/2$
Heun	$K/3$
improved Euler	$2K/3$

Discussion

To derive the second-order Runge-Kutta formulas, we write them as

$$y(x + h) = y(x) + h\,[w_1\, f(x, y) + w_2\, f(x + c_2 h, y + a_{21}\, k_1)],$$

form the Taylor expansion of $f(x + c_2 h, y + a_{21} k_1)$, and find values of the parameters w_1, w_2, c_2, and a_{21}, so that the method agrees with the second-order Taylor method. The Taylor expansion for $f(x + c_2 h, y + a_{21} k_1)$ is

$$f(x + c_2 h, y + a_{21} k_1) = f(x, y) + c_2 h\, f_x\,(x, y) + a_{21}\, k_1\, f_y\,(x, y).$$

Thus, we want the Runge-Kutta formula

$$y(x + h) = y(x) + h\, w_1\, f + h\, w_2\, f + w_2\, c_2\, h^2\, f_x + w_2\, a_{21}\, k_1\, h\, f_y \quad (12.1)$$

to agree with the second-order Taylor formula

$$y(x + h) = y(x) + h\, f + \frac{h^2}{2} [f_x + f_y\, f]; \quad (12.2)$$

where f, f_x, and f_y are all evaluated at (x, y).

Matching the terms involving f in eqs. (12.1) and (12.2) gives

$$w_1 + w_2 = 1.$$

Matching the terms with f_x gives $w_2\, c_2 h = \dfrac{h}{2}$, so

$$w_2\, c_2 = \frac{1}{2}.$$

Matching the terms with f_y gives $w_2\, a_{21}\, k_1 = \dfrac{h}{2}\, f$; since $k_1 = h\, f$, we have

$$w_2\, a_{21} = \frac{1}{2}.$$

The midpoint method is obtained by taking $w_1 = 0$ and $w_2 = 1$; this then requires that $c_2 = \dfrac{1}{2}$ and $a_{21} = \dfrac{1}{2}$.

The modified Euler method is obtained by taking $w_1 = \dfrac{1}{2}$ and $w_2 = \dfrac{1}{2}$; this then requires that $c_2 = 1$ and $a_{21} = 1$.

The Heun method is obtained by taking $w_1 = \dfrac{1}{4}$ and $w_2 = \dfrac{3}{4}$; this then requires that $c_2 = \dfrac{2}{3}$ and $a_{21} = \dfrac{2}{3}$.

12.2.3 Third-order Runge-Kutta Methods

The general form for a third-order Runge-Kutta method is

$$k_1 = h\,f(x_n, y_n),$$
$$k_2 = h\,f(x_n + c_2 h, y_n + a_{21}k_1),$$
$$k_3 = h\,f(x_n + c_3 h, y_n + a_{31}k_1 + a_{32}k_2),$$
$$y_{n+1} = y_n + w_1 k_1 + w_2 k_2 + w_3 k_3.$$

The array of parameters has the following form:

$$
\begin{array}{c|ccc}
c_2 & a_{21} & & \\[4pt]
c_3 & a_{31} & a_{32} & \\[4pt]
\hline
 & w_1 & w_2 & w_3
\end{array}
$$

The parameters for four well-known third-order methods are as follows (see Jain, 1979 for further discussion):

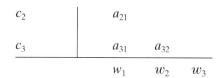

2/3		2/3		
2/3		0	2/3	
		2/8	3/8	3/8

Nystrom

1/2		1/2		
1		−1	2	
		1/6	4/6	1/6

Classical

1/2		1/2		
3/4		0	3/4	
		2/9	3/9	4/9

Nearly optimal

1/3		1/3		
2/3		0	2/3	
		1/4	0	3/4

Heun

The parameters of a third-order Runge-Kutta method satisfy (Ralston & Rabinowitz, 1978, pp. 216–217):

$$w_1 + w_2 + w_3 = 1$$
$$c_2 w_2 + c_3 w_3 = \frac{1}{2}$$
$$c_2^2 w_2 + c_3^2 w_3 = \frac{1}{3}$$
$$c_2 a_{32} w_3 = \frac{1}{6}$$
$$c_2 = a_{21}$$
$$c_3 = a_{31} + a_{32}$$

12.2.4 Classic Runge-Kutta Method

Probably the most common form of the Runge-Kutta method is the classic fourth-order method. It uses a linear combination of four function evaluations:

$$k_1 = h\, f(x_i, y_i),$$

$$k_2 = h\, f\left(x_i + \frac{1}{2}h,\ y_i + \frac{1}{2}k_1\right),$$

$$k_3 = h\, f\left(x_i + \frac{1}{2}h,\ y_i + \frac{1}{2}k_2\right),$$

$$k_4 = h\, f(x_i + h,\ y_i + k_3).$$

These four equations, together with the recursion equation

$$y_{i+1} = y_i + \frac{1}{6}k_1 + \frac{1}{3}k_2 + \frac{1}{3}k_3 + \frac{1}{6}k_4,$$

make up the method. The classic fourth-order Runge-Kutta method is described in the following algorithm.

Classic Runge-Kutta Method

Input
    f(x,y)   *right-hand side of ODE* $y' = f(x, y)$
    y0   *initial condition* $y(a) = y0$
    a   *initial value of x*
    b   *final value of x*
    n   *number of steps*

Begin computations

$$h = \frac{b - a}{n} \qquad \textit{step size}$$

y(0) = y0
For i = 0 to n−1
    x(i) = a + h i   *define grid point*
    k_1 = h f(x(i), y(i))

$$k_2 = h\, f\left(x(i) + \frac{1}{2}h,\ y(i) + \frac{1}{2}k_1\right)$$

$$k_3 = h\, f\left(x(i) + \frac{1}{2}h,\ y(i) + \frac{1}{2}k_2\right)$$

    k_4 = h f(x(i) + h , y(i) + k_3)

$$y(i + 1) = y(i) + \frac{1}{6}k_1 + \frac{1}{3}k_2 + \frac{1}{3}k_3 + \frac{1}{6}k_4$$

End

Return
    y   *vector of approximate values*

Example 12.7 Solving a Simple ODE with the Classic Runge-Kutta Method

Consider again the differential equation

$$y' = f(x, y) = x + y, \quad y(0) = 2,$$

with

$$a = 0, b = 1, n = 5, h = 0.2.$$

For comparison with the results of Euler's method, observe that this choice of n will require approximately the same number of evaluations of $f(x, y)$ as are used in Euler's method with $n = 20$.

  The graphs of the approximate and exact solutions are almost indistinguishable. The computed points and the exact solution, $y = 3 e^x - x - 1$, are shown in Fig. 12.7, and in the following table. The error is much less than for Euler's method.

Solving $y' = x + y$ with classic fourth-order Runge-Kutta method

x	Exact soln	Approx soln	Abs error
0.2	2.4642	2.4642	8.2745e-06
0.4	3.0755	3.0755	2.0213e-05
0.6	3.8664	3.8663	3.7032e-05
0.8	4.8766	4.8766	6.0308e-05
1.0	6.1548	6.1548	9.2076e-05

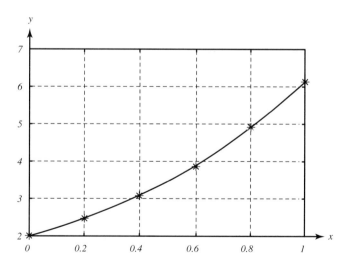

FIGURE 12.7 Solution of $y' = x + y$ with classic Runge-Kutta method, $n = 5$.

Example 12.8 Another Example of Using the Classic Runge-Kutta Method

Consider once more the differential equation

$$y' = f(x, y) = \begin{cases} y\left(-2x + \dfrac{1}{x}\right) & x \neq 0 \\ 1 & x = 0 \end{cases}$$

on the interval $0 \leq x \leq 2$ with initial value $y(0) = 0.0$. The values of the exact solution, $y = x \exp(-x^2)$ and the approximate solution at the mesh points (with $n = 10$) are shown in the following table and graphed in Figure 12.8.

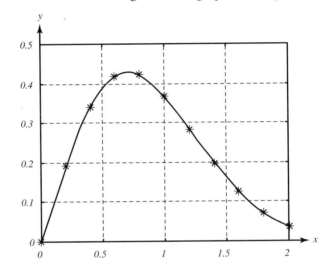

FIGURE 12.8   Classic Runge-Kutta method solution of $y' = y(-2x + 1/x)$

$y' = y\left(-2x + \dfrac{1}{x}\right)$, fourth-order Runge-Kutta method ($n = 10$).

x	Exact soln	Approx soln	Abs error
0.2	0.19216	0.19215	1.2288e-05
0.4	0.34086	0.34093	7.1314e-05
0.6	0.41861	0.41872	1.1072e-04
0.8	0.42183	0.42195	1.1763e-04
1.0	0.36788	0.36798	1.0280e-04
1.2	0.28431	0.28439	7.9678e-05
1.4	0.19720	0.19727	6.5398e-05
1.6	0.12369	0.12376	7.0105e-05
1.8	0.070495	0.070584	8.9035e-05
2.0	0.036631	0.036738	1.0716e-04

12.2.5   Other Runge-Kutta Methods

The Runge-Kutta methods described in the previous sections are only the most common, simple forms of a very extensive field of study. We write a general fourth-order Runge-Kutta method as

$$k_1 = h f(x_n, y_n)$$
$$k_2 = h f(x_n + c_2 h, y_n + a_{21}k_1),$$
$$k_3 = h f(x_n + c_3 h, y_n + a_{31}k_1 + a_{32}k_2),$$
$$k_4 = h f(x_n + c_4 h, y_n + a_{41}k_1 + a_{42}k_2 + a_{43}k_3),$$

$$y_{n+1} = y_n + w_1 k_1 + w_2 k_2 + w_3 k_3 + w_4 k_4.$$

where the array of parameters has the form

c_2	a_{21}		
c_3	a_{31}	a_{32}	
c_4	a_{41}	a_{42}	a_{43}
	w_1	w_2	w_3	w_4

The parameter arrays for two fourth-order methods are as follows:

1/2	1/2		
1/2	0	1/2	
1	0	0	1
	1/6	2/6	2/6	1/6

Classic fourth-order Runge-Kutta method

1/3	1/3		
2/3	−1/3	1	
1	1	−1	1
	1/8	3/8	3/8	1/8

Kutta's method

Higher order Runge-Kutta methods are described in a similar manner;

$$k_1 = h\,f(x_n, y_n),$$
$$k_2 = h\,f(x_n + c_2h, y_n + a_{21}k_1),$$
$$k_3 = h\,f(x_n + c_3h, y_n + a_{31}k_1 + a_{32}k_2),$$
$$k_4 = h\,f(x_n + c_4h, y_n + a_{41}k_1 + a_{42}k_2 + a_{43}k_3),$$

$$\cdot$$
$$\cdot$$
$$\cdot$$

$$k_m = h\,f(x_n + c_mh, y_n + a_{m1}k_1 + a_{m2}k_2 + \ldots + a_{m,m-1}k_{m-1}),$$
$$y_{n+1} = y_n + w_1k_1 + w_2k_2 + \ldots + w_mk_m.$$

Thus, to describe a Runge-Kutta method, we need to specify the parameters $c_2, \ldots, c_m, a_{21}, \ldots, a_{m,m-1}$, and $w_1, \ldots, w_m$. The parameters for a fifth-order method and a sixth-order method are given in the following tables (see Jain, 1979, for further discussion):

1/2	1/2					
1/4	3/16	1/16				
1/2	0	0	1/2			
3/4	0	−3/16	6/16	9/16		
1	1/7	4/7	6/7	−12/7	8/7	
	7/90	0	32/90	12/90	32/90	7/90

Lawson's fifth-order Runge-Kutta method

1/3	1/3					
2/3	0	2/3				
1/3	1/12	1/3	−1/12			
1/2	−1/16	9/8	−3/16	−3/8		
1/2	0	9/8	−3/8	−3/4	1/2	
1	9/44	−9/11	63/44	18/11	0	−16/11
	11/120	0	27/40	27/40	−4/15	−4/15	11/120

Butcher's sixth-order Runge-Kutta method

12.2.6 Runge-Kutta-Fehlberg Methods

The Runge-Kutta-Fehlberg methods use a pair of Runge-Kutta methods to obtain both the computed solution and an estimate of the truncation error. The estimate of the error can be used in programs of variable step size to decide when to adjust the step size. We outline here the most well-known Runge-Kutta-Fehlberg formulas, which combine Runge-Kutta formulas of orders 4 and 5. In general, six function evaluations are required for a method of order 5; Fehlberg developed a fourth-order method, which uses five of the function evaluations that are used in the higher order method, so the extra computational burden is slight. The parameters for the fourth- and fifth-order methods are given in the following tables:

$\frac{1}{4}$	$\frac{1}{4}$				
$\frac{3}{8}$	$\frac{3}{32}$	$\frac{9}{32}$			
$\frac{12}{13}$	$\frac{1932}{2197}$	$\frac{-7200}{2197}$	$\frac{7296}{2197}$		
1	$\frac{439}{216}$	-8	$\frac{3680}{513}$	$\frac{-845}{4104}$	
	$\frac{25}{216}$	0	$\frac{1408}{2565}$	$\frac{2197}{4104}$	$\frac{-1}{5}$

Fourth-order Runge-Kutta method

$\frac{1}{4}$	$\frac{1}{4}$				
$\frac{3}{8}$	$\frac{3}{32}$	$\frac{9}{32}$			
$\frac{12}{13}$	$\frac{1932}{2197}$	$\frac{-7200}{2197}$	$\frac{7296}{2197}$		
1	$\frac{439}{216}$	-8	$\frac{3680}{513}$	$\frac{-845}{4104}$	
$\frac{1}{2}$	$\frac{-8}{27}$	2	$\frac{-3544}{2565}$	$\frac{1859}{4104}$	$\frac{-11}{40}$
	$\frac{16}{135}$	0	$\frac{6656}{12825}$	$\frac{28561}{56430}$	$\frac{-9}{50}$	$\frac{2}{55}$

Fifth-order Runge-Kutta method

The estimated error is the value computed from the fifth-order method minus the value computed from the fourth-order method; it can be expressed directly as

$$\text{error} = \frac{1}{360} k_1 + 0\, k_2 + \frac{-128}{4275} k_3 + \frac{-2197}{75240} k_4 + \frac{1}{50} k_5 + \frac{2}{55} k_6.$$

(See Atkinson, 1989, for further discussion.)

Many approximation methods use more than one previous approximate solution value or function evaluation (of the right-hand side of the differential equation) involving approximate solution values at several previous points; such methods are known as *multistep methods*. The methods we have discussed so far use only one previous approximation and are therefore known as *one-step methods*.

The general form of a two-step method to solve the initial value problem

$$y' = f(x, y); \qquad y(x_0) = y_0$$

is

$$y_{i+1} = a_1 y_i + a_2 y_{i-1} + h[b_0 f(x_{i+1}, y_{i+1}) + b_1 f(x_i, y_i) + b_2 f(x_{i-1}, y_{i-1})]$$

where the coefficients $a_1, a_2, b_0, b_1,$ and b_2 depend on the particular method. We use the notation

$$f_{i+1} = f(x_{i+1}, y_{i+1}); \quad f_i = f(x_i, y_i); \quad f_{i-1} = f(x_{i-1}, y_{i-1}); \quad h = \frac{b - a}{n}.$$

Multistep methods are further distinguished according to whether the coefficient b_0 on the $f(x_{i+1}, y_{i+1})$ term is zero. Multistep methods in which the coefficient of the $f(x_{i+1}, y_{i+1})$ term is zero are known as *explicit methods*. An explicit two-step method has the form

$$y_{i+1} = a_1 y_i + a_2 y_{i-1} + h[b_1 f(x_i, y_i) + b_2 f(x_{i-1}, y_{i-1})]$$

If the coefficient b_0 is not zero, then the unknown y_{i+1} appears on the right hand side of the equation, necessitating an iterative solution procedure, in general. Such methods are called *implicit*. Not too surprisingly, they have some nice properties that make them important techniques and that compensate for the apparent disadvantages of the difficulty of their solution.

Multistep methods require starting values, in addition to the initial condition specified for the differential equation. For a two-step method, y_1 must be found by some other method, such as a Runge-Kutta solution; for an n-step method, the first $n-1$ values must be computed by another method.

12.3.1 Adams-Bashforth Methods

Among the most popular explicit multistep methods are the Adams-Bashforth methods. For Adams-Bashforth methods, the number of steps is the same as the order of the method. The local truncation error is one order higher than the overall order of the method. The computational procedure for the second-, third-, fourth- and fifth-order Adams-Bashforth methods are summarized here.

Second-Order Adams-Bashforth (Two-Step) Method

y_0 is given by the initial condition for the differential equation.
y_1 is found from a one-step method, such as a Runge-Kutta technique.
Then, for $i = 1, \ldots, n-1$

$$y_{i+1} = y_i + \frac{h}{2} [3 f_i - f_{i-1}]$$

Comparing this formula with the general form of a two-step method, we see that

$$a_1 = 1, a_2 = 0, b_0 = 0, b_1 = 3/2, \text{ and } b_2 = -1/2.$$

It is quite common to have $a_2 = 0$. Because the method is explicit, $b_0 = 0$.

Third-Order Adams-Bashforth (Three-Step) Method

y_0 is given by the initial conditions for the ODE.
y_1 and y_2 are found from a one-step method, such as a Runge-Kutta technique.
Then, for $i = 2, \ldots n-1$

$$y_{i+1} = y_i + \frac{h}{12} [23 f_i - 16 f_{i-1} + 5 f_{i-2}]$$

Fourth-Order Adams-Bashforth (Four-Step) Method

y_0 is given by the ODE
y_1, y_2 and y_3 are found from a one-step method.
Then, for $i = 3, \ldots n-1$

$$y_{i+1} = y_i + \frac{h}{24} [55 f_i - 59 f_{i-1} + 37 f_{i-2} - 9 f_{i-3}]$$

Fifth-Order Adams-Bashforth (Five-Step) Method

y_0 is given for the ODE,
y_1 through y_4 are found from a one-step method.
Then, for $i = 4, \ldots n-1$

$$y_{i+1} = y_i + \frac{h}{720} [1901 f_i - 2774 f_{i-1} + 2616 f_{i-2} - 1274 f_{i-3} + 251 f_{i-4}]$$

The primary use of the explicit Adams-Bashforth methods presented in this section is in conjunction with the implicit Adams-Moulton methods that we consider next. Especially for the higher order Adams-Bashforth methods, stability requirements severely limit the step size for which the method gives reasonable results. (The large negative coefficients appearing in the formula for the fifth-order Adams-Bashforth method are one indication that the method may have difficulty.)

Third-Order Adams-Bashforth Method

$$
\begin{array}{ll}
\textit{Input} & \\
\quad f(x,y) & \textit{right-hand side of ODE } y' = f(x, y) \\
\quad y0 & \textit{initial condition } y(a) = y0 \\
\quad a & \textit{initial value of } x \\
\quad b & \textit{final value of } x \\
\quad n & \textit{number of steps}
\end{array}
$$

Begin computations

$$h = \frac{b - a}{n} \qquad \textit{step size}$$

$k = h/12$

$y(0) = y0$

$$
\begin{array}{ll}
\text{For } i = 0 \text{ to } 1 & \textit{use midpoint method to start} \\
\quad z_i = f(x_i, y_i) & \\
\quad k_1 = h\, z_i & \\
\quad k_2 = h\, f\!\left(x_i + \frac{1}{2}\,h,\ y_i + \frac{1}{2}\,k_1 \right) & \\
\quad y_{i+1} = y_i + k_2 &
\end{array}
$$

End

$$
\begin{array}{ll}
\text{For } i = 2 \text{ to } n-1 & \textit{use third-order AB method to continue} \\
\quad x(i) = a + h\, i & \textit{define grid point} \\
\quad z_i = f(x_i, y_i) & \\
\quad y_{i+1} = y_i + k\,(23\, z_i - 16\, z_{i-1} + 5\, z_{i-2}) &
\end{array}
$$

End

$$
\begin{array}{ll}
\textit{Return} & \\
\quad y & \textit{vector of approximate values}
\end{array}
$$

The use of the algorithm for the Adams-Bashforth method is illustrated in the next example.

Example 12.9 Solving a Simple ODE
with an Adams-Bashforth Method

Using a simple computer program to implement the algorithm for the Adams-Bashforth three-step method to solve the simple ODE

$$y' = x + y; \qquad y(0) = 2;$$

gives the following computed values:

```
grid points
x =          [0       0.2      0.4      0.6      0.8      1     ]
AB3 solution
y =          [2       2.46     3.0652   3.8509   4.8546   6.1241]
exact solution
y =          [2       2.4642   3.0755   3.8664   4.8766   6.1548]
```

The computed values are graphed in Fig. 12.9 together with the exact solution, $y = 3\,e^x - x - 1$.

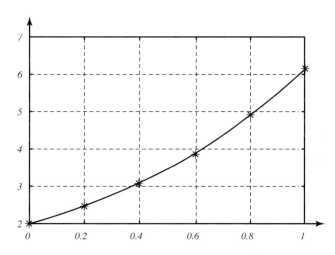

FIGURE 12.9   Solution to simple ODE using Adams-Bashforth third-order method.

12.3.2 Adams-Moulton Methods

Among the most popular implicit multistep methods are the Adams-Moulton methods. We first give the formulas for several Adams-Moulton methods. We then show how these are used together with the Adams-Bashforth methods in practice.

The coefficients of the error term are, in general, smaller for implicit methods than for the corresponding explicit method of the same order. (See summary at end of chapter.) Thus, implicit methods have less round-off error than do explicit methods.

The starting values for each method should be found from a one-step method (e.g., a Runge-Kutta method) of the same order as the Adams-Moulton method. The order of an Adams-Moulton method (global truncation error) is one order higher than the number of steps involved in the method. As with other numerical methods for ODE, the local truncation error is one order higher than the global error.

Third-Order Adams-Moulton (Two-Step) Method

y_0 is given by the initial condition for the ODE;
y_1 is found from a one-step method, e.g., a third-order Runge-Kutta method.
Then, for $i = 1, \ldots, n-1$,

$$y_{i+1} = y_i + \frac{h}{12} [5f_{i+1} + 8f_i - f_{i-1}]$$

Comparing this formula with the general form of a two-step method, we see that

$$a_1 = 1, \quad a_2 = 0, \quad b_0 = 5/12, \quad b_1 = 8/12, \text{ and } \quad b_2 = -1/12.$$

As with the Adams-Bashforth two-step method, $a_2 = 0$. Also, note that $b_0 \neq 0$, because this method is implicit.

Fourth-Order Adams-Moulton (Three-Step) Method

y_0 is given by the initial condition.
y_1 and y_2 are found from a one-step method.
Then, for $i = 2, \ldots, n-1$

$$y_{i+1} = y_i + \frac{h}{24} [9f_{i+1} + 19f_i - 5f_{i-1} + f_{i-2}]$$

Fifth-Order Adams-Moulton (Four-Step) Method

y_0 is given by the initial condition.
y_1, y_2 and y_3 are found from a one-step method.
Then

$$y_{i+1} = y_i + \frac{h}{720} [251f_{i+1} + 646f_i - 264f_{i-1} + 106f_{i-2} - 19f_{i-3}].$$

12.3.3   Predictor-Corrector Methods

In order to take advantage of the beneficial properties of implicit methods while avoiding the difficulties inherent in solving the implicit equation, an explicit and implicit method can be combined. The explicit method is used to predict a value of y_{i+1}, which we denote $y_{i+1}{}^*$. This value is then used in the right hand side of the implicit method, which produces an improved, or corrected, value of y_{i+1}.

Before considering the various ways one can combine an implicit and an explicit method of the same order to form a predictor-corrector method, we note that the implicit second-order (one-step) method known as the trapezoidal method, given by the equation $y_{i+1} = y_i + \dfrac{h}{2}[f_{i+1} + f_i]$ can also be viewed as the second-order Adams-Moulton method. (See Atkinson, 1989, p. 366.)

Second-Order Adams-Bashforth-Moulton Predictor-Corrector Method

As a simple example, we can use the second-order Adams-Bashforth method as a predictor with the second-order Adams-Moulton method as a corrector.

We begin with

y_0 given by the initial condition
y_1 found from a one-step method
Then, for $i = 1, \ldots, n-1$, compute

$$y^*{}_{i+1} = y_i + \frac{h}{2}[3f(x_i, y_i) - f(x_{i-1}, y_{i-1})]$$

$$y_{i+1} = y_i + \frac{h}{2}[f(x_{i+1}, y^*{}_{i+1}) + f(x_i, y_i)]$$

Third-order Adams-Bashforth-Moulton Predictor-Corrector Method

We can use the third-order Adams-Bashforth method as a predictor, with the third-order Adams-Moulton method as the corrector.

We begin with

y_0 given by the initial condition
y_1 and y_2 found from a one-step method
Then, for $i = 2, \ldots, n-1$, compute

$$y^*{}_{i+1} = y_i + \frac{h}{12}[23f(x_i, y_i) - 16f(x_{i-1}, y_{i-1}) + 5f(x_{i-2}, y_{i-2})]$$

$$y_{i+1} = y_i + \frac{h}{12}[5f(x_{i+1}, y^*{}_{i+1}) + 8f(x_i, y_i) - f(x_{i-1}, y_{i-1})]$$

Higher-Order Predictor-Corrector Methods

Combining an Adams-Bashforth method (as a predictor) with the corresponding order Adams-Moulton method (as a corrector) gives a predictor-corrector method of the same order.

The following algorithm computes the approximate the solution of the ODE

$$y' = f(x, y) \text{ with initial condition } y(a) = y_0$$

using the third order Adams-Bashforth-Moulton predictor corrector method.

Third-Order Adams-Bashforth-Moulton Method

Input
    f(x,y)   *right-hand side of ODE y′ = f(x, y)*
    y0   *initial condition y(a) = y0*
    a   *initial value of x*
    b   *final value of x*
    n   *number of steps*

Begin computations

$$h = \frac{b - a}{n} \qquad \text{\textit{step size}}$$

k = h/12
y(0) = y0

For i = 0 to 1   *use midpoint method to start*
    x(i) = a + h i   *define grid point*
    $z_i = f(x_i, y_i)$
    $k_1 = h\, z_i$

$$k_2 = h\, f\!\left(x_i + \frac{1}{2}h,\, y_i + \frac{1}{2}k_1\right)$$

    $y_{i+1} = y_i + k_2$

End
For in Fig. 12.95i = 2 to n−1
    x(i) = a + h i   *define grid point*
    $z_i = f(x_i, y_i)$
    $y^* = y_i + k\,(23\, z_i - 16\, z_{i-1} + 5\, z_{i-2})$ *use AB to predict*
    $z^* = f(x_{i+1}, y^*)$

$$y_{i+1} = y_i + \frac{h}{12}(5\, z^* + 8\, z_i - z_{i-1}) \qquad \text{\textit{use AM to correct}}$$

End

Return
    y   *vector of approximate values*

Note that it is not necessary to index the variables y^* and z^*, since values of the function $f(x,y)$ at y^* (the predicted value of y) are not used in the computations at the next step.

Example 12.10 Using an Adams Predictor Corrector Method

Consider again the differential equation

$$y' = f(x, y) = x + y;$$
$$y(0) = 2.$$

The approximate solution was computed using the third-order Adams-Bashforth-Moulton predictor-corrector equations with the midpoint method to start. Since the exact solution is $y = 3 e^x - x - 1$, we can find the error at each value of x where the solution has been approximated. In order to demonstrate the benefit derived from using the corrector, we also show the results we computed earlier using the Adams-Bashforth third-order method (see Fig. 12.10 as well):

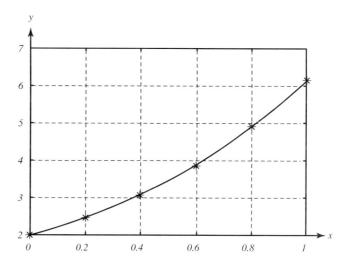

FIGURE 12.10   Solving $y' = x + y$ with a third-order predictor-corrector method.

x =   [0   0.2   0.4   0.6   0.8   1   ]

Computed results using A-B-M third-order predictor-corrector method:

y =   [2   2.46   3.0652   3.8538   4.8614   6.1365]

Values of exact solution (to five digits):

y =   [2   2.4642   3.0755   3.8664   4.8766   6.1548]

Results from Example 12.9, using Adams-Bashforth third-order method:

y =   [2   2.46   3.0652   3.8509   4.8546   6.1241]

Example 12.11 Velocity of Falling Parachutist

Consider the situation described in Example 12-A, in which the velocity of a parachutist with drag coefficient $k/m = 1.5$, $g = 32$, and $v_0 = 0$ is given by

$$m\frac{dv}{dt} = k(-v) - m\,g.$$

The parachutist reaches a terminal velocity of approximately 21 ft/sec after only about 3 seconds.

If we modify the model slightly, so that

$$m\frac{dv}{dt} = k(-v)^{1.1} - m\,g$$

we find that the terminal velocity is somewhat slower. Figure 12.11 shows the velocity of the parachutist under both models of air resistance.

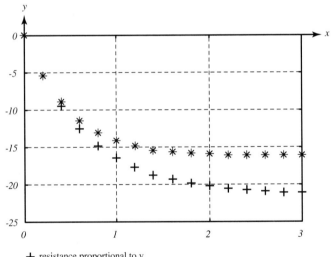

+ resistance proportional to v

* resistance proportional to $v^{1.1}$

FIGURE 12.11 Velocity of parachutist with air resistance: + denotes resistance proportional to v; * denotes resistance proportional to $v^{1.1}$.

The term "stability" is used in a variety of ways in the description of differential equations, and in particular, numerical methods for solving differential equations. For some differential equations, any errors that occur in computation will be magnified regardless of the numerical method. Such problems are called *ill-conditioned*. Other differential equations require extremely small step sizes to achieve accurate results; these problems are called *stiff*. Since these types of difficulties occur more often with higher order ODE, or systems of ODE, we postpone our discussion of stiff and ill-conditioned problems until Chapter 13.

We now consider the stability of the numerical methods presented in the previous sections. We call a numerical method *stable* if errors incurred at one stage of the process do not tend to be magnified at later stages. The analysis of the stability of a method often involves the investigation of the error for a simple problem, such as $y' = \lambda y$. If the method is unstable for the model equation, it is likely to behave badly for other problems as well, and the method is unstable. If $\lambda > 0$, the true solution grows exponentially, and it is not reasonable to expect the error to remain small as x increases. The most we could hope for is that the error remains small relative to the solution. On the other hand, for $\lambda < 0$ the exact solution is a decaying exponential, and we would like the error to also go to zero as $x \rightarrow \infty$.

12.4.1 Absolute Stabililty

If we apply Euler's method to the model equation, with initial condition $y(0) = y_0$, and to the same equation with error introduced in the form of a perturbation of the initial condition to $y(0) = y_0 + \varepsilon$, we find that the difference of the two solutions $z(x)$ satisfies the differential equation $z' = \lambda z$ with $z(0) = \varepsilon$. Applying Euler's method (with step size h) to this equation leads to the stability requirement $-2 < h \lambda < 0$. This gives the *region of absolute stability*.

In general, a method with a larger region of absolute stability will impose less restriction on the step size h. Similar analysis for the Adams-Bashforth second-order method shows that the region of absolute stability is $-1 < h \lambda < 0$. Note that although this is a smaller region than for Euler's method, the fact that the Adams-Bashforth method is higher order than Euler's method gives it some advantage. The second-order Adams-Moulton method, an implicit method, is absolutely stable for $-\infty < h \lambda < 0$. (See Atkinson, 1993, for further details.)

12.4.2 Strong and Weak Stabiliby

The stability results summarized in the previous paragraphs give some indication of the restrictions on the step size that may be necessary to achieve a stable numerical solution. We now consider more directly the stability of the difference equation that defines a numerical method. We generalize the notation introduced in Section 12.3 for a two-step method to represent an m-step method as

$$y_{i+1} = a_1 y_i + a_2 y_{i-1} \ldots + a_m y_{i+1-m} + h(b_o f_{i+1} + b_1 f_i + \ldots + b_m f_{i+1-m}).$$

The method is stable if all roots of the characteristic polynomial

$$p(\lambda) = \lambda^m - a_1 \lambda^{m-1} + a_2 \lambda^{m-2} + \ldots + a_m$$

satisfy $|\lambda_k| \leq 1$, and any root with $|\lambda_k| = 1$ is simple. It can be shown that for any method that is at least first-order accurate we must have $a_1 + a_2 + \ldots + a_m = 1$, so $\lambda_k = 1$ is a root. If the other $m-1$ roots satisfy $|\lambda_k| < 1$, the method is called *strongly stable*. If the method is stable, but not strongly stable, it is called *weakly stable*. A strongly stable method is stable for $y' = \lambda y$ regardless of the sign of λ; a method that is only weakly stable can yield unstable numerical solutions when $\lambda < 0$, as the following example illustrates. The stability analysis based on the roots of the characteristic polynomial reveals the behavior of the method in the limit as the step size becomes arbitraily small. Even a stable method can exhibit unstable behavior if the step size is too large.

Example 12.12 A Weakly Stable Method

Consider the simple two-step method

$$y_{i+1} = y_{i-1} + 2 h f(x_i, y_i)$$

and the differential equation

$$y' = -4y, \; y(0) = 1$$

for which the exact solution is $y = e^{-4x}$. If we perturb the initial condition slightly, to $y(0) = 1 + \varepsilon$, the solution becomes $y = (1 + \varepsilon)e^{-4x}$; the solution is stable since the change in the solution is only $y = \varepsilon e^{-4x}$.

However, the numerical method is only weakly stable; the characteristic polynomial is $\lambda^2 - 1 = 0$, which has roots $\lambda = 1$ and $\lambda = -1$. The numerical results for $h = 0.1$ are illustrated together with the exact solution in Fig. 12.12. Figure 12.13 illustrates the fact that a smaller step size ($h = 0.02$) delays the onset of the instability, but does not prevent it from occurring.

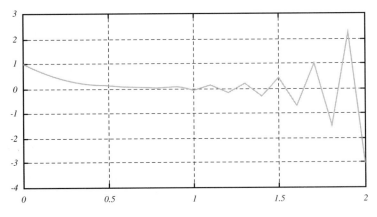

FIGURE 12.12 Solution of $y' = -4 y$ with a weakly stable method, $h = 0.1$.

Chapter 12 Ordinary Differential Equations: Initial-Value Problems

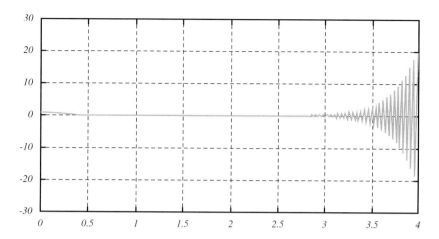

FIGURE 12.13   Instability occurs even with a much smaller step size, $h = 0.02$.

On the other hand, for the differential equation

$$y' = 4y, \, y(0) = 1$$

the weakly stable method yields acceptable results, even for $h = 0.1$, as illustrated in Fig. 12.14.

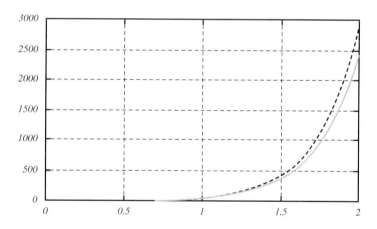

FIGURE 12.14   The solution of $y' = 4y$ with a weakly stable method, $h = 0.1$.

12.5 METHODS OF MODERN COMPUTING

We summarize the use of the built-in functions in MATLAB, Mathcad, and *Matematica*. We then consider some of the methods implemented in these functions.

12.5.1 Using Professionally Developed Software

MATLAB

MATLAB includes three functions, `ode23`, `ode45`, and `ode113`, for solving non-stiff ODE. The functions `ode23` and `ode45` implement a pair of explicit Runge-Kutta methods, second- and third-order or fourth- and fifth-order, respectively. The function `ode113` is a fully variable step size ODE solver based on the Adams-Bashforth-Moulton family of formulas of orders 1–12.

The syntax for the function call to each of the ODE solvers is the same; we illustrate it here for `ode23`. For that function, we have

$$[t, y] = \text{ode23}('F', t\text{span}, y0), \quad \text{where } t\text{span} = [t0 \ t\_\text{final}].$$

$'F'$ is a string containing the name of an ODE file. The function $F(t, y)$ must return a column vector of values. Each row in the solution array **y** corresponds to a time returned in column vector **t**. To obtain solutions at specific times $t0, t1, \ldots, t\_\text{final}$ (all increasing or all decreasing), use tspan = $[t0, t1, \ldots, t\_\text{final}]$. The initial conditions are given in the vector $y0$. There are several variations for input and also for output. More details are available in the online help provided with each function.

Mathematica

Mathematica's function `NDSolve[ {eqns}, y, {x, xmin, xmax}]` finds a numerical solution of the first-order ordinary differential equations and initial conditions given in the list {eqns}. The dependent variable is y, the independent variable is x, and the solution is obtained on the interval [xmin, xmax]. This function can also be used for higher-order ordinary differential equations.

Mathcad

Mathcad2000 implements the fourth-order Runge-Kutta method as its method for solving ODE. Mathcad2000Pro also includes functions for solving ODE with special characteristics. If the functions that define the ODE are known to be smooth, the Bulirsch-Stoer method is recommended. For ODEs that require an adaptive step size method (for example, if the solution functions for the ODE vary much more rapidly in some regions than in others), an adaptive Runge-Kutta method is provided. In addition, functions are also included for stiff differential equations; since stiffness is usually associated with higher order ODE or systems of ODE, we delay their consideration until the next chapter. The Mathdad2000Pro function `odesolve` can be used in a Solve Block structure to solve either initial value or boundary value problems.

12.5.2 Adaptive Step-Size Runge-Kutta Methods

The related problems of monitoring the truncation error and selecting an appropriate step size (and adjusting it if necessary) occur whenever we use numerical methods to approximate the solution of an ODE. One straightforward approach is to compute the solution from x to $x + 2h$, first by taking a single step of length $2h$, and again by taking two steps of length h. By taking the difference of these approximate solutions, one can obtain an estimate of the truncation error.

For Runge-Kutta there is another approach to step-size adjustment, known as the embedded Runge-Kutta formulas, or Runge-Kutta-Fehlberg methods. One reason that the classical fourth-order Runge-Kutta method is so popular is that for Runge-Kutta methods of order 5 and higher, more function evaluations are required than the order of the method (for order M, $M > 4$, either $M+1$ or $M+2$ evaluations are needed). Fehlberg found fourth-order and fifth-order Runge-Kutta methods that use the same 6 function evaluations (or 5 of the same evaluations for the fourth-order method). The coefficients for the Runge-Kutta-Fehlberg method are given in Section 12.2.6.

An alternative set of coefficients (Cash and Karp, 1990) are recommended as giving a more efficient method with better error properties. The parameters for the fourth- and fifth-order methods are given in the following tables. The estimated error is the value computed from the fifth-order method minus the value computed from the fourth-order method. See Press et al. (1992, p. 717).

1/5	1/5				
3/10	3/40	9/40			
3/5	3/10	−9/10	6/5		
1	−11/54	5/2	−70/27	35/27	
	37/378	0	250/621	125/594	0

Fourth-order Runge-Kutta-Cash-Karp method

1/5	1/5					
3/10	3/40	9/40				
3/5	3/10	−9/10	6/5			
1	−11/54	5/2		−70/27	35/27	
7/8	1631/55296	175/512	575/13824	44275/110592	253/4096	
	2825/27648	0	18575/48384	13525/55296	277/14336	1/4

Fifth-order Runge-Kutta-Cash-Karp method

12.5.3 Bulirsch-Stoer Method

The Bulirsch-Stoer method uses the idea of acceleration to combine the results of many applications of the midpoint method (with modified first and last steps) to obtain a highly accurate solution with minimal computational effort. This approach is closely related to the Richardson extrapolation for integration discussed in Chapter 11, in which the results from several applications of the trapezoid rule are combined to give a more accurate result than could be obtained just by reducing the step size for the integration. Bulirsch and Stoer used rational function interpolation to model the dependence of the true solution on the step size; this can give good approximations for some functions for which polynomial interpolation is not satisfactory. However, for smooth functions, polynomial interpolation is somewhat more efficient, and is used as the default approach in the presentation of the method in Press et al. (1992).

In using acceleration, it is highly advantageous to use a method for which the error is strictly an even function of h, that is, the error expressed in powers of the step size h contains only even powers. In this case, the order of the accelerated method increases by 2 at each stage. Gragg has shown that the error expansion for the modified midpoint method has this form.

Modified Midpoint Method

To solve

$$y' = f(x, y), \quad y(a) = y_a, \quad \text{on } [a, b], \text{ using } n - 1 \text{ intermediate points.}$$
$$x_0 = a, x_k = a + k\,h \quad (\text{for } k = 1, \ldots n)$$
$$y_0 = y_a$$

$$y_1 = y_0 + h\,f(x_0, y_0)$$
$$\text{For } k = 1, \ldots n - 1$$
$$\qquad y_{k+1} = y_{k-1} + 2\,h\,f(x_k, y_k)$$

End

$$y_n = \frac{1}{2}(y_n + y_{n-1}) + h\,f(x_n, y_n)$$

Bulirsch-Stoer-Deuflhard Extrapolation

Apply the modified midpoint method using a sequence of n steps to go from a to b, taking $n = 2, 4, 6, 8, \ldots$ Each application of the acceleration gives both an improved estimate of the solution (the extrapolated value) and an error estimate. We begin by computing the solution at x_1, starting with the modified midpoint method. Using $n = 2$, we find the solution we denote as z_2, using $n = 4$ we find z_4, and the extrapolated value $(4\,z_4 - z_2)/3$. If the error estimate indicates that the extrapolated value is not a sufficiently accurate approximation to the solution at x_1, we take $n = 6$, and extrapolate again $(4\,z_6 - z_4)/3$. The extrapolation continues until the error estimate indicates that the solution is satisfactory (or we reach an upper bound on the number of extrapolation steps allowed). When we have a satisfactory value for y_1, we go to the next subinterval (beginning the solution process with $n=2$ and $n=4$).

For a more detailed discussion, including the use of the error estimate to adjust step size, see Press et al. (1992, pp. 724–732).

Explicit One-Step Methods

Euler method (first-order, local truncation error $\dfrac{h^2}{2}y''(\eta_i)$)

$$y_{i+1} = y_i + h f_i$$

Taylor method (second-order, local truncation error $O(h^3)$)

$$y_{i+1} = y_i + h f_i + \frac{h^2}{2}g_i \quad \text{where } g_i = \frac{d}{dx}f(x_i, y_i) = y''(x)$$

Runge-Kutta methods

Midpoint method (second-order, local truncation error $O(h^3)$)

$$y_{i+1} = y_i + h f\left(x_i + \frac{h}{2}, y_i + \frac{h}{2}f(x_i, y_i)\right)$$

(this can also be viewed as an explicit two-step method with step size $H = 2h$)

Improved Euler's method (second-order, local truncation error $O(h^3)$)

$$y_{i+1} = y_i + \frac{h}{2}[f(x_i, y_i) + f(x_i + h, y_i + h f(x_i, y_i))]$$

Heun's method (second-order, local truncation error $O(h^3)$)

$$y_{i+1} = y_i + \frac{h}{4}\left[f(x_i, y_i) + 3f\left(x_i + \frac{2h}{3}, y_i + \frac{2h}{3}f(x_i, y_i)\right)\right]$$

Classic Runge-Kutta (fourth-order)

$$k_1 = h f(x_i, y_i) \qquad\qquad k_2 = h f\left(x_i + \frac{1}{2}h, y_i + \frac{1}{2}k_1\right)$$

$$k_3 = h f\left(x_i + \frac{1}{2}h, y_i + \frac{1}{2}k_2\right) \qquad k_4 = h f(x_i + h, y_i + k_3)$$

$$y_{i+1} = y_i + \frac{1}{6}k_1 + \frac{1}{3}k_2 + \frac{1}{3}k_3 + \frac{1}{6}k_4.$$

Implicit One-Step Methods

Trapezoid method (second-order local truncation error $-\dfrac{h^3}{12}y^{(3)}(\eta_i)$)

$$y_{i+1} = y_i + \frac{h}{2}[f_{i+1} + f_i]$$

(this can also be viewed as the second-order Adams-Moulton method)

Explicit Multi-Step Methods

Second-order Adams-Bashforth (two-step; local truncation $\frac{5}{12} h^3 y^{(3)}(\eta_i)$)

$$y_{i+1} = y_i + \frac{h}{2} [3f_i - f_{i-1}]$$

Third-order Adams-Bashforth (three-step; local truncation error $\frac{3}{8} h^4 y^{(4)}(\eta_i)$)

$$y_{i+1} = y_i + \frac{h}{12} [23f_i - 16f_{i-1} + 5f_{i-2}]$$

Fourth-order Adams-Bashforth (four-step; local truncation error $\frac{251}{720} h^5 y^{(5)}(\eta_i)$)

$$y_{i+1} = y_i + \frac{h}{24} [55f_i - 59f_{i-1} + 37f_{i-2} - 9f_{i-3}]$$

Fifth-order Adams-Bashforth (five-step; local truncation error $O(h^6)$)

$$y_{i+1} = y_i + \frac{h}{720} [1901f_i - 2774f_{i-1} + 2616f_{i-2} - 1274f_{i-3} + 251f_{i-4}]$$

Implicit Multi-Step Methods

Third-order Adams-Moulton (two-step; local truncation error $-\frac{1}{24} h^4 y^{(4)}(\eta_i)$)

$$y_{i+1} = y_i + \frac{h}{12} [5f_{i+1} + 8f_i - f_{i-1}]$$

Fourth-order Adams-Moulton (three-step; local truncation error $\frac{19}{720} h^5 y^{(5)}(\eta_i)$)

$$y_{i+1} = y_i + \frac{h}{24} [9f_{i+1} + 19f_i - 5f_{i-1} + f_{i-2}]$$

Fifth-order Adams-Moulton (four-step; local truncation error $O(h^6)$)

$$y_{i+1} = y_i + \frac{h}{720} [251f_{i+1} + 646f_i - 264f_{i-1} + 106f_{i-2} - 19f_{i-3}]$$

Predictor-Corrector Methods $f*_{i+1} = f(x_{i+1}, y*_{i+1})$

Second-order A-B-M method

$$y*_{i+1} = y_i + \frac{h}{2} [3f_i - f_{i-1}] \qquad y_{i+1} = y_i + \frac{h}{2} [f*_{i+1} + f_i]$$

Third-order A-B-M method

$$y*_{i+1} = y_i + \frac{h}{12} [23f_i - 16f_{i-1} + 5f_{i-2}] \qquad y_{i+1} = y_i + \frac{h}{12} [5f*_{i+1} + 8f_i - f_{i-1}]$$

Fourth-order A-B-M method

$$y*_{i+1} = y_i + \frac{h}{24} [55f_i - 59f_{i-1} + 37f_{i-2} - 9f_{i-3}]$$

$$y_{i+1} = y_i + \frac{h}{24} [9f*_{i+1} + 19f_i - 5f_{i-1} + f_{i-2}]$$

Edwards, C. H. Jr., and D. E. Penney. *Differential Equations and Boundary Value Problems: Computing and Modeling.* Prentice Hall, Englewood Cliffs, NJ, 1996.

Edwards, C. H. Jr., and D. E. Penney. *Elementary Differential Equations with Boundary Value Problems*, 3rd ed. Prentice Hall, Englewood Cliffs, NJ, 1993.

Finizio, N., and G. Ladas. *An Introduction to Differential Equations, with Difference Equations. Fourier Series, and Partial Differential Equations*, Wadsworth Publishing, Belmont, CA, 1982.

Froberg, C. E. *Numerical Mathematics: Theory and Computer Applications*, Benjamin/Cummings, Menlo Park, CA, 1985.

Garcia, A. L. *Numerical Methods for Physics.* Prentice Hall, Englewood Cliffs, NJ, 1994.

Gear, C. W. *Numerical Initial Value Problems in Ordinary Differential Equations.* Prentice-Hall, Englewood Cliffs, NJ, 1971.

Golub, G. H., and J. M. Ortega. *Scientific Computing and Differential Equations: An Introduction to Numerical Methods.* Academic Press, Boston, 1992.

Hanna, O. T., and O. C. Sandall. *Computational Methods In Chemical Engineering.* Prentice Hall, Upper Saddle River, NJ, 1995.

Jain, M. K. *Numerical Solution of Differential Equations.* John Wiley & Sons, New York, 1979.

Ortega, J. M., and W. G. Poole. *An Introduction to Numerical Methods for Differential Equations.* Pitman Publishing, Marshfield, MA, 1981.

Ritger, P. D., and N. J. Rose. *Differential Equations with Applications.* McGraw-Hill, New York, 1968.

Roberts, C. E. *Ordinary Differential Equations: A Computational Approach.* Prentice-Hall, Englewood Cliffs, NJ, 1979.

Zill, D. G. *Differential Equations with Boundary-Value Problems.* Prindle, Weber, & Schmidt, Boston, 1986.

Rice has excellent discussion of Runge-Kutta methods, and the difficulties in using simple methods for various sample problems.

Rice, J. R. Numerical Methods, Software, and Analysis. McGraw-Hill, New York, 1983.

Discussion of the methods underlying the Mathcad functions:

Cash, J. R., and A. H. Karp. *ACM Transactions on Mathematical Software*, vol. 16, pp. 201–222, 1990.

Deuflhard, P. *Numerische Mathematik*, vol. 41, pp. 399–422, 1983.

Deuflhard, P. *SIAM Review*, vol. 27, pp. 505–535, 1985.

Press, W. H., S. A. Tcukolsky, W. T. Vetterling, and B. P. Flannery. *Numerical Recipes in C; The Art of Scientific Computing*, 2^{d} ed. Cambridge: Cambridge Unversity Press, 1992.

Stoer, J., and R. Bulirsch. *Introduction to Numerical Analysis.* Springer-Verlag, New York, 1980.

For Problems P12.1 to P12.10 solve the initial value problem and compare your results to the exact solution given. Use $h = 0.5$ or $h = 0.1$.

    a.   Use Euler's method.
    b.   Use the second order Taylor method.
    c.   Use the midpoint method.
    d.   Use the classic Runge-Kutta method.

P12.1   Solve $y' = y$, $y(0) = 2$; on $[0, 1]$.
      The exact solution is $y = 2\,e^x$.

P12.2   Solve $y' = x + y$, $y(0) = 2$; on $[0, 1]$.
      The exact solution is $y = 3\,e^x - x - 1$.

P12.3   Solve $y' = -y^2$, $y(0) = 1$, on $[0, 1]$.
      The exact solution is $y = 1/(x + 1)$

P12.4   Solve $y' = 1 + x - y - xy$, $y(0) = 2$, on $[0, 1]$.
      The exact solution is

$$y = 1 + \exp\left(-x - \frac{x^2}{2}\right).$$

P12.5   Solve $y' = y\,x^{-2}$, $y(1) = 2$, on $[1, 2]$.
      The exact solution is $y = 2\exp((x - 1)/x)$

P12.6   Solve $y' = xy + x$, $y(0) = 0$, on $[0, 1]$.

      The exact solution is $y = -1 + \exp\left(\dfrac{x^2}{2}\right)$.

P12.7   Solve $y' = -2\,xy$, $y(0) = 2$, on $[0, 1]$.
      The exact solution is $y = 2\exp(-x^2)$.

P12.8   Solve $y' = x + 4\,y\,x^{-1}$, $y(1) = 1/2$, on $[1, 2]$.

      The exact solution is $y = \dfrac{1}{2}x^2 + x^4$.

P12.9   Solve $y' = 3\,x^2\,y$, $y(0) = 1$, on $[0, 1]$.
      The exact solution is $y = \exp(x^3)$.

P12.10 Solve $y' = y\cos(x)$, $y(0) = 1$, on $[0, 1]$.
      The exact solution is $y = e^{\sin x}$.

For Problems P12.11 to P12.20 solve the initial value problem and compare your results to the exact solution given. Investigate the effect of using different step sizes.

    a.   Use Euler's method.
    c.   Use the midpoint method.

    d.   Use the classic Runge-Kutta method.
    e.   Use the Adams-Bashforth-Moulton predictor-corrector method.

P12.11 Solve $y' = -y + \sin(x)$, $y(0) = 1$, on $[0, \pi]$.
      (compare the results using $n = 10, 20, 40$)
      The exact solution is $y = 1.5\,e^{-x} + 0.5\sin(x) - 0.5\cos(x)$.

P12.12 Solve $y' = y\tan(x) + x$, $y(0) = 3$, on $[0, \pi/4]$.
      Exact solution is $y = x\tan(x) + 2\sec(x) + 1$.

P12.13 Solve $y' = \dfrac{x^2 + y^2}{2xy}$, $y(1) = 2$, on $[1, 2]$.

      The exact solution is $y^2 = x(x + 3)$.

P12.14 Solve $y' = -y\tan(x) + \sec(x)$, $y(0) = 2$, on $[0, \pi/4]$.
      The exact solution is $y = \sin(x) + 2\cos(x)$.

P12.15 Solve $y' = 2\sqrt{y - 1}$, $y(0) = 5$, on $[0, 2]$.
      The exact solution is $y = 1 + (x - 2)^2$.

P12.16 Solve $y' = x + 2\,y\,x^{-1}$, $y(1) = 1$, on $[1, 2]$.
      The exact solution is $y = x^2\ln(x) + x^2$.

P12.17 Solve $y' = 4\,x\,y^{-1} - x\,y$; $y(0) = 3$ on $[0, 2]$
      The exact solution is $y = \sqrt{4 + 5\exp(-x^2)}$

P12.18 Solve $y' = x\,y^{-1} - x\,y$; $y(0) = 2$ on $[0, 2]$
      The exact solution is $y = \sqrt{1 + 3\exp(-x^2)}$

P12.19 $y' = (y + x)^2$ $y(0) = -1$
      The exact solution is $y = -x + \tan(x - \pi/4)$

P12.20 Solve $y' = \dfrac{3x}{y} - x\,y$; $y(0) = 2$ on $[0, 2]$

      The exact solution is $y = \sqrt{3 + \exp(-x^2)}$

For Problems P12.21 to P12.25 solve the initial value problem. Investigate the effect of using different step sizes, and intervals of different lengths.

P12.21 $y' = y + x^2$, $y(0) = 1$

P12.22 $y' = y + \cos(x)$, $y(0) = 1$

P12.23 $y' = y + \ln(x + 1)$, $y(0) = 1$

P12.24 $y' = y + x^{-1}$, $y(1) = 1$

P12.25 $y' = y\tan(x)$, $y(0) = 1$

A12.1 The concentration of a chemical in a batch reactor can be modeled by the differential equation

$$\frac{dC}{dt} = \frac{-k_1 C}{1 + k_2 C}.$$

Find a numerical solution for $0 \le t \le 1$.
   a. Use $k_1 = 2$, $k_2 = 0.1$, and $C(0) = 1$.
   b. Use $k_1 = 1$, $k_2 = 0.3$, and $C(0) = 0.8$.
(see Hanna and Sandall, 1995 for a discussion of similar problems.)

A 12.2 Solve the Ginzburg-Landau equation on the interval $[\,0, 3]$ for the given values of the parameter k, and initial condition.

$$\frac{dx}{dt} = k^2 x^3 - x$$

   a. $k = 1$; $x(0) = 0.7$.
   b. $k = -0.1$; $x(0) = 0.9$.
   c. $k = -0.8$; $x(0) = 0.9$.
   d. $k = 0.5$; $x(0) = 1.2$.

(Adapted from Garcia, 1994.)

A 12.3 The velocity of a body subject to the force of gravity and air resistance proportional to v is given by the differential equation:

$$\frac{dv}{dt} = g - p v$$

where g represents the gravitational acceleration (32 ft/sec) and p is the drag coefficient.
   a. Find the velocity of an arrow with initial velocity $v_0 = 300$ ft/sec, and drag coefficient $p = 0.05$.
   b. Find the velocity of a parachutist with $v_0 = 0$ ft/sec, and drag coefficient $p = 1.5$.

(See Edwards and Penney, 1993 for discussion of similar problems.)

A12.4 According to Torricelli's law, the depth y of the water in a tank with a hole in the bottom changes according to the differential equation

$$\frac{dy}{dt} = -k \sqrt{y} \, A(y).$$

$A(y)$ is the cross-sectional area of the tank at depth y. The parameter $k = a \sqrt{2 g}$, where g is the gravitational constant (32 ft/sec) and a is the area of the hole. (See Edwards and Penney, 1996 for a derivation of this equation.)
   a. Find the water depth in a tank with cross sectional area $A(y) = \pi y$; i.e. formed by rotating the curve $y = x^2$ around the y axis. Let the initial water depth be 2 ft, and the area of the hole be 0.01. When is the tank empty?
   b. Find the water depth in a tank with cross-sectional area $A(y) = \pi y^{2/3}$; i.e. formed by rotating the curve $y = x^3$ around the y axis. Take the initial water depth to be 2 ft, and the area of the hole to be 0.01. When is the tank empty?

A12.5 A simple model of the spread of disease gives $P' = k P (C - P)$, where $P(t)$ represents the number of individuals in the population who are infected, and C is the constant size of the total population. The solution of this differential equation is the logistic function. Suppose now that the parameter k fluctuates (e.g., perhaps because the population is more susceptible during certain seasons). Solve the modified problem and compare the results to those of the original model.

$$P' = (k + 0.1 \sin(t)) \, P \, (C\text{-}P);$$

$$k = 2, C = 2000, P(0) = 10.$$

A12.6 The balance in a bank account in which interest is being earned at the rate of 5%, compounded continuously and reinvested, obeys the differential equation

$$B' = 0.05 \, B; B(0) = B_0.$$

Suppose now that additional deposits are made on a regular basis, but with larger deposits made during certain months. The change in the bank balance could then be modeled by the ODE

$$B' = 0.05 \, B + C \, (\sin(2\pi \, t))^4; B(0) = B_0.$$

Take an initial deposit of $B_0 = 1000$, and a deposit schedule of $2(\sin(2 \pi \, t))^4$. Compare the balance in the account after 2 years to that given by the initial deposit and reinvestment only.

Problems A12.7 to A12.13 explore some Riccati differential equations; i.e., differential equations of the form $y' = P(x) y + Q(x) y^2 + R(x)$.

A12.7 Solve $y' = x y + y^2 + x^2$, $y(0) = 1$, on $[0, 0.5]$.

A12.8 Solve $y' = \dfrac{-1}{2} y - y^2 + \dfrac{1}{x^2}$, $y(1) = -1/3$, on $[1, 2]$.

A12.9 Solve $y' = \dfrac{1}{x} y + \dfrac{1}{x} y^2 + \dfrac{-2}{x^2}$, $y(0.1) = 1$, on $[0.1, 1]$.

A12.10 Solve $y' = \dfrac{1}{x} y + \dfrac{1}{x} y^2 + \dfrac{-2}{x}$, $y(2) = -3$, on $[2, 3]$.

A12.11 Solve $y' = y^2 + x^{-4}$, $y(1) = 0.1$, on $[1, 2]$.

A12.12 Solve $y' = y^2 + x^{-8/5}$, $y(1) = 0.1$, on $[1, 2]$.

A12.13 Solve $y' = y^2 + x^{-8/3}$, $y(1) = 0.1$, on $[1, 3]$.

Problems A12.14 to A12.16 explore some Bernoulli differential equations; i.e., differential equations of the form $y' = -P(x) y + Q(x) y^n$.

A12.14 Solve $y' = 1.5 x^{-1} y + 2 x y^{-1}$, $y(1) = 0$, on $[1, 30]$.

A12.15 Solve $y' = 6 x^{-1} y + 3 y^{4/3}$, $y(1) = 1/8$, on $[1, 3]$.

A12.16 Solve $y' = x y + y^2$, $y(1) = 0.1$, on $[0, 2]$.

EXTEND YOUR UNDERSTANDING

U12.1 Solve $y' = x^2 + y^2$, $y(0) = 1$, on $[0, 0.9]$. Discuss what happens if you try to extend the interval to $[0, 1]$.

U12.2 Solve $y' = -x^2 + y^2$, $y(0) = 1$, on $[0, 1]$.

U12.3 Solve $y' = x^2 - y^2$, $y(0) = 1$, on $[0, 1]$.

U12.4 Solve $y' = 1 - y^2$,
    a. $y(0) = 0$ on $[0, 5]$.
    b. $y(1) = 4$ on $[1, 5]$.

U12.5 Solve $y' = 4 y - 2 x^2$; $y(0) = 1/16$ on $[0, 3]$. Compare your results to the exact solution, $y = 1/2\, x^2 + 1/4\, x + 1/16$.

Problems U12.6 to U12.9 explore the application of numerical methods to differential equations for which the solution may not be unique. See a standard differential equaitons text for discussion of the conditions that guarantee the existence and uniqueness of the solution of a first order ODE initial value problem; e.g. Edwards and Penney, 1996.

U12.6 Solve $y' = y - \sin x$; $y(-\pi) = -0.5$ on $[-\pi, \pi]$

U12.7 Solve $y' = 2 y x^{-1}$; $y(-1) = 1$ on $[-1, 1]$

U12.8 Solve $y' = 2 \sqrt{y}$; $y(0) = 0$ on $[0, 1]$ compare to $y(0) = 0.001$ on $[0, 1]$

U12.9 Solve $y' = y^2$; $y(0) = 1$ on $[0, 0.5]$ compare to $y(2) = -0.5$ on $[2, 3]$

U12.10 Investigate the stability of the predictor and corrector formulas for Milne's method; this is a fourth-order method. The predictor is given by

$$y^*_{i+1} = y_{i-3} + \frac{4h}{3} [2 f_i - f_{i-1} + 2 f_{i-2}]$$

and the corrector is

$$y_{i+1} = y_{i-1} + \frac{h}{3} [f^*_{i+1} + 4 f_i + f_{i-1}]$$

The local truncation errors are $+\dfrac{14}{45} h^5 y^{(5)}(\eta_1)$, for the predictor and $-\dfrac{1}{90} h^5 y^{(5)}(\eta_2)$ for the corrector.

(See Froberg, 1985, p. 338 for further discussion.)

13

Ordinary Differential Equations: Higher Order Equations and First Order Systems

In this chapter, we extend the techniques presented in the previous chapter to higher order ODEs and systems of first-order ODEs. We begin by showing how a higher order ODE can be converted into a system of first-order ODEs. In the second section, we treat the Euler and midpoint methods for second-order ODEs and systems of two first-order ODEs in some detail to emphasize the direct relationship between each of the methods for a single ODE and the corresponding method for a system of ODEs.

For larger first-order systems, we can update all components of the solution very easily by utilizing vector notation for the unknown functions. The algorithm for each of the methods presented in the previous chapter can be applied to systems of arbitrary size with only minor modifications. Although the methods presented in this chapter are direct extensions of those seen in the last chapter, the variety of applications that can be solved is greatly expanded. We illustrate the methods using simple examples and problems, including the motion of a nonlinear pendulum, a spring-mass system, and a two-link robot arm. Sample problems describing chemical reactions are also solved.

Ordinary differential equations can be used to describe a wide variety of processes. Population growth models, predator-prey models, radioactive carbon dating, combat models, traffic flow models, and mechanical and electrical vibrations are a few of the most common applications; the list of possibilities is almost endless.

The solution of ODE initial-value problems forms the basis for the shooting method, one of the approaches to solving boundary-value problems for ordinary differential equations. The study of numerical methods for ODE-BVPs is the subject of the next chapter.

Example 13-A Motion of a Nonlinear Pendulum

The motion of a pendulum of length L subject to damping can be described by the angular displacement of the pendulum from vertical, θ, as a function of time (see Fig. 13.1). If we let m be the mass of the pendulum, g the gravitational constant, and c the damping coefficient (i.e., the damping force is $F = -c\theta'$), then the ODE initial-value problem describing this motion is

$$\theta'' + \frac{c}{mL}\theta' + \frac{g}{L}\sin\theta = 0.$$

The initial conditions give the angular displacement and velocity at time zero; for example, if $\theta(0) = a$ and $\theta'(0) = 0$, the pendulum has an initial displacement, but is released with 0 initial velocity.

Analytic (closed-form) solutions rely on approximating $\sin\theta$; the exact solutions to this approximated system do not have the characteristics of the physical pendulum, namely, a decreasing amplitude and a decreasing period. (See Greenspan, 1974, for further discussion.)

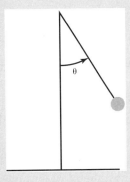

FIGURE 13.1A   Simple pendulum.

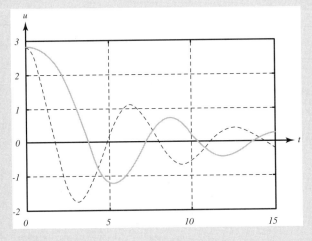

FIGURE 13.1B   Motion of nonlinear (solid line) and
linear (dashed line) pendulum.

Example 13-B Chemical Flow

A *circular reaction* involving three chemical reactions can be described as

$$A + A' \xrightarrow{\ \ k_1\ \ } B,$$

$$B + B' \xrightarrow{\ \ k_2\ \ } C,$$

$$C + C' \xrightarrow{\ \ k_3\ \ } A.$$

We assume that compounds A', B', and C' are present in excess, so that changes in their quantities can be neglected, and we simplify the notation by defining $r_1 = k_1A'$, $r_2 = k_2B'$, and $r_3 = k_3C'$; the differential equations can be written as

$$\frac{dA}{dt} = r_3C - r_1A$$

$$\frac{dB}{dt} = r_1A - r_2B$$

$$\frac{dC}{dt} = r_2B - r_3C$$

If the reaction rates are constants, the solution can be found from the eigenvalues and eigenvectors of the coefficient matrix R when the differential equation is written in matrix-vector form, $\mathbf{x}' = \mathbf{Rx}$, with $\mathbf{x} = [A, B, C]^T$ and

$$\mathbf{R} = \begin{bmatrix} -r_1 & 0 & r_3 \\ r_1 & -r_2 & 0 \\ 0 & r_2 & -r_3 \end{bmatrix}$$

This is discussed briefly in problems A5.27–A5.50. On the other hand, if the reaction rates are not constant, numerical methods may be especially useful. For example, we can take $r_2 = 2$, $r_3 = 1$, and r_1 changing from 0.1 to 10. (The units for these parameters are sec^{-1}.) The appropriate initial values of the unknown functions A, B, and C depend on the total amount of the three chemicals that is present ($Q = A + B + C$) and the rate constants; the initial values are chosen to be consistent with the equilibrium values, which are

For example, we can take $r_2 = 2$, $r_3 = 1$, and r_1 changing from 0.1 to 10. (The units for these parameters are sec^{-1}.) The appropriate initial values of the unknown functions A, B, and C depend on the total amount of the three chemicals that is present ($Q = A + B + C$) and the rate constants; the initial values are chosen to be consistent with the equilibrium values, which are

$$A = \frac{Q}{1 + r_1/r_2 + r_1/r_3}, \quad B = \frac{r_1}{r_2} A, \quad C = \frac{r_1}{r_3} A.$$

(For further discussion, see Simon, 1986, p. 118.)

A second-order ODE of the form

$$y'' = g(x, y, y')$$

can be converted to a system of two first-order ODEs by a simple change of variables:

$$u = y,$$
$$v = y'.$$

The differential equations relating these variables (functions) are

$$u' = v = f(x, u, v),$$
$$v' = g(x, u, v).$$

The initial conditions for the original ODE,

$$y(0) = \alpha_0, \quad y'(0) = \alpha_1,$$

become the initial conditions for the system, i.e.,

$$u(0) = \alpha_0, \quad v(0) = \alpha_1.$$

Example 13.1 Nonlinear Pendulum

Consider the nonlinear pendulum described at the beginning of the chapter, with angular displacement $y(x)$ given by

$$y'' + \frac{c}{mL} y' + \frac{g}{L} \sin y = 0; \quad y(0) = a, \quad y'(0) = b,$$

Choosing $g/L = 1$ and $c/(mL) = 0.3$, $a = \pi/2$, and $b = 0$, we get the second-order ODE-IVP

$$y'' = -0.3\, y' - \sin y,$$

which can be converted to a system of first-order ODEs by means of the change of variables

$$u = y$$
$$v = y'$$

The differential equations relating these variables are

$$u' = v \qquad\qquad = f(x, u, v)$$
$$v' = -0.3\, v - \sin u = g(x, u, v)$$

with initial conditions $u(0) = \pi/2$, $v(0) = 0$.

We investigate the application of Euler's method and the midpoint method to this and other systems of two first-order ODEs in the next section.

A higher-order ODE may be converted to a system of first-order ODEs by a similar change of variables. The nth-order ODE

$$y^{(n)} = f(x, y, y', y'', \ldots y^{(n-1)}),$$

$$y(0) = \alpha_0, \ y'(0) = \alpha_1, \quad y''(0) = \alpha_2, \ldots, y^{(n-1)}(0) = \alpha_{n-1},$$

becomes a system of first-order ODEs by the following change of variables:

$$u_1 = y,$$

$$u_2 = y',$$

$$u_3 = y'',$$

$$.$$

$$.$$

$$.$$

$$u_n = y^{(n-1)}.$$

The differential equations relating these variables are

$$u_1' = u_2,$$

$$u_2' = u_3,$$

$$u_3' = u_4,$$

$$.$$

$$.$$

$$.$$

$$u_n' = f(x, u_1, u_2, u_3, \ldots u_n),$$

with the initial conditions

$$u_1(0) = \alpha_0, \qquad u_2(0) = \alpha_1, \qquad u_3(0) = \alpha_2, \ldots, u_n(0) = \alpha_{n-1}.$$

We investigate the application of several of the methods from Chapter 12 to general systems of ODE in section 13.3. By utilizing vector valued functions, only minor changes are required to the algorithms presented in Chapter 12.

Any of the methods for solving ODE-IVPs discussed in Chapter 12 can be generalized to apply to systems of equations. In this section we consider systems of two first-order ODE in detail, using the Euler and Runge-Kutta methods. In section 13.3, we treat systems of arbitrary size, using vector-valued functions extensively.

13.2.1 Euler's Method for Two ODE

To apply the basic Euler's method

$$y_{i+1} = y_i + h\,f(x_i, y_i)$$

to the system of ODEs

$$u' = f(x, u, v)$$
$$v' = g(x, u, v)$$

we update the function u using $f(x, u, v)$ and update v using $g(x, u, v)$. The same step size h is used for each function (since that refers to the spacing of the independent variable x):

$$u(i + 1) = u(i) + h\,f(x(i), u(i), v(i)),$$
$$v(i + 1) = v(i) + h\,g(x(i), u(i), v(i)).$$

The process is described in more detail in the following algorithm.

Euler's Method for System of Two ODE

> *Input*
> > f(x, u, v)   *right-hand side of ODE* u′ = f(x, u, v)
> > g(x, u, v)   *right-hand side of ODE* v′ = g(x, u, v)
> > u0   *initial condition* u(a) = u0
> > v0   *initial condition* v(a) = v0
> > a   *initial value of x*
> > b   *final value of x*
> > n   *number of steps*
>
> *Begin computations*
> $$h = \frac{b - a}{n} \qquad \text{\textit{step size}}$$
> u(0) = u0
> v(0) = v0
> For i = 0 to n−1   *compute next approximate value*
> > x(i) = a + h i
> > u(i+1) = u(i) + h f(x(i), u(i), v(i))
> > v(i+1) = v(i) + h g(x(i), u(i), v(i))
>
> End
> *Return*
> > u, v   *vectors of approximate values*

Example 13.2 Nonlinear Pendulum Using Euler's Method

Consider the system of ODEs obtained from the second-order ODE for the motion of the nonlinear pendulum described in Examples 13-A and 13.1:

$$u' = v = f(x, u, v),$$

$$v' = -0.3\,v - \sin u = g(x, u, v).$$

The initial conditions are

$$u_0 = \pi/2, \text{ and}$$

$$v_0 = 0.$$

The motion for the first 15 seconds is shown in Fig. 13.2 for $n = 50$, $n = 100$, and $n = 200$. The corresponding step sizes are $h = 15/50 = 0.3$, $h = 15/100 = 0.15$, and $h = 15/200 = 0.075$. The differences in the solutions shown for these three step sizes illustrates the sensitivity of the method to the choice of parameters (such as step size). The solutions for the larger step sizes ($n = 50$, or $n = 100$) are not accurate. In order to get accurate results, we must take a fairly small step size, e.g., $n = 200$. The solution using even smaller steps is essentially the same as that shown here for $n = 200$.

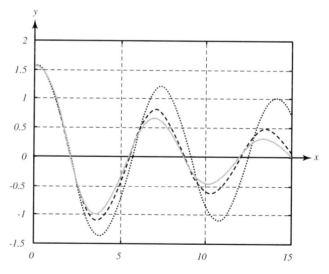

FIGURE 13.2   Solution to the nonlinear pendulum problem from Euler's method: $n = 200$ (solid line), $n = 100$ (dashed line), $n = 50$ (dotted line).

13.2.2 Midpoint Method for Two ODE

The idea in generalizing Runge-Kutta methods to systems of two equations is the same as for Euler's method; that is, we update each unknown function u and v, using the basic Runge-Kutta formulas and the appropriate right-hand side function, either f or g, from the differential equation for the unknown. To solve the system

$$u' = f(x, u, v) \qquad v' = g(x, u, v)$$
$$u(a) = u_0, \qquad v(a) = v_0$$

the formulas for the basic midpoint method,

$$k_1 = h f(x_i, y_i), \quad k_2 = h f\left(x_i + \frac{1}{2} h, y_i + \frac{1}{2} k_1\right), \quad y_{i+1} = y_i + k_2,$$

are rewritten using k_1 and k_2 to represent the update quantities for the unknown function u and calling m_1 and m_2 the corresponding quantities for the function v. We must update the function u by the appropriate multiple of k_1 or k_2 and the function v by the corresponding amount of m_1 or m_2. This means that k_1 and m_1 must be computed before k_2 and m_2 can be found. The computations for the midpoint method for a system of two ODE are given in the following algorithm.

Midpoint Method for a System of Two ODE

Input

f(x, u, v)	*right-hand side of ODE* u' = f(x, u, v)
g(x, u, v)	*right-hand side of ODE* v' = g(x, u, v)
u0	*initial condition u(a)* = u0
v0	*initial condition v(a)* = v0
a	*initial value of x*
b	*final value of x*
n	*number of steps*

Begin computations

$h = \dfrac{b - a}{n}$ *step size*

u(0) = u0
v(0) = v0
For i = 0 to n−1   *compute next approximate value*
     x(i) = a + h i
     k1 = h f(x(i), u(i), v(i))
     m1 = h g(x(i), u(i), v(i))
     k2 = h f(x(i)+0.5 h, u(i) + 0.5 k1, v(i) + 0.5 m1)
     m2 = h g(x(i)+0.5 h, u(i) + 0.5 k1, v(i) + 0.5 m1)
     u(i+1) = u(i) + k2
     v(i+1) = v(i) + m2
End
Return
     u, v   *vectors of approximate values*

Example 13.3 Nonlinear Pendulum Using the Midpoint Method

Consider again the system of ODEs obtained from the second-order ODE for the motion of the nonlinear pendulum described in Examples 13-A, 13.1, and 13.2, i.e.,

$$u' = v \qquad\qquad = f(x, u, v)$$
$$v' = -0.3\,v - \sin u = g(x, u, v),$$

with initial conditions

$$u0 = \pi/2; \qquad v0 = 0.$$

The update quantities for this problem are

$$k_1 = h\,v_i$$
$$m_1 = h(-0.3\,v_i - \sin(u_i))$$
$$k_2 = h\,(v_i + 0.5\,m_1)$$
$$m_2 = h\,(-0.3\,(v_i + 0.5\,m_1) - \sin(u_i + 0.5\,k_1))$$

with initial conditions

$$u0 = \pi/2; \qquad v0 = 0.$$

The motion for the first 15 seconds is shown in Fig. 13.3. The motion of a linear pendulum and a nonlinear pendulum is illustrated in Fig. 13.1b for a larger initial displacement.

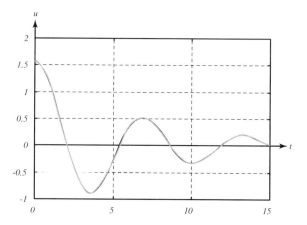

FIGURE 13.3 Oscillations of a nonlinear pendulum ($n = 50, 100,$ and 200).

Comparing the graphs of the solutions with 50, 100, and 200 subintervals shows that there is virtually no change in the solutions obtained by using more subintervals. This is in marked contrast to the results found with Euler's method in Example 13.2.

Example 13.4 Series Dilution Problem

To illustrate the use of Euler's method and the midpoint method for a system of two ODEs, consider the concentration of a dye in a two-compartment dilution process. A pure substance flows into the first tank at the same rate that a mixture leaves the first tank and flows into the second tank; the dye leaves the first tank at a rate that is proportional to the concentration. The loss from the first tank becomes the influx to the second tank, which in turn loses fluid at the same rate; thus, the volume of fluid in each tank is constant. The differential equations describing the concentration of dye in the two tanks are

$$\frac{dC_1}{dt} = -\frac{L}{V_1}C_1 \qquad \frac{dC_2}{dt} = -\frac{L}{V_2}[C_2 - C_1]$$

Taking

$$C_1(0) = 0.3 \text{ moles/liter}, \qquad C_2(0) = 0,$$
$$L = 2 \text{ liters/min}, \qquad V_1 = 10 \text{ liters, and } V_2 = 5 \text{ liters,}$$

we find the concentration in the two tanks for the first 10 minutes of the process. For comparison, we note that the exact solutions are

$$C_1(t) = C_1(0)\exp[-L/V_1)t] \qquad\qquad = 0.3\exp(-0.2t);$$

$$C_2(t) = \frac{V_1 C_1(0)}{V_1 - V_2}[\exp[-L/V_1)t - \exp[-L/V_2)t] = 0.6[\exp(-0.2t) - \exp(-0.4t)].$$

The values of C_1 and C_2 computed using Euler's method with $n = 20$ are plotted in Fig. 13.4. The exact solutions are also shown for comparison.

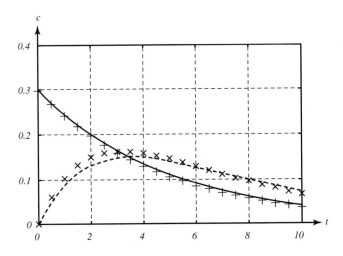

FIGURE 13.4   Concentration of dye in tank 1 (+) and tank 2 (x).

The computed results using the midpoint method are shown in Fig. 13.5,

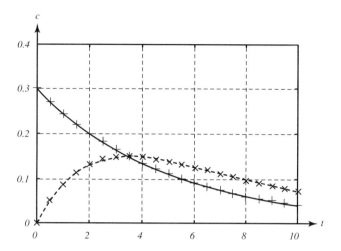

FIGURE 13.5 Concentration of dye in two compartments.

	Euler		Midpoint		Exact	
x	C_1	C_2	C_1	C_2	C_1	C_2
0.00	0.3000	0.0000	0.3000	0.0000	0.3000	0.0000
0.50	0.2700	0.0600	0.2715	0.0510	0.2715	0.0517
1.00	0.2430	0.1020	0.2457	0.0880	0.2456	0.0890
1.50	0.2187	0.1302	0.2224	0.1139	0.2222	0.1152
2.00	0.1968	0.1479	0.2012	0.1312	0.2011	0.1326
2.50	0.1771	0.1577	0.1821	0.1418	0.1820	0.1432
3.00	0.1594	0.1616	0.1648	0.1472	0.1646	0.1486
3.50	0.1435	0.1611	0.1492	0.1488	0.1490	0.1500
4.00	0.1291	0.1576	0.1350	0.1473	0.1348	0.1485
4.50	0.1162	0.1519	0.1222	0.1438	0.1220	0.1448
5.00	0.1046	0.1448	0.1106	0.1387	0.1104	0.1395
5.50	0.0941	0.1367	0.1001	0.1325	0.0999	0.1332
6.00	0.0847	0.1282	0.0906	0.1257	0.0904	0.1263
6.50	0.0763	0.1195	0.0820	0.1184	0.0818	0.1190
7.00	0.0686	0.1109	0.0742	0.1110	0.0740	0.1115
7.50	0.0618	0.1024	0.0671	0.1037	0.0669	0.1040
8.00	0.0556	0.0943	0.0607	0.0964	0.0606	0.0967
8.50	0.0500	0.0866	0.0500	0.8094	0.0548	0.0896
9.00	0.0450	0.0792	0.0498	0.0826	0.0496	0.0828
9.50	0.0405	0.0724	0.0450	0.0762	0.0449	0.0763
10.00	0.0365	0.0660	0.0407	0.0702	0.0406	0.0702

Systems of ODE may arise directly from applications such as chemical reactions, predator-prey models, and many others. They also come from the conversion of higher-order ODE into system form. The process of making this conversion is illustrated in the next example.

Example 13.5 A Higher-Order ODE

Consider the equation

$$y''' = f(x, y, y', y'') = x + 2y - 3y' + 4y''$$

with initial conditions

$$y(0) = 4, \quad y'(0) = 3, \quad y''(0) = 2.$$

The system of ODEs is

$$u_1' = u_2,$$
$$u_2' = u_3,$$
$$u_3' = x + 2u_1 - 3u_2 + 4u_3.$$

We write this system as

$$u_1' = f_1(x, u_1, u_2, u_3) = u_2,$$
$$u_2' = f_2(x, u_1, u_2, u_3) = u_3,$$
$$u_3' = f_3(x, u_1, u_2, u_3) = x + 2u_1 - 3u_2 + 4u_3.$$

For systems that come from a single higher-order ODE, the structure of the right-hand side in the previous example is a direct result of the definitions of the transformed functions. For systems of ODE in general, each of the right-hand side functions $f_1, f_2, \ldots$ may contain any or all of the indicated variables.

A system of ODE can be expressed compactly in vector notation as

$$\mathbf{u}' = \mathbf{f}(x, \mathbf{u}).$$

Since the components of the vectors, $\mathbf{u}$ and $\mathbf{f}$, are denoted by subscripts, we indicate the approximate solutions at the grid points as $\mathbf{u}_1(i)$, and so on.

13.3.1 Euler's Method for Systems

To apply the basic Euler method, $y_{i+1} = y_i + h f(x_i, y_i)$, to the system of ODE

$$u_1' = f_1(x, u_1, u_2, u_3), \quad u_2' = f_2(x, u_1, u_2, u_3), \quad u_3' = f_3(x, u_1, u_2, u_3),$$

we update the function u_1 using f_1, u_2 using f_2, and u_3 using f_3. The same step size h is used for each function. We have

$$u_1(i + 1) = u_1(i) + h f_1(x(i), u_1(i), u_2(i), u_3(i)),$$
$$u_2(i + 1) = u_2(i) + h f_2(x(i), u_1(i), u_2(i), u_3(i)),$$
$$u_3(i + 1) = u_3(i) + h f_3(x(i), u_1(i), u_2(i), u_3(i)).$$

Example 13.6 Solving a System of Three ODE Using Euler's Method

We apply Euler's method with $n = 2$ to find an approximate solution of the system of ODEs

$$u_1' = u_2$$
$$u_2' = u_3$$
$$u_3' = x + 2u_1 - 3u_2 + 4u_3$$

with initial conditions

$$u_1(0) = 4, u_2(0) = 3, \text{ and } u_3(0) = 2 \text{ on } [0, 1].$$

The solution at $i = 1$ corresponds to $x(i = 1) = 0.5$:

$$u_1(1) = u_1(0) + 0.5u_2(0) = 4 + 0.5(3) = 5.5,$$

$$u_2(1) = u_2(0) + 0.5u_3(0) = 3 + 0.5(2) = 4,$$

$$u_3(1) = u_3(0) + 0.5(x(0) + 2u_1(0) - 3u_2(0) + 4u_3(0))$$
$$= 2 + 0.5(0 + 2(4) - 3(3) + 4(2)) = 5.5.$$

The solution at $i = 2$ corresponds to $x(i = 2) = 1.0$:

$$u_1(2) = u_1(1) + 0.5u_2(1) = 5.5 + 0.5(4) = 7.5,$$

$$u_2(2) = u_2(1) + 0.5u_3(1) = 4 + 0.5(5.5) = 6.75,$$

$$u_3(2) = u_3(1) + 0.5(x(1) + 2u_1(1) - 3u_2(1) + 4u_3(1))$$
$$= 5.5 + 0.5(0.5 + 2(5.5) - 3(4) + 4(5.5)) = 16.25.$$

These computed solution values for u_3 are shown in Fig. 13.6 by "x" together with the computed results for u_1, u_2, and u_3 using $n = 10$.

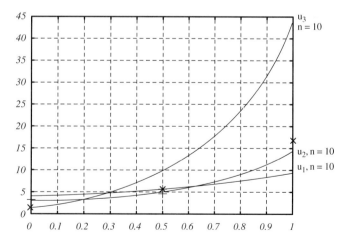

FIGURE 13.6   Solving a system of three ODE with Euler's method.

13.3.2 Runge-Kutta Methods for Systems

The idea in generalizing Runge-Kutta methods for use on systems of equations is the same as for Euler's method; that is, we update each unknown function $u_1, u_2, \ldots$, using the basic Runge-Kutta formulas and the appropriate right-hand side function $f_1, f_2, \ldots$, from the differential equation for the unknown. We now consider the midpoint method, and the classic fourth-order Runge-Kutta method for systems.

Midpoint Method

For the midpoint method, if we denote the two update parameters as k and m, then the basic second-order Runge-Kutta formulas (the midpoint method) are

$$k = h f(x_i, y_i),$$
$$m = h f\left(x_i + \frac{1}{2}h, y_i + \frac{1}{2}k\right),$$
$$y_{i+1} = y_i + m.$$

To apply these formulas to a system, we must compute k and m for each unknown function (i.e., for each component of the unknown vector $\mathbf{u}$). Note that k must be computed for each unknown before m can be found.

We illustrate the process for a system of three ODEs:

$$u_1' = f_1(x, u_1, u_2, u_3),$$
$$u_2' = f_2(x, u_1, u_2, u_3),$$
$$u_3' = f_3(x, u_1, u_2, u_3).$$

The values of the parameter k for the unknown functions u_1, u_2, and u_3 are

$$k_1 = h f_1(x(i), u_1(i), u_2(i), u_3(i)),$$
$$k_2 = h f_2(x(i), u_1(i), u_2(i), u_3(i)),$$
$$k_3 = h f_3(x(i), u_1(i), u_2(i), u_3(i)).$$

Similarly, the values of m are m_1, m_2, and m_3. Of course, to find the value of m for the first ODE, we use f_1; however, we must evaluate f_1 at the appropriate values of x, u_1, u_2, and u_3. Remembering that we are approximating the value of the unknown function employed in evaluating f makes it clear that we approximate each u using its value of k:

$$m_1 = h f_1\left(x(i) + \frac{1}{2}h, u_1(i) + \frac{1}{2}k_1, u_2(i) + \frac{1}{2}k_2, u_3(i) + \frac{1}{2}k_3\right),$$
$$m_2 = h f_2\left(x(i) + \frac{1}{2}h, u_1(i) + \frac{1}{2}k_1, u_2(i) + \frac{1}{2}k_2, u_3(i) + \frac{1}{2}k_3\right),$$
$$m_3 = h f_3\left(x(i) + \frac{1}{2}h, u_1(i) + \frac{1}{2}k_1, u_2(i) + \frac{1}{2}k_2, u_3(i) + \frac{1}{2}k_3\right).$$

Finally, the values of the unknown functions at the next grid point are found:

$$u_1(i + 1) = u_1(i) + m_1,$$
$$u_2(i + 1) = u_2(i) + m_2,$$
$$u_3(i + 1) = u_3(i) + m_3.$$

Example 13.7 Using the Midpoint Method for a System of 3 ODE

We apply the midpoint method to find an approximate solution on the interval [0,1] of the system of ODE

$$u_1' = f_1(x, u_1, u_2, u_3) = u_2$$
$$u_2' = f_2(x, u_1, u_2, u_3) = u_3$$
$$u_3' = f_3(x, u_1, u_2, u_3) = x + 2u_1 - 3u_2 + 4u_3$$

with initial conditions

$$u_1(0) = 4, u_2(0) = 3, \text{ and } u_3(0) = 2$$

With $n = 2$, we have $h = 1/2$

For this problem, the formulas for the parameters simplify to

$$k_1 = 0.5u_2(i)$$
$$k_2 = 0.5u_3(i)$$
$$k_3 = 0.5(x(i) + 2u_1(i) - 3u_2(i) + 4u_3(i))$$

and

$$m_1 = 0.5(u_2(i) + 0.5k_2)$$
$$m_2 = 0.5(u_3(i) + 0.5k_3)$$
$$m_3 = 0.5(x(i) + 0.25 + 2u_1(i) + k_1 - 3u_2(i) - 1.5k_2 + 4u_3(i) + 2k_3)$$

Finally, the values of the unknown functions at the next grid point are found:

$$u_1(i + 1) = u_1(i) + m_1$$
$$u_2(i + 1) = u_2(i) + m_2$$
$$u_3(i + 1) = u_3(i) + m_3$$

The solution at $i = 1$ corresponds to $x(i = 1) = 0.5$:

$$k_1 = 0.5u_2(0)$$
$$k_2 = 0.5u_3(0)$$
$$k_3 = 0.5(x(0) + 2u_1(0) - 3u_2(0) + 4u_3(0))$$
$$m_1 = 0.5(u_2(0) + 0.5k_2)$$
$$m_2 = 0.5(u_3(0) + 0.5k_3)$$
$$m_3 = 0.5(x(0) + 0.25 + 2u_1(0) + k_1 - 3u_2(0) - 1.5k_2 + 4u_3(0) + 2k_3)$$
$$u_1(1) = u_1(0) + m_1$$
$$u_2(1) = u_2(0) + m_2$$
$$u_3(1) = u_3(0) + m_3$$

The solution at $i = 2$ corresponds to $x(i = 2) = 1.0$

$$k_1 = 0.5u_2(1)$$
$$k_2 = 0.5u_3(1)$$
$$k_3 = 0.5(x(1) + 2u_1(1) - 3u_2(1) + 4u_3(1))$$
$$m_1 = 0.5(u_2(1) + 0.5k_2)$$
$$m_2 = 0.5(u_3(1) + 0.5k_3)$$
$$m_3 = 0.5(x(1) + 0.25 + 2u_1(1) + k_1 - 3u_2(1) - 1.5k_2 + 4u_3(1) + 2k_3)$$
$$u_1(2) = u_1(1) + m_1$$
$$u_2(2) = u_2(1) + m_1$$
$$u_3(2) = u_3(1) + m_3$$

We summarize the steps of the midpoint method in the following algorithm. In the algorithm we denote the solution vector at each step as $\mathbf{u}^{(i)}$.

Midpoint Method for a System of First-Order ODE

Approximate the solution $\mathbf{u}(x)$, of the system of ODE $\mathbf{u}' = \mathbf{f}(x, \mathbf{u})$, with initial conditions $\mathbf{u}(a) = \mathbf{u}^{(0)}$, using n steps of the midpoint method, a second order Runge-Kutta method.

Input
    $\mathbf{f}(x, \mathbf{u})$ *right-hand side of ODE $u' = f(x, u)$*
    $\mathbf{u}^{(0)}$ *initial condition $u(a) = u^{(0)}$*
    a   *initial value of x*
    b   *final value of x*
    n   *number of steps*

Begin computations

$$h = \frac{b - a}{n} \qquad \textit{step size}$$

For $i = 0$ to $n-1$
    $x(i) = a + h\,i$ *define grid point*
    $\mathbf{k} = h\,\mathbf{f}(x(i), \mathbf{u}^{(i)})$

$$\mathbf{m} = h\,\mathbf{f}\left(x_i + \frac{1}{2}h, \mathbf{u}^{(i)} + \frac{1}{2}\mathbf{k} \right)$$

    $\mathbf{u}^{(i+1)} = \mathbf{u}^{(i)} + \mathbf{m}$
End
Return
    $\mathbf{u}$ *matrix of approximate values*

The preferred orientation of the vectors $\mathbf{u}$, $\mathbf{f}$, etc. may depend on the programming language in which the algorithm is implemented, but compatibility of the orientation of the various vectors is important. If the vector $\mathbf{u}$ has only a small number of components, it may be advantageous to store the solution at each step as a row in the overall solution matrix. This would require that $\mathbf{m}$ be a row vector, which would in turn dictate that the function $\mathbf{f}$ return a row vector. Of course, the transpose of a vector or matrix may be used to change the orientation when desired or required.

The next example illustrates the use of the midpoint method to solve a system of ODEs that occur as part of the shooting method for solving boundary value problems, which is discussed in Chapter 14. This particular problem, which we revisit in Example 14.1 in the next chapter, deals with finding the electrostatic potential between two concentric spheres.

Example 13.8 Using the Midpoint Method for a System of 4 ODE

Consider the system

$$u_1' = u_2, \quad u_2' = \frac{-2}{x} u_2, \quad u_3' = u_4, \quad u_4' = \frac{-2}{x} u_4,$$

with initial conditions $u_1(1) = 10$, $u_2(1) = 0$, $u_3(1) = 0$, $u_4(1) = 1$, on the interval $[1, 2]$. Using $n = 2$ (and $h = 0.5$), we calculate the values of each component of the solution as a function of x (at $x_0 = 1$, $x_1 = 1.5$, and $x_2 = 2.0$).
First, find k for each component:

$$k_1 = 0.5(u_2(1)) = 0, \qquad k_2 = 0.5\left(\frac{-2}{x} u_2(1)\right) = 0,$$

$$k_3 = 0.5(u_4(1)) = 0.5, \qquad k_4 = 0.5\left(\frac{-2}{x} u_4(1)\right) = -1.$$

Next, find m for each component:

$$m_1 = 0.5(u_2(1) + 0.5k_2) = 0, \qquad m_2 = 0.5\left(\frac{-2}{1.25}\right)(u_2(1) + 0.5k_2) = 0,$$

$$m_3 = 0.5(u_4(1) + 0.5k_4) = 0.25, \qquad m_4 = 0.5\left(\frac{-2}{1.25}\right)(u_4(1) + 0.5k_4) = -0.4.$$

The approximate solution at $x = 1.5$ is

$$u_1(1.5) = 10 + 0 = 10, \qquad u_2(1.5) = 0 + 0 = 0,$$

$$u_3(1.5) = 0 + 0.25 = 0.25, \qquad u_4(1.5) = 1 - 0.4 = 0.6.$$

Now find k for each component:

$$k_1 = 0.5(u_2(1.5)) = 0, \qquad k_2 = 0.5\left(\frac{-2}{1.5} u_2(1.5)\right) = 0,$$

$$k_3 = 0.5(u_4(1.5)) = 0.3, \qquad k_4 = 0.5\left(\frac{-2}{1.5} u_4(1.5)\right) = -0.4.$$

Next, find m for each component:

$$m_1 = 0.5(u_2(1.5) + 0.5k_2) = 0, \qquad m_2 = 0.5\left(\frac{-2}{1.75}\right)(u_2(1.5) + 0.5k_2) = 0,$$

$$m_3 = 0.5(u_4(1.5) + 0.5k_4) = 0.2, \qquad m_4 = 0.5\left(\frac{-2}{1.75}\right)(u_4(1.5) + 0.5k_4) = -0.2286.$$

The approximate solution at $x = 2.0$ is

$$u_1(2.0) = 10 + 0 = 10, \qquad u_2(2.0) = 0 + 0 = 0,$$

$$u_3(2.0) = 0.25 + 0.2 = 0.45, \qquad u_4(2.0) = 0.6 - 0.2286 = 0.3714.$$

Classic Runge-Kutta Method

We now consider the classic fourth-order Runge-Kutta method for systems of ODE. We denote the four update parameters as **k**1, **k**2, **k**3, and **k**4 (each of which is a vector). They could easily be stored in a single matrix if desired.

The preferred orientation of the vectors **u**, **f**, etc. may depend on the programming language in which the following algorithm is implemented, but compatibility of the orientation of the various vectors is important. If the vector **u** has only a small number of components, it may be advantageous to store the solution at each step as a row in the overall solution matrix. This would require that **k**1, **k**2, **k**3, and **k**4 be a row vectors, which would in turn dictate that the function **f** return a row vector. Of course, the transpose of a vector or matrix may be used to change the orientation when desired or required.

Fourth-Order Runge-Kutta Method for a System of ODE

Input

f(x, **u**)	*right hand side of ODE* $u' = f(x, u)$
$\mathbf{u}^{(0)}$	*initial condition* $u(a) = u^{(0)}$
a	*initial value of x*
b	*final value of x*
n	*number of steps*

Begin computations

$$h = \frac{b - a}{n} \qquad \text{\textit{step size}}$$

For i = 0 to n−1

$$x(i) = a + h\,i \qquad \textit{define grid point}$$

$$\mathbf{k}1 = h\,\mathbf{f}(x(i), \mathbf{u}^{(i)})$$

$$\mathbf{k}2 = h\,\mathbf{f}\left(x(i) + \frac{1}{2}h, \mathbf{u}^{(i)} + \frac{1}{2}\mathbf{k}1 \right)$$

$$\mathbf{k}3 = h\,\mathbf{f}\left(x(i) + \frac{1}{2}h, \mathbf{u}^{(i)} + \frac{1}{2}\mathbf{k}2 \right)$$

$$\mathbf{k}4 = h\,\mathbf{f}(x(i) + h\,, \mathbf{u}^{(i)} + \mathbf{k}3)$$

$$\mathbf{u}^{(i+1)} = \mathbf{u}^{(i)} + \frac{1}{6}\mathbf{k}1 + \frac{1}{3}\mathbf{k}2 + \frac{1}{3}\mathbf{k}3 + \frac{1}{6}\mathbf{k}4$$

End

Return

u	*matrix of approximate values*

Example 13.9 Using Runge-Kutta for a Chemical Reaction Problem

Consider the circular reaction involving three chemical reactions described in Example 13-B; the differential equations are

$$\frac{dA}{dt} = r_3 C - r_1 A$$

$$\frac{dB}{dt} = r_1 A - r_2 B$$

$$\frac{dC}{dt} = r_2 B - r_3 C$$

We assume that the total quantity of the chemicals is $A + B + C = Q = 1$; the initial values of A, B, and C are chosen to satisfy the relations

$$A = \frac{1}{1 + r_1/r_2 + r_1/r_3}, \qquad B = \frac{r_1}{r_2} A, \qquad C = \frac{r_1}{r_3} A$$

for the initial rate parameters r_1, r_2, and r_3. We let $r_2 = 2$, let $r_3 = 1$, and allow r_1 to change slowly from an initial value of 0.1 according to the linear equation $r_1 = 0.1(t + 1)$. The initial values of A, B, and C are

$$A(0) = \frac{1}{1.15} = 0.8696,$$

$$B(0) = \frac{0.05}{1.15} = 0.0435,$$

$$C(0) = \frac{0.1}{1.15} = 0.0870.$$

Taking $n = 100$ subdivisions gives the concentrations illustrated in Fig. 13.7.

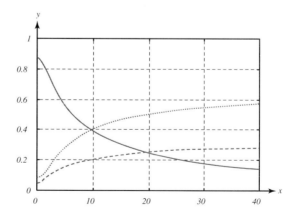

FIGURE 13.7   Concentrations of 3 reactants in circular chemical reaction. A = solid, B = dashed, C = dotted.

13.3.3 Multistep Methods for Systems

The extension of the basic two-step Adams-Bashforth method to systems of first-order ODE is accomplished in a manner very similar to that discussed for Runge-Kutta methods. In the two-step AB method, y_0 is given by the initial condition for the differential equation, y_1 is found from a one-step method (such as the midpoint method), and $y_{i+1} = y_i + \dfrac{h}{2}[3f(x_i, y_i) - f(x_{i-1}, y_{i-1})]$, (for $i = 1, \ldots, n-1$).

This can be extended for use with a system of three ODEs

$$u_1' = f_1(x, u_1, u_2, u_3) \qquad u_2' = f_2(x, u_1, u_2, u_3) \qquad u_3' = f_3(x, u_1, u_2, u_3)$$

as follows:

$u_1(i = 0), u_2(i = 0), u_3(i = 0)$ are given by the initial conditions,
$u_1(i = 1), u_2(i = 1), u_3(i = 1)$ are found from a 1-step method,

and for $i = 1, \ldots, n-1$:

$$u_1(i + 1) = u_1(i) + \frac{h}{2}[3f_1(x(i), u_1(i), u_2(i), u_3(i))$$
$$- f_1(x(i - 1), u_1(i - 1), u_2(i - 1), u_3(i - 1))],$$

$$u_2(i + 1) = u_2(i) + \frac{h}{2}[3f_2(x(i), u_1(i), u_2(i), u_3(i))$$
$$- f_2(x(i - 1), u_1(i - 1), u_2(i - 1), u_3(i - 1))],$$

$$u_3(i + 1) = u_3(i) + \frac{h}{2}[3f_3(x(i), u_1(i), u_2(i), u_3(i))$$
$$- f_3(x(i - 1), u_1(i - 1), u_2(i - 1), u_3(i - 1))].$$

Second-order Adams-Bashforth Method for a System of ODE ═══════

> *Input parameters, function, initial condition as for Fourth-Order Runge Kutta Method on p. 508.*
>
> *Begin computations*
> $h = \dfrac{b - a}{n}$ *step size*
> For $i = 0$ to 1   *use midpoint method to start*
> $x(i) = a + h\,i$
> $\mathbf{k}_1 = h\,\mathbf{f}(x(i), \mathbf{u}^{(i)})$
> $\mathbf{k}_2 = h\,\mathbf{f}\left(x(i) + \dfrac{1}{2}h, \mathbf{u}^{(i)} + \dfrac{1}{2}\mathbf{k}_1\right)$
> $\mathbf{u}^{(i+1)} = \mathbf{u}^{(i)} + \mathbf{k}_2$
> End
> For $i = 2$ to $n-1$ *use 2nd order AB method to continue*
> $x(i) = a + h\,i$
> $\mathbf{u}^{(i+1)} = \mathbf{u}^{(i)} + \dfrac{h}{2}[3\mathbf{f}(x(i), \mathbf{u}^{(i)}) - \mathbf{f}(x(i - 1), \mathbf{u}^{(i-1)})]$
> End
> *Return*
> $\mathbf{u}$ *matrix of approximate values*

Example 13.10 Mass-and-Spring System

The vertical displacements of two masses m_1 and m_2 suspended in series by springs with spring constants s_1 and s_2 are given by Hooke's law as a system of two second-order ODEs. The displacements are x_1 and x_2. (See Figure 13.8; the displacement of each mass is measured from its equilibrium position, with positive direction downward.) The ODEs are

$$m_1 x_1'' = -s_1 x_1 + s_2(x_2 - x_1),$$

$$m_2 x_2'' = -s_2(x_2 - x_1).$$

The differential equations relating these variables (functions) are

$$u_1' = u_2, \qquad u_2' = -\frac{s_1}{m_1} u_1 + \frac{s_2}{m_1}(u_3 - u_1),$$

$$u_3' = u_4, \qquad u_4' = -\frac{s_2}{m_2}(u_3 - x_1),$$

with the initial conditions

$$u_1(0) = \alpha_1, \qquad u_2(0) = \alpha_2, \qquad u_3(0) = \alpha_3, \qquad u_4(0) = \alpha_4$$

The displacement profiles of a 10-kg mass and a 2-kg mass are illustrated in Fig. 13.9. The spring constants are 100 and 120, respectively.

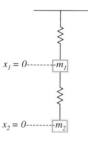

$x_1 = 0$--------m_1

$x_2 = 0$--------m_2

FIGURE 13.8 Two mass system.

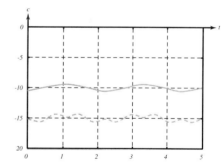

FIGURE 13.9 Displacement profiles of two masses connected by springs.

The Adams-Bashforth-Moulton (ABM) predictor-corrector methods are extended for use with systems of ODEs in a similar manner. The third-order ABM method is described in the following algorithm, and illustrated in Example 13.11. In this algorithm, recomputation of function values is avoided by defining an auxiliary variable $\mathbf{z}^{(i)} = \mathbf{f}(x(i), \mathbf{u}^{(i)})$. Although function values are not reused as extensively in the previous algorithm, a similar approach could be used for improved computational efficiency.

Third-Order Predictor-Corrector Method for a System of ODE

Input

$f(x, \boldsymbol{u})$	*right-hand side of ODE $\boldsymbol{u}' = f(x, \boldsymbol{u})$*
$\boldsymbol{u}^{(0)}$	*initial condition $\boldsymbol{u}(a) = \boldsymbol{u}^{(0)}$*
a	*initial value of x*
b	*final value of x*
n	*number of steps*

Begin computations

$h = \dfrac{b - a}{n}$ *step size*

For i = 0 to 1   *use midpoint method to start*

   $x(i) = a + h\,i$

   $\mathbf{z}^{(i)} = \mathbf{f}(x(i), \mathbf{u}^{(i)})$

   $\mathbf{k}_1 = h\,\mathbf{z}^{(i)}$

   $\mathbf{k}_2 = h\,\mathbf{f}\left(x(i) + \dfrac{1}{2}\,h, \mathbf{u}^{(i)} + \dfrac{1}{2}\,\mathbf{k}_1 \right)$

   $\mathbf{u}^{(i+1)} = \mathbf{u}^{(i)} + \mathbf{k}_2$

End

x(2) = a + 2 h

For i = 2 to n−1   *use third-order ABM method to continue*

   $x(i+1) = a + h(i+1)$ *define grid point*

   $\mathbf{z}^{(i)} = \mathbf{f}(x(i), \mathbf{u}^{(i)})$

   $\mathbf{u}^* = \mathbf{u}_i + \dfrac{h}{12}\,(23\,\mathbf{z}^{(i)} - 16\,\mathbf{z}^{(i-1)} + 5\,\mathbf{z}^{(i-2)})$ *predict*

   $\mathbf{z}^* = \mathbf{f}(x(i+1), \mathbf{u}^*)$

   $\mathbf{u}^{(i+1)} = \mathbf{u}^{(i)} + \dfrac{h}{12}\,(5\,\mathbf{z}^* + 8\,\mathbf{z}^{(i)} - \mathbf{z}^{(i-1)})$ *correct*

End

Return

   $\mathbf{u}$ *matrix of approximate values*

Example 13.11 Motion of a Baseball

Air resistance is one of the factors influencing how far a fly ball travels. In this example, we illustrate the effect of changing assumptions about the form of the air resistance. If a ball is hit with an initial velocity of [100, 45] (so that the initial condition vector is $y0 = [\ 0\quad 100\quad 3\quad 45\ ]$) and is subject to air resistance proportional to its velocity (acting on the horizontal component only), the motion can be found from a simple computer program implementing the ABM method presented in the preceding algorithm.

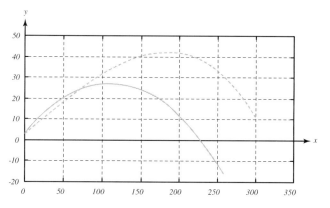

FIGURE 13.10   Flight of a baseball. Dashed line presupposes air resistance proportional to velocity in x-direction. Solid line presupposes air resistance proportional to velocity.

To take air resistance proportional to the velocity squared, we take a larger initial velocity so that the ball goes a comparable distance. We use the initial vector $y0 = [\ 0\quad 150\quad 3\quad 50\ ]$, so the initial velocity is $[150, 50]$.

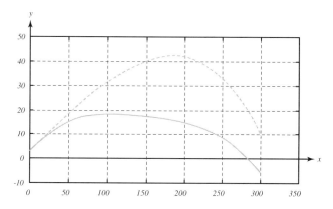

FIGURE 13.11   Flight of a baseball. Dashed line; air resistance proportional to velocity squared in x-direction. Solid line; air resistance proportional to velocity squared.

13.4   ILL-CONDITIONED AND STIFF ODE

We now consider briefly two ways in which a higher-order ODE or system of first-order ODE may have characteristics that will cause difficulties for any numerical method that is used to solve the problem.

13.4.1   Ill-Conditioned ODE

There are ODE or systems of ODE for which any error that occurs will increase, regardless of the numerical method employed. Such problems are called *ill-conditioned*. As an illustration, consider the system

$$u_1' = 2u_2$$
$$u_2' = 2u_1$$

for which the general solution is

$$u_1 = a\,e^{2x} + b\,e^{-2x}$$
$$u_2 = a\,e^{2x} - b\,e^{-2x}$$

With the initial conditions

$$u_1(0) = 3$$
$$u_2(0) = -3$$

we have $a = 0$, $b = 3$. However, for any numerical error that occurs, a component of the positive exponential will be introduced and will eventually dominate the true solution.

Ill-conditioning can also occur for a single first-order ODE, as the following problem shows. Consider the ODE

$$y' = 3y - t^2$$

for which the general solution is

$$y = C\,e^{3t} + \frac{1}{3}t^2 + \frac{2}{9}t + \frac{2}{27}.$$

If we take the initial condition as $y(0) = \dfrac{2}{27}$, the exact solution is

$$y = \frac{1}{3}t^2 + \frac{2}{9}t + \frac{2}{27}.$$

However, any error in the numerical solution process will introduce the exponential component which will eventually dominate the true solution. The exponential term is known as a parasitic solution.

13.4.2   Stiff ODE

An ODE in which there is a rapidly decaying transient solution also causes difficulties for numerical solution, requiring an extremely small step size in order to obtain an accurate solution. One source of such equations is in the description of a spring-mass system with large spring constants, hence these problems are known as *stiff ODE*. Stiff ODE are very common in chemical kinetic studies, and also occur in many network analysis and simulation problems.

As an illustration, consider the system

$$u' = 98u + 198v,$$

$$v' = -99u - 199v,$$

with initial conditions $u(0) = 1$, $v(0) = 0$.

The exact solution is

$$u(t) = 2e^{-t} - e^{-100t},$$

$$v(t) = -e^{-t} + e^{-100t}.$$

It is also possible for a single first-order ODE to be stiff, as the following problem shows. Consider the ODE

$$y' = \lambda(y - g(t)) + g'(t)$$

with $\lambda \ll 0$ and $g(t)$ a smooth, slowly varying function.

The solution is

$$y = (y_0) - g(0)) e^{\lambda t} + g(t).$$

The first term in the solution will soon be insignificant compared with $g(t)$, but stability will continue to be governed by $h\lambda$, necessitating a very small step size.

For a system of equations

$$\mathbf{y}' = \mathbf{A}(\mathbf{y} - \mathbf{g}(t)) + \mathbf{g}'(t)$$

the eigenvalues of $\mathbf{A}$ correspond to λ; if all of the eigenvalues have negative real parts, the solution will converge toward $\mathbf{g}(t)$ as $t \to \infty$.

Numerical Methods for Stiff ODE

The simplest method for stiff problems is the backward Euler method

$$y_{i+1} = y_i + h f(t_{i+1}, y_{i+1}).$$

The error is amplified by $(1-h \lambda)^{-1}$ at each step, which is less than one if $\mathrm{Re}(\lambda) < 0$. Thus, the backward Euler's method is A-stable, according to the following definition.

A method is called *A-stable* if any solution produced when the method is applied (with fixed step size $h > 0$) to the problem $y' = \lambda y$ (with $\lambda = \alpha + \beta i$ and $\alpha < 0$) tends to zero as $n \to \infty$.

Dahlquist (1963) showed that a multistep method that is A-stable cannot have order greater than two. The trapezoidal method is the second-order multistep method with the smallest error constant (see summary for Chapter 12).

Since A-stability is difficult to achieve, a somewhat less restrictive stability condition, known as *stiff-stability*, is often sufficient. Methods for stiff ODE are implicit and often require iterative techniques for their solution. Newton's method may be used, with the required Jacobian either supplied by the user, or generated numerically. (See Gear, 1971, for further discussion.)

The basic functions for solving ODE in software packages can be used for either a single first-order ODE or a system of first-order ODE. In this section we consider two methods that are especially intended for stiff ODE. We then illustrate the use of built-in functions for systems of ODE for solving a problem of robot motion.

The NAG Software Library includes three routines for general ODEs (two Runge-Kutta-Merson methods and one Adams method). The routine for stiff ODE is based on the BDF (Backward Differentiation Formula) method (see Hall and Watt, 1976, for further information).

The NIST Index groups the functions for ODE initial value problems according to their suitability for nonstiff or mildly stiff problems or methods for stiff ODE. The methods for nonstiff or mildly stiff problems are further grouped as Runge-Kutta, Adams predictor-corrector, or Bulirsch-Stoer methods. Several of the routines for stiff problems are based on either Gear's method, Backward Differential Formula methods, or the modified extended backward differentiation formulae (which have better stability properties than BDF methods).

The Matlab functions ode15s and ode23s are designed to solve stiff differential equations. The function ode15s implements a variable order method; ode23s is a low-order method. By default, the Jacobians needed by each method are generated numerically.

Mathcad2000Pro includes four functions for stiff ODE. The algorithms used in these functions are either semi-implicit extrapolation methods (extensions of the Bulirsch-Stoer methods) or Rosenbrock methods (extensions of the Runge-Kutta methods). The basic ideas are summarized briefly in the next sections.

13.5.1   Rosenbrock Methods

The Rosenbrock method is a generalization of the Runge-Kutta methods for stiff equations. The first of the practical implementations of these methods is due to Kaps and Rentrop (1979). The Rosenbrock methods are competitive with more complicated algorithms for moderate-sized systems (on the order of 10 or fewer equations) with moderate accuracy criterion (relative error of 10^{-4} or 10^{-5}).

The general idea is to find a solution of the form

$$y(x + h) = y(x) + \text{corrections},$$

where the corrections are solutions of a set of linear equations involving Runga-Kutta terms and terms depending on the Jacobian of the system. The effectiveness of the method relies on an effective embedded Runge-Katta method for step-size adjustment.

Several different forms of the update equations have been proposed; the form favored by Press et al. was originally developed by Shampine (1982).

13.5.2 Semi-Implicit Extrapolation Methods

The following method for stiff equations of the form $\mathbf{y}' = \mathbf{f}(\mathbf{y})$ is due to Bader and Dueflhard; it uses a semi-implicit midpoint rule for the extrapolation (Press et al., 1992, pp. 742–747). The method is based on the implicit midpoint rule

$$\mathbf{y}_{n+1} - \mathbf{y}_{n-1} = 2h\,\mathbf{f}\!\left(\frac{\mathbf{y}_{n+1} + \mathbf{y}_{n-1}}{2}\right)$$

The semi-implicit form comes from linearizing the right-hand side. This, together with a special first step (the semi-implicit Euler step), and a smoothing last step, forms the basic algorithm. For computational efficiency, the equations are written in terms of the change in the solution, $\mathbf{D}_k = \mathbf{y}_{k+1} - \mathbf{y}_k$.

Semi-Implicit Extrapolation

Define
$\quad \mathbf{f}(\mathbf{y})$ *right hand side of ODE*

$\quad \mathbf{J}$ *Jacobian marix,* $\left[\dfrac{\partial \mathbf{f}}{\partial \mathbf{y}}\right]$;

$\quad m$ *number of steps*

$\quad h = \dfrac{x_1 - x_0}{m}$ *step size*

First step
$$\mathbf{D}_0 = [\mathbf{I} - h\,\mathbf{J}]^{-1}\, h\,\mathbf{f}(\mathbf{y}_0)$$
$$\mathbf{y}_1 = \mathbf{y}_0 + \mathbf{D}_0$$

Compute
For $k = 1, \ldots m-1$
$$\mathbf{D}_k = \mathbf{D}_{k-1} + 2[\mathbf{I} - h\,\mathbf{J}]^{-1}\,[h\,\mathbf{f}(\mathbf{y}_k) - \mathbf{D}_{k-1}]$$
$$\mathbf{y}_{k+1} = \mathbf{y}_k + \mathbf{D}_k$$

End

Smooth the last step
$$\mathbf{D}_m = [\mathbf{I} - h\,\mathbf{J}]^{-1}\,[h\,\mathbf{f}(\mathbf{y}_m) - \mathbf{D}_{m-1}]$$
$$\mathbf{y}_m = \mathbf{y}_m + \mathbf{D}_m$$

Return
$\quad \mathbf{y}_m$

Example 13.12 Robot Motion

In this example, we illustrate the use of a built-in function (the MATLAB function `ode23`) for solving the problem of simulating the motion of a two-link planar robot arm. This is an example of a forward dynamics problem—i.e., given the applied joint torques, we solve for the resulting motion of the system. Attaining a solution involves integrating the equations of motion, which are two nonlinear coupled ODE. In order to solve the problem, a user-supplied function (called `robot2` in this example) is required to calculate the accelerations of the two-link robot (these are the systems of differential equations to be solved by `ode23`). A MATLAB script defines the various parameters needed, calls the function `ode23`, and plots the results. The MATLAB function and MATLAB script are given following the graph of the results.

The required parameters for this problem are

length of each link of the robot arm

mass of each link

initial angular position of each link

desired final angular position of each link

gravitational constant

matrices for P-D control with gravity compensation

The moment of inertia for each link is calculated from the mass and length

The unknowns for this system of ODE are

$q1$ position (in radians) of the first link

$q2$ position (in radians) of the second link

$q1\,d$ velocity of first link

$q2\,d$ velocity of second link

The differential equations make use of several quantities which depend on the masses and lengths of the links (constants), as well as the current positions of the links (found from solving the ODE). These quantities include the mass matrix, the Christoffel matrix, and the gravity vector. From these, the generalized accelerations are computed (which are the values returned by the function for the derivatives of the third and fourth components of the vector of unknowns). The derivative of the first component is the third component; the derivative of the second component is the fourth component.

In addition to plotting the position and velocity of each link as a function of time, the torques are also computed and plotted.

(See Spong and Vidyasagar, 1989, for derivation of the equations and description of the coordinate system conventions.)

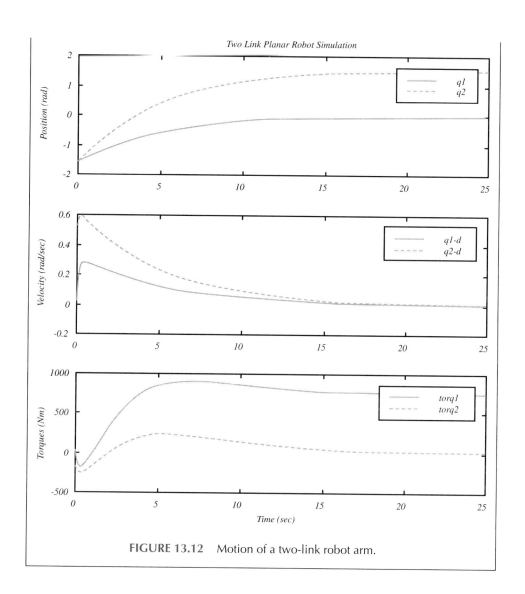

FIGURE 13.12   Motion of a two-link robot arm.

```
% S_robot_motion
% the following variables are used by the function robot2
global L1  Lc1  L2  Lc2  m1  m2  g
global I1  I2  q1_goal  q2_goal  K_p  K_v

% Set up parameters (in metric units)
   L1  = 1.0;   Lc1 = 0.5;   L2  = 1.0;  Lc2 = 0.5;    % meters
   m1  = 50.0;  m2  = 50.0;                            % kilograms
   g   = 9.81;                                         % gravity
% Set up control parameters (in metric units)
   q1_start = -pi/2;      q2_start = -pi/2;
   q1_goal  = -0.0;       q2_goal  = pi/2;
   K_p = 200.0*eye(2);    K_v = 1000.0*eye(2);

% Calculate moment of inertia for a long, slender rod
   I1 = m1*L1^2 / 12;    I2 = m2*L2^2 / 12;
% Set up values for ode23 call
   t0 = 0;   tf = 25.0;  tspan = [ t0  tf];
   y0 = [q1_start   q2_start    0    0]';
   [T, Y] = ode23('robot2',tspan, y0);
% make the output easy to look at
t = T;   q1  = Y(:,1);   q2  = Y(:,2);   q1d = Y(:,3);   q2d = Y(:,4);

% Find the required torques for each instant of time(T)
imax = max(size(T));
for i = 1:1:imax,
    phi1 = (m1*Lc1 + m2*L1)*g*cos(q1(i)) + m2*Lc2*g*cos(q1(i) + q2(i));
    phi2 = m2*Lc2*g*cos(q1(i) + q2(i));
    phi = [phi1 phi2]';
    q_dot = [q1d(i)   q2d(i)]';
    e = [q1(i)-q1_goal   q2(i)-q2_goal]';
    ed = q_dot;
    torq = -K_p*e - K_v*ed + phi;
    torq1(i) = torq(1);
    torq2(i) = torq(2);
end
% plot position vs time for both link coordinates
   subplot(3,1,1);   plot(t,q1,'-',t,q2,':');      legend('q1','q2');
   ylabel('Position (rad)');  title('Two Link Planar Robot Simulation')
% plot velocity vs time for both link coordinates
   subplot(3,1,2);   plot(t,q1d,'-',t,q2d,':');  legend('q1-d','q2-d');
   ylabel('Velocity (rad/sec)')
% plot torques vs time for both link coordinates
   subplot(3,1,3);   plot(t,torq1,'-',t,torq2,':');
   legend('torq1','torq2');  ylabel('Torques (Nm)'); xlabel('Time (sec)')
```

```
function ydot = robot2(t,y);

% Calculate the accelerations for a two-link planar robot
% Equations of motion for a 2-r planar robot
% This example was contributed by
% Pierre Larochelle, Florida Institute of Technology, 5-12-97

% This function uses the global variables

global L1  Lc1  L2  Lc2  m1  m2  g
global I1  I2  q1_goal  q2_goal  K_p  K_v

% Aliases for input states to match standard robotic's notation
  q1  = y(1);   q2  = y(2);   q1d = y(3);   q2d = y(4);

% Calculate the mass matrix [M]
  d11 = m1*Lc1^2 + m2*(L1^2 + Lc2^2 + 2*L1*Lc2*cos(q2)) + I1 + I2;
  d12 = m2*(Lc2^2 + L1*Lc2*cos(q2)) + I2;
  d21 = d12;
  d22 = m2*Lc2^2 + I2;
  M = [d11 d12; d21 d22];

% Calculate the Christoffel matrix
  h = -m2*L1*Lc2*sin(q2);
  C = h * [q2d    q2d+q1d  ;
           -q1d         0  ];

% Calculate the gravity vector
phi1 = (m1*Lc1 + m2*L1)*g*cos(q1) + m2*Lc2*g*cos(q1 + q2);
phi2 = m2*Lc2*g*cos(q1 + q2);
phi = [phi1  phi2]';

% Calculate the error vectors
  e = [(q1 - q1_goal)  (q2 - q2_goal)]';
  ed = [q1d  q2d]';

% Calculate control torque vector;
% P-D Control with gravity compensation
  tau = -K_p*e - K_v*ed + phi;

% Calculate the generalized accelerations
  qd = [q1d    q2d]';
  qdd = inv(M)*(tau - C*qd - phi);

% Generate the change in the state vector
  ydott(1) = q1d;
  ydott(2) = q2d;
  ydott(3) = qdd(1);
  ydott(4) = qdd(2);
  ydot = ydott';
```

Convert Higher-Order ODE to System of First-Order ODE

The nth-order ODE

$$y^{(n)} = f(x, y, y', y'', \ldots, y^{(n-1)}),$$

$$y(0) = \alpha_0, \ y'(0) = \alpha_1, \ y''(0) = \alpha_2, \ldots, y^{(n-1)}(0) = \alpha_{n-1},$$

becomes a system of first-order ODEs by the following change of variables:

$$u_1 = y, \ u_2 = y', \ u_3 = y'', \ \ldots \ u_n = y^{(n-1)}.$$

The differential equations relating these variables are

$$u_1' = u_2, \ u_2' = u_3, \ u_3' = u_4, \ \ldots, \ u_n' = f(x, u_1, u_2, u_3, \ldots, u_n),$$

with the initial conditions

$$u_1(0) = \alpha_0, \ u_2(0) = \alpha_1, \ u_3(0) = \alpha_2, \ \ldots, \ u_n(0) = \alpha_{n-1}.$$

Solve a System of Two ODE

$u' = f(x, u, v), \quad v' = g(x, u, v)$

Euler's Method

$$u_{i+1} = u_i + h f(x_i, u_i, v_i), \quad v_{i+1} = v_i + h g(x_i, u_i, v_i).$$

Midpoint Method

$$k_1 = h f(x_i, u_i, v_i), \qquad\qquad m_1 = h g(x_i, u_i, v_i).$$

$$k_2 = h f\left(x_i + \frac{h}{2}, u_i + \frac{1}{2}k_1, v_i + \frac{1}{2}m_1\right), \quad m_2 = h g\left(x_i + \frac{h}{2}, u_i + \frac{1}{2}k_1, v_i + \frac{1}{2}m_1\right).$$

$$u_{i+1} = u_i + k_2, \qquad v_{i+1} = v_i + m_2.$$

Solve a System of Three ODE

$u_1' = f_1(x, u_1, u_2, u_3), \quad u_2' = f_2(x, u_1, u_2, u_3), \quad u_3' = f_3(x, u_1, u_2, u_3)$

Two-Step Adams-Bashforth Method

$$u_1(i = 0), u_2(i = 0), u_3(i = 0) \text{ are given by the initial condition,}$$

$$u_1(i = 1), u_2(i = 1), u_3(i = 1) \text{ are found from a 1-step method,}$$

and for $i = 1, \ldots, n-1$

$$u_1(i + 1) = u_1(i) + \frac{h}{2}[3f_1(x(i), u_1(i), u_2(i), u_3(i)) - f_1(x(i - 1), u_1(i - 1), u_2(i - 1), u_3(i - 1))],$$

$$u_2(i + 1) = u_2(i) + \frac{h}{2}[3f_2(x(i), u_1(i), u_2(i), u_3(i)) - f_2(x(i - 1), u_1(i - 1), u_2(i - 1), u_3(i - 1))],$$

$$u_3(i + 1) = u_3(i) + \frac{h}{2}[3f_3(x(i), u_1(i), u_2(i), u_3(i)) - f_3(x(i - 1), u_1(i - 1), u_2(i - 1), u_3(i - 1))].$$

SUGGESTIONS FOR FURTHER READING

Bader, G., and P. Deuflhard. "A Semi-implicit Midpoint Rule for Stiff Systems of Ordinary Differential Equations," *Numerische Mathematik,* vol. 41, pp. 373–398, 1983.

Hall, G., and J. M. Watt (eds.). *Modern Numerical Methods for Ordinary Differential Equations.* Clarendon Press, Oxford, 1976.

Kaps, P., and Rentrop, P. "Generalized Runge-Kutta Methods of Order Four with Stepsize Control for Stiff Ordinary Differential Equations," *Numerische Mathematik*, vol. 33, pp. 55–68, 1979.

Press, W. H., S. A. Teukolsky, W. T. Vetterling, and B. P. Flannery. *Numerical Recipes in C; The Art of Scientific Computing* 2d ed. Cambridge Unversity Press, Cambridge, 1992.

Shampine, L. F. "Implementation of Rosenbrock Methods," *ACM Transactions on Mathematical Software*, vol. 8, pp. 93–113, 1982.

The suggested readings for Chapter 12 are also excellent references for the topics in this chapter. In addition, the following texts include discussion of applications of ODEs:

Ayyub, B. M., and R. H. McCuen. *Numerical Methods for Engineers.* Prentice Hall, Upper Saddle River, NJ, 1996

Greenberg, M. D. *Advanced Engineering Mathematics.* 2d ed., Prentice Hall, Upper Saddle River, NJ, 1998.

Greenberg, M. D. *Foundations of Applied Mathematics*, Prentice-Hall, Englewood Cliffs, NJ, 1978.

Grossman, S. I., and W. R. Derrick. *Advanced Engineering Mathematics.* Harper & Row, New York, 1988.

Hanna, O. T., and O. C. Sandall. *Computational Methods in Chemical Engineering.* Prentice Hall, Upper Saddle River, NJ, 1995.

Hildebrand, F. B. *Advanced Calculus for Applications*, 2d ed. Prentice Hall, Englewood Cliffs, NJ, 1976.

Inman, D. J. *Engineering Vibration.* Prentice Hall, Englewood Cliffs, NJ, 1996.

Simon, W. *Mathematical Techniques for Biology and Medicine.* Dover, New York, 1986.

Spong, M. W., and Vidyasagar, M. *Robot Dynamics and Control.* John Wiley & Sons, New York, 1989. (See p. 145, Ex. 6.4.2.)

Thomson, W. T. *Theory of Vibrations with Applications.* Prentice Hall, Englewood Cliffs, NJ, 1993.

For Problems P13.1 to P13.10 solve the initial value problem by first converting the problem to a system of first order ODE. For each solution method, investigate the effect of increasing n.

    a. Solve the system using Euler's method.
    b. Solve the system using the midpoint method.
    c. Solve the system using the classic Runge-Kutta method.
    d. Solve the system using the Adams-Bashforth-Moulton method.

P13.1 $y'' = y + x$, $y(0) = 2$, $y'(0) = 0$, on $[0, 2]$.

P13.2 $y'' = y' + y + x$, $y(0) = 1$, $y'(0) = 0.5$, on $[0, 2]$.

P13.3 $y'' = -2y' - y + x^2$, $y(0) = 7$, $y'(0) = -4$, on $[0, 2]$.

P13.4 $y'' = -4y' - 4y$, $y(0) = 1$, $y'(0) = 8$, on $[0, 4]$.

P13.5 $y'' = y + x^2 - 4x$, $y(0) = -2$, $y'(0) = 2$, on $[0, 4]$.

P13.6 $y'' = 5y' - 6y$, $y(0) = 2$, $y'(0) = 5$, on $[0, 1]$.

P13.7 $y'' = -y' + 6y$, $y(0) = 1$, $y'(0) = -2$, on $[0, 4]$.

P13.8 $y'' = -9y$, $y(0) = 1$, $y'(0) = 6$, on $[0, 2\pi]$.

P13.9 $y'' + \dfrac{-1}{1 + x}y' + \dfrac{-3}{1 + x}y = 0$, $y(0) = 1$, $y'(0) = -1$, on $[0, 2]$.

P13.10 $y'' + \dfrac{4}{1 + x^2}y' + \dfrac{2}{1 + x^2}y = 0$, $y(0) = 1$, $y'(0) = -1$, on $[0, 2]$.

For Problems P13.11 to P13.20 solve the initial value problem by the numerical method of your choice. Investigate the effect of modifying the initial conditions (for either y or y').

P13.11 $y'' + \dfrac{-6x^2}{1 + x^3}y' + \dfrac{-6x}{1 + x^3}y = 0$, $y(0) = 1$, $y'(0) = 0$, on $[0, 1]$.

P13.12 $y'' + y' - y^2 = 0$, $y(0) = 1$, $y'(0) = 0$, on $[0, 2]$.

P13.13 $y'' + y + y^3 = 0$, $y(0) = 2$, $y'(0) = 0$, on $[0, 10]$.

P13.14 $y'' = -2yy'$, $y(1) = 1$, $y'(1) = -1$, on $[1, 5]$.

P13.15 $y'' = -2(y + x)(y' + 1)$, $y(1) = 0$, $y'(1) = -2$, on $[1, 5]$.

P13.16 $y'' = \dfrac{6x^4}{y}$, $y(1) = 1$, $y'(1) = 3$, on $[1, 2]$.

P13.17 $yy'' + (y')^2 = 0$, $y(1) = 2$, $y'(1) = 1/2$, on $[1, 2]$.

P13.18 $y'' + 4x^{-1}y' + 2x^{-2}y = 0$, $y(1) = 2$; $y'(1) = -3$, on $[1, 2]$.

P13.19 $y'' - 4x^{-1}y' + 6x^{-2}y = 0$, $y(1) = 5$, $y'(1) = 13$, on $[1, 2]$.

P13.20 $x^2y'' + 4xy' + 2y = x$, $y(1) = 1/6$, $y'(1) = -5/6$, on $[1, 2]$.

P13.21 $y'' - 2x^{-2}y = 0$, $y(1) = 3$, $y'(1) = 3$, on $[1, 2]$.

P13.22 $x^2y'' - xy' + y = 0$, $y(1) = 1$, $y'(1) = 2$, on $[1, 2]$.

P13.23 $x^2y'' + xy' + y = 0$, $y(1) = 0$, $y'(1) = 3$, on $[1, 3]$.

P13.24 Solve the Bessel equation of order zero

$$x^2y'' + xy' + x^2y = 0, \ y(1) = 1, \ y'(1) = 0, \text{ on } [1, 4].$$

P13.25 Solve the Bessel equation of order one

$$x^2y'' + xy' + (x^2 - 1)y = 0, \ y(1) = 1, \ y'(1) = 0, \text{ on } [1, 4].$$

P13.26 Solve Legendre's equation for $\alpha = 1$, 2, or 3.

$$(1 - x^2)y'' - 2xy' + \alpha(\alpha + 1)y = 0, \ y(0) = 1, \\ y'(0) = 1, \text{ on } [0, 0.9].$$

P13.27 Solve the Chebyshev equation for $\alpha = 1$, 2, or 3.

$$(1 - x^2)y'' - xy' + \alpha^2y = 0, \ y(0) = 1, \ y'(0) = 1, \\ \text{on } [0, 0.9].$$

P13.28 Solve Airy's equation

$$y'' - xy = 0, \ y(0) = 1, \ y'(0) = 1, \text{ on } [0, 5].$$

P13.29 Solve the Hermite equation for $\lambda = 1$, 2, 3, or 4.

$$y'' - 2xy' + \lambda y = 0, \ y(1) = 1, \ y'(1) = 0, \text{ on } [1, 4].$$

P13.30 Solve the Laguerre equation for $\lambda = 1$, 2, 3, or 4.

$$xy'' + (1 - x)y' + \lambda y = 0, \ y(1) = 1, \ y'(1) = 0, \text{ on } [1, 4].$$

For problems P13.31 to P13.40, solve the initial value problem $\mathbf{x}' = A\,\mathbf{x}.$

P13.31

$$A = \begin{bmatrix} 3 & -3 & 2 & -1 \\ 12 & -12 & 10 & -5 \\ 15 & -15 & 14 & -7 \\ 6 & -6 & 6 & -3 \end{bmatrix}$$

a. $x0 = [1\ 0\ 0\ 0]^T$ b. $x0 = [0\ 1\ 0\ 0]^T$
c. $x0 = [0\ 0\ 1\ 0]^T$ d. $x0 = [0\ 0\ 0\ 1]^T$

P13.32

$$A = \begin{bmatrix} 1 & -3 & 2 & -1 \\ 4 & -6 & 2 & -1 \\ -5 & 5 & -8 & 5 \\ -10 & 10 & -10 & 7 \end{bmatrix}$$

a. $x0 = [1\ 0\ 0\ 0]^T$ b. $x0 = [0\ 1\ 0\ 0]^T$
c. $x0 = [0\ 0\ 1\ 0]^T$ d. $x0 = [0\ 0\ 0\ 1]^T$

P13.33

$$A = \begin{bmatrix} 3 & -3 & 2 & -1 \\ 10 & -10 & 8 & -4 \\ 10 & -10 & 9 & -4 \\ 2 & -2 & 2 & 0 \end{bmatrix}$$

a. $x0 = [1\ 0\ 0\ 0]^T$ b. $x0 = [0\ 1\ 0\ 0]^T$
c. $x0 = [0\ 0\ 1\ 0]^T$ d. $x0 = [0\ 0\ 0\ 1]^T$

P13.34

$$A = \begin{bmatrix} -9 & 9 & -6 & 3 \\ -10 & 11 & -6 & 3 \\ 3 & -2 & 4 & -2 \\ 4 & -4 & 4 & -2 \end{bmatrix}$$

a. $x0 = [1\ 0\ 0\ 0]^T$ b. $x0 = [0\ 1\ 0\ 0]^T$
c. $x0 = [0\ 0\ 1\ 0]^T$ d. $x0 = [0\ 0\ 0\ 1]^T$

P13.35

$$A = \begin{bmatrix} -2 & 3 & -2 & 1 \\ 1 & 1 & 2 & -1 \\ 10 & -9 & 12 & -7 \\ 9 & -9 & 10 & -7 \end{bmatrix}$$

a. $x0 = [1\ 0\ 0\ 0]^T$ b. $x0 = [0\ 1\ 0\ 0]^T$
c. $x0 = [0\ 0\ 1\ 0]^T$ d. $x0 = [0\ 0\ 0\ 1]^T$

P13.36

$$A = \begin{bmatrix} -13 & 12 & -8 & 4 \\ -24 & 21 & -14 & 7 \\ -14 & 12 & -9 & 6 \\ -6 & 6 & -6 & 6 \end{bmatrix}$$

a. $x0 = [1\ 0\ 0\ 0]^T$ b. $x0 = [0\ 1\ 0\ 0]^T$
c. $x0 = [0\ 0\ 1\ 0]^T$ d. $x0 = [0\ 0\ 0\ 1]^T$

P13.37

$$A = \begin{bmatrix} -11 & 6 & -4 & 2 \\ 3 & -9 & 8 & -4 \\ 18 & -19 & 16 & -7 \\ 2 & -2 & 2 & 1 \end{bmatrix}$$

a. $x0 = [1\ 0\ 0\ 0]^T$ b. $x0 = [0\ 1\ 0\ 0]^T$
c. $x0 = [0\ 0\ 1\ 0]^T$ d. $x0 = [0\ 0\ 0\ 1]^T$

P13.38

$$A = \begin{bmatrix} -36 & 30 & -20 & 10 \\ -61 & 50 & -36 & 18 \\ -34 & 20 & -25 & 13 \\ -10 & 10 & -10 & 6 \end{bmatrix}$$

a. $x0 = [1\ 0\ 0\ 0]^T$ b. $x0 = [0\ 1\ 0\ 0]^T$
c. $x0 = [0\ 0\ 1\ 0]^T$ d. $x0 = [0\ 0\ 0\ 1]^T$

P13.39

$$A = \begin{bmatrix} 30 & -24 & 16 & -8 \\ 38 & -28 & 18 & -9 \\ 6 & -2 & 0 & 0 \\ -2 & 2 & -2 & 1 \end{bmatrix}$$

a. $x0 = [1\ 0\ 0\ 0]^T$ b. $x0 = [0\ 1\ 0\ 0]^T$
c. $x0 = [0\ 0\ 1\ 0]^T$ d. $x0 = [0\ 0\ 0\ 1]^T$

P13.40

$$A = \begin{bmatrix} -28 & 24 & -16 & 8 \\ -42 & 34 & -22 & 11 \\ -10 & 6 & -2 & 0 \\ 6 & -6 & 6 & -5 \end{bmatrix}$$

a. $x0 = [1\ 0\ 0\ 0]^T$ b. $x0 = [0\ 1\ 0\ 0]^T$
c. $x0 = [0\ 0\ 1\ 0]^T$ d. $x0 = [0\ 0\ 0\ 1]^T$

A13.1 The motion $x(t)$, $y(t)$ of an object (such as a baseball), subject to the forces of gravity and air resitance proportional to velcoity, can be described by the system of second-order ODEs

$$x'' = -c\,v\,x', \qquad y'' = -c\,v\,y' - g,$$

where the speed of the object is $v = \sqrt{(x')^2 + (y')^2}$, $g = 32$ ft/s^2 , and $c = 0.002$ is a typical value for a baseball. (In mks units, $g = 9.81$ m/s^2 , and $c = 0.006$.) Solve with initial conditions $x(0) = 0$; $y(0) = 0$; $x'(0) = 100$ ft/s ; $y'(0) = 100$ ft/s. Does the ball clear a fence which is 400 ft from home plate and 10 ft tall? Investigate other initial conditions for the velocity of the ball.

A13.2 The motion of one body around another, such as a comet orbiting around the sun, can be described by the system of ODEs

$$x'' = -K\,x/r^3, \qquad y'' = -K\,y/r^3,$$

where $r = \sqrt{x^2 + y^2}$. With distance measured in AU ($1\ AU = 1.496 \times 10^{11}$ m) and time measured in years, we have $K \approx 40$ (for an object rotating around the sun). Take as initial conditions, $x(0) = 1$, $x'(0) = 0$, $y(0) = 0$, $y'(0) = 2$, and solve for $0 \le t \le 4$; investigate the effect of different values of $y'(0)$. (For further discussion, see Garcia, 1994, or Greenberg, 1978.)

A13.3 The motion of a spherical pendulum of length L can be described, in terms of its angular displacement from the vertical ϕ and its angular dispacement from the positive x-axis θ, by the ODEs

$$\phi = -2\,\phi'\,\theta'\,\cot(\theta),$$

$$\theta' = (\phi')^2 \sin(\theta)\cos(\theta) - (g/L)\sin(\theta).$$

Find the motion for the following sets of initial conditions

a.	$\phi = 0$,	$\theta = 0.2$,	$\phi' = 0$,	$\theta' = 0.2$.
b.	$\phi = 0$,	$\theta = 0$,	$\phi' = 0.2$,	$\theta' = 0$.
c.	$\phi = 0$,	$\theta = 0.2$,	$\phi' = 0.2$,	$\theta' = 0.2$.
d.	$\phi = 0$,	$\theta = 0.2$,	$\phi' = 0.01$,	$\theta' = 0.2$.
e.	$\phi = 0$,	$\theta = 0.2$,	$\phi' = 0.2$,	$\theta' = 0$.

(See Thomson, 1986, p. 275.)

A13.4 Consider a system of four blocks coupled by springs, between two walls a distance L_w apart, as introduced in Chapter 3 (A3.6). Let the unstretched lengths of the springs be $L_1, \ldots, L_5$, the spring constants be $k_1, \ldots, k_5$, and the masses of the blocks be $m_1, \ldots m_4$. The equations of motion for each block ($i = 1, \ldots, 4$) are

$$\frac{dx_i}{dt} = v_i \qquad \frac{dv_i}{dt} = \frac{F_i}{m_i}$$

where

$$F_1 = -k_1(x_1 - L_1) + k_2(x_2 - x_1 - L_2)$$

$$F_2 = -k_2(x_2 - x_1 - L_2) + k_3(x_3 - x_2 - L_3)$$

$$F_3 = -k_3(x_3 - x_2 - L_3) + k_4(x_4 - x_3 - L_4)$$

$$F_4 = -k_4(x_4 - x_3 - L_4) + k_5(L_w - x_4 - L_5)$$

Solve the system for

$L_1 = 2$; $L_2 = 2$; $L_3 = 2$; $L_4 = 2$; $L_5 = 2$; $L_w = 8$.

$k_1 = 1$; $k_2 = 1$; $k_3 = 1$; $k_4 = 1$; $k_5 = 5$, $m_1 = \ldots = m_4 = 4$.

Investigate the effect of changing various parameter values, including making the blocks of different masses. (See Garcia, 1994, p. 103 for further discussion.)

A13.5 The time-evolution of the concentrations of two components (A and C) in a nonlinear chemical reaction of the form $A + B \leftrightarrow C \rightarrow D + E$, occuring in a constant volume batch reactor, can be modeled by the equations

$$\frac{dy_1}{dt} = -r_1\,y_1\,(y_1 - K) + r_2 y_2 \qquad y_1(0) = 1$$

$$\frac{dy_2}{dt} = -(r_2 + r_3)\,y_2 + r_1\,y_1\,(y_1 - K) \qquad y_2(0) = 0$$

where y_1 is the concentration of A, y_2 is the concentration of C, r_1, r_2, and r_3 are rate constants, and the parameter K depends on the initial composition of the mixture. Solve using $r_1 = r_2 = r_3 = 1$; $K = 0$; investigate the effect of modifying these values. (See Hanna and Sandall, 1995, pp. 285 for further discussion.)

A13.6 The time evolution of the concentration of two chemical species in an oscillatory chemical system such as the Belousov-Zhabotinski reaction can be described by the Brusselator model:

$$\frac{dx}{dt} = A + x^2 y - (B + 1)\, x \qquad \frac{dy}{dt} = B\,x - x^2 y$$

The parameters A and B are positive, as are the initial conditions for x and y; investigate the solutions for various choices of A, B, $x(0)$ and $y(0)$. Consider cases where $B/(1 + A^2) < 1$; $B/(1 + A^2) > 1$; and $B/(1 + A^2) = 1$. (See Garcia, 1994, p. 98 for further discussion; the original reference is Nicolis and Prigogine, 1977.)

A13.7 A fairly general two-compartment chemical flow problem describes the concentration of two chemicals, C_1 and C_2, in two compartments with volumes V_1 and V_2 respectively. The concentrations change with time as a result of concentration-independent input into each compartment, I_1 and I_2, concentration-dependent output ($L_1 C_1$ and $L_2 C_2$) and diffusion from V_1 into V_2, $K(C_1 - C_2)$. Any of the inputs or outputs can be taken to be negative to represent flow in the opposite direction. The system of differential equations is

$$\frac{dC_1}{dt} = \frac{1}{V_1}\left[I_1 - L_1 C_1 - K(C_1 - C_2)\right]$$

$$\frac{dC_2}{dt} = \frac{1}{V_2}\left[I_2 - L_2 C_2 - K(C_2 - C_1)\right]$$

The behavior of the system depends on the relative values of the various rates and volumes. For example, let $C_1(0) = C_2(0) = 0$, $I_1 = 1$, $I_2 = 0$, $V_1 = 10$, $V_2 = 5$, and investigate the following flows:

    a. $L_1 = 2$, $L_2 = 2$, $K = 10$;
    b. $L_1 = 2$, $L_2 = 3$, $K = 20$;

find the concentration in the two tanks for the first 10 minutes of the process. (See Simon, 1986, p. 88, for further discussion.)

A13.8 For a mother-daughter radioactive decay process, we assume that for each mother atom that decays, a daughter atom is produced; daughter atoms are in turn lost at a rate proportional to their quantity. This process is described by the equations

$$\frac{dM}{dt} = -L_1 M(t), \qquad \frac{dD}{dt} = -L_2 D(t) + L_1 M(t).$$

Find the amount of each substance as a function of time if $M(0) = 10$, $D(0) = 0$, $L_1 = 2$, $L_2 = 0.1$. Investigate the effect of varying any of these values. (See Simon, 1986, p. 37 for further discussion.)

A13.9 The Lorenz equations

$$\frac{dx}{dt} = p\,(y - x) \qquad \frac{dy}{dt} = r\,x - y - xz \qquad \frac{dz}{dt} = x\,y - q\,z$$

are a well-known example of a system with chaotic behavior for certain values of the parameters. The system was studied by Lorenz in connection with the problem of finding the effect of heating a horizontal fluid layer from below. Investigate the solutions for the following values of the parameters and initial conditions.

    a. $p = 10$, $q = 8/3$, $r = 28$, $[x\ y\ z] = [1\ 1\ 2]$
    b. $p = 10$, $q = 8/3$, $r = 28$, $[x\ y\ z] = [1\ 2\ 2]$
    c. $p = 10$, $q = 8/3$, $r = 28$, $[x\ y\ z] = [2\ 2\ 2]$
    d. $p = 10$, $q = 3$, $\quad r = 18$, $[x\ y\ z] = [1\ 1\ 2]$
    e. $p = 10$, $q = 3$, $\quad r = 18$, $[x\ y\ z] = [1\ 2\ 2]$
    f. $p = 10$, $q = 3$, $\quad r = 18$, $[x\ y\ z] = [2\ 2\ 2]$
    g. $p = 10$, $q = 8$, $\quad r = 18$, $[x\ y\ z] = [1\ 1\ 2]$
    h. $p = 10$, $q = 8$, $\quad r = 18$, $[x\ y\ z] = [1\ 2\ 2]$
    i. $p = 10$, $q = 8$, $\quad r = 18$, $[x\ y\ z] = [2\ 2\ 2]$

The solutions are often plotted in the x-y plane or the y-z plane.

A13.10 Solve the classical Van der Pol differential equation for an oscillator

$$\frac{d^2 x}{dt^2} - \mu\,(1 - x^2)\,\frac{dx}{dt} + x = 0,$$

for a variety of values of the parameter μ and the initial conditions.

    a. $\mu = 0.4$, $x(0) = 0.1$, $x'(0) = 0$.
    b. $\mu = 1$, $\quad x(0) = 0.5$, $x'(0) = 0$.
    c. $\mu = 2$, $\quad x(0) = 1$, $\quad x'(0) = 1$.
    d. $\mu = 5$, $\quad x(0) = 1$, $\quad x'(0) = 0$.
    e. $\mu = 5$, $\quad x(0) = 1$, $\quad x'(0) = 1$.

A13.11 A simple predator-prey relationship is described by the Lotka-Volterra model, which we write in terms of a fox population $f(t)$, with birth rate b_f, and death rate d_f, and a geese population $g(t)$ with birth rate b_g, and death rate d_g.

$$\frac{df}{dt} = f(t)\,(b_f g(t) - d_f) \qquad \frac{dg}{dt} = g(t)\,(b_g - d_g f(t))$$

Find the populations as a function of time for the following initial conditions and parameter values.

   a. $b_f = 1, d_f = 1, b_g = 1, d_g = 1, f(0) = 2, g(0) = 2$.
   b. $b_f = 1, d_f = 1, b_g = 1, d_g = 1, f(0) = 10, g(0) = 2$.
   c. $b_f = 1, d_f = 1, b_g = 1, d_g = 1, f(0) = 2, g(0) = 10$.
   d. $b_f = 1, d_f = 1, b_g = 1, d_g = 1, f(0) = 2, g(0) = 2$.
   e. $b_f = 1, d_f = 1, b_g = 1, d_g = 1, f(0) = 10, g(0) = 2$.
   f. $b_f = 1, d_f = 0.5, b_g = 1, d_g = 0.5, f(0) = 2, g(0) = 10$.

A13.12 If two species compete for food but do not prey on each other, the populations can be described by the equations

$$\frac{dx}{dt} = x(a_1 - b_1 x - c_1 y) \qquad \frac{dy}{dt} = y(a_2 - b_2 y - c_2 x)$$

where all constants are positive; each population would have logistic growth if the other were not present. Find the solutions for the following combinations of parameter values and initial conditions.

   a. $a_1 = 2; b_1 = 1; c_1 = 1; a_2 = 10; b_2 = 10; c_2 = 1;$ $x(0) = 4; y(0) = 2$.
   b. try other combinations of parameters for which $a_2/c_2 > a_1/b_1$ and $a_1/c_1 > a_2/b_2$
   c. $a_1 = 2, b_1 = 1, c_1 = 1, a_2 = 10, b_2 = 1, c_2 = 1,$ $x(0) = 4; y(0) = 2$.

   d. try other combinations of parameters for which $a_2/c_2 > a_1/b_1$ and $a_2/b_2 > a_1/c_1$
   e. $a_1 = 2, b_1 = 1, c_1 = 1, a_2 = 10, b_2 = 1, c_2 = 10,$ $x(0) = 4; y(0) = 2$.
   f. try other combinations of parameters for which $a_1/b_1 > a_2/c_2$ and $a_2/b_2 > a_1/c_1$

A13.13 The equations for the deflection y and rotation z of a simply supported beam with a uniformly distributed load of intensity 2 kips/ft and bending moment $M(x) = 10x - x^2$, can be expressed as

$$\frac{dz}{dx} = \frac{M}{EI} = \frac{10x - x^2}{EI} \qquad \frac{dy}{dx} = z$$

where E is the modulus of elasticity, and I is the moment of inertia of the cross section of the beam. Taking $EI = 3600$ kip/ft, $y(0) = 0$ and $z(0) = -0.02$, find y and z (for $0 \le x \le 10$). (See Ayyub and McCuen, 1996, p. 239 for further discussion.)

A13.14 The shape of a cantilever beam with a uniformly distributed load of intensity w kips/ft can expressed in terms of the deflection y, the slope of the tangent to deflected shape of the beam s, the bending moment m, and the shear force v by the following system of ODEs:

$$\frac{dy}{dx} = s; \qquad \frac{ds}{dx} = \frac{m}{EI}; \qquad \frac{dm}{dx} = v; \qquad \frac{dv}{dx} = -w.$$

Taking $EI = 3600$ kip/ft, $w = 1.5$ kips/ft, and initial conditions

$$y(0) = 0, s(0) = 0, v(0) = 20 \text{ kips}, m(0) = -100 \text{ kip-ft}$$

find y and z (for $0 \le x \le 10$). (See Ayyub and McCuen, 1996, p. 260 for a discussion of a similar problem.)

EXTEND YOUR UNDERSTANDING

U13.1 Investigate the numerical solution of the ODE $y'' = 16\,y$, $y(0) = 1$, $y'(0) = -4$; using the techniques discussed in this chapter. Compare each numerical solution to the exact solution. What is the nature of the difficulty displayed by this problem?

U13.2 Compare the computational effort required in using the fourth-order Runge-Kutta method with that for the third-order Adams-Bashforth-Moulton method; use several of the previous problems to investigate these two methods.

14

Ordinary Differential Equations: Boundary Value Problems

For the higher order ordinary differential equations considered in the previous chapter, all of the required information about the solution is specified at the same point, say, $x = a$, and the solution function is sought on an interval $a \leq x \leq b$. In many important applications, the information that is known about the desired solution is given at the endpoints of the interval. Such problems are called *ordinary differential equation boundary-value problems* (ODE-BVP).

In this chapter, we consider two standard approaches to solving ODE-BVP; the shooting method and the finite-difference method. The shooting method is motivated by the example of trying to hit a target at a specified distance. In the initial-value problem for the motion of an object, both the initial position and the initial velocity are given. From the solution, the location at which the object lands can be determined. In an experimental setting, one could try different velocities, observe the landing points, and eventually make the necessary adjustments to hit the target. Fortunately, for a linear problem, this basic idea leads to a numerical method that does not rely on repeated trial-and-error corrections. For a nonlinear ODE, we obtain iterative techniques analogous to the secant method or Newton's method from Chapter 2.

The finite-difference method is based on dividing the interval of interest into a number of subintervals and replacing the derivatives by the appropriate finite-difference approximations, as discussed in Chapter 11. If the differential equation is linear, it is transformed into a system of linear algebraic equations, which can be solved by the techniques investigated in previous chapters. For a nonlinear ODE, the system of algebraic equations is nonlinear, and the methods of Chapter 7 may be used. The finite-difference approach is also very important for partial differential equations, which are the subject of the next chapter.

Example 14-A Deflection of a Beam

Several boundary-value problems arise in the study of the deflection of a horizontal beam. For example, we consider a beam (see Fig. 14.1) that is freely hinged at its ends (i.e., at $x = 0$ and $x = L$), with a uniform transverse load w and tension T. In this case, the deflection, $y(x)$, is described by the ODE boundary-value problem

$$y'' - \frac{T}{EI}y = \frac{w\,x\,(x - L)}{2\,EI}, \qquad 0 \le x \le L.$$

The physical parameters of the beam are the modulus of elasticity, E, and the central moment of inertia, I. We assume that the beam is of uniform thickness, so that the product EI is a constant. For convenience, the downward direction is taken as positive.

The boundary conditions state that the beam is supported, and therefore has no deflection, at $x = 0$ and $x = L$; i.e.,

$$y(0) = y(L) = 0.$$

The exact solution of the ODE is

$$y(x) = A \sinh(\alpha x) + B \sinh(\alpha(L - x)) - \frac{w}{\alpha^2 T} + \frac{wLx}{2T} - \frac{wx^2}{2T},$$

with $\alpha^2 = T/EI$, and $A \sinh(\alpha L) = B \sinh(\alpha L) = w / \alpha^2 T$.

However, the ODE is based on the assumption that y' is small, so that $(y')^2$ is negligible and $1/R \approx y''$. In general, the radius of curvature, R, is related to the deflection by

$$\frac{1}{R} = \frac{y''}{[1(y')^2]^{3/2}},$$

which leads to the differential equation

$$\frac{y''}{[1 + (y')^2]^{3/2}} - \frac{T}{EI}y = \frac{w\,x\,(x - L)}{2\,EI}, \qquad 0 \le x \le L,$$

for which numerical methods are important (see Jaeger, 1963, for discussion).

FIGURE 14.1   Bending of a beam.

Example 14-B A Well-Hit Ball

Many factors influence the path of a baseball after it is hit. As an example, we consider a ball hit so that it lands 300 feet from home plate after 3 seconds. We assume that air resistance acts only against the horizontal component of the flight and is proportional to the horizontal velocity, so that the motion of the ball is given by

$$\frac{d^2x}{dt^2} = -c\,\frac{dx}{dt}$$

and

$$\frac{d^2y}{dt^2} = -g.$$

The initial position is $x(0) = 0$, $y(0) = 3$, and the desired landing time is $t_f = 3$, so that $x(3) = 300$, $y(3) = 0$. We take the drag coefficient $c = 0.5$. The vertical component of the motion can be found directly by

$$y(t) = -16t^2 + 47t + 3.$$

The solution for $x(t)$ can be found by the methods of this chapter. Plotting y versus x gives the path of the ball, as illustrated in Fig. 14.2.

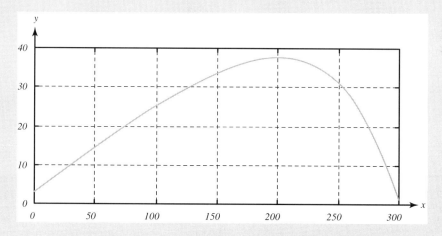

FIGURE 14.2   Flight of a baseball subject to some air resistance.

Higher order ODEs do not necessarily have all of the information about the solution given at the same (initial) point. Problems in which the value of the unknown function or its derivative is given at two different points are known as *boundary-value problems*. In particular, we investigate the second-order, two-point boundary-value problem of the form

$$y'' = f(x, y, y'), \quad a \le x \le b$$

with Dirichlet boundary conditions: $\quad y(a) = \alpha, \qquad\qquad y(b) = \beta,$
or Neuman boundary conditions: $\qquad y'(a) = \alpha, \qquad\qquad y'(b) = \beta,$
or mixed boundary conditions: $\qquad y'(a) + c_1 y(a) = \alpha, \quad y'(b) + c_2 y(b) = \beta.$
The first method we consider is based on the techniques presented in Chapter 13 for IVPs. The idea is to guess an initial value for $y'(a)$, generate a solution, and then adjust the solution so that it matches the specified value for $y(b)$. This is known as the *shooting method*. If the ODE is linear, we can solve two IVPs and form a linear combination of the solutions that will solve the BVP. If the ODE is nonlinear, an iterative process can be used. The linear case is described in the next section.

14.1 SHOOTING METHOD FOR LINEAR BVP

A linear two-point boundary value problem can be solved by forming a linear combination of the solutions to two initial-value problems. The form of the IVP depends on the form of the boundary conditions. We begin with the simplest case, Dirichlet boundary conditions, in which the value of the function is given at each end of the interval. We then consider some more general boundary conditions.

14.1.1 Simple Boundary Conditions

Suppose the two-point boundary value problem is linear, i.e., of the form

$$y'' = p(x) y' + q(x) y + r(x), a \le x \le b,$$

with boundary conditions $y(a) = ya$, $y(b) = yb$. The approach is to solve the two IVPs

$$u'' = p(x) u' + q(x) u + r(x), \quad u(a) = ya, \quad u'(a) = 0,$$
$$v'' = p(x) v' + q(x) v, \qquad\qquad v(a) = 0, \qquad v'(a) = 1.$$

If $v(b) \ne 0$, the solution of the original two-point BVP is given by

$$y(x) = u(x) + \frac{yb - u(b)}{v(b)} v(x).$$

This solution is based on the standard technique of solving a linear ODE by finding a general solution of the homogeneous equation (expressed as the ODE for v) and a particular solution of the nonhomogeneous equation (expressed as the ODE for u). The arbitrary constant A that would appear in the solution $y(x) = u(x) + A v(x)$ is found from the requirement that $y(b) = u(b) + A v(b) = yb$, which yields

$$A = \frac{yb - u(b)}{v(b)}.$$

In order to approximate the solution of the linear ODE - BVP $y'' = p(x) y' + q(x) y + r(x)$, with boundary conditions $y(a) = ya$, $y(b) = yb$, using the linear shooting method, we must convert the problem to a system of four first-order ODE-IVP, which we write as $\mathbf{z}' = f(x, \mathbf{z})$. The variables z_1 and z_2 are u and u', respectively, where u satisfies the ODE-IVP $u'' = p(x) u' + q(x) u + r(x)$, with initial conditions $u(a) = ya$, $u'(a) = 0$. The variables z_3 and z_4 are v and v', respectively, where v satisfies the ODE-IVP $v'' = p(x) v' + q(x) v$, with initial conditions $v(a) = 0$, $v'(a) = 1$.

Define the variables, z_1, z_2, z_3, and z_4

$$z_1 = u \quad z_2 = u' \quad z_3 = v \quad z_4 = v'$$

Define the ODE

$$z'_1 = z_2$$
$$z'_2 = p(x) z_2 + q(x) z_1 + r(x)$$
$$z'_3 = z_4$$
$$z'_4 = p(x) z_4 + q(x) z_3$$

Define the initial conditions

$$z_1(a) = ya \qquad z_2(a) = 0 \qquad z_3(a) = 0 \qquad z_4(a) = 1$$

In the following algorithm we denote the procedure to solve the IVP as

$$\text{ODE\_IVP}(f, a, b, w0).$$

The original problem has been converted into the appropriate system of first-order ODE-IVP as described above. The components of the solution are shown as z_1, z_2, z_3, and z_4, although a 2-dimensional array could also be used for z if desired.

Linear Shooting Method

Input
- f(x, z)   *right-hand side of system of four first-order ODE-IVP*
- a   *initial point*
- b   *end of interval of solution*
- ya   *solution at x = a*
- yb   *solution at x = b*
- n   *number of subdivision of [a, b]*

Begin computation
z0 = [ya 0 0 1]   *initial condition for system*
[z1, z2, z3, z4] = ODE_IVP(f, a, b, z0, n)   *solve the ODE-IVP system*
For i = 1 to n   *construct solution to BVP*
    y(i) = z1(i) + (yb − z1(n))*z3(i)/z3(n)
End
Return
    y

Example 14.1 Electrostatic Potential Between Two Spheres

The electrostatic potential between two concentric spheres can be represented by the second-order ODE

$$y'' = \frac{-2}{x} y'.$$

If we assume that the radius of the inner sphere is 1 and its potential is 10, while the radius of the outer sphere is 2 and its potential is 0, then the boundary conditions are

$$y(1) = 10; \quad y(2) = 0.$$

This equation can be converted to the pair of initial-value problems

$$u'' = \frac{-2}{x} u', \quad u(1) = 10, \quad u'(1) = 0,$$

$$v'' = \frac{-2}{x} v', \quad v(1) = 0, \quad v'(1) = 1.$$

which in turn becomes a system of four first order initial value problems by defining the variables $z_1, \ldots z_4$ as $z_1 = u, z_2 = u', z_3 = v, z_4 = v'$.

The differential equations become

$$z_1' = z_2, \quad z_2' = \frac{-2}{x} z_2, \quad z_3' = z_4, \quad z_4' = \frac{-2}{x} z_4,$$

with initial conditions

$$z_1(1) = 10, \quad z_2(1) = 0, \quad z_3(1) = 0, \quad z_4(1) = 1.$$

The solution of the original ODE is the linear combination of the solutions u and v, or, in terms of our system,

$$y(x) = z_1(x) + \frac{yb - z_1(b)}{z_3(b)} z_3(x).$$

The solution is illustrated in Fig. 14.3.

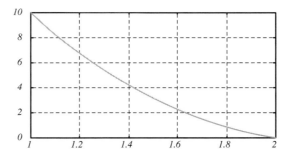

FIGURE 14.3 Electrostatic potential between two spheres.

Example 14.2 Deflection of a Simply-Supported Beam

As described in Example 14-A, the deflection of a beam supported at both ends, subject to uniform loading along its length, is described by the ODE-BVP

$$y'' = \frac{T}{EI} y + \frac{w\, x\, (x - L)}{2\, EI}, \qquad 0 \le x \le L, \qquad y(0) = y(L) = 0.$$

We illustrate the problem for the following parameter values:

$$L = 100, \quad w = 100, \quad E = 10^7, \quad T = 500, \quad I = 500.$$

The problem is linear, of the form

$$y'' = p(x)\, y' + q(x)\, y + r(x), \qquad a \le x \le b,$$

with $a = 0$, $b = L = 100$, $p(x) = 0$, $q(x) = T/EI = 10^{-7}$, and $r(x) = 10^{-8}[x(x-L)]$; the boundary conditions are $y(a) = 0$, and $y(b) = 0$.

The solution can be obtained by solving the following IVPs over $a \le x \le b$:

$$u'' = q(x)\, u + r(x), \qquad u(a) = 0, \qquad u'(a) = 0,$$
$$v'' = q(x)\, v, \qquad\qquad v(a) = 0, \qquad v'(a) = 1.$$

The solution of the two-point BVP is given by

$$y(x) = u(x) - \frac{u(b)}{v(b)}\, v(x).$$

The two second-order IVPs are converted to a system of four first-order IVPs by the change of variables

$$z_1 = u, \quad z_2 = u', \quad z_3 = v, \quad z_4 = v'.$$

The differential equations relating these variables are

$$z_1' = z_2, \qquad z_2' = 10^{-7}\, z_1 + 10^{-8}\, [x(x - L)],$$
$$z_3' = u_4, \qquad z_4' = 10^{-7}\, z_3,$$

with the initial conditions $z_1(0) = 0$, $z_2(0) = 0$, $z_3(0) = 0$, $z_4(0) = 1$. The computed solution is illustrated in Fig. 14.4.

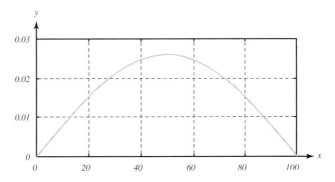

FIGURE 14.4   Deflection of a simply supported beam with uniform loading.

Example 14.3 A Simple Linear Shooting Problem

Consider the ODE

$$y'' = \frac{2x}{x^2 + 1} y' - \frac{2}{x^2 + 1} y + x^2 + 1,$$

with boundary conditions $y(0) = 2$, $y(1) = 5/3$.

      To use the shooting method for this problem, we must solve the IVP

$$u'' = \frac{2x}{x^2 + 1} u' - \frac{2}{x^2 + 1} u + x^2 + 1, \qquad u(0) = 2, \quad u'(0) = 0.$$

$$v'' = \frac{2x}{x^2 + 1} v' - \frac{2}{x^2 + 1} v, \qquad v(0) = 0, \quad v'(0) = 1.$$

Letting $z_1 = u$, $z_2 = u'$, $z_3 = v$, $z_4 = v'$, the second-order IVP become

$$z_1' = z_2$$

$$z_2' = \frac{2x}{x^2 + 1} z_2 - \frac{2}{x^2 + 1} z_1 + x^2 + 1$$

$$z_3' = z_4$$

$$z_4' = \frac{2x}{x^2 + 1} z_4 - \frac{2}{x^2 + 1} z_3$$

Initial condition for system
$z0 = [ya \quad 0 \quad 0 \quad 1]$

Initialize parameters
$a = 0$
$b = 1$
$h = (b-a)/n$
Define grid points
for $i = 1$ to n
   $x(i) = a + h*i$
end
Solve the ODE-IVP system, using any appropriate method
Use solution of system to construct solution to BVP
for $i = 1$ to n
   $y(i) = z_1(i) + (yb - z_1(n))*z_3(i)/z_3(n)$
end

For reference, we note that the general solution of the ODE is

$$y(x) = d_1 x + d_2(x^2 - 1) + x^4/6 + x^2/2.$$

The exact solution of the BVP is $y = x^4/6 - 3x^2/2 + x + 2$.

14.1.2   General Boundary Condition at $x = b$

Suppose that the linear ODE

$$y'' = p(x)\,y' + q(x)\,y + r(x);$$

has boundary conditions consisting of the value of y given at $x = a$, but the condition at $x = b$ involves a linear combination of $y(b)$ and $y'(b)$:

$$y(a) = ya; \quad y'(b) + c\,y(b) = yb.$$

As in the previous discussion, the approach is to solve the two IVP:

$$u'' = p(x)\,u' + q(x)\,u + r(x) \qquad u(a) = ya; \quad u'(a) = 0,$$
$$v'' = p(x)\,v' + q(x)\,v \qquad\qquad v(a) = 0; \quad v'(a) = 1.$$

The linear combination, $y = u + d\,v$, satisfies the conditions at $x = a$, since $y(a) = ya$. We now need to find d (if possible) so that y satisfies

$$y'(b) + c\,y(b) = yb$$

If $v'(b) + c\,v(b) \neq 0$, there is a unique solution, given by

$$y(x) = u(x) + \frac{yb - u'(b) - c\,u(b)}{v'(b) + c\,v(b)}\,v(x)$$

Example 14.4 More General Boundary Conditions

Consider the ODE from Example 14.3

$$y'' = \frac{2x}{x^2 + 1}\,y' - \frac{2}{x^2 + 1}\,y + x^2 + 1;$$

but with the boundary conditions $\quad y(0) = 1; \quad y'(1) + y(1) = 0;$
    The exact solution, $y = (x^4 - 3x^2 - x + 6)/6$, and the computed solution are indistinguishable in Fig. 14.5.

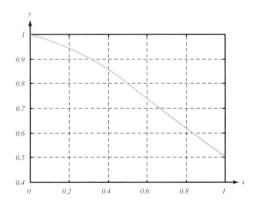

FIGURE 14.5   A BVP with a mixed boundary condition at $x = b$.

14.1.3   General Separated Boundary Conditions

Suppose that the linear ODE

$$y'' = p(x)\,y' + q(x)\,y + r(x)$$

has mixed boundary conditions at both $x = a$ and $x = b$; i.e.,

$$y'(a) + c_1\,y(a) = ya, \quad y'(b) + c_2\,y(b) = yb.$$

As in the previous discussion, the approach is to solve two IVPs, however, the appropriate forms are now

$$u'' = p(x)\,u' + q(x)\,u + r(x), \quad u(a) = 0, \quad u'(a) = ya,$$
$$v'' = p(x)\,v' + q(x)\,v, \quad v(a) = 1, \quad v'(a) = -c_1.$$

The linear combination $y = u + d\,v$ satisfies $y'(a) + c_1\,y(a) = ya$; we need to find d (if possible) such that y satisfies $y'(b) + c_2\,y(b) = yb$.

If $v'(b) + c_2\,v(b) \neq 0$, there is a unique solution, given by

$$y(x) = u(x) + \frac{yb - u'(b) - c_2\,u(b)}{v'(b) + c_2\,v(b)}\,v(x).$$

Example 14.5 Linear Shooting with Mixed Boundary Conditions

Consider again the ODE from Examples 14.2 and 14.4, i.e.,

$$y'' = \frac{2x}{x^2 + 1}\,y' - \frac{2}{x^2 + 1}\,y + x^2 + 1,$$

but with the boundary conditions $y'(0) + y(0) = 0$, $y'(1) - y(1) = 3$.

The exact solution of the BVP, $y = x^4/6 + 3x^2/2 + x - 1$, and the computed solution appear as a single curve in Fig. 14.6.

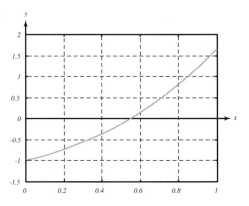

FIGURE 14.6   Solution to linear shooting problem with mixed boundary conditions.

14.2 SHOOTING METHOD FOR NONLINEAR BVP

We now consider the shooting method for nonlinear problems of the form $y'' = f(x, y, y')$ on the interval $[a, b]$. We assume that $y(a)$ is given and that some condition on the solution is also given at $x = b$. The idea is the same as for linear problems, namely, to solve the appropriate initial-value problems and use the results to find a solution to the nonlinear problem. However, for a nonlinear BVP, we have an iterative procedure rather than a simple formula for combining the solutions of two IVPs. In both the linear and the nonlinear case, we need to find a zero of the function representing the error—that is, the amount by which the solution to the IVP fails to satisfy the boundary condition at $x = b$. We assume the continuity of f, f_x, and f_y on an appropriate domain, to ensure that the initial-value problems have unique solutions.

We begin by solving the initial value problem

$$u'' = f(x, u, u'), \quad u(a) = ya, \quad u'(a) = t, \tag{14.1}$$

for some particular value of t. We then find the error associated with this solution; that is, we evaluate the boundary condition at $x = b$ using $u(b)$ and $u'(b)$. Unless it happens that $u(x)$ satisfies the boundary condition at $x = b$, we take a different initial value for $u'(a)$ and solve the resulting IVP. Thus, the error (the amount by which our shot misses its mark) is a function of our choice for the initial slope. We denote this function as $m(t)$.

The first approach we consider uses the secant method to find the zero of the error function. This allows us to treat a fairly general boundary condition at $x = b$. The second approach is based on Newton's method.

14.2.1 Nonlinear Shooting Based on the Secant Method

To solve a nonlinear BVP of the form

$$y'' = f(x, y, y'), \quad y(a) = ya, \quad h(y(b), y'(b)) = 0,$$

we may use an iterative process based on the secant method presented in Chapter 2. We need to find a value of t, the initial slope, so that solving eq. (14.1) gives a solution that is within a specified tolerance of the boundary condition at $x = b$. We begin by solving the equation with $u'(a) = t(1) = 0$; the corresponding error is $m(1)$. Unless the absolute value of $m(1)$ is less than the tolerance, we continue by solving eq. (14.1) with $u'(a) = t(2) = 1$. If this solution does not happen to satisfy the boundary condition (at $x = b$) either, we continue by updating our initial slopes according to the secant rule (until our stopping condition is satisfied), i.e.,

$$t(i) = t(i - 1) - \frac{t(i - 1) - t(i - 2)}{m(i - 1) - m(i - 2)} m(i - 1).$$

We now describe the nonlinear shooting method in the form of an algorithm. The algorithm assumes the existence of a finite-difference routine for solving a system of ODE-IVP. The BVP

$$y'' = f(x, y, y'); \quad y(a) = ya; \quad h(y(b), y'(b)) = 0$$

is converted into the IVP

$$u'' = f(x, u, u'); \quad u(a) = ya; \quad u'(a) = t$$

The method seeks to find a zero of the error function

$$m(t) = h(u(b), u'(b))$$

Nonlinear Shooting (Secant Method)

Input
  f(x, y, y')   *right-hand side of BVP: y'' = f(x, y, y')*
  [a, b]   *interval of definition of BVP*
  ya   *BC: (a) = ya*
  h(y(b), y' (b)) *BC: h(y(b), y' (b)) = 0*
  tol   *stop if abs(error) < tol*
  max_it   *stop if number of iterations reaches max_it*
Initialize first two values of u' (0)
  t(1) = 0
  t(2) = 1
Begin computation loop
test = 1
i = 1
While (test>tol)&(i<=max_it)
  If i > 2   *compute the next value of u' (0) using secant method*
  t(i) = t(i−1) − (t(i−1) − t(i−2)) m(i−1)/(m(i−1) − m(i−2))
  End
  Note that the IVP is the system z = [z1 z2], where z1 = y, z2 = y'
  z(0) = [ya t(i)]   *define current initial condition*
  Solve initial value problem
     solution is an n-by-2 matrix of values at points x1 . . . xn in [a, b]
  m(i) = h(z(n,1), z(n,2))
  test = abs(m(i))
  i = i+1
End
Return
  z = [z1 z2]   *z1 is vector of values of y*
        z2 is vector of values of y

Example 14.6 Nonlinear Shooting Method

To illustrate the use of the nonlinear shooting method, consider the BVP on $[0, 1]$
$$y'' = -2\,y\,y', \qquad y(0) = 1, \qquad y(1) + y'(1) - 0.25 = 0.$$
We start with transforming the problem to an IVP
$$u'' = -2\,u\,u'; \qquad u(0) = 1; \qquad u'(0) = t$$
and then write this as a system of two first-order ODE-IVP (using $z_1 = u, z_2 = u'$)
$$z_1' = z_2$$
$$z_2' = -2\,z_1\,z_2$$
The function that will be zero when the boundary condition is satisfied at $x = 1$ is
$$h = z_1 + z_2 - 0.25$$
We initialize the first two values used for $u'(0)$ to be
$$t(1) = 0$$
$$t(2) = 1$$
Begin iterations (initialize counter and test parameter)

if $i > 2$ compute the next value of $u'(0)$ using secant method
$$t(i) = t(i-1) - (t(i-1) - t(i-2))*m(i-1)/(m(i-1) - m(i-2))$$
end
solve the ODE-IVP
(the computed values of z_1 and z_2 at $x = 1$ are $z_1(n)$ and $z_2(n)$),
$m(i) = h(z_1(n), z_2(n))$
test $=$ abs($m(i)$)   if this is larger than the tolerance, continue

The exact solution is $y = 1/(x+1)$. The computed solution, $u(x)$, and $u'(x)$ are shown in Fig. 14.7. For the given tolerance, `tol = 0.00001`, the process converged in eight iterations.

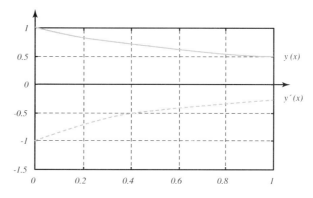

FIGURE 14.7   Solution $y(x)$ and $y'(x)$ for nonlinear shooting problem.

14.2.2 Nonlinear Shooting using Newton's Method

We next illustrate how Newton's method can be used to find the value of $y'(a) = t$ in the initial-value problem for nonlinear shooting. We consider the following nonlinear BVP with simple boundary conditions at $x = a$ and $x = b$:

$$y'' = f(x, y, y'), \qquad y(a) = ya, \qquad y(b) = yb$$

We begin by solving the initial-value problem

$$u'' = f(x, u, u'), \qquad u(a) = ya, \qquad u'(a) = t.$$

The error in this solution is the amount by which $y(b)$ misses the desired value, yb. For different choices of t, we get different errors, so we define

$$m(t) = u(b, t) - yb.$$

We need to find t such that $m(t) = 0$ (or $m(t)$ is as close to zero as we wish to continue the process). In the previous section, we found a sequence of t using linear interpolation between the two previous solutions; in order to use Newton's method, we need to have the derivative of the function whose zero is required, namely, $m(t)$. Although we do not have an explicit formula for $m(t)$, we can construct an additional differential equation whose solution allows us to update t at each iteration.

$$u'' = f(x, u, u'), \qquad\qquad u(a) = ya, \qquad u'(a) = t(k - 1)$$
$$v'' = v f_u(x, u, u') + v' f_u(x, u, u'), \qquad v(a) = 0, \qquad v'(a) = 1$$

The derivation of the auxiliary ODE is given in the discussion at the end of the section.

Nonlinear Shooting (Newton's Method) ═══════════════════════════════

> *Input*
> | | |
> | --- | --- |
> | f(x, u, u′) | right-hand side of ODE |
> | g(x, u, u′) | f_u(x, u, u′) function for auxiliary ODE |
> | h(x, u, u′) | f_u′(x, u, u′) function for auxiliary ODE |
> | [a, b] | interval for solution |
> | ya | BC: value of y(a) |
> | yb | BC: value of y(b) |
> | t(0) | initial estimate for t |
>
> For k = 1 to n
>   Solve the ODE-IVP system (convert to four first-order ODE)
>   u″ = f(x, u, u′),   u(a) = ya,   u′ (a) = t(k−1)
>   v″ = v g(x, u, u′) + v′ h(x, u, u′),   v(a) = 0,   v′ (a) = 1
>   Check for convergence
>   m = u(b, t(k−1)) − yb;
>   if | m | < tol, stop;
>   otherwise, update t:
>   t(k) = t(k−1) − m / v(b, t(k−1))

Example 14.7 Nonlinear Shooting with Newton's Method

To illustrate the use of nonlinear shooting using Newton's method, consider the ODE-BVP

$$y'' = -\frac{[y']^2}{y}, \qquad y(0) = 1, \qquad y(1) = 2.$$

The initial value problem consists of two second-order ODEs; the first corresponds to the original problem, but with the boundary condition replaced by an initial condition on the first derivative, $u'(0) = t_k$. The second ODE is an auxiliary equation that allows us to update the value of the parameter t_k. The first ODE is

$$u'' = -[u']^2 u^{-1}, \qquad u(0) = 1, \qquad u'(0) = t_k.$$

To construct the auxiliary ODE, we need the following partial derivatives:

$$f_u(x, u, u') = -[u']^2 (-1) u^{-2},$$
$$f_{u'}(x, u, u') = -2[u'] u^{-1}.$$

Thus, the auxiliary ODE is

$$v'' = v[u']^2 u^{-2} - v' 2[u']u^{-1}, \qquad v(0) = 0, \qquad v'(0) = 1.$$

Writing this as a system of four first-order ODEs, we define the components of our unknown function z as follows:

$$z_1 = u, \qquad z_2 = u', \qquad z_3 = v, \qquad z_4 = v'.$$

The ODEs are

$$z_1' = z_2 \qquad\qquad z_2' = -\frac{z_2^2}{z_1}$$

$$z_3' = z_4 \qquad\qquad z_4' = z_3 \left(\frac{z_2}{z_1}\right)^2 - \frac{2 z_4 z_2}{z_1}$$

The numerical solution and the exact solution of this ODE, $y = \sqrt{3x + 1}$, are shown in Fig. 14.8.

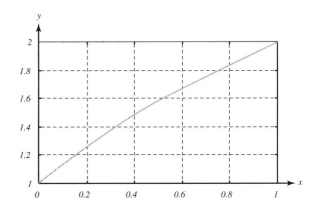

FIGURE 14.8   Solution of nonlinear shooting problem using Newton's method.

Discussion

In order to use Newton's method to find the value of the parameter t so that the amount by which the solution to the initial value problem

$$u'' = f(x, u, u'), \quad u(a) = ya, \quad u'(a) = t,$$

misses the solution to the original boundary value problem

$$y'' = f(x, y, y'), \quad y(a) = ya, \quad y(b) = ya,$$

we need to know how the error function, $m(t) = u(b, t) - yb$, varies with t. Newton's method updates t as

$$t_i = t_{i-1} - \frac{m(t_{i-1})}{m_t(t_{i-1})}.$$

We continue to use a prime to denote differentiation with respect to x, and we use a subscript to denote a partial derivative. In order to find an expression for m_t, we make use of the fact that, for the given form of boundary condition, we have $m_t(t) = u_t(b, t)$. To find u_t, we use the chain rule for partial derivatives to differentiate $u'' = f(x, u, u')$:

$$(u'')_t = f_t(x, u, u') = f_x x_t + f_u u_t + f_{u'}(u')_t.$$

Since x and t are independent, $x_t = 0$, so we have

$$(u'')_t = f_u u_t + f_{u'}(u')_t.$$

We introduce a new variable $v = u_t$ and assume sufficient continuity that we can interchange the order of differentiation with respect to x and t, so that $(u'')_t = (u_t)''$ and $(u')_t = (u_t)'$. This gives the linear ODE for v:

$$v'' = f_u v + f_{u'} v'.$$

The initial conditions $u(a, t) = ya$ and $u'(a) = t$ yield the initial conditions for v, namely, $v(a) = 0$ and $v'(a) = 1$. Thus, solving the ODE-IVP for v allows us to use the fact that $v = u_t = m_t$ to update t in the formula for Newton's method.

Shooting methods can suffer from instabilities in the IVP; however, for a nonlinear second-order ODE-BVP, the resulting nonlinear zero-finding problem depends on only one variable. Newton's method generalizes to systems more easily than the secant method, and may converge more rapidly, but requires solving twice as many ODE. In the next sections, we investigate an alternative approach to solving ODE-BVP.

14.3   FINITE-DIFFERENCE METHOD FOR LINEAR BVP

The second type of solution technique we consider for ODE-BVP is based on replacing the derivatives in the differential equation by finite-difference approximations (discussed in Chapter 11). The interval of interest, $[a, b]$, is divided into n subintervals by specifying evenly spaced values of the independent variable, $x_0, x_1, x_2, \ldots, x_n$, with $x_0 = a$ and $x_n = b$. The length of each subinterval is $h = x_{i+1} - x_i$.

The approximate solution at x_i is denoted y_i. We first illustrate the finite-difference method with a simple example.

Example 14.8 A Finite-Difference Problem

Use the finite difference method to solve the problem

$$y'' = y + x(x - 4), \quad 0 \le x \le 4,$$

with $y(0) = y(4) = 0$ and $n = 4$ subintervals. The finite-difference method will find an approximate solution at the points $x_1 = 1$, $x_2 = 2$, and $x_3 = 3$.

Using the central difference formula for the second derivative, we find that the differential equation becomes the system

$$y''(x_i) \approx \frac{y_{i+1} - 2\,y_i + y_{i-1}}{h^2} = y_i + x_i(x_i - 4), \quad i = 1, 2, 3.$$

For this example, $h = 1$. In writing out the system of algebraic equations, we make use of the fact that at $i = 1$, $y_0 = 0$ (from the boundary condition at $x = 0$), and similarly, at $i = 3$, $y_4 = 0$. Substituting in the values of x_1, x_2, and x_3 we obtain

$$y_2 - 2y_1 + 0 = y_1 + 1(1 - 4),$$
$$y_3 - 2y_2 + y_1 = y_2 + 2(2 - 4),$$
$$0 - 2y_3 + y_2 = y_3 + 3(3 - 4).$$

Combining like terms and simplifying gives

$$-3y_1 + y_2 \qquad = -3,$$
$$y_1 - 3y_2 + y_3 = -4,$$
$$y_2 - 3y_3 = -3.$$

Solving, we find that $y_1 = 13/7$, $y_2 = 18/7$, and $y_3 = 13/7$.

We note for comparison, that the exact solution of this problem is

$$y = \frac{2(1 - e^4)}{e^{-4} - e^4} e^{-x} - \frac{2(1 - e^{-4})}{e^{-4} - e^4} e^x - x^2 + 4x - 2.$$

At $x = 1$, the exact solution is 1.8341 (to four decimal places); the finite-difference solution is $y_1 = 13/7 = 1.8571$. (See Fig. 14.9.)

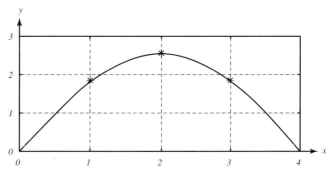

FIGURE 14.9 Small finite difference example.

We now consider the general linear two-point boundary value problem

$$y'' = p(x)\, y' + q(x)\, y + r(x), \qquad a \le x \le b,$$

with boundary conditions

$$y(a) = \alpha, \qquad y(b) = \beta.$$

To solve this problem using finite differences, we divide the interval $[a, b]$ into n subintervals, with $h = (b-a)/n$. To approximate the function $y(x)$ at the points $x_1 = a + h, \dots, x_{n-1} = a + (n-1)h$, we use the central difference formulas (Chapter 11):

$$y''(x_i) \approx \frac{y_{i+1} - 2y_i + y_{i-1}}{h^2}; \qquad y'(x_i) \approx \frac{y_{i+1} - y_{i-1}}{2h}.$$

Substituting these expressions into the BVP and writing $p(x_i)$ as p_i, $q(x_i)$ as q_i, and $r(x_i)$ as r_i, gives (for $i = 1, \dots, n-1$)

$$\frac{y_{i+1} - 2y_i + y_{i-1}}{h^2} = p_i \frac{y_{i+1} - y_{i-1}}{2h} + q_i\, y_i + r_i.$$

where $y_0 = y(a) = \alpha$ and $y_n = y(b) = \beta$.

Further algebraic simplification leads to a tridiagonal system for the unknowns $y_1, \dots, y_{n-1}$; for $i = 1, \dots, n-1$ we have

$$\left(1 + p_i \frac{h}{2}\right) y_{i-1} - (2 + h^2 q_i)\, y_i + \left(1 - p_i \frac{h}{2}\right) y_{i+1} = h^2 r_i$$

Expanding this expression into the full system gives

$$-(2 + h^2 q_1)\, y_1 + \left(1 - p_1 \frac{h}{2}\right) y_2 = h^2 r_1 - \left(1 + p_1 \frac{h}{2}\right) \alpha$$

$$\left(1 + p_2 \frac{h}{2}\right) y_1 - (2 + h^2 q_2)\, y_2 + \left(1 - p_2 \frac{h}{2}\right) y_3 = h^2 r_2$$

$$\vdots$$

$$\left(1 + p_i \frac{h}{2}\right) y_{i-1} - (2 + h^2 q_i)\, y_i + \left(1 - p_i \frac{h}{2}\right) y_{i+1} = h^2 r_i$$

$$\vdots$$

$$\left(1 + p_{n-2} \frac{h}{2}\right) y_{n-3} - (2 + h^2 q_{n-2})\, y_{n-2} + \left(1 - p_{n-2} \frac{h}{2}\right) y_{n-1} = h^2 r_{n-2}$$

$$\left(1 + p_{n-1} \frac{h}{2}\right) y_{n-2} - (2 + h^2 q_{n-1})\, y_{n-1} = h^2 r_{n-1} - \left(1 - p_{n-1} \frac{h}{2}\right) \beta$$

The following algorithm describes the steps necessary to approximate the solution vector $u(x)$ of the linear ODE-BVP

$$y'' = g(x, y, y') = p(x) y' + q(x) y + r(x)$$

with BC $y(a) = y_a$, $y(b) = y_b$, using the linear finite-difference method.

Linear Finite-Difference Method

Input
    p(x)
    q(x)
    r(x)
    [a, b]   *interval for solution*
    ya
    yb
    n   *number of subdivisions of the interval*
Compute
h = (b−a)/n
For k = 1 to n−1
    x(k) = a + h*k
    p(k) = p(x(k))
    q(k) = q(x(k))
    r(k) = r(x(k))
End
Tridiagonal system: upper diagonal U, diagonal D, lower diagonal L
For k = 1 to n−1

$$U(k) = 1 - p(k)\frac{h}{2}$$

$$D(k) = -(2 + h^2 q(k))$$

$$L(k) = -(2 + h^2 q(k))$$

End
L(1) = 0
U(n−1) = 0

Define right-hand side c

$$c(1) = h^2 r(1) - ya\left(1 + p(1)\frac{h}{2}\right)$$

For k = 2 to n−2
    c(k) = h² r(k)
End

$$c(n-1) = h^2 r(n-1) - yb\left(1 - p(n-1)\frac{h}{2}\right)$$

Solve tridiagonal system to find y
Return
    y   *vector of values of solution at grid points*

Example 14.9 Linear Finite-Difference Problem

Consider the BVP

$$y_{xx} = 2y_x - 2y, \qquad y(0) = 0.1, \qquad y(3) = 0.1e^3 \cos(3)$$

Define

$aa = 0 \qquad bb = 3 \qquad n = 300$
$y_a = 0.1 \qquad y_b = 0.1*\exp(3)*\cos(3)$

for $k = 1$ to $n-1$

$p_k = 2 \qquad q_k = -2 \qquad r_k = 0$

end
$h = (bb-aa)/n$
Define tridiagonal system
for $k = 1$ to $n-1$

$$a_k = 1 - p_k \frac{h}{2} \qquad d_k = -(2 + h^2 q_k) \qquad b_k = 1 + p_k \frac{h}{2}$$

end
$b_1 = 0$
$a_{n-1} = 0$

$$c_1 = h^2 r_1 - y_a \left(1 + p_1 \frac{h}{2}\right)$$

for $k = 2$ to $n-2$

$c_k = h^2 r_k$

end

$$c_{n-1} = h^2 r_{n-1} - y_b \left(1 - p_{n-1} \frac{h}{2}\right)$$

Solve tridiagonal system to find y
 The solution is shown in Fig. 14.10.

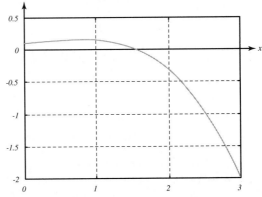

FIGURE 14.10　Linear finite-difference problem.

Example 14.10 Finite-Difference Solution for Deflection of a Beam

Consider again the deflection of a simply supported beam, described by the ODE boundary-value problem

$$y'' - \frac{T}{EI} y = \frac{w\,x\,(x - L)}{2\,EI}, \qquad 0 \le x \le L$$

where we use the specific parameter values given in Example 14.3:

$$L = 100, \quad w = 100, \quad E = 10^7, \quad T = 500, \quad I = 500.$$

Thus, the problem reduces to

$$y'' = 10^{-7}y + 10^{-8}[x(x - L)], \qquad 0 \le x \le 100,$$

with

$$y(0) = y(100) = 0,$$
$$p(x) = 0,$$
$$q(x) = 10^{-7},$$
$$r(x) = 10^{-8}[x(x - L)].$$

We let $n - 20$ be the number of subintervals.
The solution is shown in Fig. 14.11.

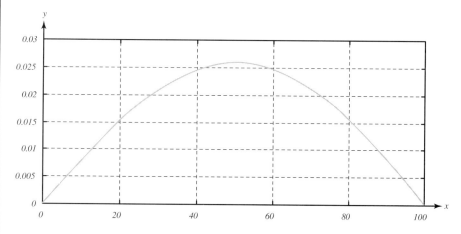

FIGURE 14.11   Deflection of a simply supported beam, using finite differences.

14.4 FINITE-DIFFERENCE METHOD FOR NONLINEAR BVP

We next discuss briefly the use of finite differences in nonlinear boundary-value problems. As has been remarked earlier, nonlinear problems are, in general, significantly more difficult than linear problems.

We consider the nonlinear ODE-BVP of the form

$$y'' = f(x, y, y'), \quad y(a) = \alpha, \quad y(b) = \beta.$$

We assume that $f(x, y, y')$ has continuous derivatives that satisfy

$$0 < Q_* \leq f_y(x, y, y') \leq Q^* \quad \text{and} \quad |f_{y'}(x, y, y')| \leq P^*$$

for some constants Q_*, Q^*, and P^*.

We use a finite difference grid with spacing $h \leq 2/P^*$. Let us apply the central difference formula for y' and y'' to obtain a nonlinear system of equations. We denote the result of evaluating f at x_i using $(y_{i+1} - y_{i-1})/2h$ for y' as f_i. The ODE then becomes the system

$$\frac{y_{i+1} - 2y_i + y_{i-1}}{h^2} - f_i = 0$$

An explicit iteration scheme, analogous to the SOR method, is given by

$$y_i = \frac{1}{2(1 + \omega)} [y_{i-1} + 2\omega y_i + y_{i+1} - h^2 f_i],$$

where $y_0 = \alpha$, and $y_n = \beta$.

If we define the parameters $z = 1/(2*(1+w))$ and $k = h^2$, the system of equations becomes

$y(1) = z*(ya + 2 w y(1) + y(2) - k f(1))$

for $j = 2$ to $n-2$

$$y(j) = z*(y(j - 1) + 2 w y(j) + y(j + 1) - k f(1))$$

end

$y(n - 1) = z*(y(n - 2) + 2 w y(n - 1) + yb - k f(n - 1))$

The remarkable result is that, for $\omega \geq h^2 Q^*/2$, the process will converge. (See Keller, 1968, Section 3.2.) In the next example, we illustrate the process for the nonlinear BVP introduced in Example 14.8.

Example 14.11 Solving a Nonlinear BVP Using Finite Differences

Consider again the nonlinear BVP

$$y'' = -\frac{[y']^2}{y}, \qquad y(0) = 1, \qquad y(1) = 2.$$

We illustrate the use of the iterative procedure just outlined, by taking a grid with $h = 1/4$, so that $x_0 = 0$, $x_1 = 0.25$, $x_2 = 0.5$, $x_3 = 0.75$, and $x_4 = 1$.

The general form of the difference equation is

$$y_i = \frac{1}{2(1 + \omega)} [y_{i-1} + 2\omega\, y_i + y_{i+1} - h^2 f_i],$$

where

$$f_i = -\frac{[(y_{i+1} - y_{i-1})/2h]^2}{y_i} = -\frac{y_{i+1}^2 - 2y_{i+1}\, y_{i-1} + y_{i-1}^2}{4h^2\, y_i}.$$

Substituting the rightmost expression for f_i into the equation for y_i, we obtain

$$y_i = \frac{1}{2(1 + \omega)} \left[y_{i-1} + 2\omega\, y_i + y_{i+1} + \frac{y_{i+1}^2 - 2y_{i+1}\, y_{i-1} + y_{i-1}^2}{4y_i} \right].$$

The computed solution after 10 iterations agrees very closely with the exact solution, as is shown in Fig. 14.12. To use a finer grid, a loop can be added to generate the equations for $i = 2, \ldots, n-1$, since only the first and last equations have a special form to accommodate the boundary conditions.

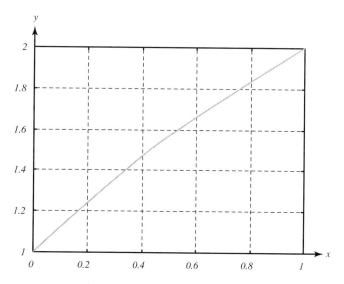

FIGURE 14.12   Solution of nonlinear ODE-BVPs using finite differences.

Some software packages, such as Mathcad, have built-in functions for boundary value problems. Others, such as MATLAB and *Mathematica*, require the user to transform the BVP into a system of IVP (using the shooting method) or into a system of finite difference equations. Software libraries, such as the NIST Index and the NAG Software Library, include routines for ODE boundary value problems.

14.5.1 Professionally Developed Routines

The NAG Software Library includes three routines for boundary value problems, each based on a finite-difference technique. One routine is designed for a system of linear first-order ODE. Another solves a system of n first-order nonlinear ODE (using Newton iteration). The third, which also treats a system of nonlinear ODE, allows for continuation. In using continuation, one describes the ODE and BVP in terms of a parameter ε; $\varepsilon = 0$ corresponds to an easy problem and $\varepsilon = 1$ corresponds to the more difficult problem whose solution is sought.

The NIST Index includes routines for multipoint boundary values problems, grouped according to linear, nonlinear, and Sturm-Liouville (eigenvalue) problems. Routines for nonlinear problems are based on a variety of techniques, including finite-differences, multiple shooting, and collocation.

14.5.2 Mathcad's Functions

Mathcad2000Pro has three functions for use in solving ODE two-point boundary value problems. The functions `sbval` and `bvalfit` convert a boundary value problem into an initial value problem; `sbval` is used for continuous problems; `bvalfit` is used if there is a discontinuity on the interval $(x1, x2)$. The function `odesolve`, which is used in a Solve Block structure, can be used for either initial value or boundary value problems.

The function `sbval` converts a two-point boundary value problem into an initial value problem, using the shooting method, with Newton's method to reduce the discrepancy between the computed solution at the end of the interval and the given boundary values at that point. This function finds the required initial values for the solution so that the solution will match the specified boundary values. In order to actually obtain the solution to the ODE, one must call `rkfixed`, or any of the other ODE-IVP solution functions.

The function `sbval` uses the shooting method with the classical fourth-order Runge-Kutta method for the solution of the initial value problems. The approach is based on using Newton's method for a nonlinear problem, as was the discussion in section 14.2.2. However, the implementation in `sbval` is more general, allowing for an arbitrary number of unknown functions, and boundary conditions which are not restricted in form. Newton's method should give the exact result in one step if the problem is linear, although a second step may be needed to improve the round-off error. See Press et al. (1992, pp. 757–759).

The function bvalfit is used in a manner similar to that for sbval; however, bvalfit is used when the derivatives (right-hand side of the differential equation) have a discontinuity at a single point xf between $x1$ and $x2$. The method is two-point shooting, in which solutions computed starting at $x1$ (toward $x2$) and starting at $x2$ (going toward $x1$), are constrained to be equal at an interior point, xf. As for sbval, bvalfit gives the initial values needed (at $x1$ and $x2$) for the solution to match at xf. The solution may be obtained by calling rkfixed, or any of the other ODE solvers.

The function bvalfit implements a two-point shooting method; see Press et al. (1992, sect. 17.2), or Keller (1968) for details.

The Mathdad2000Pro function odesolve, which is used in a Solve Block structure, can be used for either initial value or boundary value problems. A Solve Block begins with the word Given. The ODE and the constraints (initial and/or boundary values) are then typed, followed by the call to the function odesolve. The function odesolve solves a single ODE, with either initial or boundary value constraints. Boundary constraints must be specified at exactly two points. The differential equation must be linear in the highest derivative. For an initial value problem, the solution is based on the Mathcad function rkfixed (or, if desired, the user may select rkadapt), with interpolation of function values at points between those computed by the ODE solver. For a boundary value problem, odesolve calls sbval, followed by a call to rkfixed or rkadapt.

Shooting Method (for linear BVP)

$$y'' = p(x)\,y' + q(x)\,y + r(x), \qquad y(a) = \alpha, \qquad y(b) = \beta.$$

$$\text{Solve the IVP } u'' = p(x)\,u' + q(x)\,u + r(x), \qquad u(a) = \alpha, \qquad u'(a) = 0$$

$$v'' = p(x)\,v' + q(x)\,v, \qquad\qquad v(a) = 0, \qquad v'(a) = 1.$$

The solution of the original two-point BVP is (if $v(b) \neq 0$) given by

$$y(x) = u(x) + \frac{\beta - u(b)}{v(b)}\,v(x).$$

Shooting Method (for nonlinear BVP)

$$y'' = f(x, y, y'), \qquad y(a) = ya, \qquad h(y(b), y'(b)) = yb.$$

Let $t(0) = 0; t(1) = 1$; compute for $j = 1\ldots$, until $|m(j)| < \text{tol}$
    Solve the IVP $u'' = f(x, u, u')$, $u(a) = ya$, $u'(a) = t(j - 1)$

$$m(j) = yb - h(u(b), u'(b)), \qquad \text{(the error at } x = b)$$

$$(\text{for } j \geq 2) \quad t(i) = t(i - 1) - (t(i - 1) - t(i - 2))\,m(i - 1)/(m(i - 1) - m(i - 2))$$

Finite-Difference Method (for linear BVP)

$$y'' = f(x, y, y'), \qquad y(a) = \alpha, \qquad y(b) = \beta.$$

For $h = (b - a)/n$, $x(i) = a + h*i$, $p(i) = p(x(i))$; $q(i) = q(x(i))$; $r(i) = r(x(i))$, solve the tridiagonal system ($i = 1$ to $n - 1$; $y(0) = \alpha$; $y(n) = \beta$)

$$\left(a + p(i)\,\frac{h}{2}\right)y(i - 1) - (2 + h^2\,q(i))y(i) + \left(1 - p(i)\,\frac{h}{2}\right)y(i + 1) = h^2\,r(i).$$

Finite-difference Method (for nonlinear BVP)

$$y'' = f(x, y, y'), \qquad y(a) = \alpha, \qquad y(b) = \beta.$$

If there are constants Q_*, Q^*, and P^* such that $0 < Q_* \leq f_y(x, y, y') \leq Q^*$ and $|f_{y'}(x, y, y')| \leq P^*$; use a finite difference grid with spacing $h \leq 2/P^*$.
    Let f_i denote the result of evaluating f at x_i using $(y_{i+1} - y_{i-1})/2h$ for y'.

The ODE then becomes the system $\dfrac{y_{i+1} - 2y_i + y_{i-1}}{h^2} - f_i = 0.$

The iterative scheme (with $y_0 = \alpha$, and $y_n = \beta$)

$$y_i = \frac{1}{2(1 + \omega)}\,[y_{i-1} + 2\omega\,y_i + y_{i+1} - h^2\,f_i]$$

converges for $\omega \geq h^2\,Q^*/2$.

SUGGESTIONS FOR FURTHER READING

For the basic theory, see suggestions from Chapter 12. In addition, see:

Ascher, U. M., R. M. M. Mattheij, and R. D. Russell. *Numerical Solution of Boundary Value Problems for Ordinary Differential Equations.* SIAM, Philadelphia, 1995.

Fox, L. *Numerical Solution of Two-Point Boundary Value Problems in Ordinary Differential Equations.* Dover, New York, 1990.

Keller, H. B. *Numerical Methods for Two-Point Boundary-Value Problems.* Blaisdell, Waltham, MA, 1968.

Troutman, J. L., and M. Bautista. *Boundary Value Problems of Applied Mathematics*, Prindle, Weber & Schmidt Publishing, Boston, 1994.

For further discussion of applications of two-point boundary value problems, see:

Haberman, R. *Elementary Applied Partial Differential Equations with Fourier Series and Boundary Value Problems.* Prentice-Hall, Englewood Cliffs, NJ, 1983.

Hanna, O. T., and O. C. Sandall. *Computational Methods in Chemical Engineering.* Prentice Hall, Upper Saddle River, NJ, 1995.

Hornbeck, R. W. *Numerical Methods.* Prentice-Hall, Englewood Cliffs, NJ, 1975.

Inman, D. J. *Engineering Vibration.* Prentice Hall, Upper Saddle River, NJ, 1996.

Jaeger, J. C. *An Introduction to Applied Mathematics.* Clarenden Press, Oxford, 1951.

Roberts, C. E. *Ordinary Differential Equations: A Computational Approach.* Prentice-Hall, Englewood Cliffs, NJ, 1979.

For discussion of the methods implemented in Mathcad, see:

Acton, F. S. *Numerical Methods That (usually) Work*, corrected edition. Mathematical Association of America, Washington, DC, 1990.

Keller, H. B. *Numerical Methods for Two-Point Boundary-Value Problems.* Blaisdell, Waltham, MA, 1968.

Press, W. H., S. A. Teukolsky, W. T. Vetterling, and B. P. Flannery. *Numerical Recipes in C: The Art of Scientific Computing*, 2^d ed. Cambridge: Cambridge University Press, 1992.

Stoer, J., and R. Bulirsch. *Introduction to Numerical Analysis.* Springer Verlag, New York, 1980.

For Problems P14.1–P14.14, solve the boundary-value problem

    a. Using the linear shooting method.
    b. Using the finite-difference method.

P14.1 $y'' = -y,$
$y(0) = 1, y(\pi) = -1.$

P14.2 $y'' = y + x,$
$y(0) = 2, y(1) = 2.5.$

P14.3 $y'' = -2y' - y + x^2,$
$y(0) = 10, y(1) = 2.$

P14.4 $y'' = y / (e^x + 1),$
$y(0) = 1, y(1) = 5.$

P14.5 $y'' = -2 y' - 4 y,$
$y(0) = 2, y(1) = 2.$

P14.6 $y'' = -9 y,$
$y(0) = 0, y(\pi/6) = 1.$

P14.7 $y'' = y / 4 + 8,$
$y(0) = 0, y(\pi) = 2.$

P14.8 $y'' = -2 x y',$
$y(0) = 1, y(10) = 0.$

P14.9 $x^2 y'' + x y' + x^2 y = 0,$
$y(1) = 1, y(8) = 0.$

P14.10 $x^2 y'' - x y' + y = 0,$
$y(1) = 1, y(3) = 4.$

P14.11 $x^2 y'' + x y' + y = 0,$
$y(1) = 0, y(10) = 1/2.$

P14.12 $6x^2 y'' + x y' + y = 0,$
$y(1) = 2, y(64) = 12.$

P14.13 $x y'' - y' - x^5 = 0,$
$y(1) = 1/2, y(2) = 4.$

P14.14 $x y'' + y' + x = 0,$
$y(2) = -1, y(4) = 15.$

For Problems P14.15–P14.25, solve the boundary-value problem

    a. Using the nonlinear shooting method.
    b. Using the finite-difference method.

P14.15 $y'' + y' - y^2 = 0$
$y(0) = 1; y(1) = 2.$

P14.16 $y'' = 2y y',$
$y(1) = 1, y(2) = 1/2.$

P14.17 $y'' = -2 (y + x)(y' + 1),$
$y(1) = 0, y(2) = -2.$

P14.18 $y'' = -x (y')^2 - x^2 y,$
$y(0) = 1, y(1) = -1.$

P14.19 $y'' = e^y, y(0) = 1,$
$y(1) = 0.$

P14.20 $2yy'' = (y')^2 - 4 y^2,$
$y(\pi/6) = 1/4, y(\pi/2) = 1.$

P14.21 $y'' = 2y^3, y(1) = 1,$
$y(2) = 1/2.$

P14.22 $yy'' = -(y')^2 - 1,$
$y(1) = 1, y(1/2) = \sqrt{3/4}.$

P14.23 $(1 + x^2) y'' = 4 xy' - 6 y,$
$y(0) = 1, y(1) = -4/3.$

P14.24 $x^3 y'' = x^2 y' + 3 - x^2,$
$y(1) = 4, y(1) = 15/2.$

P14.25 $y'' = x (y')^3,$
$y(0) = 0, y(1) = \pi/2.$

A14.1 The steady-state temperature distribution for a rod of length L, with source term $Q(x) = 1$, and temperatures given at the two ends of the rod, is described by the BVP:

$$u_{xx} + Q(x) = 0;$$
$$u(0) = A, \qquad u(L) = B.$$

Solve for $A = 0$, $B = 100$.

A14.2 To find the steady state temperature distribution for a rod of length L, with source term $Q(x) = \sin(2\pi x/L)$, and insulated ends, solve the BVP:

$$u_{xx} + Q(x) = 0$$
$$u_x(0) = 0, \qquad u_x(L) = 0.$$

A14.3 The steady state temperature distribution for a rod of length L, with source term $Q(x) = x^2$, temperature fixed at $x = 0$, and the end of the rod at $x = L$ insulted, is described by the BVP:

$$u_{xx} + Q(x) = 0,$$
$$u(0) = T, \qquad u_x(L) = 0.$$

Solve for $T = 100$, $L = 1$.

A14.4 The steady-state temperature distribution between two concentric spheres, with fixed temperature at $r = a$ and $r = b$, is given by the BVP:

$$r\,u_{rr} + 2\,u_r = 0;$$
$$u(a) = T_1, \qquad u(b) = T_2.$$

Solve for $a = 1$, $u(1) = 0$, $b = 4$, $u(4) = 80$.

A14.5 The steady-state temperature distribution of a rod with heat source $Q > 0$ proportional to temperature, and with the temperature at the ends of the rod fixed at 0, is given by the BVP:

$$u_{xx} + Q\,u = 0,$$
$$u(0) = 0, \qquad u(L) = 0.$$

Solve for $L = 10$, $Q = (\pi/L)^2$.

A14.6 Modeling a second-order chemical flow reactor with axial dispersion leads to the ODE-BVP:

$$eP_{zz} - P_z - B\,P^2 = 0;$$
$$e\,P_z(0) = P(0) - 1; \; P_z(1) = 0.$$

Solve for $B = 7.5$, and $e = 0.1$ to find $P(1)$.
(See Hanna and Sandall, 1995, pp. 16–18.)

A14.7 The Blasius equation describes laminar boundary layer flow on a flat plate

$$f_{xxx} + f\,f_{xx} = 0;$$
$$f(0) = 0; \quad f_x(0); \quad f_x(\infty) = 1.$$

Investigate a numerical solution by approximating ∞ by some large value of x.
(See Hanna and Sandall, 1995, pp. 256 for discussion of a series approach to the solution).

A14.8 A simple model of pseudo-homogeneous, isothermal chemical reaction and diffusion in a cylindrical catalyst pellet with irreversible first-order reaction kinetics can be written (in terms of dimensionless variables) as

$$y_{xx} + \frac{1}{x}\,y_x = B\,y$$
$$y_x(0) = 0 \qquad y(1) = 1$$

Investigate the numerical solution of this problem for $B = 1$, 10, and 100.
(see Hanna and Sandall, pp. 257 to 258 for discussion of a series approach to the solution).

A14.9 Equations for the deflection (y) and rotation (z) of a simply supported beam with a uniformly distributed load of intensity 2 kips/ft and bending moment $M(x) = 10\,x - x^2$ can expressed as

$$\frac{dz}{dx} = \frac{M}{EI} = \frac{10\,x - x^2}{EI}$$
$$\frac{dy}{dx} = z$$

where E is the modulus of elasticity and I is the moment of inertia of the cross section of the beam. Taking $EI = 3600$ kip/ft, $y(0) = 0$ and $y(10) = 0$, find y and z for $0 \le x \le 10$. (See Ayyub and McCuen, 1996, p. 239.)

A14.10 The deflection of a uniform beam of length L, with both ends fixed, subject to a load proportional to the distance from one end, i.e., $w = bx$, is described by the ODE-BVP

$$EI \frac{d^4 y}{dx^4} = w(x) = b\,x,$$

$$y(0) = y'(0) = 0,$$

$$y(L) = y'(L) = 0.$$

Solve using EI = 3600 kip/ft, $L = 10$, $b = 2$.

A14.11 To find the deflection of a cantilever beam of unit length, with a distributed load, $w(x) = x$, solve the BVP

$$u_{xxxx} = x$$

with the boundary conditions

$$u(0) = u'(0) = u''(1) = u'''(1) = 0.$$

The conditions at $x = 1$ correspond to no bending moment and no shear there.

A14.12 To find the deflection of a simply supported beam of unit length, with a point load P at the midpoint, $w(x) = \delta(x - 1/2)$, solve the BVP

$$u_{xxxx} = w(x)$$

with the boundary conditions

$$u(0) = u'(0) = u(1) = u'(1) = 0.$$

EXTEND YOUR UNDERSTANDING

U14.1 Consider the numerical solutions to the BVP

$$y'' = -y;$$

$$y(0) = 0; \qquad y(\pi) = 0.$$

The exact solution is $y = A \sin(x)$ for any constant A. How do the shooting method and the finite difference method respond to the nonunique solution?

U14.2 Consider the numerical solutions to the BVP

$$y'' = -y;$$

$$y(0) = 0; \qquad y(\pi) = 1.$$

The general solution is $y = A \sin(x) + B \cos(x)$, but no choice of A and B will satisfy these boundary conditions. How do the shooting method and the finite difference method repsond to this situation?

U14.3 $y'' = \dfrac{2x}{x^2 + 1} y' - \dfrac{2}{x^2 + 1} y + x^2 + 1;$

$$y(0) = 2; \qquad y'(1) - y(1) = -3$$

This BVP has infinitely many solutions (See Roberts, 1979, pp. 347.)

U14.4 $y'' = \dfrac{2x}{x^2 + 1} y' - \dfrac{2}{x^2 + 1} y + x^2 + 1;$

$$y(0) = 2; \qquad y'(1) - y(1) = -1$$

U14.5 The finite difference method presented in the text uses the central difference approximation for y'. The linear system that is obtained in using the finite difference method is guaranteed to be diagonally dominant if the step size $\Delta x < 2/M$, where M is an upper bound on $|p(x)|$.

$$y'' = -2\,x\,y',$$

$$y(0) = 1, \qquad y(10) = 0.$$

Investigate the solution of this problem using finite differences with different values of Δx, both larger and smaller than 0.1.

U14.6 Forward differences may be preferable for the first derivative approximation in cases where $p(x) \leq 0$. Develop a program implementing this method and compare the results to those found in U14.5.

15

Partial Differential Equations

We conclude our investigation into numerical methods for solving differential equations with an introduction to some numerical techniques for solving linear second-order partial differential equations (PDEs) with constant coefficients. These equations fall into three basic categories: parabolic, hyperbolic, and elliptic. As an example of a parabolic PDE, we consider the heat equation, which describes the temperature distribution in a slender rod. A hyperbolic PDE is illustrated by the wave equation for a vibrating string. To illustrate numerical methods for elliptic PDEs, we investigate the Laplace (potential) and Poisson equations for steady-state temperature distribution in a two-dimensional region.

Numerical techniques for solving partial differential equations are primarily of two types: finite-difference methods and finite-element methods. In the first three sections of the chapter, we investigate finite-difference methods for parabolic, hyperbolic, and elliptic equations, using the heat equation, wave equation, and Poisson equation as examples. These techniques are a direct extension of the ideas presented in the previous two chapters. Replacing the partial derivatives by finite-difference approximations leads to a system of algebraic equations for the values of the unknown function at the grid points. Depending on the type of PDE and the choice of difference approximation (forward, backward, or central), the resulting equations may be solved directly or may require iterative techniques. Stability issues restrict the choice of mesh spacing for some types of problems also.

The final section of the chapter provides an introduction to finite-element methods for dealing with elliptic problems. The finite-element approach seeks to find a solution as a linear combination of relatively simple basis functions. For many elliptic problems, the solution of the PDE is equivalent to minimizing an integral over the relevant domain or, for certain problems with derivative boundary conditions, a combination of an integral over the region and an integral along the boundary. Finite-element methods are especially suitable for regions that are not rectangular. We illustrate the process using triangular subregions and basis functions that are piecewise linear on the subregions.

Example 15-A Heat Equation

The temperature in a thin rod of unit length can be described by the one-dimensional heat equation

$$u_t = c\, u_{xx}, \qquad \text{for } 0 < x < 1, \qquad 0 < t.$$

For a rod of length L, a simple change of variables can be used to transform the problem to the interval $[0, 1]$.

The initial temperature is given for each point in the rod:

$$u(x, 0) = f(x), \qquad 0 < x < 1.$$

In addition, information must be supplied describing what happens at each end of the rod. If the ends of the rod are kept at specified temperatures (by immersing each end in a fluid bath with a temperature that fluctuates with time, for example), then the boundary conditions are

$$u(0, t) = g_0(t), \qquad u(1, t) = g_1(t), \qquad o < t.$$

Other physical situations give different forms for the boundary conditions. For example, keeping an end of the rod insulated corresponds to specifying that the partial derivative u_x is zero at that end of the rod:

$$u_x(0, t) = 0 \quad \text{or} \quad u_x(1, t) = 0.$$

A third possibility is that an end of the rod is subject to convective cooling (a warm rod exposed to cooler air, for example). The corresponding boundary condition involves a combination of u and u_x at the appropriate end.

This combination of PDE, initial condition, and boundary conditions is a standard example of a parabolic PDE (see Fig. 15.1).

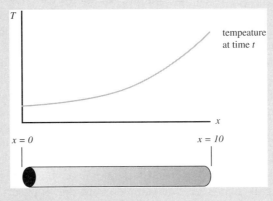

FIGURE 15.1   A rod that is cold at $x = 0$ and hot at $x = 1$.

Example 15-B Wave Equation

The motion of a vibrating string can be described by the one-dimensional wave equation

$$u_{tt} - c^2 u_{xx} = 0, \qquad \text{for } 0 < x < 1 \text{ and } 0 \leq t.$$

Problems on a more general interval may be transformed to $[0, 1]$ by a simple change of variable.

The initial displacement $u(x, 0)$ and initial velocity $u_t(x, 0)$ are given for each point in the string:

$$u(x, 0) = f_1(x), \qquad u_t(x, 0) = f_2(x), \qquad 0 < x < 1.$$

In addition, information must be supplied about the motion of the ends of the string. The string may be fixed at each end (with zero displacement), which gives the boundary conditions

$$u(0, t) = 0, \qquad u(1, t) = 0, \qquad 0 < t.$$

If the ends of the string are allowed to move in a prescribed manner, the boundary conditions have the more general form

$$u(0, t) = g_0(t), \qquad u(1, t) = g_1(t), \qquad 0 < t.$$

If an end of the string is attached to a frictionless vertical track, the appropriate boundary condition specifies that, at $x = 0$ or $x = 1$,

$$u_x = 0;$$

this corresponds to the insulated boundary condition for the one-dimensional heat equation.

More complicated boundary conditions result when an end of the string is attached to a spring-mass system. For example, the so-called elastic boundary condition is analogous to the Newton-cooling boundary condition for the one-dimensional heat equation.

This combination of PDE, initial conditions and boundary conditions, is a standard example of a hyperbolic PDE (see Fig. 15.2).

Although the one-dimensional wave equation does not usually require a numerical solution, an example will serve as an introduction to higher dimensional wave equations, wherein numerical methods are more likely to be worthwhile.

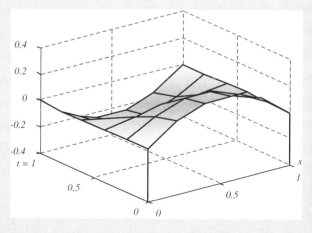

FIGURE 15.2 Vibrating string.

Example 15-C Poisson's Equation

The steady-state temperature in a rectangular plate $0 \le x \le 1, 0 \le y \le 1$ can be described by the Poisson equation

$$u_{xx} + u_{yy} = f(x, y)$$

A more general rectangular region can be transformed to this simple region by a change of variables.

If there are no heat sources (i.e., if $f(x, y) = 0$), the equation is known as Laplace's equation. Gravitational and electrostatic potentials also satisfy the Poisson equation (or the Laplace or potential equation if there are no sources).

The temperature may be prescribed along each boundary:

$$u(0, y) = g_0(y), \qquad u(1, y) = g_1(y), \qquad 0 \le y \le 1;$$

$$u(x, 0) = f_0(x), \qquad u(x, 1) = f_1(x), \qquad 0 \le x \le 1.$$

As with the one-dimensional heat equation, other possible boundary conditions include having the boundary or part of the boundary insulated, so that the directional derivative of u in the outward normal direction is zero along that part of the boundary:

$$u_x(0, y) = 0, \text{ or } u_x(1, y) = 0, \text{ or } u_y(x, 0) = 0, \text{ or } u_y(x, 0) = 0.$$

The Newton cooling boundary condition corresponds to heat flowing out at a rate proportional to the difference between the temperature of the plate and that of the surrounding medium.

The Poisson equation is a standard example of an elliptic PDE (see Fig. 15.3).

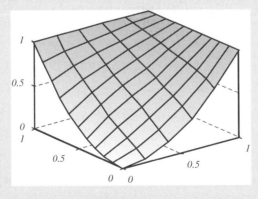

FIGURE 15.3 Steady-state temperature in a plate.

15.1   CLASSIFICATION OF PDE

Although the theory of solutions of PDEs, and many of the techniques for numerical solutions of PDEs, are beyond the scope of this book, we examine several standard techniques for the numerical solution of linear second-order PDEs involving two independent variables—either spatial variables x and y or a single spatial variable and a time variable. The general form of PDE we consider is

$$a\,u_{xx} + b\,u_{xy} + c\,u_{yy} + d\,u_x + e\,u_y + f\,u + g = 0$$

or

$$a\,u_{xx} + b\,u_{xt} + c\,u_{tt} + d\,u_x + e\,u_t + f\,u + g = 0.$$

The coefficients $a, b, \ldots, g$ may depend on the independent variables (but not on the unknown function u).

PDEs of the preceding form are normally classified into three types—parabolic, hyperbolic, and elliptic—depending on the sign of $b^2 - 4\,a\,c$. The PDE is

parabolic	if	$b^2 - 4\,a\,c = 0$,
hyperbolic	if	$b^2 - 4\,a\,c > 0$,
elliptic	if	$b^2 - 4\,a\,c < 0$.

Of course, if the coefficients are not constants, the PDE may have a different classification in different parts of the solution domain.

15.1.1   Numerical Methods for PDE

The most widespread numerical techniques for solving PDEs are finite-difference methods and finite-element methods. Finite-difference methods are based on subdividing the domain of the problem by introducing a mesh of discrete points for each of the independent variables. Derivatives are replaced by the appropriate difference quotients (see Chapter 11), and the resulting system of algebraic equations is solved by methods presented in previous chapters. There are several different finite-difference methods, depending on the type of PDE and the choice of forward- or backward-difference formulas.

Finite-element methods are based on restricting the form of the functions used (rather than the points at which the solution is sought) and finding a linear combination of these simple functions that minimizes the appropriate integral functional (which includes information from both the differential equation and the boundary conditions). For finite elements, the simple functions are required to be zero except on a small subregion of the problem domain. Finite-element methods are especially popular for elliptic problems.

A finite-difference solution of the one-dimensional heat equation

$$u_t = c\,u_{xx}, \qquad \text{for } 0 < x < 1, \qquad 0 < t \le T,$$

with initial conditions $\qquad u(x, 0) = f(x), \qquad 0 < x < 1,$

and boundary conditions $\qquad u(0, t) = g_0(t), \qquad u(1, t) = g_1(t), \qquad 0 < t \le T,$

begins with the definition of a mesh of points at which the solution is sought.

We divide the interval $[0, 1]$ into n pieces, each of length $h = \Delta x = 1/n$. The corresponding points are denoted x_i, for $i = 0, \ldots , n$. The ends of the interval are at $x_0 = 0$ and $x_n = 1$; the interior points are $x_i = i\,h$, for $i = 1, \ldots , n{-}1$.

In a similar manner, we define a mesh for the time interval, with m subdivisions, with $k = \Delta t = T/m$ and $t_j = j\,k, j = 0, 1, \ldots , m$. As with the variable x, the ends of the time interval are $t_0 = 0$ and $t_m = T$ (see Fig. 15.4).

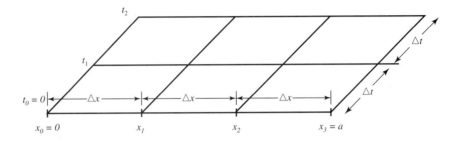

FIGURE 15.4   Spatial mesh, $n = 3$; temporal mesh, $m = 2$.

The solution at a grid point $u(x_i, t_j)$ is denoted u_{ij}. Similarly, values of the initial condition $f(x)$ at grid points are abbreviated as f_i, and values of the boundary conditions are either g_{1j} or g_{2j}. Finite difference techniques replace the partial derivatives in the PDE with difference quotients.

For the heat equation, we use the forward difference formula for u_t:

$$u_t \Rightarrow \frac{1}{k}\,[u_{i,j+1} - u_{i,j}].$$

Similarly, we replace the second derivative (with respect to the spatial variable) by the finite difference formula from Chapter 11, using the fact that the spacing between points in the x direction is h. If this difference formula is applied at the jth time step, we have

$$c\,u_{xx} \Rightarrow \frac{c}{h^2}\,[u_{i-1,j} - 2u_{i,j} + u_{i+1,j}].$$

This expression yields an explicit method that is easy to solve, but imposes restrictions on the relative values of the mesh spacing in the x and t directions. The restrictions are necessary to maintain stability of the solution, i.e., to prevent the inevitable errors in the solution from becoming larger as the calculations proceed from $t = 0$ to $t = T$.

On the other hand, if the difference is used at the $(j+1)^{st}$ time step, we have

$$c\,u_{xx} \Rightarrow \frac{c}{h^2}\left[u_{i-1,j+1} - 2u_{i,j+1} + u_{i+1,j+1}\right].$$

This expression gives an implicit method that is somewhat more difficult to solve, but that is stable without placing any restriction on the mesh spacing.

Finally, we consider the Crank-Nicolson method, which averages the second derivative difference formulas at the jth and $(j+1)^{st}$ time steps; this gives a stable method with better truncation error than the simple implicit method.

15.2.1 Explicit Method

Replacing the space derivative by the difference formula at the jth time step and the time derivative by a forward difference gives a linear system of equations for the temperature u at the grid points:

$$\frac{1}{k}\left[u_{i,j+1} - u_{i,j}\right] = \frac{c}{h^2}\left[u_{i-1,j} - 2u_{i,j} + u_{i+1,j}\right].$$

This equation can be simplified by introducing the parameter $r = \dfrac{c\,k}{h^2}$; solving for $u_{i,j+1}$, we have

$$u_{i,j+1} = r\,u_{i-1,j} + (1 - 2r)\,u_{i,j} + r\,u_{i+1,j}, \quad \text{for } i = 1, \ldots, n-1.$$

Since the solution is known for $t = 0$, we can solve explicitly for the first time step and proceed from there in a step-by-step manner.

The points that are involved in the calculations at time steps j and $j+1$ with the explicit method are shown schematically in Fig. 15.5.

The x and t meshes must be chosen so that $0 < r \le 0.5$ in order to ensure stability. This requirement is discussed further following an example.

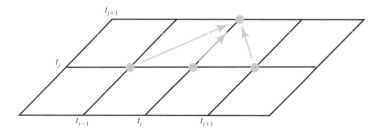

FIGURE 15.5   Temperature determined from information at previous time step.

The following algorithm computes the approximate solution of the

parabolic PDE $\qquad u_t = c\, u_{xx}, \qquad 0 < x < 1,\ 0 < t \leq T,$

with initial conditions $\qquad u(x, 0) = f(x), \qquad 0 < x < 1,$

and boundary conditions $\qquad u(0, t) = g_0(t), \qquad u(1, t) = g_1(t), 0 < t \leq T$

The algorithm returns a matrix **u**, in which the spatial variable runs down each row, and time advances from left to right. It may be more convenient to display the transpose of **u**, so that x runs from left to right, and t increases from top to bottom.

Heat Equation, Explicit Finite-Difference Method

Input

     c   *coefficient in PDE:* $u_t = c\, u_{xx}$

     T   *find solution for $0 < t < T$*

     n   *number of subdivisions of [0, 1]*

     m   *number of subdivisions of [0, T]*

     f(x)   *initial condition*

     g0(t)   *boundary condition at x = 0*

     g1(t)   *boundary condition at x = 1*

Compute parameters

     h = 1/n

     k = T/m

     $r = \dfrac{c\,k}{h^2}$

     s = 1 − 2 r

Define vector of grid points for x and evaluate the initial condition

For i = 0 to n

     $x_i = i\,h$

     $u(i, 0) = f(x_i)$

End

Define vector of grid points for t and evaluate the boundary conditions

For j = 0 to m

     $t_j = j\,k$

     $u(0,j) = g_0(t_j)$

     $u(n, j) = g_1(t_j)$

End

Find the solution at time steps j = 1, ... m

For j = 1 to m

     For i = 1 to n−1

         $u(i, j) = r\,u(i-1, j-1) + s\,u(i, j-1) + r\,u(i+1, j-1)$

     End

End

Return

     u   *matrix of solution values*

                 (or expand matrix to include IC and BC if desired)

Example 15.1 Temperature in a Rod, Explicit Method, Stable Solution

Consider the temperature in a rod of unit length given by the PDE

$$u_t - u_{xx} = 0, \qquad \text{for } 0 < x < 1, \quad 0 < t.$$

The initial temperature of the rod is $u(x, 0) = x^4$, $0 < x < 1$, and the temperatures at $x = 0$ and $x = 1$ are, respectively,

$$u(0, t) = 0, \quad u(1, t) = 1, \quad 0 < t.$$

Taking a fairly coarse mesh with $h = \Delta x = 0.2$ and the largest time step allowed for stability (so that $\Delta t = 0.02$ and $r = 0.5$) results in a simplification of the general forward difference equation $u_{i,j+1} = r\, u_{i-1,j} + (1 - 2r)\, u_{i,j} + r\, u_{i+1,j}$ to the form

$$u_{i,j+1} = 0.5\, u_{i-1,j} + 0.5\, u_{i+1,j}.$$

It is convenient to display the solution in an array with the rod extending from left to right and time progressing down the page. The values of the independent variables (x and t) at the mesh points are shown across the top of the array and down the left-hand side; the corresponding mesh index values at these points are also shown for reference. The initial and boundary conditions are shown in bold. The solution is shown in Fig. 15.6. The exact steady state solution of this problem is $u(x) = x$.

The solution for the first few time steps are given in the following table:

$x =$		0.0	0.2	0.4	0.6	0.8	1.0
t	j\i	0	1	2	3	4	5
0.00	0	**0.0**	0.0016	0.0256	0.1296	0.4096	**1.0**
0.02	1	**0.0**	0.0128	0.0656	0.2176	0.5648	**1.0**
0.04	2	**0.0**	0.0328	0.1152	0.3152	0.6088	**1.0**
0.06	3	**0.0**	0.0576	0.174	0.362	0.6576	**1.0**
0.08	4	**0.0**	0.087	0.2098	0.4158	0.681	**1.0**
0.10	5	**0.0**	0.1049	0.2514	0.4454	0.7079	**1.0**

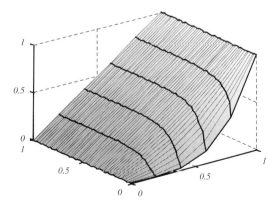

FIGURE 15.6 Temperature in a rod.

Discussion

There are two primary considerations in choosing the step sizes, h and k, for a finite difference solution of the heat equation. One issue is the effect that the step sizes have on the order of the truncation error for the method. The other important issue is the stability of the method.

Choosing Step Sizes for Higher Order Truncation Error

The finite-difference representations of the partial derivatives in the heat equation are based on the Taylor series formulas developed in Chapter 11. The partial derivative of u with respect to t is

$$u_t\,(x_i, t_j) = \frac{u(x_i, t_{j+1}) - u(x_i, t_j)}{k} + O(k) = \frac{1}{k}\,[u_{i,j+1} - u_{i,j}] + O(k).$$

Similarly,

$$u_{xx}\,(x_i, t_j) = \frac{1}{h^2}\,[u_{i-1,j} - 2\,u_{i,j} + u_{i+1,j}] + O(h^2).$$

Substituting into the PDE gives

$$\frac{1}{k}\,[u_{i,j+1} - u_{i,j}] + O(k) = \frac{c}{h^2}\,[u_{i-1,j} - 2u_{i,j} + u_{i+1,j}] + O(h^2).$$

Combining the two expressions for the truncation error shows that the truncation error for the explicit method is $O(h^2 + k)$:

$$\frac{1}{k}\,[u_{i,j+1} - u_{i,j}] = \frac{c}{h^2}\,[u_{i-1,j} - 2u_{i,j} + u_{i+1,j}] + O(h^2) + O(k).$$

If we make use of the actual form of the first term of the error, we find that

$$\frac{1}{k}\,[u_{i,j+1} - u_{i,j}] = \frac{c}{h^2}\,[u_{i-1,j} - 2u_{i,j} + u_{i+1,j}] + \frac{c\,h^2}{12}\,u_{xxxx} - \frac{k}{2}\,u_{tt}$$

$$+ \text{ higher order terms.}$$

Since u satisfies the PDE $u_t = c\,u_{xx}$, assuming sufficient continuity for the derivatives, we find by calculus that $u_{tt} = c\,u_{xxxx}$. Thus, we can obtain a method with truncation error $O(k^2)$ if we choose h and k so that

$$\frac{c\,h^2}{12}\,u_{xxxx} - \frac{k}{2}\,u_{tt} = \frac{h^2}{12}\,u_{tt} - \frac{k}{2}\,u_{tt} = \frac{1}{2}\left(\frac{h^2}{6} - k\right)u_{tt} = 0.$$

Hence, for $r = \dfrac{k}{h^2} = \dfrac{1}{6}$ the truncation error is $O(k^2) = O(h^4)$.

Restrictions on Step Sizes to Ensure Stability

The primary difficulty with the explicit method is the stability condition, which requires that

$$r = \frac{c\,k}{h^2} \leq \frac{1}{2}.$$

A numerical method is stable if errors that may be present at one stage of the computation do not grow as the process proceeds. To consider the stability of the forward difference solution of the heat equation, it is useful to express the computation in matrix-vector form. The solution at time step $j+1$, which we denote by the column vector $\mathbf{u}(\,:\,,j+1)$, is found by multiplying the tridiagonal matrix $\mathbf{A}$ by the solution at the jth time step:

$$
\begin{bmatrix}
1-2r & r & & & \\
r & 1-2r & r & & \\
& \cdot & \vdots & \cdot & \\
& & r & 1-2r & r \\
& & & r & 1-2r
\end{bmatrix}
\begin{bmatrix}
u(1,j) \\
\vdots \\
u(n,j)
\end{bmatrix}
=
\begin{bmatrix}
u(1,j+1) \\
\vdots \\
u(n,j+1)
\end{bmatrix}
$$

Suppose the true solution of the PDE at time step j is $\mathbf{U}(\,:\,,j)$ and the computed solution is $\mathbf{u}(\,:\,,j) = \mathbf{U}(\,:\,,j) + \mathbf{E}$. Then the computed solution at step $j+1$ is

$$\mathbf{A}\,(:,j) = \mathbf{A}\,\{\mathbf{U}(:,j) + \mathbf{E}\} = \mathbf{A}\,\mathbf{U}(:,j) + \mathbf{A}\,\mathbf{E}.$$

After m time steps, the effect of the error $\mathbf{E}$ has become $\mathbf{A}^m\mathbf{E}$. From matrix algebra, it follows that

$$\|\,\mathbf{A}^m\mathbf{E}\,\| \leq |\,\lambda\,|^m\,\|\,\mathbf{E}\,\|$$

where λ is the dominant eigenvalue (eigenvalue of largest magnitude) of $\mathbf{A}$. Stability is assured if $|\,\lambda\,| \leq 1$. The Gerschgorin theorem (Chapter 1) bounds the eigenvalues of $\mathbf{A}$ inside circles centered at $1-2r$; the radius of each of the largest circles is $2r$, so any eigenvalue μ satisfies

$$(1-2r) - 2r \leq \mu \leq (1-2r) + 2r;$$

thus, we are guaranteed that $-1 \leq \lambda \leq 1$
if

$$-1 \leq 1 - 4r,$$

or

$$r \leq \frac{1}{2}.$$

15.2.2 Implicit Method

Consider again the PDE

$$u_t = c\,u_{xx}, \qquad \text{for } 0 < x < 1, \quad 0 < t \le T.$$

Replacing the space derivative by a centered difference at the *forward* time step $j+1$ and the time derivative by a *forward* difference gives

$$\frac{1}{k}\left[u_{i,j+1} - u_{i,j}\right] = \frac{c}{h^2}\left[u_{i-1,j+1} - 2u_{i,j+1} + u_{i+1,j+1}\right],$$

or

$$u_{i,j} = (-r)\,u_{i-1,j+1} + (1+2r)\,u_{i,j+1} + (-r)\,u_{i+1,j+1},$$

where $r = \dfrac{c\,k}{h^2}$. This method is unconditionally stable.

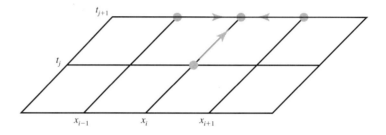

FIGURE 15.7   Values needed for computation at time $j+1$.

The points involved in the calculations are illustrated in Fig. 15.7. Unlike calculations in the explicit method, calculations for a point at the $(j+1)^{st}$ time level depend both on the results from one point at the jth time level and on other points at the $(j+1)^{st}$ level. The resulting system of equations can be solved by techniques discussed in Chapter 4. The tridiagonal system must be solved at each time step, with a different right-hand side, so LU factorization of the tridiagonal system is an efficient approach, as given in the following algorithm.

The following algorithm computes the approximate solution of the

parabolic PDE	$u_t = c\,u_{xx}$,	$0 < x < 1, 0 < t \le T,$
with initial conditions	$u(x,0) = f(x),$	$0 < x < 1,$
and boundary conditions	$u(0,t) = g_0(t),$	$u(a,t) = g_1(t), 0 < t \le T$

The algorithm returns a matrix $\mathbf{u}$, in which the spatial variable runs down each row, and time advances from left to right. It may be more convenient to display the transpose of $\mathbf{u}$, so that x runs from left to right, and t increases from top to bottom.

Input

    c   *coefficient in PDE: $u_t = c\, u_{xx}$*

    T   *find solution for $0 < t < T$*

    n   *number of subdivisions of [0, 1]*

    m   *number of subdivisions of [0, T]*

    f(x)   *initial condition*

    g0(t)   *boundary condition at $x = 0$*

    g1(t)   *boundary condition at $x = 1$*

Begin computation

h = 1/n

k = T/m

$r = \dfrac{c\,k}{h^2}$

For i = 0 to n   *Evaluate the initial condition*

    u(i, 0) = f(i h)

End

For i = 1 to n−1   *Define tridiagonal system*

    D(i) = 1+ 2 r

    A(i) = −r

    B(i) = −r

End

A(n−1) = 0

B(1) = 0

For i = 2 to n−1   *LU factorization*

    B(i) = B(i)/D(i−1)

    D(i) = D(i) − B(i) A(i−1)

End

For j = 1 to m

    R(1) = u(1, j−1) + g₀(j k)   *Define right-hand side*

    For i = 2 to n−2

        R(i) = u(i, j−1)

    End

    R(n−1) = u(n−1, j−1) + g₁(j k)

    z(1) − R(1)   *Solve lower triangular system*

    For i = 2 to n−1

        z(i) = R(i)− B(i) z(i−1)

    End

    u(n−1,j) = z(n)/D(n)   *Solve upper triangular system*

    For i = n−2 to 1

        u(i, j) = (z(i) − A(i) u(i+1, j))/D(i)

    End

End

Return

    u   *matrix of solution values*

Example 15.2 Temperature in a Rod, Implicit Method

Let the temperature in a rod (of unit length) be given by the PDE

$$u_t - u_{xx} = 0, \qquad \text{for } 0 < x < 1, \qquad 0 < t < T.$$

The initial conditions are $\qquad u(x, 0) = x^4, \qquad 0 \le x \le 1$;
the boundary conditions are $\qquad u(0, t) = 0, \qquad u(1, t) = 1, \qquad 0 < t < T.$
 Consider a fairly coarse mesh, with $n = 5$, so that $h = \Delta x = 0.2$, and take $m = 5$ and $T = 0.2$, so that $k = \Delta t = 0.04$. With these parameter values, we get

$$r = \frac{c\,k}{h^2} = \frac{\Delta t}{(\Delta x)^2} = 1.0, \text{ and the general equation}$$

$$u_{i,j} = -r\,u_{i-1,j+1} + (1 + 2r)\,u_{i,j+1} - r\,u_{i+1,j+1}$$

simplifies to

$$-u_{i-1,j+1} + 3u_{i,j+1} - u_{i+1,j+1} = u_{i,j}.$$

Note that this time step is twice as large as the maximum value that can be used for stable computations with the explicit method.

 We must find values of u at the node points $i = 1, 2, 3$, and 4 for each time step; u is given by the boundary conditions for $i = 0$ and $i = 5$. To go from the initial conditions ($t = 0$) to the solution at the first time step ($t = 0.04$) requires that the following tridiagonal system be solved:

$$
\begin{aligned}
3u_{1,1} - u_{2,1} & & & = u_{1,0} + u_{0,1} = 0.0016 + 0.0 \\
-u_{1,1} + 3u_{2,1} - u_{3,1} & & & = u_{2,0} \quad\;\; = 0.0256 \\
-u_{2,1} + 3u_{3,1} - u_{4,1} & & & = u_{3,0} \quad\;\; = 0.1296 \\
-u_{3,1} + 3u_{4,1} & & & = u_{4,0} + u_{5,1} = 0.4096 + 1.0
\end{aligned}
$$

The computed values are

$$u_{11} = 0.037033, \quad u_{21} = 0.1095, \quad u_{31} = 0.26586, \quad u_{41} = 0.55849.$$

The right-hand side for the second time step is

$$(0.037033, \; 0.1095, \; 0.26586, \; 1.55849).$$

Repeating the calculations, using the right-hand side found from the solution at the previous time step, gives the solution with values listed in the following table. The solution has almost reached its steady-state linear temperature distribution; the plot is essentially the same as is shown in Figure 15.6.

Temperature in a rod; solution for $t = 0.00$ to $t = 0.32$.

	$x = 0$	0.2	0.4	0.6	0.8	1
$t=$						
0.00	0	0.0016	0.0256	0.1296	0.4096	1
0.04	0	0.037033	0.1095	0.26586	0.55849	1
0.08	0	0.072904	0.18168	0.36264	0.64038	1
0.12	0	0.10387	0.2387	0.43055	0.69031	1
0.16	0	0.1286	0.28192	0.47846	0.72292	1
0.20	0	0.14753	0.314	0.51254	0.74515	1

Discussion

The finite-difference representations of the partial derivatives in the heat equation are as given for the explicit method, except that the second derivative is approximated at step $j+1$, rather than at step j. Thus, we have

$$u_t\,(x_i, t_j) = \frac{1}{k}\,[u_{i,j+1} - u_{i,j}] + O(k),$$

and

$$u_{xx}\,(x_i, t_{j+1}) = \frac{1}{h^2}\,[u_{i-1,j+1} - 2u_{i,j+1} + u_{i+1,j+1}] + O(h^2).$$

Substituting into the PDE and simplifying shows that the truncation error for the implicit method is the same as for the explicit method, i.e., $O(h^2+k)$.

To show that the implicit method is unconditionally stable, consider the matrix—vector form of the process, viz.,

$$\begin{bmatrix} 1+2r & -r & & & \\ -r & 1+2r & -r & & \\ & \cdot & \vdots & \cdot & \\ & & -r & 1+2r & -r \\ & & & -r & 1+2r \end{bmatrix} \begin{bmatrix} u(1, j+1) \\ \vdots \\ u(n, j+1) \end{bmatrix} = \begin{bmatrix} u(1, j) \\ \vdots \\ u(n, j) \end{bmatrix},$$

or

$$\mathbf{A}\,\mathbf{u}(:, j+1) = \mathbf{u}(:, j).$$

For analysis (but not for actual computation!), we write the latter equation as

$$\mathbf{A}^{-1}\,\mathbf{u}(:, j) = \mathbf{u}(:, j+1),$$

so that, by the same reasoning as for the explicit method, stability is assured if λ the dominant eigenvalue of $\mathbf{A}^{-1}$, satisfies $|\lambda| \leq 1$. In terms of the eigenvalues of $\mathbf{A}$, the condition becomes

$$|\mu| \geq 1,$$

where μ is the eigenvalue of $\mathbf{A}$ with the smallest magnitude.

By the Gerschgorin theorem, this condition is true regardless of the value of r. Each of the circles determined by the Gerschgorin Theorem is centered at $(1+2r, 0)$. The radii of the first and last circles are r; all other circles have radius $2r$. Thus all eigenvalues are greater than or equal to 1.

15.2.3 Crank-Nicolson Method

Using the average of the centered difference at the forward time step $j+1$ and the current time step j gives

$$\frac{1}{k}[u_{i,j+1} - u_{i,j}] = \frac{c}{2h^2}[u_{i-1,j} - 2u_{i,j} + u_{i+1,j}] + \frac{c}{2h^2}[u_{i-1,j+1} - 2u_{i,j+1} + u_{i+1,j+1}].$$

Defining $r = \dfrac{ck}{h^2}$ as before, we can write the equations as

$$-\frac{r}{2}u_{i-1,j+1} + (1+r)u_{i,j+1} - \frac{r}{2}u_{i+1,j+1} = \frac{r}{2}u_{i-1,j} + (1-r)u_{i,j} + \frac{r}{2}u_{i+1,j}.$$

A general two-stage method with weighting factor λ, for $0 \le \lambda \le 1$, gives

$$\frac{1}{k}[u_{i,j+1} - u_{i,j}] = \frac{\lambda}{h^2}[u_{i+1,j} - 2u_{i,j} + u_{i-1,j}] + \frac{1-\lambda}{h^2}[u_{i+1,j+1} - 2u_{i,j+1} + u_{i-1,j+1}],$$

or, in terms of r and λ,

$$-r\lambda u_{i-1,j+1} + (1 + 2r\lambda)u_{i,j+1} - r\lambda u_{i+1,j+1}$$
$$= r(1-\lambda)u_{i-1,j} + (1 - 2r(1-\lambda))u_{i,j} + r(1-\lambda)u_{i+1,j}.$$

The resulting system of equations can be solved by techniques discussed in Chapter 4.

The Crank-Nicolson method is unconditionally stable and has better truncation error, $O(h^2 + k^2)$, than the basic implicit method. For the appropriate choice of λ, the truncation error for the general two-stage method is $O(h^4)$; this occurs when $2r\lambda = r - 1/6$. The truncation error is reduced to $O(h^6)$ if the step sizes are chosen so that $r = \dfrac{\sqrt{5}}{10}$ and $\lambda = \dfrac{3 - \sqrt{5}}{6}$. (See Ames, 1992, p. 65, for further discussion.)

The following algorithm computes the approximate solution of the

parabolic PDE	$u_t = c\,u_{xx}$,	$0 < x < 1, 0 < t \le T$,
with initial conditions	$u(x, 0) = f(x)$,	$0 < x < 1$,
and boundary conditions	$u(0, t) = g_0(t)$,	$u(a, t) = g_1(t), 0 < t \le T$

The algorithm returns a matrix $\mathbf{u}$, in which the spatial variable runs down each row, and time advances from left to right. It may be more convenient to display the transpose of $\mathbf{u}$, so that x runs from left to right, and t increases from top to bottom.

Input

    c   *coefficient in PDE:* $u_t = c\,u_{xx}$

    T   *find solution for $0 < t < T$*

    n   *number of subdivisions of $[0, a]$*

    m   *number of subdivisions of $[0, T]$*

    f(x)   *initial condition*

    g0(t)   *boundary condition at $x = 0$*

    g1(t)   *boundary condition at $x = a$*

Begin computation

h = a/n

k = T/m

$$s = \frac{1}{2}\frac{ck}{h^2} \qquad\qquad \textit{this is } r = 2$$

For i = 0 to n   *Evaluate the initial condition*

    u(i, 0) = f(i h)

End

For i = 1 to n−1   *Define tridiagonal system*

    D(i) = 1+ 2 s

    A(i) = −s

    B(i) = −s

End

A(n−1) = 0

B(1) = 0

For i = 2 to n−1   *LU factorization*

    B(i) = B(i)/D(i−1)

    D(i) = D(i) − B(i) A(i−1)

End

For j = 1 to m

    R(1) = s g_0(j k) + (1−2s) u(1, j−1) +s u(2,j−1)   *Define right-hand side*

    For i = 2 to n−2

        R(i) = s u(i −1, j−1) + (1−2s) u(i, j−1) + s u(i+1, j−1)

    End

    R(n−1) = s u(n−2,j−1) + (1−2s) u(n−1, j−1) + s g_1(j k)

    z(1) = R(1)   *Solve lower triangular system*

    For i = 2 to n−1

        z(i) = R(i)− B(i) z(i−1)

    End

    u(n−1,j) = z(n)/D(n)   *Solve upper triangular system*

    For i = n−2 to 1

        u(i, j) = (z(i) − A(i) u(i+1, j))/D(i)

    End

End

Return

    u   *matrix of solution values*

We illustrate the use of this algorithm in the next example, which repeats the same problem as in Example 15.2. Time increases from the top of the array to the bottom of the array; x increases from left to right.

Example 15.3 Temperature in a Rod, Crank-Nicolson Method

Consider again the temperature of a rod of unit length, given by the PDE

$$u_t - u_{xx} = 0, \qquad \text{for } 0 < x < 1, \quad 0 < t,$$

with initial temperature

$$u(x, 0) = x^4, \qquad 0 < x < 1,$$

and temperatures of

$$u(0, t) = 0, \qquad u(1, t) = 1, \qquad 0 < t.$$

at $x = 0$ and $x = 1$, respectively. Take a fairly coarse mesh, with $h = 0.2$ and $k = 0.04$, so that $r = \dfrac{c\,k}{h^2}$. In this case, the general equation

$$-\frac{r}{2} u_{i-1,j+1} + (1 + r)\, u_{i,j+1} - \frac{r}{2} u_{i+1,j+1} = \frac{r}{2} u_{i-1,j} + (1 - r)\, u_{i,j} + \frac{r}{2} u_{i+1,j}$$

simplifies to

$$-0.5\, u_{i-1,j+1} + 2\, u_{i,j+1} - 0.5\, u_{i+1,j+1} = 0.5\, u_{i-1,j} + 0.5\, u_{i+1,j}$$

To find the solution at the first time step, the equations are

$$
\begin{aligned}
+\, 2\, u_{1,1} - 0.5\, u_{2,1} &= 0.5\, (u_{0,0} + u_{2,0} + u_{0,1}) &= 0.0128 \\
-\, 0.5\, u_{1,1} + 2\, u_{2,1} - 0.5\, u_{3,1} &= 0.5\, (u_{1,0} + u_{3,0}) &= 0.0656 \\
-\, 0.5\, u_{2,1} + 2\, u_{3,1} - 0.5\, u_{4,1} &= 0.5\, (u_{2,0} + u_{4,0}) &= 0.2176 \\
-\, 0.5\, u_{3,1} + 2\, u_{4,1} &= 0.5\, (u_{3,0} + u_{5,0} + u_{5,1}) &= 1.0648
\end{aligned}
$$

The solution is shown in the following table for the first five time steps. The solution has almost reached its steady-state linear temperature distribution; the plot is essentially the same as is shown in Fig. 15.6.

Temperature in a rod, solution by Crank Nicolson method

$t \setminus x$	0.0	0.2	0.4	0.6	0.8	1.0
0.00	0.00	0.0016	0.0256	0.1296	0.4096	1.00
0.04	0.00	0.034794	0.11358	0.28831	0.60448	1.00
0.08	0.00	0.078313	0.19968	0.39728	0.6714	1.00
0.12	0.00	0.11578	0.26343	0.46235	0.71491	1.00
0.16	0.00	0.14258	0.3069	0.50689	0.74231	1.00
0.20	0.00	0.16092	0.33678	0.53672	0.7609	1.00

15.2.4 Insulated Boundary

The form of the boundary conditions depends on the physical situation being described. Keeping an end of the rod insulated corresponds to specifying that the partial derivative u_x is zero at that end of the rod; i.e.,

$$u_x(0, t) = 0 \quad \text{or} \quad u_x(a, t) = 0.$$

We illustrate the modification to the explicit method for the case of the temperature of the rod given at $x = 0$, but the end of the rod at $x = a$ insulated, so that $u_x(a, t) = 0$. The recommended approach to a boundary condition specified by a derivative is to add a fictitious point to the grid; for the situation described here, we extend the grid to include the point x_{n+1} at each time step. Using the central difference formula, we find that the boundary condition $u_x(a, t)$ becomes

$$\frac{1}{2k}[u_{n+1,j} - u_{n-1,j}] = 0,$$

or

$$u_{n+1,j} = u_{n-1,j}.$$

Applying the general update equation at $i = n$ gives

$$u_{n,j+1} = r\, u_{n-1,j} + (1 - 2r)\, u_{n,j} + r\, u_{n+1,j},$$

which includes the fictitious point. Substituting the information from the boundary condition, we get

$$u_{n,j+1} = r\, u_{n-1,j} + (1 - 2r)\, u_{n,j} + r\, u_{n-1,j} = 2r\, u_{n-1,j} + (1 - 2r)\, u_{n,j}.$$

The system of equations is

$$\begin{aligned}
u_{1,j+1} &= r\, u_{0,j} + (1 - 2r)\, u_{1,j} + r\, u_{2,j}, & i &= 1 \\
u_{i,j+1} &= r\, u_{i-1,j} + (1 - 2r)\, u_{i,j} + r\, u_{i+1,j}, & i &= 2, \ldots, n - 1, \\
u_{n,j+1} &= 2r\, u_{n-1,j} + (1 - 2r)\, u_{n,j}, & i &= n.
\end{aligned}$$

For comparison, the equations for the explicit method (with u_0 and u_n given by boundary conditions) are

$$\begin{aligned}
u_{1,j+1} &= r\, u_{0,j} + (1 - 2r)\, u_{1,j} + r\, u_{2,j}, & i &= 1, \\
u_{i,j+1} &= r\, u_{i-1,j} + (1 - 2r)\, u_{i,j} + r\, u_{i+1,j}, & i &= 2, \ldots, n - 2, \\
u_{n-1,j+1} &= r\, u_{n-2,j} + (1 - 2r)\, u_{n-1,j} + r\, u_{n,j}, & i &= n - 1.
\end{aligned}$$

The standard example of a hyperbolic equation is the one-dimensional wave equation

$$u_{tt} - c^2 u_{xx} = 0, \qquad \text{for } 0 \le x \le 1 \text{ and } 0 \le t.$$

Initial conditions are given for $u(x, 0)$ and $u_t(x, 0)$, for $0 \le x \le 1$:

$$u(x, 0) = f_1(x),$$

$$u_t(x, 0) = f_2(x),$$

Boundary conditions are given at $x = 0$ and $x = 1$, for $0 < t$:

$$u(0, t) = g_0(t),$$

$$u(1, t) = g_1(t),$$

Although the one-dimensional wave equation does not usually require a numerical solution, it serves as an introduction to higher dimensional wave equations for which numerical methods are more likely to be worthwhile.

The mesh is given as before:

$$x_i = ih, i = 0, 1, \ldots, n, \quad h = \Delta x = 1/n,$$

$$t_j = jk, j = 0, 1, \ldots, m, \quad k = \Delta t = T/m.$$

As with the heat equation, there are several choices for finite-difference approximations for u_{xx} and u_{tt}; each choice yields a method with certain characteristics—explicit or implicit technique, stability requirements, and truncation error. We consider an explicit method and an implicit method, each based on central difference formulas for the second derivatives.

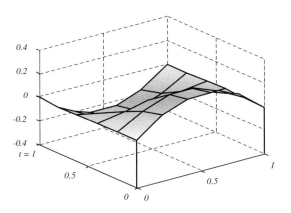

FIGURE 15.8   Vibrating string

15.3.1 Explicit Method

Replacing the space derivative in the wave equation by the difference formula at the jth time step, i.e.,

$$c^2 u_{xx} \Rightarrow \frac{c^2}{h^2} [u_{i-1,j} - 2u_{i,j} + u_{i+1,j}].$$

and replacing the time derivative by the difference formula at the ith space step, i.e.,

$$u_{tt} \Rightarrow \frac{1}{k^2} [u_{i,j-1} - 2u_{i,j} + u_{i,j+1}],$$

gives

$$\frac{1}{k^2} [u_{i,j-1} - 2u_{i,j} + u_{i,j+1}] = \frac{c^2}{h^2} [u_{i-1,j} - 2u_{i,j} + u_{i+1,j}].$$

In a similar manner to our approach for the heat equation, we define the parameter

$$p = \frac{c\,k}{h} = c\,\frac{\Delta t}{\Delta x},$$

solve for the unknown $u_{i,j+1}$, and rearrange the order of the terms on the right-hand side to obtain

$$u_{i,j+1} = p^2 u_{i-1,j} + 2(1 - p^2) u_{i,j} + p^2 u_{i+1,j} - u_{i,j-1}.$$

Since the solution is known for $t = 0$, we can solve for $u_{i,j+1}$, starting with $j = 0$. However, we do not know $u_{i,-1}$. To overcome this difficulty, we use the initial condition for $u_t(x, 0) = f_2(x)$ and replace the time derivative by the centered difference formula to give

$$u_{i,1} - u_{i,-1} = 2\,k\,f_2(x_i).$$

The equation for u at the first time step now becomes (for $i = 1, \ldots n-1$)

$$u_{i,1} = 0.5\,p^2 u_{i-1,0} + (1 - p^2)\,u_{i,0} + 0.5\,p^2 u_{i+1,0} + k\,f_2(x_i),$$

where the values of $u_{i-1,0}$, $u_{i,0}$, and $u_{i+1,0}$ are available from the initial condition $u(x, 0) = f_1(x)$. The value of u at each subsequent time step can be found from the general equation

$$u_{i,j+1} = p^2 u_{i-1,j} + 2(1 - p^2) u_{i,j} + p^2 u_{i+1,j} - u_{i,j-1}.$$

There are two stability requirements, determined by the matrix of coefficients of u at the jth time step:

1. The sum of the coefficients of the $u_{\cdot,j}$ terms must be less than or equal to 2; this is satisfied for all choices of p, since $p^2 + 2(1-p^2) + p^2 = 2$.
2. No coefficient of $u_{\cdot,j}$ is negative. (A negative coefficient on $u_{i,j-1}$ is fine.) This requires that $1 - p^2 \geq 0$, or $p \leq 1$ (i.e., $c\,k \leq h$). (For further discussion, see Ames, 1992, p. 266.)

Approximate the solution of the hyperbolic PDE

$$u_{tt} = c\, u_{xx} \qquad \text{for } 0 \le x \le 1, 0 \le t \le T$$

with boundary conditions $\quad u(0, t) = g_0(t), \qquad u(1, t) = g_1(t)\, 0 < t$
and initial condition $\qquad u(x, 0) = f_1(x), \qquad u_t(x, 0) = f_2(x)\ 0 \le x \le 1$
using finite differences.

Wave equation, Explicit Finite-Difference Method

Input
- c   *coefficient in PDE:* $u_{tt} = c\, u_{xx}$
- T   *find solution for $0 < t < T$*
- n   *number of subdivisions of [0, 1]*
- m   *number of subdivisions of [0, T]*
- f1(x)   *initial condition for* u
- f2(x)   *initial conditions for* u_t
- g0(t)   *boundary condition at $x = 0$*
- g1(t)   *boundary condition at $x = 1$*

Compute parameters
- h = 1/n   *step size for x*
- k = T/m   *step size for t*
- p = (c k/h)^2

Evaluate initial and boundary conditions
For i = 0 to n
     $u(i,0) = f_1(i\, h)$
End
For j = 0 to m
     $u(0,j) = g_0(j\, k)$
     $u(n,j) = g_1(j\, k)$
End

Solution at first time step
For i = 1 to n−1

$$u(i, 1) = \frac{p}{2} u(i - 1,0) + (1 - p)\, u(i,0) + \frac{p}{2} u(i + 1,0) + k\, f_2(i\, h)$$

End

Solution at remaining time steps
For j = 2 to m
     For i = 1 to n−1
         $u(i,j) = p\, u(i-1,j-1) + 2\,(1-p)\, u(i,j-1) + p\, u(i+1,j-1) - u(i,j-2)$
     End
End

Return
- u   *matrix of solution values*

Example 15.4 Vibrating String, Explicit Method, Stable Solution

Consider the motion of a vibrating string of unit length with both ends held fixed and an initial displacement described by the PDE

$$u_{tt} - u_{xx} = 0, \qquad \text{for } 0 < x < 1, \quad 0 < t.$$

The initial conditions

$$u(x, 0) = x(1 - x), \qquad u_t(x, 0) = 0, \qquad 0 < x < 1;$$

the boundary conditions are

$$u(0, t) = 0, \qquad u(1, t) = 0, \qquad 0 < t.$$

With a fairly coarse mesh, $h = \Delta x = 0.2$, stability requires that $p = \dfrac{\Delta t}{\Delta x} \leq 1.0$, or $k = \Delta t < 0.2$. Using the maximum allowed value of Δt (so that $p = 1$) results in a simplification of the general equation for the first time step,

$$u_{i,1} = 0.5\, p^2\, u_{i-1,0} + (1 - p^2)\, u_{i,0} + 0.5\, p^2 u_{i+1,0} + \Delta t\, g(x_i),$$

to the form

$$u_{i,1} = 0.5\, u_{i-1,0} + 0.5\, u_{i+1,0} + 0.2\, g(x_i) = 0.5\, u_{i-1,0} + 0.5\, u_{i+1,0}.$$

The initial and boundary conditions (bold), and the solution at the first time step (italics) are given in the following tabulation:

	x =	0.0	0.2	0.4	0.6	0.8	1.0
t	λi	0	1	2	3	4	5
0.0	0	**0.0**	**0.16**	**0.24**	**0.24**	**0.16**	**0.0**
0.2	1	**0.0**	*0.12*	*0.20*	*0.20*	*0.12*	**0.0**

The value of u at each subsequent time step can be found from the general equation $u_{i,j+1} = u_{i-1,j} + u_{i+1,j} - u_{i,j-1}$. The solution at the second time step (shown in italics) is shown in the following table:

	x =	0.0	0.2	0.4	0.6	0.8	1.0
t	λi	0	1	2	3	4	5
0.0	0	**0.0**	**0.16**	**0.24**	**0.24**	**0.16**	**0.0**
0.2	1	**0.0**	0.12	0.20	0.20	0.12	**0.0**
0.4	2	**0.0**	*0.04*	*0.08*	*0.08*	*0.04*	**0.0**

The solution was graphed in Fig. 15.8.

15.3.2 Implicit Method

As is the case with parabolic equations, implicit finite-difference solutions have stability advantages for hyperbolic equations also. A simple implicit scheme (Ames, 1992, p. 284) results from replacing the time derivative by the difference formula at the ith space step: $u_{tt} \Rightarrow \dfrac{1}{k^2}[u_{i,j-1} - 2u_{i,j} + u_{i,j}1]$,

and replacing the space derivative by an average of the differences at the $(j+1)^{th}$ and $(j-1)^{th}$ time steps

$$c^2 u_{xx} \Rightarrow \frac{c^2}{2h^2}[u_{i-1,j+1} - 2u_{i,j+1} + u_{i+1,j+1} + u_{i-1,j-1} - 2u_{i,j-1} + u_{i+1,j-1}].$$

The difference equation then becomes

$$u_{i,j-1} - 2u_{i,j} + u_{i,j+1} = \frac{c^2 k^2}{2h^2}[u_{i-1,j+1} - 2u_{i,j+1} + u_{i+1,j+1} + u_{i-1,j-1} - 2u_{i,j-1} + u_{i+1,j-1}].$$

In a manner similar to that for the heat equation, we define $p = ck/h$, so that

$$-p^2 u_{i-1,j+1} + 2(1 + p^2)u_{i,j+1} - p^2 u_{i+1,j+1} = 4u_{i,j} + {}^2 u_{i-1,j-1} - 2(1 + p^2)u_{i,j-1} + p^2 u_{i+1,j-1}.$$

Since the solution is known for $t = 0$, we can solve for $u_{i,j+1}$, starting with $j = 0$. However, we do not know $u_{i,-1}$. To overcome this difficulty, we use the initial condition for $u_t(x, 0) = f_2(x)$ and replace the time derivative by the centered difference formula to give $u_{i,-1} = u_{i,1} - 2 k f_2(x_i)$. The values of $u_{0,j}$ and $u_{n,j}$ are given by the boundary conditions.

The Equations for $j = 0$

$$4(1 + p^2)u_{1,1} - 2p^2 u_{2,1} = 4u_{1,0} - 2p^2 k f_2(x_0) + 4(1 + p^2)k f_2(x_1) - 2p^2 k f_2(x_2) + 2p^2 u_0$$

$$-2p^2 u_{1,1} + 4(1 + p^2)u_{2,1} - 2p^2 u_{3,1} = 4u_{2,0} - 2p^2 k f_2(x_1) + 4(1 + p^2)k f_2(x_2) - 2p^2 k f_2(x_3)$$

$$\vdots$$

$$-2p^2 u_{i-1,1} + 4(1 + p^2)u_{i,1} - 2p^2 u_{i+1,1} = 4u_{i,0} - 2p^2 k f_2(x_{i-1}) + 4(1 + p^2)k f_2(x_i) - 2p^2 k f_2(x_{i+1})$$

$$\vdots$$

$$-2p^2 u_{n-2,1} + 4(1 + p^2)u_{n-1,1} = 4u_{n-1,0} - 2p^2 k f_2(x_{n-2}) + 4(1 + p^2)k f_2(x_{n-1}) - 2p^2 k f_2(x_n) + 2p^2 u_n$$

The Equations for $j = 1, 2, \ldots$

$$2(1 + p^2)u_{1,j+1} - p^2 u_{2,j+1} = 4u_{1,j} + p^2 u_{0,j-1} - 2(1 + p^2)u_{1,j-1} + p^2 u_{2,j-1} + p^2 u_{0,j+1}$$

$$-p^2 u_{1,j+1} + 2(1 + p^2)u_{2,j+1} - p^2 u_{3,j+1} = 4u_{2,j} + p^2 u_{1,j-1} - 2(1 + p^2)u_{2,j-1} + p^2 u_{3,j-1}$$

$$\vdots$$

$$-p^2 u_{i-1,j+1} + 2(1 + p^2)u_{i,j+1} - p^2 u_{i+1,j+1} = 4u_{i,j} + p^2 u_{i-1,j-1} - 2(1 + p^2)u_{i,j-1} + p^2 u_{i+1,j-1}$$

$$\vdots$$

$$-p^2 u_{n-2,j+1} + 2(1 + p^2)u_{n-1,j+1} = 4u_{n-1,j} + p^2 u_{n-2,j-1} - 2(1 + p^2)u_{n-1,j-1} + p^2 u_{n,j-1} + p^2 u_{n,j+1}$$

Input (as listed in Explicit Finite-difference method); compute parameters as
    $h = 1/n$ *step size for x*
    $k = T/m$ *step size for t*
    $p = c\,k/h$
    $q = p\char94 2$
For i = 0 to n   *Evaluate initial and boundary conditions*
    $u(i,0) = f_1(i\,h)$
End
For j = 0 to m
    $u(0,j) = g_0(j\,k)$
    $u(n,j) = g_1(j\,k)$
End
For i = 1 to n−1   *Form tridiagonal system for first time step*
    $a(i) = -2\,q$
    $d(i) = 4\,(1+q)$
    $b(i) = -2\,q$
    $r(i) = 4\,f_1(i\,h) -2\,q\,k\,f_2(h\,(i-1)) +4\,(1+q)\,k\,f_2(h\,i) - 2\,q\,k\,f_2(h\,(i+1))$
End
$r(1) = r(1) + 2\,q\,u(0,1)$
$r(n-1) = r(n-1) + 2\,q\,u(n,1)$
$b(n-1) = 0$
$a(1) = 0$
Solve tridiagonal system to obtain u(: , 1), vector of displacements at j = 1
For i = 1 to n−1   *Form tridiagonal system for remaining time steps*
    $a(i) = -q$
    $d(i) = 2\,(1+q)$
    $b(i) = -q$
End
$b(n-1) = 0$
$a(1) = 0$
For j = 2 to m
    For i = 1 to n−1
        $r(i) = 4\,u(i,j) + q\,u(i-1,j-1) -2\,(1+q)\,u(i,j-1) + q\,u(i+1,j-1)$
    End
    $r(1) = r(1) + q\,u(0,1)$
    $r(n-1) = r(n-1) + q\,u(n,1)$
Solve tridiagonal system to obtain u(: , j), displacements at time step j
End
Return   u   *matrix of solution values*

    This implicit method has unrestricted stability (Ames, 1992, p. 285; see Ames as well for a discussion of the general three-level implicit form). The preceding implicit method corresponds to $\lambda = 1/2$, the explicit method corresponds to $\lambda = 0$, and the general method has unrestricted stability for $\lambda \geq 1/4$.

15.4 POISSON EQUATION: ELLIPTIC PDE

The standard example of an elliptic equation is the two-dimensional Laplacian or potential equation. As is often the case, we consider the PDE on the unit square, $0 \le x \le 1, 0 \le y \le 1$; problems on other rectangular regions can be transformed to this region by a simple change of variables.

$$u_{xx} + u_{yy} = 0, \quad 0 \le x \le 1, \quad 0 \le y \le 1,$$

or Poisson's equation

$$u_{xx} + u_{yy} = f(x, y), \quad 0 \le x \le 1, \quad 0 \le y \le 1.$$

The simplest boundary conditions specify the value of the function along each of the four sides of the rectangular domain:

$$u(x, 0) = f_0(x), \quad u(x, 1) = f_1(x), \quad 0 < x < 1;$$
$$u(0, y) = g_0(y), \quad u(1, y) = g_1(y), \quad 0 < y < 1$$

We define a mesh in the $x - y$ plane:

$$x_i = i\,h, \quad i = 0, 1, \ldots, n, \quad h = \Delta x = 1/n,$$
$$y_j = j\,k, \quad j = 0, 1, \ldots, m, \quad k = \Delta y = 1/m.$$

We denote the (approximate) value of $u(x, y)$ at the point (x_i, y_j) as $u_{i,j}$ and the value of the right-hand side, $f(x_i, y_j)$ as f_{ij}. Replacing the second derivatives by centered differences gives a system of algebraic equations for the function values at the mesh points:

$$\frac{1}{k^2}[u_{i,j+1} - 2u_{i,j} + u_{i,j-1}] + \frac{1}{h^2}[u_{i+1,j} - 2u_{i,j} + u_{i-1,j}] = f_{ij}.$$

However, unlike the situation with the wave equation, no information is given that allows us to solve these equations in a sequential manner. Due to the somewhat more extensive computations needed to obtain interesting results, we first present an algorithm for Poisson's equation and then illustrate the process with examples.

The first example is the potential equation problem solved earlier in Chapter 3. However, using the following algorithm, one need not form the coefficient matrix explicitly. The second example is a Poisson equation with the same boundary conditions as those for the potential equation. Gauss-Seidel iteration is built directly into the algorithm.

The following algorithm uses finite differences to approximate the solution of the elliptic PDE

$$u_{xx} + u_{yy} = f(x, y), \quad 0 \le x \le 1, \quad 0 \le y \le 1.$$

with boundary conditions

$$u(x, 0) = f_0(x), \quad u(x, 1) = f_1(x), \quad u(0, y) = g_0(y), \quad u(1, y) = g_1(y).$$

Input
- n   *number of subintervals in x direction*
- m   *number of subintervals in y direction*
- ff(x,y)   *right-hand side of PDE*
- $f_0(x)$ *boundary condition at y = 0*
- $f_1(x)$ *boundary condition at y = 1*
- $g_0(y)$ *boundary condition at x = 0*
- $g_1(y)$ *boundary condition at x = 1*

Define parameters
- h = 1/n   *step size for x*
- k = 1/m   *step size for y*
- $r = \dfrac{h^2}{k^2}$
- $c = \dfrac{1}{2\,r + 2}$

Initializations
For j = 1 to m−1   *Evaluate boundary conditions at x =0; x = 1*
    u(0,j) = g_0(j k)
    u(n,j) = g_1(j k)
End
For i = 1 to n−1
    u(i,0) = f_0(i h)   *Evaluate boundary conditions at y = 0; y = 1*
    u(i,m) = f_1(i h)
    For j = 1 to m−1
       f(i,j) = ff(i h, j k)   *Evaluate right hand side at grid points*
       u(i, j) = 0   *Initialize solution at interior points*
    End
End
For it = 1 to max_it   *Begin iterations*
    For i = 1 to n−1
       For j = 1 to m−1
          u(i,j) = r c (u(i,j+1) +u(i,j−1)) + c (u(i+1,j) +u(i−1,j)) −h^2 c f(i,j)
       End
    End
    Add test for convergence here if desired
End
Return
    u   *Matrix of solution values*

Example 15.5 Potential Equation

Consider the equation

$$u_{xx} + u_{yy} = 0, \quad 0 \le x \le 1, \quad 0 \le y \le 1.$$

with boundary conditions

$$u(0, y) = y^2, \quad u(1, y) = 1, \quad 0 < y < 1,$$
$$u(x, 0) = x^2, \quad u(x, 1) = 1, \quad 0 < x < 1.$$

The solutions after 1, 5, 20, and 50 iterations are shown in Fig. 15.9.

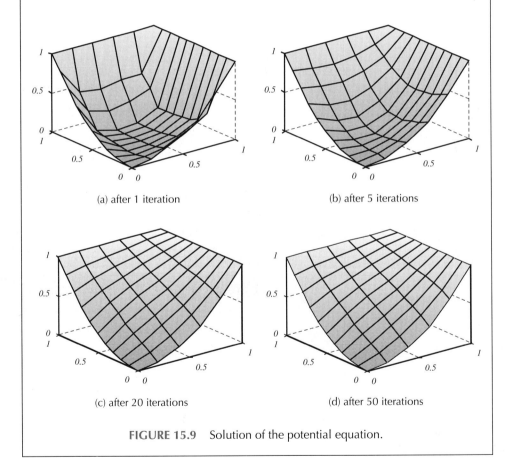

(a) after 1 iteration (b) after 5 iterations

(c) after 20 iterations (d) after 50 iterations

FIGURE 15.9   Solution of the potential equation.

Example 15.6 Poisson's Equation

Consider the equation

$$u_{xx} + u_{yy} = x + y, \quad 0 \le x \le 1, \quad 0 \le y \le 1,$$

with boundary conditions

$$u(0, y) = y^2, \quad u(1, y) = 1, \quad 0 < y < 1,$$
$$u(x, 0) = x^2, \quad u(x, 1) = 1, \quad 0 < x < 1.$$

The solutions after 1, 5, 20, and 50 iterations are shown in Fig. 15.10. The solution values change only slightly after the first 20 iterations.

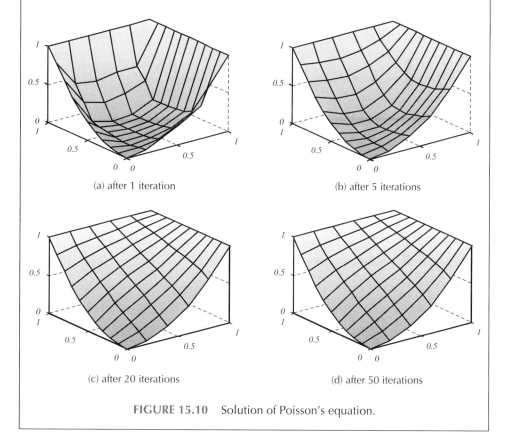

(a) after 1 iteration

(b) after 5 iterations

(c) after 20 iterations

(d) after 50 iterations

FIGURE 15.10 Solution of Poisson's equation.

Finite-difference methods for solving a two-dimensional Poisson equation

$$u_{xx} + u_{yy} = f(x, y)$$

on a rectangular region are based on dividing the domain of the problem into rectangular subdomains and approximating the solution at the mesh points. An alternative approach, known as the finite-element method, allows the domain to be divided into any convenient set of subregions (often triangular, but not necessarily of the same size). Rather than just finding the solution at the mesh or node points, an approximate solution of suitably simple form is found over the entire region. In the following discussion, we assume that the subregions are triangular.

The problem of solving the differential equation is converted into a corresponding problem of minimizing a functional that consists of an integral over the region (and, for certain types of boundary conditions, a line integral along the boundary).

In this section, we consider a finite-element solution to an elliptic PDE of the form

$$u_{xx} + u_{yy} + r(x, y)\, u = f(x, y) \quad \text{on the region } R$$
$$u(x, y) = g(x, y) \qquad\qquad \text{on the boundary of } R$$

The corresponding functional to be minimized is

$$I[u] = \iint_R [u_x^2 + u_y^2 - r(x,y)u^2 + 2f(x, y)u]\, dx\, dy.$$

A finite-element solution of the PDE is a function $U = \sum_{j=1}^{m} c_j\, \phi_j$ where the ϕ_j are called basis functions. In order to find the solution function U, we must determine the appropriate basis functions, and the coefficients c_j. Both the basis functions and the coefficients multiplying them depend on the choice of subregions.

The solution process consists of the following steps:

1. Define the subdivision of R.
   Specify the locations of the nodes $V_1, \ldots, V_n, V_{n+1}, \ldots, V_m$
   $j = 1, \ldots, n$ are interior nodes, $j = n+1, \ldots, m$ are on the boundary of R.
   Specify the nodes that define each subregion.
2. Define each of the basis functions $\phi_j, j = 1, \ldots, m$.
3. Determine the coefficients c_j that multiply the basis functions

Coefficients c_j for the basis functions that correspond to boundary nodes ($j = n+1, \ldots, m$) are chosen so that the solution U satisfies the boundary conditions at those nodes.

Coefficients c_j for the basis functions that correspond to interior nodes ($j = 1, \ldots, n$), so that U minimizes the integral $I[u]$.

15.5.1 Defining the Subregions

There are several reasons that a triangular subdivision of the region R is convenient. Triangles allow great flexibility in covering an irregularly shaped region. The use of triangular subregions also simplifies the computation of the basis functions, and the coefficients in the linear combination of basis functions, for the finite-element solution of the PDE.

In order to specify the subdivision of the region, we must know the locations of the nodes (vertices of the triangles), and also the definition of the triangular subregions in terms of the vertices that define each triangle. We also need to distinguish between nodes on the boundary of the region and interior nodes. We assume that there are m nodes, with nodes $j = 1, \ldots n$ in the interior of R and nodes $j = n+1, \ldots, m$ on the boundary of R. If the region R is divided into p triangular sub-regions $T_1, T_2, \ldots, T_p$; the vertices of these regions are the nodes, $V_1, \ldots, V_n, V_{n+1}, \ldots, V_m$.

Example 15.7 Defining the Subdivision of a Region

The region R, $0 \le x \le 3$, $0 \le y \le 3$ illustrated in Figure 15.11 is divided into four triangular sub-regions, $T_1, T_2, \ldots, T_4$. The vertices of these regions are the nodes V_1, V_2, V_3, V_4, V_5. There is only one interior node, V_1. The coordinates of the nodes are given in the matrix V. The triangles are defined by specifying the node indices of the three vertices of each triangle. Thus

$$V = \begin{bmatrix} 1 & 1 \\ 0 & 3 \\ 3 & 3 \\ 3 & 0 \\ 0 & 0 \end{bmatrix} \quad T = \begin{bmatrix} 1 & 2 & 3 \\ 1 & 3 & 4 \\ 1 & 4 & 5 \\ 1 & 5 & 2 \end{bmatrix}$$

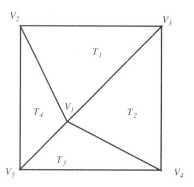

FIGURE 15.11   Square region divided into four triangular subregions.

15.5.2 Defining the Basis Functions

We now consider the basis functions ϕ_j. There is a basis function corresponding to each node. We define ϕ_j to have the following properties:

$\phi_j = 1$ at node j;

$\phi_j = 0$ at all other nodes; and

ϕ_j is linear on each triangular subdomain.

Thus ϕ_j is piece-wise planar. For each triangle that has node j as a vertex, we find a plane $z = a + b\,x + c\,y$ such that $z = 1$ at node j, $z = 0$ at the other two vertices; ϕ_j is identically zero on any subdomain that does not have node j as a vertex.

Example 15.8 Finding the Basis Functions

We now find the five basis functions ϕ_j for the region described in Example 15.8. The definition of the basis functions involves the determination of a plane that passes through three specified points. We want $\phi_j = 1$ at node j and $\phi_j = 0$ at the other nodes. The equation of the plane that is equal to one at (x_1, y_1), zero at (x_2, y_2), and zero at (x_3, y_3) has the form $z = a + b\,x + c\,y$, where the constants a, b, and c are found by solving the system

$$1 = a + b\,x_1 + c\,y_1$$
$$0 = a + b\,x_2 + c\,y_2$$
$$0 = a + b\,x_3 + c\,y_3$$

The First Basis Function
$\phi_1 = 1$ at node 1, and $\phi_1 = 0$ at nodes 2, 3, 4, and 5.

On T_1, $\phi_1 = a + b\,x + c\,y$, where   On T_2, $\phi_1 = a + b\,x + c\,y$, where

$1 = a + b + c,$ $1 = a + b + c,$

$0 = a + 0 + 3\,c,$ $0 = a + 3\,b + 3\,c,$

$0 = a + 3\,b + 3\,c$ $0 = a + 3\,b + 0$

$\Rightarrow a = 3/2, b = 0, c = -1/2.$ $\Rightarrow a = 3/2, b = -1/2, c = 0.$

On T_3, $\phi_1 = a + b\,x + c\,y$, where   On T_4, $\phi_1 = a + b\,x + c\,y$, where

$1 = a + b + c,$ $1 = a + b + c,$

$0 = a + 3\,b + 0,$ $0 = a + 0 + 0,$

$0 = a + 0 + 0$ $0 = a + 0 + 3\,c$

$\Rightarrow a = 0, b = 0, c = 1.$ $\Rightarrow a = 0, b = 1, c = 0.$

It is convenient to display the definition of ϕ_1 in the following table:

	T_1	T_2	T_3	T_4
ϕ_1	$(3-y)/2$	$(3-x)/2$	y	x

The Second Basis Function

ϕ_2 is equal to zero at node 1, one at node 2, and zero at nodes 3, 4, and 5,
$\phi_2 = 0$ on T_2 and T_3.

On T_1, $\phi_2 = a + b\,x + c\,y$, where   On T_4, $\phi_2 = a + b\,x + c\,y$, where

$\quad 1 = a + 0 + 3\,c,$ $\quad 1 = a + 0 + 3\,c,$

$\quad 0 = a + b + c,$ $\quad 0 = a + b + c,$

$\quad 0 = a + 3\,b + 3\,c$ $\quad 0 = a + 0 + 0$

$\Rightarrow a = 0, b = -1/3, c = 1/3.$ $\Rightarrow a = 0, b = -1/3, c = 1/3.$

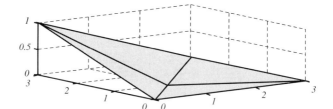

FIGURE 15.12   Second basis function.

Hence,

	T_1	T_2	T_3	T_4
ϕ_2	$(-x+y)/3$	0	0	$(-x+y)/3$

The Third Basis Function

$\phi_3 = 0$ at nodes 1, 2, 4, and 5; $\phi_3 = 1$ at node 3; $\phi_3 = 0$ on T_3 and T_4.
As with ϕ_1 and ϕ_2, we form the linear systems to find the values of a, b, and c
that define ϕ_3 on T_1 and on T_2; we find that on T_1, $a = -1/2$, $b = 1/3$, and
$c = 1/6$, and on T_2, $a = -1/2$, $b = 1/6$, and $c = 1/3$, so

	T_1	T_2	T_3	T_4
ϕ_3	$(-3 + 2x + y)/6$	$(-3 + x + 2y)/6$	0	0

Note the symmetric form of ϕ_3 on T_1 and T_2.

The Fourth Basis Function

We can exploit the symmetry of the figure to find ϕ_4 from ϕ_2 by interchanging
the roles of x and y and interchanging the triangular regions $T_1 \leftrightarrow T_2$ and
$T_3 \leftrightarrow T_4$; doing this gives

	T_1	T_2	T_3	T_4
ϕ_4	0	$(x - y)/3$	$(x - y)/3$	0

The Fifth Basis Function

$\phi_5 = 0$ at nodes 1, 2, 3, and 4, and $\phi_5 = 1$ at node 5; $\phi_5 = 0$ on T_1 and T_2. Thus

	T_1	T_2	T_3	T_4
ϕ_5	0	0	$(3 - x - 2y)/3$	$(3 - 2x - y)/3$

15.5.3 Computing the Coefficients

It is a relatively easy task to determine the coefficients c_j for the basis functions that correspond to boundary nodes ($j = n+1, \ldots, m$); they are chosen so that the solution U satisfies the boundary conditions at those nodes.

To find the coefficients corresponding to the interior nodes, we must minimize

$$\iint_R [U_x^2 + U_y^2 - r(x, y)U^2 + 2f(x, y)U]\, dx\, dy, \qquad \text{with } U = \sum_{j=1}^{m} c_j\, \phi_j.$$

The minimum occurs where $\dfrac{\partial U}{\partial c_i} = 0$, for $1 \leq i \leq n$.

This gives a linear system of equations, $\mathbf{Ac} = \mathbf{d}$, where
$\mathbf{A} = [a_{ij}], 1 \leq i, j \leq n,$

$$a_{ij} = \iint_R [\phi_i]_x\, [\phi_j]_x + [\phi_i]_y\, [\phi_j]_y - r(x,y)\, \phi_i\phi_j\, dx\, dy, \tag{15.1}$$

and

$$d_i = -\iint_R f(x,y)\, \phi_i\, dx\, dy - \sum_{j=n+1}^{m} c_j\, b_{ij}, \tag{15.2}$$

in which

$$b_{ij} = \iint_R [\phi_i]_x\, [\phi_j]_x + [\phi_i]_y\, [\phi_j]_y - r(x,y)\, \phi_i\phi_j\, dx\, dy,$$

$$1 \leq i \leq n; \quad n + 1 \leq j \leq m. \tag{15.3}$$

Note that for piece-wise planar basis functions, the partial derivatives that occur in the integrals in these equations (15.1–15.3) are just constants, so that the corresponding portion of the integral is a constant times the area of the triangular subregion. This is one of the ways in which triangular subregions simplify the computations.

Example 15.9 A Finite-Element Solution

Consider the problem $u_{xx} + u_{yy} = 0$
with boundary conditions

$$u = x/3 \text{ for } y = 0, 0 \leq x \leq 3, \quad u = y/3 \text{ for } x = 0, 0 \leq y \leq 3,$$
$$u = 1 \text{ for } y = 1, 0 \leq x \leq 3, \quad u = 1 \text{ for } x = 1, 0 \leq y \leq 3.$$

The basis functions found in Example 15.9 are appropriate for problems defined on $0 \leq x \leq 3; 0 \leq y \leq 3$, with the triangular subdivision shown in Figure 15.11.

To Find the Coefficients for the n Nodes on the Boundary

For the given region, $U(V_2) = 1$, $U(V_3) = 1$, $U(V_4) = 1$, and $U(V_5) = 0$. Since we are looking for $U = c_1\, \phi_1 + c_2\, \phi_2 + c_3\, \phi_3 + c_4\, \phi_4 + c_5\, \phi_5$ to satisfy the boundary conditions, and because each ϕ_j is zero except at node j, we must have $c_2 = c_3 = c_4 = 1$ and $c_5 = 0$.

To Find the Coefficients for the Interior Node

We have only one interior node, so we have only one coefficient to determine from the given equations. We must solve $A\,c_1 = d$, where

$$A = \iint_R [\phi_1]_x\,[\phi_1]_x + [\phi_1]_y\,[\phi_1]_y\,dx\,dy \qquad \text{and} \quad d = -\sum_{j=2}^{5} c_j\,b_j,$$

in which $\quad b_j = \iint_R [\phi_1]_x\,[\phi_j]_x + [\phi_1]_y\,[\phi_j]_y\,dx\,dy, \qquad 2 \le j \le 5.$

Because $c_5 = 0$, the calculation of b_5 is not required, but we do have a number of integrations to perform. We have used the fact that both $r(x, y)$ and $f(x, y)$ are zero in this example to simplify the expressions for A and d also.

We note, for use in the following calculations, the areas of the triangular regions:

$$A_1 = \text{area}(T_1) = 3; \ A_2 = 3; \ A_3 = 3/2; \qquad A_4 = 3/2.$$

To Find a

	T_1	T_2	T_3	T_4
ϕ_1	$(3-y)/2$	$(3-x)/2$	y	x
$[\phi_1]_x$	0	$-1/2$	0	1
$[\phi_1]_y$	$-1/2$	0	1	0

$$a = \iint_R [\phi_1]_x\,[\phi_1]_x + [\phi_1]_y\,[\phi_1]_y\,dx\,dy$$

$$= \iint_{T1} 0 + 1/4\ dx\,dy + \iint_{T2} 1/4 + 0\ dxdy + \iint_{T3} 0 + 1\ dxdy + \iint_{T4} 1 + 0\ dxdy$$

$$= 1/4\ (\text{area of } T_1 + \text{area of } T_2) + \text{area of } T_3 + \text{area of } T_4$$

$$= (1/4)(3 + 3) + 3/2 + 3/2 = 9/2.$$

To Find b_2

	T_1	T_2	T_3	T_4
ϕ_2	$(-x+y)/3$	0	0	$(-x+y)/3$
$[\phi_2]_x$	$-1/3$	0	0	$-1/3$
$[\phi_2]_y$	$1/3$	0	0	$1/3$

$$b_2 = \iint_R [\phi_1]_x\,[\phi_2]_x + [\phi_1]_y\,[\phi_2]_y\,dx\,dy$$

$$= \iint_{T1} 0 + (-1/2)(1/3)dxdy + \iint_{T2} 0 + 0\ dx\,dy$$

$$+ \iint_{T3} 0 + 0\ dxdy + \iint_{T4} (1)(-1/3) + 0\ dx\,dy$$

$$= (-1/6)(\text{area of } T_1) + (-1/3)(\text{area of } T_4) = -1.$$

To Find b_3

	T_1	T_2	T_3	T_4
ϕ_3	$(-3+2x+y)/6$	$(-3+x+2y)/6$	0	0
$[\phi_3]_x$	1/3	1/6	0	0
$[\phi_3]_y$	1/6	1/3	0	0

$$b_3 = \iint_R [\phi_1]_x\,[\phi_3]_x + [\phi_1]_y\,[\phi_3]_y\,dx\,dy$$

$$= \iint_{T1} 0 + (-1/2)(1/6)dx dy + \iint_{T2} (-1/2)(1/3)$$

$$+ 0\,dx dy + \iint_{T_3} 0 + 0\,dx dy + \iint_{T4} 0 + 0\,dx dy$$

$$= (-1/2)(\text{area of } T_1) + (-1/6)(\text{area of } T_2 = -3/4.$$

To Find b_4

	T_1	T_2	T_3	T_4
ϕ_4	0	$(x-y)/3$	$(x-y)/3$	0
$[\phi_4]x$	0	1/3	1/3	0
$[\phi_4]y$	1/3	-1/3	-1/3	0

$$b_4 = \iint_R [\phi_1]_x\,[\phi_4]_x + [\phi_1]_y\,dx dy$$

$$= \iint_{T1} 0 + 0\,dx dy + \iint_{T2} (-1/2)(1/3) + 0 dx dy$$

$$+ \iint_{T3} 0 + (1)(-1/3)\,dx\,dy + \iint_{T4} 0 + 0\,dx dy$$

$$= (-1/6)(\text{area of } T_2) + (-1/3)(\text{area of } T_3) = -1.$$

The Right-Hand Side

$$d = -[c_2\,b_2 + c_3\,b_3 + c_4\,b_4] = -[b_2 + b_3 + b_4]$$
$$= -[(-1) + (-3/4) + (-1)] = 11/4$$

The equation to be solved is

$$9/2\,c_1 = 11/4 \rightarrow c_1 = 11/18$$

The solution of the potential equation is

$$U = (11/8)\,\phi_1 + \phi_2 + \phi_3 + \phi_4,$$

which simplifies to

	T_1	T_2	T_3	T_4
U	$5/12 + 7/36\,y$	$5/12 + 7/36\,x$	$1/3\,x + 5/18\,y$	$5/18\,x + 1/3\,y$

15.5.4   Algorithms

We now give several algorithms that describe the steps needed to find a finite-element solution

$$U = \sum_{j=1}^{m} c_j \, \phi_j$$

for a PDE

$$u_{xx} + u_{yy} + r(x, y)\, u = f(x, y) \quad \text{on the region } R$$
$$u(x, y) = g(x, y) \qquad\qquad\qquad\;\; \text{on the boundary of } R$$

The corresponding functional to be minimized is

$$I[u] = \iint_R [u_x^2 + u_y^2 - r(x, y)u^2 + 2f(x, y)\, dx\, dy.$$

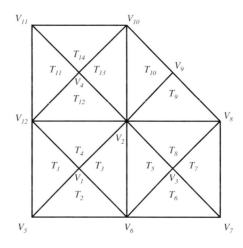

FIGURE 15.13 R, a subset of $0 \le x \le 2$, $0 \le y \le 2$, subdivided into 14 triangular subregions.

The overall solution process is comprised of the following three steps:

1) Define the geometry of the regions.
2) Define the basis functions for the given geometry.
3) Determine the coefficients c_j that multiply the basis functions.

Coefficients c_j for the basis functions that correspond to boundary nodes ($j = n+1, \ldots, m$) are chosen so that the solution U satisfies the boundary conditions at those nodes.

Coefficients c_j for the basis functions that correspond to interior nodes ($j = 1, \ldots, n$), so that U minimizes the integral $I[u]$.

Input

V	*matrix of the coordinates of the node (interior nodes first)*
n	*number of interior nodes*
m	*total number of nodes*
T	*matrix defining the triangular subregions (index of each vertex)*
p	*number of triangular subregions*

Compute, or input area of each triangle. In general, for a triangle with corners at (x_1, y_1), (x_2, y_2) and (x_3, y_3), the area is $\mathtt{Area(T) = 0.5\ det\ (TT)}$, where

$$TT = \begin{bmatrix} x_1 & y_1 & 1 \\ x_2 & y_2 & 1 \\ x_3 & y_3 & 1 \end{bmatrix}$$

Example 15.10 Define Geometry for Finite-Element Problem

For the region illustrated in Fig. 15.13, the relevant parameters are:

$n = 4$	number of interior nodes
$m = 12$	number of nodes
$p = 14$	number of triangles

Vertices (nodes) are:
$$V = \begin{bmatrix} 1/2 & 1/2 \\ 1 & 1 \\ 3/2 & 3/2 \\ 1/2 & 3/2 \\ 0 & 0 \\ 1 & 0 \\ 2 & 0 \\ 2 & 1 \\ 3/2 & 3/2 \\ 1 & 2 \\ 0 & 2 \\ 0 & 1 \end{bmatrix}$$

Triangles are
$$T = \begin{bmatrix} 1 & 5 & 12 \\ 1 & 5 & 6 \\ 1 & 2 & 6 \\ 1 & 2 & 12 \\ 3 & 2 & 6 \\ 3 & 6 & 7 \\ 3 & 7 & 8 \\ 3 & 8 & 2 \\ 2 & 8 & 9 \\ 2 & 9 & 10 \\ 4 & 11 & 12 \\ 4 & 12 & 2 \\ 4 & 2 & 10 \\ 4 & 10 & 11 \end{bmatrix}$$

Area of each triangle is 1/4, so $H = [1/4, 1/4, \ldots 1/4]$

Input parameters and arrays for the geometry
The basis function for each node has the form A + Bx + Cy on each triangle.
The information is stored in three arrays: *A(m, p); B(m, p);C(m, p);*
        row index gives the node number;
        column index gives the triangular element.
For j = 1 to m   *for each node*
  For k = 1 to p   *for each triangle*
    For i = 1 to 3   *for each vertex*
      M(i, 1) = 1   *form coefficient matrix*
      M(i, 2) = V(T(k,i), 1)
      M(i, 3) = V(T(k,i), 2)
      If T(k,i) == j   *form right-hand side*
        r(i,1) = 1
      Else
        r(i,1) = 0
      End
    End
    x = M\r   *solve M x = r*
    A(j, k) = x(1)
    B(j, k) = x(2)
    C(j, k) = x(3)
  End
End

Example 15.11 Basis Functions

Although we do not need to display the definition of each basis function, it is informative to consider briefly what the information in arrays **A**, **B**, and **C** can tell us for the region defined in Example 15.11. Each row of the matrix corresponds to a basis function, each column to a triangular element. The information about the basis function corresponding to node 1 is in the first row of matrices **A**, **B**, and **C**. Node 1 is a vertex of triangles 1, 2, 3, and 4, so the only possible nonzero coefficients for the first basis function occur in the first four rows. Specifically, the first row of the three arrays are

$$A(1,:) = [0\ 0\ 0\ 2\ 2\ 0 \ldots\ldots\ldots 0];$$
$$B(1,:) = [2\ 0\ -2\ 0\ 0 \ldots\ldots 0];$$
$$C(1,:) = [0\ 2\ 0\ -2\ 0 \ldots\ldots\ 0];$$

This code tells us that the first basis function is

$0 + 2x + 0y$ on T_1,
$0 + 0x + 2y$ on T_2,
$2 - 2x + 0y$ on T_3,
$2 + 0x - 2y$ on T_4,
0 on all other triangles.

It is easy to verify that the function defined in this way has the required values at each of the vertices.

Input
  H   *vector giving areas of triangular subregions*
  A, B, C   *arrays defining basis functions*
  c2   *coefficients of basis functions corresponding to boundary nodes*
             values determined so that U satisfies boundary conditions
Compute c1, vector of coefficient for each interior node
For i = 1 to n
    For j = 1 to n
        For k = 1 to p
            s(k) = B(i, k)*B(j, k) + C(i, k)*C(j , k)
        End
        M (i, j) = s*H^T
    End
End
For i = 1 to n
    For j = n+1 to m
        For k = 1 to p
            s(k) = B(i, k)*B(j, k) + C(i , k)*C(j , k)
        End
        G (i, j − n) = s*H^T
    End
    d(i) = − G*c2^T
End
c1 = M\d^T *coefficients corresponding to interior nodes*
Find the final solution, the vector of coefficients is c = [c1   c2]
UA = A^T*c^T
UB = B^T*c^T
UC = C^T*c^T
U = [UA UB UC]   *concatenation of matrices UA, UB, and UC*

Example 15.12 Finite-Element Solution of the Laplace Equation

We now solve the potential equation on the region shown in Fig. 15.13.
   The boundary conditions are

$u = 0$	for	$0 \leq x \leq 2, y = 0$, and $0 \leq y \leq 2, x = 0$,
$u = x$	for	$0 \leq x \leq 1, y = 2$,
$u = y$	for	$0 \leq y \leq 1, x = 2$,
$u = 1$		along the diagonal boundary.

The geometry has been defined, the areas of the triangles have been determined, and the basis functions have been computed in the previous examples. We find the coefficients of the basis functions so that $U = c_1 \phi_1 + \ldots + c_m \phi_m$ is the desired solution. The vector **c** of coefficients is the concatenation of **c1** (the coefficients corresponding to the interior nodes) and **c2** (the coefficients corresponding to the boundary nodes). The *BC* require that $U = 1$ at nodes 8, 9, and 10 and $U = 0$ at all other nodes; hence $\mathbf{c2} = [1 \quad 1 \quad 1 \quad 0 \quad 0]$. For this example, we find that $\mathbf{c1} = [\ 0.1154, \ 0.4615, \ 0.3654, \ 0.3654, \ 0, \ 0, \ 0\ ]$ so $\mathbf{c} = [0.1154, \ 0.4615, \ 0.3654, \ 0.3654, \ 0, \ 0, \ 0, \ 1, \ 1, \ 1, \ 0, \ 0]$.

The final solution is

$$U = \begin{cases}
0 & + \ 0.2308\,x \ + \ 0 & y & \text{on } T_1 \\
0 & + \ 0 & x \ + \ 0.2308\,y & \text{on } T_2 \\
-0.2308 & + \ 0.2308\,x \ + \ 0.4615\,y & & \text{on } T_3 \\
-0.2308 & + \ 0.4615\,x \ + \ 0.2308\,y & & \text{on } T_4 \\
-0.2692 & + \ 0.2692\,x \ + \ 0.4615\,y & & \text{on } T_5 \\
0 & + \ 0 & x \ + \ 0.7308 & \text{on } T_6 \\
-0.5385 & + \ 0.2692\,x \ + \ 1.0000\,y & & \text{on } T_7 \\
-0.8077 & + \ 0.5385\,x \ + \ 0.7308\,y & & \text{on } T_8 \\
-0.6154 & + \ 0.5385\,x \ + \ 0.5385\,y & & \text{on } T_9 \\
-0.6154 & + \ 0.5385\,x \ + \ 0.5385\,y & & \text{on } T_{10} \\
0 & + \ 0.7308\,x \ + \ 0 & y & \text{on } T_{11} \\
-0.2692 & + \ 0.4615\,x \ + \ 0.2692\,y & & \text{on } T_{12} \\
-0.8077 & + \ 0.7308\,x \ + \ 0.5385\,y & & \text{on } T_{13} \\
-0.5385 & + \ 1.0000\,x \ + \ 0.2692\,y & & \text{on } T_{14}
\end{cases}$$

The computed values at the nodes can be found from these formulas:

Node	x	y	U	Results from formula for
1	1/2	1/2	0.1154	T_1, T_2, T_3, or T_4
2	1	1	0.4615	$T_3, T_4, T_5, T_8, T_9, T_{10}, T_{12}$, or T_{13}
3	3/2	1/2	0.3654	T_5, T_6, T_7, or T_8
4	1/2	3/2	0.3654	T_{11}, T_{12}, T_{13}, or T_{14}
5	0	0	0	T_1, or T_2
6	1	0	0	T_2, T_3, T_5, or T_6
7	2	0	0	T_6 or T_7
8	2	1	1	T_7, T_8, or T_9
9	3/2	3/2	1	T_9 or T_{10}
10	1	2	1	T_{10}, T_{13}, or T_{14}
11	0	2	0	T_{11} or T_{14}
12	0	1	0	T_1, T_4, T_{11}, or T_{12}

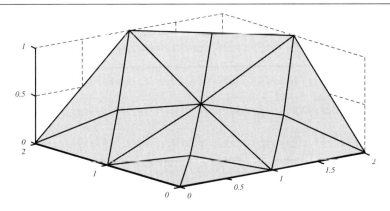

FIGURE 15.14 Solution to Poisson's equation using finite elements.

Professionally developed software packages have a variety of routines for solving
PDE. We conclude this chapter by summarizing briefly the functions in Mathcad
and MATLAB.

15.6.1   Mathcad's Functions

The function `relax` solves the linear system that arises from using the finite-
difference approximations for the partial derivatives in the Poisson PDE on a
square region in the plane. The function is called as

$$\text{relax}(\mathbf{A}, \mathbf{B}, \mathbf{C}, \mathbf{D}, \mathbf{E}, \mathbf{F}, \mathbf{U}, \text{rjac})$$

The matrices $\mathbf{A}$, $\mathbf{B}$, $\mathbf{C}$, $\mathbf{D}$, $\mathbf{E}$ give the coefficients of the linear system of equations.
The matrix $\mathbf{F}$ contains the source term for each point inside the region where the
solution is sought. The matrix $\mathbf{U}$ contains the boundary values and initial guesses
for the solution inside the region. The parameter rjac is the spectral radius (largest
eigenvalue) of the Jacobi iteration matrix.

The function `relax` is more general than the function `multigrid` (discussed
next) in that `relax` allows for arbitrary boundary conditions and does not restrict
the number of mesh subdivisions along the x or y axes (as long as the discretization
has the same number of divisions in each direction). For simplicity in the following
discussion, we take the square region to be the unit square, $0 < x < 1, 0 < y < 1$.

The PDE to be solved is of the form

$$u_{xx} + u_{yy} = f(x, y) \qquad \text{for } 0 < x < 1, 0 < y < 1$$

with boundary conditions

$$u(0, y) = g_1(y) \quad u(0, y) = g_2(y) \quad \text{for } 0 < y < 1$$
$$u(x, 1) = g_3(x) \quad u(x, 1) = g_4(x) \quad \text{for } 0 < x < 1$$

We discretize the region by taking $0 \le j \le n$ and $0 \le k \le n$. The boundary
conditions apply for $j = 0$, $j = n$, $k = 0$, and $k = n$. If the approximate solution is
denoted u, then at each point in the grid we have the discretized equation

$$a_{j,k}\, u_{j+1,k} + b_{j,k}\, u_{j-1,k} + c_{j,k}\, u_{j,k+1} + d_{j,k}\, u_{j,k-1} + e_{j,k} + u_{j,k} = f_{j,k}$$

For the standard finite difference approximations, $a_{jk} = b_{jk} = c_{jk} = d_{jk} = 1$, and
$e_{j,k} = -4$. The value of f_{jk} depends on the right-hand side of the PDE. The information about the boundary conditions is included in matrix $\mathbf{U}$.

The function returns a matrix $\mathbf{S}$, whose elements give the approximate
solution at each grid point of the region.

The function `multigrid` is generally faster than `relax` for the problems for
which `multigrid` is suitable. The method is restricted to problems with 0 boundary conditions, and the number of interior subdivisions in each direction, $n-1$, is a
power of 2. The function is called as

$$\text{multigrid}(\mathbf{M}, \text{ncycle})$$

where $\mathbf{M}$ is an (2^k+1) by (2^k+1) matrix containing the source term at each point of
the region, and ncycle is the number of cycles to be performed at each level of the
multigrid iteration. In general, ncycle $= 2$ gives good results.

15.6.2 MATLAB's Functions

MATLAB has several built-in functions that are helpful for visualizing the solutions generated by the finite-element method. The script that produces the plot in Figure 15.14 illustrates the use of the MATLAB function `trimesh`. The basic function call requires specification of the node indices for each of the triangles (in array T) and the coordinates of the vertices of the triangular regions. The coordinates are given in three arrays: one for the x-coordinate, one for the y-coordinate, and one for the z-coordinate. An additional vector may be used to define edge color; if it is not user specified, edge color is proportional to the z coordinate.

The function `trisurf` is used in the same way as `trimesh`, but plots the surface defined by the triangular elements. The MATLAB code is as follows:

```
% S_plot_15_19
% plot for region in Figure 15.19
% define triangles by giving x, y, and z coord
x = [ 0.5      1       1.5      0.5      0   1   2   2   1.5   1   0   0 ];
y = [ 0.5      1       0.5      1.5      0   0   0   1   1.5   2   2   1 ];
z = [ 0.1154   0.4615  0.3654   0.3654   0   0   0   1   1     1   0   0 ];
        T    = [ 1       5       12
                 1       5       6
                 1       2       6
                 1       2       12
                 3       2       6
                 3       6       7
                 3       7       8
                 3       8       2
                 2       8       9
                 2       9       10
                 4       11      12
                 4       12      2
                 4       2       10
                 4       10      11];
trimesh(T, x, y, z)
```

Finally, for more general polygonal regions, MATLAB has a function, `inpolygon`, to determine whether a given point is inside the polygon. The point or points to be checked are given in two vectors, **x** and **y**. The polygon is defined by two other vectors, **u** and **v**. The returned value is 1 if the point is strictly inside the polygon, 0.5 if the point is on the boundary, and 0 otherwise. The function call is `in = inpolygon(x,y,u,v)`. For example, to determine whether the points (1, 1), (2, 0), and (3, 0.5) are inside the square $0 \le x \le 2, 0 \le y \le 2$, we define

```
x = [ 1   2   3];
y = [ 1   0   0.5];
u = [ 0   2   2   0];
v = [ 0   0   2   2];
in = inpolygon(x, y, u, v)
```

The result

```
in =            1           0.5           0
```

shows that the first point is inside the square, the second is on the boundary, and the third is outside the square.

Heat Equation: Parabolic PDE: A finite-difference solution of the one-dimensional heat equation

$$u_t = c\, u_{xx} \qquad \text{for } 0 < x < 1, \quad 0 < t \le T,$$

with initial conditions $\quad u(x, 0) = f(x), \quad 0 < x < 1,$

and boundary conditions $\quad u(0, t) = g_0(t), \quad u(1, t) = g_1(t), \quad 0 < t \le T,$

utilizes the mesh $\quad h = \Delta x = 1/n, \; k = \Delta t = T/m, \text{ with } r = \dfrac{c\,k}{h^2}.$

Explicit method (stability requires $0 < r \le 0.5$)

$$u_{i,j+1} = r\, u_{i-1,j} + (1 - 2r)\, u_{i,j} + r\, u_{i+1,j}.$$

Implicit method (unconditionally stable)

$$u_{i,j} = (-r)\, u_{i-1,j+1} + (1 + 2r)\, u_{i,j+1} + (-r)\, u_{i+1,j+1};$$

Crank-Nicolson method (unconditionally stable)

$$-\frac{r}{2} u_{i-1,j+1} + (1 + r)\, u_{i,j+1} - \frac{r}{2} u_{i+1,j+1} = \frac{r}{2} u_{i-1,j} + (1 - r)\, u_{i,j} + \frac{r}{2} u_{i+1,j};$$

Wave Equation: Hyperbolic PDE: A finite-difference solution of the

$$u_{tt} - c^2\, u_{xx} = 0 \text{ for } 0 \le x \le a, \text{ and } 0 \le t,$$

with initial conditions $\quad u(x, 0) = f_1(x), \; u_t(x, 0) = f_2(x), \text{ for } 0 \le x \le a,$

and boundary conditions $\quad u(0, t) = g_1(t), \quad u(a, t) = g_2(t), \quad \text{for } 0 < t,$

utilizes the mesh $\quad h = \Delta x = a/n, \quad k = \Delta t, \quad \text{with } p = \dfrac{c\,k}{h} = \dfrac{\Delta t}{\Delta x}.$

Explicit Method (Stability Requires $p \le 1$). The general form of the difference equation is

$$u_{i,j+1} = p^2\, u_{i-1,j} + 2(1 - p^2)\, u_{i,j} + p^2\, u_{i+1,j} - u_{i,j-1}.$$

The equation for u at the first time step

$$u_{i,1} = 0.5\, p^2\, u_{i-1,0} + (1 - p^2)\, u_{i,0} + 0.5\, p^2\, u_{i+1,0} + k\, f_2(x_i);$$

Implicit Method (Unrestricted Stability). The general form of the difference equation is

$$-p^2 u_{i-1,j+1} + 2(1 + p^2)u_{i,j+1} - p^2 u_{i+1,j+1} = 4u_{i,j} + p^2 u_{i-1,j-1} - 2(1 + p^2)u_{i,j-1} + p^2 u_{i+1,j-1}$$

The equations for $j = 0$ have the form:

$$4(1 + p^2)u_{1,1} - 2p^2 u_{2,1} = 4u_{1,0} - 2p^2 k f_2(x_0) + 4(1 + p^2)k f_2(x_1) - 2p^2 k f_2(x_2) + 2p^2 u_{0,1}$$
$$-2p^2 u_{1,1} + 4(1 p^2)u_{2,1} - 2p^2 u_{3,1} = 4u_{2,0} - 2p^2 k f_2(x_1) + 4(1 + p^2)k f_2(x_2) - 2p^2 k f_2(x_3)$$
$$\vdots$$

$$-2p^2 u_{i-1,1} + 4(1\, p^2)u_{i,1} - 2\, p^2 u_{i+1,1} =$$
$$4u_{i,0} - 2p^2 k f_2(x_{i-1}) + 4(1 + p^2)k f_2(x_i) - 2p^2 k f_2(x_{i+1})$$
$$\vdots$$

$$-2\, p^2 u_{n-2,1} + 4(1 + p^2)u_{n-1,1} =$$
$$4u_{n-1,0} - 2p^2 k f_2(x_{n-2}) + 4(1 + p^2)k f_2(x_{n-1}) - 2p^2 k f_2(x_n) + 2p^2 u_{n,1}$$

The value of u at each subsequent time step can be found from:

$$2(1 + p^2)u_{1,j+1} - 4u_{1,j} - 2(1 + p^2)u_{1,j-1} + p^2 u_{2,j-1} + p^2 u_{0,j+1} + p^2 u_{0,j-1}$$

$$-p^2 u_{1,j+1} + 2(1 + p^2)u_{2,j+1} - p^2 u_{3,j+1} = 4u_{2,j} + p^2 u_{1,j-1} - 2(1 + p^2)u_{2,j-1} + p^2 u_{3,j-1}$$

$$\vdots$$

$$-p^2 u_{i-1,j+1} + 2(1 + p^2)u_{i,j+1} - p^2 u_{i+1,j+1} = 4u_{i,j} + p^2 u_{i-1,j-1} - 2(1 + p^2)u_{i,j-1} + p^2 u_{i+1,j-1}$$

$$\vdots$$

$$-p^2 u_{n-2,j+1} + 2(1 + p^2)u_{n-1,j+1} = 4u_{n-1,j} + p^2 u_{n-2,j-1} - 2(1 + p^2)u_{n-1,j-1} + p^2 u_{n,j-1} + p^2 u_{n,j+1}$$

Poisson's Equation: Elliptic PDE

Finite-difference solution

$$u_{xx} + u_{yy} = f(x, y) \qquad 0 \le x \le 1; \qquad 0 \le y \le 1.$$

with boundary conditions

$$u(a, y) = h_1(y) \quad u(b, y) = h_2(y) \quad c < y < d$$
$$u(x, c) = k_1(x) \quad u(x, d) = k_2(x) \quad a < x < b$$

utilizes a mesh in the *x-y* plane

$$x_i = a + ih, \quad i = 0, 1, \ldots n \quad h = \Delta x = (b - a)/n$$
$$y_j = c + jk, \quad j = 0, 1, \ldots m \quad k = \Delta y = (d - c)/m$$

the general form of the difference equatio is

$$\frac{1}{k^2}[u_{i,j+1} - 2u_{i,j} + u_{i,j-1}] + \frac{1}{h^2}[u_{i+1,j} - 2u_{i,j} + u_{i-1,j}] = f_{ij}.$$

Finite-element solution

$$u_{xx} + u_{yy} + r(x, y)\, u = f(x, y) \qquad\qquad \text{on the region } R$$
$$u(x, y) = g(x, y) \text{ on boundary of } R$$

seeks to minimize the functional

$$I[u] = \iint_R [u_x^2 + u_y^2 - r(x,y)u^2 + 2f(x,y)u]\, dx\, dy$$

where u is a linear combination of the basis functions.

If R is divided into p triangular subregions, $T_1, T_2, \ldots T_p$, there is a piecewise-linear basis function corresponding to each node. The basis function corresponding to node j has the value one at node j and zero at all other nodes.

SUGGESTIONS FOR FURTHER READING

Our discussion of numerical methods for partial differential equations in this chapter provides only a brief introduction to an extensive area of research and application. The following are some of the many excellent sources for further study of these topics.

Ames, W. F. *Numerical Methods for Partial Differential Equations*, 3rd ed. Academic Press, Boston, 1992.

Boyce, W. E., and R. C. DiPrima. *Elementary Differential Equations and Boundary Value Problems,* 5th ed. Wiley & Sons, New York, 1992.

Birkhoff, G., and R. E. Lynch. *Numerical Solution of Elliptic Problems.* SIAM, Philadelphia, 1984.

Celia, M. A., and W. G. Gray. *Numerical Methods for Differential Equations.* Prentice-Hall, Englewood Cliffs, NJ, 1992.

Colton, D. *Partial Differential Equations.* Random House, New York, 1988. (This text includes a brief history of PDE, pp. 49–53.)

Forsythe, G. E., and W. R. Wasow. *Finite-Difference Methods for Partial Differential Equations.* Wiley & Sons, New York, 1960.

Garcia, A. L. *Numerical Methods for Physics.* Prentice-Hall, Englewood Cliffs, NJ, 1994.

Golub, G. H., and J. M. Ortega. *Scientific Computing and Differential Equations: An Introduction to Numerical Methods.* Academic Press, Boston, 1992.

Haberman, R. *Elementary Applied Partial Differential Equations, with Fourier Series and Boundary Value Problems.* Prentice-Hall, Englewood Cliffs, NJ, 1983.

Hall, C. A., and T. A. Porsching. *Numerical Analysis of Partial Differential Equations.* Prentice-Hall, Englewood Cliffs, NJ, 1990.

Meis, T. and U. Marcowitz. *Numerical Solution of Partial Differential Equations.* Springer-Verlag, New York, 1981.

Mitchell, A. R. *Computational Methods in Partial Differential Equations.* Wiley & Sons, London, 1969.

Svobony, T. *Mathematical Modeling for Industry and Engineering.* Prentice Hall, Upper Saddle River, NJ, 1998.

Troutman, J. L., and M. Bautista. *Boundary Value Problems of Applied Mathematics.* PWS Publishing, Boston, 1994.

Zauderer, E. *Partial Differential Equations of Applied Mathematics,* 2nd ed. Wiley & Sons, New York, 1989.

The finite-element method is important in mathematics and engineering; the following references include discussion of the method from several different points of view.

Axelsson, O., and V. A. Barker. *Finite Element Solution of Boundary Value Problems.* Academic Press, New York, 1984.

Becker, E. B., Carey, G. F., and Oden, J. T. *Finite Elements: An Introduction.* Vol. 1. Prentice-Hall, Englewood Cliffs, NJ, 1981.

Davies. A. J. *The Finite Element Method: A First Approach.* Clarendon Press, Oxford, 1980.

Mitchell, A. R., and R. Wait. *The Finite Element Method in Partial Differential Equations.* Wiley & Sons, London, 1977.

Silvester, P. P., and R. L. Ferrari. *The Finite Elements for Electrical Engineers,* 3rd ed. Cambridge University Press, Cambridge, 1996.

Strang, G., and G. Fix. *An Analysis of the Finite Element Method.* Prentice-Hall, Englewood Cliffs, NJ, 1973.

Zienkiewicz, O. C., and Taylor, R. L. *The Finite Element Method,* 4th ed., Vol. 1. London: McGraw-Hill, 1989.

PRACTICE THE TECHNIQUES

For Problems P15.1 to P15.10, solve the one-dimensional heat equation using the specified finite-difference method.

    a. Use the explicit finite-difference method with $\Delta x = 0.2$ and $\Delta t = 0.01$.

    b. Use the explicit finite-difference method with $\Delta x = 0.2$ and $\Delta t = 0.02$.

    c. Use the explicit finite-difference method with $\Delta x = 0.2$ and $\Delta t = 0.1$.

    d. Use the implicit finite-difference method with $\Delta x = 0.2$ and $\Delta t = 0.1$.

    e. Use the Crank-Nicolson method with $\Delta x = 0.2$ and $\Delta t = 0.1$.

P15.1   Solve $u_t - u_{xx} = 0$, for $0 \leq x \leq 1$, $0 < t < 0.5$, with initial condition $u(x, 0) = 0$, (for $0 \leq x \leq 1$), and boundary conditions $u(0, t) = 0$, $u(1, t) = t$ (for $0 < t < 0.5$).

P15.2   Solve $u_t - u_{xx} = 0$, for $0 \leq x \leq 1$, $0 < t < 0.5$, with initial condition $u(x, 0) = x$, (for $0 \leq x \leq 1$), and boundary conditions $u(0, t) = 0$, $u(1, t) = 1$ (for $0 < t < 0.5$).

P15.3   Solve $u_t - u_{xx} = 0$, for $0 \leq x \leq 1$, $0 < t < 0.5$, with initial condition $u(x, 0) = x(1 - x)$, (for $0 \leq x \leq 1$), and boundary conditions $u(0, t) = 0$, $u(1, t) = 0$ (for $0 < t < 0.5$).

P15.4   Solve $u_t - u_{xx} = 0$, for $0 \leq x \leq 1$, $0 < t < 0.5$, with initial condition $u(x, 0) = 10$, (for $0 \leq x \leq 1$), and boundary conditions $u(0, t) = 0$, $u(1, t) = 0$ (for $0 < t < 0.5$).

P15.5   Solve $u_t - u_{xx} = 0$, for $0 \leq x \leq 1$, $0 < t < 0.5$, with initial condition $u(x, 0) = \sin(4\pi x)$, (for $0 \leq x \leq 1$), and boundary conditions $u(0, t) = 0$, $u(1, t) = 0$ (for $0 < t < 0.5$).

P15.6   Solve $u_t - u_{xx} = 0$, for $0 \leq x \leq 1$, $0 < t < 0.5$, with initial condition $u(x, 0) = \sin(\pi x) + \sin(2\pi x) + \sin(3\pi x)$, ($0 \leq x \leq 1$), and boundary conditions $u(0, t) = 0$, $u(1, t) = 0$ ($0 < t < 0.5$).

P15.7   Solve $u_t - u_{xx} = 0$, for $0 \leq x \leq 1$, $0 < t < 0.5$, with initial condition $u(x, 0) = \sin(\pi x)$, (for $0 \leq x \leq 1$), and boundary conditions $u(0, t) = 0$, $u(1, t) = 1$ (for $0 < t < 0.5$).

P15.8   Solve $u_t - u_{xx} = 0$, for $0 \leq x \leq 1$, $0 < t < 0.5$, with initial condition $u(x, 0) = x$, ($0 \leq x \leq 1$), and boundary conditions $u_x(0, t) = 0$, $u_x(1, t) = 0$ ($0 < t < 0.5$), i.e., ends insulated.

P15.9   Solve $u_t - u_{xx} = 0$, for $0 \leq x \leq 1$, $0 < t < 0.5$, with initial condition

$$u(x, 0) = \begin{cases} 0, & \text{for } 0 \leq x \leq 0.2, \\ 20, & \text{for } 0.2 < x < 0.8, \\ 0, & \text{for } 0.8 \leq x \leq 1, \end{cases}$$

and boundary conditions $u(0, t) = 0$, and $u(1, t) = 0$ ($0 < t < 0.5$).

P15.10   Solve $u_t - u_{xx} = 0$, for $0 \leq x \leq 1$, $0 < t < 0.5$, with initial condition $u(x, 0) = x^2$, (for $0 \leq x \leq 1$), and boundary conditions $u(0, t) = 0$, $u(1, t) = 0$ (for $0 < t < 0.5$).

For Problems P15.11 to P15.15, solve the wave equation using the following finite-difference schemes.

    a. Use the explicit finite-difference method with $\Delta x = 0.1$ and $\Delta t = 0.1$.

    b. Use the explicit finite-difference method with $\Delta x = 0.1$ and $\Delta t = 0.2$.

    c. Use the implicit finite-difference method with $\Delta x = 0.1$ and $\Delta t = 0.2$.

P15.11   Solve $u_{tt} - u_{xx} = 0$, for $0 \leq x \leq 1$, $0 < t < 2$, with initial conditions (string plucked in the middle, zero initial velocity)

$$u(x, 0) = 0.2 \, x, \qquad \text{for } 0 \leq x \leq 5.0,$$
$$u(x, 0) = 0.2 \, (1 - x), \quad \text{for } 0.5 < x < 1,$$
$$u_x(x, 0) = 0,$$

and boundary conditions $u(0, t) = 0$, and $u(1, t) = 0$ ($0 < t < 2$).

P15.12   Solve $u_{tt} - u_{xx} = 0$, for $0 \leq x \leq 1$, $0 < t < 2$, with initial conditions (string plucked at $x = 0.2$, zero initial velocity)

$$u(x, 0) = \begin{cases} 0.5 \, x, & \text{for } 0 \leq x \leq 0.2, \\ 0.1 - (x - 0.2)/8, & \text{for } 0.2 < x < 1, \end{cases}$$

$u_x(x, 0) = 0$, and boundary conditions $u(0, t) = 0$, and $u(1, t) = 0$ ($0 < t < 2$).

P15.13   Solve $u_{tt} - u_{xx} = 0$, for $0 \leq x \leq 1$, $0 < t < 2$, with initial conditions $u(x, 0) = 0$ and $u_x(x, 0) = 0$, and boundary conditions $u(0, t) = 0$, $u(1, t) = 0.2 \sin(t)$ (for $0 < t < 2$).

P15.14 Solve $u_{tt} - u_{xx} = 0$, for $0 \le x \le 1$, $0 < t < 2$, with initial conditions $u(x, 0) = 0$ and $u_x(x, 0) = 0$, and boundary conditions $u(0, t) = 0$, $u(1, t) = 0.2 \sin(\pi t)$ (for $0 < t < 2$).

P15.15 Solve $u_{tt} - u_{xx} = 0$, for $0 \le x \le 1$, $0 < t < 2$, with initial conditions $u(x, 0) = 0$ and $u_x(x, 0) = \sin(\pi x)$, and boundary conditions $u(0, t) = 0$, $u(1, t) = 0$ (for $0 < t < 2$).

For Problems P15.16 to P15.25, solve the potential equation using the finite-difference method with the specified mesh.

    a.   *Use $\Delta x = 0.25$ and $\Delta y = 0.25$.*
    b.   *Use $\Delta x = 0.2$ and $\Delta y = 0.2$.*
    c.   *Use $\Delta x = 0.1$ and $\Delta y = 0.1$.*

P15.16 Solve $u_{xx} + u_{yy} = 0$, for $0 \le x \le 1$, $0 \le y \le 1$, with boundary conditions $u(x, 0) = x$, $u(0, y) = y$, $u(x, 1) = 1$, and $u(1, y) = 1$.

P15.17 Solve $u_{xx} + u_{yy} = 0$, for $0 \le x \le 1$, $0 \le y \le 1$, with boundary conditions $u(x, 0) = 0$, $u(0, y) = 0$, $u(x, 1) = x$, and $u(1, y) = y$.

P15.18 Solve $u_{xx} + u_{yy} = 0$, for $0 \le x \le 1$, $0 \le y \le 1$, with boundary conditions $u(x, 0) = x$, $u(0, y) = 2y$, $u(x, 1) = 2$, and $u(1, y) = 1+y$.

P15.19 Solve $u_{xx} + u_{yy} = 0$, for $0 \le x \le 1$, $0 \le y \le 1$, with boundary conditions $u(x, 0) = x^2$, $u(0, y) = -y^2$, $u(x, 1) = x^2 + x - 1$, and $u(1, y) = 1 + y - y^2$.

P15.20 Solve $u_{xx} + u_{yy} = 0$, for $0 \le x \le 1$, $0 \le y \le 1$, with boundary conditions $u(x, 0) = x^2 + 1$, $u(0, y) = -y^2 + 1$, $u(x, 1) = x^2$, and $u(1, y) = 2 - y^2$.

P15.21 Solve $u_{xx} + u_{yy} = 0$, for $0 \le x \le 1$, $0 \le y \le 1$, with boundary conditions $u(x, 0) = x^2 - 1$, $u(0, y) = -y^2 - 1$, $u(x, 1) = x^2 + x - 2$, and $u(1, y) = y - y^2$.

P15.22 Solve $u_{xx} + u_{yy} = 0$, for $0 \le x \le 1$, $0 \le y \le 1$, with boundary conditions $u(x, 0) = x^3$, $u(0, y) = y^3$, $u(x, 1) = x^3 - 3x^2 - 2x + 1$, and $u(1, y) = y^3 - 3y^2 - 2y + 1$.

P15.23 Solve $u_{xx} + u_{yy} = 0$, for $0 \le x \le 1$, $0 \le y \le 1$, with boundary conditions $u(x, 0) = x^3$, $u(0, y) = y^3$, $u(x, 1) = x^3 - 3x^2 + x + 1$, and $u(1, y) = y^3 - 3y^2 + y + 1$.

P15.24 Solve $u_{xx} + u_{yy} = 0$ for $0 \le x \le 1$, $0 \le y \le 1$, with boundary conditions $u(x, 0) = x^3$, $u(0, y) = y$, $u(x, 1) = x^3 - 3x + 1$, and $u(1, y) = y + 1 - 3y^2$.

P15.25 Solve $u_{xx} + u_{yy} = 0$ for $0 \le x \le 1$, $0 \le y \le 1$, with boundary conditions $u(x, 0) = 0$, $u(0, y) = y^3 + y$, $u(x, 1) = 2 + x - 3x^2$, and $u(1, y) = y^3 - y$.

For Problems P15.26 to P15.35, solve the potential equation (given in P15.16 to P15.25, respectively) using the finite-element method with a mesh of 16 triangles. This mesh is similar to (an extension and rescaling of) that shown in Fig. 15.13; the triangles are defined in the matrices V and T, (compare to those given in Example 15.10.) Note that V_9 is now an interior node, the new node, V_{13} is a boundary node.

$$V = \begin{bmatrix} 1/4 & 1/4 \\ 1/2 & 1/2 \\ 3/4 & 1/4 \\ 1/4 & 3/4 \\ 0 & 0 \\ 1/2 & 0 \\ 1 & 0 \\ 1 & 1/2 \\ 3/4 & 3/4 \\ 1/2 & 1 \\ 0 & 1 \\ 0 & 1/2 \\ 1 & 1 \end{bmatrix}$$

and

$$T = \begin{bmatrix} 1 & 5 & 12 \\ 1 & 5 & 6 \\ 1 & 2 & 6 \\ 1 & 2 & 12 \\ 3 & 2 & 6 \\ 3 & 6 & 7 \\ 3 & 7 & 8 \\ 3 & 8 & 2 \\ 2 & 8 & 9 \\ 2 & 9 & 10 \\ 4 & 11 & 12 \\ 4 & 12 & 2 \\ 4 & 2 & 10 \\ 4 & 10 & 11 \\ 8 & 9 & 13 \\ 9 & 10 & 13 \end{bmatrix}$$

For Problems P15.36 to P15.40, solve the Poisson equation

a. Use the finite-difference method with $\Delta x = 0.25$ and $\Delta y = 0.25$.
b. Use the finite-difference method with $\Delta x = 0.2$ and $\Delta y = 0.2$.
c. Use the finite-difference method with $\Delta x = 0.1$ and $\Delta y = 0.1$.
d. Use the finite-element method with a mesh of 16 triangles, as described for P15.26-P15.35.

P15.36 Solve $u_{xx} + u_{yy} = 6x$ for $0 \le x \le 1, 0 \le y \le 1$, with boundary conditions $u(x, 0) = x^3$, $u(0, y) = y$, $u(x, 1) = x^3 - 3x + 1$, and $u(1, y) = -2y + 1$.

P15.37 Solve $u_{xx} + u_{yy} = 2x + 2 - 2y$ for $0 \le x \le 1$, $0 \le y \le 1$, with boundary conditions $u(x, 0) = x^2$, $u(0, y) = y$, $u(x, 1) = x^2 + 1$, and $u(1, y) = 1 + y^2$.

P15.38 Solve $u_{xx} + u_{yy} = 2x + 2 - 2y$ for $0 \le x \le 1$, $0 \le y \le 1$, with boundary conditions $u(x, 0) = x^2$, $u(0, y) = y$, $u(x, 1) = x + 1$, and $u(1, y) = 1 + y^2$.

P15.39 Solve $u_{xx} + u_{yy} = 2(1 + y)$ for $0 \le x \le 1, 0 \le y \le 1$, with boundary conditions $u(x, 0) = x^3$, $u(0, y) = y^2$, $u(x, 1) = x^3 + x^2 + 1$, and $u(1, y) = -2y^2 + 4y + 1$.

P15.40 Solve $u_{xx} + u_{yy} = \sin(\pi x)$, for $0 \le x \le 1, 0 \le y \le 1$, with boundary conditions $u(x, 0) = x$, $u(0, y) = y$, $u(x, 1) = 1$, and $u(1, y) = 1$.

EXPLORE SOME APPLICATIONS

A15.1 The telegrapher's equation, $v_{tt} - c^2 v_{xx} + 2 av_t = 0$, which governs propagation of signals on telegraph lines, is an example of a wave equation with damping. Investigate the numerical solution of this equation for a variety of initial and boundary conditions, and parameter values for a and c. (See Zauderer, 1989, or Svobodny, 1998, for discussion.)

A15.2 The standard inviscid Burger's equation,

$$\frac{\partial}{\partial t} \rho = -\frac{\partial}{\partial x} \left(\left(\frac{1}{2} \rho \right) \rho \right) = -\rho \frac{\partial}{\partial x} \rho$$

is a simple nonlinear PDE with wave solutions which describes the evolution of the density of an inviscid fluid. The generalized inviscid Burger's equation is

$$\frac{\partial}{\partial t} \rho = -\frac{\partial}{\partial x} \left(\left(a + \frac{1}{2} b \rho \right) \rho \right).$$

One application of this equation is in the modeling of traffic flow. The density of the traffic ρ depends on both density and velocity according to the equation

$$\frac{\partial}{\partial t} \rho = -\frac{\partial}{\partial x} F(\rho).$$

where $F(\rho) = \rho v(\rho) = \rho v_m(1 - \rho/\rho_m)$; that is, velocity is a linear function of density, with maximum veloc-

ity denoted v_m and maximum density denoted ρ_m. Investigate the solution of this PDE using different choices of finite-difference approximations for the partial derivatives. Take the initial density to be ρ_m for $-100 < x < 0$, and 0 for $0 < x < 500$; find the solution for $-100 < x < 500$. (See Garcia, 1994 for further discussion.)

A15.3 In the heat equation $u_t = c u_{xx}$, the parameter c is the thermal diffusivity of the material. Some typical values (cm^2/sec) are given in the following table, (adapted from Boyce and DiPrima, 1986, p. 515.)

Material	Diffusivity
silver	1.71
copper	1.14
aluminium	0.86
cast iron	0.12

Compare the termperature profile for rods of different materials, each with initial temperature of 100C and ends held at 0C.

A15.4 Compare the termperature profile for rods of different materials (see A15.3), each with initial temperature of 100°C, with one end held at 0°C and the other end insulated.

U15.1 Compare the computational effort required to solve the one-dimensional heat equation using the explicit finite-difference method, the implicit finite-difference method, or the Crank-Nicolson method. The implicit methods (both basic and Crank-Nicolson) allow a larger time step than the explicit method; how much larger does it need to be to have the computational effort be the same as for the explicit method? Investigate these questions both analytically and experimentally for some of the problems P15.1 to P15.10.

U15.2 Compare the computational effort required to solve the one-dimensional wave equation using the explicit finite-difference method and the implicit finite-difference method. The implicit method allows a larger time step than the explicit method; how much larger does it need to be to have the computational effort be the same as for the explicit method? Investigate these questions both analytically and experimentally for some of the problems P15.11 to P15.15.

U15.3 Compare the computational effort required to solve the potential equation using the finite-difference method and the finite-element method. Investigate these questions both analytically and experimentally for some of the problems P15.16 to P15.25.

U15.4 The finite-element method is well suited to domains that are more general than the simple rectangular regions illustrated in the text. Modify the domain for some of the problems given in the practice the techniques section (P15.16 to P15.25) and solve the resulting problem using finite elements.

U15.5 The finite-element method is well suited to problems in which boundary conditions are more general than those illustrated in the text. Modify a portion of the boundary condition for some of the problems given in the practice the techniques section (P15.16 to P15.25) to reflect a no-flux or insulated condition, i.e., take the outward normal to the boundary to be zero; then solve the resulting problem using finite elements.

U15.6 Consider the Poisson equation $u_{xx} + u_{yy} = f(x, y)$, $0 \le x \le 1$; $0 \le y \le 1$, with boundary conditions

$$u(x, 0) = x \quad u(x, 1) = 1 \quad 0 < x < 1$$

$$u(0, y) = y \quad u(1, y) = 1 \quad 0 < y < 1$$

Take

$$f(x,x) = \begin{cases} 1 & \text{for } (x, y) = (1/3, 2/3) \\ 0 & \text{otherwise} \end{cases}$$

Choose an appropriate mesh, and solve using the finite-element method.

U15.7 Consider the Poisson equation $u_{xx} + u_{yy} = f(x, y)$, $0 \le x \le 1$; $0 \le y \le 1$, with boundary conditions

$$u(x, 0) = x \quad u(x, 1) = 1 \quad 0 < x < 1$$

$$u(0, y) = y \quad u(1, y) = 1 \quad 0 < y < 1$$

Take

$$f(x, y) = \begin{cases} 1 & \text{for } (x, y) = (1/4, 1/2) \\ 0 & \text{otherwise} \end{cases}$$

Choose an appropriate mesh, and solve using the finite-difference method.

U15.8 Consider the Poisson equation $u_{xx} + u_{yy} = f(x, y)$; $0 \le x \le 1$; $0 \le y \le 1$. with boundary conditions

$$u(x, 0) = x \quad u(x, 1) = 1 \quad 0 < x < 1$$

$$u(0, y) = y \quad u(1, y) = 1 \quad 0 < y < 1$$

Take

$$f(x, y) = \begin{cases} 1 & \text{for } (x, y) = (1/3, 2/3) \\ 1 & \text{for } (x, y) = (1/4, 1/2) \\ 0 & \text{otherwise} \end{cases}$$

Choose an appropriate mesh, and solve using the finite-element method or the finite-difference method.

Bibliography

Abramowitz, M. and I. A. Stegun (eds.), *Handbook of Mathematical Functions, with Formulas, Graphs, and Mathematical Tables*, Dover, New York, 1965.

Achieser, N. I., *Theory of Approximation*, Dover, New York, 1993.

Acton, F. S., *Numerical Methods That (usually) Work*, Mathematical Association of America, Washington, DC, 1990. (Originally published by Harper and Row, New York, 1970.)

Ames, W. F., *Numerical Methods for Partial Differential Equations*, 3rd ed., Academic Press, Boston, 1992.

Ascher, U. M., R. M. M. Mattheij, R. D. Russell, *Numerical Solution of Boundary Value Problems for Ordinary Differential Equations*, SIAM, Philadelphia, 1995. (Originally published by Prentice Hall, Englewood Cliffs, NJ, 1988.)

Atkinson, K. E., *An Introduction to Numerical Analysis*, 2nd ed., John Wiley, New York, 1989.

Axelsson, O. and V. A. Barker, *Finite Element Solution of Boundary Value Problems*, Academic Press, New York, 1984.

Ayyub, B. M. and R. H. McCuen, *Numerical Methods for Engineers*, Prentice Hall, Upper Saddle River, NJ, 1996.

Bader, G. and P. Deuflhard, "A Semi-implicit Midpoint Rule for Stiff Systems of Ordinary Differential Equations," *Numerische Mathematik,* vol. 41, pp. 373–398, 1983.

Barrett, R., J. Donato, J. Dongarra, V. Eijkhout, R. Pozo, C. Romine, and H. van der Vorst, *Templates for the Solution of Linear Systems: Building Blocks for Iterative Methods*, SIAM, Philadelphia, 1993.

Bartels, R. H., J. C. Beatty, and B. A. Barsky, *An Introduction to Splines for Use in Computer Graphics and Geometric Modeling*, Morgan Kaufmann, Los Altos, CA, 1987.

Becker, E. B., G. F. Carey, and J. T. Oden, *Finite Elements: An Introduction*, Vol. 1, Prentice Hall, Englewood Cliffs, NJ, 1981.

Birkhoff, G. and R. E. Lynch, *Numerical Solution of Elliptic Problems*, SIAM, Philadelphia, 1984.

Bloomfield, P., *Fourier Analysis of Time Series—An Introduction*, Wiley, New York, 1976.

Boyce, W. E. and R. C. DiPrima, *Elementary Differential Equations and Boundary Value Problems*, 4th ed. John Wiley & Sons, New York, 1986.

Boyer, C. B., *The History of the Calculus and Its Conceptual Development*, Dover, New York, 1949.

Bracewell, R. *The Fourier Transform and Its Applications*, McGraw-Hill, 1986.

Brent, R., *Algorithms for Minimization Without Derivatives*, Prentice Hall, Englewood Cliffs, NJ, 1973.

Brezinski, C., *History of Continued Fractions and Padé Approximants*, Springer-Verlag, Berlin, 1991.

Briggs, W. L. and V. E. Henson, *The DFT: An Owner's Manual for the Discrete Fourier Transform*, SIAM, Philadelphia, 1995.

Bringham, E. O., *The Fast Fourier Transform*, Prentice Hall, Englewood Cliffs, 1974.

Brodie, K. W., "Unconstrained Minimization," in *The State of the Art in Numerical Analysis*, D. A. H. Jacobs (ed.), Academic Press, London, pp. 229–268, 1977.

Burden, R. L. and J. D. Faires, *Numerical Analysis*, 6th ed., Prindle, Weber & Schmidt, Boston, 1996.

Cash, J. R. and A. H. Karp, "A Variable Order Runge-Kutta Method for Initial Value Problems with Rapidly Varying Right-Hand Sides," *ACM Transactions on Mathematical Software*, vol. 16, pp. 201–222, 1990.

Celia, M. A. and W. G. Gray, *Numerical Methods for Differential Equations*, Prentice Hall, Englewood Cliffs, NJ, 1992.

Chapman, S. J., *Fortran 90/95 for Scientists and Engineers,* McGraw-Hill, New York, 1997.

Cheney, E. W., *Introduction to Approximation Theory*, McGraw-Hill, New York, 1966.

Clenshaw, C. W. and A. R. Curtis, "A Method for Numerical Integration on an Automatic Computer," *Numerische Mathematik*, vol. 2, pp. 197–205, 1960.

Coleman, T. F. and C. Van Loan, *Handbook for Matrix Computations*, SIAM, Philadelphia, 1988.

Colton, D., *Partial Differential Equations*, Random House, New York, 1988.

Conte, S. D. and C. de Boor, *Elementary Numerical Analysis*, 2nd ed. McGraw-Hill, New York, 1972.

Dahlquist, G. "A Special Stability Problem for Linear Multistep Methods," *BIT*, vol. 3, 1963, pp. 27–43.

Dahlquist. G. and A. Bjorck, *Numerical Methods*, (Translated by Ned Anderson), Prentice Hall, Englewood Cliffs, NJ, 1974.

Danzig, G. B., *Linear Programming and Extensions*, Princeton University Press, Princeton, NJ, 1963

Datta, B. N., *Numerical Linear Algebra and Applications*, Brooks Cole, Pacific Grove, CA, 1995.

Davies, A. J., *The Finite Element Method: A First Approach*, Clarendon Press, Oxford, U.K., 1980.

Davis, P. J., *Interpolation and Approximation*, Dover, New York, 1975. (Originally published by Blaisdell Publishing in 1963.)

deBoor, C., *A Practical Guide to Splines*, Springer-Verlag, New York, 1978.

Deitel, H. M. and P. J. Deitel, *C++: How to Program,* 3rd ed., Prentice Hall, Upper Saddle River, NJ, 2001.

Deitel, H. M. and P. J. Deitel, *Java: How to Program,* 4th ed., Prentice Hall, Upper Saddle River, NJ, 2001.

Deitel, H. M., P. J. Deitel, and T. R. Nieto, *Visual Basic 6: How to Program,* Prentice Hall, Upper Saddle River, NJ, 1998.

Dennis, J. E. and R. B. Schnabel, *Numerical Methods for Unconstrained Optimization and Nonlinear Equations*, Prentice Hall, Englewood Cliffs, NJ, 1983.

Dennis, J. E. Jr. and D. J. Woods, *New Computing Environments: Microcomputers in Large-Scale Computing*, edited by A. Wouk, SIAM, Philadelphia, 1987, pp. 116–122.

Deuflhard, P., "Order and Stepsize Control in Extrapolation Methods," *Numerische Mathematik*, vol. 41, pp. 399–422, 1983.

Deuflhard, P., "Recent Progress in Extrapolation Methods for Ordinary Differential Equations," *SIAM Review*, vol. 27, pp. 505–535, 1985.

Dillon, W. R. and M. Goldstein, *Multivariate Analysis: Methods and Applications*, John Wiley and Sons, New York, 1984.

Dongarra, J. J., C. B. Moler, J. R. Bunch, and G. W. Stewart, *LINPACK User's Guide*, SIAM, Philadelphia, 1979.

Edwards, C. H. Jr. and D. E. Penney, *Calculus and Analytic Geometry*, 5th ed., Prentice Hall, Upper Saddle River, NJ, 1998.

Edwards, C. H. Jr. and D. E. Penney, *Differential Equations and Boundary Value Problems: Computing and Modeling*, Prentice Hall, Englewood Cliffs, NJ, 1996.

Edwards, C. H. Jr. and D. E. Penney, *Elementary Differential Equations with Boundary Value Problems*, 3rd ed., Prentice Hall, Englewood Cliffs, NJ, 1993.

Elliott, D. F. and K. R. Rao, *Fast Transforms: Algorithms, Analyses, Applications*, Academic Press, New York, 1982.

Ellis, T. M. R., I. R. Phillips, and T. M. Lahey, *Fortran 90 Programming*, Addison-Wesley, Reading, MA, 1994.

Etter, D. M., *Engineering Problem Solving with Ansi C*, Prentice Hall, Englewood Cliffs, NJ, 1995.

Etter, D. M. and D. C. Kuncicky, *Introduction to Matlab*, Prentice Hall, Englewood Cliffs, NJ, 1999.

Eves, H., *Great Moments in Mathematics* (v. 1, before 1650; v. 2, after 1650), Mathematical Association of America, Washington, DC, 1983.

Faires, J. D. and R. Burden, *Numerical Methods*, 2nd ed., Brooks/Cole, Pacific Grove, CA, 1998.

Farin, G., *Curves and Surfaces for Computer Aided Geometric Design: A Practical Guide*, 2nd ed., Academic Press, Boston, 1990.

Finizio, N., and G. Ladas, *An Introduction to Differential Equations, with Difference Equations, Fourier Series, and Partial Differential Equations*, Wadsworth Publishing, 1982.

Forsythe, G. E. and W. R. Wasow, *Finite-Difference Methods for Partial Differential Equations*, John Wiley & Sons, New York, 1960.

Forsythe, G. E., M. A. Malcolm, and C. B. Moler, *Computer Methods for Mathematical Computations*, Prentice Hall, Englewood Cliffs, NJ, 1977.

Forsythe, G. E. and C. B. Moler, *Computer Solution of Linear Algebraic Systems*, Prentice Hall, Englewood Cliffs, NJ, 1967.

Fox, L., *Numerical Solution of Two-Point Boundary Value Problems in Ordinary Differential Equations*, Dover, New York, 1990 (originally published by Clarendon Press, Oxford, 1957).

Fox, L., *An Introduction to Numerical Linear Algebra*, Oxford University Press, New York, 1965.

Fraleigh, J. B. and R. A. Beauregard, *Linear Algebra*, Addison-Wesley, Reading, MA, 1987.

Freund, R. W., G. H. Golub, and N. M. Nachtigal, "Iterative Solution of Linear Systems," *Acta Numerica I*, Cambridge University Press, Cambridge, U.K., pp. 57–100, 1992.

Froberg, C. E., *Numerical Mathematics: Theory and Computer Applications*, Benjamin/Cummings, Menlo Park, CA, 1985.

Garcia, A. L., *Numerical Methods for Physics*, Prentice Hall, Englewood Cliffs, NJ, 1994.

Gear, C. W., *Numerical Initial Value Problems in Ordinary Differential Equations*, Prentice Hall, Englewood Cliffs, NJ, 1971.

Gill, P. E., W. Murray, and M. H. Wright, *Numerical Linear Algebra and Optimization*, Addison-Wesley, Redwood City, CA, 1991.

Golub, G. H. and J. M. Ortega, *Scientific Computing and Differential Equations: An Introduction to Numerical Methods*, Academic Press, Boston, 1992.

Golub, G. H., and C. F. Van Loan, *Matrix Computations*, 3rd ed., Johns Hopkins University Press, Baltimore, 1996.

Gragg, W., "On Extrapolation Algorithms for Ordinary Initial Value Problems," *J. SIAM Numer. Anal. Ser. B*, vol. 2, pp. 384–403, 1965.

Greenbaum, A., *Iterative Methods for Solving Linear Systems*, SIAM, Philadelphia, 1997.

Greenberg, M. D., *Advanced Engineering Mathematics*, 2nd ed., Prentice Hall, Upper Saddle River, NJ, 1998.

Greenberg, M. D., *Foundations of Applied Mathematics*, Prentice Hall, Englewood Cliffs, NJ, 1978.

Greenspan, D., *Discrete Numerical Methods in Physics and Engineering*, Academic Press, New York, 1974.

Grossman, S. I. and W. R. Derrick, *Advanced Engineering Mathematics*, Harper & Row, New York, 1988.

Haberman, R., *Elementary Applied Partial Differential Equations, with Fourier Series and Boundary Value Problems*, Prentice Hall, Englewood Cliffs, NJ, 1983.

Hager, W. W., *Applied Numerical Linear Algebra*, William W. Hager, Dept. of Mathematics, Univ. of Florida, Gainesville, FL. (originally published by Prentice Hall, Englewood Cliffs, NJ, 1988.)

Hair, J. F., R. E. Anderson, R. L. Tatham, and W. Black, *Multivariate Data Analysis*, 5th ed., Prentice Hall, Englewood Cliffs, NJ, 1998.

Hall, C. A. and T. A. Porsching, *Numerical Analysis of Partial Differential Equations*, Prentice Hall, Englewood Cliffs, NJ, 1990.

Hall, G. and J. M. Watt (eds.), *Modern Numerical Methods for Ordinary Differential Equations*, Clarendon Press, Oxford, 1976.

Hamming, R. W., *Numerical Methods for Scientists and Engineers*, 2nd ed., McGraw-Hill, New York, 1973.

Hanna, O. T. and O. C. Sandall, *Computational Methods In Chemical Engineering*, Prentice Hall, Upper Saddle River, NJ, 1995.

Hibbeler, R. C., *Engineering Mechanics: Dynamics,* 7th ed., Prentice Hall, Englewood Cliffs, NJ, 1995.

Hibbeler, R. C., *Engineering Mechanics: Statics,* 7th ed., Prentice Hall, Englewood Cliffs, NJ, 1995.

Hildebrand, F. B., *Introduction to Numerical Analysis*, Dover, New York, 1987.

Hildebrand, F. B., *Advanced Calculus for Applications,* 2nd ed., Prentice Hall, Englewood Cliffs, NJ, 1976.

Himmelblau, D. M., *Basic Principles and Calculations in Engineering*, 3rd ed., Prentice Hall, Englewood Cliffs, NJ, 1974.

Horn, R. A. and C. R. Johnson, *Matrix Analysis*, Cambridge University Press, Cambridge, 1985.

Hornbeck, R. W., *Numerical Methods*, Prentice Hall, Englewood Cliffs, NJ, 1975.

Householder, A. S., *The Numerical Treatment of a Single Nonlinear Equation*, McGraw-Hill, New York, 1970.

Inman, D. J., *Engineering Vibration*, Prentice Hall, Englewood Cliffs, NJ, 1996.

Isaacson, E. and H. B. Keller, *Analysis of Numerical Methods*, Dover, New York, 1994. (Originally published by John Wiley & Sons, 1966.)

Jaeger, J. C., *An Introduction to Applied Mathematics*, Clarenden Press, Oxford, 1951.

Jain, M. K., *Numerical Solution of Differential Equations*, John Wiley, New York, 1979.

Jensen, J. A. and J. H. Rowland, *Methods of Computation*, Scott, Foresman and Company, Glenview, IL, 1975.

Johnson, R. A. and D. W. Wichern, *Applied Multivariate Statistical Analysis*, 4th ed., Prentice Hall, Englewood Cliffs, NJ, 1998.

Kachigan, S. K., *Multivariate Statistical Analysis: A Conceptual Introduction*, 2nd ed., Radius Press, New York, 1991.

Kahaner, D., C. Moler, and S. Nash, *Numerical Methods and Software*, Prentice Hall, Englewood Cliffs, NJ, 1989.

Kammer, W. J., G. W. Reddien, and R. S. Varga, "Quadratic Splines," *Numerische Mathematik*, vol. 22, pp. 241–259, 1974.

Kaps, P. and Rentrop, P., "Generalized Runge-Kutta Methods of Order Four with Stepsize Control for Stiff Ordinary Differential Equations," *Numerische Mathematik*, vol. 33, pp. 55–68, 1979.

Keller, H. B., *Numerical Methods for Two-point Boundary-value Problems*, Blaisdell, Waltham, MA, 1968.

Kollerstrom, N. "Thomas Simpson and 'Newton's Method of Approximation': An Enduring Myth," *British Journal for the History of Science*, v. 25 (1992), pp. 347–354.

Kolman, B., *Introductory Linear Algebra with Applications*, 6th ed., Prentice Hall, Upper Saddle River, NJ, 1997.

Lancaster, P. and K. Salkauskas, *Curve and Surface Fitting: An Introduction*, Academic Press, Boston, 1986.

Larsen, R. W., *Introduction to Mathcad 2000*, Prentice Hall, Upper Saddle River, NJ, 2001.

Leon, S. J., *Linear Algebra with Applications*, 5th ed., Prentice Hall, Upper Saddle River, NJ, 1998.

Leon, S. J., E. Herman, and R. Faulkenberry, *ATLAST: Computer Exercises for Linear Algebra*, Prentice Hall, Upper Saddle River, NJ, 1996.

Lorenz, E., "Deterministic Nonperiodic Flows," *Journal of Atmospheric Sciences*, vol. 20, pp. 130–141, 1963.

Mardia, K. V., *Multivariate Analysis*, Academic Press, London, 1980.

Marquardt, D. W., "An Algorithm for Least-squares Estimation of Nonlinear Parameters," *Journal of the Society for Industrial and Applied Mathematics*, vol. 11, pp. 431–441, 1963.

Mathcad2000 Reference Manual, Mathsoft, Cambridge, MA, 1999.

Mathcad2000 User's Guide, Mathsoft, Cambridge, MA, 1999.

Meis, T. and U. Marcowitz, *Numerical Solution of Partial Differential Equations*, Springer-Verlag, New York, 1981.

Mitchell, A. R., *Computational Methods in Partial Differential Equations*, John Wiley & Sons, London, 1969.

Mitchell, A. R. and R. Wait, *The Finite Element Method in Partial Differential Equations*, John Wiley & Sons, London, 1977.

Morrison, D. F., *Multivariate Statistical Methods*, 3rd ed., McGraw-Hill, New York, 1990.

Nicolis, G. and I. Prigogine, *Self-Organization in Nonequilibrium Systems*, John Wiley & Sons, New York, 1977.

Nussbaumer, H. J., *Fast Fourier Transform and Convolution Algorithms*, Springer-Verlag, New York, 1982.

Nyhoff, L. R., *Fortran 90 for Engineers and Scientists,* Prentice Hall, Upper Saddle River, NJ, 1996.

Ortega, J. M., *Numerical Analysis—A Second Course*, Academic Press, New York, 1972.

Ortega, J. M. and W. G. Poole, *An Introduction to Numerical Methods for Differential Equations*, Pitman Publishing, 1981.

Pauling, L., *General Chemistry*, Dover, New York, 1989.

Piessens, R., E. de Doncker, C. W. Uberhuber, and D. K. Kahaner, *QUADPACK: A Subroutine Package for Automatic Integration*, Springer-Verlag, New York, 1983.

Polak, E., *Computational Methods in Optimization*, Academic Press, New York, 1971.

Powers, D. L., *Boundary Value Problems*, 3rd ed., Harcourt Brace Jovanovich, Orlando, FL, 1987.

Press, W. H., S. A. Teukolsky, W. T. Vetterling, and B. P. Flannery, *Numerical Recipes in C, The Art of Scientific Computing*, 2nd ed., Cambridge Unversity Press, Cambridge, 1992.

Ralston, A. and P. Rabinowitz, *A First Course in Numerical Analysis*, 2nd ed., McGraw-Hill, New York, 1978.

Reinboldt, W. C., *Methods for Solving Systems of Nonlinear Equations*, SIAM, Philadelphia, 1974.

Rice, J. R., *Numerical Methods, Software, and Analysis*, 2nd ed., Academic Press, New York, 1992.

Ridders, C. J. F., "Technical Note: Accurate Computation of F'(x) and F'(x) F''(x)," *Advances in Engineering Solftware*, vol. 4, no. 2, 1982, pp. 75–76.

Ridders, C. J. F., "Three-point Iteration Derived From Exponential Curve Fitting," *IEEE Transaction on Circuits and Systems,* 1979, vol. CAS-26, pp. 979–980.

Ritger, P. D. and N. J. Rose, *Differential Equations with Applications*, McGraw-Hill, New York, 1968.

Rivlin, T. J., *An Introduction to the Approximation of Functions*, Dover, New York, 1981. (Originally published by Blaisdell Publishing, 1969.)

Roberts, C. E., *Ordinary Differential Equations: A Computational Approach*, Prentice Hall, Englewood Cliffs, NJ, 1979.

Shampine, L. F., "Implementation of Rosenbrock Methods," *ACM Transactions on Mathematical Software*, vol. 8, pp. 93–113, 1982.

Silvester, P. P. and R. L. Ferrari, *Finite Elements for Electrical Engineers*, 3rd ed., Cambridge University Press, Cambridge, UK, 1996.

Simmons, G. F., *Calculus with Analytic Geometry*, McGraw-Hill, New York, 1985.

Simmons, G. F., *Differential Equations with Applications and Historical Notes,* McGraw-Hill, New York, 1972.

Simon, W., *Mathematical Techniques for Biology and Medicine*, Dover, New York, 1986. (Originally published by MIT Press, 1977.)

Singleton, R.C., "An Algorithm for Computing the Mixed Radix Fast Fourier Transform," *IEEE Transactions on Audio and Electroacoustics,* vol. AU-17, pp. 93–103, 1969.

Singleton, R.C., "A Method for Computing the Fast Fourier Transform with Auxiliary Memory and Limited High-speed Storage," *IEEE Transactions on Audio and Electroacoustics,* vol. AU-15, pp. 91–97, 1967.

Smith, D. E., *A Source Book in Mathematics*, Dover, New York, 1959.

Spong, M. W. and M. Vidyasagar, *Robot Dynamics and Control*, John Wiley & Sons, New York, 1989.

Stoer, J. and R. Bulirsch, *Introduction to Numerical Analysis*, Springer Verlag, New York, 1980.

Strang, G., *Linear Algebra and Its Applications*, 3rd ed., Harcourt Brace Jovanovich, San Diego, CA, 1988.

Strang, G. and G. Fix, *An Analysis of the Finite Element Method*, Prentice Hall, Englewood Cliffs, NJ, 1973.

Struik, D. J., *A Concise History of Mathematics*, 4th ed., Dover, New York, 1987.

Svobony, T., *Mathematical Modeling for Industry and Engineering*, Prentice Hall, Upper Saddle River, NJ, 1998.

Taha, H. A, *Operations Research, An Introduction,* 6th ed., Prentice Hall, Upper Saddle River, NJ, 1997.

Thomson, W. T., *Introduction to Space Dynamics*, Dover, New York, 1986. (Originally published by John Wiley & Sons, 1961.)

Thomson, W. T., *Theory of Vibrations with Applications*, Prentice Hall, Englewood Cliff, NJ, 1993.

Timan, A. F., C. J. Hyman, and N. I. Achieser, *Theory of Approximation*, Dover, New York, 1993.

Troutman, J. L. and M. Bautista, *Boundary Value Problems of Applied Mathematics*, Prindle, Weber & Schmidt Publishing, 1994.

Van der Pol, B., "Forced Oscillations in a Circuit with Non-linear Resistance," *Phil. Mag.*, vol. 3, pp. 65–80, 1927.

Van Loan, C. F., *Computational Framework for the Fast Fourier Transform*, SIAM, Philadelphia, 1992.

Vargaftik, N. B., *Tables of the Thermophysical Properties of Liquids and Gases*, 2nd ed., Hemishpere, Washington D.C., 1975.

Weinstock, R., "Isaac Newton: Credit Where Credit Won't Do," *The College Mathematics Journal*, v. 25, no. 3, May 1994, pp. 179–192.

Wilkinson, J. H., *The Algebraic Eigenvalue Problem*, Oxford University Press, New York, 1965.

Wilkinson, J. H. and C. Reinsch, *Linear Algebra,* vol II *of Handbook for Automatic Computation*, Springer-Verlag, New York, 1971.

Winston, W. L., *Operations Research, Aplications and Algorithms*, 3rd ed., Duxbury Press (Wadsworth), Belmont, CA, 1994.

Young, D. M. and R. T. Gregory, *A Survey of Numerical Mathematics*, vols. 1 and 2, Dover, New York, 1988.

Zauderer, E., *Partial Differential Equations of Applied Mathematics*, 2nd ed. John Wiley & Sons, New York, 1989.

Zienkiewicz, O. C. and R. L. Taylor, *The Finite Element Method*, 4th ed., Vol 1, McGraw-Hill, London, 1989.

Zill, D. G., *Differential Equations with Boundary-Value Problems*, Prindle, Weber, & Schmidt, Boston, 1986.

Answers to Selected Problems

(Most answers shown to 5 digits.)

Chapter 1

P1.1 $x = 1, y = 2$

P1.3 $x = 1, y = 1$

P1.5 $x = 1, y = 3$

P1.7   for $x_0 = 0.8$, $x_1 = 0.99957$, $x_2 = 0.90965$, $x_3 = 0.96928$; conditions of the theorem are satisfied

P1.9   for $x_0 = 0.5$, $x_1 = 0.75$, $x_2 = 0.4375$, $x_3 = 0.80859$; conditions of the theorem are not satisfied

P1.11 C_1: center $(1,0)$, radius $3/8$; C_2: center $(2,0)$, radius $1/2$; C_3: center $(3,0)$, radius 0; disks disjoint, so $5/8 \le \mu_1 \le 11/8$; $3/2 \le \mu_2 \le 5/2$; $\mu_3 = 3$

P1.13 C_1: center $(1,0)$, radius $1/4$; C_2: center $(2,0)$, radius $1/2$; C_3: center $(3,0)$, radius $1/4$; disks disjoint, so $3/4 \le \mu_1 \le 5/4$; $3/2 \le \mu_2 \le 5/2$; $11/4 \le \mu_3 \le 13/4$

P1.15 C_1: center $(1,0)$, radius $3/8$; C_2: center $(2,0)$, radius $1/2$; C_3: center $(3,0)$, radius $1/3$; μ_1 and μ_2 are within the union of the regions bounded by C_1 and C_2; $23/8 \le \mu_3 \le 25/8$

P1.17   a. 10.9; b. 11.0; c. rel error for a: $-9 * 10^{-3}$, rel error for b: $9 * 10^{-5}$

P1.19   a. $x_1 = 56.98$, $x_2 = 0.02$; b. $x_1 = 56.98$, $x_2 = 0.0176$; c. $x_1 = 56.9825$, $x_2 = 0.0175$

P1.21   a. 1.2; b. 1.1; c. 1.0666 (note, this is not better, the exact result is $\arctan(2) = 1.1071...$)

P1.23   a. 5; b. 4.5; c. 4.333... (exact result: $(2^2 - 2^0)/\ln(2) = 4.3281...$)

P1.25   a. 3.5343; b. 3.1474; c. 3.0184 (exact result is 3)

P1.27   (a. and b.) $0.92857 \le y \le 1.0714$; a. $1.9572 \le x \le 2.0429$; b. $1.9572 \le x \le 2.0429$

P1.29   (a. and b.) $1.9684 \le y \le 2.0316$; a. $2.9537 \le x \le 3.0463$; b. $2.9263 \le x \le 3.0737$

Chapter 2

P2.1 $x = 1.4142$

P2.3 $x = 2.6458$

P2.5 $x = 1.5874$

P2.7 $x = 0.49492$

P2.9 $x = 0.81904$

P2.11 $x = -2.8794$, $x = -0.6527$, $x = 0.53209$

P2.13 $x = -3.1055$, $x = 0.22346$, $x = 2.882$

P2.15 $x = 2.8063$

P2.17 $x = -3.324$, $x = -1.6197$, $x = 5.9437$

P2.19 $x = 0$, $x = 1.3333$, $x = 2.5$

P2.21   a. x alternates between 1 and -1; b. $x = 0.2541$; c. $x_0 = 0.5 \rightarrow x = 0.44853$; $x_0 = 0 \rightarrow f'(x_0) = 0$; Newton's method fails. d. $x = 0.87055$

P2.23 $x = 2.029$, $x = 4.9132$, $x = 7.9787$

P2.25 $x = -0.70347$

P2.27   a. $x = 2.4781$, $x = 3$; b. $x = 2.7368$, $x = 2.7$

P2.29 $x = 0.12313$

Chapter 3

P3.1 $x = [\ 1.1429, 1.0000, -0.7143]^T$
$= [\ 8/7, 1, -5/7\ ]^T$

P3.3 $x = [\ 1, 2, 3\ ]^T$

P3.5 $x = [\ 1, 1, 1\ ]^T$

P3.7 $x = [\ 1, 2, 6\ ]^T$

P3.9 $x = [\ -1, 2, 0, 1\ ]^T$

P3.11 $x = [\ 3, -4, -5\ ]^T$

P3.13 $x = [\ 2, 1, -1\ ]^T$

P3.15 $x = [\ 1, 1, 1, 1, 1, 1\ ]^T$

P3.17   a. $x = [\ 0, 3\ ]^T$; b. $x = [\ -1, 3\ ]^T$; without rounding $x = [\ -1.001, 3.001\ ]^T$

P3.19   a. $x = [\ 0, 5, 0\ ]^T$; b. $x = [\ 1, 2, 3\ ]^T$; without rounding $x = [\ 1.0005, 1.9995, 2.9995]^T$

P3.27 $x = [\ 1, 1, 1\ ]^T$

P3.29 $x = [\ 1, -2, 5, 8\ ]^T$

P3.31 $x = [\ 2, -5, -2, 1, -2, 2\ ]^T$

P3.33 $x = [\ -4, 3, -3, 4, 3, 3, 5, 5\ ]^T$

P3.35 $x = [\ -3, 1, -1, -2, 3, -4, -1, -1, 3, 0\ ]^T$

P3.37   a. $x = [\ 4, -4, 4, 1, 2, 3, -4, 2\ ]^T$

b. $x = [\ -2, 1, 1, 0, 3, 0, -1, 5\ ]^T$

c. $x = [\ -3, -3, -2, 0, 4, -3, 3, 1\ ]^T$

d. $x = [\ 5, 2, -4, -3, 2, -4, 0, -1\ ]^T$

P3.39   a. $x = [\ 1, 0, 2, -1, 5, -1, -2, -5, -3, -2\ ]^T$

b. $x = [\ 1, -1, -3, 4, -4, -4, -1, 2, 4, 0\ ]^T$

c. $x = [\ -2, 1, -5, 4, -1, 2, -4, 2, -2, 4\ ]^T$

d. $x = [\ 1, 0, 1, -1, -1, 4, -4, -3, -3, -3\ ]^T$

Chapter 4

P4.1   a. $L = \begin{bmatrix} 1 & 0 & 0 \\ 2 & 1 & 0 \\ 3 & 4 & 1 \end{bmatrix}$

$U = \begin{bmatrix} 1 & 2 & 3 \\ 0 & 4 & 5 \\ 0 & 0 & 6 \end{bmatrix}$

b. $A^{-1} = \begin{bmatrix} 1.5833 & -0.1667 & -0.0833 \\ -1.5417 & 1.0833 & -0.2083 \\ 0.8333 & -0.6667 & 0.1667 \end{bmatrix}$

c. $\det(A) = 24$

d. $x = [\ 1.3333\ -0.6667\ 0.3333\ ]^T$
$y = [\ 2.1944\ -2.8472\ 1.6111\ ]^T$

P4.3   a. $L = \begin{bmatrix} 1 & 0 & 0 \\ 2 & 1 & 0 \\ 1 & 2/3 & 1 \end{bmatrix}$

$U = \begin{bmatrix} 2 & 1 & -2 \\ 0 & -3 & 6 \\ 0 & 0 & -1 \end{bmatrix}$

b. $A\_inv = \begin{bmatrix} 1/6 & 1/6 & 0 \\ 0 & 1 & -2 \\ -1/3 & 2/3 & -1 \end{bmatrix}$

c. $\det(A) = 6$

d. $x = [\ 1/3\ -1\ -2/3\ ]^T$
$y = [\ -1/9\ 1/3\ -1/9\ ]^T$

P4.5   a. $L = \begin{bmatrix} 1.0000 & 0 & 0 \\ 0.5000 & 1.0000 & 0 \\ 0.3333 & 1.0000 & 1.0000 \end{bmatrix}$

$U = \begin{bmatrix} 1.0000 & 0.5000 & 0.333 \\ 0 & 0.0833 & 0.0833 \\ 0 & -0.0000 & 0.0056 \end{bmatrix}$

b. $A^{-1} = \begin{bmatrix} 9 & -36 & 30 \\ -36 & 192 & -180 \\ 30 & -180 & 180 \end{bmatrix}$

c. 4.6296e-04

d. $x = \begin{bmatrix} 3 & -24 & 30 \end{bmatrix}^T$
$y = \begin{bmatrix} 1791 & -10116 & 9810 \end{bmatrix}^T$

P4.7

a. $L = \begin{bmatrix} 1 & 0 & 0 & 0 \\ 2 & 1 & 0 & 0 \\ 3 & 4 & 1 & 0 \\ -1 & -3 & 0 & 1 \end{bmatrix}$

$U = \begin{bmatrix} 1 & 1 & 0 & 3 \\ 0 & -1 & -1 & -5 \\ 0 & 0 & 3 & 13 \\ 0 & 0 & 0 & -13 \end{bmatrix}$

b. $A\_inv = \begin{bmatrix} -0.2308 & 0.2051 & 0.3333 & 0.1795 \\ 0.0769 & 0.4872 & -0.3333 & 0.0513 \\ 0.0000 & -0.3333 & 0.3333 & 0.3333 \\ 0.3846 & -0.2308 & -0.0000 & -0.0769 \end{bmatrix}$

c. $\det(A) = 39$

d. $x = \begin{bmatrix} 0.4872 & 0.2821 & 0.3333 & 0.0769 \end{bmatrix}^T$
$y = \begin{bmatrix} 0.0703 & 0.0677 & 0.0427 & 0.1164 \end{bmatrix}^T$

P4.9 a. $L = \begin{bmatrix} 1 & 0 & 0 & 0 \\ 0 & 1 & 0 & 0 \\ 0 & 0 & 1 & 0 \\ 1/3 & -1/9 & 1/9 & 1 \end{bmatrix}$

$U = \begin{bmatrix} 3 & 7 & 4 & 0 \\ 0 & 3 & 13 & 3 \\ 0 & 0 & 1 & 4 \\ 0 & 0 & 0 & 1/9 \end{bmatrix}$

b. $A\_inv = \begin{bmatrix} -98 & 32 & -24 & 295 \\ 49 & -16 & 12 & -147 \\ -12 & 4 & -3 & 36 \\ 3 & -1 & 1 & -9 \end{bmatrix}$

c. $\det(A) = -1.0000$

d. $x = \begin{bmatrix} 205 & -102 & 25 & -6 \end{bmatrix}^T$
$y = \begin{bmatrix} -25724 & 12859 & -3159 & 796 \end{bmatrix}^T$

P4.11

a. $L = \begin{bmatrix} 1 & 0 & 0 & 0 & 0 & 0 \\ 2 & 1 & 0 & 0 & 0 & 0 \\ 3 & 4 & 1 & 0 & 0 & 0 \\ 1 & 0 & 0 & 1 & 0 & 0 \\ 0 & 1 & 0 & -1 & 1 & 0 \\ 2 & 0 & 1 & 1 & -2 & 1 \end{bmatrix}$

$U = \begin{bmatrix} 1 & 2 & 1 & 1 & 0 & 0 \\ 0 & 2 & 2 & 0 & 1 & 0 \\ 0 & 0 & 1 & 0 & 0 & 1 \\ 0 & 0 & 0 & 1 & 6 & 12 \\ 0 & 0 & 0 & 0 & 2 & 6 \\ 0 & 0 & 0 & 0 & 0 & 1 \end{bmatrix}$

b. $A\_inv =$
$\begin{bmatrix} 52.50 & -28.50 & 11.00 & -7.50 & -16.50 & -10.0 \\ -16.25 & 9.75 & -3.50 & 2.25 & 4.75 & 2.50 \\ 9.00 & -6.00 & 2.00 & -1.00 & -2.00 & -1.00 \\ -28.00 & 15.00 & -6.00 & 4.00 & 9.00 & 6.00 \\ 12.50 & -6.50 & 3.00 & -2.50 & -5.50 & -3.00 \\ -4.00 & 2.00 & -1.00 & 1.00 & 2.00 & 1.00 \end{bmatrix}$

c. $\det(A) = 4$

d. $x = \begin{bmatrix} 1.00 & -0.50 & 1.0 & 0.00 & -2.00 & 1.0 \end{bmatrix}^T$
$y = \begin{bmatrix} 100.75 & -31.625 & 17.0 & -53.5 & 26.75 & -9.0 \end{bmatrix}^T$

P4.15 a. $dd = \begin{bmatrix} 4 & 4 & 3 \end{bmatrix}$
$bb = \begin{bmatrix} 0 & 4 & 2 \end{bmatrix}$

b. $L = \begin{bmatrix} 1 & 0 & 0 \\ 4 & 1 & 0 \\ 0 & 2 & 1 \end{bmatrix}$

$U = \begin{bmatrix} 4 & 2 & 0 \\ 0 & 4 & 1 \\ 0 & 0 & 3 \end{bmatrix}$

P4.17 a. $dd = \begin{bmatrix} 5 & 3 & 2 \end{bmatrix}$
$bb = \begin{bmatrix} 0 & 3 & 3 \end{bmatrix}$

b. $L = \begin{bmatrix} 1 & 0 & 0 \\ 3 & 1 & 0 \\ 0 & 3 & 1 \end{bmatrix}$

$U = \begin{bmatrix} 5 & 1 & 0 \\ 0 & 3 & 3 \\ 0 & 0 & 2 \end{bmatrix}$

P4.19 a. $dd = \begin{bmatrix} 1 & 1 & 1 & 1 \end{bmatrix}$
$bb = \begin{bmatrix} 0 & 2 & 2 & 1 \end{bmatrix}$

b. $L = \begin{bmatrix} 1 & 0 & 0 & 0 \\ 2 & 1 & 0 & 0 \\ 0 & 2 & 1 & 0 \\ 0 & 0 & 1 & 1 \end{bmatrix}$

$U = \begin{bmatrix} 1 & 3 & 0 & 0 \\ 0 & 1 & 2 & 0 \\ 0 & 0 & 1 & 5 \\ 0 & 0 & 0 & 1 \end{bmatrix}$

P4.21 a. $dd = \begin{bmatrix} 1 & 2 & 4 & 4 \end{bmatrix}$
$bb = \begin{bmatrix} 0 & 1 & 3 & 3 \end{bmatrix}$

b. $L = \begin{bmatrix} 1 & 0 & 0 & 0 \\ 1 & 1 & 0 & 0 \\ 0 & 3 & 1 & 0 \\ 0 & 0 & 3 & 1 \end{bmatrix}$

$U = \begin{bmatrix} 1 & 4 & 0 & 0 \\ 0 & 2 & 2 & 0 \\ 0 & 0 & 4 & 3 \\ 0 & 0 & 0 & 4 \end{bmatrix}$

P4.23 a. $dd = \begin{bmatrix} 5 & 1 & 1 & 4 \end{bmatrix}$
$bb = \begin{bmatrix} 0 & 2 & 3 & 1 \end{bmatrix}$

b. $L = \begin{bmatrix} 1 & 0 & 0 & 0 \\ 2 & 1 & 0 & 0 \\ 0 & 3 & 1 & 0 \\ 0 & 0 & 1 & 1 \end{bmatrix}$

$U = \begin{bmatrix} 5 & 0 & 0 & 0 \\ 0 & 1 & 2 & 0 \\ 0 & 0 & 1 & 4 \\ 0 & 0 & 0 & 4 \end{bmatrix}$

P4.25 a. $dd = \begin{bmatrix} 1 & 2 & 3 & 4 & 5 & 6 \end{bmatrix}$
$bb = \begin{bmatrix} 0 & 2 & 3 & 4 & 5 & 6 \end{bmatrix}$

b. $L = \begin{bmatrix} 1 & 0 & 0 & 0 & 0 & 0 \\ 1 & 0 & 0 & 0 & 0 & 0 \\ 0 & 3 & 1 & 0 & 0 & 0 \\ 0 & 0 & 4 & 1 & 0 & 0 \\ 0 & 0 & 0 & 5 & 1 & 0 \\ 0 & 0 & 0 & 0 & 6 & 1 \end{bmatrix}$

$U = \begin{bmatrix} 1 & -5 & 0 & 0 & 0 & 0 \\ 0 & 2 & -4 & 0 & 0 & 0 \\ 0 & 0 & 3 & -3 & 0 & 0 \\ 0 & 0 & 0 & 4 & -2 & 0 \\ 0 & 0 & 0 & 0 & 5 & -1 \\ 0 & 0 & 0 & 0 & 0 & 6 \end{bmatrix}$

P4.27 a. $dd = \begin{bmatrix} 5 & 4 & 2 & 3 & 4 & 1 \end{bmatrix}$
$bb = \begin{bmatrix} 0 & 3 & 2 & 1 & 3 & 4 \end{bmatrix}$

b. $L = \begin{bmatrix} 1 & 0 & 0 & 0 & 0 & 0 \\ 3 & 1 & 0 & 0 & 0 & 0 \\ 0 & 2 & 1 & 0 & 0 & 0 \\ 0 & 0 & 1 & 1 & 0 & 0 \\ 0 & 0 & 0 & 3 & 1 & 0 \\ 0 & 0 & 0 & 0 & 4 & 1 \end{bmatrix}$

$U = \begin{bmatrix} 5 & 2 & 0 & 0 & 0 & 0 \\ 0 & 4 & 0 & 0 & 0 & 0 \\ 0 & 0 & 2 & 2 & 0 & 0 \\ 0 & 0 & 0 & 3 & 4 & 0 \\ 0 & 0 & 0 & 0 & 4 & 4 \\ 0 & 0 & 0 & 0 & 0 & 1 \end{bmatrix}$

P4.29 $L = \begin{bmatrix} 1.0000 & 0 & 0 \\ 0.1667 & 1.00 & 0 \\ 1.0000 & 0 & 1.00 \end{bmatrix}$

$U = \begin{bmatrix} 6.00 & 2.0000 & 2.0000 \\ 0 & 1.6667 & -1.3333 \\ 0 & 0 & -1.0000 \end{bmatrix}$

P4.31 $L = \begin{bmatrix} 1 & 0 & 0 & 0 \\ 0 & 1 & 0 & 0 \\ -1 & 0 & 1 & 0 \\ 0 & 0 & 1 & 1 \end{bmatrix}$

$U = \begin{bmatrix} -1 & 1 & 0 & 0 \\ 0 & 1 & -1 & 1 \\ 0 & 0 & 1 & 0 \\ 0 & 0 & 0 & -1 \end{bmatrix}$

P4.33

$$L = \begin{bmatrix} 1.00 & 0 & 0 & 0 & & 0 \\ 0 & 1.00 & 0 & 0 & 0 & 0 \\ 0 & 0 & 1.00 & 0 & 0 & 0 \\ 0 & 0 & 0 & 1.0000 & 0 & 0 \\ 0 & 0 & 0 & 0 & 1.0000 & 0 \\ 0.50 & 0.25 & 0 & 0.0833 & 0.0486 & 1 \end{bmatrix}$$

$$U = \begin{bmatrix} -2 & 6 & 4.0 & 0 & 0 & 0 \\ 0 & 4 & 8.0 & -0.50 & 0 & 0 \\ 0 & 0 & -0.5 & 3.25 & 1.50 & 0 \\ 0 & 0 & 0 & 1.50 & 1.75 & -3.00 \\ 0 & 0 & 0 & 0 & -3.00 & 13.00 \\ 0 & 0 & 0 & 0 & 0 & -0.3819 \end{bmatrix}$$

P4.35 a. Doolittle form

$$L = \begin{bmatrix} 1 & 0 & 0 \\ 2 & 1 & 0 \\ 4 & 3 & 1 \end{bmatrix}$$

$$U = \begin{bmatrix} 9 & 18 & 36 \\ 0 & 4 & 12 \\ 0 & 0 & 1 \end{bmatrix}$$

b. Cholesky form

$$L = \begin{bmatrix} 3 & 0 & 0 \\ 6 & 2 & 0 \\ 12 & 6 & 1 \end{bmatrix}$$

$$U = \begin{bmatrix} 3 & 6 & 12 \\ 0 & 2 & 6 \\ 0 & 0 & 1 \end{bmatrix}$$

c. $x1 = \begin{bmatrix} -1 & 2 & 1 \end{bmatrix}^T$
   $x2 = \begin{bmatrix} 2 & 1 & -1 \end{bmatrix}^T$
   $x3 = \begin{bmatrix} -2 & -2 & 1 \end{bmatrix}^T$

P4.37 Pivoting is required, Cholesky and Doolittle methods fail.

$LU = PA =$

$$\begin{bmatrix} 2 & -1 & 0 & 0 & 0 & 0 \\ -1 & 2 & -1.0000 & 0 & 0 & 0 \\ 0 & 0 & -1.0000 & 2.0000 & -1 & 0 \\ 0 & -1 & 0.6667 & -1.0000 & 0 & 0 \\ 0 & 0 & 0 & -1.0000 & 2 & -1 \\ 0 & 0 & 0 & 0 & -1 & 2 \end{bmatrix}$$

$$L = \begin{bmatrix} 1.0 & 0 & 0 & 0 & 0 & 0 \\ -0.5 & 1 & 0 & 0 & 0 & 0 \\ 0 & 0 & 1 & 0 & 0 & 0 \\ 0 & -0.6667 & 0 & 1 & 0 & 0 \\ 0 & 0 & 0 & 1 & 1.0 & 0 \\ 0 & 0 & 0 & 0 & -0.5 & 1 \end{bmatrix}$$

$$U = \begin{bmatrix} 2 & -1.0 & 0 & 0 & 0 & 0 \\ 0 & 1.5 & -1 & 0 & 0 & 0 \\ 0 & 0 & -1 & 2 & -1 & 0 \\ 0 & 0 & 0 & -1 & 0 & 0 \\ 0 & 0 & 0 & 0 & 2 & -1 \\ 0 & 0 & 0 & 0 & 0 & 1 \end{bmatrix}$$

c. solution using LU_pivot
   xx1 = 2 1 3 -1 -3 -2
   xx2 = 1 2 3 -1 -3 -2
   xx3 = 1 -1 2 -2 3 -3

Chapter 5

Results after 10 iterations

P5.1 a. m = 3.0001, v = [0.00 0.50 1.00], error = 4.5601e-05, exact = 3
   b. m = 1.0000, v = [1.00 0.00 -1.00], error = 5.8666e-05, exact = 1.

P5.3 a. m = 3.0132, v = [1.00 1.00 0.0087], error = 0.0109, exact = 3.
   b. m = 1.9768, v = [-0.9653 -0.9653 1.0], error = 0.0290, exact = 2

P5.5 a. m = 3.0240, v = [-0.0106 0.2889 1.0000], error = 0.0162, exact = 3
   b. m = 0.9990, v = [1.0000 0.9996 -0.0012], error = 0.0012, exact = 1

P5.7 a. m = 5.1521, v = [0.2367 1.0000 0.0529], error = 0.0355, exact = 5
   b. m = 3.4033, v = [0.1618 1.0000 0.7092], error = 0.3437, exact = 3

P5.9   a. m = 2.0019, v = [0.2884 1.0000 0.5730], error = 0.0012, exact = 2
   b. m = 0.9980, v = [0.2857 1.0000 0.5714], error = 5.4704e-06, exact = 1

P5.11   a. m = 4.00,   v = [1.00 0.0010 -0.9980 0.0010], error = 0.0048, exact = 4
   b. m = 1.9993, v = [0.0005 0.5002 1.00 0.5002], error = 0.0011, exact = 2

P5.13   a. m = 4.990,   v = [0.9970 1.00 0.0060 0.0030],   error = 0.0172, exact = 5
   b. m = 0.0000, v = [0.5000 1.0000 0.5000 0.0000], error = 5.6445e-15, exact = 0,
(Hint: modify the inverse power method, or see hint for P5.19 below)

P5.15   a. m = 5.00, v = [-0.6049 -0.1369 0.50 1.00], error = 2.0968, exact = 5
   after 50 iterations, m = 5.0002, v = [-0.0000 1.0000 0.2500 0.5001], error = 1.1922e-04
   b. m=1.00, v=[-0.0002 -0.0006 -0.00 1.00], error = 0.0013, exact = 1

P5.17   a. m = 4.0834, v = [-0.0005 -0.0592 0.4117 1.0000 0.5291], error = 0.1150, exact = 4
   b. m = 1.9876, v = [0.5002 -0.4829 -0.9663 0.5166 1.0000], error = 0.0353, exact = 2

P5.19   a. m = 3.0132, v = [-0.0087 0.4869 1.0000 0.7566 0.5044], error = 0.0191, exact = 3; after 30 iterations,
   m = 3.0000, v = [-0.000 0.500 1.000 0.750 0.50], error = 5.6172e-06
   b. m = -5.7135e-10, v = [1.00 1.00 -0.00 -0.00 -0.00], error = 7.7881e-07, exact = 0; converged after 12
   iterations, m = -7.0636e-12, error = 4.8669e-08.
(Hint: Apply inverse power method to B = A - 0.2I and then add 0.2 to the eigenvalue.)

P5.21   a. m = 8.7839, v = [-0.5198 1.00 0.2923], error = 0.1514;
   b. m = 8.8657, v = [-0.5198 1.00 0.2923], error = 0.1139;

P5.23   a. m = 16.6077, v = [-0.5306 1.0000 0.2966], error = 0.2326;
   b. m = 16.7373, v = [-0.5306 1.0000 0.2966], error = 0.1713;

P5.25   a. m = 45.0458, v = [-0.1743 1.0000 0.0506],   error = 0.0013;
   b. m = 45.0454, v = [-0.1743 1.0000 0.0506], error = 0.0012;

P5.27   a. m = -8.9669, v =[0.3685 -0.0528 1.00], error = 0.6893
   b. m = -8.7071, v =[0.3685 -0.0528 1.00], error = 0.6384

P5.29   a. m = 57.2864, error =1.3067;
   b. m = 58.0325, error = 0.8996;
   eigenvector for parts a. and b. v = [1.000 0.0220 0.1218 -0.6622],

P5.31   a. m = 48.2782, v = [-0.1454 1.0000 -0.1017 -0.0383], error = 0.0133;
   b. m = 48.2800, v = [-0.1454 1.0000 -0.1017 -0.0383], error = 0.0132;

P5.33   a. m = 72.0000, v = [1.0000 0.3333 -0.6652 0.6681], error = 0.0746
   b. m = 71.9997, v = [1.0000 0.3333 -0.6652 0.6681], error = 0.0746

P5.35   a. m = 33.3009, v = [-0.1043 0.4447 -0.5053 1.00 0.2490], error = 0.0637
   b. m = 33.3290, v = [-0.1043 0.4447 -0.5053 1.0000 0.2490], error = 0.0532

P5.37   a. m = 76.3303, error = 0.0742;
   b. m = 76.2918, error = 0.0502; eigenvector for parts a. and b.
   v = [0.8155 0.1067 1.0000 -0.1053 0.4252   0.0853 0.3795],

P5.39   a. m = 194.6906, error = 0.7786;
   b. m = 194.7387, error = 0.7723; eigenvector for parts a. and b.
   v = [-0.3087 1.0000 -0.6857 -0.0823 -0.5172 0.9594 0.3572 0.8342 0.0161]

P5.41   a. the QR factorization of matrix A is

$$Q = \begin{bmatrix} -0.2182 & -0.6838 & -0.6963 \\ -0.4364 & -0.5698 & 0.6963 \\ -0.8729 & 0.4558 & -0.1741 \end{bmatrix} \quad R = \begin{bmatrix} -4.5826 & 3.9279 & -5.2372 \\ -0.0000 & -1.2536 & 1.1396 \\ -0.0000 & -0.0000 & 0.5222 \end{bmatrix}$$

the upper triangular matrix

$$B = \begin{bmatrix} 3.000 & -0.6667 & -7.4535 \\ -0.0000 & 1.0000 & 0.0000 \\ 0.0000 & -0.0000 & 1.0000 \end{bmatrix}$$

has the same eigenvalues as A (on the diagonal): 3, 1, 1.

b. the upper Hessenberg matrix with the same eigenvalues as A is

$$AA = \begin{bmatrix} 1.0000 & 0 & 0 \\ -4.4721 & 3.0000 & -6.0000 \\ 0.0000 & -0.0000 & 1.0000 \end{bmatrix}$$

the upper Hessenberg matrix is converted to the upper triangular matrix

$$B = \begin{bmatrix} 3.0000 & 4.4721 & 6.0000 \\ -0.0000 & 1.0000 & -0.0000 \\ 0.0000 & -0.0000 & 1.0000 \end{bmatrix}$$

with the eigenvalues on the diagonal.
(computational effort is approximately 1/2 that needed for part a.)

P5.43   a.

$$Q = \begin{bmatrix} -0.8575 & 0.5145 & 0 \\ -0.5145 & -0.8575 & 0 \\ 0 & 0 & 1.0000 \end{bmatrix}$$

$$R = \begin{bmatrix} -5.8310 & 1.7150 & -1.3720 \\ 0 & -1.0290 & -0.3430 \\ 0 & 0 & 2.0000 \end{bmatrix}$$

upper triangular matrix

$$B = \begin{bmatrix} 3.0147 & -4.9970 & 1.4142 \\ 0.0030 & 1.9853 & 0.0041 \\ 0 & 0 & 2.000 \end{bmatrix}$$

with the same eigenvalues as A (on the diagonal):
3.0147, 1.9853, 2.0000.
   b.   the upper Hessenberg matrix with the same eigenvalues as A is A itself.

P5.47   a. $Q = \begin{bmatrix} 0.2040 & -0.4011 & 0.8930 \\ 0.9748 & -0.0013 & -0.2233 \\ 0.0907 & 0.9160 & 0.3907 \end{bmatrix}$

$$R = \begin{bmatrix} 176.4540 & 48.2165 & -22.3741 \\ -0.0000 & -0.4061 & 2.9493 \\ 0.0000 & 0.0000 & 0.8372 \end{bmatrix}$$

$$B = \begin{bmatrix} 5.1175 & 21.0988 & 182.8169 \\ -0.0056 & 3.8943 & 7.3171 \\ -0.0001 & -0.0014 & 2.9882 \end{bmatrix}$$

$$e - \begin{bmatrix} 5.1175 & 3.8943 & 2.9882 \end{bmatrix}$$

b. $AA = \begin{bmatrix} -36.0000 & -9.4939 & -5.9047 \\ 172.7426 & 44.9453 & 26.0879 \\ 0.0000 & 0.0879 & 3.0547 \end{bmatrix}$

$$B = \begin{bmatrix} 5.1175 & -23.5183 & 182.5214 \\ 0.0056 & 3.9911 & -7.3038 \\ -0.0000 & 0.0147 & 2.8914 \end{bmatrix}$$

$$e = \begin{bmatrix} 5.1175 & 3.9911 & 2.8914 \end{bmatrix}$$

P5.51   a. $Q = \begin{bmatrix} -0.4339 & -0.7071 & -0.0638 & 0.5547 \\ 0.4339 & -0.7071 & 0.0638 & -0.5547 \\ 0.7593 & 0.0000 & -0.3403 & 0.5547 \\ 0.2169 & 0.0000 & 0.9360 & 0.2774 \end{bmatrix}$

$R = \begin{bmatrix} -9.2195 & 9.2195 & -4.4471 & 4.0132 \\ -0.0000 & -5.6569 & 2.8284 & -1.4142 \\ -0.0000 & 0 & -1.1061 & 2.8504 \\ 0.0000 & 0 & 0 & 1.6641 \end{bmatrix}$

after 10 iterations, the matrix is almost upper triangular

$B = \begin{bmatrix} 3.9894 & -0.0020 & -0.3496 & 13.9731 \\ -0.0028 & 3.9995 & -0.0908 & -2.5377 \\ -0.0295 & -0.0056 & 3.0302 & 3.6283 \\ -0.0001 & -0.0000 & -0.048 & 1.9810 \end{bmatrix}$

$e = [\;3.9894 \quad 3.9995 \quad 3.0302 \quad 1.9810\;]$

b. Upper Hessenberg

$AA = \begin{bmatrix} 4.0000 & 0 & 0 & 0 \\ 8.3066 & 1.8406 & 0.8521 & -12.0333 \\ 0.0000 & -0.2169 & 3.1594 & 0.2408 \\ 0.0000 & 0.0000 & -0.0000 & 4.0000 \end{bmatrix}$

$B = \begin{bmatrix} 3.9894 & 0.2795 & -8.1193 & -11.3740 \\ 0.0296 & 3.0462 & 2.0218 & 2.6984 \\ 0.0000 & -0.0173 & 1.9644 & -2.8648 \\ 0.0000 & -0.0000 & -0.0000 & 4.0000 \end{bmatrix}$

$e = [\;3.9894 \quad 3.0462 \quad 1.9644 \quad 4.0000\;]$

P5.55   a. $Q = \begin{bmatrix} 0.1414 & -0.9899 & 0 & 0 \\ 0.9899 & 0.1414 & 0 & 0 \\ 0 & 0 & -0.5300 & -0.8480 \\ 0 & 0 & -0.8480 & 0.5300 \end{bmatrix}$

$R = \begin{bmatrix} -21.2132 & 10.1823 & -20.9304 & 0 \\ -0.0000 & -0.5657 & 5.0912 & 0 \\ 0 & 0 & -9.4340 & -0.8480 \\ 0 & 0 & -0.0000 & 0.5300 \end{bmatrix}$

$B = \begin{bmatrix} 4.0605 & 22.9972 & 9.5804 & -19.1608 \\ 0.0028 & 2.9395 & -1.0081 & 2.0161 \\ 0 & 0 & 5.0000 & -8.0000 \\ 0 & 0 & 0.0000 & 1.0000 \end{bmatrix}$

$e = [\;4.0605 \quad 2.9395 \quad 5.0000 \quad 1.0000\;]$
b. A is upper Hessenberg.

P5.57
a. $Q = \begin{bmatrix} 0.2626 & -0.6607 & 0.4048 & -0.4131 & 0.400 \\ 0.3939 & -0.5919 & -0.4048 & 0.4131 & -0.400 \\ 0.2626 & 0.1376 & -0.7625 & -0.4131 & 0.400 \\ 0.6565 & -0.3441 & -0.2353 & -0.4849 & -0.400 \\ 0.5252 & -0.2753 & -0.1883 & 0.5029 & 0.600 \end{bmatrix}$

$R = \begin{bmatrix} 7.6158 & 6.3027 & -7.6158 & 8.1410 & -2.3635 \\ 0.0000 & -2.5052 & 1.5967 & -2.6703 & 0.4405 \\ 0.0000 & -0.0000 & -2.3346 & -1.8263 & 0.3012 \\ 0.0000 & 0.0000 & -0.0000 & -2.6941 & 1.8679 \\ 0.0000 & -0.0000 & 0.0000 & 0 & 0.8000 \end{bmatrix}$

$B = \begin{bmatrix} 4.0552 & -0.0524 & 0.5977 & 1.0820 & 11.5716 \\ -0.0266 & 2.0007 & -0.0077 & 1.2381 & 3.5007 \\ -0.0591 & 0.0015 & 1.9828 & 2.7926 & 7.8998 \\ -0.0206 & 0.0005 & -0.0060 & 2.9631 & 2.7234 \\ -0.0002 & 0.0000 & -0.0001 & -0.0003 & 1.9982 \end{bmatrix}$

$e = [4.0552 \quad 2.0007 \quad 1.9828 \quad 2.9631 \quad 1.9982]$

b.
$AA = \begin{bmatrix} 2.0000 & 0 & 0 & 0 & 0 \\ -7.3485 & 3.8889 & -0.0994 & -9.7992 & -8.4256 \\ -0.0000 & -0.9938 & 3.1111 & 0.0369 & 2.2768 \\ -0.0000 & -0.0000 & 0.0000 & 2.0000 & 0.0000 \\ -0.0000 & 0.0000 & -0.0000 & -0.0000 & 2.0000 \end{bmatrix}$

$B = \begin{bmatrix} 4.0522 & 0.8587 & 5.2410 & 7.0225 & 7.6099 \\ -0.0680 & 2.9786 & 5.1388 & 6.8344 & 4.2734 \\ -0.0000 & -0.0064 & 1.9662 & -0.0450 & -0.0288 \\ 0.0000 & -0.0000 & 0.0000 & 2.0000 & 0.0000 \\ -0.0000 & -0.0000 & -0.0000 & -0.0000 & 2.0000 \end{bmatrix}$

$e = [4.0552 \quad 2.9786 \quad 1.9662 \quad 2.0000 \quad 2.0000\;]$

P5.59 a. QR_factor algorithm fails

b.

$AA =$

$$\begin{bmatrix} -8.0000 & -5.7585 & -4.9735 & -7.0216 & -3.5777 \\ 13.8924 & 11.3316 & 7.5722 & 14.1866 & 9.1423 \\ 0.0000 & -1.5418 & 1.4703 & -3.9991 & -3.0447 \\ 0.0000 & -0.0000 & -0.1684 & 1.1980 & -1.7744 \\ -0.0000 & -0.0000 & 0.0000 & -0.0000 & 3.0000 \end{bmatrix}$$

$B =$

$$\begin{bmatrix} 3.0127 & -0.7503 & -4.6326 & -3.7316 & -17.6593 \\ 0.0172 & 1.9878 & 0.8999 & 1.3603 & 22.4197 \\ 0.0000 & -0.0005 & 0.9995 & -1.7889 & 3.3341 \\ 0.0000 & 0.0000 & -0.0000 & 3.0000 & 0.7456 \\ 0.0000 & -0.0000 & -0.0000 & -0.0000 & -0.0000 \end{bmatrix}$$

$e = [\, 3.0127 \quad 1.9878 \quad 0.9995 \quad 3.0000 \quad -0.0000 \,]$

P5.61 a. $Q = \begin{bmatrix} -0.9370 & -0.1735 & 0.3030 \\ 0.1562 & -0.9844 & -0.0808 \\ 0.3123 & -0.0284 & 0.9495 \end{bmatrix}$

$R = \begin{bmatrix} -6.4031 & 2.4988 & 2.6550 \\ -0.0000 & -7.7302 & -0.6941 \\ 0.0000 & -0.0000 & 1.2122 \end{bmatrix}$

$B = \begin{bmatrix} 8.8697 & -0.0970 & -0.0000 \\ -0.0970 & 6.0033 & -0.0000 \\ -0.0000 & -0.0000 & 1.1270 \end{bmatrix}$

$e = [\, 8.8697 \quad 6.0033 \quad 1.1270 \,]$

b. $AA = \begin{bmatrix} 6.0000 & 2.2361 & -0.0000 \\ 2.2361 & 4.0000 & 3.0000 \\ -0.0000 & 3.0000 & 6.0000 \end{bmatrix}$

$B = \begin{bmatrix} 8.8697 & 0.0970 & 0.0000 \\ 0.0970 & 6.0033 & 0.0000 \\ 0.0000 & 0.0000 & 1.1270 \end{bmatrix}$

$e = [\, 8.8697 \quad 6.0033 \quad 1.1270 \,]$

P5.65 a. $Q = \begin{bmatrix} -0.5946 & -0.2057 & 0.7772 \\ 0.4460 & -0.8887 & 0.1060 \\ 0.6690 & 0.4097 & 0.6202 \end{bmatrix}$

$R = \begin{bmatrix} -13.4536 & 23.1908 & 14.7172 \\ 0.0000 & -37.8707 & 7.5864 \\ -0.0000 & -0.0000 & 1.6879 \end{bmatrix}$

$B = \begin{bmatrix} 45.0454 & -0.0239 & -0.0000 \\ -0.0239 & 20.0000 & -0.0000 \\ -0.0000 & -0.0000 & 0.9546 \end{bmatrix}$

$e = [\, 45.0454 \quad 20.0000 \quad 0.9546 \,]$

b. $AA = \begin{bmatrix} 8.0000 & 10.8167 & -0.0000 \\ 10.8167 & 23.2308 & 13.8462 \\ -0.0000 & 13.8462 & 34.7692 \end{bmatrix}$

$B = \begin{bmatrix} 45.0454 & 0.0239 & -0.0000 \\ 0.0239 & 20.0000 & 0.0000 \\ -0.0000 & 0.0000 & 0.9546 \end{bmatrix}$

$e = [\, 45.0454 \quad 20.0000 \quad 0.9546 \,]$

P5.69 a. $Q = \begin{bmatrix} -0.9742 & -0.0262 & 0.2071 & 0.0853 \\ -0.0585 & -0.5679 & -0.0084 & -0.8210 \\ -0.0390 & -0.7166 & -0.4812 & 0.5034 \\ 0.2143 & -0.4041 & 0.8517 & 0.2555 \end{bmatrix}$

$R = \begin{bmatrix} -51.3225 & -2.7084 & -4.0918 & 19.5821 \\ -0.0000 & -13.8081 & -17.0130 & -16.6594 \\ 0.0000 & 0 & -11.7395 & 35.3765 \\ 0.0000 & 0 & 0 & 3.6758 \end{bmatrix}$

$B = \begin{bmatrix} 58.0976 & -0.1146 & 0.0060 & -0.0000 \\ -0.1146 & 35.5004 & -0.5341 & 0.0000 \\ 0.0060 & -0.5341 & 23.7782 & -0.0000 \\ -0.0000 & 0.0000 & -0.0000 & 0.6238 \end{bmatrix}$

$e = [\, 58.0976 \quad 35.5004 \quad 23.7782 \quad 0.6238 \,]$

b. $AA = \begin{bmatrix} 0.0000 & -11.5758 & -0.0000 & -0.0000 \\ -11.5758 & 38.7463 & 11.6143 & 0.0000 \\ -0.0000 & 11.6143 & 8.0082 & 8.5860 \\ -0.0000 & 0.0000 & 8.5860 & 21.2456 \end{bmatrix}$

$B = \begin{bmatrix} 58.0976 & -0.1147 & -0.0000 & 0.0000 \\ -0.1147 & 35.5242 & 0.0775 & 0.0000 \\ -0.0000 & 0.0775 & 23.7545 & 0.0000 \\ 0.0000 & 0.0000 & 0.0000 & 0.6238 \end{bmatrix}$

$e = [\, 58.0976 \quad 35.5242 \quad 23.7545 \quad 0.6238 \,]$

P5.73 a. $Q = \begin{bmatrix} -0.7894 & 0.1478 & -0.2024 & -05604 \\ -0.2046 & -0.9784 & 0.0096 & 0.0267 \\ 0.4093 & -0.1021 & -0.8578 & -0.2936 \\ -0.4093 & 0.1021 & -0.4723 & 0.7740 \end{bmatrix}$

$R = \begin{bmatrix} -51.3079 & -16.5764 & 33.1528 & -33.1528 \\ 0.0000 & -17.4849 & -2.0906 & 2.0906 \\ -0.0000 & -0.0000 & -27.0651 & -20.8193 \\ -0.0000 & -0.0000 & 0.0000 & 17.2938 \end{bmatrix}$

$$B = \begin{bmatrix} 72.0000 & 0.0000 & -0.0000 & 0.0000 \\ 0.0000 & 18.0000 & 0.0000 & -0.0044 \\ -0.0000 & 0.0000 & 36.0000 & 0.0000 \\ 0.0000 & -0.0044 & 0.0000 & 9.0000 \end{bmatrix}$$

$$e = \begin{bmatrix} 72.00 & 18.00 & 36.00 & 9.00 \end{bmatrix}$$

b. $AA = \begin{bmatrix} 40.5000 & -31.5000 & 0.0000 & 0.0000 \\ -31.5000 & 40.5000 & -0.0000 & -0.0000 \\ 0.0000 & -0.0000 & 18.8471 & -3.8118 \\ 0.0000 & 0.0000 & -3.8118 & 35.1529 \end{bmatrix}$

d. $B = \begin{bmatrix} 72.0000 & -0.0000 & -0.0000 & -0.0000 \\ -0.0000 & 9.0000 & -0.0000 & 0.0000 \\ 0.0000 & -0.0000 & 35.9997 & -0.0791 \\ 0.0000 & 0.0000 & -0.0791 & 18.0003 \end{bmatrix}$

$$e = \begin{bmatrix} 72.0000 & 9.0000 & 35.9997 & 18.0003 \end{bmatrix}$$

Chapter 6

(Results shown are exact, not values after 3 or 10 iterations.)

P6.1 $x = [\, 1, 2, \ 3\,]^T$

P6.3 $x = [\, 2, 1, -1\,]^T$

P6.5 $x = [\, 0.3, 1.8, 1.7\,]^T$

P6.7 $x = [\, 6, 3, 5, 2\,]^T$

P6.9 $x = [\, 0, 1, 0, -1\,]^T$

P6.11 $x = [\, 1, 2, 3, 4\,]^T$

P6.13 $x = [\, 1, -2, 3, 2, -1\,]^T$

P6.15 $x = [\, -2, 4, -6, 2, -4, 7\,]^T$

P6.17 $x = [\, -2, 1, 4, -6, 3, 2, -4, 7\,]^T$

Chapter 7

P7.1 $x = 0.90644, y = 2.5704$

P7.3 $x = 1.38, \ \ y = 1.6335$

P7.5 $x = 1.0784, y = 1.9259$

P7.7 $x = 0.56451, y = 1.1579, \ z = 1.5299$

P7.9 $x = 1.4901, y = -0.68477, z = 0.98001$

P7.11 $x = 0.29704, y = 0.67481, z = 0.73066$

P7.13 $x = 0.33016, y = 0.47535, z = 0.60284$

P7.15 $x = 0.57627, y = 0.36755, z = 0.70639$

Chapter 8

P8.1 a. coefficients from algorithm, and polynomial

$c = 0.5000 \ \ -4.0000 \ \ 4.0000$

$p(x) = 0.5 \,(x-2)\,(x-3) -4\,(x-1)\,(x-3) + 4\,(x-1)\,(x-2)$

b. divided difference table, and polynomial

1	1		
		3	
2	4		0.5
		4	
3	8		

$p(x) = 1 + 3\,(x-1) + 0.5\,(x-1)\,(x-2)$

P8.3 a. coefficients from algorithm, and polynomial

$c = 0.0333 \ \ -0.0857 \ \ 0.0476$

$p(x) = 0.0333\,(x-9)\,(x-16)$
$\qquad -0.0857\,(x-4)\,(x-16)$
$\qquad +0.0476\,(x-4)\,(x-9)$

b. divided difference table, and polynomial

4	2		
		0.2	
9	3		-0.0048
		0.1429	
16	14		

$p(x) = 2 + 0.2\,(x-4) -0.0048\,(x-4)\,(x-9)$

P8.5 a. coefficients from algorithm, and polynomial

$c = 0.5000 \ \ -2.0000 \ \ 2.0000$

$p(x) = 0.5\,(x-1)\,(x-2) -2x\,(x-2)$
$\qquad +2x\,(x-1)$

b. divided difference table, and polynomial

0	1		
		1	
1	2		0.5
		2	
2	4		

$p(x) = 1 + x + 0.5x\,(x-1)$

P8.7 a. coefficients from algorithm, and polynomial

$c = -0.556 \ \ 0.5000 \ \ -1.5000 \ \ 1.5000$

$p(x) = -0.0556x\,(x-1)\,(x-2)$
$\qquad + 0.5\,(x+1)\,(x-1)\,(x-2)$
$\qquad -1.5\,(x+1)\,x(x-2)$
$\qquad +1.5\,(x+1)\,x\,(x-1)$

b. divided difference table, and polynomial

−1	1/3			
		2/3		
0	1		2/3	
		2		4/9
1	3		2	
		6		
2	9			

$p(x) = 1/3 + (2/3)(x+1) + (2/3)(x+1)x + (4/9)(x+1)x(x−1)$

P8.9 a. coefficients from algorithm, and polynomial
$c = 0 \quad 0.5000 \quad 0 \quad −0.1667$
$p(x) = 0.5x(x−2)(x−3)$
$\qquad −0.1667x(x−1)(x−2)$

b. divided difference table, and polynomial

0	0			
		1		
1	1		−1	
		−1		1/3
2	0		0	
		−1		
3	−1			

$p(x) = 0 + x \quad −x(x−1)$
$\qquad + (1/3)x(x−1)(x−2)$

P8.11 (Lagrange form) $p(x) = −1.5(x−2/3)(x−1)$ $(x−2) −6.75 x(x−1)(x−2) + 3x(x−2/3)$ $(x−2) −0.1875 x(x−2/3)(x−1)$

P8.13 (Lagrange form) $p(x) = −3(x−2/3)(x−1)$ $(x−2) −13.5 x(x−1)(x−2) + 10.5x(x−2/3)$ $(x−2) −0.1875 x(x−2/3)(x−1)$

P8.15 (Lagrange form) $p(x) = −(4/3)(x−0.5)$ $(x−1)(x−1.5) + 8x(x−1)(x−1.5) −4x$ $(x−0.5)(x−1.5)$

P8.17 (Lagrange form) $p(x) − 0.0055x(x−8)$ $(x−27) −0.0019x(x−1)(x−27) + 0.0002x$ $(x−1)(x−8)$

P8.19 (Lagrange form)
$p(x) = −0.0194(x+1)x(x−1)(x−2)(x−3)(x−4)$
$\qquad −0.0042(x+2)x(x−1)(x−2)(x−3)(x−4)$
$\qquad +0.0646(x+2)(x+1)(x−1)(x−2)(x−3)$ $(x−4)$
$\qquad −0.0625(x+2)(x+1)x(x−1)(x−3)(x−4)$
$\qquad +0.0222(x+2)(x+1)x(x−1)(x−2)(x−3)$

Chapter 9

P9.1 $y = 3.5 x -2.6667$

P9.3 $y = 0.1651 x + 1.4037$

P9.5 $y = 1.5 x + 0.8333$

P9.7 a) $y = 2.8 x + 1.9333$
b) $y = 1.333 x^2 + 1.4667 x + 0.6$

P9.9 a) $y = 2.3 x + 0.3$
b) $y = 0.75 x^2 + 0.05 x + 1.05$

P9.11 a) $y = -0.94 x + 0.4867$
b) $y = 2.475 x^2 -6.055 x + 1.8067$

P9.13 a) $y = -1.68 x + 0.54$
b) $y = 6.075 x^2 -14.235 x + 3.78$

P9.15 a) $y = -0.8 x + 1.6$
b) $y = -2 x^2 + 2.2 x + 1.1$

P9.17 a) $y = 0.2299 x + 0.6207$
b) $y = -0.0132 x^2 + 0.4398 x + 0.2961$
c) $y = 0.0021x^3 -0.063x^2 +0.7115x +0.1344$

P9.19 a) $y = 1.12 x + 1.26$
b) $y = 0.5696 x^2 + 1.1125 x + 0.9702$
c) $y = 0.1957x^3 +0.5718x^2 +0.955x +0.975$

P9.21 $y = 2.9679 x + 3.5467$

P9.23 $y = -3.3164 x + 0.28$

P9.25 $y = 4.0616 x - 3.8039$

P9.27 $y = -0.8182 x^2 -1.7372 x + 2.58$

P9.29 $y = 5.0052 x^2 -0.5594 x + 4.3498$

P9.31 $y = 4.1402 x -5.8261$

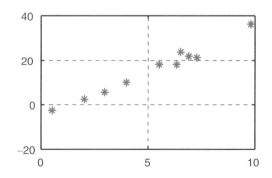

P9.33 $y = 3.9954 x^2 + 4.4814 x - 1.4743$

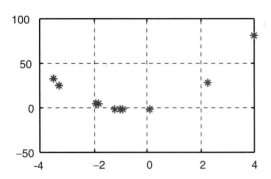

exponential (log-linear) fit; err = 8.4483e-04

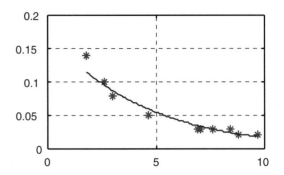

P9.35

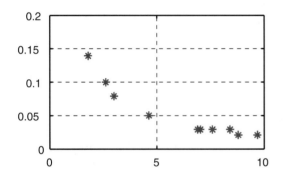

reciprocal of data

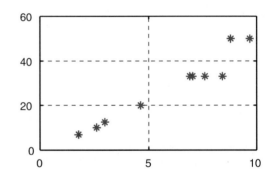

quadratic fit; err = 5.3794e-04

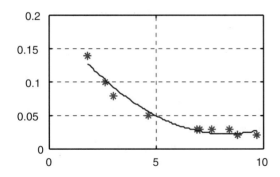

linear fit to reciprocal of data

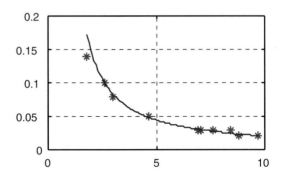

P9.37

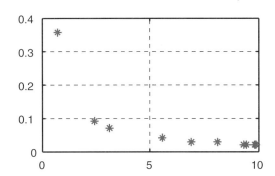

reciprocal of data

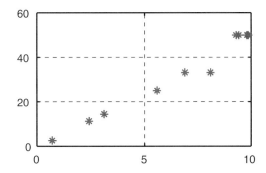

quadratic fit, err = 0.0148

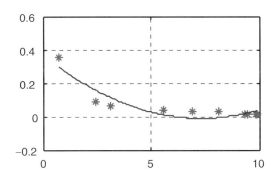

z = 1/ (5.2528 x -2.2642); error = 0.1211

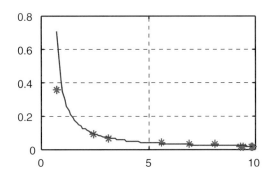

exponential (log-linear) fit, err = 0.0322

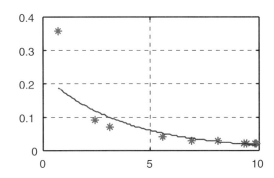

P9.39 plot data and reciprocal of data

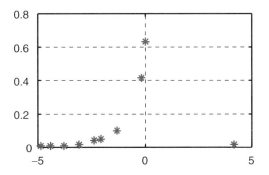

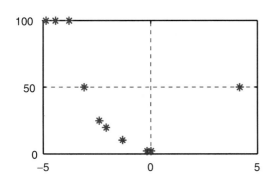

quadratic fit to reciprocal of data

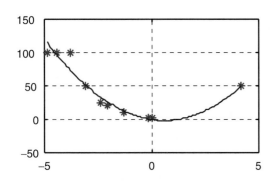

data and approximating function

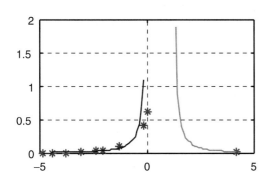

P9.41

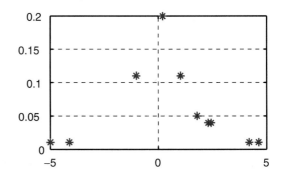

reciprocal of data

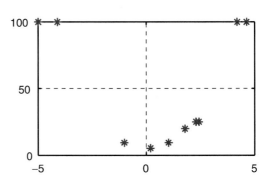

data and best-fit reciprocal of quadratic

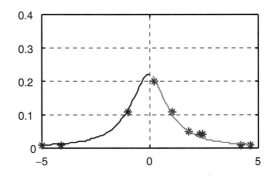

a **P9.43**
cubic fit

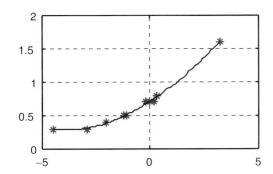

P9.45
cubic fit

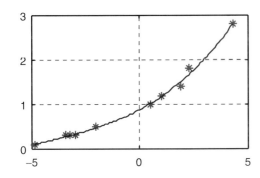

P9.47
cubic fit

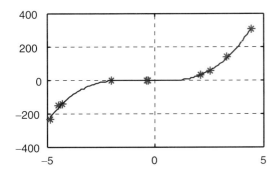

P9.49
quadratic fit

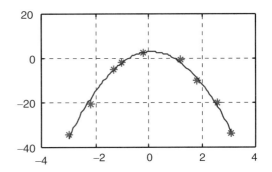

Chapter 10

P10.1 a. m = 1; a = 1/2, 1/2 b = 0, 1/2
b. m = 2; a = 1/2, 1/2, 0 b = 0, 1/2, 0

P10.3 a. m = 1; a = 1/2, -1/2 b = 0, 1/2
b. m = 2; a = 1/2, -1/2, 0 b = 0, 1/2, 0

P10.5 a. m = 1; a = 1/2,-1/3 b = 0,-1/3
b. m = 2; a = 1/2,-1/3,-1/6 b = 0,-1/3, 0

P10.7 a. m =1; a = 1/2,-4/9   b = 0,0
b. m =2; a = 1/2,-4/9,0   b = 0,0,0
c. m =4; a = 1/2,-4/9,0,-1/18 b = 0,0,0,0

P10.9 a. m = 1; a = 1/2, 1/4 , b = 0, 0.6036
b. m = 2; a = 1/2, 1/4, 0, b = 0, 0.6036, 0
c. m = 4; a = 1/2, 1/4, 0, 1/4, 0,
b = 0, 0.6036, 0, 0.1036, 0

P10.11 a. m = 1; a = 1/2, -1/2 , b = 0, -1/2
b. m = 2; a = 1/2, -1/2, 0, b = 0, -1/2, 0

P10.13 a. m = 1; a = 1/2, 1/2 , b = 0, -1/2
b. m = 2; a = 1/2, 1/2, 0, b − 0, -1/2, 0

P10.15 a. m = 1; a = 1/2, 1/3 ,   b = 0, 1/3
b. m = 2; a = 1/2, 1/3, -1/6, b = 0, 1/3, 0

P10.17 a. m = 1; a = 1/2, 4/9 ,   b = 0, 0
b. m = 2; a = 1/2, 4/9, 0,   b = 0, 0, 0
c. m = 4; a = 1/2, 4/9, 0, 1/18, b = 0, 0, 0, 0

P10.19 a. m = 1; a = 1/2, -1/4 ,   b = 0, -0.6036
b. m = 2; a = 1/2, -1/4, 0, b = 0, -0.6036, 0
c. m = 4; a = 1/2, -1/4, 0, -1/4, 0,
b = 0, -0.6036, 0, -0.1036, 0

P10.21
g = 2.0000   1.0000+ 1.0000i   0   1.0000- 1.0000i
gg = 2.0000   1.0000- 1.0000i   0   1.0000+ 1.0000i

P10.23
g = 2.0000   -1.0000+ 1.0000i   0   -1.0000- 1.0000i
gg = 2.0000   -1.0000- 1.0000i   0   -1.0000+ 1.0000i

P10.25
g = 2.0000   -0.6667- 0.6667i   -0.6667
-0.6667+ 0.6667i
gg = 2.0000   -0.6667+ 0.6667i   -0.6667
-0.6667- 0.6667i

P10.27
g = 3.00   -1.3333   0 + 0.00i -0.3333   0.0+ 0.0i
-1.3333- 0.00i
gg = 3.00   -1.3333- 0.00i 0.00- 0.00i -0.3333+ 0.0i
0.0   -1.3333- 0.00i

P10.29 g = 4.0 1.0 +2.4142i 0 1.0 +0.4142i
          0   1.0 -0.4142i   0   1.0 -2.4142i

          gg = 4.0 1.0 -2.4142i   0   1.0 -0.4142i
          0   1.0 +0.4142i   0   1.0 +2.4142i

Chapter 11

P11.1 a. df = 0.010 b. db = 0.010 c. dc = 0.010
d. dc2 = 0.040, dr = (4*dc -dc2)/3 = 0

P11.3 a. df = 6 b. db = 2 c. dc = 4 d. dc2 = 6.6667;
dr = 3.1111

P11.5 a. df = 0.20 b. db = 0.3333 c. dc = 0.25
d. dc2 = 0.25; dr = 0.25

P11.7 a. 25 b. 21.7789 c. 22 d. 21.6411 e. 21.4043

P11.9 a. 0.4083 b. 0.4056 c. 0.4056 d. 0.4055
e. 0.4054

P11.11 a. 1.5000 b. 1.5675 c. 1.6667 d. 1.5708
e. 1.5000

P11.13 a. 1.1667 b. 1.2075 c. 1.2222 d. 1.2092
e. 1.2000

P11.15 a. 1.3090 b. 1.4172 c. 1.3727 d. 1.4241
e. 1.4434

P11.17 a. 1.6089 b. 1.6520 c. 1.5507 d. 1.6528
e. 1.7365

P11.19 a. 5.4807 b. 5.2799 c. 5.2894 d. 5.2725
e. 5.2541

Chapter 12

P12.1
c. yy = 2.00   2.2100   2.4421   2.6985   2.9818
3.2949   3.6409   4.0231   4.4456   4.9124   5.4282

d. yy = 2.00   2.2103   2.4428   2.6997   2.9836
3.2974   3.6442   4.0275   4.4511   4.9192   5.4366

P12.3
c. yy = 1.00   0.9098   0.8343   0.7704   0.7155
0.6679   0.6263   0.5895   0.5567   0.5274   0.5011

d. yy = 1.00   0.9091   0.8333   0.7692   0.7143
0.6667   0.6250   0.5882   0.555   0.5263   0.5000

P12.5
c. yy = 2.00   2.1905   2.3630   2.5194   2.6618
2.7916   2.9104   3.0194   3.1197   3.2122   3.2979

d. yy = 2.00   2.1903   2.3627   2.5191   2.6614
2.7912   2.9100   3.0190   3.1192   3.2118   3.2974

P12.7
c. yy = 2.00   1.9800   1.9212   1.8271   1.7030   1.5559
1.3933   1.2230   1.0524   0.8878   0.7343

d. yy = 2.00   1.9801   1.9216   1.8279   1.7043   1.5576
1.3954   1.2253   1.0546   0.8897   0.7358

P12.9
c. yy = 1.00   1.0008   1.0075   1.0265   1.0648   1.1310
1.2375   1.4028   1.6569   2.0505   2.6732

d. yy = 1.00   1.0010   1.0080   1.0274   1.0661   1.1331
1.2411   1.4092   1.6686   2.0730   2.7182

P12.11
d. yy = 1.00   0.7843   0.7040   0.7061   0.7564   0.8187
0.8635   0.8697   0.8242   0.7227   0.5683

P12.13
d. yy = 2.00   2.1237   2.2450   2.3643   2.4819   2.5981
2.7129   2.8266   2.9394   3.0512   3.1623

P12.15
d. yy = 5.00   4.2411   3.5621   2.9618   2.4416   2.0013
1.6411   1.3608   1.1605   1.0403   1.00

P12.17
d. yy = 3.00   2.9667   2.8724   2.7355   2.5755   2.4158
2.2757   2.1670   2.0921   2.0464   2.0218

P12.19

d. yy = -1.00 -0.8884 -0.8298 -0.802 -0.7924 -0.791
-0.7898 -0.7807 -0.7539 -0.6952 -0.5809

(P 12.21-25, Results for ABM3, n = 10)

P12.21
yy = 1.0000 1.1053 1.2236 1.3588 1.5144 1.6948
1.9047 2.1492 2.4342 2.7658 3.1513

P12.23
yy = 1.0000 1.1099 1.2409 1.3946 1.5727 1.7770
2.0097 2.2736 2.5714 2.9063 3.2820

P12.25
yy = 1.0000 1.0050 1.0203 1.0465 1.0851 1.1385
1.2101 1.3049 1.4311 1.6015 1.8376

Chapter 13

P13.1
a. uu = 2.0000 2.0000 2.0800 2.2480 2.5152 2.8963
3.4100 4.0796 4.9336 6.0068 7.3413

b. uu = 2.0000 2.0400 2.1688 2.3995 2.7491 3.2394
3.8980 4.7587 5.8638 7.2649 9.0257
exact, y= 1.5*exp(x) + 0.5*exp(-x) -x;

P13.3
a. uu = 7.0000 6.2000 5.4400 4.7376 4.1050 3.5503
3.0789 2.6940 2.3975 2.1903 2.0724

b. uu = 7.0000 6.2200 5.4951 4.8350 4.2465 3.7346
3.3028 2.9534 2.6878 2.5069 2.4112
exact, y = exp(-x) + x exp(-x) + x^2 - 4 x + 6

P13.5
a. uu = -2.00 -1.20 -0.7200 -0.6624 -1.1296 -2.2404
-4.1463 -7.0507 -11.2329 -17.0808 -25.1355

b. uu = 2.00 -1.360 -1.1616 -1.5471 -2.7004 -4.8751
-8.4344 -13.9072 -22.0705 -34.0707 -51.6013
exact, y = -exp(x) + exp(-x) - x.^2 +4*x -2

P13.7
a. uu = 2.0000 1.8000 1.6200 1.4580 1.3122 1.1810
1.0629 0.9566 0.8609 0.7748 0.6974

b. uu = 2.0000 1.8100 1.6381 1.4824 1.3416 1.2142
1.0988 0.9944 0.9000 0.8145 0.7371
exact, y = 2 exp(-x)

P13.9
a. uu = 1.0000 0.8000 0.6800 0.6200 0.6097 0.6446
0.7241 0.8502 1.0272 1.2615 1.5613

b. uu = 1.0000 0.8400 0.7402 0.6918 0.6912 0.7384
0.8364 0.9907 1.2094 1.5028 1.8838

P13.11
midpoint method,
uu = 1.0000 1.0000 1.0060 1.0242 1.0616 1.1271
1.2332 1.3985 1.6508 2.0322 2.6053

P13.13 Solution is similar to y = 2 cos(2x), fairly
large n required for nice solution.

P13.15
midpoint method,
uu = 0 -0.6400 -1.2115 -1.7331 -2.2222 -2.6902
-3.1443 -3.5889 -4.0269 -4.4601 -4.8899

P13.17
midpoint method,
uu = 2.0000 2.0494 2.0976 2.1447 2.1908 2.2360
2.2803 2.3237 2.3664 2.4083 2.4494

P13.19
Euler's method,
uu = 5.00 6.3000 7.8200 9.5803 11.6016 13.9047
16.5106 19.4407 22.7163 26.3591 30.3906
exact, y = 2 x^2 + 3 x^3

P13.21
Euler's method,
uu = 3.00 3.3000 3.6600 4.0745 4.5399 5.0535
5.6134 6.2183 6.8670 7.5587 8.2928

midpoint method,
uu = 3.00 3.3300 3.7147 4.1507 4.6356 5.1677
5.7456 6.3684 7.0351 7.7452 8.4982
exact, y = 2 x^2 + 1/x

P13.23
midpoint method,
uu = 0 0.5400 0.9834 1.3495 1.6532 1.9060 2.1169
2.2929 2.4397 2.5619 2.6631

P13.25
midpoint method,
uu = 1.00 1.0000 0.9622 0.8807 0.7569 0.5975
0.4130 0.2162 0.0208 -0.1595 -0.3125

P13.27
midpoint method,
x = 0 0.1000 0.2000 0.3000 0.4000 0.5000 0.6000
0.7000 0.8000 0.9000

a = 1, uu = 1.0000 1.0950 1.1799 1.2541 1.3169
1.3668 1.4015 1.4169 1.4055 1.3505

a = 2, uu = 1.0000 1.0800 1.1168 1.1071 1.0475
0.9337 0.7605 0.5204 0.2016 -0.2192

a = 3, uu = 1.0000 1.0550 1.0126 0.8717 0.6364
0.3176 -0.0655 -0.4803 -0.8718 -1.1323

P13.29
midpoint method, on [1, 3]
k = 1, uu = 1.000 0.980 0.8999 0.7172 0.3441
-0.4089 -1.9740 -5.3898 -13.2966 -32.7878 -84.0125

k = 2, uu = 1.000 0.960 0.8006 0.4442 -0.2615
-1.6323 -4.3614 -10.0592 -22.6926 -52.6169 -128.4744

k = 3, uu = 1.000 0.940 0.7021 0.1810 -0.8179
-2.6792 -6.2099 -13.2143 -27.9828 -61.3645 -142.5102

k = 4, uu = 1.00 0.920 0.6044 -0.0724 -1.3264
-3.5583 -7.5656 -15.0492 -29.8918 -61.5631 -134.6992

Note, using larger n shows that solutions actually decay more rapidly than results above indicate.

P13.31

a.

t	x1	x2	x3	x4
0	1.0000	0	0	0
0.1	1.2855	1.2707	1.6848	0.6997
0.2	1.5438	2.7317	3.8321	1.6441
0.3	1.7775	4.4741	6.6155	2.9190
0.4	1.9890	6.6179	10.2687	4.6398
0.5	2.1804	9.3235	15.1057	6.9627
0.6	2.3536	12.8053	21.5499	10.0981
0.7	2.5102	17.3510	30.1713	14.3305
0.8	2.6520	23.3476	41.7391	20.0436
0.9	2.7803	31.3158	57.2908	27.7552
1.0	2.8964	41.9575	78.2258	38.1647

b.

t	x1	x2	x3	x4
0	0	1.0000	0	0
0.1	-0.2855	-0.2707	-1.6848	-0.6997
0.2	-0.5438	-1.7317	-3.8321	-1.6441
0.3	-0.7775	-3.4741	-6.6155	-2.9190
0.4	-0.9890	-5.6179	-10.2687	-4.6398
0.5	-1.1804	-8.3235	-15.1057	-6.9627
0.6	-1.3536	-11.8053	-21.5499	-10.0981
0.7	-1.5102	-16.3510	-30.1713	-14.3305
0.8	-1.6520	-22.3476	-41.7391	-20.0436
0.9	-1.7803	-30.3158	-57.2908	-27.7552
1.0	-1.8964	-40.9575	-78.2258	-38.1647

c.

t	x1	x2	x3	x4
0	0	0	1.0000	0
0.1	0.1903	1.0803	2.5897	0.6997
0.2	0.3625	2.3692	4.6508	1.6441
0.3	0.5184	3.9557	7.3563	2.9190
0.4	0.6594	5.9585	10.9390	4.6398
0.5	0.7869	8.5365	15.7123	6.9627
0.6	0.9024	11.9029	22.0987	10.0981
0.7	1.0068	16.3442	30.6679	14.3305
0.8	1.1013	22.2463	42.1885	20.0436
0.9	1.1869	30.1290	57.6973	27.7552
1.0	1.2642	40.6932	78.5937	38.1647

d.

t	x1	x2	x3	x4
0	0	0	0	1.0000
0.1	-0.0952	-0.5402	-0.7948	0.6502
0.2	-0.1813	-1.1846	-1.8254	0.1779
0.3	-0.2592	-1.9778	-3.1782	-0.4595
0.4	-0.3297	-2.9793	-4.9695	-1.3199
0.5	-0.3935	-4.2683	-7.3561	-2.4813
0.6	-0.4512	-5.9515	-10.5493	-4.0491
0.7	-0.5034	-8.1721	-14.8339	-6.1653
0.8	-0.5507	-11.1231	-20.5942	-9.0218
0.9	-0.5934	-15.0645	-28.3487	-12.8776
1.0	-0.6321	-20.3466	-38.7969	-18.0824

P13.33

a.

t	x1	x2	x3	x4
0	1.0000	0	0	0
0.1	1.2855	1.0138	1.0659	0.2325
0.2	1.5438	2.0713	2.2897	0.5408
0.3	1.7775	3.1993	3.7161	0.9445
0.4	1.9890	4.4291	5.3993	1.4674
0.5	2.1804	5.7973	7.4047	2.1391
0.6	2.3536	7.3473	9.8117	2.9959
0.7	2.5102	9.1308	12.7170	4.0828
0.8	2.6520	11.2099	16.2382	5.4548
0.9	2.7803	13.6596	20.5188	7.1798
1.0	2.8964	6.5705	25.7336	9.3412
0	0	1.0	0	0

P13.35

b.

t	x1	x2	x3	x4
0	0	1.0	0	0
0.1	0.3321	1.0679	-1.0418	-0.9589
0.2	0.7377	1.0345	-2.4739	-2.1003
0.3	1.2332	0.8202	-4.5103	-3.5485
0.4	1.8383	0.2996	-7.4663	-5.4783
0.5	2.5774	-0.7224	-11.809	-8.1414
0.6	3.4801	-2.5466	-18.232	-11.9044
0.7	4.5827	-5.6338	-27.7692	-17.306
0.8	5.9294	-10.6863	-41.96	-25.1414
0.9	7.5743	-18.7694	-63.096	-36.587
1.0	9.5833	-31.4941	-94.603	-53.390

P13.39

d.

t	x1	x2	x3	x4
0	0	0	0	1.0000
0.1	-0.9515	-1.2072	-0.1605	1.0952
0.2	-2.1405	-2.9905	-0.6687	1.1813
0.3	-3.3964	-5.1759	-1.5203	1.2592
0.4	-4.4481	-7.4084	-2.6306	1.3297
0.5	-4.9407	-9.1499	-3.8157	1.3935
0.6	-4.4804	-9.7182	-4.7867	1.4512
0.7	-2.7098	-8.3817	-5.1684	1.5034
0.8	0.5868	-4.5112	-4.5472	1.5507
0.9	5.3622	2.2172	-2.5515	1.5934
1.0	11.1882	11.5937	1.0376	1.6321

P13.37

c.

t	x1	x2	x3	x4
0	0	0	1.0000	0
0.1	-0.2673	0.9647	2.7103	0.2569
0.2	-0.3566	2.2283	4.7373	0.6605
0.3	-0.3556	3.8099	7.2624	1.2748
0.4	-0.3141	5.7966	10.5250	2.1888
0.5	-0.2593	8.3361	14.8398	3.5262
0.6	-0.2047	11.6412	20.6240	5.4580
0.7	-0.1566	16.0026	28.4345	8.2203
0.8	-0.1169	21.8114	39.0189	12.1377
0.9	-0.0856	29.5929	53.3841	17.6562
1.0	-0.0616	40.0525	72.8899	25.3870

Chapter 14

P14.1

a. xx = 0 0.0245 0.2158 0.4069 0.5984 0.7917 0.9881 1.1844 1.3808 1.5761 1.7686 1.9598 2.1512 2.3443 2.5406   2.7370 2.9333 3.1290 3.1416

   yy = 1.0000 1.1602 2.3767 3.5062 4.5098 5.3554 6.0100 6.4336 6.6100 6.5334 6.2148 5.6711 4.9197 3.9798 2.8726 1.6550 0.3737 -0.9177 -1.0000

b.

   x = 0   0.3142 0.6283 0.9425 1.2566 1.5708 1.8850 2.1991 2.5133 2.8274 3.1416

yy = 1.0000 0.9527 0.8113 0.5899 0.3103 -0.0000 -0.3103 -0.5899 -0.8113 -0.9527 -1.0000

P14.3

a. xx = 0 0.0078 0.0703 0.1328 0.1953 0.2578 0.3203 0.3828 0.4453 0.5078 0.5703 0.6328 0.6953 0.7578 0.8203 0.8828   0.9453 1.0000

yy = 10.0000 9.8856 9.0118 8.2076 7.4679 6.7877 6.1629 5.5892 5.0630 4.5807 4.1393 3.7357 3.3673 3.0316 2.7263 2.4494 2.1989 2.0000

b.

x =	0	0.1	0.2	0.3	0.4	0.5	0.6	0.7	0.8	0.9	1.0

yy = 10.00 8.6195 7.4117 6.3564 5.4361 4.6352 3.9400 3.3386 2.8207 2.3772 2.00

P14.5

a. xx = 0   0.0078 0.0703 0.1328 0.1953 0.2578 0.3203   0.3828 0.4453 0.5078 0.5703 0.6328 0.6953 0.7578 0.8203 0.8828 0.9453 1.0000

   yy = 2.0000 2.0626 2.5109 2.8698 3.1444 3.3406 3.4647 3.5235 3.5236 3.4720 3.3756 3.2410 3.0747 2.8828 2.6711 2.4452 2.2099 2.0000

b.

x =	0	0.1	0.2	0.3	0.4	0.5	0.6	0.7	0.8	0.9	1.0

yy = 2.0   2.6998 3.1742 3.4469 3.5446 3.4958 3.3286 3.0709 2.7483 2.3844 2.0000

P14.7

a.

xx = 0 0.0245 0.2209 0.4172 0.6136 0.8099 1.0063 1.2026 1.3990 1.5953 1.7917 1.9880 2.1844 2.3807 2.5771 2.7734 2.9698 3.1416

yy = 0 -0.2445 -2.0309 -3.5283 -4.7511 -5.7110 -6.4173 -6.8768 -7.0940 -7.0710 -6.8075 -6.3010 -5.5466 -4.5370 -3.2625 -1.7108 0.1330 2.0000

b.

x =	0	0.3142	0.6283	0.9425	1.2566	1.5708	1.8850	2.1991	2.5133	2.8274	3.1416

yy = 0   -2.7723 -4.8234 -6.2039 -6.9479 -7.0738 -6.5847 -5.4685 -3.6976 -1.2284 2.0000

P14.9

a.

xx = 1.0000 1.0547 1.2377 1.4401 1.6452 1.8509 2.0579 2.2666 2.4770 2.6898 2.9058 3.1264 3.3428 3.5558 3.7669 3.9774 4.1884 4.4013 4.6172 4.8378 5.0655 5.2910 5.5159 5.7406 5.9637 6.1871 6.4128 6.6430 6.8803 7.1137 7.3424 7.5692 7.7962 8.0000

yy = 1.0000 0.9192 0.6588 0.3889 0.1364 -0.0923 -0.2945 -0.4664 -0.6049 -0.7074 -0.7720 -0.7975 -0.7846 -0.7379 -0.6624 -0.5627 -0.4437 -0.3101 -0.1671 -0.0199 0.1260 0.2579 0.3713 0.4617 0.5255 0.5615 0.5687 0.5465 0.4949 0.4191 0.3256 0.2191 0.1046   0

b.

x =	1.0000	1.7000	2.4000	3.1000	3.8000	4.5000	5.2000	5.9000	6.6000	7.3000	8.0000

yy = 1.000   0.1872 -0.4242 -0.6985 -0.6096 -0.2622 0.1543 0.4474 0.5007 0.3157 0

P14.11

xx = 1.0000 1.0703 1.2503 1.4541 1.7018 2.0047 2.3813 2.8604 3.3916 3.9541 4.5166 5.0791 5.6416 6.2041 6.7666 7.3291 7.8916 8.4541 9.0166 9.5791 10.0000

yy = 0   0.0456 0.1489 0.2458 0.3407 0.4306 0.5127 0.5833 0.6314 0.6592 0.6707 0.6711 0.6635 0.6504 0.6333 0.6134 0.5914 0.5680 0.5437 0.5188 0.5000

b.

x = 1.0000 1.9000 2.8000 3.7000 4.6000 5.5000 6.4000 7.3000 8.2000 9.1000 10.0000

y = 0   0.3919 0.5626 0.6360 0.6599 0.6565 0.6374 0.6090 0.5752 0.5384 0.5000

P14.13

a.

x = 1.0000 1.0078 1.0703 1.1328 1.1953 1.2578 1.3203 1.3828 1.4453 1.5078 1.5703 1.6328 1.6953 1.7578 1.8203 1.8828 1.9453 2.0000

y = 0.5000 0.5066 0.5634 0.6290 0.7049 0.7931 0.8958 1.0157 1.1557 1.3194 1.5106 1.7339 1.9941 2.2971 2.6490 3.0568 3.5284 4.0000

b.

x = 1.0000 1.1000 1.2000 1.3000 1.4000 1.5000 1.6000 1.7000 1.8000 1.9000 2.0000

y = 0.5000 0.5937 0.7117 0.8615 1.0531 1.2987 1.6136 2.0164 2.5297 3.1804 4.0000

P14.15

a.

x = 0   0.0078 0.0703 0.1328 0.1953 0.2578 0.3203 0.3828 0.4453 0.5078 0.5703 0.6328 0.6953 0.7578 0.8203 0.8828 0.9453 1.0000

y = 1.0000 1.0048 1.0438 1.0846 1.1274 1.1724 1.2199 1.2702 1.3235 1.3803 1.4408 1.5055 1.5750 1.6496 1.7300 1.8168 1.9110 2.0000

P14.17

a.

x = 1.0000 1.0078 1.0703 1.1328 1.1953 1.2578 1.3203 1.3828 1.4453 1.5078 1.5703 1.6328 1.6953 1.7578 1.8203 1.8828 1.9453 2.0000

y= 0   -0.0213 -0.1848 -0.3376 -0.4819 -0.6193 -0.7508 -0.8776 -1.0005 -1.1201 -1.2370 -1.3516 -1.4645 -1.5759 -1.6863 -1.7958 -1.9048 -2.0000

P14.19

b.

x = 0   0.0078 0.0703 0.1328 0.1953 0.2578 0.3203 0.3828 0.4453 0.5078 0.5703 0.6328 0.6953 0.7578 0.8203 0.8828 0.9453 1.0000

y = 1.0000 0.9853 0.8736 0.7712 0.6773 0.5911 0.5119 0.4393 0.3727 0.3119 0.2563 0.2058 0.1601 0.1190 0.0823 0.0499 0.0215 0.0000

P14.21

b.

x = 1.0000 1.0078 1.0703 1.1328 1.1953 1.2578 1.3203 1.3828 1.4453 1.5078 1.5703 1.6328 1.6953 1.7578 1.8203 1.8828 1.9453 2.0000

y = 1.0000 0.9922 0.9343 0.8828 0.8366 0.7950 0.7574 0.7232 0.6919 0.6632 0.6368 0.6124 0.5899 0.5689 0.5494 0.5311 0.5141 0.5000

P14.23

b.

x = 0   0.0078 0.0549 0.1019 0.1490 0.1963 0.2449 0.2974 0.3536 0.4133 0.4758 0.5383 0.6008 0.6633 0.7258 0.7883 0.8508 0.9133 0.9758 1.0000

y = 1.0000 0.9983 0.9801 0.9488 0.9046 0.8477 0.7767 0.6863 0.5751 0.4416 0.2870 0.1191 -0.0600 -0.2483 -0.4436 -0.6439 -0.8471 -1.0514 -1.2550 -1.3333

P14.25

x =   0 0.0078 0.0703 0.1328 0.1953 0.2578 0.3203 0.3828 0.4453 0.5078 0.5703 0.6328 0.6953 0.7578
0.8203 0.8828 0.9453 1.0000

y =   0 0.0180 0.1611 0.3011 0.4356 0.5631 0.6829 0.7947 0.8988 0.9958 1.0861 1.1703 1.2491 1.3229
1.3923 1.4577 1.5195 1.5708

Chapter 15

P15.1

Solution at t = 0.5

a.	0	0.0683	0.1444	0.2364	0.3523	0.50
b.	0	0.0682	0.1443	0.2363	0.3522	0.50
c.	0	3.9062	-15.6250	29.6875	-25.625	0.50 (unstable)
d.	0	0.0693	0.1461	0.2381	0.3533	0.50
e.	0	0.0682	0.1443	0.2365	0.3521	0.5000

P15.3

Solution at t = 0.5

a.	0	0.0010	0.0016	0.0016	0.0010	0
b.	0	0.0008	0.0012	0.0012	0.0008	0
c.	0	-44.2775	27.3650	27.3650	-44.2775	0 (unstable)
d.	0	0.0053	0.0086	0.0086	0.0053	0
e.	0	0.0005	0.0016	0.0016	0.0005	0

P15.5

Solution at t = 0.5

a.	0	0.0000	0.0000	0.0000	0.0000	0
b.	0	-0.0029	0.0048	-0.0048	0.0029	0
c.	0	-19809	32052	-32052	19809	0 (unstable)
d.	0	0.0000	-0.0000	0.0000	-0.0000	0
e.	0	-0.0621	0.1004	-0.1004	0.0621	0

P15.7

Solution at t = 0.5

a.	0	0.2012	0.4020	0.6020	0.8012	1.00
b.	0	0.2009	0.4008	0.6015	0.8005	1.00

c. 0   39.0625 -171.8750 334.375   -299.375 1.0 (unstable)

d. 0   0.2081   0.4129   0.6127   0.8078   1.00

e. 0   0.1985   0.3991   0.6022   0.7952   1.00

P15.9

Solution at t = 0.5

a. 0   0.0825   0.1335   0.1335   0.0825   0

b. 0   0.0724   0.1000   0.1171   0.0618   0

c. 0   90250   -120000   87790   38130   0 (unstable)

d. 0   0.4058   0.6610   0.6660   0.4141   0

e. 0   0.5248   -0.2946   0.3233   0.1623   0

P15.11

a. oscillations most easily shown graphically
b. unstable

P15.17

a.	0.00	0.0000	0.0000	0.0000	0.00
	0.00	0.0547	0.1172	0.1797	0.25
	0.00	0.1172	0.2422	0.3672	0.50
	0.00	0.1797	0.3672	0.5547	0.75
	0.00	0.2500	0.5000	0.7500	1.00

P15.19

a.	0.0000	0.0625	0.2500	0.5625	1.00
	-0.0625	0.0547	0.3047	0.6797	1.1875
-	0.2500	-0.0703	0.2422	0.6797	1.2500
-	0.5625	-0.3203	0.0547	0.5547	1.1875
-	1.0000	-0.6875	-0.2500	0.3125	1.0000

P15.21

a.	1.00	1.0625	1.2500	1.5625	2.0000
	0.9375	0.9688	1.1562	1.4687	1.9375
	0.7500	0.7813	0.9688	1.2812	1.7500
	0.4375	0.4688	0.6563	0.9688	1.4375
	0.0000	0.0625	0.2500	0.5625	1.00

P15.23

a.	0.0000	0.0156	0.1250	0.4219	1.0000
	0.0156	0.1719	0.3438	0.6094	1.0781
	0.1250	0.3438	0.4844	0.6250	0.8750
	0.4219	0.6094	0.6250	0.5469	0.4844
	1.0000	1.0781	0.8750	0.4844	0.0000

P15.25

a.	0.0000	0.0000	0.0000	0.0000	0.0000
	0.2656	0.2656	0.1875	0.0157	-0.2344
	0.6250	0.6406	0.4844	0.1406	-0.3750
	1.1719	1.2031	0.9687	0.4531	-0.3281
	2.0000	2.0625	1.7500	1.0625	0.0000

Index

Nonlinear functions of several variables, finding zeros of, 241–254, (264–266). *See also* Newton's method, Fixed point iteration, Minimization

Nonlinear pendulum. *See* Pendulum

Nonlinear shooting method. *See* Shooting method

Nonlinear system from geometry, 242, 244–245

Normalized floating point system, 15

Numerical differentiation, 3, 407. *See also* Differentiation, numerical, Difference formulas, Backward difference formula, Central difference formula, Forward difference formula

Numerical linear algebra, 3, 95–124, 131–169, 175–197, 207–235

Numerical integration, 3, 407. *See also* Trapezoid, Simpson, Gaussian quadrature, Midpoint, Romberg, Newton-Cotes

Numerical round off, 3. *See also* Error, round off

Nystrom method for ODE, 463

O

ODE. *See* Differential equation, ordinary

Oil reservoir modeling, 324, 337, 342

Operation counts. *See* Flops

Orbit, (526). *See also* Elliptical orbit

Order (big-Oh), 14. *See also* Convergence, order of; Error, truncation

Order of equations
effect on accuracy, 26–27, 106
effect on convergence, 217, 221

Ordinary differential equations
boundary value problems, 529–558. *See also* Shooting, Finite difference
initial value problems, 449–528. *See also* Taylor, Euler, Runge Kutta, Adams Bashforth, Adams Moulton, Adams Bashforth Moulton
stability, 479–481
stiff, 514–515

Orthogonal functions, 348–352

Orthonormal functions, 348

Orthogonal polynomials, 348–352. *See also* Gram Schmidt process, Legendre polynomials

Ostrowski Theorem, 226

Over relaxation, 222. *See also* SOR

Overflow, 17

P

Pade approximation, 323, 354–356, 363, (367). *See also* Rational function approximation

Parabolic PDE, 563. *See also* Heat equation

Parametric curves, 269, (318–319)

Parasitic solution, 514

Partial derivatives, 415

Partial differential equations (PDE), 3, 559–608. *See also* Heat equation, Wave equation, Poisson equation, Finite element method

Partial pivoting, See Pivoting, row

Pascal, Blaise, 2

PDE. *See* Differential equations, partial

Pendulum
nonlinear, 492, 494, 497, 499
spherical, (526)

Permutation matrix. *See* Matrix

Persian mathematics, 1

Piecewise planar function. *See* Basis function

Piecewise polynomial interpolation, 267, 297–306, (314–316)
cubic, 300–306
linear, 297
quadratic, 298–299

Pivot
column, 99
element, 99
row, 99, 119

Pivoting, row, 95, 107–111, 124

Planetary orbits, (526). *See also* Elliptical orbit

Poisson equation, 207, 208, 214–215, 562, 584–587, 603. *See also* Elliptical PDE

Polak Ribiere method, 2

Polynomial, 3. *See also* Interpolation

Polynomial interpolation, 267, 270–289, 311, (314–319). *See also* Lagrange interpolation polynomial, Newton interpolation polynomial

Population growth, 325, 340

Potential (Laplace) equation, 208, 214, 559, 586, 592–594, (606). *See also*, Elliptical PDE

Positive definite matrix, 226

Power method, 178–187, 197, (199–201)
accelerated, 181, 197
basic, 175, 178–180, 197
inverse, 175, 184–187, 197
shifted, 182, 197

Power spectrum, 397, 401, (404–406)

Precision, 16

Predator-prey problems, (528)

Predictor-corrector methods. *See* Adams-Bashforth-Moulton methods

Pythagorean theorem, 54

Q

QR factorization, 95, 160–164, 170. *See also*. Householder, Givens, Hessenberg

QR method for eigenvalues, 175, 188–195, (201)

Quadratic equations, Babylonian solution, 1

Quadratic formula, effect of round off, 19, (51)

Quadratic least squares. *See* Least squares approximation

Quadratic spline, 298–299, 312, (314)

Quadrature, Gaussian, (265), 407, 433–438, 443, (446)

Quazi Newton methods, 258–261

R

Radiation flux, (320)

Radix-2 FFT. *See* FFT

Rate of convergence. *See* Convergence

Rational function approximation, 323, 354–356, 363

Rational function interpolation, 267, 294–296, 312, (315–316)

Rayleigh quotient, 181–183, 197

Regula falsi, 53, 61–64, 70–71, 89, (91). *See also* false position

Reinsch, 2

Relative error. *See* Error, relative

Relaxation. *See* SOR

Riccati equation, (490)

Richardson extrapolation, 416–417, (444), 454, 484

Ridder's method, 2, 86, 440

Robot, motion of, 243, 250, (265), 518–521

Romberg integration, 430–432, (444), (446), (447)

Root finding. *See* Bisection, Regula falsi, Secant, Newton, Muller
Round off error. *See* Error, round off
Rounding, 18
Rosenbrock methods, 516
Row pivoting. *See* Pivoting, row
Runge, Carl, 2
Runge function, 288–289, 295, 304
Runge Kutta methods, 2, 449, 457–469, 485, 504–509
    adaptive step-size, 483
    for systems, 504–509, (524)
    fourth order, 464–467
    higher order , 468
    second order, 457–462
    third order, 463
Runge-Kutta-Fehlberg methods, 469, 483

S

Saturated oxygen, (320)
Scaling, 111
School enrollments, (321)
Secant method, 4, 53, 61, 65–71, 89, (91), (94), 539
Shooting method, 532–544, 554
    linear, 532–538, 554
    nonlinear, 539–544, 554
Significant digits, 14
Simplex
    method for linear programming, 230–234
    search, 260
Simpson, Thomas, 2
Simpson's rule, 407, 421–423, 428–429
Solving equations of one variable. *See* Bisection, Fixed point iteration, Muller, Newton, Regula falsi, Secant
Solving systems of linear equations. *See* Gaussian elimination, Gauss Seidel, Jacobi, SOR
SOR method, 207, 210, 222–227, 235, (237–238)
    conditions for convergence, 226–227
Spline interpolation, 133, 267, (269), 297–306, 312, (318–319). *See also* Cubic spline
Spring, (92)
Spring-mass system. *See* Mass-spring system
Stability, 479–481, 515
    absolute, 479

finite difference methods for PDE, 569, 573, 574, 579
Milne's method for ODE, (490)
strongly stable method, 479–481
weakly stable method, 479–481
Steady state heat distribution. *See* Heat equation
Steepest descent method. *See* Minimum of function
Stopping conditions, 13, 57, 62, 65, 73, 80, 179, 184, 188, 192, 195, 210, 213, 219, 223, 229, 247, 252, 255, 261
Stiff ODE, 514–515
Straight line approximations. *See* Newton, Regula falsi, Secant, Trapezoid
Successive over relaxation. *See* SOR
Successive underrelaxation, 222
Symmetric power method, 181
System of linear equations. *See* Gaussian elimination, Jacobi, Gauss Seidel, SOR
System of nonlinear equations. *See* Newton's method, Fixed point iteration
System of ordinary differential equations. *See* Differential equations, system

T

Taylor, Brook, 2
Taylor methods, 449, 451–456, 485. *See also* Euler's method
Taylor approximation, 353
Taylor polynomial, 3, 15
Taylor series, 22
Telegrapher's equation, (607)
Temperature conversion data, (366)
Temperature in a rod, (557). *See also* Heat equation
Termination conditions. *See* Stopping conditions
Theorems
    Fixed point convergence, 11
    Fixed point convergence in R^n 254
    Gerschgorin circle, 12, 48
    Newton's method convergence, 77
    Ostrowski, 226
    Secant method convergence, 69

Thermal diffusivity, (607)
Thirteen-point formula, 415
Thomas method, 124. *See also* Gauss-Thomas
Three-point difference formulas, 411–413
Torricelli's law, (489)
Trace, 183
Traffic density, (607)
Trapezoid method for ODE, 485
Trapezoid rule, 8, 9, 33, 34, 48, (51), 407, 419–420, 426–427 ,
Tridiagonal system, 112–117, 133, 148, 301
Trigonometric approximation, 372–382, (404)
Trigonometric interpolation, 372–382, (404)
Trigonometric polynomial, 372
Truncation error. *See* Error
Truss, forces on, 97, 103, 110, (130)
Tukey, 3
Two point boundary value problem. *See* Boundary value problem
Two link robot arm. *See* Robot, motion of

U

Underflow, 17
Updating
    sequential, 218
    simultaneous, 211
Upper Hessenberg matrix. *See* Hessenberg
Upper triangular matrix. *See* LU, QR

V

Van der Pol equation, (527)
Vapor pressure, (320)
Viscosity, (320)

W

Water draining, (367), (489)
Wave equation, 561, 578–583, 602. *See also* Hyperbolic PDE
Waveforms for musical instruments, 370, 398, (404)
Word, 16

Z

Zeros of a function. *See* Nonlinear function

Author Index